WARRIOR STATESMAN

WARRIOR STATESMAN

THE LIFE OF MOSHE DAYAN

ROBERT SLATER

ST. MARTIN'S PRESS

New York

Design by Judith Dannecker

Library of Congress Cataloging-in-Publication Data

Slater, Robert
    Warrior statesman : the life of Moshe Dayan / Robert Slater.
        p.   cm.
    ISBN 0-312-06489-6
    1. Dayan, Moshe, 1915–1981.   2. Statesman—Israel—Biography.
3. Generals—Israel—Biography.   4. Israel—Armed Forces—Biography.
5. Israel—Politics and government.   I. Title.
    DS126.6.D3S57   1991
    956.9405′092—dc20   91-20425
    [B]   CIP

First Edition: September 1991

10 9 8 7 6 5 4 3 2 1

TABLE OF CONTENTS

FOREWORD

THE BLACK EYEPATCH dominated Moshe Dayan's appearance, like some dark, spidery animal wrapped around his face. With its thin straps sliding over his bald head and upper cheek, the oval eyepatch jarred, dismayed, overwhelmed. The message conveyed was unmistakable: This man has been through hell and survived.

He had survived by a miracle. When in 1941 a French soldier fired at him, the bullet pierced Dayan's field glasses and ripped out his left eye. That injury was the turning point of Moshe Dayan's life.

He had believed that he was going to die. He did not. Nor did he become a helpless cripple, as he feared he would. Until then he had been a soldier, and he wanted to return to soldiering. Gradually he overcame the handicap of being one-eyed and took part in some of the most dramatic events in modern history. By virtue of his deeds—and the black eyepatch that he wore after the shooting—Moshe Dayan became one of the most well-known figures of our era. He was instantly recognized no matter how far he traveled from home. If people did not recall Dayan's name, they did remember his country. "Israel, Israel," they would shout out at him. And he would smile back.

He became a key figure in the building of the state of Israel, shaping and leading its army, directing three of its wars, helping at the end of his career to shape the country's first treaty with an Arab state. No other Israeli leader served in leadership roles for as long as Moshe Dayan did:

He was in the headlines constantly as far back as 1948, when he served as commander of Jerusalem; and he remained in the headlines thirty-three years later, trying to make a political comeback. He was his country's most visible symbol. Just as his eyepatch became a symbol of the man, so too did the eyepatch come to symbolize the state of Israel. It symbolized Israel's nerve and its awesome military strength, but it symbolized too the wounds that were inevitably inflicted on the Jews in Israel.

Dayan's life and achievements took on great meaning for the Jewish people. The first child born on the first kibbutz, proud, independent leader of a Jewish army, hero of fiercely fought but highly successful wars, Dayan became the symbol of the new Jew, able to stand on his own feet, willing to defend himself against all enemies. Oddly enough, he saw himself not so much as a representative of the modern Jewish people but as one of a long line of generations of Jews that went back thousands of years. The plight of his parents' generation, whether it was the Holocaust or other lesser travails, interested him far less than how his Jewish ancestors lived in the desert in the early ages.

Still, it was his lot to defend the Jewish people in Palestine, and he found that he was very good at it. Indeed, Moshe Dayan was born to the battlefield. He found war exciting, and could not get enough of it. He made the military the centerpiece of his life. It bothered him little that he constantly exposed his life to risk. Living on the edge of death stimulated him, made him feel that he was living life to the fullest.

Above all else, Moshe Dayan was a warrior, one of the most sparkling of his era. An extraordinary soldier, he was imaginative, courageous, spirited. His whole approach to the military was to be unorthodox. He used that same approach in building the Israel Defense Forces, teaching his soldiers: Always be different, unconventional, always challenge the rules, never go by the book; above all else, retain the element of surprise.

It was Dayan who shaped his country's army, set its battle standards, insisted that all that mattered in wartime was whether a soldier could and would fight, not how he looked or how he marched. Due largely to Dayan, the Israel Defense Forces (IDF) grew into a menacing juggernaut, one of the mightiest military engines in the world.

He was as contemptuous of the rules in other walks of life as he was in the army. Rule breakers often wind up in jail or at least cast aside by society. Not Moshe Dayan. He had proven his worth as a soldier, a negotiator, a military leader. That, at least in his view, gave him a license to thumb his nose at rules and conventions. Pillaging national treasure became legitimate. So did consorting with all sorts of women. Feeling special, Dayan acquired a self-confidence that bordered on cockiness, arrogance: Only he knew what was best for his country, how to deal with the Arabs, when to fight, when to withdraw.

Often he was right, and for that he was immensely admired. Often he sniffed at tradition and convention, and for that he was resented. Because he was a military hero, he got away with such behavior. Many were awed by his genius. Just as many despised him. He was Israel's most controversial and colorful leader. Though he was controversial, many Israelis found Dayan's attitude toward life worth emulating. Hence, Dayan's most important qualities found their way into the personalities of many Israelis: his spirit of defiance and irreverence, his love of informality, his disdain for frills, discipline, and rules.

He loved to write. He wrote highly descriptive and thoughtful school compositions at an early age. Later, he produced diaries and a number of memoirs. He always wrote poetry. He was constantly thinking, taking in his surroundings and trying to make sense of them. He believed that he deserved a place in history and so he rushed to get all of his thoughts and memories down on paper.

He left his imprint on the shape of the country, upon its people, upon its policies toward others. In large measure due to Moshe Dayan, Israel adopted an aggressive stance against the Arabs from the outset. Others cautioned moderation, trying to negotiate with the Arabs rather than fight them. Dayan saw this as unrealistic, irrelevant, dangerous.

Dayan's activism protected the nation: He believed that Israel, small and surrounded by a hundred million hostile Arabs, had no choice but to act aggressively, to seize the initiative in battle, and to thrust quickly into the enemy's territory. In this manner, the Arabs would be kept at bay.

They were. As chief of staff of the army in the 1956 Sinai campaign and as minister of defense in the 1967 Six Day War, Dayan presided over great military victories. On the eve of both wars Dayan had the foresight to realize that Israel had no choice but to enter battle. Thanks to that foresight, a tiny land stood tall, and a country whose survival had seemed in doubt projected an image of strength and solidity.

When the 1948 and 1956 wars ended, Israel retreated into its smallness, avoiding the political risks of retaining large chunks of Arab territory. With its back to the wall on the eve of the 1967 encounter, the country decided that being so small made the country unacceptably vulnerable. After the Six Day War and the capture of vast amounts of Arab land, Israel opted for maintaining strategic depth, for keeping its forces in Arab lands. Only peace would cause their removal. Dayan saw the great advantages of this policy and he promoted it relentlessly. He overlooked the long-range cost.

Israel took on the role of neighborhood bully, oppressor, occupier, creating images that would harden. No one was more responsible for those images than Dayan. As a result of the Six Day War, Dayan had been elevated to the stature of a demigod in Israel and abroad. He was given credit for rescuing Israel from potential disaster. As the most powerful figure in the country after the Six Day War, he was able to shape Israel's postwar world. He chose to set the country on a course of long-term occupation. He decided that it was in Israel's best interest to dig deep roots into East Jerusalem, the West Bank, the Gaza Strip, Sinai, and the Golan Heights. He sought to demonstrate to the Arab inhabitants that Israel's occupation was benign, that it was possible for the Arabs to get along with the Israelis. Yet he was not prepared to give the Arabs what they most wanted: an assurance that Israel would leave their lands immediately.

Few national leaders have risen so high and then fallen so low as Moshe Dayan. Thanks to him the country reflected an exuberant self-confidence after 1967. It believed its own myths: that the Israel that had devastated the Arabs in the Six Day War would easily deflect any Arab military attack; that the Arabs, knowing of Israel's overwhelming might, would not dare take up arms. It was delusion on a grand scale, as the surprise attack by the Egyptians and Syrians beginning the Yom Kippur War of 1973 was to show. Dayan went from savior to scapegoat, bearing the brunt of the blame for the catastrophic events of that October. Those who had worshiped at his feet a mere six years before now condemned him as a murderer and villain.

Other men might have withdrawn from public life to suffer their humiliation quietly. To be sure, Dayan was deeply affected by the public's excoriation. He grew furious at accusations that he had not done enough to prepare the country for war, that he had not seen war coming. If he had to accept blame, others in the government should too. Not feeling guilty, he refused to drift away from public life quietly. When Prime Minister Menachem Begin asked him to become foreign minister in 1977, three and a half years after the Yom Kippur War, Dayan happily agreed. It was his chance to contribute to peace, to be active again. His instincts told him that the prospects for peace with the Arabs had improved and he wanted to be part of whatever peace negotiations ensued. To his good fortune, he did not have to wait long. Once Egyptian president Anwar Sadat came to Jerusalem in November 1977, six months after Dayan became foreign minister, the Camp David peace process began. It culminated in the signing of the Israeli-Egyptian peace treaty in March 1979. Dayan played a significant role in bringing that treaty to fruition. Thus, he ended his life as peacemaker.

I first came upon Moshe Dayan shortly after arriving in Israel in December 1971. He was minister of defense, recent hero of the Six Day War, the most illustrious star in Israel's firmament. As the Jerusalem correspondent for United Press International, I covered Dayan during the Yom Kippur War and its aftermath. Later, when I was working for *Time* magazine, I covered the last years of Dayan's career as part of my general coverage of Israel. Often he was inside some building holding crucial, secret talks—with Henry Kissinger or Jimmy Carter, or with Golda Meir and other Israeli leaders. And I was outside, waiting with other journalists for Dayan to emerge and give us a few words. Other times I saw him at press conferences and public speeches.

I found it slightly unprofessional when some of my news colleagues called Dayan a legend. I had never met a legend and had never been sure who would qualify. Dayan was, nonetheless, a daunting figure. He seemed utterly self-confident, totally unapproachable, a force and power in his own right who, while not prime minister, towered above other Israeli leaders. When he had something to say, he did so, oblivious of the possibility that he might be contradicting government policy. Often, through such utterances, he was trying to determine policy. I recall listening at a briefing once to Foreign Minister Abba Eban's spokesman assail Defense Minister Dayan for holding just such an independent view on some topic. "How could this happen?" I asked naively. "That's Dayan. What can we do?" the spokesman replied forlornly.

Having written biographies of two other Israeli leaders, Yitzhak Rabin (1977) and Golda Meir (1981), I came around to the idea that Dayan would make a wonderful subject for a biography. Two Israeli authors, Naphtali Lavie and Shabtai Teveth, had written biographies of Dayan in midcareer: Lavie's was *Moshe Dayan: A Biography* (London: Vallentine, Mitchell, 1968); Teveth's, *Moshe Dayan* (London & Jerusalem: Weidenfeld & Nicolson, 1972; New York: Houghton-Mifflin, 1973). After Dayan died in the fall of 1981 it struck me that a full-length biography on him was worth doing.

I saw Dayan frequently at public speeches and news conferences, and interviewed him on occasion, the last time six months before his death in March 1981. I was working for *Time* magazine. His memoirs on the Camp David peace process, *Breakthrough*, had just been published, and he was about to embark on his final campaign for the Knesset. Unfortunately, *Time* decided not to run the interview and I faced the unpleasant task of informing Dayan. "They've thrown it in the garbage," he said to me with a mixture of distaste and resignation.

While researching this book I've often thought back to my last meeting with him. This was not the Moshe Dayan I had gotten to know over the years, but a shell of the man. At times those close to Dayan asked me whether I thought I could capture "the real Moshe." To be honest, I was not quite sure what was meant by the question. Was this the real man, at the end of his career, still craving to be in the spotlight? Or was the real Moshe Dayan the man who strode through the gates of the Old City that June day in 1967, a conquering hero? What of the broken, dismal figure who emerged from the Yom Kippur War of 1973? My own sense is that there was no real Moshe Dayan, but rather a very complex, intriguing personality whose impact on his nation and on the world was very large indeed. My task as biographer was to convey that personality in all its complexity throughout the stages of his life. That task was made all the more challenging by the voluminous amount of detail Dayan and others close to him left behind on the public record: his memoirs, his daughter Yael's, his former wife Ruth's; then too, Dayan's speeches, press conferences, and interviews.

I chose to go beyond all of these and conduct in-depth interviews with many of those who were familiar with Dayan. Often I interviewed the same person several times. It became clear to me that, nearly a decade after his death, his acquaintances still held a special place in their hearts for Moshe Dayan. Members of the immediate family gave me hours of their time, as did political and military figures who had worked with Dayan. For many of those interviewed, recalling Dayan was an emotional experience: Some exhibited joyful nostalgia, some pain and bitterness. However they felt, it became important, sometimes crucial, that they speak of Dayan, that they contribute their assessment of him to this project. Israeli cabinet ministers put aside their busy daily schedules for me. I thank all of those who participated.

The following people were interviewed: Avraham Adan, Shimon Agranat, Yosef Almogi, Meir Amit, Alfred Atherton, Shlomo Aronson, Yosef Avidar, Uri Avnery, Aharon Barak, Haim Baram, Chaim Bar-Lev, Neora Bar-Nor, Mordechai Bar-On, Michael Bar-Zohar, Yitzhak Ben-Aharon, Uri Ben-Ari, Mordechai Ben-Porat, Meron Benvenisti, Nahman Betser, Udi Betser, Ron Ben-Yishai, Irving Bernstein, Avraham Biran, Zvi Brenner, Zbigniew Brzezinski, Aryeh Brown, Moshe Carmel, Jimmy Carter, Yoseph Checanover, Amnon Cohen, Mulla Cohen, Assi Dayan, Rahel Dayan, Ruth Dayan, Yael Dayan, Abba Eban, Arie Lova Eliav, Michael Elkins, Azriel Eynav, Walter Eytan, Ben Feller, Yehoshua Gavish, Shlomo Gazit, Israel Gefen, Eitan Haber, Amos Hadar, Yehoshafat Harkabi, Yossi Harel, Meir Har-Zion, Chaim Herzog, Mordechai Hod, Yigal Hurvitz, Anwar Khatib, Yehiel Kadishai, Teddy Kollek, Eliahu

Lankin, Naphtali Lavie, Sam Lewis, Moshe Lissak, Danny Matt, Ha-
dassah More, Aryeh Naor, Uzi Narkiss, Yuval Ne'eman, Aryeh Neh-
emkin, Dan Pattir, Benny Peled, Yohanan Pelz, William Quandt,
Yehoshua Raviv, Meir Rosenne, Eliakim Rubinstein, Akiva Sa'ar, Harold
Saunders, Rachel Schwartz, Zvi Schwartz, Iska Shadmi, Michael Shashar,
Zalman Shoval, Joseph Sisco, Avino'am Slutzky, Israel Tal, Dan Tol-
kowski, Zvi Tsur, Yehuda Tubin, Cyrus Vance, Martin Van Creveld,
Raphael Vardi, Ezer Weizman, Gad Ya'acobi, Amnon Yannai, Oded
Yannai, Aharon Yariv, Haim Yisraeli, Binyamin Zarhi, Rehavam Ze'evi,
and others who wished to remain anonymous.

In addition to a valuable series of interviews I conducted with Rahel
Dayan, I was fortunate to receive from her a number of unpublished
letters Moshe Dayan wrote to her over the years.

I wish to thank Carol Sutherland for the many hours she put into this
project, identifying important material in Hebrew and then translating
it; Meena Ben-Harosh for transcribing numerous taped interviews; and
Lisa Miller for transcribing taped material. I also thank Miriam Slater
for translating Hebrew-language poetry and compositions from Dayan's
childhood. I am grateful to all who assisted me at libraries and archives
in Israel, among which were the Knesset library in Jerusalem, the Israel
Defense Forces archives in Givatayim, the American Culture Centers
in Tel Aviv and Jerusalem; the American Jewish Committee library in
Jerusalem; the archives at Nahalal; the archives at *Ma'ariv* and *Yediot
Aharonot* in Tel Aviv, and the *Jerusalem Post* in Jerusalem. I thank also
Avner Falk for allowing me to see the English translation of his Hebrew-
language book: *Moshe Dayan: The Man and the Myth. A Psychoanalytic
Biography* (Jerusalem: Cana Publishing House, 1985).

Veteran Israeli journalist Haim Baram read the manuscript and provided me with a host of insights into Israel's complex political scene. I
thank him especially.

To my colleagues at the *Time* magazine Jerusalem Bureau: Jon Hull,
Jamil Hamad, Ron Ben-Yishai, and Marlin Levin, I offer my thanks for
your encouragement and help. I especially wish to thank Jean Max, our
office manager, for her continuous help throughout the project.

I am also grateful to the following publishers for permission to quote
from these works: Weidenfeld & Nicolson Ltd (London): *My Father, His
Daughter*, Yael Dayan, 1985; *Destination Peace*, Gideon Rafael, 1981;
Breakthrough, Moshe Dayan, 1981; and *On Eagles' Wings*, Ezer Weiz-
man, 1976. Ballantine Books, a division of Random House, Inc.: *Among
Lions*, J. Robert Moskin, 1982. Farrar, Straus & Giroux, Inc.: *The Power
and the Principle*, Zbigniew Brzezinski, 1983. HarperCollins Publishers:
In Search of Identity, Anwar Sadat, 1978.

My editor Bill Thomas has improved this book in many ways and for that I thank him. I wish also to thank Adam Goldberger for his efforts as copy editor. For their tolerance and patience, I thank Miriam, Adam, and Rachel, my three children.

Above all, I thank my wife Elinor for being the first to tell me that I should do this book, for making numerous suggestions throughout the research and writing, and mostly, for being at my side.

❖ 1 ❖

To a New Land

MUD UP TO THEIR ankles; flies buzzing around their faces; endless hours of working the soil; disease; this less-than-romantic picture awaited the thousands of Russian Jews who ventured to Palestine at the turn of the twentieth century. Anguished by anti-Semitism in the old country, they were eager to find refuge in new surroundings. For many, the pioneering life was simply too harsh, and they soon left Palestine. The hearty, determined ones, the visionaries, stayed on, among them Moshe Dayan's parents, Shmuel and Dvorah. In Russia Jews had become rabbis or peddlers, butchers or tailors. Now in a new land, they yearned to become New Jews, to reshape their Jewish identities. Simply by looking down at their feet they found a new ideology. Once the synagogue had been the focus of their Jewish lives. Now their inspiration would come from the soil. The hoe and the sickle suddenly took on mystical properties; planting seeds replaced prayer. And not just that. Taming the land became crucial, not just for building a new life but for carving out a homeland.

But what kind of homeland? Certainly not one that merely transported the ghetto and the piety and the peddlers. Though sovereignty remained a far-off dream, socialism and its attendant goal of equality burned deeply inside these Jewish immigrants. When they did achieve statehood a mere four decades later, this tiny band of tough-minded, zealous farmers and ideologues and fledgling soldiers, this Mayflower generation of the state of Israel, dominated the political and social and economic leadership. By then the mud and the flies and the disease had bequeathed to this aristocracy of the land a conviction that they were this new country's elite.

No one thought himself more aristocratic, more an authentic voice of this founding generation, than Moshe Dayan's father, Shmuel Dayan. The dour-faced son of a poor, religious-minded Russian family, he found little ennobling about poverty or piety. Shmuel had been born in 1890 into one of the three hundred Jewish families in Djeskov, near Kiev in the Ukraine. Largely merchants who sold fish, farm implements, and shoes to the peasants, the Jews of Djeskov kept to themselves, finding piety the strongest shield against their precarious existence. Three generations of Dayans had lived under one roof, poorer than many of their Jewish acquaintances in the town. Thanks to one inhabitant, the house was a magnet, drawing visiting rabbis and others. It was as if someone had hung a shingle on the door saying Wisdom Dispensed Here. The man whose wisdom was sought, whether on personal, business, or religious subjects, was Rabbi Pinhas Dayan, Shmuel's grandfather, Moshe Dayan's great-grandfather. Rabbi Dayan led a devout life, head buried in a sacred Jewish text, prayer shawl wrapped around his neck, and a silk yarmulke atop his head, even when he slept. Undoubtedly he possessed the same kind of charisma exhibited by his great-grandson, for Shmuel reported, "Everyone would come to shake the rabbi's hand or just touch his fingertips, and would go away feeling comforted and with hope of better days ahead."[1] Rabbi Dayan was the latest in a long line of Jewish luminaries within the Dayan family: From one of them on Shmuel's father's side, Reb Eliyahu, who had been a religious judge or *dayan*, the family acquired the name Dayan.

Shmuel's father Avraham was a sorrowful figure. During childhood he was attacked by a bull, which left him with a limp for life; and he was pressured into marrying a poor orphan whom he did not love. He had no more luck in commerce. Trying his hand at selling raisin wine to the poor, Avraham was too frightened to wander down to the cellar to get the wine bottles. Here was one trait which grandson Moshe did not inherit. Failing as a grocer, Avraham became an itinerant peddler, aided at times by his two sons, Shmuel and Eliyahu.

Shmuel's first Zionist stirrings came while reading pamphlets that contained the urgings of Jewish pioneers in Palestine, appealing to Russian Jews to emigrate. After the crushing burdens of poverty and anti-Semitism, Shmuel found the Zionist pioneers' message to be "like a good ointment for my bones."[2] With six hundred rubles in savings, and accompanied by Eliyahu, the eighteen-year-old Shmuel embarked in 1908 on the voyage to Palestine.

MOSHE DAYAN'S MOTHER made a similar voyage, but not until five years later. Dvorah Zatulovsky was born in the same year as Shmuel and came from the Kiev region as well, but there the similarities abruptly end. Djeskov had an active Jewish life; not so Prochorovka, with only one Jewish family—the Zatulovskys. Moreover, in contrast with ne'er-do-well Avraham Dayan, Dvorah's father Yehiel Ze'ev was a man of stature and wealth. The owner of a lumberyard along the banks of the Dnieper, he was also a Hebrew scholar who had published a book on Jewish defense efforts in the Ukraine during the seventeenth-century pogroms.

At age fifteen, during the 1905 Russian Revolution, Dvorah joined the *Narodniki* in their protest against the czarist regime, indifferent to the risks. The Narodniki were a socialist movement that sought support among the peasants. Three years later, Dvorah enrolled as a student in the Faculty of Education at the University of Kiev. Romantically attracted to a professor, she thought of marrying him, but never did. Enraptured with the Russian novelist Tolstoy, Dvorah took the train to his home at Yasnaya Polyana when he died in 1910. She said, "In every person's life there comes a moment when he wishes to bid the sun stand still. That was my moment."[3]

Searching for another such magical moment, Dvorah set off the following year for the Bulgarian front, where she served as a volunteer nurse. Russia supported Bulgaria, which had just attacked Turkey. Happily identifying with the subjugated Bulgarians at first, Dvorah soon decided this was not her war, the Russians were not even her own people. Sensing her life was in error, she abandoned the university and instead spent the winter of 1912 searching through her father's library. Eventually she came upon a letter written to Yehiel Ze'ev by Vladimir Tiomkin, the representative of the Lovers of Zion movement in Palestine, and "every word fell on fertile soil."[4] So, twenty-three years old, and against her parents' wishes, she sailed on the *Princess Olga* in January 1913 for Palestine.

That act alone—pulling up stakes in one country and moving to another—told a good deal about the characters of Dvorah Zatulovsky and Shmuel Dayan. They were independent, stubborn, driven. To survive in the Holy Land, they would need such traits as armor against the harshness, and as sources of strength during the times of adversity.

ARRIVING IN PALESTINE in 1908, Shmuel Dayan confronted the harshness and adversity soon enough, including the lack of jobs, and competing
for the few jobs that were available against Arabs with far greater farming
skills. He finally secured work in the barley fields at Petach Tikvah, but
suffered from the flies and then from malaria, a disease with frightening
symptoms: chattering teeth, dry tongue, excruciating weakness. Un-
daunted, he pursued the Zionist ideal of working the land, trying to get
the work that had been going to the Arabs at the same wages.

For the next three years, Shmuel moved around, binding wheat
sheaves, digging irrigation ditches, and nurturing an interest in public
affairs. In his first year in Palestine he sponsored a meeting in Ein Ganim
to support the moderately socialist Jewish newspaper *Hapoel Hatzair*
(Hebrew for "Young Worker") and then walked barefoot all the way to
Jaffa to deliver the cash he had collected, along with the protocols of the
meeting to the newspaper editors. After laboring all day at Ein Ganim,
he turned his room into a clubhouse where friends could learn Hebrew,
read about the burgeoning Jewish labor movement in Palestine, and
debate what kind of society they wished to build. In time Shmuel graduated from building houses and picking fruit to proper farm work. Purchasing an old five-chambered Turkish pistol and a cartridge belt in Jaffa,
he headed north to Yavniel, where for six months he engaged in plowing,
sowing, reaping, and threshing. An Arab *keffiyeh* wrapped around his
head, his pistol on his hip, he could not have been happier: "I burst into
song. Here I was ploughing the soil of the land of Israel. What more
could my soul want?"[5]

Perhaps a permanent home. The opportunity arose when in 1911 he
joined Degania, an experimental community on the southern edge of
Lake Kinneret (the Sea of Galilee), as a hired hand. The entire settlement
comprised only two stone buildings: a two-story one with eight rooms,
where the settlers lived; and a single-story one for the dining room,
kitchen, bakery, showers, and storehouse. For the eleven members of
this, the Jewish community's first kibbutz, Degania was as much an idea
as a place, requiring the tiny settlement to place the group above the
individual, extolling egalitarianism and collective decision making. Here,
though, utopia was less a goal than physical survival.

Most of Degania's settlers wanted to abandon their past practice of
wandering from place to place, developing tracts of land and then turning
them over to permanent settlers. They wished to stay put and to make
Degania into a model for future Jewish settlements—by depending only

on their own Jewish labor. It would not be easy, not in that searing heat at 650 feet below sea level. Shmuel Dayan, however, thought they could contribute more to the Jewish settlement drive by sticking to their itinerant life. A power struggle erupted and Shmuel's followers urged that he take over from Yosef Bussel as Degania's farm manager; when Shmuel and his allies forced the issue at a kibbutz general meeting, Bussel agreed to bring Shmuel in as comanager. Though he appeared to be settling down, Shmuel continued to favor moving from place to place.

DEGANIA WAS ABOUT to get a visitor. Following her week-long voyage from Odessa to Jaffa early in 1913, Dvorah Zatulovsky had arranged to meet Israel Bloch, one of the Degania settlers, upon her arrival. When he did not turn up, she struck up an acquaintance with Israel Betser at the port. He brought her to his kibbutz, Merhavya, where she remained for three months. Once Dvorah ascertained that Bloch had returned to Degania—he had been buying cows in Beirut for the kibbutz—she took the train to Zemach, at the foot of Lake Kinneret, then made her way to nearby Degania by foot. Shmuel Dayan took a liking to her at once.

Dvorah had problems adjusting, displaying little affection for the hard work and congeniality that were considered essential traits for a model kibbutznik. Nor was she enraptured with the philosophizing about Zionism or the talk about remaking oneself into a New Jew. Esteeming Russian culture and literature, she spoke neither Hebrew nor Yiddish, the favored tongues of the kibbutz. However brave the new experiment, it was all a bore to her. Asked to bake bread for the fifty Degania settlers, she showed sufficient disdain for that task to be consigned to the less pleasant farming chores: patching old sacks together, rooting up weeds, and working on the threshing floor. Degania had every reason to turn down Dvorah's application for membership; but the real reason for her rejection had to do with Shmuel's romantic feelings toward her. To assure that no one else would steal Dvorah's heart, Shmuel hit upon a ploy that at first defied logic: He would insist that she leave the kibbutz. Shmuel successfully argued that the presence of Dvorah and two other new female arrivals had kept the men from working diligently. Accordingly, her membership bid rejected, Dvorah went off to Sejera (later Kefar Tavor), where she studied Hebrew, having decided it was crucial to know if she was going to carry on in Palestine. She wrote frequently to Shmuel. When he went to Beirut to seek medical treatment for an ear infection brought on by a mosquito bite, Dvorah spent her entire savings on a one-way boat ticket to be with him. She checked into a cheap hotel, spending most of her time at Shmuel's beside. They became engaged, and in her new status, Dvorah was welcomed into Degania as a full member.

Toward the end of 1913 both Shmuel and Dvorah became ill. Dvorah was suffering from malaria and infectious bronchitis; Shmuel's chronic ear and nose infection had not been cured by the Beirut doctors. The couple thought it wise to leave Palestine briefly. Borrowing funds from his brother Eliyahu, Shmuel sailed in December from Haifa to Trieste and then on to Vienna, where he hoped to obtain medical treatment. The following month, Dvorah sailed to Odessa and from there went on to Prochorovka to be with her parents. While in Vienna, Shmuel worried that Dvorah might succumb to her parents' pressure to stay in Russia. He wrote to her that "the city is attractive and life is easy there. . . . But we shall not abandon the land, for without work on the land there is no pleasure in our lives."[6]

Shmuel planned to meet Dvorah in Russia, but to enter his native country he needed to get his hands on a false passport, grow a full beard, and travel under an assumed name. Having failed to report for military service in the Russian army back in 1910, he now had to avoid the czar's police. Dvorah had hoped to meet Shmuel in his native town of Djeskov; but her parents insisted that she remain at home. Dvorah was torn between returning to Palestine and staying with her parents. As she wrote on April 25, 1914, a few months before the start of World War I: "If I elope from home, my conscience will lacerate me for having run away and left my father to suffer alone. How long is this going to last?"[7] Eventually, Shmuel walked the snow-covered route of nineteen miles from Djeskov to Prochorovka. Overcoming her guilt about leaving her parents, Dvorah left with Shmuel for Odessa, from where they sailed to Haifa in July, this time to stay.

Marriage was now on their minds. For Shmuel, this was a shocking about-face. He had once scorned the institution, with its pregnancies and babies, as a hindrance to the development of kibbutz life. He also felt it kept the women from their farm work. Now he was in love. In September he and Dvorah were married. A *shochet*, or ritual slaughterer, came by cart from the nearby settlement of Menahamiya to perform the wedding. The marriage canopy was a blanket tied to poles usually used for holding up orange trees. For the ceremony, which took place on the banks of the Jordan River, Dvorah wore a white dress that she had sewn herself.

The following spring Dvorah felt her first birth pains. The first step the nurses took was to lock the door and shutters to keep the recently arrived locusts from entering. Settlers passing outside heard Dvorah's moaning. Intent upon being nearby, Shmuel arranged for another settler to take his guard duty in the fields. As dawn began on May 4, 1915, Moshe Dayan came into the world. He was named after a nineteen-year-old member of Degania, Moshe Barsky, who had volunteered to get medicine for Shmuel the year before. While en route Barsky had been shot and killed by six Arabs.

Moshe Dayan was the first baby born in Degania and the first baby born in an Israeli kibbutz—but he was not the first kibbutz child. That distinction went to Degania's Gideon Baratz, who had been born two years earlier in Tiberias. Unlike his parents, Moshe was born into a Jewish environment, at least in his immediate surroundings. Later it occurred to him that in this respect his childhood was far easier than that of his parents.

He was undeniably a most difficult infant. He was a howler from birth—so much so that Dvorah was forced to take him down to the Jordan River in the evenings so that his screaming would not wake up others. He was also sickly. By his second summer, in 1916, he had contracted an eye disease called trachoma. Making matters worse, Dvorah was barely fit to take care of herself, let alone an infant. Yet, during that same summer of 1916, virtually blind from her own bout with trachoma, she traveled around the countryside by cart in search of medical treatment for her infant. His welfare came first, this frail little child whom she nicknamed Moussa, Moussik, and Moussinka. She chafed at efforts to alleviate the wear and tear of motherhood: When Gideon's mother, Miriam Baratz, proposed that she and Dvorah share in the supervising of their two babies, Dvorah grudgingly agreed. Two weeks later, Dvorah begged out of the arrangement, preferring to give one hundred percent of her time to little Moshe.

While away from Degania seeking medical treatment in Jaffa for Moshe, Dvorah did not have the heart to write to Shmuel the full drama of Moshe's maladies. Still, their common suffering, mother and child, was evident from what she did reveal. He was happy and likable and made people laugh, she wrote. He seemed intelligent, and knew many words. Sometimes he grabbed a pencil and wrote the words "Daddy" and "Home" on a piece of paper as if he were writing to Shmuel. His illness made him restless, and to keep him quiet Dvorah told him story after story. She could not deny that the child's smaller eye was crossed and the difference between it and his healthy eye quite noticeable.

Little Moshe's sickliness persisted. During the summer of 1918, only three years old, he contracted pneumonia. One photograph from that period, of Moshe standing between his parents at Degania, shows a sickly child, slightly chubby, with his left eye drooping and nearly closed. With no hospital in Tiberias, Shmuel and Dvorah took a room in the Wingert Hotel in Tiberias. They endured nine days of hell. Moshe lay motionless, thin and pale, his eyes shut. Fearing the worst, his parents took turns waving wet towels over the child's bed. To Dvorah the endless night brought only horror: "Will he survive? The heart contracts with fear. Here, look, he's not breathing. What shall I do? Without my being aware of it, my desperate cry comes through and tears apart the quiet of the night: 'Miriam, come here, he's going to die!' "[8] Finally, Shmuel told Dvorah to listen, the boy was saying something in a weak voice: "Mommy, they're singing." Indeed, the muezzin was calling Muslims to morning prayers from the minaret of his mosque—and Moshe was alert enough to hear it!

Upon a doctor's advice, Dvorah took Moshe away from the hundred-degree temperature of Tiberias to a cooler clime father north in Metulla. There Moshe made enough of a recovery for Dvorah to contemplate their return to Degania. The settlement sent a horse and cart. Mother and child left Metulla early one morning to avoid the midday sun. The scorching heat was the boy's enemy. When the horses suddenly became violent and broke the harness shaft, Dvorah and Moshe were forced to wait on the roadside while the driver did repairs. Dvorah grew frantic. She had to flee the sun. Making her way on foot to Rosh-Pinna, twelve miles to the south, she swept through the fields, clinging to the tiny child, her mind enflamed by the maddening thought that she might collapse. Her torment grew: The boy was breathing with difficulty. She wanted to stop, but that was impossible. She must reach safety. Sweat poured down Dvorah's face and covered her eyes. Suddenly, she was overwhelmed by an agonizing weakness. She lapsed into an unconscious state.

When she awoke, she was shocked into reality by a peasant woman who was sprinkling cold water on her. She had no idea where she was nor who her savior had been. How much time had elapsed? Where was Moshe? She found herself and Moshe inside a house, reclining on a cold stone floor covered with a mat.

Eventually reaching Degania, Dvorah was stymied in her search for medical treatment of Moshe's persistent trachoma. Though Turkish forces in Palestine were in retreat after taking a drubbing from General Allenby's British forces, it remained dangerous to move about the country. Once the war was over, Dvorah reached Jerusalem, early in 1919. Mother and child were in separate places for a time, Dvorah in the Rothschild Hospital getting help for a kidney ailment, Moshe at Dr. Aryeh Feigenbaum's Ophthalmic Hospital for his trachoma. She soon learned the good news that Moshe's trachoma would not require surgery and was treatable with daily massages of copper sulfate. Dvorah decided to use the time to teach Moshe how to read and write—in Hebrew.

By the time she and Moshe returned to Degania that summer, Shmuel and some other Degania settlers had grown weary of kibbutz life and wanted to establish a less collectivized commune that they would call a moshav. They had not minded pooling the farming and marketing efforts; but they yearned for more privacy in their personal lives. That June Shmuel attended a convention of the Hapoel Hatzair party at the Kinneret work farm and pushed through a resolution calling on the party to establish the Jewish community's first moshav.

Meanwhile, Degania was about to expand: To accommodate a fresh influx of immigrants, the kibbutz decided to split into two adjoining settlements, Degania A and Degania B. Shmuel Dayan was put in charge of establishing Degania B and of assuring its security. Its early days were extremely difficult. By April 1920 Arabs were rumored to be readying attacks on Jewish settlements in the Jordan Valley, including Degania B. Shmuel's inclination was to stay and fight; others, fearing the outcome of an Arab attack, urged retreating to Degania A. When the Arabs attacked Degania B on April 24, Shmuel ordered his fourteen men to man battle positions. Some chose to retreat. Shmuel agonized over what to do. Deserters, he believed, deserved to be shot; but that was out of the question. Besides, he himself ultimately realized the futility of remaining. Before departing, Shmuel poured kerosene on the wall of the settlement's wooden building and ignited it.

The four-year-old Moshe, back at Degania A, watched the flames. He did not understand what was happening. But he sensed that it was something bad for his father and his settler friends. In time, that image of the conflagration of Degania B sharpened in Moshe Dayan's mind as a costly lesson in how not to fight the Arabs. For Shmuel, the pain of defeat was more immediate, and was made all the more ignominious when he learned that at the nearby Jewish settlement of Menahamiya it had taken only ten Jewish fighters to save that commune. (Degania B was given a new lease on life a year later when Shmuel turned the settlement over to a new group that included Levi Eshkol, a future prime minister of the state of Israel.) As an adult, Moshe Dayan retained a highly selective mixture of memories from those days in Degania. The hot climate, the dust, and the painful way the elements affected his eyes mixed with a happier collection of memories: visits to nearby Zemach, populated in those days with several thousand Arabs; the railroad station; the shops; the jingle of coins in his pocket meaning that he could buy lemonade, halvah, or candy. Yet the strongest memory remained the horrifying scene of Degania B alight in flames while its fifteen fighters beat a hasty retreat. He never spoke about what that scene really meant to him, but his silence spoke volumes. He would find a better way; he would not permit the Arabs to get the upper hand against him.

While waiting for the Twelfth Zionist Congress, scheduled to meet in Europe in September 1921, to approve financing for the first moshav, the three Dayans moved to Tel Aviv. Shmuel worked in the agricultural center of the Hapoel Hatzair party; Dvorah delivered letters to hard-to-find new immigrants for the Missing Relatives Bureau. Moshe was sent to kindergarten each morning. In the afternoons his parents locked the apartment's door and windows, fearing that he might wander off. Their fears were well founded. Once, Moshe had broken all the windows trying to escape. For that, the boy received a whipping from his father. Iron bars were added to the windows. Binyamin Zarhi, whose father and Dvorah Dayan were cousins, recalled seeing Moshe for the first time then, thin, with little holes on his face, suffering from malaria. Zarhi thought the boy energetic, eager to take control of things.[9] Shmuel and Dvorah soon took jobs helping to build the Haifa-Nazareth road, breaking up rocks into smaller stones and gravel. At night they slept in tents near the construction site. Learning that her parents were about to immigrate to Palestine, Dvorah preferred not to greet them in a roadside tent: Thanks to a schoolteacher friend, she and Moshe moved into a Haifa school.

Shmuel's dream—that first moshav—was about to become a reality. Alloted only thirty-two thousand Egyptian pounds by the Zionist Congress, less than they had hoped, Shmuel and six other settlers had incentive enough to set up stakes immediately. The site was to be on a hill called Mahlul in Arabic, several miles from Nazareth at the western approach to the Jezreel Valley. Their spirits sagged upon hearing the sad history of the place from an old man on the site. German immigrants had tried to settle there but had all died soon thereafter; Arabs next tried but suffered the same quick fate.

"What makes it impossible to live here?" asked a prospective settler.

"Bad wind and bad water," the old man answered. "If anyone drinks this water, his belly swells up and in three days he is dead."

Glancing at the graves in a nearby cemetery, Shmuel and the others wondered why their luck should be any better. Just then the youngest of the group yelled out, "We are glad to be alive, aren't we?" The others understood the question as a call to battle. "We will settle here," another shouted quickly.[10]

And so on September 10, 1921, the seven men spent their first night near where Nahalal would be built. They spoke in whispers and avoided lighting fires—to prevent an Arab attack. Ten days later, Shmuel journeyed to Haifa to pick up Dvorah and Moshe. The three Dayans made their way to Nahalal, first by train, then on foot. The parents took turns carrying Moshe, weak from one of his recurrent fevers. With its bubbling spring, lemon and fig trees, and its merciful shade, the new moshav looked beautiful to Dvorah. Never mind the checkered history of the site or its malaria-breeding swamps. Shmuel noticed them but he and his friends were determined to succeed; swamps could be drained with some hard work and perseverence. The twenty-one pioneers would need both in full measure. They quickly set up seven tents, plus a kitchen and dining hall in a hut. Their first general meeting lasted three days and during that time a seven-member village council was chosen and the principles of the moshav were agreed upon. They would live by their own labor, speak only Hebrew, and help one another in times of need. None of this, however, mattered to six-year-old Moshe. He longed for Degania, where he had left close friends, where he could wander down to the main road and watch the cars go by. Here at Nahalal he looked up at strange faces and stranger surroundings.

He had little time to dwell on this. Rumors grew that the Arabs planned to attack Nahalal to mark the fourth anniversary of the Balfour Declaration, British foreign minister Arthur Balfour's letter of November 2, 1917 to Lord Rothschild, the president of the British Zionist Federation, promising a Jewish homeland in Palestine. Anticipating the assault on Nahalal, the male settlers sent the women and children away. Dvorah and Moshe went to Nazareth, a two-hour walk from the new settlement, and remained there until May 1922. Dvorah took Moshe to a clinic every day for treatment of his trachoma. Eventually it was cured. A kindergarten provided the boy with his first formal year of education. He progressed in reading and writing and showed a talent for drawing. He enjoyed solitude, happy to remain aloof from the games other children played. Though Dvorah and Moshe lived in the midst of friendly Arabs, the Jewish children made sure to walk in pairs around the Nazareth streets. When Arab youngsters taunted Moshe and his friends, it was he who proposed picking a fight with the older Arabs—to show them that taunting did not pay. He must have sensed that any display of weakness had its price.

Moshe wanted very much to return to Nahalal but when he wrote as much to his father, Shmuel disheartened the boy by sending him a letter dripping with ideological fervor. He wrote of walking that morning behind his plow, the first European plow to work this land. That made him ponder when Jews plowed the land two thousand years before, before they were driven out of the land and sent into exile. That thought led him to dwell on the past one hundred years when Jews dared to return to rebuild their land. Shmuel promised his son that when Moshe grew up they would work the land side by side. If Jewish fathers and sons in Palestine were to act similarly, the father wrote, this would assure Jewish control over the land forever. Undoubtedly this well-intentioned message was not at all what Moshe wanted to hear. He had asked for something practical, a father's approval for a son to come home. Instead he received a bombastic, sentimental statement that must have seemed largely irrelevant. Later in life, Moshe recoiled at the same kind of lofty rhetoric that came pouring in great streams from the lips of his father's generation.

By the spring of 1922 Moshe and Dvorah had returned to Nahalal. The Arabs had not attacked the settlement and it was deemed safe for those in Nazareth to return home. The settlers—now numbering eighty families—had moved out of their tents into huts, and then into cottages. A well-known architect, Richard Kauffmann, had designed Nahalal's new look, placing the settlers' homes in a circle around the center; a certain distance from the circle was a twenty-acre plot of land given to each family for farming. Some features of kibbutz life were retained: Farm facilities were jointly owned and the marketing of produce and the purchasing of supplies was handled cooperatively. Just as Degania became the model for later kibbutzim, so too did Nahalal serve as a precedent for the network of Israel's moshavim. The Dayan cottage had a living room, two bedrooms, kitchen, porch, and a bathtub on the kitchen floor, but an outdoor facility served as the bathroom. When Moshe was eight years old, Shmuel, at Dvorah's insistence, built an add-on to the porch that became the boy's room; he lived in it until his wedding in 1935.

This then was Moshe Dayan's milieu as a child. He was surrounded by families who possessed a special ruggedness, a doggedness that had been born out of their passage from the hardships of Russia to the rigors of Palestine. These founders of Nahalal knew, no less than did the single-minded idealists in the kibbutzim, how they wished to live. While the settlers at Degania and other egalitarian communes in Palestine were quite prepared to submerge their personalities into the whole, Nahalal's residents wanted none of that: They wanted to reserve for themselves the right to decide how to lead their own personal lives.

Apart from his parents, the person who had the greatest influence on young Moshe was a man who arrived one evening at Nahalal a year after its founding. He wore glasses and was dressed in a Russian shirt with a fringed belt tied around his middle. His name was Meshulam Halevy. Hired to teach the moshav's fifteen children, including Moshe, he held classes in the living room of his hut. The youngsters could not get enough of him. His instruction in the Bible had the greatest impact on the children. Meshulam did not simply teach the Bible. He infused each pupil with an infatuation with their Jewish roots. It was as if Meshulam had invented a time machine that could transport the children of Nahalal back thousands of years, to the places where the towering figures of the Bible walked.

From Meshulam's tutoring, Moshe came to appreciate some of the similarities between the present day and the biblical age. The surrounding Jezreel Valley, Mount Gilboa, and the River Jordan were all mentioned in the Bible. The modern-day bedouins, who lived off their sheep, goats, cattle, camels, and asses, emulated Abraham, the first Patriarch. The young Moshe began to identify himself as part of this biblical tradition; he was a link in a chain that carried back thousands of years, of the same people, speaking the same language, emulating the same patterns of work and life. In time, he developed a particularized view of the Bible, identifying with its warriors, and disdainful of the Patriarchs for having fought few battles, for avoiding killing, weapons, blood, casualties. These were not the kind of men about whom one wrote tear-filled poetry. He took special note that the Patriarchs did not exploit their few military successes by seizing enemy territory or settling in it. Their worst sin of all, in his view, was their constant habit of getting themselves out of bad spots by seeking a peaceful resolution. One could almost think that Moshe Dayan might condemn the Patriarchs as weaklings.

MESHULAM DIVIDED the youngsters into three age groups, Moshe, seven years old, was put with the oldest group—the seven- to nine-year-olds. Teaching the "Curriculum for Municipal Schools," which had been proposed by the Education Committee of the Jewish Agency, seemed illogical to Meshulam. The children should learn how to live on a moshav, not prepare themselves for a university. He taught them the Bible, nature, and geometry. That would suffice. The whole outdoors was Meshulam's classroom: He took the children on long hikes, explaining the plants and animals to them. He carried a magnifying glass and a botanical handbook. Always he pointed out the biblical significance of the places he visited. His special expertise lay in painting, music, and poetry. Suddenly the youngsters were performing as a choir or an orchestra. Tone deaf, Moshe did not qualify for the choir. He tried to play a triangle in the orchestra but he would either hit it too early or too late. Meshulam wisely persuaded him to drop out of the orchestra. Above all, Meshulam urged the children to think independently. He suggested that they write for the "Village Children's Newspaper" and keep private diaries. Moshe Dayan's fifth-grade diary remained a treasured memento of Meshulam's for years, its pages yellowed, passages filled with spelling mistakes. The young Moshe wrote vividly and philosophically. Between the lines one could sense his personal struggle with trying to find a place among his peers. In one entry, Moshe wrote: "Slowly the children assemble. There is a suggestion that we go to the wood. As for me, I don't agree with this. There is another suggestion to have our photographs taken, but this depends on Meshulam. We have our photographs taken. The pictures don't come out. We hang about. There is nothing to do." Later his thoughts become deeper, if a bit vague: "In my opinion, every human being has to have an aim in life and he should carry it out exactly. The aim should lead him in the right path."[11] Putting one's innermost thoughts on paper distressed Moshe. Fearful that others would get their hands on his diary, he was cautious about what he confessed: "There are things worth talking and writing about, but they are things that it's not a good idea to make public and for that reason I'm not writing about them. I'm afraid people will read them. Shalom."[12]

Moshe was not Meshulam's favorite. That honor fell to another student, Dov Yermiya, who was two years older than Moshe. Dov was good-looking, played the violin at school parties, and was well-liked by the class, the girls in particular. Meshulam could not help but cast favor on the boy, inducing a jealous Moshe to search for ways to bring Dov down to size. When Dov's father placed his son on his shoulders so that the boy's clothes would not get soiled, Moshe waited patiently for Dov to be put down—and then proceeded to beat the child up. Dov did not fight back but relied upon Meshulam to break up the fisticuffs. Moshe's link with Dov did not end with schoolboy antics. In later years Moshe Dayan met a woman who was married to Dov Yirmiya—and again the two men were at odds with one another.

The fisticuffs were part of Moshe's efforts to be accepted by his schoolmates. So too was his overwhelming self-confidence: From an early age he believed that he knew better than others what was right, and he was not afraid to tell them so. Once, Moshe and his Nahalal schoolmates played a game of soccer against youngsters from a nearby Arab village. When Moshe's team came close to scoring a goal, Benyamin Brenner (who had replaced Meshulam Halevy temporarily) would whistle a foul for the Arabs' side—to preserve some balance in the scoring—until Moshe exploded at him. Brenner was not objective. He was whistling at the wrong time. For that insubordination, Brenner tossed Moshe out of the game.[13]

To his misfortune, Moshe's schoolmates were not overly impressed with him. They found him to be more concerned for himself than for others. And so they looked to others as leadership material, especially

Moshe Betser (who was killed on board a British troopship in 1943) and Amnon Yannai from the senior class; Dov Yirmiya from the junior class; and Nahman Betser, Moshe Betser's younger brother. Though Moshe Dayan possessed a forceful character, he also had trouble expressing himself verbally, and that damaged his popularity. When he spoke, he sounded confused, disorganized, almost as if he were putting his thoughts together as he spoke. He had no such difficulty expressing himself on paper: his diary entries reveal a youngster who wanted not merely to be accepted. He wanted to lead: "I feel I'm getting back into things, that I will hold the reins that guide the children in my hand. . . . I feel more and more that the children are like clay in my hands."[14] Yet another diary entry shows Moshe, in the fifth grade, wrestling with how to assert himself above the crowd: "I see that if I want to be among the most diligent pupils, then I mustn't devote myself to writing essays or to painting. I have to devote myself to one thing because I will always have free time for essays when I want."[15]

He found that he could attract the attention of his school chums by engaging in projects around the settlement. He built his own grafting shed and his own apple nursery; his seedlings were in large demand. But the applause died down too quickly for him. So he indulged in the not-so-charming habits of teasing the girls and picking on older boys. That hardly encouraged his classmates' affection. When it came time to hold class elections, Moshe received fewer votes than the other candidates. Plain and simple, the others found his unfriendliness, his fawning attitude toward some boys, and his bullying, unappealing. He picked on girls as readily as on boys, and never understood what was wrong with using his physical strength to overcome a helpless young female. When one schoolgirl finally spat at him after he had pinned her to a wall, he asked her in great shock why she had done such a thing. Older, larger boys did not intimidate him and if he thought that someone had caused him to lose face, he would challenge that person to a fight. The class got so fed up with Moshe's bullying that they ganged up on him: After throwing him to the ground and stomping on him, they vowed not speak to him for a month.

Shmuel and Dvorah's less-than-esteemed status at Nahalal rubbed off on Moshe and added to his problems with his schoolmates. The Dayans were regarded as slightly disreputable, especially since Shmuel engaged in that most unworthy of pursuits—politics. His real "crime," however, was in overlooking his responsibilities to his farmland. Taking a cue from his father, Moshe often seemed unenthralled with farming—virtually a sin against humanity at Nahalal. The Nahalal settlers took note that Moshe was the only child who had refused to lead the mules to his family's farm plot to eat the first harvest of barley at the moshav; they also would not forget that he had once spread earth over the ground to make it appear that he had been hoeing diligently. Worst of all, few could understand why Moshe needed his own room. For reading and thinking, Shmuel lamely explained to them. But why, the others asked, did a farmer need time to read and think? When Moshe's parents sought approval to hire an English teacher for their child, the settlement turned them down, fearing that once Moshe learned English, he would leave Nahalal. Another source of friction was the frequent commotion at the Dayan household, a veritable social center to which visitors who knew Shmuel from his public life frequently flocked.

His classmates had to admit that Moshe had a rich imagination and a gift for writing. Moshe drew special inspiration from the Russian literary masters. Even before he had learned to read, he was listening to his mother read to him in Hebrew from Dostoyevski, Tolstoy, Pushkin, and Chekhov. When he could read, he devoured their works on his own, relying upon Hebrew translations. Dostoyevski's *Crime and Punishment* was his favorite. Not surprisingly, given the Russian literary influence, the youngster revealed a melancholy, almost morbid mood in his poetry, his troubled response to an uncertain world. One such poem, "The Song of the Harp," was published in the school newspaper when Moshe was ten years old:

> *He plucked the harp so slow,*
> *He plucked a song of woe.*
> *He sat in the tent alone,*
> *In the tent, the wanderer's home.*
> *The tree above his head*
> *Bowed too, as mourning the dead.*
> *The trees all swung and swayed,*
> *By the light of the stars, bright-rayed.*
> *And the harp still played and played.*
> *Beginning, alone and afraid.*

At first it was rejected because Moshe's classmates found the first line unclear; when Meshulam explained the line to the class and praised the whole poem lavishly, the class accepted it for publication. In essays that Moshe wrote for the newspaper, Moshe's thoughts were fanciful yet contemplative and brooding. He was a ten-year-old with the attitudes of a forty-year-old. One example: "Everyone has his star in the sky; everyone has his guardian angel in the sky and for everyone who likes to go outside on a cold winter night as the wetness seeps through his body, wrapped in a coat or his sweater, gazing long hours at the sky, gazing and gazing, everyone like this has a star in the sky, and I too have my star in the sky." Another: "It's raining. Light rain. And I'm sitting and writing, sitting curled up and all wrapped up in my writing. My teeth are fastened together and I'm writing. Only at a time like this can you write so deeply when it's totally quiet in a room. . . ."

For one of the children's newspapers in June 1927 Moshe showed acute powers of description in writing an essay called "The Hangman":

> The hangman walks, his mind full of thoughts, and he re-members . . . as though it happened just this moment. . . . He was then eight years old, and it was a time of rioting, and the king . . . was cruel to his subjects, and the people desired a republic . . . and his father too was among the rebels. One day as he was lying in bed half asleep, his father came to his bedside, kissed his forehead, looked piercingly into his eyes, and asked: 'Shall you renounce your father's teachings?' And he was young then and could not under-stand. Now he is a hangman. Hangman! The words crush and stab . . . he was twenty years old, arrested for having murdered a man, and sentenced to death . . . And he agreed to be a hangman . . . But what is the matter? A stone is pressing upon his heart, pressing and beating down upon him, and he goes into a tavern to drink. Inside, everything is dirt and squalor, vomiting drunkards, and he drinks. The drink is strong, but his emotions are sevenfold stronger.

Indeed, he was a very grown-up twelve year old.

SIGNIFICANTLY, Moshe's first personal encounters with Arabs were ami-able. On school outings he and the other children visited nearby springs and conversed with the Arabs, picking up a few words of Arabic, learning about their ways. When an Arab youngster, Wahash Hanhana of the Arab el-Mazarib tribe, displayed interest in Jewish farming methods, Moshe happily showed the boy what a European plow looked like and let him try it out himself. From such idyllic moments, Moshe soon sensed that his fellow Jews were better off than the Arabs. He found the Arabs enchanting and he respected their stoicism and their innate dignity. Shmuel Dayan felt none of these things. Encountering Arabs, their faces wrapped in a *keffiyeh* so that only their noses and eyes were exposed, Shmuel would say to his son: "Look, they have the eyes of murderers."

But Moshe knew better, knew that his father was freely associating the eyes of the Arabs with the eyes of the Russian police. Moshe found he had no trouble getting along with Arabs. He believed that Jews and Arabs were not inherently different and that no good reason existed for regarding Arabs as superior or inferior to the Jews.

Moshe's first violent confrontation with Arabs occurred when he was twelve years old. While he and some friends were on a horseback ride they came upon four young Arabs guarding a herd of cattle grazing on Nahalal's fields. Without hesitating, Moshe cracked his whip on his horse, and headed straight for the herd, scattering the cattle in all directions. One Arab guard dragged Moshe off his mare and, with help from the other Arabs, beat him badly. Moshe's friends had gone for help and, upon their return, found him bathed in blood. He felt little remorse. "Don't get excited about it," he told the others. "Learn a lesson from it. Next time we'll bring sticks instead of whips. They won't dare trespass on our land again." The episode gained Moshe a reputation for bravery and decisiveness among his young acquaintances, but among Nahalal's elders he was thought reckless.

FOR FARMBOYS at Nahalal, education was not the most critical thing in life. Indeed, it was not at all clear how Moshe and the other children would be able to further their education, if at all, after Meshulam Halevy's primary school. That problem was resolved when, in 1926, a farm school for girls was established at Nahalal by the Women's International Zionist Organization (WIZO). Its first headmistress was Hannah Meisel-Shochat, a stern-looking woman who wore thin metal glasses and a scarf on her head. The school was meant to furnish young women eighteen years and older with the necessary preparation to aid their husbands in farming life. At first, boys were excluded from the two-year course, largely because of their mischievousness. Young Moshe Dayan was a primary offender. When he was fourteen years old, a boy two years older came to live with relatives at Nahalal. He had been kicked out of schools for wild behavior and his family hoped he would settle down. He did not: He began beating up the Nahalal children, girls as well as boys.

It was time for Moshe Dayan to take charge. "It's not right that this fellow tries to gain control," Moshe told his schoolmates, hoping to organize a group who would teach the outsider a lesson. "If we all get together we can defeat him." One eager recruit, Avino'am Slutzky, gave the group its name, Habibi—Hevrat Birionim Yehudim B'Eretz Yisrael. In English, the Society of Jewish Hooligans in the Land of Israel. Moshe organized the boys for a surprise attack against the boy after choir. They beat him to a pulp and for a while the youngster acted less aggressively. Again, Moshe plotted against the troublemaker, this time planning to trick him when he and the other boys were attending a lecture at the WIZO girls school. It was winter and a room was set aside for the boys' muddy boots while they attended a lecture in socks. Ordinarily, the problematic youth would scamper home after such a lecture to avoid a beating from Moshe and his friends; but this time, Moshe arranged for the youth's boots to be removed. After the lecture, the angry youngster asked Slutzky where his boots were. Avino'am went in search and came back—but with only one muddy shoe. Was this one? he asked. Nodding yes, the boy was greeted harshly with a slap of the muddy shoe across his face. Executing the rest of the plan, Moshe and the others jumped on him.

Habibi ruled the roost—at least for a while. No matter how much Mrs. Meisel-Shochat complained to the Nahalal village committee, the boys delighted in stealing the best apples and plums from the school orchards and breaking into the school kitchen to get at the puddings. Seeking revenge for being kicked off school grounds, the boys broke the windows of a classroom. Unprompted, the ringleader of the group—young Moshe Dayan—showed up at the headmistress's office to apologize and to promise to pay for the damage. Sensing that the boy was being truthful and that he possessed leadership qualities, Mrs. Meisel-Shochat agreed to accept him as a pupil for the fall of 1929. Most of Meshulam Halevy's other students chose farm work instead of further studies. A myth grew up that Moshe was the only male student in the girls' school— a myth perpetuated by none other than Shmuel Dayan. But it was merely a myth.

MOSHE'S FATHER invested little time in helping to run the Dayan household. Shmuel Dayan felt hemmed in by life at Nahalal and drew himself increasingly into public affairs, undertaking frequent missions abroad on behalf of the Palestine Jewish community's labor movement. He was saddled with guilt over his inability to stay on the farm. All of that idealism, all of that ideology about getting one's hands dirty and engaging in independent labor, mattered for little in practice. Shmuel did not find farm life very exciting and he yearned to escape. Dvorah gave birth to a daughter named Aviva on February 21, 1922 and a son named Zohar on April 8, 1926. But neither of those events discouraged Shmuel's wanderlust. During 1924 and 1925 he engaged in a tireless search for the financing of Jewish settlement on Rothschild-owned lands on the Horan plateau in Transjordan.

All the while Dvorah was struggling valiantly with the farming chores and child raising, but finding the burden too demanding. After Aviva's birth several years earlier Dvorah had begged the Nahalal villagers to establish a kibbutz-style children's home so that she and other working mothers could free themselves of part of the child-raising chores; her idea was scorned. Dvorah's day began at 4:00 A.M. milking the cows and lasted until 9:00 P.M. But Shmuel's absence was felt: The tomatoes and eggplants rotted in the fields, she had to borrow money to buy medicine and seeds, and a ton and a half of grain went unsold.

Moshe did his share of the farm chores but he never truly liked them. To avoid farm chores, Moshe would sleep late in the morning. When he did the chores, he often excelled. Once, the man who tended cows at Nahalal was away sick and no one could be found to bring one particularly dangerous cow outside of his stall for milking. Then Moshe came along and asked what was the matter. Suddenly, the youngster jumped over a six-foot wall and into the cow's stall. He grabbed the cow by the nose and shouted to the others. "Open the door. What's the problem?" Those who watched Moshe take charge of the difficult cow suggested that this was not simply an illustration of a relaxed and confident farmer. It was an early example of Moshe Dayan's personal courage.

Unable to spare Shmuel the grisly details of farm life, Dvorah wrote to Shmuel, explaining that she had no clothes for the children and that he was badly missed. Her letters had no impact on her itinerant husband. He was off in his own world and his letters reflected a man who seemed to have forgotten that he had a wife and children back home on the farm. As the Jewish holiday of Hanukkah approached in 1925, Dvorah employed Moshe in her campaign to lure Shmuel home. "I'm sure you will send us something," the boy wrote, "but it will not take your place. A holiday without a father is not a holiday." Unwilling to leave Europe, Shmuel had the bright idea that Dvorah, Moshe, and Aviva would come live with him. Well into her third pregnancy, Dvorah would have none of it. Shmuel only returned home in the summer of 1926, several months after the birth of his son Zohar.

Toward his mother, Moshe felt pity. He esteemed the noble manner with which she carried her burden. He was grateful to her for giving him an intellectual curiosity, a literary streak, a love of reading, and a desire for solitude and reflection. Toward his father, Moshe dared not write in later years what he truly felt and so he wrote almost nothing. When others wrote that he and his father did not get along, Moshe became furious. Yet those who wrote this came uncomfortably close to the truth.

The difficulties with his father actually began when Moshe was a small boy. One night when Moshe was five, Shmuel locked Moshe in the Degania chicken coop for not doing what he had been told to do. "You will stay here until you obey," Shmuel told the boy. Strange sounds emanated from the chicken coop. Jackals prowled around outside. Moshe was shivering from the cold. He was frightened, but he did not give in. After a number of hours his father set him free—"without my obeying him," Moshe proudly and defiantly noted later.

Shmuel had no real rapport with Moshe. When the boy spoke to him, tried to convince him of something, he refused to listen, refused to acknowledge every once in a while that his son just might be right. That rubbed Moshe the wrong way. He had little respect for his father's mind: Moshe felt he was always talking in nonsensical formulas, always spouting truisms, unopen to argument. It was different with Dvorah. She was open to discussion. Sometimes she showed Moshe that his arguments were wrong, and sometimes she even admitted that he was right.

Dvorah had come to Palestine thinking of herself as a revolutionary. She had a keen mind, a great love of literature, and a talent for writing, but she devoted her life to the farm and her children, unable to fight off the yoke of troubles Shmuel had left for her while he traveled. She felt herself a martyr, and admitted to herself on reflection that she had little chance of fulfilling her own intellectual ambitions. Fed up by the late 1920s with Shmuel's insistence on staying away from home for long periods, Dvorah sought to take one small step. She began writing articles for *Dvar Hapoelet,* the Hebrew-language working women's newspaper. She called her first article "My Immigration" and her editors liked what she did well enough to offer her a post on the newspaper's editorial board. She accepted even though it meant leaving the children at home on their own while she ventured off to Tel Aviv for meetings. Dvorah continued to press Shmuel to return home; she and Moshe even wrote to him in the United States, where he had gone to promote Zionism among American Jews. They threatened not to send letters anymore unless he promised to return at once. The threats were in vain.

Moshe was now fourteen years old, and taking cognizance of the world around him. Arab riots in Hebron and at the Western Wall in Jerusalem in 1929 aroused his interest. When the British sent a royal commission to Palestine to gather testimony on what could be done to alleviate the tensions, Moshe followed the probe through the newspapers with mounting interest. Reading each word of the testimony, he would then pass judgment on who had spoken well and who had not. It was the first evidence of his budding interest in politics.

♦ 2 ♦

UNSHEATHING THE SWORD

MOSHE DAYAN handled a gun for the first time at the age of ten. As long as the Arabs sought to take over fields belonging to the Jewish settlements, a youngster from Nahalal needed to be as familiar with a rifle as with a hoe. At first Moshe was permitted to watch his father clean his German carbine, covertly wrapped in an oiled cloth. Then Shmuel allowed him to clean and later load it. Finally, father and son took tin cans and empty bottles and Moshe had his first target practice. Boys Moshe's age learned how to shoot, but they had little chance to use anything other than a pistol.

Shooting was a skill Moshe would soon need. Mounting Arab attacks against Jews had led the yishuv, the Jewish community in Palestine, to form a defense organization called the Haganah ("Defense") in June 1920—clandestine from the start because the British prohibited Jews from carrying arms. Throughout the 1920s and 1930s, yishuv leaders debated how much force to use against the Arabs. The relative quiet of the 1920s had lulled yishuv leaders into giving defense efforts a low priority. Many of these leaders opposed the use of force except for self-defense.

Opposition lessened after the violent Arab assault on Jewish worshipers at the Western Wall in Jerusalem on August 23, 1929 and, a few days later, the Arab massacre of fifty-nine Jews in Hebron. Worried that Jewish settlements around the country could face similar Arab violence, the

Haganah brought Nahalal under its wing; so at the age of fourteen, Moshe Dayan, proud and pleased, was recruited into this secret group. He was given instruction in handling a pistol and in judo. His first post was as a sentry to warn Nahalal's adults, engaged in secret training, if the British were approaching.

More exciting work was in store. Along with four other Nahalal teenagers, Moshe learned military equestrianship from two members of Nahalal who had served in the Russian army. He looked less than soldierly in his short pants and sandals, but the rifle slung over his left shoulder was enough to give Moshe a military appearance. His four fellow equestrians were Nahman Betser, Avino'am Slutzky, Amnon Yannai, and Dov Yermiya. When bedouin tribesmen brought their goats to pasture on Nahalal's wheat fields, the five boys on horseback went into action. Their escapades won them a certain local fame. Usually when the boys, screaming and brandishing their whips, came upon the trespassers, the bedouin shepherds would flee, leaving their flocks behind. Once, a shepherd remained behind, seemingly oblivious of the stones the boys were throwing at him or to the whip Moshe was cracking over his head. Moshe was about to strike the youngster but pulled back when he realized to his great surprise that the shepherd was none other than his Arab friend Wahash. Moshe beat a hasty, embarrassed retreat.

Meanwhile, he put in long hours with the Haganah, pleased that it offered a way out of the drudgery of farm life, and carried with it a prestige and dignity that milking cows did not. He was perfectly willing to invest late evenings in his Haganah work. All Dvorah could do was pour her heart out in letters to Shmuel about this fifteen-year-old youngster who had fallen totally under the influence of the "Martial Law," in the ambiguous phrase used by Dvorah to describe the Haganah's efforts.

The Haganah was taking defense matters more seriously because, by the early 1930s, the rules of the game between Jews and Arabs were changing: Trespassing disputes, once the dominant source of their conflict, had given way to politically motivated Arab assaults. Arab nationalist concerns were awakened by a demographic fact: The Jews were becoming a majority in Palestine. Jews from Poland and Germany streamed in to avoid oppression: In the mid-1930s 165,000 European Jews settled in Palestine. The change in Arab sensibilities became all too apparent to the Nahalal settlers when, in December 1932, an Arab threw a bomb into the hut of Yosef Ya'akobi, one of the Dayans' neighbors. The bomb killed Ya'akobi's eight-year-old son at once; the next morning Yosef died of his wounds. Though Shmuel Dayan had hammered away at convincing his son that all Arabs were violent and, given the chance, would attack the Jewish settlers, Moshe thought such a generalization overly simplistic: He exhibited curiosity about what really drove the Arabs to violence. Rather fearlessly, he visited the Arab village of Zippori near Nazareth, the headquarters for the very Arabs who had attacked the Ya'akobi home. Moshe wanted to believe that Jewish-Arab comity could prevail despite such wicked men. Toward his Arab neighbors he held positive, friendly feelings, valuing the Arabs as hard workers who were devoted to the land, as he was. Their way of life appealed to him. He had no doubt that peaceful co-existence was possible between Jew and Arab. Such optimistic views were in striking contrast with the attitude expressed by many other members of the yishuv, who did not really like the Arabs and viewed them strictly as adversaries. They had no time or taste for their culture nor any wish to get close to them.

MOSHE DAYAN displayed an early distaste for politics and political parties, which he equated with the excessive verbiage of the older generation of yishuv politicians. This attitude placed him in growing disfavor with the political establishment. Sparking matters was the attempt by Hanoar Ha'oved, the Histadrut's youth arm, to organize a branch in Nahalal. (The Histadrut was a powerful labor federation that became the leading political institution of the yishuv.) Moshe and his young friends at the settlement resisted the overture, bothered by a feeling that Hanoar Ha'oved was designed for children from the city. When labor movement leaders learned of this rebuff, they dispatched Israel Galili, a founder of the youth arm, to try to get Moshe and his friends to change their minds. Galili got nowhere. The appearance of an article in the movement's journal attacking the Nahalal youth for lacking character, public-mindedness, and displaying "destructive negativism" added fuel to the fire. When Moshe responded with his own article in the journal, defending the spirit of Nahalal, he quickly became an unofficial spokesman for Nahalal's youngsters and other moshav youngsters in the yishuv. By the summer of 1933, the labor movement's three-year-old political party, known as Mapai—Mifleget Poalei Eretz Yisrael or the Land of Israel Workers' Party—was busy trying to recruit the Nahalal youngsters to join. Though Moshe and some of the other young people at Nahalal had misgivings, the recruiting campaign was successful.

IT WAS A GRAMOPHONE and some records that boosted Moshe's social life. Shmuel had purchased the items in the United States. Once Moshe's friends heard about the acquisitions, they flocked to the Dayan home, particularly on Friday evenings and Saturday afternoons. A sixteen-year-old Nahalal girl named Chaya Rubinstein was Moshe's first romantic interest. Too shy at first to approach her, he eventually asked her for notes from school lessons he had missed. They began preparing lessons together and one day he asked her home to listen to records. During one of her visits he whispered in her ear, suggesting they go for a walk. A mild reprimand followed: If Moshe wanted to come for a walk with her, Chaya asserted formally, he would have to ask her properly. When he did so, they began taking walks that lasted for hours. By the spring of 1932, however, the romance had cooled and he had stopped seeing Chaya.

A year later, during the summer of 1933, a serious romance developed between Moshe and one of the students at the WIZO agricultural school at Nahalal. Yehudit Wigodsky, nicknamed Yuka, was older and taller than Moshe but he was thoroughly taken with her. She had graduated from the school that summer and then returned to live in her parents' home in Rishon l'Zion. It was a happy coincidence for Moshe that he had been offered work in Tel Aviv, permitting him to be closer to his girlfriend. Throughout 1933 Moshe had engaged in various kinds of labor, which included helping to build the first forty permanent houses at Nahalal. He found the construction work exhausting, particularly as he was expected to pitch in with farm chores as well. The pay was meager, so when the houses were completed that autumn and the engineer of the housing project offered Moshe and seven other Nahalal young men higher-paying jobs in Tel Aviv, they accepted. During the day Moshe erected scaffolding at building sites in Tel Aviv and neighboring Ramat Gan. During the evenings he studied draftsmanship, algebra, and geometry at the Technion Night School and the Popular University.

He had more on his mind than just studies. Often after work he took the bus to Rishon l'Zion; he and Yuka would then return to Tel Aviv by bus, for a movie or a walk on the beach. He took the bus twice more later in the evening, escorting Yuka home to Rishon, then returning to his own home in Tel Aviv. Each of those four bus rides took an hour. All this traveling led Moshe to believe—as opposed to the prevailing attitude among other young men—that marriage was essential. Some of Moshe's friends lived with their girlfriends, but being of a somewhat puritanical bent in these early years, he had remained a virgin and believed in the sanctity of the family unit. As for Yuka, she too liked the idea of marriage, but believed she was too young. She preferred to wait. Faced with that, Moshe changed hs mind about taking a vow of chastity before marriage: He encouraged Yuka to sleep with him. When she said no, he gave her an ultimatum: Either they were to get married or, failing that, sleep together. Otherwise, he would leave her. Ultimately, they split up, but agreed that it would be only temporary—to test their true feelings for one another. Their separation, however, became permanent, most likely because Yuka wanted to spare herself the drudgery of being married to a farmer.

AS MUCH AS HE liked the tranquillity that farm life signified, Moshe Dayan was not fated to be a farmer. He was born to participate in life around him, to shun the passive existence represented by the hoe and the sickle; above all, to engage his natural curiosity in the problems that hovered over his fellow Jews and the local Palestinian Arab population like a coming storm. The first real indication of Moshe's desire to engage himself in the larger sweep of life was the journey he embarked upon in September 1934, a journey that was as much a rite of personal passage as it was a hike through the desert.

Returning to Nahalal that summer from Tel Aviv, he found that there was free time between the plowing and the sowing for some adventure. The journey was not meant to take place in the desert at all. It was instead planned as a hike to Mount Hermon in the north; but when so few of the other Nahalal youngsters were prepared to join Moshe on the trip, out of concern for the rising tension between Jews and Arabs, it was scrapped. Moshe then turned to a pair of youngsters in a lower class, Binyamin Zarhi and Baruch Zemel. They agreed upon a far more ambitious itinerary, to hike south via Beit-Shean, following the Jordan River to Jericho, then along the Dead Sea to Sedom (biblical Sodom); westward to Hebron, Beersheba, and aiming for Gaza on the Mediterranean coast. The danger-filled travel plan sent shudders through the Nahalal settlers, who urged the commune's security officials to cancel the trip. Moshe and his two friends were determined to proceed.

Taking two canteens each, one camera, hard-boiled eggs, tins of sardines, extra clothes, a map, and five Palestinian pounds, they set off. Throughout their first day of travel they were forced to drink large quantities of water due to the incredible heat. By nightfall, when they had reached a wadi near the northern end of the Dead Sea, the boys' canteens were nearly empty. They realized they must get themselves to the Jordan River, though it would mean venturing perilously close to a bedouin camp. Moving carefully toward the river, they accidentally wound up in the middle of that very camp. Moshe's companions wanted to make a dash for safety but he insisted they stay. He shouted a familiar Arabic greeting, *"Ya zalame, ya zlam, ya nass!"* ("Oh men, oh man, oh people.") Gazing at the boys' leather canteen straps, the bedouins thought they were policemen and remained quiet. Moshe and his friends discovered an old Arab shaking with fear inside a tent. He gave the boys water. Returning to the main road, Moshe and his friends quickly fell asleep.

Awakening, the boys headed westward toward the Jiftlik Valley but, losing their way, they entered Wadi Fatsa'el and were now in worse trouble than before: Low on water, they were unclear how far they were from the Jordan. At this point in the tale, accounts of the participants vary: In Moshe Dayan's version, as recounted in *Story of My Life,* the three boys came upon an Arab shepherd and his flock. When they asked for water, he escorted them to a nearby bedouin encampment. There they were brought to the tent of the chief, Emir Diab, given water, and advised for their own safety to accompany one of the bedouins who happened to be traveling by donkey to Jericho. They did so, and from Jericho moved on to Sedom. Binyamin Zarhi, however, recalled that when the three boys approached a bedouin spring at Jiftlik, the emir of the bedouins suddenly appeared on horseback, carrying a rifle. He aimed the gun at the boys and asked what they were doing.

"There is a blood revenge going on between Jews and Arabs," he said menacingly.

Zarhi and Zemel stammered in fear. Moshe, however, ignored the Arab's words and the pointed gun: He broke into a big smile and greeted the horseman "good morning" in Arabic, acting as if he were meeting an old friend. Moshe then whipped out a camera and took a picture of his newly won friend. Before they knew it, the boys were being served coffee, pita, and cheese.[1] Both Dayan and Zarhi agreed later that the emir offered the boys a young Arab escort on to Jericho.

Determined to continue on the trip, Moshe soon needed the same diplomatic skills. Approaching Jericho, the three boys and the bedouin escort encountered two Arab policemen who grew suspicious at finding three Jews annd a bedouin. They beat up the bedouin just to show him who was in charge, and then searched the boys' belongings, figuring they were illegal Jewish immigrants. Preparing to take the "illegals" to the Nablus police station, the policemen were taken aback by Moshe's declaration in Arabic that they were not illegal immigrants and would not go with them.

Moshe asked one of the policemen his name.

"Jabber," the man replied.

Moshe gave this a moment's thought. "Are you related to the Jabber who works for the Nahalal police?"

"Indeed I am. He is my brother."

That broke the ice. Suddenly they exchanged friendly handshakes.

After the bedouin left them, the boys moved on to Kalya on the northwestern tip of the Dead Sea. There they met someone who had been a baker at Kibbutz Degania. He advised them to scrub their plans to travel south to Sedom. A group of Jewish hikers had headed there recently and had not been heard of since. Taking the advice—at least for the time being—the boys hitched a ride on Kalya's bus to Jerusalem. The next morning, they took an Arab bus to Hebron, where they planned to set out on foot for Sedom. But they rerouted themselves, taking an Arab taxi to Beersheba and then a bus to Gaza. No sooner had they arrived at Gaza port than they were arrested by Arab policemen who suspected them of being illegal Jewish immigrants. Moshe was not intimidated: He asked the interrogating officer for his name and wrote it in a notebook. Eventually freed, the boys reached Tel Aviv, where Moshe decided that their adventures were worth recording for posterity, an early example of his keen sense of public relations. Getting some newspaper coverage would, he reasoned, garner the boys some well-earned prestige back home in Nahalal. The three boys arrived at the building of the newspaper *Davar;* but Moshe waited outside. With a large pimple on his chin he was in no mood to see strangers. So the other two boys recounted the tale to Zalman Shazar, assistant editor of *Davar*, and later president of the state of Israel from 1963 to 1973. Shazar listened intently and proceeded to write a news story that appeared on the front page of the newspaper the next day—September 17, 1934. By the time the three boys had returned to Nahalal, families and friends had passed the *Davar* story around—and, as Moshe had hoped, he and his friends were local heroes.

A new woman student from Jerusalem began her relationship with Moshe Dayan in the summer of 1934—only neither one of them knew it. Ruth Schwartz had arrived at Nahalal to attend the WIZO agricultural school. But just before school was to start, she had attended a summer camp at Nahalal for members of the Socialist Youth Movement. She had been cautioned by her kibbutznik camp adviser to pay no attention to the young fellows from the moshav—"and especially, see that you stay away from the boys of two families here—the Dayan family and the Uri family." Ruth had only a vague idea what the Dayan and Uri boys looked like. When a young man whom she believed to be an Uri lectured the camp on the structure of the moshav, she was suitably impressed with his message and with his personal style. She was interested in getting to know him, despite her adviser's warning. What she did not know until later was that the speaker was Moshe Dayan.

They did not meet then—they were sitting at opposite ends of the bonfire. Nor did they meet at the next campfire. But a few weeks later, when Ruth arrived for the opening of the school, she managed to meet "this Uri fellow." In the coming weeks she learned more about him—

for one thing that his real name was Moshe Dayan—and what she found out, she liked. Whatever he said seemed important, he smelled good, a fresh and clean aroma "like that of fresh milk and new mown hay."[2] He was different from the other young men: He had plowed a frozen field before daybreak, he could handle a scythe and knew how to make things grow. She found him intelligent and handsome. His love of Tolstoy and Dostoyevski moved her. They became better acquainted when the WIZO school and Nahalal formed a "Committee of Two" to organize joint sports events: Moshe and Ruth. Though they never planned a single sports event, they did find it a useful excuse to spend more and more time together.

Ruth was falling in love with Moshe, and at the same time drawing closer and closer to the Dayan household. She met Moshe's father Shmuel and watched in shock at the way he drank nine cups of tea in one sitting. Dvorah, looking as though she had stepped out of a Russian novel, made the stronger impression on her. Ruth loved the literary discussions— and adored the food: the fresh salads, the home-baked bread, the rich farm cream and butter. When Dvorah offered to pay Ruth to take over the scrubbing and darning while she attended meetings of the Working Womens' Council in Tel Aviv, Ruth accepted. This angered Moshe. He disliked his mother's absences and grew annoyed that his mother had created a business connection with his girlfriend.

BY THE END of 1934 the nineteen-year-old Moshe had settled into farm life, discovering that plowing the land was not enough: It had to be defended as well. Until now he had largely avoided violent encounters with Arabs. But the very act of tilling the soil near Nahalal brought him into confrontation with the neighboring el-Mazarib bedouin tribe. Led by Binyamin Zarhi, Moshe and others started to plow land bordering on Wadi Shimron, believing they had a perfect right to farm this land: The Jewish National Fund had, after all, purchased it from an Arab landowner, allocating the land to Nahalal. The bedouins challenged that right. Along the slopes above, members of the el-Mazarib tribe, including Moshe's friend Wahash, gathered in growing fury to watch the Jewish farmers down below. Reinforced with Arabs from the nearby village of Mahlul, the bedouins pelted Moshe and the other farmers with rocks, leading Moshe and his group to toss their own rocks. Someone struck Moshe on the head with a club. He fell to the ground unconscious. Had the attacker been Wahash? Moshe would later write that he had that impression. Others believed it had been someone else. At any event, Moshe was put on a horse and returned to Nahalal, where, upon recovering consciousness, he reported that he had completed his mission. Only then was he prepared to have someone dress the wound. He recuperated at first in the infirmary, then at home, and finally at a convalescent home in Jerusalem. Once again, Moshe had been involved in an incident that was on the lips of everyone at Nahalal—and other settlements as well. Moshe Dayan drew no special military lessons from the encounter. He was still very much a novice in the art of fighting.

MOSHE HAD NO DOUBT that he wanted Ruth to be a part of his future. He faced one obstacle: her parents. They had hoped their daughter would marry a university graduate with a bright future rather than a farmer from Nahalal with little education. They resigned themselves to Moshe—and then encouraged him to get an education. Moshe and Ruth were unsure of where to live. Ruth was devoted to the kibbutz way of life but Moshe, despising the kibbutzim, pictured the two of them dwelling on one of the new tension-filled border settlements. When Ruth picked up an infection that winter, she went home to Jerusalem for two weeks. Moshe wrote to her every day, describing how difficult his work routine was, but he had a fire, a kettle, a letter from Ruth, and Dostoyevski: "How he purifies one with his concept of suffering."[3] Then he urged her to forgo thoughts about living on a kibbutz: "You'll just end up ruining your life. You'll marry some fool, have six children, and then get divorced."

Ruth did not doubt that she wanted to spend the rest of her life together with Moshe. For young settlers, though, marriage was for later. Remarkably, Ruth encouraged Moshe Dayan to marry another woman! For years Moshe and Ruth never mentioned the story of Moshe's first marriage, and only in 1972, when Ruth published her memoirs, . . . Or Did I Dream a Dream?, did the truth emerge. They had remained silent all that time not out of embarrassment but indifference. For them, Ruth's initiative just did not seem important. However, the story is important given Ruth's relationship with Moshe at the time. Ruth and Moshe, after all, appeared to be headed for marriage. Ruth's proposal to find Moshe a wife, if implemented, might well have prevented Ruth from marrying her true love. In making the proposal Ruth thought she was just being charitable and Zionist.

In a sense she was. The bride in question was a German Jewish woman named Wilhelmina—no one recalls her last name—who had been living in Haifa, a friend of Ruth's German roommates at school. It was the spring of 1934 and Wilhelmina possessed a temporary permit to remain in Palestine; when it expired in the fall, she would be forced to return to Nazi Germany, unless she could find a husband. Marrying someone Jewish from Palestine would enable her to stay. It all seemed so perfect to Ruth, who, figuring that her Moshe was a suitable guinea pig for this piece of fiction, suggested to him that he marry Wilhelmina. Moshe was disinterested in marrying anyone, let alone Wilhelmina. He had never met her and he understood that she was unattractive, ten years his senior, and spoke only German. Then of course he was romantically involved with Ruth.

Moshe had an obligation to marry the young woman, argued Ruth, if only to help build and strengthen the country. Moshe grudgingly caved in. Delighted, Ruth contacted Wilhelmina and the rabbi in Nahalal, and a date was set. After arriving in Nahalal by bus from Haifa, Wilhelmina was greeted by Ruth, who introduced her to Moshe. The prospective bride and groom could not exchange a word—Ruth did some translating between Hebrew and German. After the ceremony, Wilhelmina, now protected against being tossed out of Palestine, headed back for Haifa; Moshe went back to the cow shed.

He was determined to get away from Nahalal, perhaps to get more schooling. Ruth's parents, thinking this a good idea, presented Moshe and Ruth with a gift: a trip to England. There was only one problem. Moshe and Ruth could not travel as an unmarried couple, it was not done. Ruth's parents insisted that the young couple—Moshe was twenty years old, Ruth sixteen—marry before going abroad. Moshe, however, was already married. If Moshe and Ruth were to wed, Wilhelmina had to be located, and speedily. Ruth's altruistic deed had implications for her relationship with Moshe. Had the German woman left the country without informing Moshe of her whereabouts, he would not have been able to divorce her and would have been committing bigamy had he tried to marry Ruth. Luckily for Ruth and Moshe she was located, and Moshe and Wilhelmina Dayan were divorced with the same suddenness and indifference that they married.

Moshe and Ruth married on July 12, 1935. The day held special significance for the Dayan family: This was the same day that Ruth's parents had married twenty years earlier; it would also be the same day on which Moshe and Ruth's three children would marry. That morning Moshe had harvested grapes especially for the wedding celebration. He then donned khaki trousers, khaki cap, sandals, and a short-sleeved shirt. Nahalal's rabbi Zechariah performed the ceremony. Attending were such Jewish luminaries as Dr. Arthur Ruppin, a founding father of Jewish farming settlement in Palestine; Dov Hos, a senior figure in the Jewish Agency; and Moshe Sharett, then head of the Jewish Agency's Political Department. Moshe had invited the el-Mazarib tribe, but at a council to discuss the invitation, some members of the tribe believed it best not to attend. For one thing, Arabs did not routinely show up at Jewish weddings; for another, some worried that they would be attacked in revenge for the injury they had inflicted upon Moshe the previous winter. The tribe's elders, who had concluded that Moshe Dayan was a man of great bravery, a genuine hero, thought it nonsense that he would harm the tribe. So they came to the wedding.

At the start, one of the tribesmen, Abdullah Mustapha, shook Moshe's hand to make a *sulha*, a gesture of peace. With that over, the bedouins made their presence felt. They leaped on their horses, shouting and laughing, every once in a while firing off their guns in the air to mark the celebration. They danced the *debka*, as a flute played in the background. Unbeknownst to them, the new bride, having made a startling discovery, was off engaged in—farm work! In the excitement everyone had overlooked that the cows had to be milked. Ruth put on her shorts and a work shirt and rushed over to the cow shed.

MOSHE DISLIKED receiving wedding gifts, but he could not turn down Zvi and Rachel Schwartz's offer to finance their boat trip to England and provide them with a monthly allowance of fifteen British pounds. The Schwartzes had an ulterior motive. They hoped Moshe would study and return with a good knowledge of English. On his British-Palestinian passport Moshe described himself as a farmer, five feet eight inches tall, with black hair and brown eyes.

Following the wedding, he and Ruth set sail for Marseilles on the S.S. *Marietta Pasha;* they took the train to Paris, then London. Moshe was an unprepared tourist. When a porter offered to carry his luggage, he refused; when apprised of the custom of putting his shoes outside the door of his Paris hotel room to be polished, he declined. By the time he and Ruth had arrived in London that September, several of Zvi Schwartz's contacts had begun trying to help Moshe secure a place in a British university. Moshe's credentials were unimpressive. He was a graduate of a two-year course at the girls' school at Nahalal and he did not possess a secondary-school diploma.

For Ruth, their arrival in London was a homecoming. She had lived there for seven years as a child while her parents were studying at London University. She needed little time for adjustment. She was fluent in English and quickly found a job teaching Hebrew. For Moshe, however, their six-month stay in England was a disaster. According to Ruth, he hated the whole experience.[4] This first departure from home killed Moshe

Dayan's appetite for such journeys. Though his public career in later years required extensive travel, he never liked being abroad: He constantly compared foreign styles, facilities, and food unfavorably to what he had been accustomed to back home. From the moment Moshe and Ruth rented an apartment in Finsbury Park, he found London distressing. His eyes began to hurt him from the dirty fog, and lacking English, he could not find part-time work. A farmboy down to the soles of his sandaled feet, Moshe did not take to wearing shoes, nor could he get used to putting on a coat, a tie, or an overcoat. Rebelling against English dress codes, he reverted to his native style: open-necked shirt, trousers, and sandals. He could not completely ignore the cold London winter. He grudgingly wore shoes instead of sandals, and an overcoat, but without the jacket underneath. When Ruth urged the headmaster at the religious school where she taught Hebrew to hire Moshe, he said no on two counts: Moshe did not wear a skullcap (as was required at the school) nor did he possess sufficient English. His inability to master English gnawed at him. He disliked having to be dependent upon Ruth for basic conversation and asking directions.

He had little inclination toward academic life either. Thanks to Zvi Schwartz's connections with Harold Laski, the English political theorist who lectured at the London School of Economics, and Chaim Weizmann, the head of the Jewish Agency, Moshe was accepted at the London School of Economics. Laski and Weizmann also arranged for him to study agriculture at Cambridge once he passed entrance examinations. He did take some correspondence courses at the London School of Economics but found them of no value and of little interest. Shmuel Dayan, in his letters to Moshe, very cleverly sought to instill a sense of guilt about Moshe's leaving the deteriorating Nahalal farm. The elder Dayan chided his son for taking up the easy life—pocketing a monthly allowance without having to work for it. Ruth wanted to remain in London. She urged Moshe to take the university entrance examinations, but he had little incentive to remain. Later he claimed that he had truly wanted to study but the lack of a high-school degree had held him back. From what is known about how little Moshe enjoyed living abroad, such an assertion seems disingenuous.

In March 1936 Moshe and Ruth returned to Palestine. What encouraged Moshe to return was the news that some of his friends planned to build a new farm settlement on a hill called Shimron, just a half-hour walk from Nahalal; the new one hundred–acre kibbutz outpost would overlook the moshav. What with the built-in constraints at Nahalal—a scarcity of space and the proviso that only one son could take over the parents' farm—it was only natural that these, the other sons of Nahalal, would want to set up their own commune. There, they would farm and help defend the growing yishuv.

THE YISHUV was growing. It had numbered only 60,000 in 1919 but had swelled to 350,000 by 1935. The British had allowed the Jewish populace to establish a Va'ad Leumi—a National Council—as well as a Jewish Agency. The Agency was to work with the British in implementing the pledge of the Balfour Declaration to establish a Jewish national home. The Arabs looked upon that declaration as an infringement of their own rights in Palestine; at best, they were prepared to view the document as entitling the Jews to a limited Jewish minority in the Holy Land. To the British, the Jews were to blame for the increase in Jewish-Arab tension in Palestine, if only because they insisted on the right of immigration. By way of demonstrating that the country was large enough for Jews and Arabs to live together, no matter how many Jews arrived from abroad, the yishuv encouraged Jewish youngsters to establish settlements in the remote and hazardous segments of Palestine. Accordingly, between 1936 and 1939 thirty-six "stockade-and-tower" settlements were built, so called because of their fortifications and the thirty-six-foot-high watchtowers, topped by searchlights, which ringed the settlements.

The Arabs were beginning to stir from their slumber. Between 1936 and 1939 the Arab Revolt occurred, a bloody period when Arab assaults against the yishuv claimed the lives of 550 Jews and left 2,500 other Jews wounded. Some 2,200 Arabs were killed by British and Jewish forces along with 140 British. Beginning in April 1936 the Arabs started to riot under the command of the mufti of Jerusalem, Haj Amin el-Husseini, and the Arab Higher Committee. For the next three years the assaults continued, as Arabs killed Jews on the streets and carried out raids against the outlying Jewish settlements. The few thousand feckless British did little to interfere, no match for the lightly armed and fast-moving Arab guerrillas. The only force keeping the Arabs at bay was the twenty-five thousand–strong Haganah. Realizing that they alone could not contain the Arabs, the British reluctantly permitted the Haganah to guard the Jewish farm settlements around the country. For some time they also supplied the Haganah with light weapons.

In July 1937 the six-member Peel Commission, appointed by the British to improve Jewish-Arab relations in Palestine, issued a 404-page report, recommending that the British Mandate be replaced by separate Jewish and Arab states. Though dismayed at the small amount of territory conceded to them, the Jews grudgingly accepted the plan; at least the Jews were pleased to have some control over immigration. The Arabs were contemptuous of the plan and immediately stepped up their armed assaults.

The yishuv was split in its thinking over how to deal with the mounting Arab violence. Some, including Shmuel Dayan, urged self-restraint, believing that cooperation with the British would lead the British to side with the yishuv against the Arabs. Others, led by David Ben-Gurion, chairman of the Jewish Agency Executive, wanted a more aggressive approach and urged the strengthening of the Haganah. When the Arabs began attacking the Iraq Petroleum Company's pipeline that ran through the Jezreel Valley to the port terminal at Haifa, the British unleashed a campaign to suppress Arab guerrilla warfare. Reluctantly, the British also agreed that several thousand Jews (secretly members of the Haganah) could form a new Jewish defense group called the Supernumerary Police. The creation of this settlement police force bolstered the Haganah by giving weapons training to the Haganah men.

Also in that year, in May, searching for a compromise, the British announced a White Paper that would permit fifteen thousand Jews to immigrate annually to Palestine over the following five years, after which further Jewish immigration would be halted altogether. Prior to this, immigration had been unlimited. Jewish land purchase would be scaled back dramatically. For the yishuv leadership, the White Paper was tantamount to the renunciation of the Balfour Declaration.

THE SIX FOUNDING members of Shimron, none more than twenty-two years old, lived at first in five huts when the settlement was founded. Ruth joined the four other young women in housekeeping chores: cooking, laundry, mending, and taking care of the vegetable garden. Moshe and Ruth were the only married couple in the settlement. He found kibbutz life not to his liking—"emotional partnership, sociability and absolute egalitarianism were not in keeping with my nature."[5] While Ruth was told that she would eventually be accepted as a full member, Moshe was given only "candidate" status and was placed on a six-month trial. He found the provisional status demeaning—and inconsequential. He eventually agreed to the candidate role. Still, on August 12, 1936, he sat on his camp bed in Afula, where he had been serving with the British, and wrote to Nahman Betser, the dominant figure in the Shimron group: "I cannot and do not wish to be in the position of being tested . . . if you believe in my capability and good will—fine. If not— then not. I may not succeed in conforming to the ideal you have set for yourselves, though personally I don't think that should be necessary. What is important is that one sincerely wishes to live an honest life within the group, that one should support the continuing development of the society and the settlement, work hand in hand with the others, not look for the easiest work or the best position, and that one should be frank and open with everyone. That, in fact, is all. Keep well, Moshe." There is in this personal testament an early, crucial glimpse into Moshe Dayan's personality. He had no wish to be tested, did not wish to be held to anyone else's standard. He should be accepted for what he is—or not accepted. He asked nothing more.

Life at Shimron developed into a routine for Moshe and Ruth. From the oak logs, Moshe built furniture for their small room. Ruth worked in the sheep pen; Moshe did night guard duty. When he finished at 3:00 A.M. he headed for the kitchen to prepare eggs for himself and an onion omelet with potatoes on the side for Ruth. He would then wake her. Ruth would then eat, and milk the goats. Moshe fell asleep. The commune brought in some income from afforestation work, supplied by the Jewish National Fund under contract, in the nearby Nazareth hills.

That routine ended in March 1937 for Moshe. It was then that he drifted away from Shimron and began his life of soldiering. His task was to serve as a guide for the British army units stationed in Afula in the Jezreel Valley in the heart of Palestine. He joined the British soldiers on their patrols as they tried to protect the Iraq Petroleum Company pipeline that stretched through the valley to the port terminal at Haifa. One of the main lifelines of the British empire, the pipeline was a popular target for Arab attacks. Dayan was paid eight Palestine pounds a month. Most of the week he lived in a British army camp in Afula, going home one night a week to Shimron. Though he was passing through the first serious stage in his military career, he envisaged the work as only a temporary assignment, not as a factor that would keep him from setting up his own home with Ruth. To his great sorrow, he was passed over for the post of regional commander at Shimron despite the fact that he was regarded as the best-suited militarily. The post carried with it the chance to attend the Haganah platoon leaders' course during the summer of 1937—something Dayan very much wanted to do, but now could not. Popularity counted more in the selection. Nahman Betser was chosen. For the next eight months, until December 1937, Dayan served with the King's Own Scottish Borderers and then with the Yorkshire Fusiliers.

The pipeline, just a foot or so underground, was an easy target: The Arabs would spill oil on the ground near the pipe, fire their rifles, puncturing a hole in the pipe, then heave a flaming weighted sack at the spot. The conflagration could last for days. The British were inept: They did no serious reconnaissance work, and they patrolled the pipeline without varying their routine, enabling the Arabs to learn the patterns without difficulty. Even small details such as the need for lightweight uniforms escaped their attention. It was a painful but vital lesson for Moshe Dayan. To fight saboteurs who knew the terrain, who moved stealthily on foot, who could hide among the local population, it took imagination, cunning, deception. "It became clear to me that the only way to fight them was to seize the initiative, attack them in their bases, and surprise them when they were on the move."[6] In those few sentences, Moshe Dayan encapsulated the basic elements of the military doctrine that guided the emerging Jewish military forces; these were the same tactics—seizing the initiative, carrying the battle to the enemy's bases, the element of surprise—that became crucial underpinnings of the Israel Defense Forces.

Dayan was still tentative about military life. He was only twenty-two years old and already disillusioned with army life, already disgusted by the endless violence. He simply wanted to go home. "There's a big maneuver tonight," he wrote to Ruth, "and I'm very worried that I'm going to be in charge, and it's hard to make it come off right. It's not so important whether I'll succeed; all I want is to be finished with all this. It's so boring. . . . When will there be peace? All I want is quiet, and all there is is terror, terror which we must fight. What will be the end? It's better not to think about that. . . ."[7] Indeed he really wanted to get away from all the troubles in Palestine. He and Ruth considered signing on a ship; he would work as a deckhand, she would be in the kitchen. When they applied, however, to the S.S. *Zion*, they were rejected as too old.

WITH MOSHE away a good deal of the time, Ruth struck up a close relationship with Nahman Betser, Moshe's erstwhile schoolmate and now the leading figure of Shimron. Dayan was in love with Ruth when they married and for some time afterward. His letters to her during the 1930s reflect that love: "I miss you so much and I am miserable. . . . I feel strongly that . . . I must take care of you. . . ."[8] Yet their love could not patch over the obvious differences in outlook. Ruth sympathized with the kibbutz way of life, but Moshe did not believe in groups and communes. He wanted them to have their own home. Kibbutz life also meant taking part in the social life of the community, singing, dancing, decision making, sharing in the chores, and collective child raising. None of that was for Moshe. He was too introspective, too individualistic, too little of what is called today a team player.

No wonder that Ruth drifted toward Nahman Betser. He was the very embodiment of the kibbutznik, a strong, silent type who was content living a collectivized life. As Ruth drifted away from Moshe, Nahman's shoulder was there to cry on. During Moshe's absences she began walking with Nahman on his nightly guard patrols. When she went off on visits to Tel Aviv, Nahman wrote her letters.

Many years later, Ruth insisted that the words "platonic" and "sort of an idealistic love affair" best described her link to Betser.[9] Yet, according to someone who knew Dayan, as far as Dayan was concerned, Ruth was romantically involved with Betser. From her own description of the episode in her memoirs, there is ample evidence that Ruth realized the potential cost to her marriage of this crying on Nahman's shoulder. However strong her feelings for Nahman, she was not prepared to end her brief marriage to Moshe for him. However, at one point Ruth had actually left Shimron and gone to Hanita where Nahman was a Haganah instructor. Yossi Harel, then a close acquaintance of Ruth, noted: "One evening Ruth moved to the tent of Nahman Betser. It was very strange to me. I knew that she was married to Moshe but she left him and went to Hanita. A week later, Moshe came with a tender and picked Ruth up and she went with him."[10]

Pressure grew on Ruth to make up her mind—Nahman or Moshe. Nahman Betser's brother Moshe argued that out of fairness to his brother, she should drop one or the other. She had already decided not to abandon Moshe—as long as he would have her. Tormented by this unhappy triangle, Ruth decided to cut off her relationship with Nahman. She wrote two letters, one to Moshe, the other to Nahman. To Moshe she professed feelings of love: "You've made me not know what to do about Nahman, whether to write him or not, or send you the letter first to be censored. No wonder I cry . . . I love you to distraction. . . . But why write all this? I know you won't believe me. Probably you think I've myself a boyfriend here. . . ." She wrote Moshe that while she loved him completely and belonged to him alone, she also loved Nahman in a way. She conveyed the same message to Nahman.

Unbeknownst to her, Moshe intercepted the two letters, recognizing Ruth's handwriting. He opened both letters and then sent them back to her, adding a note that the one to Nahman was "warmer and more lyrical."[11] Nahman left Shimron in April 1938 and moved to a kibbutz in the Beit-Shean Valley. Some of Shimron's settlers blamed Moshe and Ruth for forcing the departure of the community's leader. Soon after, Ruth became pregnant for the first time. Ruth's relationship with Nahman Betser, occurring soon after Moshe and Ruth were married, has been largely overlooked as a contributing factor in the downfall of the Dayan marriage. Yet Moshe may well have been scarred by the discovery that

Ruth and Nahman had become close. Ruth, for her part, rejected the notion that Moshe used the fact of her relationship with Betser as an excuse for his later womanizing. As Ruth noted, "Moshe was going with women before [my relationship with] Nahman. I didn't write about it. I didn't think it was important. Moshe had girlfriends from the day I met him. It wasn't something new. He was always away and he always had someone."[12]

ENDING HIS STINT at Afula in December 1937, Dayan returned to Shimron and was soon promoted to sergeant; he was also appointed commander of one of the mobile guards, with six men under him, a relatively large force for the time. His was one of three mobile guard units in the Nahalal district. Dayan was given a light truck. The job comprised daylight patrols and night ambushes between Jewish settlements and Arab villages. As part of the most active Haganah units, a certain fame accrued to Dayan and his men. With fame, an individualistic streak came out. On one occasion, Dayan's British commander, Lee Marshall, ordered him to find his six constables and rush to the Nazareth mountains to help put out a raging forest fire. He refused to follow the order, giving no explanation. In later years, Dayan would still not divulge what had motivated this insubordination except to speculate that perhaps the heat of the day had given him reason not to burden his constables who were, after all, only making six British pounds a month. The British demoted Dayan from sergeant to private.

Demotion or not, the Haganah had plans of its own for Dayan. It sent him to a six-week platoon commanders course in Bet Yannai in December 1937. One of fifty-two students, Dayan impressed others in the course with his physical toughness, his sense of humor—and his brains. In every exercise, large or small, he managed to devise some unusual tactic that had escaped the instructors' notice. The study of military theory left him yawning. He wanted to be out in the field and to learn through his own experience.

It was at Bet Yannai that Moshe Dayan and Yigal Allon were thrown together for the first time. Yosef Avidar, who later held senior command positions with the IDF in the early 1950s, was commander of the course. He recalled Dayan and Allon as the two best students under him, excelling in field exercises and in commanding others under them. The course was designed to acquaint the men with field awareness. They learned how to move in day and night. Dayan became a deputy company commander after the course. Allon, born at Kefar Tavor in the Galilee three years after Dayan, was the grandson of Russian immigrants who had founded the first Jewish settlement in the Upper Galilee, Rosh-Pinna, in 1882; Allon had helped to found Kibbutz Ginnosar on the Sea of Galilee in 1937. In later years, a fierce competition would develop between the two for the senior positions of the army and government.

But in 1937 Dayan was still tentative about soldiering: "I won't emerge from this as an officer," he wrote Ruth back at Shimron. "I'll finish this course and that's that. Because geniuses like me, there are plenty of. At least, that's what they say."[13]

A few Haganah leaders had grown exceedingly bitter that Jewish settlements exercised little initiative in defending themselves against Arab attack. At Bet Yannai, and later at a six-week course at Ju'ara, Dayan met one such leader and immediately fell under his spell. His name was Yitzhak Sadeh. Sadeh had been born in 1890 in Lüblin, Poland, into a respected Jewish family. He became a sergeant in the czar's army during World War I—the highest rank a Jew could attain. Just before emigrating to Palestine, he had commanded a company in Petrograd. In 1936 Sadeh had organized a small, unofficial mobile unit with young volunteers from the Jerusalem Haganah branch. Trained and led by him, the Nodedet ("Patrol") tracked down and ambushed guerrilla bands around Jerusalem, rather than wait passively for them to attack. Its hands tied by the self-restraint controversy, the Haganah leadership did not support Sadeh's brief but enlightening experiment. After he became chief of staff of the Haganah he played a major role in switching Haganah tactics from self-defense to active defense. Don't wait for the Arab marauder, he used to say, don't wait to defend the kibbutz. Go after the person attacking you, take the offensive. This was Yitzhak Sadeh's doctrine.

Sadeh, though his activist doctrine had an impact on the thinking of the "can-do" Haganah people, was stymied by the fact that the Haganah still thought in terms of defending the settlements for the most part, relying on towers and stockades, fence patrols for the exterior lands, and three- or four-man guard posts. Sadeh wanted to build up a Jewish army of small guerrilla bands but few supported him. It was only when an outsider by the name of Orde Wingate advocated much the same strategy that the new doctrine was adopted.

Sadeh was an earlier version of everything that Moshe Dayan the soldier would become: He was full of ideas and he demanded great daring of the men under him, daring that others would call recklessness. Having learned at the feet of Yitzhak Sadeh, it was like a cold shower for Dayan to take part next in a British course for sergeants at the British military camp of Sarafend near Tel Aviv. What he learned there, he hated. British military thinking, as far as he was concerned, may have been good for running the empire, but it had no real relevance for what was going on in and around Nahalal and the Jezreel Valley. The highly disciplined inspection parades, the stress on polished boots and smart dress—of what use was all that when trying to deal with merciless Arab marauders?

To Dayan, all that mattered in soldiering was becoming the best fighter possible. Accordingly, he acquainted himself with the tools of the trade. As a youngster he had taken great pride in showing his friends the secret hiding place of his father's gun. Later, he felt at home at the shooting range. Though small-framed, he had the physical strength of men taller and heavier, but what distinguished him from others was his mind, processing and analyzing military information, taking hold of a problem and searching for quick, effective solutions. The problems often had to do with being weak, or at least seeming to be weak and thus being unable to overcome the strong. As Avino'am Slutzky noted, Dayan simply dismissed the idea that the weak inevitably were doomed to defeat: "There was none of this, the weak against the strong. That factor didn't exist with him. He looked for a way to defeat the other person, the way a good chess player does. He searched for weaknesses on the part of his opponent."[14] It is no surprise then to find that Moshe Dayan was a fine chess player. He played most intensively while at Shimron; when he was not actually engaged in a game he would sit at the side watching friends play. Avino'am Slutzky, a chess partner of Dayan's from that period, went on to become the chess champion of the Jewish settlements in 1946. What struck Slutzky was that Moshe Dayan adopted the same tactics on the chessboard that he did on the battlefield: "From the very beginning of the game, Moshe wanted to attack without making any preparation. In chess as in war, you have to hold your heavy fire for later, and protect your queen. Moshe was impatient. From the very start of the game he would play foolishly. He would go into battle at once. He wanted bloodshed. Others with whom I played were more cautious. But Moshe—he was a commando in chess!"[15]

Meanwhile, at Shimron, members were formulating the nature of their commune. Dayan, like many others, found the rules confining. He was dismayed when the supplies committee rejected his request to buy a coat for Ruth. Though Shimron was not meant to be the members' permanent site—they would soon move on to Hanita farther north on the Lebanese frontier—its settled atmosphere bothered Moshe. As he wrote to Rachel Schwartz, "Your generation, and my parents, has already built up this country. What is there left for people my age to do? Here where we're sitting now, right next to Nahalal, everything is already civilized. The best we can do at this point is to go to some unsettled point near the northern border. Or else to the Negev. . . ."[16]

In fact, in September 1938, when some members of Shimron began

planning to establish their permanent site at Hanita, Moshe and Ruth
returned to Nahalal, where they wanted to set up their own home with
their own farmland. At first they moved into the Dayan household (by
now a concrete house had taken the place of the wood-frame hut). Relations were at best strained. Moshe and Ruth were eager to set up their
own farm. Shmuel and Dvorah looked askance at some of Ruth's behavior.
They believed she would have been better off making cheese and butter
rather than sewing dresses. They disliked the bourgeois gifts she received: a crude washing machine from her parents; a boxer dog from
relatives in Vienna. Moshe loved the dog and named it Lava. Shmuel
felt that having a personal relationship with a dog was a most bourgeois
act; one day he simply shot the dog! Soon thereafter, Moshe and Ruth
moved into their own hut, which they occupied until 1944.

DURING A LULL in the Arab Revolt, between December 1936 and May
1937, sixteen new Jewish settlements had been established in northern
Palestine. But such efforts were suspended by the fall of 1937, when
Arab attacks intensified. Jewish settlement efforts were only renewed
with the plan to establish Hanita in March 1938. This was to be Moshe
Dayan's most important military encounter against Arabs to date. An
overt political act, the Hanita project was part of the yishuv's program
to place four or five Jewish settlements along the northern border of
Palestine; it was feared that without Jewish settlement in the western
Galilee, the borders of any future Jewish state would not include this
region.

Though the settlers of Shimron had been designated as the eventual
inhabitants of Hanita, its actual establishment on March 21, 1938, was
undertaken by the Haganah. During the early months of 1938, Arab
groups in Lebanon had intensified their assaults across the frontier into
Palestine. Settling Hanita became an important priority as a means of
keeping these gangs from penetrating into the country. Surrounded by
Arab villages, this was an area where no Jews had settled before. Establishing Hanita would prove that Jewish settlement under such difficult
conditions could work. Everyone expected violence at the outset. For
that reason, the Haganah organized a force of nearly five hundred men
under Yitzhak Sadeh; he in turn chose as his two deputies Moshe Dayan
and Yigal Allon. The competition between Dayan and Allon was only in
its beginning stages. To appreciate how keen was their rivalry, a photograph from Hanita survives and shows Sadeh standing between Dayan
and Allon. Allon and Sadeh are smiling; Dayan has a satsified but un-
smiling look. In later years, sharp-eyed observers would note that Dayan

had made sure to place himself on slightly higher ground so that anyone looking at the photograph would get the impression that he was senior to Allon. It was all imaginary, but then again Dayan was already playing with his image. As for Allon, he too sought to create the impression that Dayan was no match for him. To anyone who asked about their early competition, he said dismissively: "I taught Moshe Dayan how to throw a hand grenade."

The fighting at Hanita marked the most important operation undertaken by the Haganah until then. Arriving at the bottom of the hilltop site, the "settlers" left their vehicles on the road and then climbed the rocky slopes, carrying material for the wooden watchtower and perimeter fence. Their hope was to have enough equipment in place that first day so that the site could be protected during the evening against the expected Arab attack. A strong wind and the sheer amount of equipment delayed them—by evening they had not even put up the tents. By midnight, the Arabs opened fire from two nearby hills. Sadeh, aggressiveness driving his every military instinct, wanted to form his men into an attack force and move against the Arabs. He put the proposal to Ya'acov Dori, Haganah commander of the northern region, but was turned down. Later, Dayan would recall Sadeh's attempt to move "beyond the fence" as the model behavior of a soldier leading his forces in battle. But sadly, Sadeh's bold military thinking had yet to penetrate the upper echelons of the Haganah's leadership. The shooting carried on for an hour and twenty minutes, during which the Arabs managed to kill two of the Hanita force and wound several others before fleeing across the Lebanese frontier.

For the next three days, work on the settlement progressed while the Arabs regrouped their forces. Then, on the fourth day, while the Hanita unit was building an access road, the Arabs opened fire and again they fled. Over the next few weeks, in an effort to accelerate work on the new settlement, Dayan was enlisted to drive workers from Nahariya on the Mediterranean coast back and forth in an armored car that was fitted with steel plates on its sides. Once the main fortifications were in place, Sadeh disbanded the force; Dayan returned to the Jezreel Valley to resume command of the supernumerary mobile unit. Until it was permanently settled later in 1938, Hanita served as a Haganah defense and training base.

ARMED WITH IMPATIENCE, sensing the way the battle was shaping up, Dayan feared that the Jewish settlements were heading for a fall unless they whipped themselves into fighting shape. Their defenses were weak and they were little more than sitting ducks, a set of big, fat targets waiting to be attacked and decimated. The lesson to be learned from this static, passive military strategy was a fairly simple one: The only way the Jewish settlers were going to keep the Arab enemy at bay was to take the fight to him, to surprise the Arabs in their own bases, and give them a thrashing before they could muster their own forces for an assault. It was self-evident to Moshe Dayan—but not to the Jewish settlements. They believed in their static defenses, in the impregnability of their fences. Dayan was determined to show them otherwise. While commanding a Haganah NCO course at Kibbutz Alonim in 1938, Dayan ordered his men to mount an "assault" against the Haganah base at Ju'ara, heavily protected to conceal what was going on there from the British. The guards had orders to shoot anyone trying to break in. Some of Dayan's men were hesitant to try this live exercise but he persuaded them. One evening he and his men managed to penetrate the perimeter fence and— without a shot being fired at them—to enter the base. They had not even been noticed. Later, Ju'ara's security unit complained that Dayan had acted unfairly by penetrating under the fence, as if fairness were part of the rules of warfare. Amused, Dayan believed that the only thing that counted was achieving the mission—and he had done that.

Not satisfied with the way others, particularly the British, were training soldiers, Dayan set down what he believed was important in a manual which, though never officially published by the Haganah, served as a crucial forerunner in the development of Haganah fieldcraft instruction. Rejecting British-style training, with its emphasis on a soldier's appearance and behavior, Dayan stressed in the booklet that what mattered was not how a soldier looked, but what he knew. He had to know the terrain, how to exploit its features, he had to know how to guard properly, how to shoot accurately, how to infiltrate and set ambushes, how to cut gaps in a fence, how to crawl speedily, how to sneak up on a target without being noticed. He had to know how to throw hand grenades and how to dress appropriately so that moving around would be easier. He sent the booklet on to Ya'acov Dori, who was then head of the Haganah's Instruction Department in Haifa. Dori, greatly impressed with Dayan's text, saw in it the first written exposition of the emerging doctrine laid down by Yitzhak Sadeh and adopted by Dayan—the doctrine that rejected static defense in favor of attack.

MOSHE DAYAN had few genuine heroes. One of them—a non-Jew—was a British officer named Charles Orde Wingate who arrived in Palestine in September 1936 and quickly displayed sympathy for the Zionist enterprise. More than anyone else, Wingate would inspire Dayan in forging the tactics that he would later use in the building of the Israel Defense Forces. Born in India to a Scottish family, Wingate served in Palestine as an intelligence officer. With a deep love for the Bible, he viewed the many Jewish settlements and kibbutzim as living evidence of the Bible's prophecies about the redemption of Zion. As a youngster he had been looked down upon, made to feel that he was a failure; in Palestine, he realized the Jews had been treated like that for hundreds of years, and here they were building a homeland. He felt that he could identify with such people. Moreover, when he examined the young men in the kibbutzim, he truly believed they would make better soldiers than even the British. All they needed was proper training. To doubtful yishuv leaders who wondered just what this British captain had read about the Jewish cause in Palestine, Wingate told them that there was only one important book on the subject of Zionism, and he was totally familiar with it—the Bible.

Wingate taught Dayan military tactics, but he also taught him a code of life. The basis of that code was that there was always a way to reach a goal, and often, unorthodox means were the most fruitful way. It was a code that allowed its adherent to slip and slide in and around the normal rules of society. Indeed, it provided a kind of carte blanche for avoiding those rules.

What distinguished Orde Wingate and made its mark on Moshe Dayan was his sheer audacity in believing that he could teach the Haganah soldiers how to defeat the Arabs. He seemed slightly unhinged to them— "mad and maddening" in Moshe Dayan's apt phrase.[17] Wingate was slovenly in appearance, rude, abrasive, and fearless. What does not emerge from most accounts of the Bible-carrying Wingate is his utter ruthlessness. He could shoot an Arab on the spot to make an example to others who would not talk. He would strike soldiers who had not been fully prepared for battle. His military approach was clearly iconoclastic, and if it required someone a little crazy to project a new way of thinking, no one among the Jewish community seemed to mind. Indeed, as Dayan and the others got to know Wingate, their affection for him knew no bounds. The Haganah men called him Hayedid (the Friend) and realized there was a lot to be said for his conviction that the best defense was attack. In teaching the Haganah men to be professional fighters, in giving future Israeli army commanders such as Moshe Dayan and Yigal Allon their first formal training, he was helping to build the future Israeli army. Every leader in the IDF was in effect a disciple of Wingate's, none more so than Moshe Dayan.

Before Wingate would undertake an action in Palestine he read the appropriate biblical passage, trying to find evidence for an ancient Jewish victory in the locale of an upcoming Jewish attack.

An adventurer in the tradition of "Chinese" Gordon or Lawrence of Arabia, Wingate was convinced that the only way the yishuv could counter Arab violence was by building its own army. Throughout the 1920s and early 1930s such an idea was greeted with derision by the moderate elements of the yishuv and the Haganah. But by 1938, Wingate's vision made sense.

Wingate met Moshe Dayan for the first time while making the rounds in search of improving ways to combat Arab terror. One day shortly before sunset Wingate showed up at Shimron. He had a heavy revolver on his side and a small Bible in his hand. Dayan's most singular impression was the way the man stared at him, an intense and piercing look that was unforgettable: "He looked you straight in the eye as someone who seeks to imbue you with his own faith and strength."[18] Wasting no time, he gathered Dayan and the others together in the Shimron dining room, speaking to them in heavily accented Hebrew. The group asked him to switch to English and he complied. He explained his personal military doctrine, one that he had developed during his experiences in guerrilla warfare in the Sudan. He believed in relying upon small, highly mobile forces that could launch large-scale attacks. Above all, he believed in diversion and deception. (He put the taillights on the front of the cars under his command to trick the enemy into thinking he was going in the opposite direction!) Unlike his fellow British soldiers, he could not have cared less about parade drills. All that he demanded was that the men keep their rifles clean. Exploiting the darkness was an essential part of this trickery. He talked about the techniques he had picked up in setting night ambushes and proposed there and then that he lead them in an ambush that very night. Calling for a map, he astonished the men by proposing that, rather than their usual practice of laying an ambush near the approaches to a Jewish settlement, they should choose as their proposed ambush site a place that was near an Arab village. In this manner, they could reach out and attack the enemy, and not wait for him to attack them first in their homes. Dayan remembered how shocked he and the others were at hearing this British officer lecture them on a subject they felt they knew something about—fighting the Arabs. They felt more than shock. They were amused at his arrogance.

Their amusement soon turned to admiration. Wingate chose as his target the crossroads near the Arab village of Mahlul, a few miles away. Grabbing their weapons, the men dashed off with Wingate. Even before they reached the target, he was teaching them new tricks: traveling along the ridges of the hill, not on the paths; placing himself at the lead, rather than the usual two trackers. Dayan had intended to put himself at the head of the group as one of the trackers, but Wingate announced he would be at the front: "I know how to wage war and you don't," he said with great self-assurance. Dayan glanced at this seemingly fragile, thin British officer and wondered how he was going to manage to climb over rocks, through bushes, all at a hearty pace. But by dawn Wingate had not flagged; never did he ask the men to rest, never did he slip. Reaching the target, Wingate divided his men into two groups and placed them one hundred yards apart. If and when the Arabs appeared, they would be trapped in the middle, enabling the men to attack from both sides. The lesson had been learned—on paper. That first night, no Arabs moved out of the village on the attack. The point was nevertheless clear. What Wingate had taught Dayan and the others—the "emerge from the fence" strategy—was not new: Sadeh had the same idea. Where Sadeh had been unable to convince his superiors of the wisdom of the approach, Wingate, by what Dayan termed his positiveness and his stubborn lack of compromise, won converts. He taught Jewish soldiers that it was possible to fight at night and in that manner to outdo the Arabs. He insisted that the Arabs were scared stiff of the night and the Jews could succeed by exploiting this weakness.

After an assault, Wingate and the settlers returned to the Shimron dining hall. They fried omelets and potatoes on the primus stove and made tomato salad. Off in a corner Wingate sat naked, Bible in hand, eating raw onions. The man was different. "Judged by ordinary standards," Dayan wrote, "[Wingate] would not be regarded as normal. But his own standards were far from ordinary. He was a military genius and a wonderful man."[19]

Dayan joined Wingate in a number of ambushes against Arab foes from Galilee to Bethlehem. Writing to Ruth, he recorded one of these assaults with great pride: "Yesterday we went out on an action, about seven of us, and met eighty Arabs. Our boys were a bit nervous and so didn't shoot absolutely straight. But don't worry, it's not dangerous. . . . Really, don't worry. I'm writing you about this only because you may read about it in the papers and be alarmed. Captain Wingate was here and will be coming for a week. Otherwise nothing new. I haven't slept for forty-eight hours and must go out again tonight. But just don't you worry." He closed the letter: "Everybody thinks our action was quite good. Captain Wingate praised our operation and we may be getting a citation. After all, we were just seven and there were eighty of them. Our boys behaved wonderfully."[20] Significantly, the letter reflected a new sense of excitement toward military life. Dayan no longer agonized in his letters about how much longer he would have to participate in the fighting. He now took for granted that he had no choice but to take part.

In July 1938 Wingate commanded a group of Haganah men from Kibbutz Hanita on a raid against Arab guerrillas based in a neighboring village. Soon thereafter, he persuaded his British superiors to let him build up a counterguerrilla force under his command, to be called the Special Night Squads (SNS). Secretly, Wingate hoped to make these squads the nucleus of a burgeoning Jewish army. The British agreed to the SNS because they thought that such a force could protect the Iraq Petroleum Company pipeline from Arab sabotage. To organize the squads, Wingate met with Haganah intelligence officers and then turned to the Jewish settlements for recruits. British soldiers also took part. Dayan was never actually a member of these squads. Wingate's influence over him was nevertheless powerful. In setting up these squads, Wingate demonstrated to Dayan the effectiveness of the retaliatory raid, in which small units of specially selected, highly trained soldiers would penetrate deep into Arab territory under the cover of darkness, destroy a few homes and sometimes kill known terrorists, and return home before daylight. Through Wingate's tactics, the Arabs learned that they could not move anywhere they pleased in total safety. Wingate's efforts worked. In time, Arab attacks against the pipeline ceased.

In the end Wingate was simply too unorthodox for the British, too pro-Zionist—and in time he was recalled to London. On the eve of his departure from Palestine, his commanders put into his personal file that he was a good soldier, but a security risk as far as Palestine was concerned. He put Jewish interests above all interests and therefore he should not be allowed back.

During World War II he practiced his ideas on a much larger battlefield, in Ethiopia and Burma. Commanding his famous Chindits in 1944, Wingate was killed in a plane crash in the Burma jungles. Ben-Gurion paid him the highest compliment by saying that had he lived, Wingate would have been the natural choice to command the Israel Defense Forces during the 1948 War of Independence.

✦ 3 ✦

TROUBLE WITH

THE BRITISH AND FRENCH

MOSHE DAYAN'S career stalled: incarceration; the agony of being on the inside when all hell was breaking loose outside; not knowing when he would be free. That was to be Dayan's fate in the fall of 1939. The storm signals occurred abruptly enough. The British decision to issue its infamous White Paper on May 17 of that year ruptured the uneasy alliance between London and the yishuv. Once again the Haganah was forced to adopt a pose of secrecy, an underground existence that raised anew the specter of possible confrontation with the British. The first indication that the British had disengaged from their partnership with the Haganah came that fall. Moshe Dayan was one of the victims.

In August the Haganah had asked Dayan to serve as an instructor in field tactics in a platoon commanders' course at Yavniel, four miles west of Degania. One of the other instructors was Yigal Allon. To avoid detection by the British, the Haganah pretended that it was operating a physical education program under the auspices of the Hapoel sports federation. Things went smoothly until October 3 when, during a lecture on tactics, two British security officers appeared at the entrance of the tent. The lecturer hastily switched to the subject of track and field. After listening briefly, the officers searched the camp, discovering a rifle under a mattress. They departed without saying a word. Sensing danger, Haganah headquarters swiftly ordered the "sportsmen" to evacuate the camp and regroup at Kibbutz Ein Hashofet near the western edge of the Jezreel Valley.

The trainees split into two groups. The one under Yigal Allon's command, with seventeen Haganah men, had no difficulty reaching Ein Hashofet. Having gathered all the weapons, the second group under Moshe Carmel broke camp at 2:00 A.M., trailing four hundred yards behind their guides, Moshe Dayan and Mordechai Sukenik. A British-sponsored patrol of fifteen Arabs riding in five pickup trucks accosted the two guides, but the Arabs appeared to accept their story that they were mere hikers. Sukenik won a nod of approval after showing the patrol his firearms license. The Arabs departed, but when warned of the larger group's presence by a nearby Arab shepherd, they quickly surrounded the other forty-one members of the Haganah course, taking them into custody. Dayan and Sukenik were rounded up shortly afterward. Why did these two not alert the others that a patrol was in the vicinity? Dayan unconvincingly defended his and Sukenik's diffidence by contending that the two of them firmly believed that the patrol would not stumble upon the others. A larger question remains: How was it possible for only fifteen Arabs to surround and take control of forty-three Haganah men? Still, Dayan and the others remained optimistic as they made their way in two trucks to Acre Prison. Although Arabs had arrested them, they believed they would be released when the British learned of the misunderstanding. They should have known better.

Hoping that Moshe would show up on Friday, October 5—it was the Jewish holiday Simhat Torah—Ruth waited in vain on the main road near Nahalal. She was furious at Moshe for not coming home and at the Haganah for keeping him from home. Only on the following day did she hear from him, albeit indirectly. A man from a nearby village approached her and gave her a note on a small piece of paper: "Ruth, we have been arrested and taken to Acre on a seemingly minor charge. I hope it will end well. Kisses to you and Yael. See you soon—your Moshe."

A few days later, Ruth contacted an attorney in Haifa. He explained that if found guilty of the charges of possessing weapons illegally, Moshe and the others could be hanged.

The forty-three Haganah prisoners arrived at the Acre Prison, built in the eighteenth century by the Turks and resting on top of five hundred-year-old Crusader foundations. Hands on one another's shoulders, they were immediately placed in a detention room. If interrogated, they had decided to supply only their names and ages; they would also ask for an attorney. Their goal was to convince the British guards that members of a sports club had been accidentally arrested. Within moments a few policemen entered the room and asked who spoke English. Zvi Brenner, one of the four prisoners who did, was the first taken for questioning.

"Death! Death!" The three British interrogators screamed that word repeatedly as they kicked Brenner, beat him with their batons, and shined a spotlight on his face. His screams carried to the next room, where Dayan and the other forty-one prisoners were kept. Their proximity was deliberate. The questioners persisted. Brenner would not break. The guards sought out another English-speaker. They came upon Moshe Dayan. He walked into the interrogation room and felt the contempt of his questioners almost at once. Unless he answered their questions, he would be executed. Bearing arms was, they noted, a capital offense. Dayan's captors learned that he had a wife and daughter (Yael had been born the previous February). They stepped up their verbal torture. His daughter would be orphaned and would have to spend her life knowing that her father had been a common criminal. Never before had Dayan confronted such danger. Even when he had stared down the armed bedouin sheikh Emir Diab in the Jordan Valley five years earlier, he had not been under such a physical threat. He could not win over these men with a cheerful smile, as he had the sheikh. Dayan wondered whether there might not be some advantage to revealing a little bit about themselves, if only to prevent the others from suffering. The questions came with the same arrogance and contempt. Where had they gotten their arms? "I don't know," Dayan said, knowing such a terse and evasive answer would not suffice. Were they members of the Haganah? Yes, he admitted. Was that not a terrorist organization? No, said Dayan calmly. Why, the British and the Haganah had at one point fought side by side. A pair of British warders moved toward Dayan, their truncheons poised to strike him. He spoke quickly and with determination. If they hit him— or for that matter any of his friends outside—they would have to understand that other Haganah members on the outside would exact revenge. Dayan then returned to the theme of common Haganah-British purpose. Did they not understand that a man named Adolf Hitler was out there doing damage both to the British and the Jews? Why turn on one another when there was work to do—together—to foil this evil figure? Dayan's emotional plea worked wonders. The men dropped their truncheons to their sides and permitted him to return to the others. No one else was beaten. Most of Dayan's fellow prisoners regarded what he had done as correct, even as a sign of personal leadership. Moshe Carmel did not. He argued that Haganah men had to keep tight lipped, or else there would be no way of knowing what they had divulged.

Spared physical harm, the Forty-three, as they came to be known in yishuv lore, still faced the unappealing prospect of a trial on charges of illegally possessing arms: One of them, Avshalom Tau, was charged as well with pointing his gun at his captors. Dayan and the others could not let themselves believe they would get anything but a light sentence. The ghastliness of his prison existence led Dayan to dwell on what his family meant to him. "If sometimes . . . I wear an irritable face, or it seems to you that I don't live family life fully enough," he wrote to Ruth with an obvious sense of guilt about the past, "if only I could convey to you one thousandth part of the love I feel for both of you at night, if you could only feel what you both mean to me."[1]

Having his family see him through the prism of prison life did little to boost his spirits. Dayan was a proud young man: Even if his being incarcerated had been a mistake, even if the Haganah's purpose in carrying weapons was perfectly justified, it was degrading and unmanly to have his family see him in a prison uniform and move, slavelike, when his British masters ordered him about. The first visiting day—Saturday, October 14—proved frustrating and humiliating for Dayan. He and the others were lined up in a shallow ditch divided from their visitors by barbed wire. Only two visitors per prisoner were permitted. Even after friends and relatives climbed on concrete platforms they could only see the heads and upper parts of their loved ones. Ruth and Dvorah were there, as was eight-month-old Yael, an "illegal" visitor who broke away at one point and began crawling toward the barbed wire. The commotion—prisoners and visitors yelling back and forth at one another: Arab guards shouting "Yallah, yallah" (Arabic for "Hurry up!)—made visiting day a nightmare for Dayan. Yael's presence particularly anguished him. Was it healthy for an infant to see her father dressed in prison clothes? He asked Ruth to leave her home next time "because I'm not sure I won't start literally to cry when I see her on the other side of the wire fence."[2] No matter how distasteful prison was, Dayan did not accept preferential treatment for himself, even though, thanks to Ruth's aggressiveness and high official contacts, this might have won him freedom. Ruth was prepared to visit England to try to seek a royal pardon but was refused a visa.

Rather than devastate him, prison life uplifted Dayan. Not that he found it tolerable or easy. He did not. From the 180 letters written during his Acre incarceration, one senses that he came to view prison almost as a badge of honor. "It is clear to me," he wrote to Ruth, "that life is divided into two categories, that of the free man, and that of the prisoner. Anyone who hasn't experienced both has lived only half a life."[3] Dayan found prison conditions harsh, but what bothered him more than anything else was "the certain knowledge that one can do nothing except obey the orders of the Arab warder and carry them out immediately."[4]

Eight days after writing that letter—on November 6—the trial of

Dayan and the other forty-two Haganah prisoners began in a military camp near Acre. It was a major event: Represented among the accused were the elite families of the yishuv; Dayan confidently believed that he would receive no more than a one-year sentence, just enough time, he figured, to complete *Gone With the Wind.* He asked Ruth to provide him with a copy. Ruth had wanted the attorneys to ask the military court to judge Moshe and Mordechai Sukenik separately. Dayan would not hear of it. The accused sat on benches, their legs in chains, with the attorneys seated at tables to the left and right. The "illegal" arms were placed on exhibit, rifles on the floor, grenades and ammunition on a bench. A British major served as prosecutor; three British officers were the judges. Among the three defense attorneys was Dayan's father-in-law, Zvi Schwartz. The prosecutor contended that the men had broken the law and should therefore be punished. The defense attorneys countered that one could not overlook the purpose behind the military training of the Forty-three—to take up common cause with the British in their fight against Nazi Germany. Leniency was in order. Among those testifying for the defense was Moshe Dayan. To Ben Feller, who was covering the trial for the *Palestine Post* (later the *Jerusalem Post*), Dayan was "correct," deferring to the court, but clinging to a strong sense of pride. He acted as if he had nothing to hide, and he and his colleagues had been defending the Allied cause.[5]

After five days of courtroom drama, the three officers handed down their judgment: guilty. Moshe Dayan and the others were sentenced to ten years in jail. Avshalom Tau was given life. A harsh verdict, but not harsh enough for the British officers milling around the court. "Fancy freeing them in ten years," whispered one. "Put them against the wall and shoot them." No longer the accused, the Forty-three were now convicts, made to parade out of the courtroom in chains and taken back to Acre Prison. There they donned prison uniforms and—the most degrading experience of all to Dayan—had their heads shaved.

Prison conditions were dismal. Dayan and the others were thrown into a long, dark cell with only two small windows that looked out onto the courtyard; mattresses were strewn on the floor. Each prisoner had two thin blankets. Two pails had been placed at the opposite sides of the room, one for drinking water, the other to be used as a toilet. The prisoners' daily routine began with ten minutes of exercise, then breakfast, work, two meals, at 11:00 A.M. and 3:00 P.M., and, winding up the day, fourteen hours confined to their cell. Three times a day the warders lined up the prisoners for a roll call, counting each one by tapping him on the head with a stick.

Almost immediately, the Forty-three saw the need to organize themselves. A prisoners' committee was chosen, with Moshe Dayan as one of three members. He was responsible for contact with the prison administration and the Jewish institutions on the outside. Ya'acov Salomon was in charge of activities within the cell; Moshe Carmel, who had been deputy course commander, handled general affairs. Dayan fought to improve prisoners' conditions when justified. Because of his efforts, the prisoners were permitted to work only half a day and use the other half to study, to receive writing material and books, and to keep their lights on until 8:00 P.M. Through bribery and smuggling, the Forty-three managed to increase their contact with the outside.

It was in prison that Moshe Dayan's leadership qualities became apparent. Few had befriended him as a youngster or wished to see him in charge of anything. Within the Haganah, his military and organizational skills had thrust him into junior command positions, but nothing more. Now, within the Acre Prison walls, under the great strain and tension of prison life, when the weak were inclined to shrink and the strong prevail, he was counted among the strong. "You can't imagine how much the guys here like and respect me," he wrote to Ruth. "This has never happened to me in other groups I've found myself in previously and all because of the cheek and resoluteness with which I talk to the policemen and the administration, and because of our good organization and ability to keep in good spirits."[6]

He displayed such temerity toward the guards because he was racked with guilt about being on the inside, missing the military struggle outside. To soothe those who worried about him he masked his true feelings by writing cheerful letters that made prison sound, if not benign, then at least tolerable. His parents needed calming down. Conjuring up nightmarish visions of Russian jails, they imagined their son going through some special kind of hell. Dayan knew better and he told them so. "You seem to think that being in prison here is like the descriptions in Dostoyevski . . . or as it used to be in Turkish times, but it is not. Certainly our room is not particularly beautiful or luxurious, but up to now, at any rate, our food and clothing have been satisfactory, everything is reasonably clean, and we are not badly treated. We have even managed to get rid of the lice."[7] In truth, prison life took its toll on Dayan physically. He appeared thin and gaunt, in need of a few good meals.

Good news came toward the end of November, when Chaim Weizmann appealed for leniency on behalf of the Forty-three to Field Marshal Lord Ironside, the British chief of the Imperial General Staff. The field marshal was receptive: He told Weizmann that such men, the followers of Orde Wingate, should be given medals, not jail sentences. He halved their prison sentences. Avshalom Tau's life sentence was reduced to ten years. Only partially salved, Dayan and his prisonmates demanded their freedom. On November 28, the yishuv called a general strike in an effort to arouse sympathy for the Haganah men; movie houses and theaters closed down and the Hebrew-language newspapers did not publish that day.

It did not help. All one could do was to ease the prisoners' burden. Shmuel Dayan tried. In December, soon after the Haganah men had been moved into four separate cells, he disguised himself as an assistant to the prison's meat supplier and sneaked in to tell his son that Ironside had agreed to review the case within six months. Ruth brought Yael to see her father on her first birthday, February 12, 1940. He appeared in brown prison clothes, with a grubby-looking beard and a sad look on his face. "That was the only time I saw Moshe humble," Ruth said many years later, the image of him with his head bowed, as if guilty of something, still fresh in her mind.[8] She asked the deputy chief warder, Captain Grant, to let her husband have a close look at Yael. He refused. Dayan scolded Ruth for making such a request.

Getting along with others in the prison was crucial. Dayan knew how to do this. When thirty-four members of the Irgun Zvai Le'umi ("National Military Organization"), the right-wing dissident underground group, showed up after being charged for possessing arms, he agreed to make joint presentations of demands to the British on behalf of the Haganah and the Irgun prisoners. Relating to the Arab prisoners was more complex. It occurred to Dayan that both they and the Forty-three were in jail for a similar reason: committing nationalist acts. Though their peoples were on a collision course with one another on the outside, inside they might be able to find common cause. Should he hate these people? he wondered. It seemed so much easier to accommodate oneself to a peaceful coexistence. Thus he and the Arabs joined one another for Jewish and Muslim festivals alike.

The yearning to be free remained intense. With so much time on his hands, Dayan daydreamed about his future, acknowledging in his letters to Ruth that prison life had changed his view of his future—once he was set free.

> Basically, I think that my demands on life are minimal. If once I thought that social activities were central, that one should search for "fun" and "content," that in order to find life satisfactory one should be active and perhaps even a leader, today I ask for much less. The subject is happiness, and to achieve it I imagine a way of life—We are sitting in our cozy room, listening to the radio, reading a good book

> or poetry. Yael rolling on the rug and you are knitting. We
> sip tea and talk. . . . I know this is an exaggerated romantic
> idyllic picture, but these are my daydreams.[9]

It was only natural that a prisoner would long, not for an active life, not
to be a leader, but for the domestic bliss portrayed in Dayan's letter. It
was, of course, the last thing in the world that he wanted. He was in
fact a man of action, not someone who longed for the home fires. For
the moment it was important to assure his family that he had no further
desire to roam, to engage in battle. "I could be the village driver, or a
watchman, a builder or a farmer, in a kibbutz or a moshav, even a trade
union functionary, as long as I can have the peace of family life, the good
books and the two of you," he wrote to Ruth.[10]

Prison life seems to have addled his brain. This man who had detested
kibbutz life so much, who had little good to say about yishuv politics,
was now expressing an eagerness to become a kibbutznik or a trade union
functionary!

In February 1940, five months after the Forty-three had arrived at
Acre Prison, they were transferred to Mazra'a camp, a few miles north
of Acre. Conditions improved: The mattresses were more comfortable;
they slept in huts; there were utensils for food; and they were able to
work at the nearby experimental agricultural station thinning out wheat
and spreading fertilizer. Ruth and Yael had greater access to Dayan.

Improved conditions were not a substitute for freedom. As the spring
approached, Dayan and the other forty-two grew increasingly irritated—
first and foremost at their Jewish friends on the outside who, they believed, were not doing enough to seek their release.

AROUND PASSOVER a rumor spread around the camp that the British
were under pressure to establish a Jewish unit within the British army.
That cheered the Forty-three. Surely the British would want to release
Jewish prisoners so that they could take part in the new unit. Nothing
happened.

For Dayan, each day added new frustrations. He made necklaces from
fruit pits, put together olive-wood picture frames, and sought to improve
himself so that when he was free he would be better equipped to deal
with the world. He wrote letters to Ruth in English for practice. He
read O. Henry's short stories, some Shakespeare, and John O'Hara's
Appointment in Samarra. As he turned the pages, he thought gloomily
of the pledge by Lord Ironside to reexamine the Forty-three's case within
six months. The deadline was fast approaching and no word had come.

British forces were being routed in Europe and forced to evacuate. Meanwhile Moshe Dayan and his cellmates remained in jail.

The Jewish Agency's Political Department decided on a new tactic. They abandoned the policy of seeking collective release for the Forty-three and sought the release of individuals. Perhaps the British might be willing to release those individuals who had cooperated with the British army. The Agency, however, neglected to notify the Forty-three of the change in tactic. Among the Forty-three, only Moshe Dayan favored the new tactic. Few were surprised that he had taken this view, with his strong family connections and his past record of cooperation with the British. Disregarding Dayan, the others rejected the new policy. Dissension among the group was intensified a few days later when a letter from Ruth to him was discovered, informing Dayan that his release was imminent, that the required papers had already been signed by the district commissioner in Nazareth. Dayan could not convince the others that he had been unaware of the attempt to free him. Nonetheless, he emphatically defended the idea of seeking personal releases. "I don't see any problem with this," he argued. "No one forced us to enter jail altogether, and we don't have to leave it together. I would be happy for anyone who could be saved."[11] He must have sounded hypocritical to the others: It had been Dayan who had prevented other prisoners from being beaten by the British; it had been Dayan who, as their representative, had sought to broaden the rights of *all* prisoners. No longer was it one for all, all for one. The Forty-two no longer let Dayan serve as their liaison with the prison authorities.

The policy of seeking individual releases failed, but the future of the whole group brightened. Rumors again circulated in January 1941 that the British were willing to expand the number of Palestinian Jewish volunteers to the British army. Perhaps they would want the Forty-three to serve. To draw attention to themselves, Dayan and the others decided to stage a hunger strike on March 1, 1941, but this drastic course became unnecessary. On February 16 Dayan and the other forty-two men were officially notified that the next morning they would be set free. No one slept that night. At dawn their clothes returned; the men collected around the entrance to the camp, where their palms were stamped with a release symbol.

Then Moshe Dayan went home. He had been in prison for sixteen months.

Upon his release, Dayan was so furious with the British for keeping him in prison that he vowed not to help them win the war. Twenty-one years later he displayed more charity toward his captors. He even said that he had learned to admire the British because of his prison experience: "I would wish everybody to be treated in prison as the British treated me. The officers, sergeants and privates treated us in a way that was correct, sympathetic and civilized. I am sure that they did this not because somebody told them to, but because that was how British people behaved, how they were."[12]

IT WAS ONLY twenty miles from Acre to Nahalal—but it had taken sixteen months to make the trip. Dayan was back to being a farmer, working in the cow shed and the poultry run, plowing the fields. He drove a beer truck and then a tractor just to be closer to home. He was now living his daydream. When farm work slackened, he took odd jobs in Nahalal, mixing concrete, building troughs, laying floors. At night he went on guard duty. He spent time with his daughter Yael.

This postprison interlude lasted three months. Storm clouds from World War II were gathering over the Middle East, with potentially dangerous implications for Palestine and the yishuv. For Moshe Dayan, it meant a return to soldiering. This time Palestine was threatened with a pincer action as Nazi-collaborationist Vichy forces appeared ready to swoop down from Syria to attack northern Palestine; and to the south, Rommel's Axis forces were advancing toward the Egyptian frontier in preparation for an invasion of Palestine. Faced with these threats, the British felt obliged to utilize Jewish underground fighters of the Haganah.

In May 1941 the Haganah had organized a countrywide mobile force of full-time soldiers to defend the Jewish settlements against Arab attacks and to serve as a reserve force for the British army. The most senior Haganah officer, Yitzhak Sadeh, was called upon to head that new force. It was called the Palmach, a shortened version of Plugot Mahatz (Shock Companies). One day in May Sadeh had shown up at Moshe Dayan's home in Nahalal with a new assignment. Dayan was to be one of the first two company commanders of this commando corps. The other was Yigal Allon. At first the two companies were to be the main element of the special force. But they were soon given new orders—to join the British invasion of Syria.

That invasion was set to begin on Saturday evening, June 7. The operation that Dayan's company would undertake was part of the larger Allied effort to destroy the threat from Nazi-collaborationist Vichy forces from the north. His company was attached to the Australian spearhead. Just prior to the actual invasion, it was to cross the frontier to take control of the two bridges near the village of Iskanderun, six miles to the north of the Palestinian frontier. Seizing those bridges would keep the French from blowing them up and slowing the Allied thrust.

The advance party moved out from Kibbutz Hanita in northern Palestine, numbering sixteen in all: ten Australians, five Jews, and one Arab. One of the Jews was Moshe Dayan. The Australians had a few machine guns, rifles, and revolvers; the Jews had scraped together a tommy gun, a few rifles, pistols, and hand grenades. They lacked detailed maps of the targeted area. Dayan took for his tracker a Circassian who had once been the leader of an Arab terrorist gang. That may have appeared a strange, even risky choice; but he was convinced it was far better to use a gang leader or even a murderer than a simple Arab shepherd or fellah. Gang leaders and murderers would act with courage and skill, whereas a shepherd or fellah might run away at the first sign of trouble. Still, as Dayan was told, the man's wife and children were held hostage in a Haifa hotel during the operation to ensure that the Circassian would not harm Dayan's men once in Syria.

It took two hours to reach the frontier. "Well, we've invaded," Dayan joked to the others. "Now we can go back home." For four more hours they walked, eventually climbing to the ridge above their target. It was 2:00 A.M. and in only two more hours the first unit of the main invasion force was due. Whipping out binoculars, Dayan took in the Mediterranean coast, Iskanderun, and the two bridges. He split the sixteen men into two units. One he led to the northern bridge, the other he sent to the southern bridge. After Dayan's group had crawled near the bridge, they waited for instructions from one of the Australian officers on how to proceed with the attack; none came. The only murmur from the Australians was to advise Dayan to keep his finger on the trigger in case their guide betrayed them. Dayan leaped forward with his guide toward the northern bridge and then toward the southern one, finding neither one guarded or mined. Essentially, Dayan's mission was over—all that was required of him was to guard the bridges for the two remaining hours until the main contingents reached them. Leaving others on alert, Dayan promptly lay down in a roadside ditch and went to sleep.

He awoke several hours later at first light, immediately sensing that something was wrong: Where was the main invasion force? He heard shots off in the distance. He decided that he must evacuate his men immediately. Did Dayan genuinely believe, as he insisted in his 1976 memoirs, *Story of My Life,* that the situation he and his men faced was desperate and that a speedy exit was necessary? Or, sensing boredom rather than any real peril, might Dayan have simply yearned for something more exciting than protecting a pair of irrelevant bridges? The evidence suggests adventure, rather than fear, motivated him. In a memo to his Haganah superiors soon after the operation, he indicated that he was bent on doing something. Whatever his reason, it was a fateful decision, one that nearly cost him his life.

Dayan's guide remembered that a police station was located only a mile to the south; even if manned by two or three policemen, it could be captured, eliminating one dangerous source of gunfire. Leaving a few men behind to guard the bridges, Dayan took his unit to an orange grove near the two-story building, from where they spotted not the mere handful of local police they had expected, but an entire unit of French troops. When the French opened machine-gun fire on their visitors, Dayan and his men crouched behind a low stone fence at the edge of the orange grove; the grove was near a road, on the other side of which was the police station. Pinned down, with its ammunition about to run out, Dayan's force was in serious trouble. They had only one choice, and that was to try to seize the police station. Dayan grabbed a box of explosives and tossed a hand grenade that landed on the terrace of the police station, an eighty-foot bull's-eye that effectively silenced one of the machine guns. He then instructed one of the Australian officers to cover him and Zalman Mart, one of Dayan's Jewish recruits, while the two ran across the road. The Australians were firing repeatedly at the building's doors and windows, enabling Dayan and Mart to reach the other side of the road safely. The two attackers took cover under the terrace. The shooting from the building ceased for a moment, and Dayan exploited the quiet to dash back for the box of explosives. He set it against the building, and when the box exploded, his comrades surged forward. Dayan lobbed a grenade through the upper pane of a door and after it went off, he and Mart rushed the building with a burst of gunfire that killed two French soldiers. On the floor two others, a French officer and a soldier, lay dead. The air was heavy with dust and the smell of gunpowder. Dayan and Mart moved to a second room, where eight armed and two unarmed French soldiers were sitting, their hands covering their ears, bewildered at their plight of surrendering to such a small company. Dayan and Mart easily took them prisoner. The battle for the police station—at least this dramatic first phase—was over.

The French prisoners told Dayan a remarkable tale. The police station was in fact the main headquarters of the French Vichy forces in the region. Some of those Vichy forces had already deployed themselves near the Palestinian frontier, erecting roadblocks and designing ambushes on the main highway to protect against the expected invasion from the south. All of this was crucial intelligence for the Allied invasion troops and so Dayan instructed Zalman Mart to take one of the French motorcycles and try to reach friendly forces. Aside from the intelligence, Dayan wanted to impart the message that he and his men required an early rescue before the nearby French overwhelmed his men. Mart set out, but when his tires were shot out not far from the police station, he had to return.

All that Dayan and his soldiers could do was try to defend themselves and hope that the Allied force would arrive in time. They did have some luck in that the police station was stocked with weapons, including a machine gun that was placed on the building's roof. Dayan chose to take a position behind that machine gun. The only cover he had, and it was poor indeed, was a twelve-inch-high ledge around the roof. It was shortly after 7:00 A.M., June 8, when the first French reinforcements showed up and surrounded the building. The French fired and Dayan turned the machine gun on them. Then, hoping to locate the source of the firing, he lifted to his eyes field glasses he had taken from a dead French officer. He had just about gotten them into focus when disaster struck.

A rifle bullet smashed into the binoculars. Parts of the field glasses' lens and metal casing went into Dayan's left eye. Sections of two fingers of his right hand were torn off by the bullet as well. As he fell backward (ironically, on a French flag), Dayan lost consciousness.

He came to after a moment. Mart was the first to discover that Dayan had been wounded. Noticing that the metal casing of the field glasses had lodged in Dayan's eye, he tried to dislodge it. No luck. Dayan had the presence of mind to implore Mart to cease trying, thinking perhaps that the casing might block further bleeding. Mart placed a handkerchief on the wounded eye and bandaged Dayon's fingers.

Mart asked Dayan how seriously he thought he was wounded.

"If I can reach a hospital within three hours, I'll live," he answered, knowing full well that reaching British forces for medical treatment was well nigh impossible for the time being. Dayan sized up his predicament soberly: He believed that he was going to die soon.

With the battle raging, all that could be done was to take some blankets and turn them into a makeshift stretcher on which he was placed and lowered to the ground floor. One of the Australian soldiers, convinced that Dayan would die from loss of blood without immediate aid, proposed to him that they turn him over to the French for medical care.

Dayan said no. "If I die, I die, but I don't want to be a prisoner." His mind went back to Acre. That particular agony was still fresh in his mind. Enough was enough.

Incredibly, Dayan's force gave him a chance to survive, and not as a prisoner. Thanks to the machine gun on the roof and a mortar, also retrieved from the French earlier, his men held back the French for the next six hours. Finally, the advance Australian unit of the invasion force arrived. The building was secure. The second and final phase of the battle for the police station was over. Dayan's life hung in the balance.

PLACED ON A CAPTURED French truck along with two wounded Australian soldiers, Dayan was driven to Rosh Hanikra. The journey was slowed by the invasion convoys heading in the opposite direction. From Rosh Hanikra, he was taken to a hospital in Haifa, arriving shortly before dark—twelve hours after being shot.

As Dayan lay in Rothschild Hospital, Italian planes carried out bombing runs on Haifa. The hospital was in danger of being hit. Dayan, trapped inside, sought the truth from the doctors about his chances.

"Two things are certain," came a physician's reply. "You've lost an eye and you'll live. What is not clear is the condition of your head, with so many bits of glass and metal embedded in it." Dayan needed immediate surgery. His wife's signature was necessary but she was nowhere to be found. The doctors delayed operating. Finally, they had to begin. Otherwise it might have been too late.

The surgery revealed that the left eye could not be saved. All that could be done was to remove all the metal and glass fragments and close up the empty socket.

Ruth arrived during surgery. She had been incorrectly informed by a Haganah man that Dayan's injury was only to his hand and was not serious. Borrowing a car and a driver (she could not drive herself), Ruth hurried to Haifa. There, she learned that her husband had forty pieces of shrapnel in his head. She could feel only gratitude that he was alive at all. After surgery, Dayan's head was wrapped in bandages, as were both hands. A tube had been inserted through a hole in the bandages above his nose. His nostrils were kept open with safety pins to keep him from choking.

Would Dayan be blind? Brain-damaged? Perhaps even both? Such worries crossed Ruth's mind as she approached his bedside after surgery.

But Dayan's mind was still lucid.

"Will I be able to see?" he asked Ruth.

"Yes. But with only one eye."

Ruth knew that she had to get her husband out of this place, out of Haifa. Bombs were falling nearby. She had already spent one night in an air-raid shelter to protect herself and Yael. Where could she take her husband? She immediately thought of Jerusalem. With its special status as a holy city, it would be spared aerial bombing. As soon as it grew quiet, Ruth placed Dayan in the backseat of her mother's Morris and traveled with him to Jerusalem's Hadassah Hospital.

Dayan's battle wounds and the flight from Haifa were not the only shocks he endured. Ruth had some news. Waiting for a quiet period, she told him that she was pregnant with their second child.

Dayan went into a rage.

"Who is going to hire a man with one eye?" he asked, betraying a fear that he had become invalided for life. "It's impossible. I'm not going to be able to support my family. We can't have the child." His words tore through Ruth. It was too late for second thoughts.

So Moshe Dayan, turned into a one-eyed man by a French bullet, would have to accommodate himself to fathering another child. In time, he would have to adjust to a whole variety of changes wrought by that bullet. No change would be more earthshaking for him, more bewildering, than the moment he put on the black eyepatch for the first time. He wore it to protect those he did not know from that embarrassing split second of having to confront the ghastly, scarred sight of an empty socket where his left eye should have been. Conversely, he felt no need to shield his closest friends or family from viewing the deformity. Only at home was he comfortable enough to remove the eyepatch.

Why the two faces of Moshe Dayan? Why shield the public from his real self, but not his close friends and family? One must surmise that even at this early moment in his career, when few of his peers knew who he was, Moshe Dayan was, however unconsciously, seriously concerned about his public image, about making sure that that image would be as memorable as possible.

The use of the eyepatch showed an instinctive flair for public relations. He would have preferred that the injury to the eye had not occurred. Eventually, when all the surgery failed, when it became apparent to him that he was stuck with the eyepatch for good, Dayan sought to make the best of a bad thing: He made it the essential part of his personal appearance, the mark of identity people remembered more than his thin dark hair, his thick, farm-hardened fingers, or his roundish face, seemingly too large for his squat, stubby figure. The eyepatch did not melt into the background, it reached out and grabbed the onlooker. It said: "The wearer of this item has done something that others have not done."

Indeed, Moshe Dayan could lay claim to some extraordinary deeds. He had shown great courage and initiative on the battlefield, thus emerging as one of the yishuv's few heroes of World War II. While all the Jewish guides who had taken part in the invasion of Syria were considered heroes, Dayan displayed the qualities of an authentic warrior. Perhaps if he had stayed behind and guarded those irrelevant bridges, had waited for the Australians to present themselves, he could have saved his left eye. He would then not have achieved fame, the fame that comes from military exploits, from storming police stations against great odds, from firing cannons on rooftops when retreat might have seemed more prudent.

Though a small operation in the wider perspective of World War II, Dayan's seizure of the French police station in Lebanon electrified his fellow Jews. The Hebrew-language newspapers carried front-page stories about his injury. On June 10, *Davar*, for example, wrote, "In Nahalal, as in all other settlements, everybody is showing sympathy for relatives and friends of Moshe Dayan (son of Shmuel Dayan) who was wounded on Saturday night during the advance into Syria and Lebanon." His popularity soared, helped along by the praise lavished on him by his Australian comrades-in-arms. "That boy scout son-in-law of yours," one Australian officer told Rahel Schwartz while visiting Dayan, "if there's anything he doesn't know about military matters, it isn't worth knowing."[13]

Any number of genuine heroes would emerge from the yishuv; but no one was lionized in quite the same way that Dayan was. The eyepatch conferred so much glory on its wearer that some had trouble believing that Dayan had not dreamed it up as a crafty publicity stunt. Once, in 1960, an Israeli soldier wrote to Ruth Dayan, asking her to help resolve a dispute with his army buddies who had insisted that Dayan's eyepatch was a clever public relations gimmick, and that he had in fact never been injured. They were sure because one day a newspaper photo of Dayan showed him wearing the eyepatch over the left eye, while in another newspaper photo it was over the right eye. Gimmick or injury? Ruth pointed out that sometimes newspaper photos are inadvertently reversed.

For all the glory that the eyepatch would signify, Dayan suffered tremendously from his injury. He endured endless pain, particularly a pounding in his head that kept him awake at night. To dull his pain Dayan took tranquilizers. The doctors instructed him to take only a few a day, but he lied to them, as did Ruth: Sometimes he took eighteen a day.

HE WAS TO BECOME one of the most famous military commanders of the twentieth century, in part because of his eyepatch. In the days and weeks after his eye injury, however, Dayan's hopes of quickly returning to the battlefield were short lived. His damaged hand required that the fish-oil bandages be changed daily. He had to keep tubes in his nose for some time. Pus trickled from his eye socket. The remaining shrapnel in his head gave him splitting headaches. His fingers were paralyzed. Relieved of his command, Dayan dwelt on the possibility of serving in the British army. But as what? A night watchman? Feelings of self-pity overwhelmed him: self-pity, induced by the problems of adjusting to his new life, blurred vision, difficulties in reading, spilling things he tried to pour, exploring the dark with only one eye; self-pity, made worse by the growing realization that he would never be able to soldier again, that perhaps Yigal Allon (made deputy commander of the Palmach in 1943) might outshine him; self-pity, devouring him because he had a pregnant wife and a better chance of remaining a cripple without a skill than of being a breadwinner. Such emotions erupted in Dayan's mind like tiny explosions, making the constant headaches seem even worse.

What could he do? There was always the Palmach. The most he could expect would be to train others; yet to do that he would have to agree to the Palmach's kibbutz-oriented regimen: three weeks of each month laboring on a kibbutz with board and lodging in return; the fourth week reserved for military training. He had never been a man of the kibbutz. Now was no time for him to start. His heart and soul belonged to the moshav, to Nahalal; there, his father needed help with the farming; there, if anywhere, Moshe Dayan felt he was needed and wanted.

Eventually he began to manage better with only one eye: He learned to read without glasses; drive a car by gauging distances; accustom himself to the dark by taking long walks. He fell on occasion, but in time he learned how to keep his balance. Even with the eye injury, Dayan was determined to remain within the military framework.

Salvation came a few weeks after he was out of the hospital from the man who lived on the ground floor of his Jerusalem home: Reuven Shiloah, director of special services in the Jewish Agency's Political Department. Now that David Ben-Gurion had steered yishuv policy back toward cooperation with the British, it was only natural that the Jewish Agency develop close contacts with British intelligence. The Agency's Political Department had been created in order to facilitate those contacts. Shiloah asked Dayan to come work for him: Dayan's assignment would be to oversee the establishment of a small underground network of transmitting stations that would relay intelligence information to the Allied forces in the likely event that the German forces overran Palestine. Throughout the summer Dayan worked on the "Palestine Scheme," as the British called it; the Haganah referred to the PS as "Moshe Dayan's private network."

Jerusalem became the central exchange of the network, with subsidiary locations around the country. On September 26 a three-month course began for twenty radio operators, one of whom was Ruth (she was not very good at it). The British paid for all the equipment and for Dayan's salary of twenty British pounds a month plus five pounds for renting a large four-room apartment in Jerusalem (which doubled as the central exchange). The network produced fifty operators.

Dayan was eager to expand the network's efforts. On October 20, he proposed yet another contingency plan, this one calling for the training of individuals who could pass as Arabs or Germans and who would spy for the British after a German conquest of Palestine. To this the British initially said no. But the following July 1942 they in effect accepted the idea by permitting the creation of an Arab and German platoon within the Palmach.

The German advance on Palestine never materialized. Part of Dayan's plan was, however, carried out later in the war. Haganah members conducted operations behind Nazi lines in Europe, seeking to rescue Jewish survivors and Allied pilots who had bailed out over Nazi-occupied sections.

The Nazis and their Holocaust against the Jews played less of a role in the molding of Moshe Dayan's political thinking than it did in the thinking of other Israeli leaders, particularly two Israeli prime ministers, Menachem Begin and Yitzhak Shamir. Dayan's writings are almost bare of any reference to the Holocaust. He very likely found it difficult to relate to so sweeping a defeat for the Jewish people.

Toward the end of August 1942 Dayan traveled to Baghdad. The reasons for this trip are unclear. He had asked the driver of a convoy of buses belonging to a Jewish transport cooperative if he could go along as the second driver. The cooperative had been chartered by the British army to drive an Indian battalion to Iraq, then return to Palestine with an English unit that was replacing the Indian one. When the Haganah learned that Dayan planned to visit Iraq, he was asked to take three suitcases of small arms to the Baghdad Haganah cell. That cell had been trying to help Jews there defend themselves against local Arabs. The journey took three days. When the bus finally arrived at a British military camp twenty miles outside of Baghdad, Dayan was ordered to remain in the camp for his own safety, complicating his plans. He sneaked through the camp fence on bare feet, wearing only shorts and an undershirt. Reaching the highway safely, he was momentarily stymied by the prospect of getting through the police checkpoints. He noticed that the police were checking anyone who was not an Arab. Taking off his eyepatch, he tried to blend in with the local inhabitants. When a convoy of donkeys carrying farm produce passed by, he reached for a branch from a bush and began prodding one of the slower donkeys, turning himself into a member of the caravan.

Once inside Baghdad, Dayan realized that he would have trouble seeking out his Haganah contact in the designated place, the Hotel Umayyad, because of his run-down appearance and dirty clothes. He was right. A janitor, noticing his clothes and his one eye, tried to chase him off the premises. After much arguing and, no less important, a financial bribe, Dayan persuaded the man to seek out Enzo Sereni, the local Haganah official. Finally, Dayan and Sereni met. A quick wash in Sereni's hotel room and Dayan was off on a tour of the city with Sereni as his guide. They visited a museum, but Dayan quickly became bored. He had not yet developed a keen interest in antiquities. During a visit to the Jewish Quarter that evening, Dayan was approached by some Jewish activists who begged him to smuggle two young Polish Jewish refugees into Palestine. Dayan accepted the challenge before returning to the camp.

The following night Dayan once again made his way surreptitiously into Baghdad, this time taking the suitcases of weapons to his Haganah friends. He returned to the camp with the two Polish youngsters, dressed as British officers. Upon his return to Palestine, Dayan delivered the two youngsters to Kibbutz Maoz Chaim and then went on to Nahalal.

With no German invasion, Dayan's espionage units remained unemployed, the men disgruntled at being unable to play a combat role. Dayan wanted something to do as well, and when nothing was forthcoming he resigned from the network. The Jewish Agency leadership urged him to withdraw his resignation. He did so half-heartedly. He was still welcome around the planning tables of the Haganah, but few paid much attention to him. For one thing, he was out of step with the consensus among Palestinian Jewry that suggested that Jewish statehood would come only with the aid of the British, that ultimately Britain would implement the Balfour Declaration. Nonsense, thought Dayan. The yishuv had to rely upon itself, no one else. It must build up its military strength for the forthcoming battle. If negotiations with Palestinian Arabs could prevent that war, all the better. But no one else would come to the rescue of the Jews. Of that Dayan was certain.

He spent the next two years—from September 1942 to the summer 1944—living in a prefab hut on Shmuel and Dvorah's farm at Nahalal. It was very crowded. Moshe and Ruth shared a small room with Yael and Ehud, who had been born on January 31, 1942. The roof leaked but Shmuel refused to pay to have it repaired. "Moshe will fix it," he said. Moshe, it turned out, was too busy growing tomatoes.

Plagued by his eye injury and his difficulty in adopting a clear-cut political line, Dayan remained in the shadows. The Palmach employed itself in illegal immigration work; the Haganah prepared for the coming battle with the Arabs; but Dayan remained aloof. Both the Palmach and Haganah sought out leaders with a particular brand of politics: the Palmach had its connections to the left-wing Ahdut Avoda party; the Haganah, to the more centrist Mapai. Dayan, politically neutral, found no welcome embrace in either camp. Nor did he seek one out. To have won membership in the senior ranks of either group would have meant taking an active political role, and Dayan was not prepared for that.

In 1944 Moshe and Ruth acquired their own farm, Number 53 on the Nahalal circle. They were able to make the purchase thanks to a 4,400–pound sterling gift from Zvi Schwartz that covered most of the 4,000-pound cost of the farm plus a 1,400-pound mortgage. Moshe and Ruth had a small two-room house, still with no toilet facilities inside. Of the three Dayan children, Moshe was the only one engaged in farming; Zohar (nicknamed Zorik) and Aviva were in the British army; Zorik was in the Jewish Brigade, serving in Italy and Belgium; Aviva was a nurse and later an army driver in Egypt. Moshe and Ruth had no livestock, so they purchased some cows. In fact all they had at first were some citrus groves. But Dayan built a chicken run and obtained some turkeys, involving himself in the same kind of rugged farm work that he had known as a youngster. German shepherds were around; and a mule called Lord that they hitched to a two-wheel cart for transportation; and chicks, a donkey, and small rabbits. Ruth was again pregnant.

With a farm and a growing sense of self-assuredness, Dayan raised no fuss about the new arrival. All in all, with few of the pressures of military life, the years between 1944 and 1948 marked a supremely happy time for both Moshe and Ruth. There was less adventure in Dayan's life now, and his involvement in public affairs was only minimal. The seasons were marked not by military engagements but by the planting of tomatoes in the summer, cauliflower in the fall. Their third child, Assaf, was born on November 23, 1945. Ruth had wanted the baby to be born at home, but Moshe insisted on her going to the hospital in Afula. To get there they had to violate a night curfew imposed by the British.

Though simple by many standards, the Dayan household contained certain items that gave the family a slight edge over others at Nahalal. The children had a radio and toys and were carefully dressed; each one had shoes, boots, and sandals. Like the other children at Nahalal, Dayan's youngsters quickly became acquainted with everyday farm life. Whenever a cow gave birth, Dayan made a point of having Yael on hand, even if it meant awakening her. He invested time in other forms of education as well: Dayan made sure to recite the recently published poetry of Natan Alterman and Avraham Shlonsky to the children.

In late 1943, intrigued by their nationalist zeal, Dayan held a series of meetings with leaders of the right-wing Irgun. Menachem Begin's Irgun had recently become engaged in terror against the British, an out-and-out violation of Haganah policy at the time, which was to devote all yishuv resources to the fight against the Nazis. Dayan seemed torn, in sympathy with the Irgun's goals but displeased by its methods. It was those methods which got in the way of Dayan falling in step with Irgun leaders when they proposed a joint military effort. The Irgun approached Dayan knowing that Dayan was interested in weakening the British. Dayan met with Eliahu Ravid and Eliahu Lankin, both members of the Irgun's high command. Dayan listened as they urged him to join a new underground group called Am Lohem (Hebrew for "Fighting People"). Its goal would be to place combatants from the Haganah, Palmach, Irgun, and Stern Group together under one fighting banner. Dayan rejected the offer. He could side with the motives of the right-wing groups, Dayan explained, but he could not defy British authority. Nor could he withdraw from the Haganah so easily.

Still, he was keenly interested in meeting the Irgun leader, Menachem Begin. From the latter's recollection of their meeting around that time, the two men got on wonderfully. Dayan spoke about his combat in Syria. Begin liked what he heard, liked that Dayan did not boast. Begin took Dayan's matter-of-fact portrayal of his combat to be a sign of his courage. Begin later described Dayan as one of the Haganah's most important officers. Dayan noted appreciatively that Begin's men were demonstrating that it was possible to take on the British. The Irgun deserved praise for that. Nonetheless, Dayan and Begin concluded no agreement; they found no way to resolve their differences.

Dayan still found the Irgun compelling. After it blew up the offices of the British secret service in three large towns in Palestine in March 1944, Dayan appeared at Eliahu Ravid's house to learn about the technical details of the operation. Eliahu Lankin, the Irgun commander of the Jerusalem area, gave Dayan a briefing. "Our leaders disagree with each other," Dayan told Lankin and Ravid, "but we, the soldiers, don't have to get involved in the argument."

Unfortunately for Dayan, he would soon get involved. One day in 1944 Eliyahu Golomb, then the head of the Haganah, arrived in Nahalal, and insisted that Dayan come to Tel Aviv to take on full-time work in intelligence for the Haganah. Let him rest a little while longer, Ruth begged Golomb, just for a year. Golomb was insistent. He promised that the new assignment would last no more than three months. Dayan, however, remained in Tel Aviv for a year, living with Ruth in a series of run-down hotel rooms while Yael and Ehud went to school.

Dayan's assignment turned out to be one of the most controversial of his career. He was asked to take a leading role in the suppression of the Irgun and the smaller right-wing dissident group called the Stern Group. Intense debate occurred within Haganah circles about how to deal with the dissident groups' terror. An ultimatum was decided upon: Either they ceased their activities—or the Haganah would be forced to take measures against them. Complicating matters, the Irgun and Stern Group refused to act unilaterally.

Clearly, Dayan would have preferred a more neutral assignment, since the effort at suppression pitted Jew against Jew; but despite these misgivings, he grabbed the chance to return to the fray. Dayan's role in this effort remains murky, and no wonder. In later years, leaders of the Haganah, the Irgun, and Stern Group would be forced to work side by side—in politics, in war, in all sorts of ways. Everyone preferred to forget the time when one side hunted down the other—when the Haganah proclaimed a hunting season, or Saison, against these right-wing troublemakers. That Saison lasted from October 1944 until the summer of 1945. It was a nasty time, when Haganah men snooped on Irgun and Stern Group dissidents, hunted them down, and turned them over to the British. Jew against Jew—not exactly what Theodor Herzl had in mind when he called for the creation of a Jewish state; nor David Ben-Gurion, when he envisioned the future state of Israel. To achieve that state, Jews would have to fight the British, the Arabs, but not one another.

It is not hard to imagine why Moshe Dayan and other Haganah men later remained tight-lipped about their role in the Saison. There was nothing to gain from elaborating, nothing at all. Dayan's precise role in this affair has never been spelled out. Eliahu Lankin believes that Dayan was one of the ringleaders of the Saison: "Dayan talked nicely but was no better than the rest of those who kidnapped our boys."[14] From the 1967 Six Day War onward, Dayan would serve in governments with the one-time Irgun leader, Menachem Begin. The two men sensed an identity of purpose in each other. Neither had reason to look back.

DURING THE SUMMER of 1944, Dayan dabbled in politics but only grudgingly. It was soon after the historic split in Mapai: the Ahdut Avoda (United Labor) faction had broken away from Mapai, opposing Ben-Gurion's insistence on focusing on partition as a means of attaining Jewish statehood. Berl Katznelson, the Mapai ideologue, tried to rally young people who had not yet joined any party to form a "young circle" in Mapai. Accordingly, he asked Dayan to come from Nahalal to the founding meeting of the "young circle" in Haifa. Dayan did so, feeling a bit lost. "Look, friends," he said, "politics is not for me and I am not cut out for politics. If you want me just to decorate the stage at the foundation meeting, I'll come, because Berl has asked me to. But don't expect any political activity on my part."[15]

DESPITE HIS EYE INJURY, few thought of Moshe Dayan as a cripple. Few believed that his military days were over. Those who recalled his exploits in Syria were eager to recruit him for positions of command. One opportunity arose soon after the war, when a number of Haganah officers grew angry that the Haganah was not doing enough to avenge British acts against the yishuv. Representing these officers, Iska Shadmi journeyed to Nahalal in search of someone to lead them in their own effort. He sought out Moshe Dayan. He knocked on Dayan's door at 2:00 A.M.

Shadmi got right to the point: "We want you to head our group. We have to do something that will move the Haganah."

For fifteen minutes Dayan listened. Then he began. He told Shadmi he sympathized with what he and the others wanted to do. But there was a catch.

"If you take me as your commander I will be a disaster for you. I have a reputation among the British as someone who 'breaks through fences.' The first time your group has weapons, the British will come to me. They will understand that Moshe Dayan is cooking up something. So I think you have made the wrong choice."

What did he suggest as an alternative? Dayan said tersely: "I like to suggest only what I take upon myself to do. I will leave that with you." In the end, Shadmi managed to exact a promise from Haganah leaders that more would be done against the British.[16]

IF ZIONIST POLITICS was alien to most of the young members of the yishuv during this postwar period, that was not the case with Dayan. He had no interest in leaving the military for a life of public affairs. Even had he wished to, his father's generation was still very much in political control of the yishuv. Still, Dayan held strong political convictions, the most important of which was that Jews in Palestine should strive for their own state. Zalman Shoval, who had been a politician in his own right and Dayan's chief political lieutenant, recalled meeting him for the first time in 1946 while camping, along with other members of Shoval's scouting group, Hatzofim Habonim, near Nahalal. Their first encounter was abrupt: The Nahalal boys under Dayan's leadership "attacked" the camp, engaging in ninety seconds of stone throwing, a routine habit of Jewish "fighters" aimed at testing the alertness of their colleagues. Later Dayan sat around the campfire and talked about the future Jewish state, leaving an indelible impression on Shoval: "Here was a young man who talked to us in our language. He talked about the creation of the Jewish state, not as something which was up on the clouds, but as an absolute certainty."[17]

Dayan's first real leap into Zionist politics came at the Twenty-second Zionist Congress in Basel, Switzerland, in December 1946. He went there as an observer as part of the Mapai delegation, as did twenty-three year-old Shimon Peres, both representatives of Mapai's Young Guard. One of the official delegates was Shmuel Dayan. The congress was to debate two conflicting strategies related to how the yishuv should deal with the British. The activist strategy was espoused by David Ben-Gurion, who favored disconnecting the yishuv from the British in preparation for the creation of the Jewish state. The moderate approach was championed by Chaim Weizmann, who thought the yishuv could only benefit by cooperating with the British. Zealously supporting Ben-Gurion's view was Moshe Dayan. At an internal meeting of the Mapai delegation he insisted that the activist approach should apply not only to defense matters but to all Zionist aims, especially land settlement and immigration. The speech was Dayan's first exposure before a large public group. Most importantly, Ben-Gurion later expressed his agreement with Dayan's broad definition of activism. That compliment was, to the fledgling Dayan, a critical step forward in his political advancement. Dayan had less luck with another idea he advanced. Seeking ways to put pressure on the British to allow Jews to immigrate to Palestine, he proposed that British-run immigrant camps abroad be burned down to dramatize the problem and thus force the British to bring the interned Jews to Palestine. The proposal was given little attention.

The truth was that Dayan was not eager for a role in politics, but David Ben-Gurion wanted young blood brought into the Zionist movement to win the youngsters over to his activist line. So he insisted that young members of the Zionist movement be allowed to participate, if not in the senior positions then as official observers. At Basel, Dayan came up against the older generation of Zionist politicians and did not much like what he saw. Writing to Nahman Betser, who was in Nahalal, on December 14 from Switzerland, he noted admiringly the work of those from Palestine who were smuggling Jewish survivors of the Holocaust into Palestine. These were the real workers, and not the veteran orators who did little else but shout and seek applause.

After the congress Dayan went to Paris for an eye operation. The hospital was in a convent; the nurses were nuns. However much fame Dayon gained from the eyepatch, he found the attention that it drew to him dismaying. Rather than have to worry about awkward reactions wherever he went, he preferred staying at home. "It is difficult for a normal-eyed person to understand how unpleasant it is to be the constant object of curious stares and whispers," he wrote.[18] It was his heartfelt wish to walk down a street or attend a movie without attracting any interest. The doctor planned to graft a piece of bone into Dayan's eye socket and then give him a glass eye. Unfortunately, the operation failed. Reacting to the surgery poorly, Dayan ran a high fever for four days, hallucinating. The doctors were convinced he was near death. He lay for a month, attended to by French-speaking nuns as well as Ruth and Re'uma (Ruth's sister, who married Ezer Weizman). He could not swallow food. His body was in the throes of rejecting the transplant. Making matters worse, the room was unheated. The advice Ruth received from one nun was most unexpected: "I can't understand why you remain in that chair, madame. Why don't you get into the bed and keep Monsieur warm?"[19] Dayan soon recovered.

Returning home in February 1947, Dayan was soon appointed to a high-ranking post within the Haganah—staff officer for Arab Affairs with the rank of major. Though the rank was low compared to others of his generation, the post represented a significant leap forward in his career: For the first time he was part of the Haganah's national command. Only during the second part of that year, after Ben-Gurion appointed Israel Galili head of the Haganah's national headquarters and Ya'acov Dori chief of staff did plans for Israel's war of independence begin in earnest. At that stage Dayan was called up to begin full-time work in Arab intelligence in his staff post.

Though the title, staff officer for Arab Affairs, sounded good, frustration pursued Dayan in the new post. Overlapping bureaucracies weighed on him. His was not the only yishuv institution dealing with Arab affairs. The Jewish Agency's Arab Department took an interest in the subject as well. Then too, his powers were limited. He could advise, but he had no direct command over soldiers. That was left to others. Because of his derring-do in Syria, his eyepatch, and the publicity surrounding his antics, Dayan had acquired a certain reputation within the yishuv. He was a rising star, and others in the intelligence service responded with jealousy; they were not about to take his proposals seriously.

His task was to recruit agents who could filter out information about the plans of Arab cells in Palestine. At that time, these cells were the yishuv's principle enemy. Once the actual Israeli War of Independence began in the spring of 1948, these groups joined with the invading armies. Throughout 1947, the cells undertook increasingly violent action against the Jewish community. Using the same approach as he had in choosing trackers during the 1941 invasion into Syria, Dayan believed it was crucial to pick men who knew the Arab terrorist cells. He wanted no amateurs. His efforts paid off handsomely as the intelligence he was able to acquire helped Israeli forces in various campaigns in the north.

On November 29, when the United Nations' General Assembly voted to partition Palestine into a Jewish and an Arab state, Moshe Dayan was home at Nahalal. He lifted Yael out of her bed while Ruth picked up Ehud (Assaf, still a baby, was left asleep). They dressed quickly and went to the Nahalal community hall to join the dancing, kissing, embracing, and crying. The night-long festivities were tinged with sadness: The partition resolution almost certainly meant war with the Arabs, and the burial of many Jewish fighters. Indeed, the day after the United Nations vote, eight Jews were killed. Had the Arabs been willing to implement the UN resolution peacefully, the Jews most likely would have welcomed the creation of an Arab state, but negotiations over implementation never took place. Refusing to accept the UN resolution, the Arab states prepared themselves for war with the new Jewish state. For the next five and half months, the Arabs tried to nullify the partition resolution, not even waiting for the birth of the new Jewish state. Arab attacks against the yishuv increased with every passing day, as rural settlements, towns and interurban transportation were assaulted. Though some voices were raised urging that the establishment of the state be delayed, David Ben-Gurion and others were adamant, believing that under any circumstances a fight with the Arabs was unavoidable, and unless the Jews won, there would be no Zionist enterprise, no Jewish immigration, and no Jewish settlement.

Moshe Dayan's name is missing from the history books covering the earliest phase of Arab-Jewish fighting during 1948. He sat on the senior councils of planning but held no combat role. The men in the field shared the limelight, such as there was, and, while the Haganah had created seven new brigades and the Palmach had enlarged itself so that it now stood at three brigades, Dayan was not offered command of as much as a battalion. He was in fact home a great deal, milking cows at Nahalal.

During this period Dayan served as one of Ben-Gurion's advisers. He participated in the high command's deliberations on policy toward the Arabs. One key discussion in early January was attended by Ben-Gurion, Moshe Sharett, Israel Galili, Yigael Yadin, Yigal Allon, Yitzhak Sadeh, and Moshe Dayan. At issue was a recent Palmach retaliatory raid against an Arab village in the Galilee. Was it justified for the Jews to inflict heavy causalties on the Arabs? The high command had tried to follow a policy of moderation in its retaliatory raids in regions that had been relatively quiet, such as this one. But on December 18, twelve Arabs from the village of Hassas had been killed in a retaliatory raid, among them a woman and four children. None of that bothered Dayan. He supported harsh reprisals despite the price. Several others at the meeting, including Ben-Gurion, criticized the action, but Dayan said, "The action in Hassas had the desired effect; the villagers have made peaceful approaches to us."

Dayan also spoke up in favor of storming Jaffa and inflicting a major blow against local Arabs there. He believed that limited retaliatory action achieved nothing, lowering Jewish prestige in Arab eyes and reducing Jewish deterrent capabilities: "All our actions in Jaffa from the first day of the war until now have served only to ruin our prestige, and we haven't given the answer we could. There are places—Haifa, for example— where retaliatory action has achieved the desired effect, sometimes by chance. If we stop Arab transport throughout the country and blow up buses in Balad-a-Sheikh, that's a direct hit at Balad-a-Sheikh because they can't live without buses; they need them to get to work, 3,000 people travel from there every day. An action like that has no value if carried out in Ramle, because there the people aren't dependent on buses." As for the Negev, Dayan suggested "initiating a battle and killing one or two hundred Arabs."

Dayan's hawkish approach represented the minority view; the dominant attitude was in favor of maintaining a low profile, gathering strength, and postponing decisions until the British had departed the country. In time Dayan's tack became official policy, but only after a painful experience in March: It was then that the Haganah failed in the Battle of the Roads and convoys to Yechiam, Gush Etzion, Atarot, Har Tov, and Jerusalem were routed. By early April the high command went on the initiative, as evidenced by Operation Nachshon and the Battle of Mishmar Ha'emek.

The dangers were everywhere. One night in early April Dayan was called to Jerusalem on a certain assignment. The city had been under heavy siege for months. Carrying Ruth's basket of Nahalal eggs and cream for delivery to the Schwartzes, Dayan flew in a Piper Cub, and was supposed to stop at a kibbutz near the Dead Sea before reaching Jerusalem; word came that the kibbutz had fallen under Arab siege. Dayan's whereabouts were unknown for two days. Ruth was convinced that Moshe had been killed. When she learned that the Kastel, an Arab hilltop village five miles west of Jerusalem, had been the focus of a battle from March 31 to April 9, and that it had been taken by the Palmach at a price of 250 Jewish dead, she cried all night and the next morning. She assumed he must have been among the dead. She begged a Haganah acquaintance to place a phone call to Ben-Gurion. Surely, he could find out what Dayan's situation was. But Ben-Gurion had no news. He tried to calm Ruth by suggesting that he would have heard by now if the news had been bad. Ben-Gurion was right. The next day Dayan traveled out of Jerusalem safely.

Mid-April brought monumental tragedy to the Dayan family. Moshe's brother Zorik had been a platoon leader in the northern front's Carmeli Brigade and had taken part in a four-day battle resisting an attack on Kibbutz Ramat Yohanan, east of Haifa, by the Druze, the Arabic-speaking sect who had drifted away from Islam. On the second day of the battle, April 14, he participated in an assault against the Druze. He did not return. Upon hearing that Zorik was missing, Dayan rushed to Ramat Yohanan to search for him on the battlefield, but the fighting was too intense to allow a search. Once the fighting ended with a Jewish triumph over the Druze, others located Zorik's body. The sad truth was then learned: He had led his soldiers on an attack on an enemy position only to receive a bullet in his forehead. (Even the death of his brother would not prevent Dayan from advocating in the 1950s that officers lead their men into battle.) Dayan went with Israel Gefen, Aviva's husband, to the kibbutz dining room, where the bodies of the dead fighters were laid out. Without Gefen he was concerned that he might break down at the sight of his dead brother. Dayan identified Zorik from scars and a mended broken arm. Stoically, he did not collapse.[20] Zorik had died at the age of twenty-two; he left his wife Mimi and a baby named Uzi.

Zorik's death was a shock to the Dayan household. He had always been Dvorah's favorite child. After his death she would suffer a black depression for a long time. Dvorah said very little to her remaining son whenever they met. Dayan attributed her distance to Zorik's loss. The loss of Zorik had a frightening effect on Yael: She imagined that if death could come to her uncle, then why not to her father? Dayan could do nothing to ease her fears. He told her that he had gotten his bullet, and had survived it. Now, he said, he knew how to avoid bullets and he had no intention of being hit again.

A few days after the Ramat Yohanan battle, the enemy Druze communicated to Dayan that they were prepared to stop fighting the Jews. Dayan agreed to meet them, despite the fact that some of them had been involved in his brother's death. When he appeared at the meeting, the Druze feared that they had been led into a trap because Dayan was undoubtedly intent upon revenge. To the Druze, the concept of a blood revenge was very real; but for Dayan it was not. "Since you have come to make a pact with us, I forgive you for spilling blood of my blood," he told them, and then he raised a glass of wine and toasted, "To Life." He explained that his intention was not revenge, but to turn the Druze into friends—and if not that, then neutrals. Displaying no great emotion, Dayan told them it was in their interest to defect from the Syrian army, which had treated them as a minority and given them no sense of security. They were better off joining the Jewish forces. Negotiations ensued and the relieved Druze promised to remain on the sidelines in the forthcoming fighting. As a result of this meeting, Dayan became a hero to the Druze. Moreover, their decision to sit out the fighting helped Jewish forces in the forthcoming battles.

On April 22, a few weeks before statehood was declared, Dayan was handpicked by David Ben-Gurion for a delicate assignment. A day earlier Haifa had been conquered by Jewish forces, who had begun looting the Arab sector of the city. Dayan had the task of preventing further looting and administering abandoned Arab property such as cars, refrigerators, and store goods. He ordered that anything the Jewish army could use be transferred to army warehouses; the rest would go to Jewish agricultural settlements that had been attacked by Arabs. This thankless task made for a sorry episode. Some would criticize Dayan for taking part in the looting of Haifa. He himself must have ached at the thought that others were enjoying command positions while he, still regarded by his superiors as disabled because of his eye injury, was busy cleaning up someone else's mess. But not for long. A war was about to start—and, as would always be the case, Moshe Dayan would not allow himself to be any place other than the battlefield.

✦ 4 ✦

COMMANDO AT WORK

EIGHTEEN YEARS after Israel's War of Independence, recalling the heavy casualties and the mishaps, David Ben-Gurion confessed that, in retrospect, he would have preferred Moshe Dayan as chief of staff during that war. Had Dayan held that post then, the IDF might have achieved more, and the map of Israel might have been different. "It's a pity that I did not know Moshe Dayan at the beginning of the war. I had a feeling that efforts were being made to keep him away from me. Nevertheless, I managed to become acquainted with him in the end, and I'm glad of it, for he gave me no reason to be disappointed in him."[1] (Ben-Gurion had met Dayan before 1948, most notably at the Zionist Congress in Basel two years earlier. Evidently, the prime minister did not mean to suggest that he had not known Dayan before, only that he had been unaware of his military skills at the war's start.)

Oddly enough, the one man who would have been expected to agree with this long-delayed assessment thought Ben-Gurion all wrong. Moshe Dayan sensed immediately that Israel's chief of staff during the 1948 fighting—Ya'acov Dori—might well take umbrage at the Old Man's remarks. Four days after the *Haboker* interview he wrote to Dori, noting that Ben-Gurion's remarks "exceeded all limits of what is permissible even in error." Dayan explained, "There is no doubt about the fact that at the time of the War of Independence, I was not mature enough for the post of C-of-S, or even for a lesser position on the staff, and those military actions and judgments I cooked up later were based on things I learned from my elders and betters and were the fruit of extended activity and a process of gradual development."

Noble words on Dayan's part. Deeply honest, too. Others did have more command experience—Ya'acov Dori, Yigael Yadin, Israel Galili, even Yigal Allon—and hence were the natural choices for leadership roles in the 1948 war. But Dayan did have a gift for sizing up the battlefield and for figuring out how to defeat the Arabs while keeping Israeli casualties to a minimum, that others did not possess. He was correct, as he observed in his letter to Dori, that he was not ready to assume a position of top leadership in the 1948 fighting—he was thirty-three years old and it was still others' turn. So 1948 would not be his war but rather a testing ground, a laboratory in which he would try out the military doctrines that were brewing in his head. In some ways, he would succeed. In some other ways, he would embroil himself in controversy. He would in time come to symbolize the military arm of the state of Israel; he would have greater impact on the development of that military arm than anyone else. The road to this achievement began, in many respects, on the battlefields of this war, battlefields that Moshe Dayan, critically wounded seven years earlier, had doubted he would ever see.

For seven years the question of whether Dayan could participate in soldiering had persisted. A one-eyed man might have turned into an invalid. Dayan had worried from 1941 that such would be his fate. Since then, he had sought to live as normal a life as possible. While he was struggling with that challenge, those of his generation were steadily advancing. Could Dayan catch up to them? Just how active could he be? Those were the questions that haunted him on the eve of Israel's War of Independence. Until now, he had remained on the periphery of combat, assuming posts in administration. What he wanted most was to take on a combat role. He knew in his heart, as the yishuv prepared for its ultimate test, that he was capable.

UNTIL THE EARLY part of 1948, most of the Jewish military effort had been devoted to trying to clear and hold the main roads that connected the different parts of the yishuv. As long as the British were around, the Haganah could not make an all-out effort to conquer the roads themselves; so they settled for defending individual convoys. The first major battle for a city occurred in Tiberias; there the Arab lower town fell to the Haganah on April 18, three weeks before the May 14 statehood declaration. Four days later, on April 22, the Arab quarter of Haifa was taken. Safed in northern Israel fell on May 10; three days later Jaffa surrendered.

By the first two weeks of May, the Haganah's goals had largely been achieved: Jewish towns and settlements in the northern Negev, the coastal plain, and the valleys of the Galilee were essentially secured; the Arabs, for their part, still held the central part of the country from Galilee to Judea and Samaria, including the mountain ridges around Jerusalem, which was still the real thorn.

SHORTLY BEFORE Israel's declaration of statehood in mid-May, Yitzhak Sadeh had been appointed commander of the Eighth Armored Brigade. Sadeh discovered that there was a shortage of suitable commanders. He was delighted to learn that Major Moshe Dayan was available and eager for a command: the same Dayan who had wanted to storm the Arabs at Hanita in 1938, who had found guarding a pair of bridges a bore and so had taken on an entire French unit in Syria three years later. On May 17 David Ben-Gurion wrote in his diary: "Moshe Dayan has been charged with organizing a commando for the Central Front."

Three days before, Ben-Gurion had proclaimed the birth of the Jewish state at a special session of the Jewish National Council. With Jerusalem under siege, council members gathered in Tel Aviv for the historic declaration. At midnight the British were due to leave Palestine. The Jewish leaders knew that once the British left war with the Arabs was inevitable. Within hours of Ben-Gurion's historic announcement, expeditionary armies of the Arab states attacked the new state. They came from Lebanon, Syria, Iraq, Transjordan, and Egypt; Saudi soldiers fought under Egyptian command. The Arabs had the military advantage, partly because of their overwhelming numbers and partly because of their ability to acquire heavier arms than the new state of Israel could. Against these armies, the Haganah could muster only light arms, homemade armored cars, and a few light training planes. David was fighting Goliath.

Meanwhile, as Moshe Dayan began to organize his new battalion, disastrous events occurred in the Jordan Valley: Syrian forces, entering Israel after midnight May 14, had been shelling the valley's kibbutzim, threatening their survival. It seemed only a matter of time until those forces overran the Deganias. Haganah headquarters decided to release Dayan from his duties as head of the commando battalion and appoint him commander of the Jordan Valley sector; that sector extended from Ein Gev on the eastern shore of the Sea of Galilee, to areas north of Beit-Shean. Dayan's closest friends were convinced that he deserved more than this post of battalion commander. This new appointment in the Jordan Valley put Dayan on the way toward such a promotion.

Dayan began at a disadvantage. He had been told to carry out special operations behind enemy lines as well as to support efforts in the Jordan Valley—yet local soldiers did not fall under his command. Golani Brigade commander Moshe Montag remained independent. Still his appointment had an air of urgency and he was cast in the role of a potential savior. Yigael Yadin, the acting chief of staff who replaced the ailing Dori, sent a second telegram to Montag ordering him to place at Dayan's disposal whatever he needed to do his job. Easier said than done.

The new sector commander arrived at the Deganias soon after dark. Loaded in his antiquated Haganah-owned car were three crude antitank weapons. Accompanying Dayan was a Gadna company of sixteen- and seventeen year olds who had yet to taste battle.

What Dayan found upon his arrival was an army in shambles and about to be defeated. Syrian forces, pouring down from the Golan Heights, were hoping to sweep through the Jordan Valley kibbutzim, and by the time of Dayan's arrival, were by and large succeeding. In Zemach at the southern tip of the Sea of Galilee, early that Tuesday morning, the Syrians had attacked one of the two Golani Brigade companies, which was under strength with only four hundred men. The Syrians captured the strategic police station, forcing the Golani unit to retreat, leaving dead and wounded behind. Members of nearby Sha'ar Hagolan and Massada had been forced to abandon their kibbutzim. All that stood between the Syrians and the rest of the yishuv, to the north, west, and south, were the Deganias.

Angered and frustrated at having too little authority over the troops, Dayan made a quick inspection of the front line. Matters were near catastrophic. Better, he thought to himself, to figure out what needed to be done. He could deal with the problems of breaking the chain of command later—if later came. Dayan did not know that only twenty hours remained before the Syrians were to launch their final attack. One hope of staving them off was dashed when a company from the Yiftach Brigade tried to recapture the police station at Zemach, but failed. In Tel Aviv on Wednesday a three-man delegation from Degania A, Degania B, and a third Jordan Valley kibbutz, Kinneret, went to implore the new prime minister David Ben-Gurion for more men and arms. When told none could be spared from other sectors, one of the delegation burst into tears. All Ben-Gurion could do was send them to Yigael Yadin; the acting chief of staff tried to encourage them by noting that Moshe Dayan had been appointed Jordan Valley sector commander.

At Zemach, the Syrian force comprised an infantry brigade; thirty tanks and armored cars; artillery; and air support. The Israeli fighters had only Molotov cocktails, antitank bazookas, and small arms. What they lacked in heavy arms they tried to make up in enthusiasm: Volunteers, some individually, some in groups, began to show up. Dayan learned from Montag that four French-made 65-millimeter guns, vintage 1914, were due any time. They would be the first artillery to be used by Jewish forces. Their arrival was delayed by a squabble between Ben-Gurion and Yadin: The prime minister wanted to keep the four cannons for besieged Jerusalem while the acting chief of staff insisted they go north. (On May 20, the Jewish Quarter of the Old City of Jerusalem fell to the Arab Legion.) Ultimately, they compromised by allowing the World War I pieces to be sent to the Jordan Valley fighting—but for no more than twenty-four hours!

Throughout Wednesday all efforts were aimed at erecting a solid defense perimeter that would thwart the expected Syrian assault on the two Deganias. Dayan concentrated on closing gaps in the defense arrangements at Degania B. He ordered men to take up positions at Beit Yerach, an archaeological mount just north of Degania. It was a key decision: While placing men there thinned out the defense line, the effect was to put Degania defenders on the flank of the Syrian attack. He instructed the men to abandon efforts at digging deep ditches and focus on locating the best firing positions. By this time, some Israelis were suffering from the hot sun and from thirst. Cheer up, Dayan told them: The Syrians had no shade, no trees.

The full-scale Syrian attack finally came on Thursday, May 20, at 4:15 A.M. It began with artillery shelling and mortar bombing. Thirty minutes later the Syrians moved their tank and infantry elements forward. Syrian tanks reached the fences of the two kibbutzim. One Syrian tank broke through the fence of Degania A, penetrating into the courtyard. Israeli soldiers leaped out of the trenches and tossed Molotov cocktails at the tank. It burst into flames, killing the crew. A second tank nearby met the same fate. Sometimes at a distance of only a few yards, the Degania defenders managed to silence the encircling tanks near the kibbutz. During the battle the 65-millimeter cannons had arrived, and they would be operational by noon. They had great range, and made incredible noise. Dayan was cautious about using the cannons: better not to rush into battle with the heavy armor until it was absolutely necessary—the shells were far too precious. Dayan sent word to Degania B that only if they felt their situation was desperate would he authorize the cannons' immediate firing. The settlers reported back that their situation was desperate. Fire the cannons!

When Ahya Ben-Ami, Dayan's messenger, returned from Degania B to Kinneret, he reported to Dayan that he was not sure if the Syrians had actually entered the kibbutz courtyard but he was certain that if they wished to do so, they could. Dayan then sent Ben-Ami to instruct the artillery officer nearby to fire the cannons. At first the shells were not on target. One cannon broke down. But the other three, once they found their targets, proved sufficient. Their noise was so deafening that the Syrians had apparently panicked and fled Zemach, after only forty shells had been fired. Altogether, five hundred shells were unleashed. Thirty Syrian soldiers lay dead. But had the Syrians really departed from Zemach? Instinctively, Dayan wanted to see for himself, despite the great risk. Had Syrian soldiers still been lurking in the shadows of the village, Dayan would have been an easy target. Nonetheless, at nightfall, joined by others, he drove to Zemach. It was crucial for him to know if the Syrians had retreated to Zemach or had stationed themselves farther to the east. He found Zemach empty and abandoned.

The lesson of Zemach would stay with him for years. A few Israeli shells and the Arabs had retreated in a panic, the deafening noise frightening them away. All that it seemed to take, Dayan would say later, was for someone to bang on a tin can and the Arabs would scatter like birds. From his experience in the Jordan Valley, Moshe Dayan believed the shaky generalization that Arabs shared some type of genetic defect that made them afraid of combat, that it was only necessary to fire a few shells onto the battlefield and they would instantly flee. As military philosophy, it had the obvious advantage of easing the mind of any commander who was about to confront sizeable Arab troop formations. But as tactical doctrine, the generalization was defective: No one could guarantee that the Arabs would automatically scatter every time they heard someone make a loud noise.

Where had the Syrians gone? Some had positioned themselves on Tel el Kasr near the southeastern edge of the Sea of Galilee, using their field guns to bombard the Jordan Valley settlements. Without artillery that could reach the spot, the Israelis were at a disadvantage. Dayan figured out what to do. He organized nine volunteers, mostly from the Nahalal region, and instructed them to take two small boats and row across the Sea of Galilee under cover of darkness. Reaching shore at Kibbutz Ein Gev, they made their way toward the Syrian position, creeping the last few dozen yards up the hill. The unit planted explosives that destroyed the artillery battery. Convinced that they had been assaulted by a large Israeli force, the Syrians retreated to the east. Recalling the eventful evening, Avino'am Slutzky, one of the volunteers, credited Dayan with the brainstorm: "Probably no other officer would have thought of such a thing."[2] That same night the shelling on Degania and Zemach stopped.

The Jordan Valley fighting showed that much work needed to be done to make these untrained men into real soldiers. Everywhere Dayan turned, he found another lesson that had to be learned: The wounded had been left with no one able to tend them; too many weapons proved unworkable; the Jewish settlements had not prepared themselves adequately for defense—they required more trenches, more arms. Yet, despite all these defects, Israeli soldiers had held out against an Arab army. That was the most heartening lesson.

FRESH FROM THE BATTLE for the Deganias, Dayan returned to Tel Aviv fired with enthusiasm and eager to take up command of his Eighty-ninth Mechanized Assault Battalion. He figured that defeating the Arabs would be no real problem, especially if Zemach was any model. "With a few jeeps and machine guns, we can take care of the Arab armies and put things in order," he boasted to Yitzhak Sadeh.

Before he could worry about the jeeps and machine guns, though, Dayan had to assemble a battalion. He had carte blanche from military headquarters to select whomever he wished for the elite, risk-prone Eighty-ninth. In some cases, soldiers abandoned their units after hearing that it was Moshe Dayan who would be in charge. In other cases, soldiers who left their units "voluntarily" for Dayan's sometimes spent a few days in jail. Dayan loved such tales: If someone was willing to disobey an order to join his combat unit, that soldier was right for the Eighty-ninth! Four companies were being formed. One was from among kibbutz and moshav farm settlements; joining Dayan were his childhood friends Nahman Betser, Binyamin Zarhi, and Israel Gefen. Another, headed by Akiva Sa'ar, comprised Tel Aviv residents. The third, headed by Dov Granek, drew its members from the dissident Stern Gang. The fourth was made up of volunteers, largely South African Jews.

Based at the former British army camp at Tel Litvinsky (now Tel Hashomer), near Tel Aviv, the Eighty-ninth was designed to fight independently of the rest of Sadeh's Eighth Brigade. Meant to operate behind enemy lines, the battalion would have to make up for its distinct lack of equipment with imagination and daring. At first it was forced to move entirely by jeep with no armor, no support weapons. At a later stage, a support company was added, moving largely by half-track. Because of Dayan, the unit was informal: It had no badges for ranks; no one saluted; the uniforms were homemade; morale was almost euphoric. Headquarters insisted on a certain amount of physical exercise but the men grumbled so Dayan did not force them to do it.

Dayan viewed his role as battalion commander in very narrow terms. He was not an administrator; that he left to subordinates; he would take charge of the way his men fought, period. He and his deputy Yohanan Pelz, a veteran of the Jewish Brigade in the British army, met over a cup of coffee for the first time in a Tel Aviv coffee house. Pelz was already on his guard about Dayan. When he had informed Yitzhak Sadeh that he was about to become Dayan's deputy, the brigade commander said, "All right. Go ahead. But I don't envy you." Dayan and Pelz came from different worlds: Pelz had the formal and stiff appearance of someone who had just stepped out of the British army officers' mess; Dayan, with his sandals and unbuttoned shirt, was the picture of Israeli informality.

Dayan wanted Pelz to handle administration. "I am essentially a fighting man and have no patience with such things. If you could take them off my hands, I'll take you on gladly." Pelz squeezed out a grudging promise from Dayan that he would be able to do some fighting as well—and that was that. Dayan involved himself heavily in recruiting for the battalion. He seemed like the perfect commander, holding his men's respect while demonstrating an interest in them personally as well.

Dayan conveyed his message by example. He quickly acquired a reputation as an unorthodox individualist who had no time for other people's rules. Naturally, his personal code of ethics was adopted as the battalion's. If grabbing off men from other units was acceptable practice, then why not the "borrowing" of equipment? Members of the battalion stole civilian jeeps and drove them to their base, where they hastily painted them khaki and affixed army license plates. Such behavior might have lasted for some time had Dayan's soldiers not been caught outside the government press office at the Ritz Hotel in Tel Aviv taking a jeep that happened to belong to a foreign correspondent named Arthur Koestler.

Ever the prankster, still a grown-up graduate of the Habibi, the Society of Jewish Hooligans, Dayan liked to impress the boys with his I'll-do-things-my-way stunts. Leaving the base in his jeep, he would scream, "Just watch this," and then floor the accelerator, race past the sentry, and grudgingly stop thirty meters outside the gate when the sentry shouted after him, demanding to see his papers. Once, a sentry stood up to Dayan, refusing to look at his papers until he backed up to the gate. Dayan refused to budge; the sentry threatened to shoot the battalion commander. This *High Noon* scene suddenly ended when Dayan sped off, threatening to shoot the sentry back.

While others such as Pelz were trying to impose some discipline on the battalion, Dayan did his best to make a mockery of such efforts. For Pelz, a former British army officer, discipline was essential for a soldier. Pelz insisted, for example, that firearms not be discharged in the camp. To his great surprise, one day Pelz heard shots coming from the dining hall. Rushing there, he found Dayan surrounded by his Nahalal buddies, shooting through a window at birds. Dayan was testing out a new pistol he had recently acquired.

"Moshe, what are you doing?" asked an agitated Pelz. "You are ruining whatever I have done to instill some sort of basic discipline."

"Don't be silly," Dayan replied. "There is no discipline here. There is nothing to ruin anyway." And he laughed.

Against Pelz's orders, Dayan also permitted the soldiers to drive home jeeps with wireless radios. One soldier took a jeep home and returned to the base with the wireless damaged—after Pelz had said no, and Dayan yes. Pelz complained to Dayan, only to be told: "It's not so important. Instead of bothering me, get it fixed. The energy that you spend quarreling with me, you could have fixed that jeep twenty times over."[3]

THROUGHOUT HIS CAREER, Moshe Dayan would display an ambiguous attitude toward the political right—never more so than in his strange involvement in the *Altalena* affair of late June 1948. While others among the Haganah were reluctant to take on the Irgun and Stern Gang in open confrontation, Dayan had shown during the Saison that he shared no such concern. Yet he had entered into dialogue with Menachem Begin and others; he had expressed admiration for their goals. Once again, when the call came to square off against the dissidents, Dayan did not refrain; yet the lack of enthusiasm with which he accepted the assignment, and his unaccounted-for absence from the battlefield during parts of the affair, suggest that Dayan indeed had reservations about his participation. With his highly refined political antenna operating, he apparently understood that history would not judge anyone too sympathetically who had the blood of other Jews on his hands.

ON JUNE 20, while he was still putting the finishing touches on his new battalion, Dayan was suddenly called to the headquarters of his brigade commander, Yitzhak Sadeh. Sadeh informed Dayan that the Irgun had brought a ship, the *Altalena*, laden with arms, to Israeli shores. With nine hundred recruits aboard, it was anchored off Kfar Vitkin, twenty-three miles north of Tel Aviv; its precious armaments, including five thousand rifles, were being unloaded in order to equip the Irgun. Though the Irgun and Stern Gang had long advocated harsher steps against the Arabs and the British, and had at times acted independently, yishuv leaders had been confident that with the establishment of the Israeli government on May 15, the two dissident groups would willingly fall under its jurisdiction.

By the time of the first truce on June 11, the Irgun had promised to dissolve the military wing of its organization and hand over its weapons to the army. That promise had been kept save for Jerusalem. The Irgun's goal was to land men and weapons during the truce and send them to Jerusalem and to Irgun troops who were incorporated within the army. This would constitute a particular act of defiance of the new Israeli government's rule, especially after the June 11 cease-fire, which included a pledge by Israel and the Arab states not to introduce new arms into the region. Though both sides secretly violated this agreement, the Israeli government felt that the *Altalena*'s arrival could not be tolerated.

The off-loading of the arms threatened to bring civil war down on the new state. To Ben-Gurion, the solution, painful as it seemed, was clear: The off-loading had to be stopped; the Irgun had to be destroyed as an independent body.

It was not easy to find troops willing to take part in the action. This was the Saison all over again except instead of tracking down dissidents and turning them over to the British, this time the policy was to prevent Jewish arms from reaching Jewish fighters, by shooting to kill, if necessary.

IN LOOKING FOR troops who were both loyal and prepared to take action against fellow Jews, General Headquarters turned to units of the Alexandroni Brigade. They refused to take part. Approached next was Yitzhak Sadeh's Eighth Brigade. Sadeh turned to Dayan's Eighty-ninth Battalion for the task. After summoning Dayan and explaining to him what was happening, Sadeh said simply, "It has to be dealt with."

"I am no expert in the complicated relations between the Irgun and the government," replied Dayan. "But I do not doubt my obligation to comply with an order."

According to Yohanan Pelz, Dayan ordered him to take whatever elements of the Eighty-ninth he could muster and head for Kfar Vitkin, where the *Altalena* was anchored. Dayan told Pelz to sink the ship if necessary: "You can shoot, kill and everything else."

Pondering the order, Pelz replied, "Moshe, I cannot do it. I lost all my family in the Holocaust and I cannot shoot another Jew, whatever he might be. I just can't do it. You can send me against Arabs, but not against Jews. I will not shoot another Jew and I will not order any troops to shoot at other Jews."

Pelz's words deeply upset Dayan: "You are a soldier. You were the one who told me about British army discipline. I am ordering you to go."

"I am not going to do it," Pelz said again. "It's against my conscience." He informed Dayan he would take the matter up with Sadeh.

Displaying sympathy, Sadeh said that he would not force Pelz to go.

As an aside, Pelz asked: "Incidentally, Moshe Dayan is the battalion commander. Why doesn't he go? Why does he preach sermons to me? If he's so hot for executing orders unconditionally?" Sadeh did not answer him. He just grinned.[4]

With Pelz unwilling to take part, Dayan summoned the battalion and told them that the Irgun had encircled Kfar Vitkin and its people were off-loading arms. "We have to attack with force." Dayan then had Uri Bar-On's company, comprising men from the farm settlements, set out for Kfar Vitkin. He joined them at dusk.

WHEN HE ARRIVED, he found that the Irgun had deployed on the beach, including two battalions that had deserted frontline positions to come to the rescue of the *Altalena*. At first Dayan thought it would be possible simply to surround the Irgun soldiers and force them into a quick surrender.

Some have suggested that Dayan transferred authority over the Eighty-ninth to Uri Bar-On during the afternoon of June 21 prior to the battle, but eyewitness accounts suggest that Dayan was very much involved in the fighting that ensued that evening.

Dayan's battalion called upon the Irgun to give up. But a battle began and two of Dayan's men were killed and another six wounded. Israel Gefen, who was at the battle, recalled Dayan's role, leading the battalion's charge trying to seal off the beachhead: "This was the first time I saw how fearless he was. They opened with heavy fire, machine guns and anti-tank missiles. He stood there in my half-track, an armored vehicle, totally ignoring the danger." When the shooting had died down, according to Gefen, Dayan learned where the Irgun leaders were, and broke through a barricade in order to reach them. Though he faced tommy guns, Dayan never stopped. His comrades advised him not to provide such a welcome target.

"If they hit me," said Dayan, "then they'll stop this military action." They did not hit him. He hammered out an agreement with Menachem Begin and Ya'acov Meridor, the Irgun leaders, by which they would surrender the *Altalena's* arms, but the accord quicky fell apart and the ship set sail for Tel Aviv. It was then that Dayan was summoned to Ben-Gurion's headquarters and asked to take on a mission to the United States.[5]

All of the accounts of Dayan's behavior during the *Altalena* action note one yawning gap in the record. During the evening of June 21, Dayan set off for Nahalal with Ruth, apparently to bid farewell to his parents before he departed for the United States. Yet he did not leave the country for a whole week. Where was Dayan from June 21 until his departure for the United States on June 28? More precisely, why did he leave the scene of the *Altalena* battle seemingly on the pretext that he was being sent abroad if he was not to leave Israel until a week later? Once again, his public relations instincts may have led him to conclude correctly that hanging around on the Kfar Vitkin beach would do him no good, placing him at the head of a unit whose sole purpose appeared to be killing other Jews. Dayan could not have known that the *Altalena* affair would haunt the country for years, that it would become one of the most anguishing episodes in its history, but his instincts were sufficiently refined to understand that his best tactic was to leave the scene as quickly as possible, using the trip as an excuse. In later years, he said as little as possible about his own role on the beach. He understood that silence was best for his image.

Civil war was averted when Menachem Begin called off his men and gave up the struggle. Fourteen men had been killed and the *Altalena* had been sunk by gunfire. The *Altalena* affair led to the final dissolution of the Irgun's military wing: Irgun units within the army were disbanded and their men dispersed to other units.

Dayan was soon thereafter summoned to General Headquarters and told to undertake an assignment that, in retrospect, sounds strange. He was to accompany the body of Col. David Marcus back to the United States for burial. Another young Haganah officer, Yossi Harel, would be going along too. This was strange, because Dayan had been in the midst of preparing the Eighty-ninth Battalion for further fighting; strange, too, because Dayan ranked as one of the Israeli army's most promising young commanders. The kind of mission he was about to do presumably could have been given to a number of other military men with less involvement in combat than Dayan.

Still Dayan was chosen. The mission was a sad one. David Marcus had been an American Jewish army officer who had graduated from West Point and had an outstanding record in World War II. In early 1948 he had volunteered for the Israeli army under the assumed name of Mickey Stone. On May 28, eight days after the Old City had fallen, Marcus/Stone had been appointed commander of the Jerusalem front. Just eleven days later, a few hours before the first cease-fire was to take effect on June 11, he was killed, accidentally shot by an Israeli sentry. The sentry had mistaken him for an enemy soldier after Marcus had left his tent during the night. In his will, he had asked to be buried at West Point. Alex Braude, a lodger in Dayan's flat in Jerusalem in 1942, and Marcus's aide, proposed that Dayan and Harel be escorts on behalf of the Israeli army.

The first problem Dayan and Harel faced was what to wear. They were both lieutenant colonels; but, given the newness of the Israeli army, they had no uniforms yet. The two men would have to improvise. Dayan took Harel to a store on Allenby Street in Tel Aviv; it made uniforms for British soldiers. A salesman guessed what the Israeli uniform should look like: the two men chose dark green jackets, belts, khaki shirts, epaulettes, and berets. A further complication arose because the ranks had not yet been designed. Improvising as she went along, Ruth Dayan embroidered the ranks of her husband and Harel during the long flight on June 29 to the United States.

The twenty-six–hour flight was made in a chartered plane that conveyed racehorses and thus had no seats. Dayan and Harel decided the coffin was the best place to sit and sleep; placing their blankets over it, they turned the coffin into both a seat and bed. While the plane was refueling in Paris, Dayan received a cable from Ben-Gurion. The message was very peculiar. It ordered Dayan back to Israel at once. Ben-Gurion's behavior is difficult to explain. Eager to recapture the fallen Old City of Jerusalem, he was determined to relieve David Shaltiel as commander of the Jerusalem area and replace him with Dayan. But why had Ben-Gurion not simply kept Dayan from going on the trip? The answer is unclear. At any rate, Dayan defied Ben-Gurion's order. Given the respect Dayan had for Ben-Gurion, Dayan's behavior is odd as well. How could he disobey a direct order from his commander in chief? How could he carry on to the United States on an assignment thoroughly disconnected from the fighting in Israel when the prime minister wanted him home to lead men in battle? Dayan provided no real justification. He simply carried on his business, acting as if Ben-Gurion's cable was nonexistent. Dayan reached the United States on July 2.

Upon arriving at West Point Dayan had a special request for Teddy Kollek, who had been head of the Haganah mission in New York since 1947. Making deals for arms to be sent to Israel, Kollek was in close touch with a number of Jewish veterans from World War II. Dayan wanted Kollek to find one of them who could discuss military tactics. The future mayor of Jerusalem would have liked Dayan to sit down with American officers who had expressed an interest in serving in the Israeli army. Dayan shrugged off such a proposal. "We don't need officers," he argued. "We need people who can teach fighting." Kollek put Dayan in touch with someone who would make a tremendous impression on Dayan. Abraham Baum had been working for the Haganah mission headquartered in Hotel 14 in New York, interviewing American volunteers for military service in Israel. Incongruously, the Copacabana, the well-known New York night spot, was downstairs. Baum had served in the

American Fourth Armored Division under Col. Creighton Abrams, who later became the commanding general in Vietnam. Dayan listened intently as Baum explained how he had led a small task force sixty miles behind German lines near the end of World War II. Baum's mission was to try to rescue 1,291 American prisoners. His superiors instructed him to push as fast as he could toward this camp, using only armored cars and half-tracks—no tanks, no artillery or air support. Hence, Baum instructed his platoon commander: "If we see a German, we open up with everything we have in all directions." On March 27, 1945, the force crossed the Saale River and soon broke into the POW camp. But it was attacked, and lost half of its men and vehicles. Baum was taken prisoner. Ten days later, a large American force liberated the POW camp. Task Force Baum, while not achieving all of its goals, did manage to get to the prison camp.

Its heroics struck a responsive chord in Dayan. Baum described to Dayan how Task Force Baum made sure to unleash enormous amounts of firepower whenever Germans appeared. "You wouldn't believe it," Baum said. "It worked. I don't know what you're doing in Israel, but I suggest that the moment you come to an obstacle, you open fire in all directions with whatever you have, machine guns, mortars. You should shoot and drive, shoot and drive."

Dayan listened intently. He knew that Israeli battle tactics had been designed to reduce casualties, and, accordingly, afforded the soldiers little opportunity to make the big breakthroughs against the enemy. He smiled at Harel. "This is it." It was as if Baum had just given him a prescription for victory in Israel. If, within the huge American army, there was room for a commando unit such as Task Force Baum, all the more reason for a unit such as the Eighty-ninth Battalion. Perhaps that was what impelled Dayan to boast to newsmen during his American visit that the Israeli army could capture all of Palestine in four to six weeks if fighting were to resume at the end of the cease-fire. In later years, Dayan would adapt the lesson of Task Force Baum as one of the key doctrines of the Israel Defense Forces: the use of small, mobile forces in a large-scale action.

Baum's comments on the need for speed and mobility in combat also made a durable impression on Dayan. Drawing upon his World War II experience, Baum gave Dayan a list of dos and don'ts: Don't use preliminary reconnaissance patrols a day or two in advance of the attack, since the information gained was usually insignificant, and the element of surprise was lost. Go straight to the attack; meanwhile, let the reconnaissance unit move ahead, observe, sense, feel out the situation, and report back. Make sure that you are moving all the time. Have the commander direct the action from the front line; in this way he can determine for himself what is happening rather than rely upon second-hand reports. If there's a road, use it. Use a large force to do a small mission and try to give the impression that your force is larger than it is. Attack in narrow formations; the ideal are single-line columns. Use firepower not so much to kill, but to frighten. Don't hold reserve troops back; use them as part of the main battle. Use infantry to occupy; armor should be kept mobile and ready to counterattack.

Much as he would have wanted to spend more time in the United States, Dayan felt obliged to return, since he had received another cable from Ben-Gurion imploring him to return to Israel as quickly as possible. Kollek arranged for Dayan to fly back on the same plane: This time the cargo was boxes containing the first Israeli bank notes—hot off the American presses. Dayan was a guard.

Landing a few hours before the end of the first cease-fire on July 9 at Ein Shemer, halfway between Tel Aviv and Haifa, Dayan's plane came under fire from Arab snipers. He called it later "amateur shooting, nothing serious." By now Dayan was ready to lead his troops in battle. That battle was not long in coming. The United Nations mediator, Count Bernadotte of Sweden, had unveiled a peace plan during the first truce: It would have awarded all of the Galilee to the Israelis with the Negev going to the Arabs; Jerusalem would have remained under United Nations authority. Both Arabs and Jews rejected the formula; it became clear that when the twenty-eight–day truce came to an end on July 9, fighting would resume.

Dayan planned to head straight for Tel Hashomer, get a night's sleep, and begin working with his battalion the next morning. It did not quite work that way. Entering the gates of the base, he spotted his battalion heading for Kfar Syrkin, ten miles northeast of Tel Aviv, from where it was to move out the next morning to Operation Danny.

In early phases of the war, the Israelis had pursued largely static tactics: Forces remained in defensive positions, keeping to the axis of movement, not veering from the lines of advance and retreat carefully mapped out for them. Commanders, conscious of their meager arms and their inexperienced soldiers, favored softening up the target first; they deployed their forces in preparation for an advance while still a long distance from the target. Such tactics had the advantage of keeping casualties low, but because of this approach, the Israelis lacked momentum, lacked the capability of gaining clear-cut victories over the Arabs. Morale sagged. A more dynamic approach was needed.

Thus Operation Danny. It was to be the Israeli army's first major effort after the first truce ended. Its aim was to push the Arab Legion out of its positions eleven miles from Tel Aviv and thus eliminate the threat to cut the nation in half. The first phase of the operation was to take Lod and Ramle, then capture Latrun and Ramallah on the way to lift the siege of Jerusalem.

Commanding Danny was Yigal Allon, head of the Palmach. At his disposal were forces from the Harel and Yiftach brigades with the Kiryat and Eighth Armored brigades in support. Also attached to Danny were elements of the Alexandroni and Etzioni brigades. Yitzhak Sadeh's Eighth Armored Brigade had orders to take Lod Airport as well as to take advantage of Israeli military successes to the east near the military camp at Beit Nabala. The Yiftach Brigade was to form the southern flank of the pincer movement.

Within the bulge of Lod and Ramle were one hundred thousand Arabs and thousands of troops. The Arab forces wanted to link up with the Egyptian army at Ashdod, twenty-three miles south of Tel Aviv, and, by so doing, cut Tel Aviv off from the southern part of the country. To defeat the Arab strategy, the Israelis deployed their troops in a pincer movement in order to cut the Lod-Ramle bulge off from Arab forces holding Latrun.

At nightfall on July 9, 1948, the Yiftach Brigade began clearing several Arab villages. A battalion of tanks under Sadeh's Eighth Armored Brigade advanced to the north, and took the Lod airport. These two pincer movements were to join at Ben Shemen, the Jewish children's village that had been isolated for months.

The original plan called for the tanks of Sadeh's Eighth Brigade to provide close fire support to breach the fortifications on the perimeter of the Lod-Ramle bulge. Dayan's Eighty-ninth Battalion, operating as part of Sadeh's armored brigade, was supposed to storm the villages and fortified positions northeast of the bulge, providing it with commanding positions overlooking Lod and the nearby airport. Its specific assignment was to take two enemy postions around the Arab villages of Tira and Kula—part of the advance enemy line in this sector. Tira, to the south, was not quite three miles from the airport and could be hit by enemy guns. Just two miles south of the airport was the town of Lod that was entirely under Arab control.

Fighting for the first time as a battalion, the Eighty-ninth had moved at the break of dawn on Saturday July 10, heading for Kula. Dayan doubted his troops would be required to fight at Kula: Once the Arabs learned that the Israelis were on the march, he believed, they would scatter like birds! But Kula was a tough battle. The Arabs did not flee the first time a few shots were fired. Visibly annoyed, Dayan had wanted his troops to unleash a massive display of firepower, but that had not been Pelz's plan. Dayan got in touch with Akiva Sa'ar and told him it was time to abandon the soft approach. Sa'ar should storm Kula; Dayan would take a company and storm Tira. But first he planned to see Pelz. Before he could do that, Dayan was called away.

At ten o'clock that morning, Dayan was summoned to Ben-Gurion. Upon landing the day before, Dayan had received yet one more message from Ben-Gurion urging him to appear. Dayan excused himself on the grounds that he had a battle to command. He found Ben-Gurion troubled, largely about Jerusalem. He still hoped to replace Shaltiel with Dayan.

The offer to become the commander of Jerusalem must have been flattering to Dayan. Again Dayan had the temerity to say no to the prime minister, noting that his new battalion had only that morning been engaged in a difficult battle. More fighting was expected. A commander could not leave his men in such a situation. In the face of such arguments, Ben-Gurion told Dayan he would renew the request at a later stage.

Learning that his battalion had already reached a spot near Deir Tarif, Dayan headed northeast toward Petach Tikvah, racing his jeep through fields in search of a shortcut. He found himself in a mine field, and genuinely feared for his life. He had no choice but to rest until dawn. He slept for the first time in forty-eight hours. With daylight he could see the tracks of vehicles on the path, and making sure to keep his wheels in their ruts, he reached one of his detachments after an hour.

In Dayan's absence, Pelz had taken over command of the battalion. By 1:00 A.M., Sunday, July 11, he had fallen asleep under an olive tree at Tira, and left orders to be awakened at 4:30 A.M. But Dayan arrived at 3:30 A.M., leaned over him, and began asking what had happened while he was gone. It was then that Pelz informed Dayan that in his absence the Eighty-ninth had been given the task of capturing Deir Tarif.

Pelz spread out maps and showed operational orders. Dayan glanced at them but made no comment. Dayan was outraged: Why had the Eighty-ninth been forced to get involved in the capture of Deir Tarif? During the battalion commander's absence, Pelz had abandoned Dayan's plan of taking each enemy position one by one; rather, Pelz had the battalion move along separate routes of approach. Some were to go to Tira in the north, others to Deir Tarif in the south. According to Israel Gefen, one of Dayan's men, the troops, fearing that Pelz's plan would lead to heavy casualties, had waited impatiently for Dayan to return. A sudden feeling of resentment overcame Pelz at the nerve of this inexperienced soldier who was about to retake command of the battalion. Finally, Pelz begged off, saying that he had only one more hour to sleep.

When Pelz awakened, he saw great commotion all around. Vehicles were moving. Some reported that Dayan had taken the battalion and left Pelz all alone in Tira. Pelz, however, recalled that, upon awaking, he found Dayan and asked him what was going on. Dayan took his deputy by the arm over to a jeep and spread a map out. Fresh in Dayan's mind were the lessons that Abraham Baum had passed on to him in New York. Dayan wanted to move the battalion in a single column as a "concentrated iron fist" and thrust forward in a quick dash à la Task Force Baum. Dayan had noted in his memoirs, *Story of My Life,* that Pelz had assigned some soldiers to nothing more dramatic than guard duty in Arab villages that had already been captured. (One of Baum's rules called for infantry, not mobile armored units, to perform such duties.) Dayan canceled the plan.

"Look," he said to Pelz, "this thing that you have planned is good for a regular army, it's no good for us. I spoke to a lot of people in America who have battle experience and the main thing in a battle like this is momentum. Let your men move, break through, and keep going like hell. And they will run. You don't know the Arabs, I know them. You take a brass plate and hammer and beat the brass plate with the hammer and they will run like hell. They will run when they hear a lot of noise."

According to Aryeh Nehemkin, one of Dayan's soldiers, his men were jubilant at Dayan's return; they had felt a sense of confusion until he arrived. With the battalion commander in place, things began to move. Tira fell, and Deir Tarif was in the process of being taken. Taking Beit Nabala to the east would have been considerably more difficult, as the Eighty-ninth was at a sizable arms disadvantage. Sensing that, Dayan took in the panorama from the protection of some orange groves, and noticed that the key Arab town of Lod was just three and a half miles away along land that was flat. What, he thought to himself, if we employ a small holding force to tie down the local Arab Legion units here at Deir Tarif, and send the rest of the battalion on to Lod? If we attack from the east—from Arab lines—we would likely find that part of town unfortified.

Time was running out, however. The attack would have to be done quickly, when the Arabs at Lod least expected it. But was the battalion capable of conquering Lod? Physically, it was not up to full strength. But the men had battle experience and their equipment was growing. Their half-tracks afforded them mobility and accurate marksmanship.

Lod was no small village: How could soldiers with just a few vehicles expect to tackle the well-armed Arab forces there and capture an entire town? Still, Dayan believed that the timing and the opportunity were right. Calling his company commanders together, he said to them, in a tone that suggested he was half joking, "Let's finish up here and make for Lod." Dayan's men believed that he was kidding.

HE WAS NOT. Before contemplating the capture of Lod, the battalion had to ensure that Deir Tarif was fully under control. As Dayan began to prepare his men for a further push toward the village, he was suddenly called to the signals center, where Mulla Cohen, commander of the Palmach's Yiftach Brigade, was on the line. (In fact, Cohen was asking to speak to the head of the Eighty-second Tank Battalion.)

Dayan knew that Cohen's brigade was one of the two arms of a pincer (this battalion was the other arm), but he had no idea where Cohen's men were fighting. Yiftach was supposed to play the dominant role in carrying out Operation Danny; it was supposed to capture Lod. Cohen was calling to get help for one of his units that had become pinned down under heavy fire in an orange grove southeast of Lod. Hearing Dayan on the line, Cohen asked him to send some troops to support his flagging unit. This was a golden opportunity for action. Perhaps, Dayan thought, he could exploit Cohen's plight as an excuse to embark on a bolder strategy than originally planned for his men. Dayan promised to send his men to rescue Cohen's after the conquest of Deir Tarif was complete.

Dayan want to climb to the top of a hill to survey the situation, but Akiva Sa'ar tried to warn him off, arguing that the hill was under continuing artillery fire and Jordanian snipers were around. Dayan took no heed and asked his driver to take him to the hilltop. They parked behind a pile of boulders, with Sa'ar right behind them. Dayan looked down and saw several disabled Israeli vehicles stuck on the side of the hill. He also noticed an abandoned Jordanian armored car lying on its side, its near-side wheels in a ditch. The armored car would be a great addition to the battalion; he made immediate plans to get it into service. The Jordanians were shelling and sniping anyone who tried to get near the armored car. Dayan was convinced that a combination of shrewdness and luck—and a tow cable—could bring off the heist.

When a lull came, Dayan got into a half-track and called out to a mechanic, "Will you join me, even if it's risky?"

"Sure, with you there's no risk."

To his men, Dayan exemplified the ideal soldier, largely because of his remarkable bravery. Dayan sometimes questioned whether he was really brave, or whether he had some instinct that always guided him to safety. "By now, the lack of one eye was no handicap for me. Even in the dark I did not stumble; my legs found their own way. At the sound of shot or shell, I felt no instinctive recoil, and when I thought about this later I found it was not courage but simply a physical indifference to the noice of incoming fire and the climactic burst. Even when hits were close, kicking up dirt which sprinkled my face, I felt little danger. Rather the reverse: once you could see where the shells were falling, you could avoid them."[6]

Even after the armored car was rescued, repairs had to be made to the engine, the gun, and the radio. Nobody could quite figure out how to shoot the thing. Finally, someone from a nearby artillery unit was summoned to explain how it worked. An hour later, Dayan chose the crew for what he dubbed the "Terrible Tiger." Somebody enscribed on its gun barrel in chalk the phrase, "Straight to the point." On its side was the phrase, "The Nahalal-Amman Express."

By now Deir Tarif had grown quiet. Dayan's battalion was gaining enthusiasm and self-confidence. If Dayan were to ask his men to take another enemy concentration, they would accept gladly. But would they be ready to take a whole town? Dayan had no wish to ask brigade head-quarters for approval. He knew the operational orders and disregarded them. Here Dayan was not only usurping the role of Yiftach, but he was also challenging Yigal Allon, a Palmach commander and a quasi-rival of Dayan's since 1938. Operation Danny was Yigal Allon's baby. Today it is hindsight to argue that Dayan was acting to foil Allon. No one spoke in such terms at the time, but in retrospect, Moshe Dayan was having a field day at Yigal Allon's expense. Palmach members would not let Dayan forget it for years.

The battlefield realities permitted Dayan to dream up his bold plan. The men of Yiftach were limping, his were marching. He was not plan-ning to wait for his superiors to command. He would take the initiative. So it was on to Ben Shemen, the Jewish settlement halfway between Beit Nabala and Lod. This was the next target before an attack upon Lod. Along the approach road Dayan's battalion came under heavy fire. They simply backed off and searched for another route, this one through the fields. At another point Arabs opened fire, but a burst from a machine gun on one of the jeeps sent them scurrying. The arrival of Dayan's battalion in Ben Shemen was a minor miracle for the inhabitants. They had been cut off from the rest of the Jewish population and surrounded by hostile Arabs. Dayan noted that from Ben Shemen his troops would have the advantage of not facing an Arab front in making their way to Lod. This side of Lod was largely free of Arab soldiers. "This is an opportunity that won't return," Dayan told his unit commanders. Dayan held up a map of Lod and pointed a finger at it. "We're going to attack Lod. We'll enter from here, drive through the city and leave from there. Clear?"

The question remained whether the battalion would be physically strong enough to launch the assault. Available to Dayan were only 150 soldiers. Of the battalion's original 400 men, 250 had been combat troops, but 100 had dropped from the roster since its formation; another 150 held service posts. Dayan planned to employ twenty jeeps mounted with machine guns, six half-tracks, and the Tiger. Arrayed against the battalion were an unknown number of Arab irregulars as well as two regular Arab Legion companies, possessing cannon-bearing armored cars and artillery.

Dayan determined that the Tiger would lead; then would come the half-track company, followed by a second half-track company, with the jeeps at the rear. Dayan would be with the first half-tracks, an early precedent for a battlefield norm he would insist upon in later years: The field commander must run ahead with his troops. If the Tiger or any of the half-tracks fell in action, the others in the column were to find a way around them and continue to advance. The plan, once inside the town of Lod, was to keep firing left and right in order to create panic and engineer a quick surrender. The first company was ordered to turn right, the second left, with the jeeps searching for cover behind stone fences or the courtyards of buildings. Dayan knew enough not to have the jeeps race around the streets; they were too exposed. In the event that the enemy managed to stop the column from advancing at any point, the rear vehicles, those not directly engaging the enemy, were to spread out and, exploiting their firepower, storm the enemy's positions from all sides. Speed was critical, he told his men: It would lessen their chance of being hit and heighten the enemy's fear. The battalion, Dayan said, would have to run over the enemy, crush him in spirit and body.

Dayan had supreme confidence in his men. He believed that with the proper skills and confidence, all battles should be won. "There was always some fold in the ground along which we could advance, some rock which afforded cover, and a surprise and judicious military tactic which could give us the advantage over the enemy."[7]

When Dayan had finished his pep talk the men had no questions. It was time to go into battle. The dangers were great. The battalion lacked armor that was ordinarily required to take a town the size of Lod. Moreover, the raid would occur in broad daylight. The Eighty-ninth possessed some firepower and much enthusiasm.

Some time before Dayan's attack began at 6:20 P.M., units of the Yiftach Brigade launched their attack on the southeastern quarter of Lod. "Storm through!" Dayan ordered over his walkie-talkie. "Beat them. Smash them!" It only took the battalion a hundred yards of advance before it was spotted. Though the Arabs fired at them, Dayan ordered his men not to respond. "Carry on. Move," he shouted. "No stopping for anything. The column must not stop under any circumstances."

A few moments later the Tiger halted and fired, knocking out two enemy positions. A few hundred yards farther on the column stopped. The main defense lines of the enemy were hailing machine-gun fire at the half-tracks with great ferocity. The entire battalion began firing, as the jeeps moved to either side of the road. While the jeeps aimed accurately at their targets, the column became static; just ahead the road was impassable, cut by an antitank ditch.

Dayan left his scout car and went from one half-track to another.

"What if the road is mined?" anxious drivers asked him.

"Then," Dayan answered with customary aloofness, "you'll be blown sky high."

He approached the Tiger. The half-tracks had ceased moving. They preferred to rely upon the armored car.

Just then Dayan noticed that the Arabs were fleeing. This was the moment to move ahead. He found a side track that ran off the road through the fields. It seemed passable. He ordered the Tiger's commander to cease firing and to move along the track. It might be mined. But he would have to take that risk.

Dayan returned to his half-track. As the half-tracks moved, the men aboard kept firing their machine guns on either side. Soon they had crossed the enemy's main defense line. They had entered Lod.

Heavy fire came from the police station, but the Tiger kept firing. The track was free of mines. At the crossroads, the Tiger turned right—according to the plan. But the first half-track company, which was supposed to follow also to the right, carried on straight. It was forced to fight on its own, advancing and firing and reaching the city square.

The second half-track company and the jeeps followed it. In short, the commandos, rather than splitting up as had been planned, remained together—except for the Tiger, which was now all alone. Arabs who had retreated from positions already overrun by the Israeli soldiers continued to fire and hurl hand grenades, but soon the Eighty-ninth reached the center of town and the Arab firing died down.

Israel Gefen, who took part in the battle for Lod, described those moments: "We did it in a sort of gung ho way, riding through the main street with all we had, surprising them. . . . The soldiers greatly appreciated Dayan's courage and adored him because his approach was to go in force, overwhelm the enemy, gain local superiority in both firepower and mobility. And get where you are going before the enemy knows where you are."[8]

The local Arab Legion commander came out of his headquarters in the Lod police fortress. Eyeing a tank he thought he recognized, the

Arab commander waved at it and cheered, thinking it was the vanguard of reinforcements for his troops. When two Israeli jeeps approached, he ran into the fortress, locking the gates behind him.

Save for the Tiger, the whole battalion proceeded in the direction of Ramle. Upon reaching the police station on the Lod-Ramle road, surprising a company of the Arab Legion inside, the first half-track company got past the station without drawing a shot. But by this time the Arab Legion rained strong fire at the second company and the jeeps; the Legion soldiers fired their heavy machine guns on the police station's tower and through openings on the top floor. An Arab threw a grenade that exploded inside a half-track, wounding everyone in it. The rest of the battalion drove on. Dayan wanted to stop the vehicles of the first company ahead of him, but the radio set no longer worked. He used hand signals, he shouted (by now his voice was hoarse), but nothing worked. Finally, after reaching the Ramle railroad station on the Jerusalem road, he was able to stop the column. Catching up with the first company in Ramle, Dayan learned the reason for its wild dash: Akiva Sa'ar's driver explained that the clutch on his half-track had failed. He could not stop.

They had reached Ramle—by accident!

The other vehicles in the column simply followed the lead half-track.

"What are you doing here?" Dayan asked Sa'ar.

"By mistake, we've captured Ramle."

"It can't be."

"Look," said Sa'ar, pointing in one direction, "the Muslim cemetery. The railroad station is on the left. Perhaps from here it's worth going on to Latrun."

It was a heady thought. The commandos had already outdone themselves. Just forty-seven minutes and they had stormed through two critical Arab towns and suffered very few casualties. Dayan might have wished to carry forward, but when a message arrived in which his men at Deir Tarif pleaded for help, he was forced to stop. Dov Granek radioed Dayan that he and his unit, which had been kept behind at Deir Tarif, had come under attack by the Arab Legion. Several of Granek's men were missing. And the Arab Legion had retaken Deir Tarif. Dayan replied that only after he had finished up in Lod and Ramle could he send reinforcements.

If Granek could not hold his position, Dayan told him, he should fall back to Tira. The next day the battalion would retake what had been given up. Granek was displeased. He sounded as if he was waiting for Dayan to urge him on.

"Perhaps I could organize the rest of my men and try and retake it myself now?"

Dayan got the hint. "Commandos or not commandos?"

"What? What?"

"Are we a commando battalion or not?"

"Commandos," shouted Dov. "Commandos. We attack."

"Take the salient from the east."

"Right."

IT WAS TIME to take account of the losses. The jeep unit had suffered four dead. Some of the wounded men from the half-track detachment were in serious condition. While the battalion was bandaging the wounded and replacing flat tires, word came that Arab armored cars were heading toward them from a nearby Arab Legion encampment. Arabs at the police station were still firing mortars at the column as well. Dayan had the column move ahead until it reached a turn in the Ramle-Latrun road. Urging the men to rush, Dayan arranged for the wounded to be put in a half-track; the column then moved off.

Dayan's own vehicle was moving on two flat tires with an engine that was puttering and coughing.

"We're driving on the tire rims," shouted Dayan's driver at him. "Perhaps we should jump. We can escape through the trees here."

"Yossele," Dayan screamed back at him, "pretend that you are driving a train. Put it into first, and just go a little slower."

The driver obeyed, and Dayan's half-track plodded along, the water in the radiator boiling. As other elements of the column passed Dayan, he was virtually on his own. Suddenly an Arab Legion armored car showed up near the corner of a side street off the Ramle road. Someone in the car fired a two-pound gun at Dayan's half-track, but missed. Had he scored a direct hit, the half-track and Dayan would have been wiped out. Dayan quickly got his radioman (who happened to be the son of the rabbi who performed the Dayan wedding in 1935) to turn his machine gun on the Arab Legion car. The car fled.

Dayan returned to the police fort between Lod and Ramle. To retrieve the dead and wounded, enemy positions in the police station had to be silenced. That accomplished, the battalion returned to Lod. There the Israeli column dealt with enemy fire from the police station, with the help of the Tiger and a pair of half-tracks, the only Israeli vehicles free to fight. All of the other undamaged vehicles were employed in pushing those that had been hit. Dayan's battalion lost nine men and suffered seventeen wounded. After one more swing through the town, the men headed for the exit of the city toward Ben Shemen. At the exit they met elements of the Yiftach Brigade, which had arrived to mop up and occupy the town. Dayan's storming of Lod and Ramle, and the subsequent return through the two towns, had allowed the Yiftach Brigade to take advantage of the panic of the Arab residents (most of Lod's inhabitants fled during that panic). The town of Lod surrendered to the Yiftach Brigade. The following day Ramle surrendered and was occupied by units of the Kiryat Brigade. Eager to get help for his wounded, Dayan ordered his battalion to return to its base at Tel Hashomer. He did not seek approval from Operation Danny headquarters or from his Brigade commander, Yitzhak Sadeh. He just gave the order on his own.

At once a debate began over who captured these critical towns, Allon's Palmach or Dayan's commandos. In Rome, Ruth Dayan purchased a copy of the *Daily American* and saw a headline indicating that General Allon had captured Ramle and Lod. There was not a word about Dayan.

Dayan, however, attributed the fall of Lod and Ramle to the fact that his men had, through their storming of the town, sown confusion and caused a panicky flight of Arabs from both cities. Supporting Dayan on this point was none other than Maj. Adib el-Kassem of the Arab Legion. In June 1952, while he and Dayan were attending an advanced course in England, the Jordanian officer praised the courage of Dayan's troops. He particularly noted how their action had demoralized the inhabitants and spread panic among them.

The fall of Lod and Ramle were significant blows to the Arabs because it marked the turn of the tide against Jordan: Once the fortified positions northeast of Lod and Ramle fell to the Israelis, the Arab threat to Tel Aviv was ended, and freedom of movement between Tel Aviv and Jerusalem was assured. Another bonus involved Israel's fight against the Egyptian army, which had reached Ashdod. The Egyptian army's right flank was suddenly exposed by virtue of the Israeli triumph in the Lod area. The Lod-Ramle victory meant that the IDF could release large numbers of troops to enter the fighting for Jerusalem.

It was a stirring moment for Moshe Dayan. David Ben-Gurion called it the greatest of Israel's victories, though he had misgivings about the way Dayan conducted himself: "This is not the way to fight a war." Nonetheless, the prime minister did not waver from his intention to appoint Dayan commander of Jerusalem. As usual, others, particularly Palmach officers, griped about Dayan's behavior, but some of them grudgingly acknowledged that the Eighty-ninth had acted well, as Yigal Allon put it, with "great daring." Lod and Ramle were the baths of fire for Dayan's military tactics. Building on what he had learned from Abraham Baum, from Orde Wingate, and from Yitzhak Sadeh, Dayan had for the first time performed as the commander of a major operation. He had followed the pattern of Task Force Baum, grouped his men in a single column, forced them to move quickly and to move forward at all costs, pushed them to use as much firepower as possible. The results were astonishing. The Arabs had not fled at the sound of a few shells, but flee they did. Dayan had taken a minimum of casualties. His performance did not elevate him into the ranks of the senior commanders of the War of Independence, but it did rank him among the most valiant and imaginative of Israel's field commanders.

After sleeping for a few hours at Tel Hashomer, Moshe Dayan was awakened and given a message to report to the chief of operations, Maj. Gen. Yigael Yadin, at General Headquarters. Offering some kind words about the battalion's effort in Lod, Yadin instructed Dayan to take his men south, to join the Givati Brigade in seeking a breakthrough to the Negev. The fighting there had started close to the expiration of the first cease-fire on July 8 and would persist for ten days until a second cease-fire took effect. The Egyptians had been holding a line that ran from the Mediterranean coast eastward and was based on the Majdal-Faluja road. Thus they had cut the country in two, splitting the north from the south. Along that forward line, the Egyptians had built fortified positions on the east-west road leading from Beit Guvrin via Faluja to Ashkelon. The Israeli strategy was to capture three Egyptian bases: Givati's infantry units would handle the two army bases of Hatta and Bet Affa. The Eighty-ninth's target was Karatiya; it was farther south than Hatta and Bet Affa and would have to be reached by crossing the Egyptian lines.

The plan was for the Eighty-ninth to capture Karatiya and then for a Givati company, following behind it, to occupy the spot. Karatiya was the most challenging of the three targets and the key to the Negev breakthrough. Units from the Negev Brigade, coming from the south, were to capture Bir Abu-Jabber, Kaukaba, and Huleikat. A major purpose of the Dayan-Givati attack was to connect up with those Negev Brigade units in the south. Time for fighting was running out for the Israelis; at any time a second cease-fire might be declared.

Dayan told Yadin of his battalion's condition: the half-tracks, badly hit, needed service; casualties had reduced the unit's fighting capability (Dayan's deputy, Yohanan Pelz had been wounded; Uri Bar-On and Akiva Sa'ar, two of Dayan's best company commanders, were in hospital). The battalion had only 221 combat-ready men. Ammuniton was desperately low: The Tiger had only six shells left. (Later, unable to secure more ammunition for the Tiger from headquarters, Dayan "appropriated" twenty two-pound shells left behind in a grove near his forward encampment at Masmiya.) Yadin asked Dayan whether he felt the battalion could manage the breakthrough to the Negev. Dayan said yes. Yadin ordered him to do so, promising that after the next cease-fire the battalion would be refurbished. Yadin did assure him of another six half-tracks and four scout cars. Ben-Gurion, who was both prime minister and defense minister, requested that Dayan see him: He was determined to send Dayan to Jerusalem but agreed to postpone the decision until after the Negev combat. He told Dayan that as soon as a second cease-fire took effect, he would become Jerusalem front commander.

DAYAN, however, wanted to be in the midst of battle, to have a chance to triumph. His exuberance for battle was never more clear than when he confronted the battalion commanders of the Givati Brigade.

"Where is Karatiya?" he asked upon entering the room, pointing to a map lying on a table.

Someone pointed out the Eighty-ninth's target on the map.

"By the way," offered Dayan, "I'll capture Faluja as well."

That statement was greeted with great consternation. Here was an officer who had no connection with the Givati Brigade, storming in, seeking to impress everyone, boasting that he would mop up the Egyptians all by himself. Raphael Vardi, who was present at that meeting, thought Dayan "a little bombastic, pompous." Faluja? Few in the room thought Dayan would even be able to take Karatiya. Shimon Avidan, then commander of the Givati Brigade, convinced Dayan to forget about Faluja.[9]

Dayan set up his forward base on July 15 in an orange grove near the Masmiya crossroads, thirty miles south of Tel Aviv, thirteen miles north of the front. That evening came orders from the Givati Brigade that Dayan's battalion was to take Karatiya two evenings later. Sensing that his armored cars would have more difficulty fighting at night, Dayan tried, in vain, to have the order altered to a day battle. To prepare for the fighting, Dayan sent a reconnaissance patrol near Karatiya to probe for the best access route. Coming under fire, it retreated without finding one. Hence, the battalion would not know about the special problems crossing the deep ravine of Wadi Mufared. The battalion's maps showed Wadi Mufared negotiable for vehicles. Dayan therefore included it in the access route. What the map did not show was that the wadi was quite deep and had high, steep banks on both sides.

One critical lesson Dayan had learned from the Lod fighting was to have infantry units move along with the armor in order to exploit the enemy's first shock. Those infantry units could then establish themselves within the enemy's areas before it recovered. Dayan managed to persuade Shimon Avidan to provide the Eighty-ninth with an infantry com-

WARRIOR STATESMAN: THE LIFE OF MOSHE DAYAN   105

pany; it was to meet Dayan's men in Wadi Mufared—prior to the attack on Karatiya.

On the afternoon of July 17, Dayan informed his men that the attack would begin at 10:00 P.M.: The battalion was to depart from the abandoned village of Juseir, break into the Faluja airstrip, then cross the Majdal-Faluja road; it would then advance to the wadi south of the Karatiya mound, and then, either by vehicle or foot, launch the actual attack. "Until we get to the wadi," the battalion commander said forcefully, "there is only one rule: break through and move, fire and move." Dayan instructed the men to proceed quickly, laying down constant fire at their flanks, particularly at the airstrip and road.

Dayan was troubled by taking part in a battle with the Givati men: They seemed tired, worried. He was also critical of the Givati battalion commander for stationing himself at a rear base.

And so the Eighty-ninth went into battle again. Two reconnaissance jeeps were at the front. Then came the Tiger and two companies of mechanized infantry. Dayan took his place in the fifth vehicle in the column, the second half-track of the first mechanized company.

Soon after setting out, one half-track went over one of the battalion's own mines. Following the principle of not stopping for any reason, the men left the damaged vehicle behind. The column came under enemy fire—mortars and machine guns—within a half hour, as the first vehicles approached the airstrip.

Preferring to hold their fire, Dayan's men waited until they were 150 yards from the enemy positions. Then the column opened up with all it had. Soon several enemy posts were abandoned. The commandos crossed the airstrip without casualties. The next goal was the Majdal-Faluja road, the hardest part of the trek. Egyptian flares helped to pinpoint the Israeli soldiers, making them a perfect target for the artillery, mortar, and machine-gun fire that rained down on them. Then tragedy struck the Tiger. Its gunner, Yosef Bentowitz, a resident of Nahalal, stood up in his turret in order to direct his fire. He was immediately killed. Some of the half-tracks took hits as well; six of Dayan's men were wounded seriously.

But the jeeps moved along untouched. Reaching the main road, still under heavy fire, the battalion cut across fields to the south, losing one homemade armored car in negotiating a steep embankment. Traveling south along a dirt track, they reached the wadi and looked for the track that crossed it. But the map had been incorrect. There was no track. And climbing the wadi's steep walls was impossible.

Karatiya lay on top of a mound only a third of a mile away, but it might as well have been on the moon. Dayan's battalion could not move forward. All the while the Egyptians kept pouring mortar and machine-gun fire at the column. Dayan might have considered retreating from the wadi, but that would have meant scrubbing the mission—an impossible thought.

The mood of the soldiers turned quarrelsome, restless. While the wounded were tended to, some men searched for a way out of the wadi. Dayan was under great pressure from his company commanders. He had to decide what to do—and quickly. If they were to retreat, better to do so now rather than later, if only because of the wounded. Dayan would not give up. He had to find a way to capture Karatiya.

What if it were possible to dig their way out of the wadi? Perhaps that would work. He ordered the men to begin digging into the embankment. Could they make a path for the vehicles to get out of the ravine? It was a monumental job—and would have to be done under mortar and machine-gun fire—but it was their only hope of carrying out the mission. Dayan found the man for the job, a platoon commander named Amos Abramson from Yavniel. Dayan liked the fact that he seemed less harried by the impasse.

While Abramson busied himself organizing the dig, Dayan went to the opposite side of the wadi, wrapped his head in his Arab *keffiyeh,* and went to sleep!

In later years, senior commanders in the IDF would recall the famous sleep of Moshe Dayan in that ravine and wonder how one could justify such behavior in the midst of a battle. How could one justify the snooze when reviewing this battle in later years at the military staff college? Was it an example of calm under fire? Or reckless irresponsibility? In any event, it was a remarkable thing to do, with his troops under fire, and unsure of how they were going to extricate themselves from a dangerous positon. However it was interpreted in later years, at the time, Dayan's forty winks sent a signal to his men that he had no intention of aborting the mission. For that reason alone, morale soared. Israel Gefen, who was there, recalled that the men said to themselves, "The boss is sleeping. There's nothing to fear."[10]

Awaking, Dayan gave the diggers another thirty minutes before the first vehicles were to move. Those that could not get through at that stage would have to be left back; their crews would join other vehicles.

"At 4:00 A.M., we advance on Karatiya," Dayan barked to his commanders, "with whichever vehicles manage to get out by then." By this time, the Givati occupying unit had caught up with the Eighty-ninth and had fallen in behind the others in the wadi. First the reconnaissance unit drove through, then the Tiger, the jeeps, and five half-tracks. On these were the men, weapons, and ammunition of the other vehicles that had to be left behind.

Nearing Karatiya, Dayan's commandos prepared for the final push. Proceeding to a point two hundred yards from the village, the half-tracks moved out right and left, laying down fire from mortars and machine guns. The Tiger advanced toward the mound, shelling the summit. Enemy fire was weak, and as the jeeps drove to the flanks, the half-tracks entered the village, capturing it without suffering any wounded.

Meanwhile, the Givati Brigade captured Hatta, but failed to take Bet Affa, taking heavy casualties. With the capture of Karatiya and Hatta that night, a wedge had been driven into the Egyptian line. The Negev was no longer detached from the north. At 6:00 A.M., just two hours after the attack on Karatiya, Dayan's battalion left that village, heading back to its base via Hatta.

The Egyptians actually blasted Karatiya with twenty-five–pounders and mortars two and a half hours later but by then Dayan's men were already on their way north. Only the infantry company had remained in Karatiya. Once again Dayan was accused of pulling his troops out too quickly. This time it was Shimon Avidan, the Givati Brigade commander, who charged that Dayan, in leaving Karatiya too early, had breached discipline. Yadin instructed the military attorney general to arraign Dayan for insubordination two days after the July 18 attack on Karatiya. Once Dayan was questioned, however, he explained himself convincingly to his interrogators. The case was dismissed.

Finally Dayan had to accept David Ben-Gurion's long-standing request and leave the Eighty-ninth. As the victor at Lod and Karatiya, Dayan took satisfaction at his battalion's exploits. But he had already seen enough of battle and too many acquaintances fall. He had asked the question in the 1930s: When will it end? The answer was still not apparent. He visited Aryeh Nehemkin and Micha Ben-Barak in the hospital, two of his men who had suffered eye wounds. Dayan had no trouble expressing sympathy: "Boys, for all that's worth seeing in this wretched world, one eye is enough."

❖ 5 ❖

SOLDIER TURNED DIPLOMAT

WITH THE SECOND cease-fire taking effect on July 19, Israel still remained on the defensive along the Egyptian front in the south. But in the north, it had gained control of most of the Lower Galilee. A new Moshe Dayan had emerged at this time. In his new role as Jerusalem front commander, he would have to forgo swiftness for patience, brashness for delicacy, rubbing shoulders with the boys in the field for the fine decor of regal surroundings. He was about to become a diplomat.

Nothing in Dayan's past had prepared him for this role. Diplomacy required thinking, talking, and waiting. Dayan would learn the trade of the diplomat on the job. He would look at the real diplomats and wonder if they really knew what they were doing. Often, he doubted they did.

If diplomacy was difficult, it also had its rewards. One was the limelight. He had resisted taking command of Jerusalem despite the urgent pleas of David Ben-Gurion in part because he was convinced that it was on the battlefield that he could make his name. He wanted to remain the commander of commandos, not rush into a desk job, even though it would give him a more senior position in the army. Yet the command he was about to take on would bring him the very recognition he had been seeking all along. He gained that recognition by being associated with one of the most controversial cities on earth, and, by being Moshe Dayan: a figure who, by virtue of his ability to turn a phrase, his seemingly natural self-confidence, and that ever-present black patch, made for good newspaper copy.

So Moshe Dayan moved to Jerusalem. As the commander of the Jerusalem front he automatically became conmmander of the Etzioni Brigade. For the first time he became an international celebrity, and he remained one for the rest of his life.

DAVID BEN-GURION had always admired the commando, the fighter, the warrior in Dayan. He wanted a warrior for Jerusalem, especially for the peace process that might soon begin. Since the prospect arose that Israel and Jordan would be negotiating with each other, the prime minister wanted Moshe Dayan in the delegation because he symbolized the strength of the Israeli army, the resolve of the Israeli government not to give up valuable territory, and the Israelis' willingness to fight for what they believed was rightfully theirs.

None of these calculations mattered to the men of Dayan's Eighty-ninth Battalion. They were furious that their commander was about to be taken from them. Some had left their units to fight with Moshe Dayan; all had risked their lives in battle under him. Despite attacks made on Dayan's conduct, these men loved him. And they wanted to continue to fight under his direct command. Some petitioned David Ben-Gurion to change his mind: Dov Granek led a delegation to the prime minister. Unless Dayan remained as commander of the Eighty-ninth, members of the delegation threatened to detach themselves from the commando battalion and follow Dayan to Jerusalem. Ben-Gurion was astonished, not only at their loyalty to their commander but also that a Lehi man such as Granek felt so loyal to Dayan. He needed Dayan in Jerusalem. In the end, only two men from the Eighty-ninth joined Dayan in Jerusalem.

BY THE TIME Moshe Dayan finally arrived in Jerusalem on July 23, large-scale military action to recapture the Old City was out of the question. David Shaltiel had made one last effort a few weeks earlier to break into the Old City, but he had failed. No one, not even Moshe Dayan, could get troops ready for another assault. There was just no time. The diplomats were meeting in New York at the United Nations General Assembly and Security Council, pressuring the combatants to lay down their arms. A United Nations observation force was already in place and beginning to assure that the smallest shooting incident caused an international storm. The Swedish diplomat, Count Folke Bernadotte, who was not known as a supporter of the state of Israel, was trying to work out a long-range settlement. The peacemakers were at work. The soldiers were too weary to take up the fight again.

The cease-fire had frozen the military situation in a way partially disadvantageous to Israel: The Old City remained in Arab hands; Mount Scopus on the eastern side of the city, while under Israeli control, was precariously located within Arab-held land. The corridors linking the Jewish sectors of Jerusalem with one another were exposed to enemy fire. Two agreements had been signed just before Dayan took over the Jerusalem command. One, negotiated by Count Bernadotte and signed on July 7 by the outgoing Jerusalem military commander, David Shaltiel, was known as the Mount Scopus Agreement. It called for Scopus to be demilitarized and to fall under United Nations supervision. The second accord, arranged two weeks later with Lt. Col. Abdullah el-Tel, the Jordanian commander of the Arab sector of Jerusalem, declared a cease-fire in force and called for a status quo in the no-man's land that divided the two lines.

Dayan retained the gut instinct of the commando. He still wanted action. The Etzioni soldiers were fed up with war. They had been in too much street fighting, had witnessed too many artillery barrages, too much sniping. They had suffered too much defeat. Even had they overcome the fatigue and the weariness with fighting, they were not really combat fit. After the fatigue had come the demoralization. Then the verbal sniping. About all they could agree on was the need to get rid of David Shaltiel as their commander. A return to the battlefield would not be a popular idea.

One incident in particular brought this home to Dayan. It occurred during his first patrol to Kibbutz Ramat Rahel on the southern side of Jerusalem, overlooking Bethlehem; the kibbutz had exchanged hands a number of times during the fighting. Travel to the kibbutz was via armored car only. There was not one available when Dayan wished to go. So he set out on foot and ordered that when one did become available, it be sent on afterward to bring him and the five other officers accompanying him, back. The armored car trailed behind Dayan's group. They heard shots fired to their rear and quickly realized that the armored car was the target. Racing back to it, they discovered that the driver had been wounded. Dayan ordered everyone to get into the armored car; one officer said no, it was too dangerous to do that. Why not carry on by foot as they had been doing? Dayan grew irate.

Aren't you men ashamed? he screamed. A soldier drives here just to take us back, and gets wounded, and now we will send him back along the road while we walk safely in the trench? Go ahead, walk back through the trench, he sniffed at them. He would take the car!

After visiting troops in their posts, Dayan realized that holding these static positons with their narrow firing slits through the cold Jerusalem winter could hardly inspire men for battle. Valuable time for training was being lost as well. He ordered intensive training for the soldiers, hoping that if battle had to come, they would be ready. He was not certain they would be.

Meanwhile, Dayan moved his entire family from Nahalal to Jerusalem, against his father's better judgment. Shmuel Dayan viewed moshav ideals as good, city life as bad. The grandchildren should have remained at Nahalal, but Dayan did not want to spend so much of his time away from them and Ruth. "We're husband and wife," he told his father. "Who knows what can happen when you are separated. We are a family, and we'll stick together." In later years it would sound strange to hear these words from Moshe Dayan.

Dayan would have preferred living in a small house. But Ruth wanted one in which entertaining was possible. Given their social obligations, she was of course right. The house she and Moshe chose, however, was steeped in controversy. Known as the Abkarius Bey house, it had once belonged to an Arab. Yael Dayan thought of it as a palace. It had many rooms, painted in different colors, and long corridors. Moshe and Ruth felt awkward about moving into the house. Ruth had convinced herself she would never use property once owned by Arabs who had fled because of the war. Yet here she was doing just that. Because an Arab had fled from it, the house was now in the possession of the Custodian of Enemy Property. To assuage her guilt, she wrote down everything that she used, making a promise to herself that she would return it all if and when the owner returned. It was a promise she fretted about and so did the rest of the family, particularly Yael, who worried that one day the real owner would return and order them all out. But no one ever came.

The accommodations were not very safe: They were fully exposed to Jordanian artillery fire from within the Old City; at times, gunfire would hit the eastern side of Dayan's house, sending him and his family into the safety of the cellar. Naturally, the family decided to spend most of their time on the quieter western side of the house. By virtue of his central military role in the holy city, Dayan now became Jerusalem's Number One Host. He still eschewed formality. When he was greeted at the entrance of his new headquarters by an officer who saluted and introduced himself as his aide-de-camp, Dayan startled him by saying, "You were—until this minute."

The Dayans managed to turn their controversial home into a social center, as foreign correspondents, Foreign Office people, and friends dropped in for tea and an update on current events. Rarely were there fewer than fifty for Friday tea. Unwilling to sit next to the same person through an entire dinner, especially if that person forced him to converse in English, Dayan insisted on buffet service. Even when he was the host, Dayan found the crowd sometimes too stifling: On occasion he would be the last one to arrive for his own parties; or he might disappear in the middle. Social occasions, with their small talk, always bored him.

Nonetheless, Friday afternoons at the Dayans quickly became the focal point of Jerusalem social life. The house turned into an alternative head-quarters for the brigade, with drivers and other officers adding to the commotion. On the tables were maps, binoculars, and revolvers. One frequent visitor, Ezer Weizman (who married Ruth's sister Re'uma), noted that on Fridays the Dayans' "door never closed, as visitors bustled in and out; Jerusalemites, soldiers, UN observers, and just plain citizens and friends. One always found a marvelously informal atmosphere there. Drinks and cakes on the table. Assi dashing around between everyone's legs and Udi under the table. It was a cheerful household, a kind of total disorder together with an air of hospitality that charmed anyone who ever enjoyed the company of its occupants and their adorable children."[1]

Dayan was lord of Abkarius Bey—and made sure everyone knew it. Telling people what to do came natural to him. Only the maid Simcha appeared able to establish her authority over Dayan. The rest of the family circled in orbit around him.

With the war winding down for the time being, Dayan was able to spend more time with his family. Because of rationing, food was short. Exploiting his senior position, Dayan took a jeep and guided his family to deserted fruit orchards around Jerusalem in search of ripe figs and grapes. He was seemingly immune to fear. While the family sat in dugouts with soldiers on trips to outlying posts, Dayan would walk along the horizon at the top of a ridge. Thanks to a full moon, he was an easy target for snipers. "Get down!" the soldiers shouted. He did not listen. Bullets pinged on nearby rocks. No matter. It did not stop Dayan from having his family tag along on these visits. Yael had total confidence in her father's judgment. It was all marvelous fun for her, particularly when, during visits to Israeli positions, he would let her gaze through binoculars at Jordanian soldiers. She noticed their red and white *keffiyehs*—and their guns. If she was not tall enough to peer through an observation hole, her father made sure to lift her up. As long as he was by her side, she had no reason to fear.

In Jerusalem, Dayan's military activity was limited to only two battles, neither successful. The first was on August 17: Dayan ordered an attack on Government House Hill, overlooking the Old City. Taking that crucial target would aid the Israeli army in encircling the Old City as a prelude to its capture. When the Arab Legion violated the neutrality of Government House, Dayan thought the time ripe to try to take control of the place despite the existence of the cease-fire. In approving the mission, Ben-Gurion laid down two constraints: Dayan was given only twenty-four hours to carry out the attack, and he could not enter the UN-occupied Government House or its fenced surroundings. Dayan's operations officer, Hillel Fefferman, reported that a patrol had uncovered Jordanians entrenched on the southeastern side of the hill. The patrol had come under small-arms and mortar fire. On the southern side, held by the Egyptians, the patrol had encountered no gunfire. They decided to attack from the southern side. Fefferman said it would be impossible to hold the hill without taking Government House itself. Meir Zorea, who commanded the Beit Horon Battalion in the brigade, proposed that the soldiers take Government House only if they ran into difficulty. Though Dayan had already agreed with Ben-Gurion and Yadin that his men would refrain from taking the building, he must have understood the military necessity of including Government House in the operation, but his military record in the past few months had clearly placed his superiors on alert. He had carried out a daring raid against Lod, but had been accused of bypassing brigade plans and of pulling out too early; then, he had swiftly taken Karatiya, and was again charged with leaving the scene of the battle before he should have. For the latter he had nearly been court-martialed. Little wonder then that Dayan was under pressure to follow orders this time. More over, as brigade commander, he was in a more senior position than on the earlier occasions. Commandos could act like commandos, and get away with a lot. But the commander of the Jerusalem sector, closer to the top decision makers, had no such privilege.

So Dayan stood his ground, refusing to allow Government House to be a target. As night fell on August 17, Zorea sent two companies to try to entrap the House. He remained at the nearby suburb of Talpiot from where he could keep in touch with the men on the wireless. Arab irregulars, shooting fiercely from atop the hill at Zorea's soldiers, inflicted heavy Israeli casualties. Again, Zorea pleaded with brigade headquarters to allow him to storm Government House. Oddly, Dayan could not be found for an hour. Just as he appeared uneager to hang around during the controversial *Altalena* affair, he may have decided that little was to be gained from entering into the disputes that were bound to erupt over this doomed battle. Fefferman was unprepared to give his approval to assault Government House without hearing from Dayan first. By daybreak, all such talk of capturing Government House was academic, as the Arab irregulars had taken firm control of the crest. The only choice was to retreat to avoid further casualties. Fefferman, supported by Dayan, urged Zorea to withdraw, and he and his men did. Casualties were heavy: nine Israeli dead, another twenty-one wounded, and five taken prisoner. Exploiting their victory, the Arabs proclaimed that no less than fifty Israeli soldiers had died in the battle, including a brigade commander and a deputy division commander.

Dayan, at a briefing afterward, castigated the Bet Horon soldiers for not fighting more aggressively. Zorea thought Dayan was too hard on the men. Dayan was upset with Zorea as well, condemning him for remaining behind while his soldiers went into battle on their own. Dayan felt that the outcome might have been different had Zorea been present on the battlefield. In rebuttal, Zorea argued that few of his soldiers would have been able to sense his presence at night; while, back at the command post, he had better control of the whole unit. Zorea lashed out at Dayan for being absent during that critical hour of fighting. Fefferman left the briefing angry at Dayan, and afterward urged Zorea to join him in seeking Dayan's dismissal as brigade commander. Zorea would have none of that plot. Fefferman was soon replaced as operations officer and put in charge of the brigade's armored-car battalion.

For the next few months, Dayan worked hard to train the brigade; he tried as well to persuade Ben-Gurion to let his soldiers take on the Egyptians in the south, near Bethlehem and Hebron. Not until October 15 and the start of Operation Yoav, aimed at expelling the Egyptians from the Negev, did Dayan get the prime minister's go-ahead. Once again, Ben-Gurion limited Dayan's military efforts to only twenty-four hours. Dayan's mission was actually part of a larger effort being conducted in the Hebron region. For four days the Palmach's Harel Brigade had been successfully battling the Egyptians at Hebron, preventing them from supporting their fellow troops in the Negev. At the tail end of the Harel action on October 21, Dayan got the green light to conduct Operation Wine Press, which was meant to capture Bethlehem. Dayan would have preferred advancing along the main road, but the Etzioni Brigade would have been overpowered by the Arab Legion. So Dayan thought of taking an indirect route, going through the nearby mountain village of Beit Jalla, a natural barrier only lightly fortified by a company of Egyptian troops. By successfully assaulting Beit Jalla, Etzioni would bypass the Jordanian soldiers on the main Bethlehem-Jerusalem road. This situation was tailor-made for Moshe Dayan. Time was the problem: Another United Nations–imposed cease-fire was due to begin the next day.

Dayan's plan was for his soldiers to go down one steep slope and then climb an even steeper one. No easy trick; but, he reasoned, if they could overcome the mountain, the Israelis would have little trouble with the Egyptians. It was the Jordanian soldiers whom Dayan truly respected, not the Egyptians. With the fall of Beit Jalla, the way would be cleared to take Bethlehem, with Hebron to follow. Given the challenging task of scaling the mountain and taking its crest was the Moriah Battalion, headed by Dayan's comrade-in-arms from the Syrian invasion, Zalman Mart. Assigned to guard the flanks were Meir Zorea's Beit Horon Battalion and Hillel Fefferman's Sixty-fourth Armored Car Battalion.

Perhaps because he placed too much trust in Zalman Mart, or perhaps because he was under such great time pressure, Dayan allowed the mission to go forward without sending a reconnaissance patrol to determine the best route for the Moriah soldiers to ascend the second hill. A severe price would be paid for that error. Some terraces on the slopes were five meters high, but to Dayan, scaling difficult mountain routes was not the issue as long as the Egyptians remained true to form. He remembered his experience at Zemach. He would simply get out his tin can and bang on it a few times. Then the Egyptians would flee. Dayan chose a quarry near the West Jerusalem suburb of Bayit Vegan for his command post; from there he would be in radio contact with his troops.

The two flanking units made their way without trouble, but Mart's battalion, comprising six companies, confronted a stronger enemy than expected. One Egyptian machine-gun position knocked out the entire point company. After one Israeli soldier was killed, other soldiers had no will to carry on the fight. How different were these soldiers from Dayan's Eighty-ninth. This was no Task Force Baum. Mart's soldiers shouted to him through the wireless—he was two hundred meters behind the point with the third company—that there was nothing more that could be done. Light rifle fire peppered the lengthy, snakelike column. All Mart could report to Dayan was that in the confusion and heavy gunfire he was not certain the Israelis would be able to extricate themselves. He asked his brigade commander for permission to withdraw.

Dayan was startled to hear such defeatist talk.

"You know how important this action is. I don't have to explain it to you."

Mart was the field commander. The decision whether to retreat was his. With an air of resignation in his voice, Dayan said laconically, "You must decide what is to be done." Mart gave the order to withdraw. A single Egyptian machine-gun position had kept the Moriah soldiers from moving forward.

Trying to salvage the situation, Dayan sought Ben-Gurion's permission to have another chance to conquer the villages south of Jerusalem on the way to Beit Jalla. Most of the General Staff supported Dayan's proposal, but the prime minister said no. He worried that even if Beit Jalla were taken, Israel would merely have to return it under United Nations pressure.

Beit Jalla became a stain on Dayan's record. All the old charges surfaced. He was inept at military planning. He took on the enemy even when he should have restrained himself. His commandolike tactics may have worked at Lod and Karatiya, but they were not a prescription for success in every case.

As opposed to his harsh treatment of Hillel Fefferman, Dayan avoided blaming Zalman Mart. Dayan had an unusual relationship with Mart: The man had saved his life in Syria in 1941. Seven years later, no matter what the justification, Dayan would have had a hard time taking Mart to task for a mission for which Dayan had overall responsibility. Dayan even extended faint praise toward Mart: He had launched the attack; he had done the best that he could. Still, Mart's military career never recovered from Beit Jalla. When he retired from the Israeli army at the age of fifty-one in 1968, he was a lieutenant colonel, the same rank he had held in 1948.

ALTHOUGH HIS MILITARY skills had won him the appointment as Jerusalem commander, Dayan became involved in diplomacy quickly. The war in and around Jerusalem had wound down; what was left was to keep the violence at a low level and work toward a permanent peace. At first, Dayan did so without much enthusiasm. For a farmer from Nahalal, the transition to Jerusalem was jarring, what with the continuous meetings and arguments, cocktail parties, and dinners. Dayan was at his happiest when he visited the front, dashing out from his office to the soldiers' posts, which were sometimes only yards from the Arab lines. Still, it fell to him to negotiate local arrangements with his military counterpart, Lt. Col. Abdullah El-Tel of Jordan, and to deliberate in the utmost of secrecy over possible national accords with the Jordanian monarch, King Abdullah.

In the process, Dayan began to work closely with Prime Minister Ben-Gurion. The two men had had intermittent contact since the December 1946 Basel Zionist Congress. Ben-Gurion obviously liked Dayan, and Dayan sensed something unique in the prime minister. He thought him superior to the other politicians. He was impressed with his wisdom, his leadership, and his vision.

As THE SUMMER wore on, the diplomatic wheels began turning faster, Count Folke Bernadotte, the United Nations mediator, had paid a visit to Jerusalem on August 10. He was promoting a peace plan that would have revised the November 1947 Partition Resolution by giving Jerusalem to the Arabs; the 1947 plan only called for the internationalization of the holy places in Jerusalem.

Bernadotte was back in Jerusalem that fall. But, as he was driving on September 17, he was shot by three men in a jeep. The attackers were never found, though suspicion was immediately cast on the Stern Group; its leaders denied doing the deed. The assassination accelerated the merging of the Stern Group (which had retained an independent status in Jerusalem) into the Israeli army.

Fighting continued on the other fronts. During the fall and early winter of 1948–49, Israel had the Arabs on the defensive. Mid-October saw the Egyptians pushed out of Beersheba. Later that month, Arab forces were driven out of the Galilee. In the final week of December and the first week of January 1949 the final battles of Israel's War of Independence were fought. Eventually, Egypt was repelled from within Israel and IDF forces pursued Egyptian soldiers across the frontier into Egypt itself.

In Dayan's effort to make sure that Jerusalem remained quiet, he developed a warm relationship with his Jordanian counterpart, Lt. Col. Abdullah el-Tel. The two men struck up an unusual "friendship" toward the end of August 1948 when U.S. Marine Corps Gen. William Riley, the head of the United Nations observer teams, asked the Egyptian, Israeli, and Jordanian army representatives to meet with him in the Assyrian monastery near the Jaffa Gate of Jerusalem's Old City. Riley wanted to demilitarize the area around Government House, where UNTSO was located. That meeting ended in a deadlock, and a second meeting, on September 5, seemed to be headed in the same direction. Present were four Israeli officers and four Jordanian officers as well as six United Nations observers. Dayan became so annoyed with what he perceived as the nitpicking of one of the United Nations men, an American name Col. Carlson, that he proposed to el-Tel that they go off and negotiate on their own. To everyone's surprise, the Jordanian accepted, and they went into the next room. Thus began Moshe Dayan's first secret negotiation with an Arab official. The two men managed to settle matters in a mere fifteen minutes! They returned to the meeting and read their points of agreement into the protocol. One of those points was Dayan's idea that he and el-Tel establish a direct phone line between them without having to go through the UN—the first hot line in the Middle East.

Whenever shooting broke out, Dayan would go to the phone and he and el-Tel would try to settle the matter quickly. Among the meetings they arranged were secret Israeli-Arab talks, first between the two of them, then between Dayan and King Abdullah. Dayan and el-Tel would sometimes meet in the Assyrian convent near the Jaffa Gate, or in the Mandelbaum house on the outskirts of Mea Shearim, or standing between the front lines amid land mines at the foot of the Old City.

On November 30, Dayan signed a "complete and sincere" cease-fire agreement with Jordan's el-Tel. (Ralph Bunche later ribbed Dayan, suggesting to him that it had not been necessary to include the word "sincere" in an international agreement.) The accord provided for a fortnightly convoy of food supplies through the Arab lines to Mount Scopus, the Israeli enclave in East Jerusalem that had not fallen to the Arabs in earlier fighting. Relations between Israeli and Jordanian officials grew even warmer in the coming days when Ruth Dayan danced with a Jordanian diplomat at a United Nations Christmas party at Government House. The day before, her son Assi had been lost near the border; he had wandered away from their maid Simcha. "Don't worry, Mrs. Dayan," said Ruth's Jordanian dancing partner, "If he should ever wander over to our side, we'll treat him like a little prince."[2]

But for the Jordanians, getting too close to the Israelis was threatening. Once, when Ruth Dayan was photographed with el-Tel, he persuaded the photographer not to publish the picture. Although he did not mind being seen in public with Moshe Dayan—that was business—being photographed with Ruth might give the impression that el-Tel actually enjoyed being with Israelis. In the same spirit el-Tel once asked Dayan to have the Israeli press attack him for his anti-Israeli hostility so that he could keep up his reputation in Jordan. El-Tel hoped that these Israeli press attacks would bolster his image as a rabid Arab nationalist and help him win the support of young Arab Legion officers who opposed the moderate, pacific policy of the king. Dayan arranged for such an article to appear on December 26; it noted that the Arab Legion hoped to "clear" Jerusalem of Jews and it attacked el-Tel for his "extremism" and "anti-Jewishness."

One day soon after the November 30 agreement, el-Tel had good news for Dayan. The king had authorized him to negotiate with the Israelis on an array of subjects involving Jerusalem and nearby Bethlehem, Latrun, and Ramallah. Jordan's proposals were based on exchanging territory and sharing control. Dayan knew that Prime Minister Ben-Gurion was prepared for some territorial alterations if it meant attaining a peace agreement with the king. But joint control of Jerusalem was out of the question. On the day before the November 30 accord had been signed, el-Tel had proposed that Israel give Jordan the Arab Katamon Quarter in Jerusalem's New City; in exchange, Jordan would turn over the Jewish Quarter of the Old City. Ben-Gurion refused. He did not want to yield Katamon. To break the impasse, Dayan proposed that the Tel Aviv–Jerusalem railroad, part of which passed through Arab territory, be reopened.

Then on December 5, the Jordanian commander proposed that Jordan give up part of Latrun and the region would be administered by a mixed Jordanian-Israeli police force. In return, Israel would grant a number of Arab refugees the right to return to Lod and Ramle. Jordan also insisted that the Israelis permit them the use of the Jerusalem-Bethlehem road as far as the Jaffa Gate to the Old City in Jerusalem.

At this time hopes for a peace settlement with Jordan were rising. On December 10 Dayan gave el-Tel a note from Eliyahu Sasson of the Foreign Ministry, inviting King Abdullah to open peace talks with Israel. Two days later Dayan and Sasson, accompanied by el-Tel, held a meeting with Dr. Shwkat el-Setti, the king's physician, at the Jaffa Gate in Jerusalem. Dayan made it clear to Dr. el-Setti that talks were only useful if aimed at turning the cease-fire into a lasting peace. On December 22 Ben-Gurion authorized Dayan to notify el-Tel that Israel was opposed to simply talking about interim arangements; it wanted a real peace treaty. In that context, all outstanding issues—including the opening of the railway line, the road to Bethlehem, and electricity supplies to Jerusalem—could be resolved.

A week later, on December 29, el-Tel informed Dayan by phone that Abdullah had apointed him his royal representative to draft a peace plan with the Israelis. The negotiations for the peace plan would have to be conducted in the greatest secrecy. If word leaked that Jordanian officials, including the king, were contemplating making a peace with Israel, the prospects for a peace treaty would diminish. There was a real danger that the Jordanian negotiators might become targets for assassination as well.

Despite the obvious risks, the peace talks were to begin the next evening, December 30. Ben-Gurion selected Dayan and Reuven Shiloah of the Foreign Ministry to represent Israel. El-Tel asked Dayan to dress in civilian clothes and bring maps and relevant documents. Dayan and Shiloah had been charged by Ben-Gurion to keep the talks going even if they failed to bear fruit—in order to keep the truce with Jordan alive. The Israeli negotiators were to take no definitive stand on the question of Jordan's annexing the West Bank. They were to seek to retain the eastern border of the Negev along the Arava Valley up to and including the Red Sea port of Eilat; and to propose Jordanian access rights to Gaza.

They were to deny Jordan a political hold over Ramle and Jaffa and avoid promising that Arabs could return to Lod. Finally, if Jordan raised the issue of the Negev, they were to indicate they were not empowered to discuss it.

The first meeting held on December 30 was ceremonial and only at the second encounter on January 5, 1949, held near the Mandelbaum Gate in Jerusalem, did they begin to discuss substance. El-Tel presented Jordan's proposals: The king wanted a corridor linking Jordan and Egypt through the Negev; in Jerusalem, he sought all of the Old City except for the Jewish Quarter, Katamon, the German Colony, Talpiot, and Kibbutz Ramat Rahel.

After the session, Dayan told Ben-Gurion that it was pointless to pursue the talks. Ben-Gurion's directive was to keep talking. Israel needed peace more than the Jordanians, the prime minister said. Dayan phoned el-Tel to agree to a third meeting. Over the phone, Dayan passed on his personal distaste for Jordan's proposals, suggesting that if Jordan did not change its positions, war might recur. Meanwhile, on January 7, Israel had soundly routed the Egyptians in the final battle of the War of Independence, sending Egypt's invasion force from the Negev into eastern Sinai as the IDF pursued them aggressively.

The Israeli victory in the south made the Jordanian king more pliable. On January 11, he told el-Tel to invite "the doctor's friend" (meaning Sasson) and "one-eye" (meaning Dayan) for talks with Abdullah personally. On January 13, the day before the third meeting was to occur, el-Tel phoned Dayan to say that King Abdullah wanted to demonstrate his desire for peace by inviting the Israeli commander and Sasson for talks at his El-Shuneh Palace, two miles east of the Allenby Bridge.

On the same day armistice negotiations between Israel and Egypt began on the island of Rhodes with Dr. Ralph Bunche, United Nations mediator, as chairman. Once Egypt signed an armistice agreement, Israel was theoretically free to act against Jordan militarily, had it the heart and energy. Israel might have sought to take over those areas being discussed at the negotiating table, a move Moshe Dayan would not have opposed. But David Ben-Gurion had presided over a war that was essentially over, and that had assured Israel its political independence. The prime minister thought it best to be practical at this stage: Israel, if it were going to develop as a nation-state, would have to set aside its military claims, and give preference to the pressing domestic tasks awaiting it. Moreover, while the other Arab countries never talked about signing a peace treaty, Abdullah actually seemed willing to consider entering into one with Israel.

DAYAN MET WITH Jordan's King Abdullah twelve times. These were the first high-level contact he would have with an Arab political leader. The talks led to some substantive results for Israel, and Moshe Dayan would play a significant role in attaining some of them, but negotiating with the king fell short of Dayan's hopes. No peace treaty would emerge. Israel would have to remain vigilant, to face the distinct possiblity that more blood would have to be shed before real peace came.

The first of Moshe Dayan's visits to Abdullah's palace occurred on January 16. Getting to the meetings, held in great secrecy, was risky. Driving the Israelis on the one-hour car trip through Arab lines, el-Tel had to sneak his cargo past Arab Legion guards. He simply yelled out from a distance, "It's Col. Abdullah el-Tel" to assure guards that he should be allowed through. He never gave them a chance to examine his car too closely. To disguise himself, Dayan at times donned a red-checkered Arab Legion *keffiyeh,* at times dark glasses without the eye-patch.

That first talk and a second one on January 30 produced no agreement. Abdullah sketched a scenario in which he would be ready to negotiate a peace treaty after an armistice agreement had been signed between Israel and Jordan. After the armistice accord the king would host an opening ceremony for the final peace talks, hosted by the king at his El-Shuneh Palace; direct Israeli-Jordanian negotiations would then begin without United Nations involvement. Abdullah even suggested the composition of the Israeli negotiation team: Sharett, Sasson, and Dayan.

Negotiations with the king were routinely a long, drawn-out affair. He would greet the Israelis in a large, oblong meeting hall. Before getting down to business, they would dine for a leisurely hour, engage in political gossip, then play chess or listen to poetry readings. When the king read poetry, Dayan was supposed to offer flattery. When the two men played chess, he was expected to lose gracefully and feign surprise at the king's unexpected moves. None of this prenegotiation play pleased Dayan; he grew impatient with Abdullah's habit of starting the substantive talks only after midnight. Urging patience, Eliyahu Sasson explained that such were the Arabs' customs, and Dayan had best try to get used to them.

To Abdullah's right, when they were permitted to be present, sat Jordan's prime minister and other cabinet members. To his left sat the Israelis. Opposite the king and below him were junior advisers. The meetings opened with the king sending his warm greetings to Israel's president Chaim Weizmann, to Prime Minister David Ben-Gurion, to

Foreign Minister Moshe Sharett. He asked after Golda Myerson as well, but could not bring himself to wish her well. While acting head of the Jewish Agency's political department, she had met secretly with the king first on November 17, 1947; then again on May 11, 1948. He was angry at her now for not agreeing to his demand that she and her colleagues put off plans to establish a Jewish state.

THE FORMAL NEGOTIATIONS for a cease-fire between Israel and Jordan were to begin on March 1 in Rhodes. Heading the Israeli side was Reuven Shiloah. Moshe Dayan had been appointed on February 27 as Shiloah's deputy. It was not clear until the last minute whether Dayan would be able to attend the talks. Once again, he was in a controversy over the question of obeying military orders.

The occasion had been Tu Bishvat, the Jewish festival celebrating the planting of trees. On this day in early February new forests were to be planted in memory of the War of Independence dead. Sha'ar Hagai, where the road to Jerusalem enters the hills before the ascent to the Holy City, was selected for the main ceremony. Israel's leaders, political and military, would be there and it would be necessary to protect them against Arab attack. Zvi Ayalon, the central front commander, instructed each formation under his command, including Dayan's Etzioni Brigade, to send one guard unit. Dayan thought Ayalon's concern was exaggerated and he refused to send a guard unit despite a second demand. As Dayan had predicted, the ceremony passed without incident. Ayalon thought Dayan's behavior reprehensible and insisted he be court-martialed for disobeying orders. Ayalon stayed in the post of central front commander even after Dayan rose above him in rank in the early 1950s, causing Ayalon to remark that it was "much easier to serve under Moshe than to have him serve under you."

The three-man court examining Dayan's behavior in the Tu Bishvat incident felt that he had made some justifiable arguments and his special position as Jerusalem commander might have made his refusal understandable—but in the end, he was found guilty of disobeying orders. Unable to fall back upon precedent for such cases, since the IDF was still in its infancy, the court could not decide on a reasonable punishment.

The court had no wish to prevent Dayan from attending the Rhodes talks but could not avoid meting out some kind of punishment. Dayan himself proposed a solution. He would be given a temporary demotion from lieutenant colonel to major. Few were informed of the demotion at the time and, in order to salvage Israel's dignity at the Rhodes talks, Dayan did not have to alter the rank insignia on his military uniform—

he was given a temporary rank of lieutenant colonel in order to be on the same level with his Jordanian counterpart across the peace table.

At the Rhodes talks, Col. Ahmed Sudki el-Jundi headed the Jordanian delegation. Dr. Ralph Bunche presided over the negotations, held in the Yellow Room of the Hotel des Roses. Just a week before, Bunche had successfully concluded the Israeli-Egyptian armistice accord amidst hope that it would serve as model for the present talks with Jordan.

A minor diplomatic flap threatened to end the talks before they got very far. At the initial session, Bunche had planned to introduce the two delegations to one another. The Jordanians arrived first and took their seats; when the Israelis arrived, Bunche asked Colonel el-Jundi if he would stand up so that he could be properly introduced to Reuven Shiloah; el-Jundi refused. That prompted Sharett back in Jerusalem to cable Dayan and Shiloah to inform Bunche that unless the Jordanians alter their "boorish manner" the negotiations would cease. Later, Colonel el-Jundi apologized, saying it was a misunderstanding, that he had thought the formal introductions were to occur at the end of the session, not the start. Dayan believed him.

All the childish spats over etiquette did not really matter. Dayan understood quickly enough that the Rhodes talks were mere window dressing, that the actual negotiations were going to be conducted behind the scenes, between King Abdullah himself and senior Israeli officials. Knowing that, Dayan still found el-Jundi and his compatriots frustrating negotiating adversaries: They would not veer from their orders from Amman, to the point where if a cable arrived garbled, they would ask for a recess so they could obtain the exact wording. Both Ralph Bunche and the Jordanians thought Dayan a formidable negotiator, but with little to do, he took long walks and went sight-seeing.

On March 18 Dayan was back in Jersualem. At 6:30 P.M. that evening he met with Abdullah el-Tel at the Mandelbaum Gate, where he pressed the Israeli demand to control the Wadi Ara area south of Haifa, as well as the nearby hills, once Iraqi troops pulled out of these areas. Iraq intended to evacuate its soldiers from Palestine and permit the Arab Legion to replace them. Israel, however, would never agree to such a development. King Abdullah realized that and seemed prepared to forgo some parts of the Iraqi-held territory in Palestine. Israel had refused to discuss the subject at Rhodes. The king invited Walter Eytan, director-general of Israel's Foreign Ministry, on March 19 to meet with him on the matter.

At the session with the king, Dayan told Abdullah: "Now we are in position for war. If we are to have peace, we must have more defensible positions. With the Iraqis we were there as enemies. With you we shall be there as friends." For that reason Israel needed these strategic areas below Haifa. The meeting was short, over by 10:00 P.M., with the king promising to mull over the Israeli proposals. The king then sent a "ministerial committee" to meet with the Israeli negotiators at the Mandelbaum Gate on the night of March 22. The two sides went home without a decision. The Israelis went to see the king the next day. Following a huge five-course dinner, the talks began. The king insisted that he was being forced to make great sacrifices. Dayan replied that Israel too had been asked to make sacrifices: He and two military members of the Israeli delegation (Yadin and Yehoshafat Harkabi) had lost brothers in the war; the Israelis had not wanted this war and it would not have begun at all if Jordan and the other Arab states had not attacked. Now that the war had occurred, Jordan would have to accept responsibility and conclude the pact. And, indeed, by 3:00 A.M., agreement was reached. Maps were signed. Dayan had managed to improve Israel's positions along the borders of the Arab Triangle (Tulkarem-Jenin-Nablus) and to ensure the security of the highway that joined the coastal strip to the valleys inland through Wadi Ara and the railway line from Tel Aviv to Jerusalem.

The king gave the Israelis gifts. Dayan received a revolver. The king handed a rose to each Israeli before they departed and proclaimed: "Tonight we have ended the war and brought peace."

Dayan flew back to Rhodes, where on April 3 he signed the armistice agreement for the Israelis. The *Jerusalem Post* called the signing "a solemn moment," though it should have been a joyous one. Gen. John Bagot Glubb (Glubb Pasha), commander of the Arab Legion, signed for Jordan, as did el-Jundi.

The Israeli-Jordanian armistice accord was not the first Israel had signed with the Arab states. After the Egyptian armistice signed in late February had come Lebanon on March 23; that summer Syria signed on July 20. During three meetings in April, Dayan negotiated with Jordan to implement the armistice accord. The most difficult aspect was dividing the no-man's-land around the Government House compound and the Tel Aviv–Jerusalem railway line, which passed through the southern part of Jerusalem. Dayan succeeded in maintaining Israeli control over the railway by obtaining a five-mile stretch of the rail line in no-man's-land near Beit Safafa. In exchange, Israel ceded several Arab villages in northern Jerusalem to Jordan. Ben-Gurion was thrilled. He credited Dayan with a great diplomatic victory. Dayan was pleased too: Essentially, he had been able to win at the negotiating table what his men had failed to gain at Beit Jalla the previous October. The Jordanians and Israelis agreed to divide the no-man's-land around Government House equally, but under pressure from the big powers, the decision was nullified, and Government House was kept under a UN flag.

On June 9 Dayan was assigned by the IDF's General Staff to lead the Israeli delegation to the Mixed Armistice Commissions (MAC), which supervised the armistice accords. Dayan remained in that post until he was appointed commander of the southern front the following October 25. By and large both sides adhered to the armistice agreements, though, much to Israel's disappointment, they did not lead to peace treaties. As it became clear that Jordan was not interested in a peace treaty, Dayan grew eager to improve upon Israel's frontier with Jordan. He was against engaging in a full-scale war, but he felt that if the other side began shooting, Israel should exploit matters to improve its strategic position. He had misgivings about the power of diplomacy to attain results for Israel. "If only the men of the Foreign Ministry were like the tanks of the IDF, all Israel's international problems would be solved," he said.[3]

In two cases, Israeli believed the Armistice accords were not being carried out: the guarantee of free Israeli access to the Jewish holy places and to the Mount Scopus enclave in Jerusalem, and the demilitarized zones on the Syrian frontier. With regard to the latter complaint, Dayan thought the Israelis had a perfect right to establish civilian settlements in part of the demilitarized zone with Syria, and pressed Ben-Gurion for his support. Not until September 1949 did Ben-Gurion concur with Dayan that farm settlements could be continued in the demilitarized zone; the prime minister insisted, however, there be no attempt by Israel to build up the demilitarized zone militarily. With respect to Mount Scopus, Dayan was eager to use the army to assure Israeli access. In a memo to the chief of staff on September 22, 1949, Dayan said that while Mount Scopus is in Arab territory, when Israel agreed to the Israeli-Arab cease-fire line, Jordan had accepted that the Israelis would have free access to Mount Scopus. If the Jordanians denied such free access, Israel would cease to recognize the cease-fire line. Dayan sought to illustrate what he meant by noting that Israel had recognized a wall, but only if there were a door in that wall for the Israelis; if the Jordanians shut the door, Israel would stop recognizing the wall. It would in fact break through the wall.[4]

Dayan, furious, took the case to Ben-Gurion. He told the prime minister Mount Scopus could be taken within three hours. Otherwise, he argued, Israel would be surrendering the rights it had won at Rhodes. Ben-Gurion asked Dayan if he thought this action could provoke Jordan into a large retaliation. Dayan doubted it: Jordan would treat it as an isolated episode. Ben-Gurion felt the time was not right, that Israel was better off taking up the urgent domestic tasks of absorbing the thousands of immigrants who were streaming to Israel's shores. Priority had to be given to internal development, the building of new farm villages, urban centers, and the improvement of existing settlements. Ben-Gurion insisted that Israel would not be built simply by turning the army loose on its enemies: "On no account. The war is over. The most important thing now is to bring Jews to Israel and settle them. Jerusalem will wait. Her day will come."

Many years later, Dayan gave grudging credit to Ben-Gurion for understanding that using a military option was not always wise: "It was more important to him to teach Jews about agriculture and how to delouse children than to renew war. I would not be capable of such a decision."[5]

THE JERUSALEM appointment had given Moshe Dayan the international stage. The world's eyes were always on Jerusalem and whoever served as its leader automatically became a celebrity. Even though Dayan's meetings with Abdullah were kept secret at the time, he was accorded the status of one of Israel's important figures. As commander of Jerusalem, he had one privilege that few other Israeli leaders enjoyed: He could speak to the press directly. He, Yigael Yadin, and Ya'acov Dori were the only three army officers given that right. Dayan was emerging from under the shadow of his famous father.

Hence, he was undoubtedly thrilled at the first real international coverage of his exploits when on July 18, 1949, *Life* magazine published an article called "Army Rallies Israeli Spirit." It featured a picture of Dayan with a caption: "One-eyed young Lieut. Col. Moshe Dayan, commander at Jerusalem, is an Israeli hero."

While Dayan might have objected to the article's palpable suggestion that the IDF was being exploited by the country to inculcate nationalism in its citizenry, its portrayal of him as a future political leader could not have displeased him. About Dayan *Life* wrote: "At every opportunity, the government invites the army out to flex its muscles for the citizens. The traditon of the hero is encouraged. The handsome young soldier with the eye patch [referring to the photo of Dayan] lost his eye fighting for Britain against Vichy forces in Syria during World War Two, but he also fought hard against the Arabs and now, besides being commander at Jerusalem, is regarded as a possible future prime minister." When Israeli politicians learned of *Life* magazine's suggestion that Israelis regarded Dayan as a future prime minister, a good deal of nervous laughter was heard. How could such a preposterous idea even be raised in public? some in Israel asked. Did not everyone know that David Ben-Gurion was still in his prime? And, even if he should pass from the scene tomorrow, a whole generation of senior Israeli politicians, far more polished in the art of politics than Dayan, was around and eager to take over. The only one not laughing that hard was Moshe Dayan.

DAYAN CONTINUED to meet King Abdullah, sometimes at El-Shuneh, sometimes in Amman, to negotiate postarmistice differences and search for a possible peace treaty. He had a flair for diplomacy and the king certainly appreciated that. Getting to Amman was far more difficult for Dayan than the trip to El-Shuneh: For one thing, there was not enough time to go to Amman and return the same evening. So he would remain overnight. Meeting the king late in 1949 and early in 1950, Dayan and Reuven Shiloah actually began drafting an Israeli-Jordanian peace treaty. But the king got cold feet after British officials urged him not to rush into a peace treaty with Israel as long as the other Arab states, especially Egypt, had not done so. While leaving Jerusalem's El Aksa Mosque after Friday prayers on July 20, 1951, the king was assassinated by a Palestinian Arab.

Moshe Dayan had learned the hard way that it was possible to work out details of an armistice accord, but not a peace treaty. Israel's independence had been made secure by these armistice accords, but the underlying conflict would not easily go away.

✦ 6 ✦

MOVING UP THE RANKS

WHAT KIND of an army should Israel build? Now that the War of Independence was over, that question had to be addressed. David Ben-Gurion was certain about the kind of army he did not want: one led by all those Palmach youngsters. Yes, they were good fighters. Yes, their leader, Yigal Allon, was a superb commander. It had been Allon and his Palmach-oriented staff that had routed the Egyptians at the tail end of the war. By right the Palmach commanders—Yigal Allon, Israel Galili, and Yitzhak Sadeh—should have been given the senior positions in the new Israeli army. Yet they believed in ideologies that were irrelevant to army life: They wrapped themselves in the left-wing embrace of the newly formed Mapam party; they clung to the kibbutz not merely as their home base but as a style of life that superseded all. They were too independent for Ben-Gurion's taste. He wanted a legion of warriors, not a workers' army. He wanted a disciplined band of soldiers, not a peculiar fraternity of separatists caviling from within. Gnawing at the prime minister was the conviction that, however well the Palmach men fought, they were not capable of conducting the kind of large-scale war Israel might be required to fight, the kind of war that could be expected to start all over again—against Egypt, Syria, Iraq, or Jordan, or all of them together.

Sensing Ben-Gurion's misgivings about the Palmach, its leaders, Allon, Galili, and Sadeh, had little affection for the prime minister. To them, he was a political centrist with no special regard for the kibbutz. The men of the Palmach grew bitter at Ben-Gurion for disbanding the Palmach in November 1948; and their bitterness turned into hostility when the prime minister ordered Yigal Allon to pull Israeli forces back from the Sinai after chasing the Egyptians out of Israel later that winter.

Though he sometimes claimed that he was the last of the Palmachniks, Moshe Dayan had carved out for himself a reputation independent from Yigal Allon's troops. Though sometimes an unconventional soldier, Dayan, unlike other Palmach members, conformed to the conventions of exhibiting loyalty to only one master—the Israel Defense Forces. Dayan's politics were styled after Ben-Gurion. More importantly, David Ben-Gurion saw in Dayan someone apart from the Palmach, with impeccable political credentials (Dayan was the highest-ranking and one of the very few senior officers who identified with Ben-Gurion's Mapai party). It did not matter to Ben-Gurion that Dayan hardly looked like a soldier, with his baggy pants, his unshined shoes, his socks that fell around his ankles. The war had hardened his physical appearance. His once-boyish face now appeared slightly more rugged. He moved with more authority, more self-confidence. He still had those cherublike cheeks, but his smile had become lopsided, as if he wished to convey a permanent state of cynicism. Dayan understood the art of soldiering as few others did. With a little more polish, a little more opportunity to take on senior leadership roles, Dayan might become Israel's top soldier. At that moment, David Ben-Gurion needed new blood in the command posts of his burgeoning army.

However much Ben-Gurion wanted Dayan for a senior post in the army, the war's end gave Dayan the opportunity to consider a career outside of the military. He had tasted public life, and liked it. Indeed, Dayan was a candidate on the Mapai list for the first Knesset elections held on January 25, 1949, given the number ten slot. He was described on the official list published six days earlier as "soldier, Nahalal." In the Israeli political system of proportional representation, candidates are chosen by the party; voters cast their ballots for a party, and parliamentary seats are allotted to each faction according to its share of the total vote. Heading the list of Mapai candidates was Ben-Gurion; Moshe Shertok (Sharett) was number two; Golda Meyerson (Meir) number six; and Shmuel Dayan number seventeen. At some point after the official list was presented Dayan dropped out of the election. The reason is obscure. However, one veteran Mapai politician, Yosef Almogi, recalled that Mapai leaders may have worried that the voters would react unfavorably to a father and son appearing on the same list, presumably figuring that Shmuel Dayan had "arranged" for his son Moshe to acquire a high place on the Knesset list of candidates.[1] Mapai, winning 46 Knesset seats (out of a possible 120), secured the highest number of seats and formed the first Israeli government. Had Dayan not resigned, he would have been a member of the first Knesset.

However, Ben-Gurion was able to convince Dayan to remain in the army; on October 21, 1949, Dayan, thirty-four years old, became a major general. Four days later he was appointed commander of the southern front, replacing Yigal Allon. (At nearly the same time—on November 9—Yigael Yadin became chief of staff, replacing Ya'acov Dori.) Ben-Gurion had whispered the southern commander appointment to the General Staff when Allon was abroad. For the first time since they had appeared in that famous photograph at Hanita with Yitzhak Sadeh sandwiched in between them, Moshe Dayan had soared ahead of Yigal Allon. To his friends and admirers, Allon was a heroic figure, the finest soldier and leader to have emerged from the ranks of the Palmach, destined for greatness. For them, Moshe Dayan's appointment to the General Staff stabbed Allon in the back. At their urging, Allon and other Palmach colleagues quit the Israeli army. In later years, Allon's friends wished he had been more independent of his Palmach loyalties at the time and had stayed in the IDF. By leaving he cleared the path for his longtime rival, Moshe Dayan, to shape the IDF as he saw fit.

SERVING AS the southern front commander posed a formidable task for Dayan. The area under his command was nearly half the size of the entire country. Its southern boundary was the front against Israel's most implacable enemy, Egypt. Although his command headquarters were south of Rehovot, where he spent a few nights a week in a one-room trailer, Dayan continued to live in Jerusalem.

Friday afternoon open houses were held at the Schwartzes. Independent as ever, Moshe Dayan intended to make his own personal imprint on the new post. Assembling his staff, he sought to give the impression that Yigal Allon's men were welcome to continue. Allon's deputy, Yitzhak Rabin, thought the front commander was being disingenuous. Rabin, acting commander of the front in Allon's absence, was in charge of turning over the command to Dayan. Rabin did not doubt that Dayan would prefer to be rid of him as well as all the Palmachniks. This feeling was strengthened by their first talk, in which Dayan appeared cautious and aloof—and frank. Dayan informed Rabin that he was no longer needed.

Dayan's first task was to decide where he could leave his mark. In this postwar period he would have little chance to lead soldiers into battle.

Shocked and shattered by the 1948 war, the Arabs had retreated into a shell, too wounded and dazed to contemplate large-scale action against Israel. The victors too had little enthusiasm for renewing the fighting. After the long struggle, with its many casualties, the nation's leaders wanted to leave fighting behind. It was time to put down the swords and pick up the the plowshares, time to think about nation building.

Israel was ready to affirm its raison d'être by welcoming into its midst the hundreds of thousands of Jews from Hitler's Europe and North Africa and the Persian Gulf who needed immediate shelter. This "ingathering of the exiles" brought 686,739 immigrants to the Jewish state in the first three and half years, doubling the population. When they arrived, the immigrants needed homes and jobs. Essentially a peacetime army now, the IDF was regarded as a crucial instrument in absorbing these immigrants into the society, largely because no other institution could command resources and manpower as well as the army. While others in the IDF were skeptical about using the army for such purposes, Dayan understood that armies can serve valuable peacetime functions, perhaps no less important than their battlefield efforts.

Fortunately, Dayan had a direct channel to the senior man in government. Within two weeks of his appointment as southern front commander, Dayan was visiting David Ben-Gurion in Tel Aviv. He caught the prime minister awake late at night, preparing his speech for the next day at the inauguration of the Weizmann Institute of Science. Dayan said he had only one question: Did the prime minister want him to become involved in the civilian development of the Negev?

Yes, the prime minister answered quickly.

Dayan began immediately by ordering his officers to turn over certain IDF facilities to new immigrants for housing. During the harsh winter of 1950, Dayan made sure to provide food and medical attention for new immigrants, and assured them proper access to roads, phones, and radio communication. It amused him that some of the immigrants seemed to take the treatment they were getting from the IDF for granted, as if the army was not putting itself out in any special way for them. Even if unappreciated, Dayan saw no other way. This was Zionism and brotherhood at its best, he thought.

One of Dayan's first steps as southern front commander was to encourage members of the Negev's kibbutzim to farm their lands up to the frontier in order to avoid open, neglected areas that could become inducements to raiders from the other side. He promised the kibbutzim military assistance where needed, including the use of army vehicles. Zvi Tsur, chief of staff for the southern command, argued that the vehicles belonged to the Israeli army, not to some kibbutz. If the government thought more vehicles were needed for the kibbutzim in the south, let it earmark civilian ones for such use. Dayan retorted that many military vehicles were parked idly at the bases. To wait for the government bureaucracy to help the kibbutzim would take too long. As commander, he could order the military vehicles to the kibbutzim. Exasperated by Dayan, Zvi Tsur asked to be transferred—and became assistant director of military operations.

NO MATTER how much he invested in the southern settlement Dayan remained convinced that they were not equipped to defend themselves against Arab assaults. Others in the IDF's senior planning machinery disagreed with him and a fierce debate arose over the question of the role of these settlements in the country's southern defenses. Championing the settlements at the time was the deputy chief of operations, Yuval Ne'eman (later a renowned physicist and leader of the right-wing Tehiya party). In 1950 Ne'eman proposed to the General Staff that the southern settlements be propped up as major elements in the nation's defensive network in the south. Because Israel had no strategic depth, he asserted, turning the settlements into fortifications would create a decent strategic alternative. Under his plan, the country would build "hedgehog" settlements—named after the hedgehog, which defends itself by raising its hair and closing itself in.

To Moshe Dayan, the existing settlements were incapable of defending themselves. He conjured up the image of sausages (as opposed to Ne'eman's hedgehogs) and contended that just like sausages, the settlements' houses, lined up alongside one road, would be chopped to pieces in wartime. He insisted that it would not be possible to train the newly arriving immigrants to defend these settlements successfully. Dayan had already begun a system of IDF mobile patrols to guard the Negev against Arab infiltrators. When Chief of Staff Yigael Yadin backed Ne'eman's philosophy Dayan had to give way. As a consolation, the Negev settlements were not built with a one-street plan.

DAYAN ADOPTED a peaceful pose grudgingly. He believed that the War of Independence had not really ended, and that Israel required further military actions to improve its strategic situation. He favored conquering the West Bank and the Gaza Strip as a way of dealing with the Arab infiltration problem. He also laid plans for the conquest of Sinai. (Avraham "Bren" Adan, Dayan's operations officer, went with Dayan to the frontier, where the two men would search for possible penetration points.)[2] These aggressive actions, Dayan believed, would deter the Arabs from further military pursuits. He questioned the value of formal peace accords with the Arabs. Since the Arabs had no real interest in peace with Israel, he asserted, Israel's most prudent step would be to take military action to improve its strategic position. He proposed a military campaign that would bring Israel all of the territory up to the Jordan River. Replying to Dayan, Foreign Minister Sharett said, "The State of Israel will not get embroiled in military adventurism by deliberately taking the initiative to capture territories and expand." World opinion would simply not stand for it, said Sharett with an air of finality.

Dayan believed that he had an ally in David Ben-Gurion. After all, the prime minister still worried that the British might try to take the Negev away from Israel and give it to Egypt or Jordan, enabling the two countries to have a land bridge connecting their two countries. Dayan had again misread the subtleties of Ben-Gurion's thought. When he tried to tell the prime minister about his efforts to strengthen military security in the south, Israel's leader interrupted, saying that security did not mean military efforts alone, it meant making the desert bloom and establishing Jewish towns and farm settlements in the Negev.

Despite their differences of opinion, Ben-Gurion's door was always open to Moshe Dayan. This relationship not only saved time; it produced some surprising results. A prime example was the case of the 2,700 Arabs of the coastal town of Majdal, adjoining Ashkelon near the Gaza Strip. After the war, these Arabs found themselves within Israeli boundaries, cut off from their sources of employment as textile workers or farm laborers in and around Gaza. They were under military administration and out of work. Meeting with Dayan, they asked to be relocated to the Gaza Strip. When Dayan found little enthusiasm among the General Staff for the idea, he went directly to the prime minister and secured his approval. Dayan informed the senior officers in his command that military rule in Majdal had been canceled. To Dayan's chagrin, the General Staff informed him that he only had the power to recommend such an action, that it was the Chief of Staff who made such decisions. So, as Dayan put it, "I exhumed the body from its grave, restored Military Government to an empty Majdal, and reburied it next day with General Staff approval, thereby meeting the meticulous standards of army protocol."[3]

MOSHE DAYAN became enchanted with the desert, the colors, the vegetation and particularly the space and freedom it offered. Sometimes he grabbed his intelligence officer, Capt. Rehavam Ze'evi, and the two would plunge into the desert and not be seen for several days. Or he traveled with his daughter Yael, then eleven years old. She put on an Arab *keffiyeh* round her head and her father enchanted her with bedtime stories about Abraham, Jacob, Joseph, and Moses. He explained to her that the desert was a harsh place, no water, no shade, no way to make a living, and the biblical Hebrews of that day relied upon God for their salvation. According to Dayan, it was the very harshness of the desert that had brought his ancestors to monotheism. At the end of their journeys, Dayan would give his daughter a note for her teacher, explaining that she had been absent from school "for special reasons."

Dayan constantly searched for an excuse to get away from his desk. Sometimes he attached himself to army reconnaissance patrols, crossing the frontier into the Sinai. Smugglers or hostile bedouin tribes took shots at him. Once, Dayan and Ze'evi joined a patrol of six vehicles to search for the route to the biblical Kadesh-Barnea in eastern Sinai. Hearing a commotion, they realized they were near the Egyptian outpost at Kusseima at the Negev-Sinai frontier. They waited for the Egyptian soldiers to react.

The Egyptian commander sent an officer to inform Dayan that he had crossed over into Egypt by mistake and should return. Dayan playfully tried to insist that the Egyptians were actually on Israeli soil, according to Dayan's map. While his "hosts" were arguing with one another, Dayan quietly withdrew. The incident passed peacefully, but the next day the Israeli chief of staff, Yigael Yadin, heard about Dayan's adventure and, concerned that the southern front commander might be captured, ordered him the next day to cease such behavior.

FOR MANY REASONS, the combat standards of the Israeli army had fallen dramatically soon after the 1948 war. The war had provided a laboratory for the IDF, a trial-and-error experiment on a large scale in how to conduct oneself on the battlefield. Much of what the Israeli army did had been improvised, the instinct for survival the main driving force. In 1948 the IDF had not deployed formations larger than companies or battalions. Turning raw recruits—the thousands of new immigrants streaming into the country—into the best possible soldiers would have to wait until after the war. Who would undertake the required training? Many of the most talented officers had left the IDF's ranks. The battle-hardened instructors, who could have passed on their valuable war experience to a new generation of Israeli soldiers, went home, convinced that the Arabs would not fight again for a long time. Why bother building up the army? For those who stayed behind, training new immigrants not tempered for the rugged conditions of army life led to constant frustration. Then too there were equipment shortages. One of the army's finest soldiers, Meir Har-Zion, put his finger on the problem: "There was a problem of survival. The IDF was in a very bad situation. We were at the level of the Syrians, perhaps a little worse."[4]

The incident which, above all others, provided an early warning signal for Dayan occurred toward the end of 1950, while he was on vacation with his family in Turkey. It concerned the Kilometer 78 marker on the Eilat road and raised fears among many that war might be around the corner again. Jordan claimed that the Israelis who were building this road had penetrated Jordanian territory at Kilometer 78. Blocking the road, Jordanian troops put up a sign saying, in Arabic and Hebrew, HASHEMITE KINGDOM OF JORDAN. ROAD CLOSED. In their armored cars, they then stationed themselves on the nearby hills. Eager to avoid a full-scale war with Jordan, the Israeli General Staff ordered the southern command to shoo the enemy away and open the Arava road. "You can frighten the Jordanians, but not attack them," the acting prime minister, Eliezer Kaplan, told Chief of Staff Yadin. (Kaplan had temporarily replaced Ben-Gurion, who was in Greece.) Dayan was summoned home, perhaps because the southern command was slow in taking action, or perhaps because the chief of staff was concerned about possible complications.

Arriving at Kilometer 78 the next morning, Dayan found his troops, a mechanized battalion from an armored brigade, doing everything but breaking through the barrier. He flew over Jordanian lines, noticing that there were only a few armored vehicles of the Arab Legion and no tanks or artillery around. Upon landing, Dayan sent an Israeli officer in a jeep carrying a white flag to the Jordanians, demanding that they remove the barrier so Israel could use the road. Israel would fire only if fired upon. Dayan made clear that Israel would abide by whatever decision the Mixed Armistice Commission (MAC) made regarding Jordan's complaint. The Israeli officer returned with Jordan's rejection. Dayan then ordered the Israeli unit to open the roadblock by force and to keep on driving and only open fire if the Jordanians fired. The half-tracks cleared the barrier. The Arab Legion did not respond—until the next morning. Again the road was blocked, and again the Israeli mechanized column opened the barrier. This time the Jordanians opened fire, hitting one of the Israeli vehicles. Dayan ordered the column off the road and mortars were fired. Two Jordanian armored cars were quickly hit. The fighting ended. Subsequently, in 1951 the MAC awarded that section of the road at Kilometer 78 to Jordan; the Israeli General Staff was forced to hand over the stretch to Jordan and began building a parallel section to the west.

For Dayan, the brutal lesson was in the "dithering, indecisive" manner in which the armored brigade acted. He reported his assessment to his superiors in the IDF; big changes were necessary.

INASMUCH AS 1950 was a quiet year for the IDF, it could begin to make those changes by building up its training programs, including those for its senior officers. Though these officers had fought in the war, they had received no real training for their jobs as senior commanders, no training in running large formations, no training in armor or artillery. There was much to learn. Yigael Yadin had the bright idea of having some of the twenty-four- and twenty-five year olds give the brigade and front commanders some lessons in battlefield theory. Reversing the usual situation, the IDF launched a training program in which the subordinates would instruct their commanders. Course commanders were Yitzhak Rabin and Chaim Bar-Lev, both future chiefs of staff.

One of their prize students was Moshe Dayan. For nine months in 1950–1951 Dayan became a student of military tactics. He turned command of the southern front over to his deputy and plunged into schoolwork. He did not have an easy time—nor did his instructors have an easy time with him. They taught the "school solution," the classical way of dealing with this battlefield situation or that. Dayan listened to this orthodoxy and thought it irrelevant for combat on the Arab-Israeli battlefield. The "school solution" could teach what move to make when arrayed against certain kinds of military equipment; but it could not provide what to do under the peculiar constraints imposed by warfare in the Middle East. Dayan liked to defy the "school solution" for no other reason than his belief that military tactics should not be static, predictable, or routine. If the instructors said the best move was to go right, he would advocate going left. Although it was always difficult to pin down Moshe Dayan's military principles, he had one overriding belief: Be as different as possible from one time to another. Do not allow the enemy the luxury of being able to predict your actions. Uri Ben-Ari, who became one of the IDF's leading tank commanders, spent some time with Dayan in the first battalion commanders course in 1950; and then, soon after, Ben-Ari was chief instructor of the brigade commanders course in which Dayan was a student. "Whenever the majority thought the best solution was defense," remarked Ben-Ari, "Dayan urged offense, or mixed offense and defense."[5] The course commanders did not pay too much attention to Dayan, but in later years those who were with him at the time, such as Chaim Bar-Lev and Uzi Narkiss, credited Dayan with a sense of vision and innovation that no one else displayed.

Narkiss, an instructor in the brigade commanders course during the summer of 1951, remembered one exercise that illustrated Dayan's iconoclasm. The "students" were taken to the field and asked to decide on the best deployment for a brigade facing south. The site was near the two main crossroads leading from the Gaza Strip—east to Iraq-Suewidan and north along the coastal road. The "school solution" was to deploy around the two crossroads, leaving Kibbutz Yad Mordechai and other border settlements nearby outside the defense perimeter. Dayan was outraged, arguing that the Egyptians would have no trouble taking the settlements. "The raison d'être of the Israeli army," Dayan told the class, "is to defend our settlements, and not the contrary." Dayan insisted that Israel's defense had to be deployed right on the border of the Gaza Strip. The commanders calmly explained that military theory required that the proper place to deploy the defense was on two crossroads. The instructors suggested that for this theoretical exercise, Dayan should imagine the area empty of settlements. Dayan could not be persuaded. The instructors eventually bowed to Dayan's greater wisdom and the exercise was altered to include Yad Mordechai and the other new settlements within the defense line. More importantly, Dayan's view later became IDF military doctrine.

BY 1951 the Arabs had begun to recover from the war. The fedayeen, "self-sacrificers" in Arabic, salaried volunteers largely recruited from the Gaza refugee camps, began raids, mostly on civilian Israeli settlements throughout the country. Beginning in 1951, Israeli casualties began to mount: 137 that year, most of them civilians; 147 in 1952; 180 in 1953. Though the infiltrators appeared bent on robbery, Israeli morale sagged. Soon, the poorly fortified settlements were targets. Travel to and from the settlements became dangerous, whether due to ambushes, mortar attacks, or land mines. City dwellers stayed put. Youth groups refrained from their customary hikes. The IDF was criticized for not keeping the peace.

One of the most embarrassing incidents occurred on May 2, 1951, when the Syrians interfered with a large Israeli project to drain the Huleh swamps north of the Sea of Galilee. Crossing the Jordan, the Syrians captured Tel el Mutilla, a village situated in the demilitarized zone on the western bank of the Jordan. The two sides battled for the turf over and over again. The IDF sent an infantry unit to dislodge the Syrians but the Israeli attempts were inept and the Syrians easily held them off; finally more troops were sent and after four days of fighting the Syrians were expelled. Twenty-seven Israelis were killed. Considering how few

Syrians were holding the hill, it had taken the IDF too long, and had cost too many lives.

Though Tel el Mutilla did not fall within his jurisdiction, Dayan went there to ask local commanders what had happened. The widespread view at General Headquarters was that Tel el Mutilla was a fiasco. Dayan, however, suggested that the high number of casualties was not the relevant factor. True, too many Israelis had died, but the soldiers had displayed the perseverance he wanted to see in the Israeli soldier. Still, the impression spread that not one IDF battalion was prepared for combat. Something had to be done. Tel el Mutilla was a turning point. It had finally dawned on the IDF that an urgent need existed to improve fighting standards.

IN THE SUMMER of 1951 Moshe Dayan was playing war games. The first regional command-level exercise, known as Maneuver B, was held on August 29. It was designed to test how the IDF would fare against a surprise Egyptian attack. Dayan's southern command played the Green state—the Egyptians. Zvi Ayalon's central command troops played the Blue state—the Israelis. Dayan and Ayalon prepared for war differently. Ayalon took his entire staff, a kitchen truck and headquarters caravan, plus several command cars and jeeps on a journey that took days. Dayan went by himself, driving alone in his jeep, looking for food—dates, grapes, melons—in the process familiarizing himself with the terrain.

Because the cost of the war games was so high, following the rules was considered essential; otherwise the IDF's senior command would be unable to learn from the exercise. The plan was for Dayan's Greens to carve out an initial success; in the next stage, the Blues were to halt the Greens' march; and finally, the Blues were supposed to counterattack. The battle was to last thirty-six hours. Blue commander Zvi Ayalon was told that he had another seventy-two hours before Dayan's Greens would begin their assault.

Ayalon—and the senior echelons of the IDF—had not taken Moshe Dayan into account. The commander of the Greens coyly asked himself what would happen if the assault were to begin before the seventy-two hours expired? Might that not gain for Dayan's troops a precious element of surprise, despite the gross violation of the rules of the war game? The idea intrigued him.

It intrigued the Seventh Armored Brigade as well. Until then armor had been considered a mere supporting element of infantry within the IDF. No one had paid much attention to it; no one had suggested that armor might play an independent or even dominant role in a battle. The men of the Seventh believed that, given a chance, armor could prove its value. They were the first standing armored brigade of the IDF. Their commander was Uri Ben-Ari, and among them were Avraham "Bren" Adan, Shmuel "Gorodish" Gonen, and others who became senior IDF armor commanders in later years. They were fanatical about the importance of tanks in battle; Dayan gave them their first opportunity to show themselves off.

The Greens were supposed to wait in the Beersheba area for three days and then move. Waiting only one day, Dayan ordered the Seventh Brigade to make a breakthrough forty-five miles south of Beersheba, bypassing certain enemy units as part of the general need to thrust forward. Ayalon's troops were panic-stricken. "Unfair," they complained to the war games judges. All that the judges could do was to order the Egyptians to halt. By then it was too late. They had "vanquished" the enemy.

Chief of Staff Yigael Yadin was not amused. "That's not the way armor operates," he told Uri Ben-Ari. "You don't break through and leave the enemy and his fortifications behind you. You move forward only after you have cleared the enemy out behind you."

Dayan thought Yadin's explanations amusing—and irrelevant. To Dayan, it was Ju'ara 1938 all over again. Except that, rather than penetrating fences, Dayan was jumping the gun. He answered his critics: "In war, nothing is fair. Because either you kill your enemy. Or your enemy kills you." At the close of the maneuver, Dayan drew a cartoon and showed it to the central command staff. He had drawn a wild young fox, insignia of the southern command, standing victoriously atop a dying toothless lion, the central command insignia. Below was written: "Better a live fox than a dying lion." The day that the exercise ended, a Piper Cub dropped thousands of leaflets with this Dayan cartoon over Ayalon's positions. (Dayan, the live fox, drew inspiration for this craftiness from the founder of the Palmach, Yitzhak Sadeh. Dayan himself recognized the connection between himself and Sadeh at a memorial meeting for Sadeh on August 24, 1953, at Givat Brenner. Dayan called Sadeh, who had died the year before, "the father of lawlessness." Following the rules was not the issue, Dayan suggested; achieving the intended goal was.)

THE RULE BREAKER will ask himself: Are there times when I should play along? And what are those times? Dayan asked himself these questions through poetry. Indeed, it is likely that he enjoyed writing poetry because it afforded him an opportunity to express views that he knew he dared not express in more overt ways. His poetry also expressed a constant ambivalence about getting involved or remaining detached. His poem "The Owl and the Fox," perhaps the most famous of the Dayan poetry, reflects these feelings. He wrote the poem at the conclusion of Stage A of the battalion commanders course in the spring of 1951. In that poem he saw himself as the fox, lean, hungry, employing practical wisdom. The owl, in this case, was the IDF Training Division. Dayan, the fox, wants the owl to let him "take over" the teaching at the school so that he can impart his far more practical wisdom. Reading the poem, one feels Dayan's disenchantment with the instructors.

> So, suitably armed with pencil and paper,
> Take down the relevant exercise data:
> Tel Aviv's conquered, Haifa's a shambles,
> Through Negev and Galilee the enemy ambles.
> Jerusalem's in flames like so many candles.
> You're the commander, with fifty-five aides
> You're to move out, deploy, finalize raids,
> To wrap around, mechanize, foil, and outflank,
> The target, objectives, positions of tank.
> In local localities, on this side or that,
> To fire trajectories high, low and flat
> Infilade, defilade, reporting-line too,
> Knock out the enemy with the famous one-two.

Five months later in the summer of 1951 at a party marking the end of the advanced course, he wrote another poem called "The Fox's Swan Song," acknowledging that he found it imprisoning to be in uniform, having to obey rules and orders. In the poem, he insisted that the course had done him little good, and "A general I'll never be." "I love when they call me 'Moishe,' And suffer when they call me Sir."

DAYAN LEFT on October 26, 1951, for six months of study in England and France. During a three-month course at the Senior Officers' School at Devizes in England, he concentrated on armor for the most part. The whole experience was a far cry from life in the IDF: Dayan was given a "batman," someone who woke him in the morning, served him tea, and polished his shoes. He found the British officers, some of whom had served in the Middle East, correct, but unfriendly. They had no special liking for Israelis or Jews. Dayan found it interesting, so much that he asked Chief of Staff Yigael Yadin if he could remain to take some extra courses. Yadin said no.

When Dayan was in England, the British newspapers carried an article about a British officer who had been accused of taking bribes from Israel during the 1948 War of Independence. During a recess in the lectures, British officers grilled Dayan as if he were on trial, taunting him, asking whether he did not feel shame as an Israeli. On the contrary, Dayan retorted, it was the British officer who sold his army's weapons who should feel the shame; not Israelis who had purchased weapons, weapons that were used to defend their lives and their country. Following the course, Dayan underwent yet one more unsuccessful eye operation, this time in Paris.

Upon returning home on April 27, 1952, Dayan was offered the dual position of deputy chief of staff and chief of operations. On the face of it, the offer should have elated Dayan. These were two of the highest positions in the IDF. It was logical that the man who was number two to Chief of Staff Yigael Yadin would one day be a prime candidate for chief of staff. That did not impress Dayan. Dayan felt strongly that he possessed a unique role within the IDF and he was not about to dilute his independence by becoming "number two" to anyone. Dayan refused Yadin's request, saying that he was not suited by temperament to be a deputy. Yadin did not try to change Dayan's mind. He called Mordechai Makleff back from London in late May to resume his job as deputy.

Dayan was then appointed northern front commander. In that task, he would have his own command, and enjoy the kind of independence he wanted. Within Dayan's northern command were frontiers with three Arab states. Lebanon, Syria, and Jordan, frontiers that had been largely tranquil since the signing of the armistice agreements. Dayan knew this territory from his youth; and only recently he had wrestled with the frontier problems with Syria through his work on the Mixed Armistice Commission.

Dayan began by assigning the command's chief of staff, Chaim Bar-Lev, to prepare a war game, staging an attack against a fortified target— along the lines of what Dayan had learned while in England. Quickly Dayan realized that a morale problem existed within his troops: Some officers believed they were doing the country a favor by remaining in the army. This feeling was encouraged by the attitude of the General Staff, which offered officers sizable material benefits as an inducement. At an early stage, Dayan gathered his officers in the canteen and startled them by saying that he had no wish for any to remain under duress, or because he felt he was doing the state of Israel a favor. If anyone wanted to switch to another unit, that was fine with him. No one left. Two who stayed were Bar-Lev and Ariel Sharon, the command's intelligence officer. (Dayan once told Sharon that the only effective intelligence officer was one who knew the terrain better than Dayan did himself.) At that time, few senior officers spoke to their junior officers in tones such as Dayan had. Word spread that Dayan had given his men a gentle ultimatum, and in short order, other senior officers were adopting the same tack.

During these relatively peaceful times, Dayan was able to preside over an ample number of field exercises and instill in his men a new enthusiasm for soldiering. At times it took only the clever turn of a phrase. He once summarized an exercise by saying that neither side had won for it was impossible for the IDF to defeat the IDF. During one exercise, when one of his brigade commanders told headquarters that his own headquarters were surrounded, Dayan asked him how he knew. The officer noted that the enemy force had cut off his headquarters from the main part of the brigade. If that was the case, Dayan told him, it may be that it is your opponent who is surrounded. Being surrounded was not necessarily something physical. An Israeli officer should act as if it is not he who is surrounded, but his enemy.

The outlines of Moshe Dayan's approach toward commanding his men became clearer during this period. When he gave orders, they tended to be general, vague, leaving his subordinates room for maneuver. He himself had been a junior commander and he knew the value of permitting as much independence as possible for lower-level officers. Once, in November 1952, however, the results of such an approach proved bewildering to Dayan. It began when Dayan walked into Ariel Sharon's office to inform his intelligence officer that two Israeli soldiers had crossed over to Jordan by mistake while on a patrol and were being held captive in Amman. Was it possible, Dayan asked, to capture some Jordanians in order to trade them for the two Israelis? Dayan never spelled out what he meant by "some Jordanians." That was left to Sharon to figure out. He told Dayan he would check.

At the Sheikh Hussein Bridge near the Israeli kibbutz Ma'oz Chaim east of Beit-Shean, Sharon spotted a small police station in Jordan. Suddenly three Jordanians led by their sergeant began heading in Sharon's direction. Sharon began waving at them to get their attention and the Jordanians approached to find out what he wanted. Sharon managed to take two of them hostage, then left the absent Dayan a note: "Moshe— The mission is accomplished. The prisoners are in the cellar. Shalom, Arik."

Ecstatic at Sharon's audacity, Dayan particularly liked the fact that Sharon had not insisted on written orders from him. Such behavior, Sharon wrote later, was "vintage Dayan. Typically he would convey his intentions in an ambiguous way, leaving plenty of room for initiative and interpretation. The recipient of the order—me in this case, as in plenty of future cases—would then take it on himself to do whatever he felt had to be done, with the widest freedom of action. If the result was a success, fine. But if it was a failure, well then, the responsibility was not his but yours."[6]

On December 7, 1952, Dayan was appointed chief of the Operations branch of the General Staff. Mordechai Makleff became chief of staff on the same day that Dayan took on his new assignment. Makleff had wanted Rabin named deputy chief of staff and chief of operations, but Dayan had Ben-Gurion on his side. Again, Dayan had no interest in the post of deputy chief of staff. He refused the title. Makleff did not get along with Dayan. The chief of staff liked order. Dayan did not.

Dayan lived in a small apartment with the family not far from headquarters. Once again, members of Dayan's family realized the cost of being part of his family. Yael felt excluded, frustrated that she seemed to have go through channels to get to her father.

Ever the independent spirit, Dayan disdained the staff officers immediately under him and gathered around him eight of his most trusted military acquaintances, men such as Uzi Narkiss, Meir Amit, and Assaf Simhoni, Dayan think-alikes, men who did not operate according to the usual rules. Dayan felt an affection for them and dubbed them "tfutsot zayan," a crude Hebrew expression roughly translated as the "screw-you guys." With this phrase he wanted to convey the group's unconventional military thinking.

The army had to become leaner. Manpower had to be cut. Soldiers were to be taught how to fight. That would be the number-one priority. At a senior commanders conference, Dayan heard officers complain about a shortage of shirts in their unit. He tossed the complaint right back at them. He did not care about shirts. He only wanted to know if there were enough rifles. If a soldier tried to chew Dayan out over bad conditions in the mess hall, he was ready: Had they ever heard of Garibaldi? Well, he did not even have a mess hall.

Dayan loathed discipline except when it pertained to the battlefield. "Fighting dogs are not trained with blows," Dayan used to say when upset at the exaggerated, overformal methods of discipline or by the capricious punishments meted out in the IDF. When others in the General Staff required soldiers to wear their berets on all occasions, Dayan forgave forgetful soldiers, making sure they understood he thought such orders silly. He hated formality and disliked being kept from subordinates. He made a point of eating in the regular headquarters officers' mess, where lieutenant colonels and more junior officers ate. Often, to get a waiter's attention, he would toss a slice of bread rolled into a ball at the waiter. Trying to be "one of the boys," he made sure that no one ever forgot Moshe Dayan's visit to a base.

Favoring informality, he grudgingly wore pressed uniforms and polished shoes for parades and public appearances. While Yigael Yadin was trying to instill some formality and etiquette into the IDF, Dayan hardly cared. (Once Yadin asked him to leave the room and fix an unbuttoned shirt pocket.)

Dayan had a thing about oranges. He loved to pick them, loved to eat them. Whenever he saw an orange grove, he raced over to it and grabbed as many oranges as he could carry. Once, he was visiting a base near Tel Aviv, where the unit had not heard about Dayan's distaste for stuffiness. Sure enough, there was an honor guard standing there ready to receive him. Just as the sergeant major went to raise his hand in salute, Dayan tossed him an orange, yelling, "Catch!" The sergeant major was stunned, some said so stunned that soon thereafter he resigned from the army. The orange-tossing story made the rounds with lightning speed, doing wonders for Dayan's reputation. Anything that suggested that the top brass did not like such stiffness was welcome news.

Dayan could certainly prove exasperating. Once in 1952, the General Staff had launched a road safety campaign and issued orders to the military police to arrest anyone going above seventy kilometers an hour regardless of rank. The commander of the military police was forced to report to Yigael Yadin that Dayan had been caught going 120 kilometers (seventy-five miles) an hour. Yadin ordered Dayan court-martialed. The commander noted that when the MP halted Dayan and said, "Sir, didn't you notice that you were driving one hundred twenty kilometers an hour?" Dayan replied, "Excuse me, I have only one eye. What do you want me to look at, the speedometer or the road?" Yadin liked that retort so much that he ordered Dayan let go.

MEANWHILE, the poor showing of the IDF in border incidents persisted. From early in 1953 those incidents had increased, and reprisal raids, though small in scale, had not been successful. Sometimes the Israeli unit would return without carrying out its mission after only one or two men had been killed or wounded. Dayan, as chief of operations, understood the potentially disastrous implications: If the IDF failed in minor border skirmishes, how would it be able to stand up to the Arab armies if full-scale war occurred?

The ill-fated Israeli attack on Falama illustrated the dilemma. More than any other incident in this period Falama was a warning signal that the IDF was faltering. The incident occurred on January 23, 1953, in the Jordanian town of Falama, just inside the Arab Triangle, between Kalkilya and Tulkarem. An Israeli infantry battalion belonging to the Givati Brigade was supposed to blow up a Jordanian police station inside the village, but coming under fire, retreated without accomplishing its goal, suffering one Israeli killed and five wounded.

Waiting for the battalion just across the armistice line were Dayan, then chief of operations, and two other senior officers from the General Staff. The incident haunted Dayan. He asked himself how was it that the army could not even reach a house or a well? He vowed that this kind of soldiering would not recur. Falama would be a turning point for him. "Jewish cleverness," that formula for simply outfoxing the Arabs, no longer could be relied on. Something more was needed.

Dayan called a meeting in Tel Aviv of all officers from company commander level. At that meeting he barked out new orders that would have a profound effect upon the IDF. First, commanders were to prepare their exercises with the aim of engaging in frontal attack, of paying with the mission in lives—and they were to shun such clever schemes as flanking, surprise, or attacking deep into the rear of the enemy's lines. Second, the battalion commander would be one of the two scouts so he could decide what to do. Third, and most importantly, a unit was never to return without fulfilling its task. No matter what happened to the unit, no matter how much firepower rained down on its men, the mission had to be completed. Finally, he laid down the revolutionary rule that no officer was to suspend an attack on penalty of dismissal unless his unit suffered a casualty rate of more than fifty percent. This harsh edict clashed with the IDF principle of reducing casualties to the minimum. Dayan did not consult the chief of staff about the fifty percent casualty policy.

Mordechai Makleff said in retrospect he would not have worded the policy in quite that way, though he shared Dayan's view that the IDF must do more to build itself up as a fighting force. Dayan's fifty percent casualty rule was never issued as a formal order, but everyone knew that Dayan meant what he said. Yehoshafat Harkabi, head of military intelligence from 1955 to 1959, once heard Dayan ask an officer who had come back from a raid, "Why didn't you die? Why did you come back alive?"[7] Yes, they knew what Dayan meant, all right. Dayan was waiting for Ariel Sharon to return from a raid at the end of February 1955; they met at Kfar Azah near the frontier of the Gaza Strip. Dayan asked Sharon how had it gone. The men had accomplished their mission, Sharon said, but there had been heavy losses. Dayan looked at him and said, "The living are alive and the dead are dead."[8] For as long as the unit had combat power, it was to continue fighting. Dayan did not need to threaten the men with the consequences if they failed to carry out their mission.

Unless they had some very satisfactory explanation, they would not be in Moshe Dayan's army very long.

Falama was not the only IDF failure: In August 1953, the paratroop battalion returned from an action and reported that it had completed its mission; Dayan headed there with a bottle of brandy to toast its success only to find the next day that the only "enemy dead" the paratroopers had actually killed were an ass and two cows. Also, a platoon had been instructed to blow up a well in the Gaza Strip, but lost its way; the next morning it realized that it had never even crossed the armistice line, wandering in circles all the time.

Dayan entered into debates with others about Falama and its significance. Falama was due, Dayan believed, to officers who refused to lead their troops in battle. Problems of this nature had not happened during the 1948 war because Israeli soldiers were defending their homes; the very survival of the infant state of Israel was at stake. In that situation soldiers naturally were prepared to make sacrifices. In what Dayan termed an aggressive war, in which the option to retreat existed as in the case of retaliatory raids—soldiers fought, not for their homes, but for their commander, for their comrades-in-arms, or for the honor of their unit.

In such situations, the will to fight was not always a certainty. Soldiers might lose their enthusiasm. Commanders could too easily order their men to retreat. There had to be clear orders. That was what Dayan had proposed. Accurate maps and innovative plans were important, he told senior army officers, but if soldiers were not prepared to risk their lives, all was lost. Soldiers must be prepared to follow through on their mission even when the odds seemed not to favor its success. The only way to assure that soldiers would behave in this way was to have the commander up front.

How could one instill such zeal in the Israeli army? By trying to teach these values to each and every soldier? Perhaps. But that seemed impractical, some said unattainable. What about creating a model that by its example would help influence the rest of the army? That sounded more sensible. But what kind of model? And what could guarantee that others would learn from it?

Ultimately, the answer to all the questions came: "One Hundred and One." The phrase became synonymous with the new, aggressive, determined Israeli army, and with the most important approach used by the IDF in battling its enemy during the early 1950s. "One Hundred and One" meant retaliatory raids, based on the biblical concept of an eye for an eye. If the enemy struck at Israel, he must know that Israel would retaliate in kind. Not with all of its might, but with a small group of men who would pick out their target carefully, destroy that target, and return to base undetected.

The actual start of 101 came in Jerusalem in the late summer of 1953, after numerous border incidents. It had been the Jerusalem Reserve Brigade commander, Col. Michael Shaham, who had conceived the idea. An Arab from Nebi Samuel had vowed to kill one hundred Jews. Shaham wanted to blow up his house, but no unit in his brigade was capable of carrying out such a mission. He solved the problem, temporarily at least, by creating a team of the best fighters from the 1948 war and choosing Ariel Sharon, one of his own battalion commanders, to lead the mission. Though the first mission was hardly a success—they failed to blow up the Arab's house—Sharon's men proved that a village could be penetrated. Writing to Chief of Staff Mordechai Makleff, Shaham proposed that a secret unit of skilled and devoted volunteers under Ariel Sharon be established as part of the Jerusalem Reserve Brigade, specializing in guerrilla actions across the border. As the Arab assaults against Israelis mounted, the need for such a unit was growing. Secrecy was key, for it would be crucial for the Israeli government to deny responsiblility for the unit's reprisal raids.

When he heard about the idea, Moshe Dayan was reluctant. At first he thought little of taking forty men or so out of an army of fifty thousand and relying upon them exclusively for special missions. Dayan feared that once this special unit was given responsibility for such tasks and raised to an elite status, as would inevitably occur, the entire army's morale and fighting level would suffer. Why not make the entire IDF one large commando unit? Dayan asked. As chief of operations, Dayan clearly had less clout than the chief of staff, and since Makleff liked the idea, it was adopted. In time, Moshe Dayan became a zealous convert and embraced 101 with warmth and approval.

The need for retaliatory raids sprang from grim statistics: From 1949 to 1954, an average of one thousand infiltrations occurred per month, mostly along the Israeli-Jordanian frontier. Some 513 Israelis were killed along the frontier during this period. Criticism was rife. No one had trouble coming up with excuses for the Israeli army's inability to suppress this violence. It was the fault of the senior officers. No, it was the fault of the junior officers. No, it was the fault of the foot soldiers. The equipment was faulty. Not enough training. Enough, said Dayan. Everyone was responsible.

The reprisal policy was based upon the assumption that Israel was not powerful enough to keep the Arabs from infiltrating. By engaging in retaliatory raids after these infiltrations, the Israelis might deter the Arabs from future efforts. Thus, Dayan explained in a talk to army officers:

> We cannot prevent every water pipe from being blown up nor every tree from being uprooted. We cannot prevent the murder of workmen in a citrus grove or of families fast asleep in their beds. But we can set a high price for our blood. A price too high for the Arab world, the Arab armies and the Arab governments to pay. We can force the inhabitants of Arab villages to oppose the gangs passing through their villages and refuse to assist them. We can make sure that Arab army commanders will adhere strictly to their border obligations rather than be defeated in clashes with our units. We can force the Arab governments to forbear their power politics against Israel by transforming it into a weapon of weakness.[9]

Chosen to head the unit was Shaham's candidate: Ariel Sharon, then a young student in the School of Oriental Studies at the Hebrew University in Jerusalem and a reserve battalion commander. Dayan admired Sharon and another of 101's men, Meir Har-Zion. Both had some of the same qualities (guile, boldness, informality) that Dayan possessed. Selected for the unit were forty men, whose dress code was casual—short pants, caps, berets, *keffiyehs*—but whose armory was not (tommy guns, Molotov cocktails, commando knives). No one wore any ranks; they were, after all, supposed to be just an ordinary band of civilians. They were in fact a clandestine fraternity of guerrilla fighters and no one liked that guerrilla atmosphere surrounding the unit more than Moshe Dayan.

The secret unit went into action for the first time in September 1953. Its target was the bedouin Azazma tribe, several hundred of whom had been crossing the southern frontier freely, carrying Egyptian identification cards, and sniping at IDF patrols. Sharon's 101 assigned sixteen men to take to their jeeps and command cars, and push the bedouins back into the Sinai. Appearing on the spot to congratulate the men after their first succcessful mission was Moshe Dayan. It was then that he met Meir Har-Zion for the first time under circumstances that were less than friendly: A large black bird had perched itself on the carcass of a camel, a casualty of the recent fighting. Dayan knelt down and aimed a rifle at the new arrival. Suddenly a tall youngster in short pants, with a mountain of bushy hair, grabbed Dayan's arm and shouted. "What are you doing? That's an eagle. There are only thirty pairs of them left in the country."

At first Dayan was angry; but, calming down, he decided that Cpl. Meir Har-Zion deserved his respect for such behavior.

The more Dayan learned about Har-Zion, the more he liked. Of Har-Zion, Dayan wrote: "He was the most courageous soldier and the finest reconnaissance man in the Israel army. . . . His remarkable accomplishments in battle were due not only to his doing everything better than anyone else but to his doing it differently."[10] After Har-Zion had served only four days in the officers training course, Dayan decided the six-month stint would be a waste of time for him. He immediately promoted Har-Zion to captain. Dayan called Har-Zion "our greatest warrior since Bar Kochba."

KIBYA on October 14, 1953 was the first real test for 101. The Israeli raiding party had managed to cross into Arab territory, strike at the village of Kibya, crush the enemy's defenses, and inflict heavy damage. The public relations price, however, was stiff. A Jordanian raid against the Israeli village of Kfar Yahud had precipitated the attack; the invaders had hurled a hand grenade into a house, killing a mother and two children. Although infiltrators had killed 124 Israelis in the recent past, that murder in Kfar Yahud turned public opinion in Israel against the Arab assaults. The Arab Legion commander was nervous and urged Israel not to retaliate, saying the Jordanian government would punish the raiders. Attending a large maneuver in the north on the morning of Octorber 13, Dayan and other Israeli leaders decided that a strong reaction was needed.

Kibya was across from Kfar Yahud and the IDF knew it was a base for infiltrators. Dayan's order at first was for fifty houses to be destroyed as part of an Israeli assault against three Jordanian villages, Shukba, Nahhalin, and Kibya. Sharon was put in overall charge of the operation, both of the 890th Paratroop Battalion, and 101. The paratroopers were to deal with the main goal of the mission in Kibya, destroying the houses; 101 was to provide supporting action, blocking and raiding Nahhalin and Shukba. Despite his order to blow up fifty houses, Dayan worried that the IDF might suffer more casualties than necessary. He advised Sharon that if the going got tough, he could simply blow up a few houses and then come back. Sharon at first held his unit's fire (of the 103 men assigned to the mission, 80 entered Kibya). That induced the Jordanians to stop firing and retreat in confusion. Assuming that Kibya had been abandoned, Sharon's soldiers blew up forty-two buildings. Once that occurred, the mission ended at 3:30 A.M., with Sharon's forces suffering no losses.

"There's no one like you!" Dayan told Sharon upon his return.

Indeed, there was not. It turned out that Sharon's men had overlooked the fact that some people might be inside the destroyed houses. Later, the gruesome discovery was made that the Israelis had killed sixty-nine civilians, half of them women and children. Dayan was described as upset, but not apologetic. Unlike others in the senior echelon of the IDF, Dayan was not repelled by what had happened. After all, he reasoned, 101's soldiers had not deliberately sought to kill these civilians. It had been an accident. He preferred to look at the bright side, to note with satisfaction that 101 had acheived its goal. It was the first time since Tel el Mutilla that an IDF unit had fully accomplished its mission. Dayan was won over to the basic concept of 101: that one small, elite unit could rebuild morale throughout the army by obtaining results. It was no small task, but the results at Kibya suggested it might be possible. In time, the idea proved worthy, but some worried about its implications. David Ben-Gurion, among others, worried that "Dayan's private army," as some began to call the soldiers in 101 (and its successor, 202), so filled with arrogant esprit de corps, could at some time try to stage a coup against the civilian government. The proposition seemed nonsensical to most, and in fact nothing of that sort ever occurred. Still, the fear lingered.

On October 18, after a three-month leave, Ben-Gurion returned to his posts of prime minister and defense minister, and had to figure out what to say, if anything, on the subject of Kibya. He essentially lied, broadcasting a statement assuring that "not a single unit" had been away from its base during the night of the Kibya attack. He placed responsibility for the assault on Israeli settlers living near the frontier. Behind the scenes, the IDF issued new orders: In future operations, Israeli soldiers, even at the risk of their own lives, would have to guarantee that women and children were not potential targets. To reinforce those guarantees, the IDF prohibited 101 from using such lethal and imprecise weaponry as artillery, mortars, and hand grenades. After becoming chief of staff in December, Dayan insisted that reprisal raids be conducted only against military targets, not Arab villages and civilians living there.

Dayan had given his backing to 101 and to the effort to build morale throughout the IDF. The question remained how 101 could ease the infiltrations. Would the Israeli army be required—and prepared—to take up arms again in a full-scale war?

✦ 7 ✦

TOP SOLDIER

BY THE END of 1953, the post of chief of staff was alluringly close. David Ben-Gurion had been prepared to elevate Moshe Dayan for some time. They were kindred spirits, mentor and protégé, two men who, if they differed here and there on tactics, held a common view about what was good for their country. Ben-Gurion was eager to appoint Dayan. All did not go smoothly, however. A coalition of Mapai veterans, including Golda Meir, Zalman Aranne, and Moshe Sharett, sought to block the appointment by raising a series of accusations against Dayan that by then were hauntingly familiar: He was reckless, disorganized, undisciplined, and worst of all, a partisan. It was Shimon Peres, appointed deputy director general of the Ministry of Defense in 1952, who managed to convince Ben-Gurion to disregared these charges: "You can trust Dayan 100 percent. He'll turn the IDF into a fighting force."[1]

At the age of thirty-eight, Moshe Dayan had reached the zenith of his military career. In the previous few years, he had started to improve combat standards in the IDF—what for him was unquestionably the most important mission of the General Staff. Now he was in charge. He would have the opportunity to give that task the top priority he felt it deserved. Only twelve years earlier he had strong doubts that he would ever be able to pursue an active life; he even contemplated being a cripple. He had overcome his handicap; indeed, the very fact that he had been injured and now wore the eyepatch worked to his advantage.

Steadily, he had climbed the ranks of the IDF, shoring up Degania, fighting as a commando at Lod and Karatiya, turning into a diplomat in Jerusalem; then taking time out to study military tactics, assuming commands in the south, then the north, finally taking charge of operations for the IDF. He would begin what he considered his most important work. "He really thought that the most important thing he did was the day he became chief of staff and really reshaped the army," said Rahel Dayan, his wife from 1973 until his death in 1981. "That's when his life started, coming into a kind of destiny that was awaiting him."[2]

Dayan was officially appointed chief of staff at a ceremony on December 6, 1953. Ben-Gurion embraced the outgoing chief of staff, Makleff, and then handed the letter of appointment and the chief of staff's red, blue, and gold pennant to Dayan. The ceremony concluded with the lighting of the candles for the sixth night of Hanukkah and the singing of the traditional Hanukkah hymn "Maoz Tsur." At the conclusion of the ceremony Ben-Gurion pinned on Dayan's badge as Israel's number-one soldier. One government official observed matter-of-factly to Dayan that, now that he was the chief of staff, he would have to change his partisan approach and become respectable, more restrained. He would have to create a new Moshe Dayan. Peering at the official with as much contempt as he could muster, Dayan suggested that he was wide off the mark. "I will not change. The image of the chief of staff will."

The Dayan appointment was the prime minister's last official act before retiring to his Negev kibbutz, Sde Boker. Exhausted from the strains of the prime ministership, Ben-Gurion had shocked his countrymen by resigning in mid-October. Moshe Sharett became the new prime minister and Pinhas Lavon defense minister.

Above all else, Dayan knew that he could not guarantee that Israel would be at peace for much longer. Two days after he took over as chief of staff, Dayan spoke to graduates of the officers training course, telling them that they had some difficult times ahead: "You will come face to face with the Arabs of Palestine, who bear in their hearts the memory of the defeat of the War of Independence and the hope of a second round. The government of Jordan is helping them reorganize and turn their villages into bases for actions against Israel. When world public opinion sees fit to condemn the action at Kibya and the state of Israel, there are many who take up the cause; but when the time comes to defend the capital of Israel and the Knesset, which is situated only a few hundred meters from the border, you alone will bear this responsibility."

As he began the new job, Dayan was sure of one thing: The IDF had to change, and change fast. This was not the late 1940s, when Israel could sit back and relax, convinced that the Arabs were no longer a substantial threat. By their constant and costly raids in the early 1950s, the Arabs had sent a signal that they would only be satisfied when the state of Israel no longer existed. Because the Arabs were not yet ready to launch a second full-scale round, they sought to chip away at Israel's morale by a slow but steady war of nerves along the frontiers, sending raiders into Israel on lethal missions aimed at injuring and killing as many Israelis as possible. To combat such deeds, Dayan had to shape the Israel Defense Forces into a far more aggressive fighting machine. He would have to reshape the IDF on matters big and small.

Dayan decided to start with a strategy he understood well: He utilized the power of images better than anyone around him. He had not deliberately set out to propagate images, but wearing the black eyepatch projected such a forceful image of heroism, mystery, and suffering that he had internalized the value of appearances. Dayan began with the image of the chief of staff. Until now whoever had been chief of staff had been thought of by many as a rather aloof, mysterious individual, someone who kept his distance from ordinary soldiers, who enjoyed the accoutrements of power, the large office, the fancy desk, the aides. Such trappings, Dayan believed, might be justified for large armies without enemies at the gates, but not for tiny, poorly equipped Israel with one hundred million Arabs waiting and planning. Dayan believed that for Israel's sake, for the IDF's sake, the chief of staff had to project not a regal image, but a democratic one, not an image of aloofness, but one of closeness and caring. Only in that way could the IDF make sure that its number-one resource, its soldiers, would do their best on the battlefield. Only by creating a people's army in which the lowest foot soldier felt that everyone, from the chief of staff on down, was sacrificing for the overall cause, could the IDF triumph. No one understood this better than Moshe Dayan.

He began by discarding any impression among rank and file soldiers of the chief of staff as the Distant Authority. That first night Dayan phoned Shlomo Gazit, head of the chief of staff's bureau, and gave him his first instructions. They concerned the physical appearance of the chief of staff's office. Until then, the office had been large, the desk set back from the front door, a not so subtle reminder to the visitor that one had to go far to reach this aloof, powerful figure. Dayan wanted to send a different message to his soldiers, that even if he was their boss, he was one of them. When a soldier or an officer visited the chief of staff, Dayan wanted him to feel he was paying a call, not on some supreme power, but on just another officer in the field. It was not, however, popularity Dayan was after. He simply wanted to get closer to his men.

He told Gazit to get rid of the large desk that Makleff had been using.

He asked that a standard IDF field table be found, the kind found in any headquarters tent: a wooden board resting on legs with an army blanket covering it. Dayan refused to take over the large chief of staff's office; he turned it into a conference room and set himself up in a smaller room next door, vacated by Makleff's aide-de-camp (whom Dayan unceremoniously fired as part of his campaign to cut down the chief of staff's entourage). He refused air-conditioning. He wanted to get rid of the fleet of limousines being used by senior IDF officers, but jeeps, he found, would have cost more; so, swallowing hard, he kept the fancy cars. It was not just the chief of staff and senior officers who tightened their belts. No longer would the IDF supply overcoats: Reservists would have to bring their own. Fewer officers would be sent to study in foreign military schools. IDF bakeries, laundries, and canteens were done away with as well as cavalry and carrier-pigeon units. Whatever money there was, Dayan insisted, would be spent on acquiring weapons.

The strongest image Dayan conveyed was far more subtle. It was the image that change was afoot, that the army had begun to refashion itself, that nothing was sacred anymore, that the country's survival was at stake, and Moshe Dayan was going to assure that the nation's most important institution met the test.

The same self-assuredness that allowed Dayan to take such bold steps in refashioning the army led him to believe in his centrality to his country's destiny. To make sure that his deeds would not be forgotten, he became preoccupied with the task of recording history as he was, as he felt, making it. The idea of writing a daily diary had been suggested to him by Shlomo Gazit, his head of bureau, who had chided Dayan for failing to record immediately his impressions of his secret encounters with Jordan's King Abdullah. What Gazit said made sense. So at the end of one day, Dayan closed his door and wrote a few lines. By the next evening, when it came time to enter his thoughts into the diary, Dayan turned to Gazit with a forlorn look and declared with finality, "I don't have the patience. From now on you do it." So Gazit did. When Mordechai Bar-On became head of bureau in 1956, he managed to complete seven volumes of the diary, meticulously detailing Dayan's every activity.

Just as he tired quickly of writing the diary, Dayan tended to shun all administrative work as uninteresting and unhelpful. No matter how high he rose in the chain of command, he was not a deskman, not someone who could tolerate being chained to an office. Sitting behind that desk, Dayan would read that something interesting had occurred and within fifteen minutes he was boarding a helicopter to go see for himself. "With paperwork you cannot carry out assaults or lead armies," he told a graduating class of the Military High School in Haifa. Rather than spend hours over documents, Dayan preferred to use the time for thinking. Accordingly, he asked his staff to decide what papers he absolutely had to see, and which not. He disliked holding too many meetings. Dayan decided carefully on a day-to-day basis with whom he would talk; but if he wished to speak to someone, he didn't care if the man was on the other side of the country. Shlomo Gazit was once on a visit to the north and received a phone call from Dayan's office that he could hardly hear. Dayan wanted him in his office in a half hour. He told the office a half hour was impossible, so Dayan said, "OK, two hours." So Gazit canceled everything and showed up.[3]

Dayan's habit was to choose the most important area to deal with and leave the rest to his staff. Once, after spending a month or so working on the following year's budget, he told his aide for finances to come back in eleven months when it would be time to deal with next year's budget. Disbelieving Dayan, the aide showed up the next day, expecting other assignments from the chief of staff. Other Dayan aides tried to explain to him that indeed this was the way Dayan worked. Still skeptical, he approached the chief of staff—and was berated by Dayan for coming before the appointed date.

Above all he wanted to be with the men in the field, to make sure that they were in a state of combat readiness and were being treated well by their superiors. He needed to see for himself what was happening so that he did not have to rely on secondhand reports. He hated someone else telling him what he thought the chief of staff should know, should learn. Few soldiers who botched an operation were about to admit as much in a written report to their superiors. Dayan understood that only too well, which was one more reason why he had to be on the scene. He especially liked being around when there was action. He wanted to be there at the precise moment that the men returned from an operation, to hear what happened from them first, to sense whether they had performed well or not, and to let men who had just gone into battle know their chief of staff was very much a visible, concerned presence.

When Dayan talked to soldiers, even the lowest ranking, he talked to them as if they were his equals. His self-deprecatory sense of humor worked because he commanded respect, because the soldiers knew he too had been in action, that he had been a foot soldier once. Soon it became fashionable for other members of the General Staff to show up after an action and chat with the boys just back from battle.

Some surprise visits by the chief of staff worked to the advantage of his hosts. During one such visit, soldiers who had been out on a night action complained that they returned to base to find the kitchen closed; Dayan was furious. Why should soldiers in the rear get a good night's sleep when combat soldiers were out on an action? He immediately ordered that any combat soldier back from a night exercise or action should get a hot meal. During a visit to an armored unit one night, Dayan found that because of shortages soldiers had to forgo sugar in their tea. He awakened the chief of the quartermaster branch at home and insisted that he or one of his assistants deliver three sacks of sugar to the unit at once! He demanded to see the signed receipt for the sugar, proof of delivery. An officer appeared at the chief of staff's office the next day with the tank commander's note: "Received, items: three sacks of sugar." If such on-the-spot orders from the chief of staff led to confusion, to administrative chaos, nothing could have bothered Dayan less. What mattered was that his soldiers felt that someone was up there watching over them.

He especially enjoyed catching soldiers unawares, not after they had spent a week preparing for his visit. Woe to the soldier who was not alert and on duty when the chief of staff showed up unexpectedly. The soldiers quickly learned to respect Moshe Dayan as serious and efficient. Discovering after some action that an officer had acted unsoldierly, Dayan was not above dismissing him on the spot. There were no second chances. Though soldiers may have considered Dayan cold and heartless for such impulsive behavior, his sudden surprise visits spurred soldiers to perform better. The message spread quickly that at any given time the chief of staff might be peeking over the shoulders of soldiers engaged in an operation. This encouraged the men to fight aggressively and to complete the mission. At times, officers would complain to David Ben-Gurion that Dayan did not exhibit sufficient warmth, and that he was excessively rigid. "They say that you're harsh and that you keep your distance from people," the Founding Father observed to Dayan once. To which Dayan replied that the Bible (in 2 Sam.) spoke of the sons of Zeruiah being hard as well, but they were also of great importance to King David in establishing and widening his kingdom.[4] Essentially, Dayan's point was that to be a successful military leader, one could not worry about popularity, one had to be firm and unyielding at times; naturally the "victims" of his policies would be displeased. For example, Dayan's attempts to democratize the IDF and to do away with some frills were bound to irritate some who liked the benefits of the old system. Such irritation should not deter a military leader from doing what he thinks best. In order to achieve victories on the battlefield, "Dayan had to harden his heart and retire into his inner fortress," noted Mordechai Bar-On.[5]

He chose officers by one standard only: their daring. An officer had to serve as an example to his soldiers. He had to demonstrate to them that he was prepared to take whatever risk he asked of them. The effect on other officers and soldiers was extraordinary. Generals who otherwise would have raced into a bomb shelter joined their troops in battle, lest Dayan call them cowards.

While commanding the Gaza Strip front, where Egyptian artillery fire was routine, Raphael Vardi received word that the chief of staff planned to visit. Vardi tried to talk him out of it. "Look, we can't have the Egyptians rejoicing tomorrow that they have wounded our chief of staff."

"We can't have the chief of staff refusing to go somewhere where IDF soldiers routinely go," answered Dayan. "I will do exactly what the soldiers do."

He insisted on touring the frontier in a command car rather than a half-track—because the soldiers went out on their patrols every day in command cars.[6]

Dayan took so many risks on the battlefield that it became clear he was not just demonstrating courage to induce his soldiers to fight. He actually believed he had a lucky star watching over him. "When I go into battle," he said, "I am 100 percent sure I will win and come out safely. I believe, with my luck and skill, that I'll manage between the bullets and they will not get hold of me. You have to feel that way or you'll never come out of it. . . . During battle when I see shells exploding around me, I am able to be calm. . . . Most people, when they hear a shot, their body jerks, mine doesn't. I'm not proud of that, but when I hear bullets whistle, I know it's not birds singing, but I have no physical reaction."[7]

If Dayan had one wish, it was to mold each youngster in the Israeli army into a fighter, into someone with the mental resources and the physical conditioning to operate effectively on the battlefield. As his secretary, Neora Bar-Nor, noted: "If you were prepared to be a fighter, he was ready to forgive everything. If you looked like a general, but you sat in the rear and sent your soldiers into battle, he was ready to kill you."[8] Very little else mattered to Dayan except turning out combat-ready soldiers. Not the discipline. Not the fancy parades. Not the bureaucracy. Every once in a while, Dayan would encounter an entire unit being disciplined, being told to salute a wall because one soldier had forgotten to salute; he would discover an entire unit running with beds on their backs because someone's gun had not been polished. He was contemptuous of such collective discipline, particularly if it was not directly connected with soldiering: "The state and the parents have given us these boys and they want us to make them fighters, not soldiers."

Fighters, not soldiers. But how does an army turn a raw recruit into someone who will not retreat at the first sound of gunfire, who will calmly, professionally assess a battlefield situation, and deal with his enemy as efficiently as possible? Dayan had learned about a concept known as "Follow me" during a visit to American military bases in 1954. A year later Dayan spelled out the idea in a lecture: "The commander is not 'the most valuable man in the unit,' who must be protected from injury. The most valuable thing for a unit is the enemy objective. . . . Controlling a unit does not mean a wordy communication given personally or in writing. . . . The chief means is leadership: the order 'Follow me!' " Elsewhere, Dayan noted that when an officer called out "Follow me," "his men must feel there is no road but forwards. To achieve this, an officer must use any means at his command. Personal example will probably be the most efficient way. Every officer . . . should be able to lead a commando unit any time the occasion warrants it. The thousands of officers who train and study in the army should know that unless they accept the challenge they will not be retained. I would rather an officer be criticized for many personal shortcomings but be called 'a real fighter' by his men, than be universally praised for his virtues, but qualified with the phrase, 'but he's hardly a fighter.' "[9]

A price would be exacted on the battlefield: The IDF suffered a high rate of fatalities among its senior officer corps, but by virtue of this policy foot soldiers fought aggressively and confidently.

In May 1955 Dayan sought to make sure his soldiers understood this point, by firing a young career officer who had ordered a soldier to undertake a dangerous action while staying behind in safety. An Israeli vehicle had become stuck close to the Israeli frontier with the Gaza Strip and had come under heavy Egyptian fire. Rather than go himself, the officer in charge sent a driver to retrieve the vehicle. A few days later, Dayan explained that he would not have dismissed the officer had he concluded that the risk was too large, and that it was better to abandon the vehicle than to endanger lives. Once he chose to take bold action in an attempt to save the vehicle, the officer should have advanced with his troops. "Officers of the Israeli army do not send their men into battle," Dayan told an IDF audience at the time, "they lead them into battle." Colleagues of the officer in question rallied to his side. They insisted to Dayan that the officer had been an otherwise fine soldier, and that dismissing him would cause irreparable damage to morale among the other men in his unit. Dayan stood his ground, explaining to the Golani Brigade commander Iska Shadmi under whom the officer had served: "This officer doesn't interest me that much. He is simply a victim of my policy. I have to cut a few heads off in order to create a different army." Shadmi urged Dayan to talk with some of the senior commanders in the brigade who found his decision to dismiss the officer unjust. At that session, Dayan commented that "People go into battle. One is killed, the other isn't. That's fair? In war one can step on a mine at any time. This officer has become a victim of my war within the IDF to create new standards of fighting. You might say that he fell in battle, not on a mine, but on Dayan. I'm the mine." In the end, Dayan bowed partially to the wishes of the officer's comrades-in-arms. Rather than dismiss him from the army, the chief of staff had the officer removed from the brigade and stripped of his post as company commander.[10] That compromise, in Dayan's eyes, did not weaken his message: The "Follow me" concept would become IDF doctrine.

Moreover, in order to assure that the soldier would fight, the army had to show him that it was unwilling to treat him like so much cannon fodder. For that reason, soon after becoming chief of staff, Dayan laid down the rule that no dead or wounded were to be left behind in enemy territory.

Dayan was determined to put the best men in the battlefield. Until he was chief of staff, the practice had been to send those who could not read Hebrew-language manuals to be fighters; the literate ones were assigned to the technical services. Dayan changed that: The brightest recruits were placed in combat duty.

Rejuvenating the army was another major goal of Dayan's. Vivid images of elderly generals hanging on forever in European armies sent chills through him. He wanted none of that for the IDF. So aging veterans were either dismissed or left the army of their own accord, getting the message that the chief of staff preferred young blood. Officers were quickly promoted. In the most revolutionary step, Dayan ordered officers to retire at age forty. He called the postarmy phase the "second cycle." To ease the pain, the chief of staff arranged that pensions, which until then had been given only to those over the age of sixty-five, would go to army retirees at once. Dayan wanted a young army, not old people who he felt were essentially stale and unimaginative. He also sensed that he could control young men better, that the older men were less willing to adapt to his radical ideas. The "second cycle" policy was greeted derisively at first. How would these forty-year-olds find work? Would they make enough to support their families? Politicians worried that if the chief of staff could send the army's older generation out to pasture, might he not, after entering politics, try to send political veterans into early retirement as well?

SOLDIERING offered little chance for hobbies. Still, Moshe Dayan around this time became absorbed in a pursuit that reflected part of his very essence—the study of archaeology. The pursuit of their past had intrigued many Israelis and archaeology became a national pastime. The fact that Dayan was a soldier provided him with the time and excuse to hang around promising archaeological sites. Had he been a lawyer with an office in Tel Aviv, he once noted, he would have gone home at two in the afternoon to drink a glass of whiskey, and never gone to dig in wadis. Dayan was not religious, but growing up in the land of the Bible, and becoming familiar with the sights and sounds and smells that had roots in the early days of the Jewish people, had an impact upon him. Dayan not surprisingly became excited at the prospect of uncovering his past. He enjoyed the physical aspect of the work, being close to nature, digging into the ground, churning the rock and dirt over—and then finding something that was thousands of years old, yet seemed familiar. This was no mere intellectual exercise for Dayan. His love for archaeology was closely linked with the physical act of being in touch with the earth, the stones, the dirt. His daughter Yael noted: "This hobby became a consuming preoccupation, at times an obsession. I think the philosophy behind it, the spiritual justification—like the learning in depth about the subject—was secondary. At first, it was the physical pleasure of digging, the almost childish joy of discovery, and the wonderfully primitive creation of a bond between himself and his own history."[11]

Even without the controversy that would eventually attach itself to Dayan's digging, he would have become the country's most famous amateur archaeologist. It is not entirely clear when Dayan acquired an interest in archaeology. Once he did so, however, that interest exploded quickly into an all-consuming passion. Israel Gefen, Dayan's brother-in-law, believed that Dayan's interest first arose during the 1930s, after Dayan and another youngster from Nahalal uncovered important relics at nearby Bet She'arim. Those relics were but the tip of the iceberg. Soon thereafter, in 1936, world-renowned archaeologist Benyamin Mazar and the Israel Exploration Society dug at the site and unearthed more evidence of the ancient town of Bet She'arim, where in A.D. 200 the Sanhedrin, Supreme Court of the Jewish people, conducted its meetings.[12]

Dayan himself dated his interest in archaeology to one winter day in 1954 when he took his son Udi, then nine years old, with him to shoot wild pigeons in the south. Arriving at Tel es-Safi, an archaeological mound halfway between biblical Gezer and Lachish, father and son started to chase the birds hovering over the mound, when Dayan noticed some jars sticking out of a mud wall in a nearby wadi. At first Dayan thought little of them, believing they were ordinary Arab jars. What struck his curiosity was their color—they were red, not the usual black. Taking one home to Tel Aviv, he promptly asked a friend to assess the jar's significance, if any. The jar was indeed quite a find—dating back to the ninth century B.C., the period of the Hebrew Kings. Returning to the wadi for further study the following Saturday, Dayan came upon spouts of ancient oil lamps, potsherds, broken bricks of loam, pieces of small flasks, and handles of large jars that had been used to store grain. As he held the items in his hands, images grew in his mind of ancient civilizations buried under the roads and houses, the fields and trees, civilizations of his own Jewish people.

The chief of staff as amateur archaeologist—it made perfect sense to Moshe Dayan. Later controversies would erupt, but Dayan had found an avocation that a one-eyed person could pursue without too much strain. As time went on Dayan became a greater expert in the subject. He had a dexterity that enabled him to take the relics and piece them together into a whole. Whenever he came across potsherds, he would take them back to his garden at his house in Zahala, a suburb of Tel Aviv to which the Dayan family had moved in 1953. There, taking glue and plaster of paris, he would stick the shards together, applying acid to clean away the layers of stone. For him, it became more than a hobby. Dayan could see a deeper, near-mystical meaning behind his work. "Putting these broken vessels together, fashioning them anew and returning them to the shape given them by the potters and housewives three, four or five thousand years ago, gives me something of the feeling of creation."[13] Apart from that feeling, Dayan genuinely sensed a kinship with the people who had lived in the ancient cities. Though the comment was a slap in the face at just about everyone who considered him a friend, he once declared that his digging made him feel more in the presence of those who lived in olden days than when he entered the homes of the living. He liked to stick his head into a hole in which the people of some ancient Jewish town had lived, to look at their kitchen, to finger the ashes left from long ago, to feel the fingerprint that the ancient potter felt on the vessel. On one Saturday he enticed Ezer Weizman to crawl through a tunnel in Jerusalem in search of relics. They came upon broken pottery and part of a skull. Dayan pounced on the ancient items as if they were gold. Weizman was slightly less enthused.

"Moshe, for God's sake, look at us, crawling around. Why are you picking through old bones?"

"Idiot," Dayan replied, "You don't understand? These (pointing to the skull) are the bones of a Jew who saw the Second Temple!"

By all accounts, Dayan was a superb archaeologist. Though his critics in later years would excoriate him for "pillaging" national treasures (and such charges played a monumental role in the Israeli public's verdict on Dayan), the commonly held view of Moshe Dayan as archaeologist was unfailingly complimentary: It was said that he had a keen sense of where to dig, and when he reached a site, he had the diligence and patience of a prospector looking for gold.

MOSHE DAYAN's role in one of Israel's greatest controversies, the Lavon Affair, was rooted in the chief of staff's relationship to Defense Minister Pinhas Lavon. That relationship took shape during 1954, a difficult year for Israel. Egypt was increasing her blockade against Israeli ships and cargoes through the Suez Canal and the Gulf of 'Aqaba. While no Israeli ships could pass through the canal, Egypt permitted nonstrategic cargoes carried in non-Israeli vessels to go through every once in a while. Then at the end of 1953, Egypt placed a complete ban on all cargoes to and from Israel. Meanwhile, terrorist infiltrations were on the rise. Prime Minister Moshe Sharett and Defense Minister Lavon disagreed on how Israel should handle the increased hostility: Sharett favored diplomacy, Lavon wanted military action.

At first Dayan was pleased with Lavon's appointment as minister of defense, figuring he would give added weight to the activist approach that he and Ben-Gurion favored and that contrasted with Moshe Sharett's moderation. Dayan had little patience for the moderation diplomats such as Sharett espoused.

By February 1954 Dayan started to sense an unpleasant side to Lavon's personality. He had a tendency to overlook the chief of staff, to act as if he believed he as minister of defense should run the army—without Dayan's meddling. Dayan, needless to say, was appalled at such behavior. Nonetheless, Lavon reserved the right to meet with senior officers without informing Dayan. He was also prepared to sponsor military actions that Dayan had vetoed. Around this time Dayan and Shimon Peres, director general of the Ministry of Defense, visited Ben-Gurion at Sde Boker and complained about Lavon's rash actions. Matters came to a crunch later that year.

Dayan wanted to purchase the French AMX tank. Without informing Dayan, Lavon sought to divert funds from Dayan's tank project and to purchase heavy mortars which, as Dayan had been convinced, were defensive weapons that would not strengthen Israel's attack capability. Believing that he had supreme authority over Dayan, Lavon refused to discuss the matter with the chief of staff.

Then came June 14. It was then that Dayan visited Ben-Gurion in the hospital. Dayan described Lavon's attempts to cancel the purchase of French AMX tanks and of his going behind the chief of staff's back to make contacts with senior staff officers. Dayan wrote Lavon a letter of resignation the next day. Three days later Lavon visited Ben-Gurion in the hospital and promised to mend fences with Dayan. Lavon invited Dayan to lunch and blamed their differences on some unidentified member of the Defense Ministry; in short, he did not want Dayan to resign. They shook hands after the meal, and Dayan remained chief of staff. It was apparently impossible for Lavon to clash with a genuine military hero such as Dayan. Lavon backed down on the AMX tank issue and Dayan's order for the tanks was eventually filled.

This then was the unfriendly backdrop to the Lavon Affair that focused on a special services unit set up during the 1948 war by a Foreign Ministry department; its purpose was to conduct activity in enemy countries. (Most details of the affair were kept from the public thanks to the heavy blue penciling of the military censor.) At some point the IDF gained control of the unit and Defense Minister Lavon decided that it would be worthwhile activating it for special missions. Dayan sensed the problems involved in Lavon directing such special missions. He warned one of the officers in charge of the unit to be careful about him. In July 1954, while Dayan was away in the United States on a three-week visit to army bases, the unit carried out small sabotage actions in Cairo and Alexandria. Its purpose apparently was to cause the destruction of certain American and British institutions in Egypt, especially in Cairo, endangering British and American lives. The expected public outcry in Britain and the United States was supposed to be sufficient to cause Britain to change its mind about pulling out of Egypt and giving up its protection of the Suez Canal. In this way, Egypt's Nasser would be restrained from unleashing war against Israel. The sabotage efforts went awry when eleven of the espionage group were caught, arrested, and tried. Some received long jail terms; one member committed suicide and two others were executed on January 1, 1955.

Dayan's role in the decision making remains unclear. Some have suspected that he was actually shown the plan, but the evidence for that is highly circumstantial. It rests on little more than the suspicion that Dayan's visit to the United States at the precise time that the espionage unit was carrying out its activities may have been more than just coincidence, that he may have known enough of the plan to encourage his speedy departure abroad. That visit has been offered as evidence that he was "out of the loop," uninvolved in the decision making. The manner in which Dayan left for his visit, however—he contended that he went as the guest of the Pentagon to tour army installations, but the Pentagon did not confirm that—suggested to some otherwise. In any event, Dayan was permitted to tour the installations at his own expense.

The question of who gave the order to send the espionage team into action haunted Israeli political life for years. According to Benjamin Gibli, the director of military intelligence, Lavon had given him the final approval during a meeting on July 16 at General Headquarters. By then the espionage unit had already begun its series of attacks against the installations. That would mean that Gibli had received Lavon's approval after the start of the operation on July 2—and after it had failed. While in the United States, on July 19, Gibli sent Dayan a report mentioning that the go-ahead had been given for the Egyptian operation.

It is not clear why Gibli had told Dayan all this on July 19 when the first bombs had exploded in Egypt on July 2—ten days before Dayan left Israel. Some have suggested that Gibli may have written the letter to prove that Dayan could not have known about the operation until he was abroad. What has struck some as significant, however, is Dayan's seemingly mild reaction when he heard about the operation. He made no frantic phone call to Lavon or Sharett to protest the move, or to demand that it be called off. He simply burned the letter, as required by security regulations. Naturally enough, Dayan felt the minister of defense, and not the chief of staff, should be held ultimately responsible for any military blunder—so Dayan demanded that Lavon be fired.

Returning from abroad, Dayan rushed to Ben-Gurion to tell him about the events that had occurred. "Moshe Dayan arrived at Sde Boker this afternoon," Ben-Gurion noted in his diary on August 24. "He told me about the astonishing order issued by Lavon, while he, Dayan was abroad. The operation ordered failed, he said, and it should have been known that it would fail."[14] Dayan, who viewed Lavon as a threat, told the director of military intelligence that unless Gibli blamed the defense minister, Gibli himself could become the scapegoat. Thus at a General Staff meeting on November 1 Gibli in essence launched the Lavon Affair by pronouncing that Lavon had given the order.

Israel became obsessed with uncovering the identity of who had given the order. Was it the senior army officer responsible for the unit? Or the defense minister? The senior officer blamed Lavon; Lavon blamed the officer. A two-man inquiry panel was unable to determine who gave the order. Lavon's government and Mapai colleagues felt he should go and so on February 2, 1955, he resigned. Eighteen days later, Ben-Gurion once again became minister of defense (and the following November, prime minister). The officer in charge of the unit also lost his job.

Dayan succeeded in avoiding damage to his career with good reason. To his credit, there is every indication that he opposed the controversial operation. Just as he had managed to evade being censured for the Saison and the *Altalena*, Dayan's instinct was to steer clear of involvement in this sticky mess, one more indication of his continuing ability to avoid potentially damaging mine fields.

MOSHE DAYAN apparently began thinking in early 1955 about unleashing a major attack against the Arabs, but he never voiced such an opinion in public—never in direct terms. The frustration he felt toward diplomatic efforts that were getting nowhere was evident in the tone of his words: "No international question has been so much discussed and so little solved," he wrote in January 1955. He was willing to give the diplomats a chance, but ultimately he knew that Israel could rely only upon the IDF. "The Israel Government and its defense forces will not neglect any idea or opportunity which seems likely to offer hope of a remedy [to the infiltrations]." In the end, he hinted at Israel taking military action. "Until [there is a solution] the Israel Defense Forces will face a heavy task, and face it virtually alone as the solitary effective means for safeguarding Israel's physical integrity."[15]

Accordingly, morale building within the IDF became even more important. Still determined to turn the entire army into one big commando unit, Dayan sensed that the time had come for Unit 101 to become less independent, to fit more directly into the army's organization chart. Hence Dayan ordered that 101 be merged with the paratroopers into a single unit. In this way, 101, this "hothouse for heroes," as Ben-Gurion called the unit, would influence the paratroopers, who would influence the entire IDF. The merger became official on January 4, 1954. Commanding the new, enlarged unit—now called 202—was Ariel Sharon. By 1956 the paratroopers unit had been enlarged to brigade size. The chief of staff urged members of the General Staff and commanders from other units to join 202 on reprisal raids, to get an idea of how this elite group behaved. Officers from 202 were transferred to other units as well in the hope that they would spread the word.

As part of the effort to make all IDF troops into battle-hardened soldiers, Dayan adopted a technique he had heard about during his visit to army units in July 1954: There he was told that the U.S. Army had introduced a requirement that officers had to go through paratrooper training. As soon as he returned to Israel, Dayan insisted that all IDF officers take a paratroop course—including the entire General Staff, even the chief rabbi. Pinhas Lavon, still the defense minister then, was aghast at the suggestion, worried that senior officers might be hurt and thus lost to the army. When the chief of staff let it be known that he too intended to jump, Lavon thought the idea outrageous. Did he not realize his own importance? Lavon asked in a note to Dayan. Returning the note to him, Dayan added in handwriting that his importance depended upon his remaining independent rather than a puppet on a string. On January 4, 1955, Sharon, as commander of the paratroopers, awarded paratroop wings to Dayan.

From January 1954 until December 1955, Dayan gave 202 all of the combat assignments. The first large-scale operation mounted by the paratroopers came on Feburary 28, 1955, when Israel attacked an Egyptian army camp near Gaza City, killing forty Egyptian officers; ten Israelis died. That April, the Egyptians established fedayeen or suicide squads: seven hundred guerrillas in all, operating under the aegis of Egyptian intelligence headquarters in Gaza. Meanwhile, Ben-Gurion and Dayan were rejecting diplomatic solutions and Dayan was slowly winning support for a militant posture.

"So you want a war?" Ben-Gurion said to him in the middle of 1955.

"No, no," said Dayan. "I'm not in favor of our beginning a war, but I shall object to concessions of any sort, and if the Arabs ask for war, they shall have it. If the Syrians open fire on us when we try to divert the Jordan waters, our reply will be war."

Fears persisted that Dayan was leading the country into war. To some, renewed fighting was unwanted, in part because of the rise to power of Gamal Abdel Nasser in Egypt, thought at first to be someone with whom Israel might be able to negotiate a peaceful settlement. Nasser, the head of the so-called Free Officers, took control of the Egyptian government on July 23, 1952, and forced King Farouk into exile. For a brief time the officers appointed Gen. Mohammed Neguib as their leader. He was deposed and Nasser became supreme. Nasser's extreme Arab nationalism, combined with his quest for the leadership of the Arab world, left little doubt eventually among Israelis that he was no friend. In the late summer of 1955 the debate over how to deal with Egypt was at its height. Dayan and Sharett, the outgoing prime minister, squabbled over how aggressive Israel should be in dealing with frontier penetrations in the south. Following one such Arab raid, Dayan had ordered Israeli soldiers to attack an Egyptian fortress in the Gaza town of Khan Yunis. Sharett thought enough was enough and called them back. According to one account, Ben-Gurion sent his military aide, Col. Nehemia Argov, to meet Dayan on August 30 at the jump-off point near the Gaza Strip and told him in Ben-Gurion's name to rescind the orders. Dayan canceled the operation and resigned as chief of staff the next day after learning of Sharett's intervention.[16] Meeting with Ben-Gurion, Dayan, and a few senior cabinet colleagues, Sharett apparently hoped that Ben-Gurion would back him and warn Dayan that his planned attack was inadvisable. Ben-Gurion did no such thing. According to Gideon Rafael, who was at the meeting, "Dayan made a strong case for the policy of retaliation as the only effective means with which to stem the tide of Arab aggression. He claimed that the repeal of the orders harmed the morale of the forces. Sharett tried to soothe him, explaining again the special conditions that had prompted him to intervene and assuring him of his readiness to authorize actions if circumstances warranted them. Dayan insisted that Nasser must be taught lessons which he as a military man would understand. Diplomatic goodwill messages intended to improve him were useless." Rather than warn the chief of staff off the planned assault, Ben-Gurion asked him to relate how he intended to carry it out. It was premature to provide details, Dayan said. Ultimately, the chief of staff retracted his resignation and carried out the Gaza attack.[17]

Gamal Abdel Nasser, the Egyptian leader, announced on September 27 that Cairo had signed a commercial agreement with Czechoslovakia exchanging Czech arms for Egyptian cotton and rice. Egypt was to get two hundred MiG-15 jet fighters, fifty Ilyushin bombers, 300 Soviet-made medium and heavy tanks, 200 armored personnel carriers, and a wide variety of other military equipment. Enough, Ben-Gurion believed sorrowfully, to annihilate Israel within two days. This marked a major acceleration of the arms race in the Middle East, tipping the balance heavily against Israel, both in quantity and quality. Perhaps the most ghastly implication of the arms deal from Israel's perspective was the virtual certainty that Egypt was bent on war now that it was able to launch the dreaded "second round."

Cairo also announced in October 1955 that it had extended its blockade to the air, forcing Israel's national airline El Al to avoid flying over the Straits of Tiran and causing a suspension of its flights to Africa. The arms deal spurred Ben-Gurion to form a government quickly and get ready for war. Dayan had been vacationing in Paris. On October 19, Ben-Gurion cabled him to come home at once. The defense minister wanted the chief of staff to report on secret arms-purchase talks Israel was holding with the French.

The trip home had a substantial impact on Moshe Dayan's personal life. It was during that return trip that he met Rahel Rabinovitch. She had traveled to Europe to get away from her unhappy marriage, planning to spend three months going from Paris to London to Rome. While in Rome she decided to cut short her trip. In the airport lounge, while she was saying hello to Jerusalem friends who were also on her flight, she noticed Moshe Dayan walk past her. She had seen him a few times before, once walking on the street with Ruth, another time at the wedding of Ezer and Re'uma Weizman. Rahel took her seat in the rear of the plane. It was uncomfortable and narrow so a Jerusalem attorney whom she knew offered to switch seats with her; his seat was next to Moshe Dayan's. The attorney introduced them. She sat down; Dayan was reading Josephus Flavius and he started talking to her about the book. Lunch was served. He asked her if she had a quarter for a beer and she gave him one. She was young and beautiful, and Dayan was instantly taken with her. Later, after much conversation, he asked her, "If I call you, will you give me a cup of coffee?" Rahel said sure. So he took her phone number. "I don't know if it was 'love at first sight,' " Dayan said later, "but since I have known Rahel there has not been another person whose company I desired to the same extent or with whom I wanted (in the same degree) to share happiness and sorrow."[18]

The conversation on the plane affected Rahel deeply as well. "By the time I reached Israel I knew that my life had changed completely, not that I was in love or something like that. Somehow I felt that my life would not continue the way it was. I didn't quite understand how or what I felt, but I knew I was a different person. Now it sounds silly. At the time it didn't." Years later she remembered what had attracted Dayan to her: "He had a wonderful head. He had a beautiful . . . very attractive head. He never had much of a figure, but he had a very attractive appearance, and actually when you saw him, you never thought of how he looked, the rest of him, you just saw a head, but this is the external part. I found in him a kindred spirit."[19]

Their romance began a few days after their fateful plane ride, after Dayan phoned Rahel. He saw her frequently, before and after official meetings, whenever he had spare time. Rahel recalled seeing Dayan five or six times a day when she moved to Tel Aviv in 1966: "We never hid. It was difficult for him. Life wasn't simple. We never said, 'All right, we'll go into a place where no one will see us.' He said, 'why should I hide?' "[20] Their romance did not become a public issue at first. When Ruth eventually realized that Dayan was carrying on, she became distraught.

THE DAY AFTER Dayan returned from abroad, Ben-Gurion ordered him to prepare to capture the Straits of Tiran including Sharm el-Sheikh, Ras Nasrani, and the islands of Tiran and Sanafir, even though Israel could not really contemplate such a step until it obtained sufficient equipment.

The following month the Czech arms began flowing to Egypt. Dayan and the General Staff calculated that Egypt would need six to eight months to absorb the equipment. So an Egyptian attack was forecast any time from late spring to late summer of 1956. Israel had precious little time to close the arms gap. To whom could it turn? Not the United

States or Great Britain, the most likely sources. They refused to sell arms to Israel. France was the only other choice, but it was prepared to sell nothing more lethal than the light AMX tank. Faced with no alternative, Israel planned to acquire these, taking into account that it could also recondition some old American tanks from World War II surplus stores in Europe. Fighter planes were a large question mark. Again, only France seemed a likely supplier. The French and Israelis had common enemies: Nasser was helping the Palestinians against Israel, and the Algerian rebels against France.

Israel continued to prod Egypt. On November 2 came a major operation, an Israeli attempt to dislodge an Egyptian infantry force that had occupied and fortified a stronghold at Sabha within the El Auja demilitarized zone. Sabha was the first combat mission given to any unit other than the elite Unit 202 and was carried out by the first infantry brigade, the Golani, along with the paratroopers.

Dayan was eager to go on the attack, but he was conscious of the Egyptian military advantage. On November 27 he told the Associated Press that "The prospects of Israel to win in a war against any Arab state, or even against Egypt alone, are becoming less and less from month to month, to the extent that Egypt is getting heavy Czech equipment and is training her army to use it." Just how difficult it was for Dayan to refrain from unleashing war against Egypt was illustrated during one Israeli assault against Egypt around this time. Dayan and Uzi Narkiss were standing on a hill inside Egypt not far from Nitzana in the south. An operation was in progress. It was 3:00 A.M.

"Ben-Gurion," said Dayan, "would love now for Nasser to counterattack."

Narkiss asked why.

"Because then we could launch a large operation."

"You can do it by yourself, you can provoke him."

"No," said Dayan, "this [more moderate operation] is exactly what Ben-Gurion wants. And I can't do something contrary to his will."[21]

The chief of staff thought Israel could overcome its equipment disadvantage by undermining Egyptian plans. He wrote a memo to Ben-Gurion on November 10 in which he proposed major reprisal raids against Egypt or Egyptian-directed acts of violence; conquering the Gaza Strip (not only a terrorist base, but a likely launching pad for an Egyptian invasion against Israel); and preparing to take Sharm el-Sheikh in order to break the blockage of the Gulf of 'Aqaba. Three days later Dayan spoke to Ben-Gurion, urging military action as quickly as possible. Dayan thought the Egyptian threat was immediate: He suggested that the prime minister establish an emergency war administration of the army, recalling Yigael Yadin and making him chief of staff, and appointing Mordechai Makleff chief of operations, and Yigal Allon northern front commander. Dayan would take over as southern front commander or any other field command. The proposal was somewhat out of character for Dayan for it suggested a sense of self-doubt, a shrugging off of responsibility when the going got tough.

If Dayan had momentary questions about his own ability to lead the army, David Ben-Gurion did not. He wasted no time in telling Dayan what he thought of part of his proposal. Whether war came or not, there was no way he was going to get rid of him as chief of staff. Fearing that the international community, particularly England and the United States, would not abide an Israeli preemptive action against Egypt, the prime minister hesitated about going to war. Later, on November 13, Ben-Gurion asked Dayan to hold off taking any action on Sharm el-Sheikh until the closing days of January 1956. He made clear to his chief of staff he still hoped Nasser could be provoked into starting a war. There was little support in the government for mounting a preventive war; indeed, it adopted a formal decision rejecting a preventive war and postponing for an unspecified time Operation Omer, which had been designed to open the Straits of Tiran.[22]

Dayan was disappointed in Ben-Gurion. The chief of staff felt, according to Shimon Peres, "that BG had not done his best with the government. He [Dayan] felt . . . that if BG had dug his heels in as he should, his natural authority would have enabled him to mobilize the required majority [for military action to unblock the Straits]."[23]

The government's disinterest in taking on Egypt at this stage plunged Dayan into depression. Speaking to an Agence France Presse correspondent on December 1, 1955, he warned that an "explosion" along the Egyptian border could be avoided only if Israel received arms in quantity and quality sufficient to counterbalance the strength gained by Egypt in the Czech arms deal. And in a letter to Ben-Gurion on December 5, Dayan expressed disappointment with the government's reluctance to act. He noted that the failure to act meant that Israel was relinquishing its freedom of shipping.

With Israel focusing its diplomacy on acquiring arms from the United States and other Western countries, the IDF was engaging in actions that were detrimental to that aim. The Syrians had been firing from the slopes of the Golan Heights down on Israeli patrols and fishing boats on the Sea of Galilee, and finally, on December 11, Israel unleashed its own counterattack. The Israeli paratroop brigade and a company of the Golani infantry brigade knocked out all the Syrian positions along the northeastern shores of the lake. Fifty Syrian soldiers were killed, thirty taken prisoner. Israel lost six men, and twelve were wounded. Though United Nations truce observers had declared Israel sovereign over the Sea of Galilee, the Kinneret action disrupted Israeli efforts to get arms from Washington. Dayan was assailed for expanding the action behind the limited operation Ben-Gurion had suggested. Israel did not go to war against Egypt right away, but from February 1955 until October 1956, it carried out fifteen major reprisal raids against military camps, police fortresses, and outposts in Egypt, Jordan, and Syria. The last and perhaps the most significant was against the Jordanian police fortress near the border town of Kalkilya on October 10, 1956—less than three weeks before the Sinai campaign.

✦ 8 ✦

WAR AND COLLUSION

WAR SEEMED inevitable; the "second round" that the Arabs constantly had been threatening was imminent. Egypt and Syria had allied themselves in a joint military command in recent months. The Czech arms deal gave Egypt the means to go on the offensive, to try again to eradicate the Jewish state. Many believed that, strengthened with tanks and planes and other modern weaponry, Egypt, in league with Syria, Jordan, and Iraq, would try to erase the "stain" of 1948, to drive the Jews into the sea. One hundred million Arabs massed against the tiny, beleaguered state with its few million people. Unlike the romantic and satisfying biblical story of David and Goliath, the cards seemed to be stacked in favor of the powerful giant.

Until the masses of weapons could be absorbed in Egypt's armory, Nasser's strategy in the winter of 1955–56 was to gnaw away at Israel's morale, engaging in constant acts of terror against Israel's civilian population, and serving notice that the enemy existed and would not go away. By January 1956 tension had risen to new heights along Israel's frontiers with Jordan and Egypt, but especially along the Gaza Strip. Nearly every day fedayeen raiders crossed into Israel to attack Israelis. One of the worst incidents occurred at Kfar Habad, an Orthodox religious village eight miles east of Tel Aviv. Arabs attacked a synagogue filled with children at prayer, killing a teacher and five boys, and wounding several others. In all of 1956 Arab attackers killed 54 Israelis and wounded

129, a substantial increase from 1954, when 33 were killed and 77 wounded.

Moshe Dayan had been pressing David Ben-Gurion to take military action and had won him over to his side but the more moderate ministers in the government insisted that diplomacy be tried a bit longer. That forced the chief of staff to rely upon reprisal raids as the main IDF response to Arab terror. As long as the Arabs chose to penetrate Israel's frontiers, they had to understand that a price would be exacted from them. Dayan changed tactics slightly: Rather than hit back every time, he became more selective, using more firepower than in the past. Meanwhile, Dayan decided to strengthen the country's defenses. Frontline settlements were reinforced and fortified; new settlements were quickly built around strategically vulnerable areas such as the Nitzana demilitarized zone; the civil defense was reorganized; vast mine fields were prepared.

If Israel was going to prepare itself for large-scale war, it still had to acquire arms from abroad. That became a top priority. The French, as noted, were the most likely source. The French socialist left had warm feelings toward socialist Israel. The French right worried along with Israel over the threat of pan-Arabism, especially with the Algerian war of liberation at its peak. Egypt had evinced support for the rebel Algerian FLN. During Dayan's visit to France, in August 1954, he was greeted by the French chief of staff, Gen. Augustin Guillaume. At a ceremony on the grounds of French Army Headquarters at Les Invalides, the French general conferred on Dayan the decoration of commander of the French Legion of Honor, one of France's highest decorations. (The irony may not have been lost on the recipient, who just thirteen years earlier had lost his eye due to a French bullet.) Dayan urged the French to sell arms to Israel, alluding to their common enemy, the Arabs: "You are on the home front; while we are on the firing lines. Don't you think that when the front lines are ablaze the arms should be transferred from the home front to the forward positions?" The question was hardly rhetorical.

The French indeed were interested in selling arms to Israel. The first twelve Mystere warplanes from France arrived in April 1956, providing the IDF with warplanes that were regarded as superior to the Soviet-made MiGs being sent to Egypt. Israel hoped to obtain more tanks from France as well.

If war came, Dayan wanted to make sure that Israel would win. Yet the price of victory bothered him. He correctly judged that the single most important problem confronting the young state was how to live with the Arabs. Was killing them the answer? Was engaging in a major war with them every few years a formula for peaceful coexistence? The generation of Dayan's parents had learned to be on guard against the Arab pillager, the marauder, the terrorist. That generation saw the Arabs as little more than murderers. Moshe Dayan, in that spring of 1956, wondered whether it was necessary to treat every Arab as if he were a terrorist, as the faceless enemy.

To even ask such questions went against every rule for a country at war. Forcing such moral considerations upon one's countrymen at a time when their loved ones and friends were being cut down seemed almost unthinkable. Yet that is what Moshe Dayan did. In doing so, he laid the foundation for the way much of the outside world would think of Israel, not as a nation that hated its enemies, but as one which felt it had no choice but to fight them. Coming from anyone else, the thought would have had the sound of treachery. Coming from Israel's chief of staff, it had the ring of truth.

Dayan first aired such thoughts against the backdrop of fresh whisperings of peace. United Nations Secretary General Dag Hammarskjöld was optimistic. Hammarskjöld was then journeying throughout the Middle East, seeking an Egyptian promise to end fedayeen raids. The Egyptian leader appeared to promise the peacemaker that cross-frontier raids would cease.

The bubble of optimism, however, burst. On April 27 Dayan visited Nahal Oz, a kibbutz located across from the Gaza Strip, where he had been especially impressed with the kibbutz secretary, a Tel Avivian named Roi Rutenberg. Roi and some friends had helped to establish Nahal Oz after completing their army service. Soon after Dayan's visit disaster struck the kibbutz. On April 29 Roi was shot and killed by an Egyptian border patrol. It seemed only fitting that Dayan should give the eulogy for Roi.

The eulogy on that May 1 at Roi's graveside was almost as remarkable for what Moshe Dayan did not say as for what he did. He did not attempt to ignite Israeli passions against the perpetrators of this violence. Instead, he urged Israelis to try to understand what the root of this violence was, to exhibit some compassion for a people who had been upstaged and outshone by the Israelis. Rarely had a military leader displayed such sensitivity toward his enemy. Part of Dayan's eulogy expressed the frustration of knowing that peacemakers such as Hammarskjöld had not yet brought peace: "Roi's blood cries out to us and accuses us only, for a thousand times have we sworn that our blood shall not be spilled in vain, and yet we allowed ourselves only yesterday to be cajoled into listening and believing. And meanwhile Roi was murdered from ambush." Then

Dayan raised questions that no Israeli leader had dared to ask; he uttered out loud what few in his country would have dared to say publicly.

> Today, let us not condemn the murderers. What do we know of their fierce hate for us? For eight years they have been living in the refugee camps in Gaza, while right before their eyes we have been turning the land and the villages in which they and their forefathers lived into our own land. We should demand his (Roi's) blood not from the Arabs of Gaza, but of ourselves. . . . Let us make our reckoning today. We are a generation of settlers, and without a helmet or a gun barrel we shall not be able to plant a tree or build a house. Let us not be afraid to see the enmity that consumes the lives of hundreds of thousands of Arabs around us. Let us not avert our gaze, for it will weaken our hand. This is the fate of our generation. The only choice we have is to be armed, strong and resolute, or else our sword will fall from our hands and the thread of our lives be severed. The light in [Roi's] heart blinded him, and he did not see the slaughterer's knife. The longing for peace defeated him, and he did not hear the sound of murder.

The purpose of such stirring rhetoric was to alert the country to the hidden meaning of the political conflict, that what lay around the corner was not Armageddon, not the Final Battle between the Israelis and the Arabs. What lay in store were countless years of struggle tinged with the hope that somehow the two peoples would come to their senses. Only then would they realize they had no choice but to live with one another.

After the April violence Dayan asked himself whether Israel's policy of embarking on retaliatory raids was worth pursuing. It had long bothered him that such raids did not provide Israel with the chance to capture Arab territory with which Israel might later bargain for peace. He had grown increasingly convinced that the reprisal attacks simply did not work, did not deter the Arabs from engaging in raids against Israel. Adding to the frustration was the price paid in the lives of Israeli soldiers (fifty in 1955, sixty-three in 1956). He advocated changing the nature of these reprisal attacks: In the future the IDF would try to capture objectives on Arab soil, then bargain for Arab promises of security in that region. Such new toughness smacked of mere provocation to cabinet ministers whose main aim in life was preventing a second round with the Arabs. Dayan found no support for his boldness at the cabinet table.

Such cool treatment did not preclude Dayan from preparing the IDF for what he considered the coming war. With the retaliatory policy proving itself insufficient, with the Arabs getting stronger each day, the notion that Israel should unleash a preemptive strike against the Arabs looked more and more attractive to the chief of staff. Dayan's generals thought the idea madness. Since the end of the 1948 War of Independence, they had assumed that in the next Israeli-Arab war, it would be the Arab side that would begin hostilities. War planning, for the Israeli generals, became a matter of absorbing the first blow, of making sure that any Arab invasion would be successfully blocked by the standing army, supported by the reservists mobilized in time to reach the frontiers; only after this blocking action was successful would Israel take the offensive. Uzi Narkiss, then director of operations, presented such advice to Dayan. "He was furious," Narkiss remembered. "He insisted that after the first phase of mobilization, we should counterattack immediately." That seemed preposterous to Narkiss and the General Staff, who were unable to understand how an army in the midst of defending itself against an invasion would have the time or energy to counterattack.

Dayan was not fazed. He had a commando's mentality. Armies did not defend, they attacked. Armies did not sit back on their haunches, they moved forward. The IDF under Moshe Dayan was not about to let some invading Arab forces dictate the nature of its strategy. Task Force Baum, the Eighty-ninth Battalion, 101, 202, the IDF, all synonyms for the same thing: forward, attack, conquer! To make sure his army was ready for what he had in mind, Dayan ordered those elements that would take part in a preemptive strike to be strengthened as quickly as possible: the air force, the paratroopers, and the mobile assault forces.[1]

To take the offensive, Israel needed weapons. Israel's efforts to exploit France's pro-Israel sympathy began in earnest in June 1956. Because obtaining arms was so crucial, and because Moshe Dayan was an experienced negotiator, he spent a good deal of his time in the next few months engaged in conversations with the French. At first Israel sought arms from France but the relationship soon blossomed into a secret alliance. Joined by Yehoshafat Harkabi, the chief of military intelligence, and Shimon Peres, director general of the Ministry of Defense, Dayan boarded a French Nord plane on June 22 at a small airfield near Tel Aviv. Twelve hours later, they landed near Paris and were escorted to an ancient castle surrounded by a garden and a wall. The three days of talks began at once. The French delegation was headed by Louis Mangin, political adviser to the defense minister. The Israelis and French found common cause in the need to topple Egypt's Nasser from power. Aware that he could not commit his country to such a goal without formal government approval, Dayan nonetheless assured his French hosts that Israel was prepared to join the French in such an effort. After the French made clear they were willing to provide Israel with the necessary equipment to fight Egypt, Dayan was ecstatic. An Israeli-French military connection had been forged.

Soon thereafter, Egypt's Nasser played into Israel's hands inadvertently by way of some fresh adventurism against the French and British. Buoyed by a new confidence because of the Czech arms deal, he shocked everyone by announcing on June 26, before a crowd of tens of thousands at Cairo's Independence Square, that he had nationalized the Suez Canal. Almost at once, Dayan received word from the Israeli embassy in Paris that France's defense minister Maurice Bourges-Maunoury had asked Israel for a quick appraisal of Egypt's military strength. The embassy had the clear impression that the French were preparing themselves for military action against Egypt.

DVORAH DAYAN's failing health distracted the chief of staff during the early summer. On June 3 her doctors had discovered that she had cancer of the liver and lungs that had been rapidly spreading. She required extensive medical care. Her husband Shmuel wanted her to spend her final days at Nahalal. Their son disagreed, believing she would be better off in a hospital. The chief of staff convinced his father, but not easily. Taking time away from his duties, Dayan spent a good deal of time at his mother's bedside. The physical pain took its toll on Dvorah's mind. Even though what she uttered must have caused her son much anguish, Dvorah poured out her innermost feelings to him: "May you come back in the morning and find me dead, that will be a salvation for me and a gift to you." Her son's courage on the battlefield had left a great impression on her. Her disease twisted her mind into scornful thoughts: He might be brave in combat, but could he have withstood such physical pain? "Brave Moshe, if this had happened to him, he would put a bullet in his temple." Then she begged him to find a way to relieve her suffering. "Moussik, you are brave, the brave one, you can do anything—and to take this suffering and this pain away from me, can't you do that?"

On July 28, the chief of staff had managed to find some free time, away from his mother's bedside, away from his official duties. He was digging for antiquities near the Gaza Strip. The General Staff heard the news first. A Piper Cub was sent to locate him. Rather than land the plane, the pilot simply threw a bundle with a note to the ground. It said that Dvorah Dayan had died. She was sixty-six years old. In keeping with his aloofness from most Jewish ritual, Dayan did not observe the

Jewish custom of mourning by spending the next seven days at home. Instead, he rushed off to another meeting with Prime Minister Ben-Gurion.

DAYAN HAD little doubt what Nasser's bold move meant for Israel. War. The only questions were: When would it come? Would Israel be prepared? Writing to Yael, then in New York, the chief of staff hinted that the country would have to gear itself for fighting. "The retaliation raid, as a policy, has outlived its usefulness. The surprise element is gone, and we are thinking of other ways to maintain security. I won't bore you with details, but I'll let you know not when I want you home, which is yesterday, but when I think you should come."[2]

Nasser's July statement gave Dayan the chance to put some other military options before the prime minister. The proposals were daring, perhaps too daring for Ben-Gurion:

- Capturing the Sinai and then offering to establish control over the Suez Canal.
- Seizing Sharm el-Sheikh, thus lifting the Egyptian blockade of the Straits of Tiran.
- Capturing the Gaza Strip, Egypt's probable launching pad for the next war.

Ben-Gurion was sympathetic, but nervous. Why not wait for the arrival of the promised arms?

The IDF was ready, the chief of staff suggested, arms or no arms.

Yes, said the prime minister. But at what cost? Wait a while, he cautioned Dayan, let the arms come, let them be integrated into the IDF. Then you will get your war, a war that will be shorter and cost fewer lives than one launched now.

Dayan hated when someone urged patience on him. But this was the prime minister. He had no choice. Still, the Old Man's hesitancy did not put a brake on Israel's military planning. Dayan interpreted the prime minister's remarks as a challenge to get the IDF ready for war as expeditiously as possible.

One vital question was how would the state of Israel fight the coming war. Would Israel rely on the infantry with its mobility and speed to subdue the Egyptians, or on the massive firepower afforded by armor? Through lack of choice, the IDF had been an army of the jeep, the command car, and the half-track. Tanks had been a luxury, and when attempts were made to integrate them into the Israeli army in the early 1950s, the results were unspectacular. Too many tanks broke down, too many failed to reach the front line in time. And yet no self-respecting military officer would deny that a modern army needed tanks and their firepower to truly crush an enemy. Speed and mobility were proper tactics when an army's playthings did not supersede the jeep and the half-track.

This question—the tank versus infantry—had been hotly debated in the IDF of late. Because the chief of staff had been the army's most prominent commando, because he had inculcated into his soldiers the belief that to the swift belongs the victory, the debate still tipped in favor of the infantry. Dayan had bitter memories of tanks not having an impact in battle in 1948, of breaking down. But the armor men—Chaim Laskov, head of the Armored Corps, and Uri Ben-Ari, head of the Seventh Brigade, and others—had been winning over converts in recent days. They had convinced Dayan that the General Staff should once and for all deliberate and decide the issue.

The chief of staff agreed to a meeting in the presence of the prime minister on September 1 to discuss the issue. Then Ben-Gurion would decide. Dayan had been clever. This was his turf. The forty officers of the General Staff, for the most part, were in his pocket. Indeed, the day-long "debate" merely showed that most in the room supported Dayan, only a handful Laskov. Sitting tight-lipped throughout the day, Ben-Gurion invited Laskov around for a chat and instructed him to comply with the wishes of the majority.

As the IDF debated tanks and infantry, the French were moving toward a fateful decision. Nasser's nationalization order required a sharp response—they began thinking of a joint military operation with the British and the Israelis. The French and the British would concentrate on seizing the Suez Canal and getting rid of Nasser. The Israelis would play a major role in the fighting—especially in legitimizing the British-French thrust against Egypt.

On September 1 came the first hint that France might be serious about coordinating military action with Israel: Dayan received a "Most Immediate" signal from Israel's military attache in Paris indicating that the French vice-admiral Pierre Barjot believed that Israel should be invited into the burgeoning venture. (Britain's general Sir Charles Keightley, commander of British land forces in the Middle East, had already been named head of Operation Musketeer, the impending Anglo-French action, with Barjot as his deputy.) The cautious message did not specify how much cooperation France intended. Ben-Gurion instructed Dayan to respond that in principle Israel was ready to cooperate, even if it included a military operation. The prime minister offered to send Dayan to Paris in secret to learn more of French intentions.

ALL THE WHILE Arab terror did not cease. This put Israel in a dilemma. When fedayeen crossed the frontier and killed Israelis, the biblical injunction "an eye for an eye" made great sense. Moshe Dayan saw a grander design unfolding. If Israel was about to go to war against Egypt, in alliance with France and Great Britain, then the rules of war must apply. A key rule was to surprise one's enemy. The more reprisal raids against Egypt, the more Cairo would suspect that Israel was about to launch a major war. Israel's interest, therefore, was in keeping the Egyptian frontier quiet. This was not an easy task, not when Arabs were killing Israelis as they were that September.

The terror came from Jordan in mid-September. Arabs crossed the Jordan Valley and killed a tractor driver near Beit-Shean. Others killed four Israeli archaeologists across the frontier from Bethlehem. A day later, Arabs shot and killed a woman and her daughter. Israel felt it had no choice but to respond. It did; but significantly, all four of the major raids between September 12 and October 10 were against Jordanian targets, not Egyptian ones.

When Dayan witnessed the Israeli blood that had been spilled, he cried out for greater reprisals. Ben-Gurion, sympathetic with his intentions, still advised caution. For Dayan the most anguishing moment on a battlefield since his brother Zorik had fallen in 1948 came on September 12. It was then, during the Israeli reprisal raid against the Jordanian town of Rahawah north of Beersheba, that Meir Har-Zion was seriously wounded. A Jordanian bullet caught the twenty-one-year-old Israeli in the neck and he dropped to the ground, unable to breathe. Waiting on the Israeli side of the frontier, a mile from the site of the raid, Dayan chased after the ambulance carrying the critically injured Har-Zion to the Beersheba Hospital. Dayan was crestfallen. He had sent Har-Zion and others like him into battle, knowing the risks they took. His insistence that soldiers exhaust the mission, that officers lead their men, enhanced those risks considerably. Dayan was adamant about remaining by Har-Zion's bedside. Mordechai Bar-On, Dayan's head of bureau, recalled that Har-Zion suddenly came to life, opening his eyes and smiling, when he sensed the chief of staff nearby. Har-Zion did not recall Dayan's presence but Mordechai Bar-On clearly recalled Dayan breaking down and weeping at the site of his comrade.[3] Har-Zion survived the bullet and to this day thinks of Moshe Dayan in cosmic terms: "I was small, he was big," he said simply.[4]

DAYAN SPENT a good part of September rallying his commanders for the expected war: The General Staff's war plans in the south were dusted off and studied; training for tank crews and pilots was accelerated. Dayan asserted in midmonth that Israel had no intention of reaching the Suez Canal or of involving itself in the British-French aspect of the dispute. It was not the nationalization of the Suez Canal that concerned Israel, but rather the Egyptian blockade of the Straits, the Fedayeen raids emanating from the Gaza Strip, and the Egyptian soldiers in the Sinai. If the French (and British, perhaps) could help Israel resolve these issues, Israel would not object.

Meanwhile, Downing Street was getting cold feet. Israel informed the French that they could count on Israel for joint action against Egypt even without British participation. The French responded by inviting Israel for talks on the venture.

On September 25 Ben-Gurion instructed Dayan to travel to Paris along with Peres, Transport Minister Moshe Carmel, and Foreign Minister Golda Meir. Ben-Gurion insisted that both Great Britain and the United States agree to any joint Israeli-French mission: The United States had to promise not to impose sanctions against Israel; Britain was not to aid any Arab state should it seek to rescue Egypt.

The Israeli delegation left for Paris on the evening of September 28. Two days later the talks began at the Montparnasse home of Louis Mangin, political adviser to Defense Minister Maurice Bourges-Maunoury. Representing the French were Foreign Minister Christian Pineau; Bourges-Maunoury; Abel Thomas, director general of the Defense Ministry; and Gen. Maurice Challe, deputy to the chief of staff for air force affairs.

Pineau proposed the joint venture occur in mid-October, when the Mediterranean would be calm and the United States would be tied up with its presidential elections. Still, the British remained skittish. No matter, said Pineau. Israel could launch a war—and France could later join in. Or, if Israel objected to that, France and Israel could initiate a war together. Responding to the French foreign minister, the Israelis spoke enthusiastically in favor of a joint Israeli-French operation, concerned largely about the unpleasant prospect that Britain might join Jordan in a joint attack against Israel in reprisal. To a lesser degree, Israel worried that Washington might impose economic sanctions against Jerusalem or that the Soviets might send troops in aid of Egypt.

For practical reasons, the French preferred Israel to begin the war. In this way, the British would be more likely to join at an early stage. British participation was critical, the French insisted, because the more sophisticated British bombers could inflict damage on Cairo's airfields which the French planes could not.

The French were still reluctant to give a final go-ahead, unnerving Moshe Dayan: It made military planning difficult. Part of the French reluctance to commit themselves to a joint mission with Israel was rooted in their patronizing view of the Israeli army. They simply doubted that the IDF could deliver the goods. This view was partly due to Moshe Dayan's brutal honesty about his own soldiers. At an early stage in the talks, Dayan explained to the French chief of staff Paul Ely that the IDF was composed largely of reservists. When Dayan informed him that there was not sufficient equipment for them, so that they had to use civilian vehicles and wear their own civilian overcoats in winter, the Israeli chief of staff could sense that Ely "was conjuring up a picture of a civilian army of the eighteenth century, capable perhaps of mounting the barricades with their flags, but not of conducting a desert campaign with armored vehicles and coping with the maintenance of long supply lines."[5]

Sensing the French mistrust of the IDF, and trying to convince his prospective military partners that the IDF could do far more than mount barricades with flags, Dayan exuded a self-confidence that positively frightened the French.

Just how long would it take Israel to reach the Suez Canal? one of the French asked.

That, said the chief of staff, depended entirely on the speed of the vehicles at his army's disposal. But he believed it could be done—in four days!

Shlomo Gazit, Dayan's chief aide, was there when Dayan uttered his offhand remark, and recalled the utter disbelief with which it was greeted.

No wonder the French thought Dayan's remark a bad joke. They had been working on plans for an attack on Egypt for the past three months, and as of yet nothing had seemed workable. Then along came this upstart of a country, this upstart of a chief of staff, telling them, the French, how he was going to lead his forces through the entire Sinai in just four days!

General Challe was the first to try to rip Dayan's theory apart.

"Let's assume that you have managed to conquer the whole of Sinai— and it doesn't matter to me at the moment if it takes a day more or less— for how long, in your opinion, could you remain there and hold the Suez Canal bank?"

Dayan scratched his head, as if weighing the question carefully.

"In truth I must admit that your question is essentially a political one. And I strongly recommend that you bring it up again at the meeting you are about to have with Ben-Gurion. I can only deal with these matters in their military aspect. From the military aspect, if the IDF is required to hold the bank of the Canal, we can do that for 300 years at least!"[6]

Dayan spoke in Hebrew. His Israeli colleagues burst into laughter. The French just sat there, stupefied.

Then came the translation. General Challe sat pensively for a moment. Then he too exploded into laughter.

Suddenly the ice was broken. The French began to believe that the Israelis could deliver. General Challe became enamored of Israel's feisty, utterly self-confident chief of staff.[7] Later, General Challe confided to an Israeli diplomat that he credited Dayan, so clear and dynamic compared to the sluggish British, with inspiring his delegation to believe that Musketeer could materialize.

When the talks resumed after lunch, Dayan's buoyancy clearly had affected the mood. Dayan went one-on-one with the tall, thin, gray-haired French chief of staff Paul Ely, who had lost the use of one hand. Dayan used the afternoon to bolster Ely's confidence that Israel could handle its part of the venture even if the British stayed out. He turned over a list of equipment Israel needed, including tanks, half-tracks, trucks with four-wheel drive, bazookas, and transport planes. Israel, Dayan assured Ely, would be ready to launch an attack by October 20.

At the close of the talks, it was agreed that a French delegation would accompany the Israelis back to Israel to check whether the French would be able to use Israeli bases should the British sit out the mission. (In the case of British participation, the French would be able to use bases on Cyprus.)

Israel's attitude toward the forthcoming operation differed in some important ways from that of the British and French. Both Britain and France needed a pretext for involvement; Israel did not. Both Britain and France wanted to depose Nasser; but Israel could achieve its war aims without getting rid of the Egyptian ruler. Britain and France were willing to "allow" Israel to start the war so that they could exploit the turmoil for their own purposes; but Israel had to begin the war.

On the evening of October 2, Dayan, back in Israel, gave an early warning order to the General Staff to prepare for imminent war against Egypt. Estimated date: October 20, eighteen days from then. Estimated time of the campaign: three weeks. The French delegation, now in Israel, had its mandate widened to check whether Israel could absorb the new equipment it had asked for and to determine whether Israel could indeed carry out its part of the planned military operation. Uzi Narkiss, then a senior officer in the General Staff, arranged for the delegation to tour air force and paratrooper bases so they could judge whether Moshe Dayan had misled them with his claims at the Paris talks. Dayan was afraid to give the French the impression that Israel was so poorly off in weapons that France would have to supply the IDF with huge stocks of armaments.

The French asked Narkiss how much material Israel needed. Narkiss mentioned 300 half-tracks, 150 Sherman tanks, and some other items. Then Dayan entered the room. How much did you ask for?

When Narkiss told him, Dayan was taken aback. He feared that the French would automatically say no to such high numbers and report back to Paris that the Israeli army was in such bad shape that it needed restocking from beginning to end.

"I didn't approve any of your figures," Dayan barked. "Please ask for fifty percent less."

Narkiss, somewhat embarrassed, passed on Dayan's thinking to the French. "He thinks that 150 tanks are too much and he would like to have 75," Narkiss said. "What do you think?"

To Narkiss's shock, the French agreed to 150.[8]

The French delegation accepted Dayan's assessment that Israel's biggest difficulty was in moving rapidly through the desert. Accordingly, instructions were given to supply Jerusalem with Bren carriers, tanks, trucks with front-wheel drive, tank trailers, and fuel tankers for aircraft.

DAYAN PUT the army on a war footing. He ordered home all officers overseas on training courses, and that preparations for mobilization begin. Secrecy was paramount: The preparations were explained away as a response to the possible introduction of Iraqi troops into Jordan.

On the morning of October 3 Dayan received a memorandum from a hesitant Ben-Gurion, expressing fresh fears that without British intervention, Israel's cities might be bombed. Until this moment, the prime minister had carefully avoided accepting or rejecting the Israeli-French venture. Later that morning, Dayan and Peres saw Ben-Gurion, who informed them he was considering writing to French prime minister Guy Mollet to express doubts about the operation.

Pleading with Ben-Gurion, Dayan asked him to wait at least until after the French delegation had concluded its visit and had weighed in with its suggestions. The concern about Egypt bombing Israeli cities, Dayan said, was exaggerated. The French, even without the British, could make sure that Egypt's air force would be sufficiently crippled to prevent such bombing. Israel's air force, even if small, could defend the country in such a situation. It made little sense to abandon Israel's historic chance to deal with its fundamental security problems in league with a major ally.

Nonetheless Ben-Gurion continued to be wary.

"How can we agree to such an operation. We'll have losses that go into the thousands."

Dayan reassured the prime minister: "I promise you, Ben-Gurion, that we won't have more than 250 losses in battle."

"Really? Indeed, you mean it? How do you know?"

"I know the Israeli forces. I know the Egyptian forces. I know the terrain. I know the character of the war which we are planning. You don't have to worry."

"You promised me, remember."

Later, Shlomo Gazit asked Dayan how he dared risk making such a forecast. "Listen, if we go to war, I'm not sure. If we win, my prediction about Israeli losses will be forgotten. If we lose, it doesn't matter any more, but this may serve to change Ben-Gurion's mind."[9]

Still at issue was the question of whether Israel and France would open the war at the same time or Israel would start first. Israel wanted a simultaneous beginning: The French landings would tie up Nasser's troops, preventing them from reinforcing the Egyptians in the Sinai after Israel began its attack. Still, the French were not certain they could join Israel at the outset.

The next day, October 4, the prime minister met Dayan in Jerusalem and authorized him to continue operational plans for the Israeli campaign, which was to be called Operation Kadesh. Kadesh was the final stopping point of the Israelites in the Sinai wilderness on their way to the Land of Israel. The French delegation returned to Paris. Israel had a French promise to begin the supply of equipment immediately. Their military staffs would start the coordination of war plans as well.

With precious little time at his disposal, Dayan was inundated with a thousand little details, making sure that soldiers were in place, worrying that the equipment was workable, that spare parts could be found if necessary. Modern warfare was complicated, and Moshe Dayan was beginning to sense just how complicated when he appeared before the Ordnance Corps three days later, on October 7, and listened to the myriad problems. Reflecting on his frustration at how many technical problems needed to be resolved before war could begin, he asked his diary: "Where, oh where, are the good old days of the simple wars when as the hour of battle approached, the commander got on his white horse, someone blew the trumpet, and off he charged towards the enemy!"[10]

The next day, October 8, Dayan had the basic outlines of Israel's strategy in place: The goal would not be to kill as many Egyptians as possible but rather to aim at their army's collapse. As much equipment and weaponry as possible should be seized. Enemy positions would be bypassed where possible and frontal attacks waged only where necessary.

"Our units must press forward and not stop to clean up isolated enemy positions," he wrote in his diary. "There is no need to fear that Egyptian units who are bypassed will launch a counter-attack or cut our supply lines. We should avoid analogies whereby Egyptian units would be expected to behave as European armies would in similar circumstances."[11]

Israel's dilemma over how to deal with Arab terror worsened. On October 4, five workers traveling to the potash plant at Sedom were killed in an ambush. Dayan prepared to mount a reprisal raid but Ben-Gurion scrubbed the plan, arguing that it was better to appear less aggressive to make sure the Egyptians were caught off-guard by Operation Kadesh.

The Arabs would take this for weakness, Dayan argued. He appeared correct when five days later two Israeli farm laborers were murdered by raiders from Jordan.

Ben-Gurion's temporary moderation was put aside and on the night of October 10 the IDF launched a major attack on the Jordanian Arab Legion police fort near the frontier town of Kalkilya. Hastily planned, the assault on the fort led to the loss of eighteen Israeli lives, including eight officers, and another fifty wounded, among them fourteen officers. The assault unit came under heavy Jordanian attack on its way home and had to be extricated by other forces. In the postmortem Dayan exchanged bitter words with Ariel Sharon, commander of the operation, over what went wrong. Both men accused the other of mistakes. Dayan felt that Sharon had unwisely ordered his men deep into Jordanian territory without adequate provision for their safe return; Sharon contended that Dayan, by not giving his approval to some of Sharon's proposals, had kept the paratroopers from taking control of all the key points around Kalkilya.[12] During that same review, Dayan asserted that such raids no longer had any value. To his diary, he confided that "it is clear to all of us that we have reached the end of the chapter of night reprisal actions."[13] He believed that the IDF had lost the element of surprise, that after every murder committed in Israel the Arabs knew they would be targeted for retaliatory action—and so they prepared themselves properly, inflicting heavy damage on the Israeli units.

The Kalkilya reprisal raid may have convinced the Arabs that Israel would not take terrorist attacks lying down; but politically it had the immediate negative effect of worsening Israel's relations with Great Britain, allied as it was with Jordan, at a crucial point in the planning for the forthcoming war in the south.

By mid-October the Israelis could still not be sure that Operation Kadesh would go forward. Ben-Gurion had sent a cable to French prime minister Guy Mollet, asking for further talks in Paris. Before Mollet received the Ben-Gurion cable, he sent one of his own on the evening of October 18, with a French invitation for secret Israeli-French-British talks in Paris. Ben-Gurion decided that he would fly to Paris in a few days, taking Dayan and Peres along.

Meanwhile, on October 20 the British and French met. The British indicated their readiness for joint action against Egypt. The British presented the French with a two-paragraph statement that provided for Anglo-French intervention after the Egyptian and Israeli fighting reached the canal area. The British promised that they would not aid Egypt if war broke out between Israel and Egypt. The French were urged to pass the statement on to the Israelis. Ben-Gurion and Dayan learned of this remarkable document on the eve of their Paris journey. To the Israeli prime minister, the British proposal, while a certain step forward in that Britain was now on board, was still a recipe for disaster for Israel: The Jewish state would have been branded the aggressor, Great Britain and France, saviors. Dayan was more understanding of the British. Britain and France, he told Ben-Gurion, did not need Israel to knock out the Egyptian air force; they had five hundred planes and could accomplish that on their own. What they did need was Israel to provide the pretext for their entry into the war. This meant that Israel had some leverage with both countries. Why not exploit that leverage? Passing up the British proposal was to miss a once-in-a-lifetime chance. As long as the French used their air force to protect Tel Aviv and Haifa, Israel could afford to open hostilities in the knowledge that the French and British would join within a few days and seize the canal zone. Ben-Gurion remained unconvinced.

The French sent a plane for the Israeli delegation; it arrived in Tel Aviv on Sunday morning, October 21. To Dayan's surprise, two members from the earlier French delegation showed up at his office at 11:00 A.M. to negotiate the "scenario," the French phrase in which Israel would open hostilities, giving the French a pretext for their entry. Dayan asked them if France would employ its air force within the first twenty-four hours if Israeli cities were bombed. The French said no, for that would spoil the "scenario." Dayan grew irate. He could not stand the way the French kept using the word "scenario" nor could he tolerate the ease with which the French were prepared for the Israelis to do the hard work and for the French and British to come in later and kick them out. An infuriated Dayan lashed out at them: If Israel fought Egypt alone, that was one thing; Israel would then be forced to defend its cities as best as it could. If there was a joint effort, however, and Israeli planes were unable to defend Israeli cities (because they were away laying the groundwork for the Anglo-French assault on the canal zone), it was not acceptable that Israel's partners would remain aloof simply to protect the "scenario." Eventually, the French proposed stationing some French air squadrons in Israel in case Israeli cities needed defending.

With that compromise, Dayan and Ben-Gurion embarked that evening on their secret journey. Mordechai Bar-On, head of Dayan's bureau, went along. Dayan made sure to tell no one what he was up to. The forthcoming meetings at Sèvres were so sensitive that for years Dayan did not refer to them. (Even when he published his *Diary of the Sinai Campaign 1956* in 1966, he omitted mention of the sessions. The diary's chronology awkwardly jumped from October 21 to October 25, with Dayan noting only that there had been "numerous . . . contacts and clarifications with people overseas." In 1976, when he published his memoirs, *Story of My Life*, Dayan finally wrote about Sèvres at length.)

The car taking the Israeli delegation to Lod Airport near Tel Aviv had blinds drawn over the windows. In the car behind were the two French officials. During the trip to Lod, Dayan told Ben-Gurion of the visit of the two Frenchmen and that they were urging Israel to agree to the British plan. When he heard this, Ben-Gurion wanted to scrub the flight. Standing near the plane, the prime minister turned to the two Frenchmen and said: "If you are thinking of pressing the British proposals upon us, the only useful thing about this trip will be the opportunity to meet your prime minister." Deplaning in France, Dayan wore dark glasses, Ben-Gurion a wide-brimmed hat; they stepped into cars without official markings and were whisked away. Ben-Gurion and an aide stayed at a villa in Sèvres, on the outskirts of Paris. Dayan, Peres, and Bar-On stayed in the Reynolds Hotel in Paris, registering under assumed names. Though he was still wearing dark glasses, trying to conceal who he was, Dayan could not quite discard his true identity. He signed the register "Moshe Dya"; this was not exactly a perfect cover.

The French-Israeli talks were held at the Sèvres villa, the home of an important French family close to Defense Minister Bourges-Maunoury. After they rested a few hours, the first meeting began at 4:00 P.M. Representing the French were Prime Minister Mollet, Foreign Minister Pineau, and Bourges-Maunoury; Ben-Gurion, Dayan, and Peres represented the Israeli side. For the next three hours the men talked, with Ben-Gurion trying to remain at the general level and the French pressing to take up the proposed military campaign. Injecting a note of urgency, the French suggested that every day that Israel and France delayed made Nasser stronger and tightened his links with the Soviets. France could not keep its army on full alert much longer: Either the attack would start in a few days, or France would be forced to withdraw. Bourges-Maunoury reiterated France's pledge to have her warships patrol Israel's coastline and have French air squadrons stationed in Israel. Shimon Peres put forward an idea. He had mentioned it to Ben-Gurion but had his backing only for raising the idea, nothing more. Israel would send an Israeli vessel from Haifa to Port Said, which the Egyptians would undoubtedly stop and prevent from going through the canal. This could provide a good pretext for war. The French demurred, saying that it was too late to bring up new ideas. That would only give the British further reason to delay, or shelve the whole affair.

Later the British leadership joined in. Selwyn Lloyd, Great Britain's foreign minister, arrived, meeting at first with the French delegation for a briefing. The French returned to the Israelis without the British. An atmosphere of deadlock haunted the negotiating table. Ben-Gurion was still unwilling to agree to the British plan and talked disconsolately of leaving for Israel the following morning. The French, equally disheartened, spoke of disbanding their Suez-ready units by the end of the week. Perhaps hoping for a miracle, French foreign minister Pineau read out the British plan once again, this time in more detail than stated on earlier occasions: Israel would start military action against Egypt and reach the canal within forty-eight hours. Sometime during those forty-eight hours an Anglo-French ultimatum would be given to Egypt and Israel insisting on their withdrawal from the canal area; if Egypt rejected the ultimatum, the Anglo-French operation would be undertaken with the aim of capturing the canal zone and overthrowing Egypt's Nasser. Britain would bomb Egyptian airfields. Only if Israel attacked Jordan would the British come to Jordan's rescue.

That evening, representatives of the three countries—Israel, France, and Britain—met together for the first time. The talks lasted until midnight. Lloyd reiterated that the British were prepared for military action along the lines of the Anglo-French plan. Ben-Gurion noted that he had already said no to the plan outlined by Lloyd: It had too many disadvantages for Israel. His country would be labeled an aggressor, and its cities might be bombed by Egypt. Israel simply would not act preemptively against Egypt.

DAYAN TOOK the floor to note that Ben-Gurion had said what Israel would not do. He wanted to talk about what Israel would do. Israel was prepared to launch a reprisal action near the canal against Egypt as a way of getting the war started. The action could occur at 5:00 P.M.; the British and French could then issue a demand that evening that the Egyptians evacuate their forces from the canal zone and demand of Israel that it not advance beyond the canal. Israel, said Dayan, could accept that kind of demand from Britain and France. If Egypt refused, British and French air units would begin bombing Egyptian airfields the next morning.

If accepted by the parties around the negotiating table, Dayan's bold idea would mean that Kadesh and Musketeer could be carried out. The idea came from Dayan because that was the kind of military man he was, more a strategist than a foot soldier, more able to see the grand design than to worry about the nitty-gritty. He no longer had the patience or interest in the tiny details of soldiering. Once, he was so fascinated and preoccupied with those details that he composed an entire field manual on the subject. Now, he thought largely of how to start a war—and how to end it. Always his ideas had an element of surprise and deceit, always they were designed to sow confusion among the enemy.

Dayan was almost as concerned about how Ben-Gurion would react as the French and British. "I did not dare glance at Ben-Gurion. . . . I thought he would jump out of his skin. But he restrained his anger, though not his squirming, and all I heard was the scraping of his chair."[14] He had not broached the idea with Ben-Gurion in private. Perhaps that was just as well. Lukewarm about the entire affair, the prime minister might have discouraged Dayan from raising it. The French could not quite believe that Dayan was speaking on his own. "I know how you fellows work," Christian Pineau sneered at Dayan.

The truth was that Ben-Gurion was still not wholly on board. He kept referring to the idea as "Dayan's plan," as if to show that he wanted to keep some distance from it. Significantly, Britain's Lloyd did not rule out the reprisal raid idea, urging that it must be a genuine act of war, and not some small-scale action. Only in that way would the British ultimatum seem justified and Britain not appear an aggressor. The Israeli chief of staff assured him that a definite act of war would take place. Lloyd then mentioned that perhaps the time could be shortened between the British ultimatum and Britain's taking up arms: The British could give their ultimatum the following morning and twelve hours later take action (i.e., thirty-six hours after Israel's paratroop raids began). Ultimately, Ben-Gurion and Lloyd, though stating extreme positions at the outset, had reached the beginnings of a compromise by midnight. Lloyd then left for London to convey the new "Dayan plan" to Prime Minister Anthony Eden. Elated at the prospect of a breakthrough, Dayan phoned Rahel Rabinovitch and gleefully told her: "It's very secret and it's wonderful. I have a fantastic plan."[15]

Dayan's "fantastic" plan called for dropping a paratroop battalion at the Mitla Pass at dusk. He had selected Mitla because it was close enough to the Suez Canal (thirty miles) for the British to say that the canal had been endangered and far enough away from the massive Egyptian troop concentrations elsewhere in Sinai for the paratroopers not to be at grave risk. During the thirty-six hours before Britain and France joined in the fray, the IDF would do little other than have a brigade rush to the Mitla to rescue the paratroopers if need be. Deploying a paratrooper battalion, a mechanized brigade, and air squadrons, Israel would meet the British test of committing a "real act of war." The Mitla drop would confuse the Egyptians, who would have to decide, with an Israeli brigade in central Sinai and paratroops at Mitla, whether Israel intended a full war. Once it became clear that Egypt had mistakenly regarded the paratroop drop merely as a reprisal raid, and had responded only phlegmatically, the IDF could then launch its major three-pronged ground attack into Sinai. Dayan assumed the Egyptians would react sluggishly and uncertainly. But if they did not, under the worst circumstances, the Mitla paratroopers could be evacuated and no one would think that anything other than a reprisal raid had occurred. Only Dayan could have gotten away with such a plan. Any other member of the General Staff would have been berated for proposing such a risky idea.

At first the British were skeptical. Britain's Lloyd sent word to the French that he could not agree to "Dayan's plan"; it was not a full-scale act of war and it called for too little time between the start of the operation and the Anglo-French attack on Egyptian airfields (the British wanted forty-eight hours lest their ultimatum seem to lack credibility). This was an improvement from Britain's earlier wish to intercede only after Israel reached the canal in three or four days. But Ben-Gurion insisted that the gap be only twenty-four hours.

As Pineau planned to leave for London, Ben-Gurion had still not made up his mind whether to back the Suez campaign. Disappointed by the meetings thus far, the Israeli leader seemed displeased that both Britain and France still thought of Israel as a junior partner. Dayan could not decide whether Ben-Gurion was sincerely fearful of threats to Israeli cities, or whether he was seeking a reasonable excuse to back out of the plan on other grounds. Dayan sought to persuade Ben-Gurion to adopt his plan: There was no reason to fear what might happen during the thirty-six hours before the British joined in, he said. Ben-Gurion countered that Dayan's plan to use only a limited number of paratroopers behind enemy lines might backfire, they might be cut off, as had happened to the blocking unit at Kalkilya two weeks earlier. The Israeli public's reaction to the heavy casualties suffered in the Kalkilya raid did not augur well for what would happen if the paratroop unit also became cut off, and suffered many casualties. True, Dayan said, the public was grieved over Kalkilya, but more because it had not curbed Arab terrorism than because of the heavy losses. Operation Kadesh had the virtue of seeking to eliminate Arab terror once and for all.

With Pineau in London, Dayan and Peres tried to take the evening off. They visited a Montmartre striptease joint, but Dayan found it difficult to concentrate on the women on stage. They went to a bistro for coffee and upon departing heard someone say in excellent Hebrew: "Hey, boys, did you see who just passed? Moshe Dayan and Shimon Peres. I wonder what's up? It must be something secret, for Dayan is hiding behind dark glasses." So much for secrecy. Returning to his hotel, Dayan focused on Ben-Gurion, who still worried about the lack of American support for the plan. The prime minister had even suggested that the plotters delay their war until after the American presidential elections and then try to secure agreement from the new American president. Ben-Gurion also worried whether Britain would remain loyal to Israel, or rush to help Jordan and Iraq, and whether Egypt would bomb Israeli cities.

On October 24, at 11:30 A.M., Ben-Gurion summoned Dayan and Peres for another round of consultations. The prime minister was sitting in the garden of his house. He asked Dayan to go over his plan. The chief of staff searched for a piece of paper. Peres pulled out a cigarette pack and handed it to Dayan. On it, Dayan drew the triangular-shaped Sinai Peninsula. He marked it with three arrows: The center one pointed west, through the middle of Sinai (for the paratroopers heading for Mitla and the mechanized brigade that would link up with it); a parallel arrow above it indicated the movement of other armor through northern Sinai; a third arrow suggested the advance southward of the mobile force that would take Sharm el-Sheikh. Dayan was glad he did not have an actual map. The improvised one on the cigarette box could not have shown the mountains, sand dunes, or wadis—making the plan looking easy to implement. Dayan was encouraged at Ben-Gurion's interest. The prime minister took out his own piece of paper with questions he had written specifically for this meeting, questions largely about what Britain and France might do under various circumstances and one about how Israel could assure the world that it had no interest in territorial expansion. Dayan felt increasing confidence that Ben-Gurion would back the plan. He responded that D-Day would be 5:00 P.M. Monday, October 29. The British and French would have their D-Day Wednesday at dawn when they would begin bombing Egyptians airfields. Finally, as the consultations were ending around 2:00 P.M., Ben-Gurion acknowledged, "Moshe's plan is good. It saves lives."

At 4:00 P.M. Pineau returned from London, and announced that British representatives would soon be arriving. The British were still demanding a "full-scale act of war" but they were now prepared to advance the timetable and begin fighting at 4:00 A.M. on Wednesday; in other words, a gap of thirty-six hours. When the British arrived, they gathered around a circular table to hear, not "Dayan's plan," but the same idea now proposed as Israel's plan. By 7:00 P.M. a draft agreement was typed: It called for Israel to launch a "large-scale attack" during the afternoon of October 29. The next day Britain and France would send appeals (the word ultimatum was not used) to Egypt and Israel to withdraw to ten miles from the canal. If after twelve hours, either government did not respond to the appeal, Anglo-French forces might "take the necessary measures" to assure the demands were met. If Egypt said no, the Anglo-French force would attack Egyptian forces early Wednesday morning. Ben-Gurion looked over the draft, and put it in the inside pocket of his jacket. Dayan left the conference room and sent a "Most Immediate" signal to General Headquarters in Tel Aviv. "Good prospects for Operation Kadesh soonest. Mobilize units immediately. Ensure secrecy in mobilization. Activate deception to produce impression that mobilization aimed against Jordan because of entry of Iraqi forces. Leaving midnight tonight, arriving tomorrow morning."

On the plane back home, Dayan wrote a series of orders and guidelines for the General Staff and field commands to be issued soon after his arrival. He returned to Israel at midday October 25 and drove directly to General Staff headquarters. He had changed three important points in Israeli military plans. Instead of indicating that the aim of the war was "destroying the forces of the enemy," he now made it "to confound the military array of the Egyptian forces and bring about their collapse." Others on the General Staff favored using massive firepower to destroy as many Egyptian soldiers as possible. Dayan did not. He thought slaughtering Egyptians counterproductive; it would harm the possibility of future rapprochement between the two countries. Capturing crossroads would be sufficient to defeat the enemy. No, said the others, that would only cause the Egyptians to fight elsewhere. Dayan had his way.

He changed the site where the war would start: Instead of beginning with the capture of northern Sinai, the operation would start on the Nakhl-Mitla axis with the paratroop drop at Mitla. The third change affected the use of the Israeli air force. The campaign had originally called for Israel to open with an Israeli air attack, but now the air force would only carry the paratroopers to the drop point and maintain a state of alert in its airfields.

Only a handful of Israelis knew of the existence of the Sèvres conference, among them Foreign Minister Golda Meir and Finance Minister Levi Eshkol. Now Dayan would have to widen the net a bit. When

Dayan convened the General Staff to announce the imminent campaign that evening, he asked northern front commander Yitzhak Rabin and central front commander Zvi Tsur to leave the room saying that "we are going to be engaged in a war with Egypt."[16]

Then to those remaining he said, "This plan is very simple. We will begin with the Mitla. We will drop there and then we'll see. If it goes OK with the French, fine. If not, then the paratroopers will come back, and the Egyptians will think it is a retaliatory raid."

Without going into great detail about Israel's collusion, Dayan said simply that Britain and France might attack Egypt. If they did, "We should behave like the cyclist who is riding uphill when a truck chances by and he grabs hold. We should get what help we can, hanging on to their vehicle and exploiting its movement as much as possible, and only when our routes fork should we break off and proceed along our separate way with our own force alone."[17]

He then set in high gear the mobilizing of one hundred thousand men. Dayan ordered the intelligence branch to accelerate rumors that Iraqi troops had moved into Jordan and to leak word that Israel was about to attack Jordan. Israeli troops were moved openly to the northern and eastern borders facing Syria and Jordan. The combat units who would fight the real war in the south were moved clandestinely to their staging points. Some soldiers were given leaves so that on the Jewish sabbath of Saturday, they would be conspicuously at home. Bolstering Israel's confidence was the knowledge that its ground and air forces had nearly doubled their strength in the final days before Sinai. There was the good news from Israeli intelligence that, of the one hundred new MiG fighters in Egypt, only thirty were operational; of the fifty Ilyushin bombers, only twelve were in use; of two hundred new Soviet tanks in Egyptian hands, only fifty were in service. Most of the pilots and tank crews who had been assigned to man the new weapons were still in Soviet training schools. Still, Egypt could field one hundred thousand troops. On the plus side for Israel, however, was an undeniable fact, culled from a variety of Israeli reprisal raids: The Egyptians had always run and panicked if caught by surprise.

Israel's plan to go to war went before the cabinet on Friday, October 26. When Dayan saw how easy it had been for Ben-Gurion to win the cabinet's approval on this day, he thought back to December 1955, and only wished the prime minister had tried harder then to seek cabinet approval for war against Egypt. Had Israel acted on its own then to open the Straits of Tiran, Dayan believed, it might have avoided a year of Arab terror.

THE OBJECT of the war that Israel was about to launch was to neutralize the Egyptian threat and put a stop to the fedayeen attacks from the Gaza Strip. It was also designed to secure control of Sharm el-Sheikh in order to break the Egyptian blockade of the Gulf of 'Aqaba. Dayan set a time limit of seven to ten days for finishing the Sinai campaign.

The battlefield on which the war would occur was twenty-four thousand square miles of vast desert, mostly empty. It was inhabited by forty thousand bedouin nomads and had just a scattering of small villages. The northern part was filled with meandering sand dunes; the south had some impassable mountain ranges with peaks rising to nine thousand feet. The Mitla and Gidi passes, which crossed the Sinai from north to south, were the main thoroughfares in the southern Sinai.

Dayan's mood on Monday, October 29, the day Israel went to war, was, as Rahel Rabinovitch noted, "euphoric." As was her frequent habit, she had come to Tel Aviv to see him. They had an early lunch. As she got into a taxi for the trip home, he sounded somewhat more on edge: "Go right back home." She thought the "order" strange, coming from him. But she complied. She sensed a special mood in him. "He was like somebody who is in thin air."[18]

Dayan still viewed the infantry as the major factor in the battlefield, not the tank. Having won that debate on September 1, he had wanted the infantry to form the breakthrough units, using half-tracks and other vehicles. He still had little confidence that the tanks could reach the front on chains. It had been Dayan's plan to have Uri Ben-Ari's Seventh Brigade use tank transporters from Beersheba to the frontier and from there move in the wake of the infantry. Ben-Ari told southern front commander Assaf Simhoni that this made no sense. Simhoni persuaded Dayan. Shortly before the war, Dayan permitted the tanks to concentrate on the frontier, ready to move out at once.

Final preparations took place at 1:30 P.M., two hours before the scheduled offensive, when Israeli Mustangs flew over Sinai and cut the overhead phone lines using their propellers and wings while flying only four yards from the ground. At 3:30 P.M., a squadron of sixteen Israeli Dakota transport planes crossed the Negev frontier and slid under the Egyptian radar. Then they rose to 1,500 feet—parachute jumping height—just two minutes before 395 soldiers from Ariel Sharon's 202nd Paratroop Brigade leaped from the planes. At 4:59 P.M. they hit the ground at the Parker Memorial near the Mitla Pass. Operation Kadesh had begun. They had come down on a spot largely free of Egyptian forces. The forty-five thousand Egyptian soldiers in the Sinai were deployed far away.

By 7:30 P.M. the Israeli paratroopers had reached positions a mile from the eastern approaches to the Mitla and began to dig in. That morning Dayan had met with Ben-Gurion and worked out with him what the IDF spokesman would announce. Dayan insisted that it should be firm and threatening but not reveal Israel's true intentions. The announcement was issued at 9:00 P.M. and noted that "the IDF entered and engaged fedayeen units in Ras el-Nakeb and Kuntilla and seized positions west of the Nakhl crossroads in the vicinity of the Suez Canal. The action follows the Egyptian military assaults on Israeli transport on land and sea, designed to cause destruction and the denial of peaceful life to Israel's citizens." The statement was designed to inform the world that Israel's action in the Sinai was another retaliatory raid, nothing more. The ruse worked better than expected. Nasser could not figure out what the Israelis were doing in a place where there were so few Egyptians. Why would they want to fight against sand dunes?

Meanwhile, that same night the other battalion of Sharon's brigade grouped itself on the Jordanian frontier as a decoy. It then suddenly picked up stakes and in nine hours crossed sixty-five miles of the Negev desert where it reached the Israeli frontier near Kuntilla in Egypt. Learning that an Israeli battalion had crossed over into Egypt, the Egyptian soldiers began to scatter. Thrusting further into the Sinai, the Israeli column reached the Thamad stronghold, where it defeated the enemy after only forty minutes of fighting.

By that point Sharon's battalion had only two out of thirteen tanks operable, reinforcing Dayan's fears that tanks would have a hard time in the soft sands of the desert. Determined to reach the Mitla Pass as quickly as possible, Sharon left the disabled equipment behind. Next, his soldiers defeated the Egyptians in a twenty-minute battle at Nakhl, eventually linking up with their comrades-in-arms at the Mitla. While Sharon's men were moving forward, elsewhere along the front, the Fourth Brigade was taking Nakeb that evening and the crossroads of Kusseima the next morning.

Leaving Brig. Gen. Meir Amit, the deputy chief of staff, back at headquarters to handle the administrative side of the war, Dayan arrived at Kusseima to mingle with the troops. This was to be characteristic of him throughout the war. He had little to do with the administrative side of the war. He preferred it that way. He wanted to be in the field, to find out how things were progressing. He wanted to be able to change course on the spot, not to have to hear secondhand dispatches far from the scene. Staying in Tel Aviv, he would be under the thumb of Ben-Gurion and the other politicians. They would be telling him what to do, second-guessing him all the time. Most of all, he believed that by being on the battlefield, he could influence the troops, let them know that the chief of staff was around and cared about them.

His style played havoc with the staff in headquarters. Yehoshua Gavish, head of operations during the war, noted caustically that Ben-Gurion could not find Dayan during the five days of the war. "We ran the war without a chief of staff," Gavish noted. "We couldn't get him on the radio."[19]

Being in the field made Dayan more glamorous, more of a celebrity. He placed himself in situations that reporters loved to cover. He would have been less interesting behind a desk than he was ducking bullets with the troops. Dayan instinctively understood that if things went well in the field, and he was there, the press would turn him into the celebrity of the war. He was right.

He gave very few orders during the war itself, but he was ubiquitous, driving around in what he called the "chief of staff's unit," a six-wheel command car escorted by another with signals equipment. When luck was with him, he was able to go into battle with the troops, usually behind the first battalion. When he joined Israeli soldiers heading toward El Arish, Chaim Laskov, the division commander, was actually behind Dayan in the convoy.

Dayan did not care that his behavior was causing chaos in headquarters. To his diary he wrote: "I returned to GHQ command post each night, but of course my non-appearance during the day makes things difficult and upsets the orderly organization of the work. In the field there is a radio transmitter with me all the time and I am in constant contact with GHQ, but my staff officers complain that this is not enough. They may be right, but I am unable, or unwilling, to behave otherwise."[20]

Afterward, Dayan never quarreled with any of the decisions Amit was forced to make on his own. Amit did not find the situation easy. Amit explained: "I wouldn't say he was the easiest person to work with because of all his edges. You had to read his intentions ahead of time and operate accordingly. You had to develop a sixth sense from that, because he didn't have patience to explain to you. You had to understand it either from past experience or from all kinds of facts and bits and hints."[21]

THE BEGINNING of the war was going well. Dayan reached a field telephone and called to Rahel. His voice was filled with excitement. "If only the English bastards will get in as they promised, then this is going to be fantastic."[22]

Dayan had predicted that the Egyptians would flee once the Israeli war machine moved forward and he was proven correct. He had hoped that it would be Degania all over again, that upon hearing the noise of the tin can the Arabs would scatter. They did.

On the second evening of the war, Dayan visited Yael at an IDF training camp. He promised her a trip to the Sinai on her first leave and told her to "be a good soldier." Bad news followed: The British air attack on the Egyptian airfields—scheduled for dawn the next day, Wednesday—was postponed until the evening. In bed with the flu in Tel Aviv, Ben-Gurion was furious and anxious. He feared for the paratroopers holding the Mitla. Should he withdraw them? The Kalkilya raid echoed in his mind. He had no wish for these paratroopers to be similarly trapped. The chief of staff visited and brought some good news. Sharon's armored column had trekked and fought their way for twenty-eight hours through the Sinai and had now joined up with the paratroopers at Mitla.

What about the British? Ben-Gurion asked. Were they going to fulfill their promise?

Dayan doubted that the British and French would let Israel down, but even if they did, Ben-Gurion must permit Israel's war plans to continue unaltered. Worried, the prime minister nodded his head. The phone call from French prime minister Guy Mollet, assuring him that the delayed air attack would begin definitely the next evening, had encouraged the prime minister.

That same Tuesday evening, Britain and France issued an ultimatum to both Israel and Egypt to cease fighting and withdraw to a distance of ten miles from the Suez Canal on either side. Failure to comply within twelve hours would lead Britain and France to intervene militarily. Israel agreed. Nasser did not. At the same time American president Dwight Eisenhower was cabling Ben-Gurion to withdraw Israeli troops. The Israelis ignored the cable. Washington sought an emergency session of the United Nations Security Council; when it met, an American-sponsored resolution calling for a cease-fire and the withdrawal of Israeli troops from the Sinai was introduced. Britain and France later vetoed the American resolution.

The twelve-hour ultimatum was over Wednesday morning; but still throughout that Wednesday, the British and French did not bomb Egyptian airfields. The collusion plan had called for Israel to fight alone throughout Monday evening and Tuesday; then, thirty-six hours after the Israelis began the war, the British were supposed to have bombed the Egyptian air force and other installations—by Wednesday morning. In fact it took forty-eight hours. The planes that were due to take off from Cyprus on the bombing missions were mysteriously delayed, forcing

Israel to fight some of its major battles under threat of the Egyptian warplanes. Only at 7:00 P.M. on Wednesday, fourteen hours behind schedule, did the British and French planes finally bomb Egyptian airfields.

Despite the failure of the British and French to keep to schedule, Dayan's war machine fared very well. The only exception was Abu Agheila. The task force comprising the Fourth and Tenth infantry brigades and the Seventh Armored Brigade had headed for Abu Agheila, fifteen miles west of the Israeli frontier. Upon arriving they met fierce resistance. Toward the end of Monday evening the Fourth Infantry Brigade was to have taken Kusseima, but by dawn it was still bogged down with fighting. The slow progress disappointed the overall commander of the Sinai force, Brig. Gen. Assaf Simhoni. He approached Dayan to ask if he could rescue the Fourth. Dayan felt obliged not to reveal the collusion plans to Simhoni. The chief of staff ordered him to stay put, saying only that Israel faced certain political constraints. "For me, as a general, that's stupid," Simhoni replied, boiling with anger. Violating Dayan's orders, Simhoni went ahead and on Tuesday morning ordered the Seventh Brigade to rescue the Fourth and to mop up the resistance at Kusseima. Simhoni's "rescue" of the Fourth was superfluous. To Dayan, it was essential to preserve the myth that Israel was still engaged in nothing more than a reprisal raid and to keep large numbers of Israeli tanks from the Sinai arena until the British and French began their part of the mission. Simhoni should not have moved his tanks until Wednesday, by which time the full collusion plan would have been implemented.

Arriving at his command post Tuesday morning, Dayan learned that Israeli armor was heavily involved in Sinai. The action no longer could be described as a mere retaliatory raid. Furious, Dayan finally explained why he had wanted him to stay put until Wednesday. Replying, Simhoni asserted that he, as a commander, could not permit himself to be dependent upon some other country's forces entering the battle. Simhoni's violation of orders posed a severe problem for Moshe Dayan. Should he have the tanks withdrawn? Was it still possible to preserve the myth of the reprisal raid? If Israel's real game was discovered too early, the lives of the 395 men at the Mitla Pass might be in much greater danger.

Despite the risk, Dayan did not feel he could give orders for his soldiers to retreat. He wrote in his diary, "I could not avoid a sympathetic feeling over the hastening of the brigade into combat even before they were required. Better to be engaged in restraining the noble stallion than in prodding the mule."[23] Unwilling to restrain noble stallions, Dayan resignedly left the armored brigade in Sinai, fully aware that its presence might encourage the Egyptians to think Israel was bent on full-scale war.

He ordered to send his three brigades—the Seventh, Fourth, and Tenth—against the Egyptians frontally from east to west along the the Abu Agheila–Um Katef line.

ON WEDNESDAY at 7:00 A.M. Dayan was munching on tomatoes and cucumbers at a base. Ezer Weizman, commander of an air base at the time, came upon the chief of staff heading for a Piper Cub. Weizman asked him where he was going. To the Mitla Pass, said the chief of staff. Weizman thought to himself that "everything is hanging by a hair, and the chief of staff wants to fly to the Mitla?"

Somewhat taken back, Weizman told his brother-in-law, "My good man, you're not flying to any Mitla! I've just come back from there, and there are MiGs hovering around. If you want to, give us the order to attack the Egyptians from the air. I can understand that. But you have no business flying there."

They argued, and eventually compromised: Weizman would fly Dayan to Abu Agheila, where a battle was raging. Pressure had been mounting in the United Nations for a cease-fire and Dayan was eager to have Israeli troops take Um Katef and the nearby Um Shihan (part of the Abu Agheila stronghold) as quickly as possible. Then Israeli forces could break through into Sinai on the central sector. Though Israeli forces had advanced into Sinai elsewhere, they were moving on dirt tracks; by taking Um Katef, they could move on asphalt road, which would be far better for moving supply convoys.

The battles for Um Katef and Abu Agheila did not go well. Assaults were not coordinated properly, as overeager officers rushed enemy defenses in half-tracks before support tanks could arrive. Dayan acknowledged that he was partly at fault by insisting that the attacks be carried out hastily. At Abu Agheila, the infantry inched along, taking casualties under heavy artillery fire. By early afternoon Dayan ordered one commander to launch an attack in the Abu Agheila region before darkness, but by 6:00 P.M. the Israelis had made little progress. Dayan fired the commander on the spot.[24] Dayan replaced him, as he put it, "with an officer who would charge into hellfire." An hour later Abu Agheila was in Israeli hands.

At Abu Agheila Dayan learned the hard way that his old theory of mobility—of relying upon jeeps and trucks filled with soldiers—was of little use when confronting an enemy firmly dug in at a main crossroads. The Israeli breakthrough came as a result of the tanks' firepower.

Even without the British and French joining the battle on time, the Seventh Brigade fought and won major armored battles, seizing Abu

Agheila, the nearby Ruweifa Dam, Bir Hasanah, Jebel Livni, and Bir Hammah, in the process moving closer and closer to the Mitla Pass. After heavy fighting, Israeli forces had secured control of the three southern routes through the Sinai: Nakhl-Mitla, Jebel Livni, and the southwesterly route through Bir Hasanah.

THE MOST controversial battle of the war occurred that same day at the Mitla Pass. From the moment Ariel Sharon had linked up with the paratroopers at Mitla, he barraged the General Staff with pleas to let him engage the nearby Egyptians. Dayan answered with an emphatic no. Such an assault was not part of Sharon's orders. To make sure his orders were understood and obeyed, the chief of staff sent Lt. Col. Rehavam Ze'evi, chief staff officer of the central command, in a special plane to meet with Sharon at the Mitla. After the two men talked, Ze'evi agreed that Sharon could send a reconnaissance patrol into the Mitla on condition that it not engage the enemy.

According to Dayan, Sharon did not put together a patrol: He organized a fully equipped combat unit.

Moving forward into the Mitla, the "patrol" came under fire from Egyptians on both sides of the pass. Assuming that Egyptian resistance would not increase, Sharon's troops moved forward. A bitter seven-hour battle ensued. The Israelis captured the pass, killing 150 Egyptians, but 38 Israelis died and another 120 were wounded.

Despite the eventual capture of the pass, Dayan thought the bloody exercise a disaster. To Dayan, it might have been justified if the brigade's mission had been to reach the Suez Canal. Since its orders were to move on to Sharm el-Sheikh, but avoid getting any closer to the canal, the Mitla could easily have been bypassed.

As in the case of Simhoni, Dayan had trouble coming down too harshly on Ariel Sharon. So he reported in his *Diary of the Sinai Campaign 1956*. Was not this one more example of having to restrain the noble stallion? Though angry that his orders had been disobeyed, the chief of staff empathized with Sharon's decision to attack, recalling how, as a battalion commander in June 1948, he himself had decided to take Lod against the orders and better judgment of his superiors. Sharon was merely practicing what Dayan had preached all along: Only the commander on the spot could decide what was best for his men and for the conduct of the war in his arena. What annoyed Dayan the most was not the battle that had ensued but the fact that he had been misled into believing that only a patrol was being sent. He was disappointed that the paratroopers did not bring the issue of whether to attack to him directly. The chief of staff blamed the paratroopers for faulty judgment in misunderstanding the size of the Egyptian force they had to face. It was inconceivable, though, that Dayan could bring himself to punish those "noble stallions."

An investigation was held. Dayan had appointed Maj. Gen. Chaim Laskov, head of the Armored Corps, to direct the probe. Under questioning, Sharon insisted that he had been operating with proper authority and that Ze'evi had in fact not limited the size of the patrol. Sharon argued that under any circumstances he would have had to move his force to a more secure spot; remaining at the eastern end of the Mitla was becoming dangerous. The battle had developed as it had, not according to the patrol's plan, but because the patrol had been forced to rescue Israeli soldiers who had become trapped. Dayan was not convinced by this argument, and brought Sharon before Ben-Gurion as the final arbiter. The prime minister asked Sharon whether he did not think that the Mitla operation had been unnecessary. Sharon could only say, "Now, as we sit here, it is possible to think that way, but under the circumstances there was no alternative." Ben-Gurion, sensing that the controversy was too complex to settle, declined to arbitrate between the two men. Dayan chose not to charge Sharon with any offense nor did he relieve him of command of his brigade.

Other than the Abu Agheila and Mitla difficulties, the war had gone remarkably smoothly for the Israelis. By the end of Wednesday most of the Egyptian resistance had ended. Beginning that evening, the fighting focused on the northern Sinai sector as Israel attacked Rafah at the southern end of the Gaza Strip, seeking to break through to the approach to El Arish. On Thursday the United Nations General Assembly began its emergency session and adopted an American resolution calling for an immediate cease-fire. It had no effect. By 10:30 A.M. Chaim Bar-Lev's Twenty-seventh Brigade began advancing toward El Arish. Dayan was with the brigade as it moved along a tarred road through the sand dunes, encountering little opposition. Only at the El Jeradi salient, halfway to El Arish, did the brigade engage in battle lasting an hour. So taken with the skill of the unit commander was Dayan that he promoted him on the spot. With the battle over, Dayan fell asleep in the sand, only to be awakened by the ear-shattering noise of Egyptian shells falling not far away. By nightfall Thursday, Dayan and Bar-Lev's brigade reached the outskirts of El Arish.

After checking the cables that night, the chief of staff ordered the Ninth Infantry Brigade to move on to Sharm el-Sheikh and the Eleventh Infantry Brigade to capture the Gaza Strip. The following morning, Friday, at 6:00 A.M., the soldiers entered El Arish.

Egyptian troops—or so it seemed—had left the night before, leaving behind large quantities of military equipment. The Israelis, however, were handicapped by a troubling lack of intelligence. No one knew whether the Egyptians had totally abandoned the place. Having fought hard on the way, the soldiers began to relax, exploring, entering houses. Soldiers quickly surrounded Dayan, asking for autographs on their maps, ID cards, bandages, cigarette packets, and pictures of Nasser.

Dayan wanted to tour the town, perhaps to search for some antiquities. Bar-Lev tried to talk the chief of staff out of this risky adventure. When Bar-Lev realized that Dayan would not be deterred, the brigade commander offered the chief of staff a half-track. Dayan brushed the suggestion aside, asked for a command car, and went on his tour.

He returned only half an hour later, ashen faced. His driver had been shot and killed by an Egyptian sniper. "I think I'll stay here for the time being," Dayan said meekly to Bar-Lev. At 11:00 A.M., Dayan left in a Piper Cub for Tel Aviv. He asked the pilot to fly low enough so that he could watch the Israeli armored columns heading for the Suez Canal. The plane flew low as per his orders, low enough for Egyptian troops still at large outside El Arish to fire and nearly hit Dayan's plane.

Back in Tel Aviv, Dayan found Ben-Gurion recovered from the flu. The jubilant chief of staff reported on the successful Rafah and El Arish battles, adding that British naval vessels were now patrolling near Sharm el-Sheikh. An element of mistrust of the British still persisted. Dayan asked Ben-Gurion whether he thought the British navy might shell Israeli forces on the land.

"About the British [navy]," Ben-Gurion said, "I do not know, but about the British Foreign Office I am prepared to believe anything."

By Friday Israel was fast closing in on most of its objectives. Bar-Lev's Twenty-seventh Armored Brigade had completed the conquest of the central axis of Kusseima–Jebel Livni–Ismalia. Meanwhile, Israeli forces had taken the Gaza Strip.

The last Israeli task, assigned to Avraham Yoffee's Ninth Brigade, was to conquer Sharm el-Sheikh. By 5:00 A.M. Friday the brigade was on the move. Eager to bolster the Ninth Brigade, Amit wanted to move Sharon's paratroopers from the Parker Memorial to Sharm. Dayan was nowhere to be found. Confident that Dayan would support him and fearful that a cease-fire would go into effect before Sharm could be captured, Amit took it upon himself to order Sharon's men to move out. At midnight Friday a battalion of the 202nd Brigade reached Ras Sudar on the Gulf of Suez, then headed south to Sharm el-Sheikh.

After false reports arrived at headquarters in Tel Aviv proclaiming Sharm el-Sheikh in Israeli hands, Dayan lost patience and flew off on

Saturday morning, November 3, to find the Ninth Brigade. He located it still forty-five miles from Sharm; he then moved on to E-Tor on the west coast of the Sinai across from the Suez Canal.

In the early morning hours of Sunday the General Assembly again demanded that Israel, Britain, and France cease hostilities. Israel agreed on the condition that Egypt complied. The British and French were furious: If Egypt and Israel ceased fire there would be no excuse for their (Anglo-French) intervention. Both Britain and France urged Ben-Gurion to wait before agreeing to the cease-fire. The prime minister reluctantly acquiesced.

Dayan had flown to E-Tor, where he had planned to meet the Ninth Brigade to ensure it would attack Sharm that day; the brigade was not there. It was in fact still fighting its way down to Sharm from Eilat, a 250-mile trek. By this time, the paratroop battalion was heading for Sharm. Unable to commandeer a plane, Dayan, trying to catch up with the paratroopers, was forced to take ground transport. If Sharm had not yet been taken by the Ninth Brigade, he would order the paratroopers to take it alone—and he intended to be right there with the lead soldiers.

Setting off in several civilian vehicles left by the Egyptians, Dayan took a few Israelis as escorts and headed for the advancing paratroopers on the road skirting the Gulf of Suez. After thirty miles Dayan's tiny convoy began to pass thousands of Egyptian soldiers coming from the direction of Sharm el-Sheikh, withdrawing northwest toward Suez. The Egyptians looked frightened, but they were armed. They could have torn the chief of staff and his companions to shreds, but they were either too tired, too wounded, or too unimpressed with the people passing in the vehicles. At one point Dayan stood up on the open rear of his vehicle to get a better view. He ordered his men not to shoot the Egyptians. That might start a skirmish. Some of the Egyptians did not even bother to move aside: Dayan's convoy had to move around them. This time, Dayan was quite conscious of the risk he was taking.

Soon he came upon the trucks and half-tracks of the paratroop battalion. He was still racing against time, trying to place Sharm in Israeli hands before the United Nations could adopt a cease-fire resolution. To his great joy, he arrived in Sharm at 8:00 A.M. Monday, only to find that three hours earlier it had been captured by the Ninth Brigade. There had been little resistance. Shortly thereafter he found his friend Aryeh Nehemkin, one of the commanders. Dayan gazed at the Israeli soldiers and looked at the beautiful scenery, so far from home, so significant to the state of Israel.

"Look at what a crazy world this is," the chief of staff said to Nehemkin with a big smile. "Look at where we have gotten to. The two of us sitting on a beach at Sharm el-Sheikh. Two boys from Nahalal are sitting here."

Soon he found the Israeli flag flying from an Egyptian gun emplacement. He put in a call to Rahel and could not contain his enthusiasm. "I'm going to give you a country from the (Mediterranean) sea to the Jordan."[25]

It was a moment Dayan would always remember. The conquest of Sharm meant that the Egyptian blockade would be lifted. One of the main purposes of the war had been achieved. Whatever the cost, the country would now understand why Dayan had urged the government to go to war.

Yet, even as he realized the meaning of Israel's victory, Dayan could not help but worry at the danger that might be lurking from the sea. British vessels were nearby. Despite the collusion, Dayan—and Ben-Gurion too—wondered what Great Britain might do next.

Dayan took Nehemkin aside after they had finished a meal and, pointing to the water, warned him: "Don't be surprised if the English start shooting at you from the sea and try to destroy you. Get your soldiers ready. Don't let them sit in the water. They should be prepared [for a possible British attack].

"The English regret the agreement we made with them. . . . They are having second thoughts and I fear very much that they won't be content over our capturing these places. I am afraid they will try to get us out."[26]

Still, the Israelis had reason to celebrate.

A victory parade was held in Sharm at which Dayan told the Ninth Brigade: "For eight years, the Arabs headed by Egypt prepared for a new war of destruction against Israel. Their armies were equipped with modern weapons, and this summer, the blockade of our economy and of our sea and airway was tightened. The preparations of the Arab states under Egyptian command to annihilate Israel were complete. In the wake of fighting between October 29 and November 5, we crushed the Egyptian army in Sinai and assured our ships and aircraft the freedom to reach the city and port of Eilat. During this week of fighting, on land, in the air and on the sea, two Egyptian divisions and armored units supporting them were destroyed by us." He added that Israel had taken more than five thousand Egyptian soldiers prisoner in contrast to less than twenty Israeli soldiers taken by Egypt.

Yet even in the immediate afterglow of victory Dayan looked to the future. "We are still too tired to be able to evaluate the military significance of the Sinai War. We have triumphed, but we are not too drunk with victory to realize that even with the whole Sinai peninsula in our hands and the fighting over, the battle has not yet ended. We are tired, but not exhausted."

That same evening Dayan arrived at Ben-Gurion's home in Tel Aviv to report that Sharm had been captured and occupied and the Sinai campaign completed. Earlier in the day, the Soviet premier, Nikolay Bulganin, had issued vague threats to France and Britain and a very specific threat to Israel that the Soviet Union would destroy it unless their troops were removed from Egypt. Ben-Gurion was not shaken. His soldiers had fired their last shots, and achieved all their goals. The war was over.

"And I suppose you can't stand it, eh?" he asked Dayan half in jest, half in seriousness.

Israel had achieved its three major goals in the war: winning freedom of shipping for its vessels in the Gulf of 'Aqaba; ending the fedayeen terror; and neutralizing the threat of attack on Israel by Egypt, Syria, and Jordan. A large victory celebration was held after the war at the Dan Hotel in Tel Aviv. Dayan entered the party still sweaty and messy from the Sinai campaign. He was exuberant: "The whole thing worked just the way we planned it. We planned it for six days, and it took just six. We really finished up the Egyptians in four days, but it took six to occupy the whole peninsula."[27]

Only on Monday, November 5, did Operation Musketeer begin seriously with the dropping of the first British and French paratroopers at Port Said, where the following day Anglo-French seaborne forces completed the conquest. France, England, and Israel quickly came under Soviet pressure to withdraw. On November 14 the Kenesset approved a cabinet decision to withdraw from the territories captured in the Sinai pending a satisfactory accord with the United Nations Emergency Force (UNEF). Dayan did what he could to delay the withdrawal, hoping that something would prevent it altogether. He argued that the UNEF and the Security Council resolution would not stop the Egyptian army from coming back to Sinai and the Gaza Strip. The British and French evacuated the Suez Canal Zone on December 22. Such a step was painful and humiliating to the two countries whose clearly felt need to assert themselves as major political powers had faltered miserably. With none of their strategic or political objectives accomplished, England and France were left unpleasantly exposed as being totally dependent upon Washington both strategically and economically.

OPERATION KADESH had been Moshe Dayan's war, from start to finish. He had wanted it, had planned it, had personally conducted some of its most important battles. He had figured out the best way to start the fighting. He had correctly predicted—and convinced Israel's European allies—that Israel could do the job swiftly and efficiently. He had minimized the importance of armor at first; but he had adapted to the reality on the battlefield. He had displayed an ability to make decisions during wartime that, right or wrong, impressed others. Small decisions. Big decisions. He had estimated the fighting ability of his enemy correctly. Little that the Egyptians did surprised him.

The Israeli mauling of the Egyptian army was impressive. Dayan, in just six days, had taken care of a quarter of the Egyptian army: two infantry divisions, one armored brigade, and many smaller units, including several independent tank companies. Israel had killed three thousand Egyptian soldiers, captured another seven thousand, and destroyed twelve Egyptian jets. Its own losses were comparatively small: 180 soldiers dead; another 700 wounded. Its war booty was impressive: one hundred tanks (many of them heavy Soviet T-34s), nearly two hundred artillery pieces, small arms by the thousands, and enough fuel to supply Israel's civilian needs for a year.

Effrontery had been Moshe Dayan's watchword in military planning, dating back to the 1930s. It was all there for the military historians to ponder: the value of the indirect approach (Mitla); the virtue of exhausting the mission (Abu Agheila); the bulldozer tactics (the early battles in northern Sinai). Of course, not all had gone smoothly. Errors had been committed. The call-up had been too slow. Not enough civilian vehicles had been requisitioned. Assaf Simhoni's premature attack had lost the IDF the element of surprise. The Mitla paratroopers had disobeyed orders. Dayan concealed none of these things. (The question of whether Dayan should have disciplined Simhoni after the war became moot when the Sinai force commander was killed in a plane accident at the war's end. Simhoni had been preparing a staunch defense of his action at the time; he probably would not have needed it. Dayan was unlikely to take action.)

Ten years later, when Dayan published his *Diary of the Sinai Campaign 1956*, he felt confident enough in his handling of the war to admit that some mistakes had been made. He was raked over the coals for that admission. Commanders do not diviulge the things that go wrong on the battlefield, he was told. Moshe Dayan did. And in doing so, he offered the army and the country the chance to make sure those errors did not recur.

The proof of the war's success was Israel's collective ability to breathe a little easier after the years of tension and terror. For the next ten years the country enjoyed a period of unprecedented quiet along its frontiers. The Arab terror virtually ceased. The number of Israeli civilians killed by Arab terror attacks fell, often to less than ten a year, and even, in some years, to less than five. Israeli ships reached Eilat unhampered. The Arab states—Egypt, Jordan, Iraq, Syria—remained dormant. During this tranquil decade, the IDF used the time to build up its own strength. In the three years after the Suez campaign, the IDF did not carry out a single action. It was, many said, the most glorious epoch in the history of the state.

For all these reasons, Moshe Dayan emerged a hero and an international celebrity. Nowhere was this more true than in France, where it was said that he was one of that country's most popular personalities. "He is an amazing tactician," proclaimed the commander of the U.S. Marine Corps, "and I'd hate to see him on the enemy's side." Military experts heralded him as a master of mobile desert warfare. His thinking, they said, combined the genius of Montgomery and Rommel. Senior staff colleges around the world studied the Sinai campaign as a textbook case of how to deal with an enemy quickly and successfully.

HE WAS A HERO and a celebrity—and that made it hard to keep secrets about his relationships with other women. One day soon after the war an Italian journalist approached Ruth Dayan as she walked up the steps to the lobby of the Dan Hotel in Tel Aviv. The journalist said he had a personal question on a subject that everyone in the lobby was talking about. "They're all waiting for the final word, and I want to be the one to get it."

"All right, then, let's have it."

"Well," said the journalist, "I'd like to be the first to know about your divorce."

Perhaps he was confusing her with someone else, she said. She tried to shrug the newsman off with a light joke: She would ask her husband about the question. "Call me tomorrow," she said, then added quickly, "I haven't the slightest idea what you're talking about."

She in fact did not, but she did not wait long to find out. Confronting her husband that night, she got her answer. He acted surprised by her ignorance of his romances, then expressed annoyance, presumably for her ignorance. Ruth went to work the next morning as usual but thought how nice it would be to have a nervous breakdown, lock herself in a room, close the shutters, and remain there alone.

Instead, she donned dark glasses for the next four months. "Out-wardly," she wrote, "nothing had happened, and I was the wife of the conquering hero, met with joy whenever I arrived at some hopelessly muddy village. I think it was this—the realization that my double role gave so much to others—that helped me to carry on."[28]

Meanwhile Rahel, who had been close to Dayan for two years, tried not to put pressure on Dayan to divorce Ruth, but she found it hard to understand how he could stay married to her: "When I met Moshe, his feelings toward Ruth were close to hate. . . . I didn't want him to get a divorce. I was planning to arrange my life in such a way that as long as I live, I will live that way. He used to say, 'I cannot divorce her against her will because I married her when she was [very young] and she's the mother of three children. How can you throw away a woman you had three children with and divorce her?' Until today I don't accept that."

When she would bring up the subject of divorce, Dayan deflected her questions. Still, Rahel said she could not understand how he could feel as he did toward her and remain married to Ruth.

"That's good," Dayan answered her, "so you don't understand it."

"But this is unfair."

"I'm not the minister of fairness. I didn't say I was going to be fair."

Knowing how Dayan felt, Rahel developed a rationale for not leaving him: "I wanted the status quo. I wanted time to stop. . . . I wanted nothing to change. . . . We had difficult times, but we had such a won-derful relationship . . . that any change might bring—I was scared that the slightest change would rock the boat and I didn't want the boat to rock. . . ."[29]

DAYAN WAS BITTER that the IDF had been forced to leave the Sinai. With Egypt unwilling to negotiate peace, Israel had no guarantee that the IDF would not have to fight again in the Sinai. Leaving at this juncture, with no firm guarantees of Egypt's peaceful intentions, seemed to him foolish. Dayan made a point of being in the last half-track to leave El Arish on January 15, 1957, when the IDF pulled out of the Sinai town. Gaza was occupied for a bit longer. Ezer Weizman had offered to fly Dayan to El Arish, where he would join the retreating Israeli forces. Dayan asked Weizman to circle over one or two sites that he had singled out for archaeological digs. Landing at El Arish, they found the town filled with Israeli troops in full battle gear, their faces unhappy, assem-bling in a column of fifteen half-tracks for departure. "Anyone who knows Moshe's face when he's angry could see that he was burning with fury," wrote Weizman. "I asked him to return with me in the Piper. He refused. . . ."[30]

When he was asked why he had come to El Arish to witness the evacuation of the Israeli forces from Sinai, Dayan said, "Officers must eat all the rations they receive in the Israeli army, the palatable as well as the bitter."

Four and a half months after the war, the IDF completed its evacuation of the Sinai, on March 16, 1957. Egypt did not regain Sharm el-Sheikh or the Gaza Strip; both were under United Nations control. Egypt's Nasser said that he would allow Israel freedom of shipping through the straits; and he would end terrorism against the Jewish state. He was not willing, however, to enter into a peace treaty with the Jewish state.

On the day that the IDF left Sharm el-Sheikh, Dayan, acutely aware of all the newsmen around, said, "Just smile. Let's not make it a tragedy, and don't let them think we're upset." Rumors flew that Dayan had threatened to resign in protest against the IDF withdrawal from Sinai. At a General Staff meeting on March 10, two days after the withdrawal was completed, Dayan declared that those rumors were without foundation.

Nonetheless, in the spring, on the first Memorial Day for the soldiers killed in the Sinai campaign, Dayan published an Order of the Day criticizing the government for pulling out of the Sinai. *Ha'aretz,* the Israeli daily newspaper, editorialized against Dayan for his remarks, accusing him of ignoring the basic tenets of a democracy: The military censor banned the editorial from publication; and even after *Ha'aretz* appealed that decision to the Censorship Committee, the ban stood. Interestingly, the censor had not sought to squelch the chief of staff's criticism of the government, but *Ha'aretz*'s public criticism of the chief of staff. When an Israeli academic, Dina Goren, tried to publish details of the incident in 1971 as part of her doctoral dissertation, the censor again intervened. Three years later, Dr. Goren finally won approval to publish the details. By then, Dayan was a mere Knesset backbencher with little power to influence the censor.[31]

Moshe Dayan, age five, with his parents Shmuel and Dvorah. (Courtesy of Rahel Dayan)

On horseback, age sixteen. (Courtesy of Rahel Dayan)

Above: Left to right: Dayan, Yitzhak Sadeh, and Yigal Allon at Hanita in 1938. (Courtesy of Rahel Dayan)

Left: The photo of Dayan taken for his road and railroad pass issued on March 15, 1939. (Courtesy of Rahel Dayan)

Below: Dayan (second from left) with fellow inmates in Acre prison. He was imprisoned by the British from October 1939 through February 1941. Four months later, Dayan lost his left eye to a Vichy bullet while fighting under British command. (Courtesy of Rahel Dayan)

Above: On July 2, 1948, Dayan (rear left of coffin) arrived in the United States as part of a mission to escort the body of Colonel David Marcus. The timing seemed curious, as the War of Independence was not over, but while there Dayan held discussions with a former American army officer named Abraham Baum whose bold strategic thinking made a deep impression. (Courtesy of Israel Press and Photo Agency)
Below: "Storm through! Beat them! Smash them! No stopping for anything!": Dayan addressing part of the 89th Battalion two hours before the attack on Lod, July, 1948. (Courtesy of Akiva Sa'ar)

Above: The diplomat: Dayan shaking hands with Abdullah el-Tel, the Jordanian officer with whom Dayan negotiated the status of Jerusalem during the War of Independence. (Courtesy of Rahel Dayan)

Right: Dayan with Akiva Sa'ar, one of his officers, in Jerusalem, September, 1948. By this time Dayan was demonstrating diplomatic skills that surprised those who thought of him as an uncontrollable hothead.

Above: Dayan was part of the delegation to the Rhodes talks in early March, 1949. The United Nations-sponsored talks were mere window dressing for a secret armistice agreement Dayan negotiated later with King Abdullah of Jordan. (Courtesy of the Israel Government Press Office)

Left: Parachute training for all officers was part of Dayan's plan for upgrading the Israel Defense Force (IDF) in the early 1950s. (Courtesy of Rahel Dayan)

Above: Ruth and Moshe Dayan. (Courtesy of Rahel Dayan)

Right: Dayan was accompanied by his son Assi and his parents, Dvorah and Shmuel, as he prepared to board a plane for the United States where he was to embark on a tour of American military bases on July 11, 1954. (Courtesy of the Israel Government Press Office)

Below: Dayan attended a rally for Israel at Yankee Stadium during one of his trips to the United States in the 1950s. He is flanked by Abba Eban, right, and Eleanor Roosevelt. (Courtesy of Rahel Dayan)

Dayan with Natan Alterman in the winter of 1955–56. (Courtesy of Rahel Dayan)

Dayan's contempt for Israeli laws governing private archaelogical digs outraged his opponents. He is pictured here searching for antiquities on September 19, 1956. (Courtesy of A. Suesskind and S. Lavie)

With the troops at Sharm el-Sheikh, November 6, 1956. Israel won a crucial victory here during the Sinai Campaign. (Courtesy of the Israel Government Press Office)

Left to right: Teddy Kollek, Prime Minister David Ben-Gurion, Moshe Dayan, Shimon Peres, and Chaim Laskov, at Laskov's swearing-in as chief of staff on January 29, 1958. (Courtesy of the Israel Government Press Office)

Wading through a river in Vietnam in the summer of 1966. Dayan was critical of American military strategy, if not the war itself. (Courtesy of Rahel Dayan)

Below: The Politician: Addressing a Labor Party gathering in the 1960s.* (Courtesy of Michael Friedlin)
*Front row: second from left, Shimon Peres; fourth from left, Gad Ya'acobi; next to Ya'acobi are Yitzhak Rabin, and to his left is Golda Meir. Abba Eban is in the third row, far right.

Dayan was as adept at public relations as he was on the battlefield. He is pictured here conducting a press conference at the Bet Sokolov, Tel Aviv, June 3, 1967. (Courtesy of the Israel Government Press Office)

Dayan, flanked by Uzi Narkiss (left) and Yitzhak Rabin entering the Old City of Jerusalem on June 7, 1967. Dayan carefully staged this historic photograph. The consequences of taking the Old City and the West Bank were not fully appreciated in the heat of battle. (Courtesy of the Israel Government Press Office)

Above: Dayan, Uzi Narkiss, and Rehavam Ze'evi (with sunglasses) in conversation with the Arab keeper of the Cave of Machpelah in Hebron on June 8, 1967. (Courtesy of the Israel Government Press Office)
Right: Prime Minister Levi Eshkol (in dark beret) with Dayan and David Elazar (crouching) on the northern border, June 10, 1967. (Courtesy of the Israel Government Press Office)

Dayan with the Mayor of Hebron, Mahmed Ali Jaberi. Dayan believed that fair treatment of the Arabs in the occupied territories was an important component of Israeli security policy. (Courtesy of Daniel Rosenblum, Starphot News and Photo Agency)

Above: Rahel Dayan in October, 1967. (Courtesy of Rahel Dayan)

Dayan and Rahel's wedding, June, 1973. (Courtesy of Rahel Dayan)

Below: Dayan and Rahel in the archaeological garden at their home in Zahala the day after their wedding. (Courtesy of Rahel Dayan)

Prime Minister Golda Meir, with Dayan, speaking to the troops on the Golan Heights, November 21, 1973. (Courtesy of the Israel Government Press Office)

Dayan and Rahel with Henry and Nancy Kissinger. (Courtesy of *B'machane*, Tel Aviv)

Irving Bernstein, a senior United Jewish Appeal official, with Rahel and Yael Dayan at the house in Zahala. (Courtesy of Rahel Dayan)

Above: Dayan's negotiating skills proved crucial to the success of the Camp David Accords. He is shown here meeting with Egyptian President Anwar Sadat in Sadat's cabin during the meetings at Camp David in September 1978. (Courtesy of the Israel Government Press Office)

The delegations took a trip to Gettysburg during a break in the negotiations. (Starting third from left): Sadat, President Jimmy Carter, Menachem Begin, Dayan, Ezer Weizman, and Rosalyn Carter. (Courtesy of The White House)

The American and Israeli delegations at Camp David. From left around the table: Begin, Carter, U.S. Secretary of State Cyrus Vance, U.S. National Security Advisor Zbigniew Brzezinski, Vice President Walter Mondale, Ezer Weizman, Dayan. (Courtesy of the Israel Government Press Office)

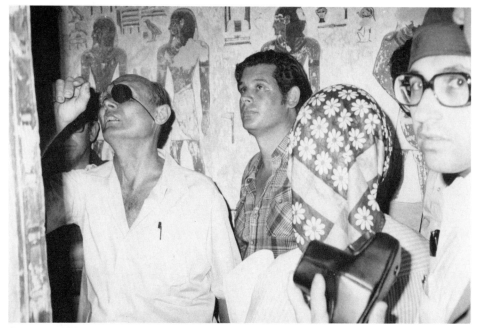

One personal benefit for Dayan of the accord with Egypt was the opportunity to study the splendors of Egyptian antiquities. He is pictured in a tomb in Upper Egypt in July, 1979. (Courtesy of the Israel Government Press Office)

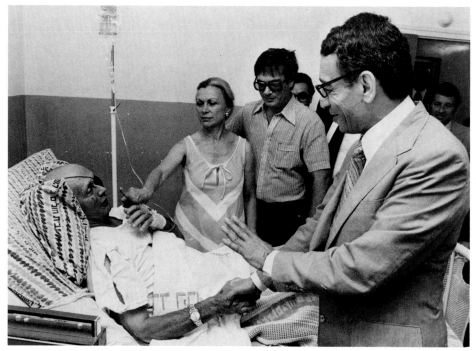

Boutrus Ghali, a senior Egyptian official, greets Dayan in Tel Hashomer Hospital. (Courtesy of Uzi Keren)

❖ 9 ❖

THE EMERGENT

POLITICIAN

DAYAN WAS ABOUT to take off his uniform. He would make the transition from commander in chief of the army to student, then from student to politician. No longer would he have the power to issue orders—and to fire someone for not carrying out those orders. Now he would have to lobby, cajole, engage in powerful oratory. If no one listened, if his proposals died on the vine, he could fire no one. For Moshe Dayan, the transition from chief of staff to politician took place slowly, and it was as traumatic for him personally as it was controversial for the country. Trauma indeed, for what does a chief of staff, recently lionized as a war hero, do for an encore?

In May 1957 he would turn forty-two years old, which was two years past the age that he, as chief of staff, had asserted was the proper one for retirement from the army. How he despised an army of elderly generals, growing fat and telling old war stories. He could not allow himself to become one of those.

Dayan planned to serve as chief of staff until January 1958, completing his term. Thanks to the Israeli triumph of October 1956, the year 1957 had been the country's first reasonably peaceful period since immediately after the War of Independence. In one of his rare public pronouncements, made that May at a ceremony in Zemach, Dayan was still expressing dismay at Israel's withdrawal from the Sinai. He noted that the Sinai campaign had removed the danger of an Egyptian attack against Israel for the next several years. What no one could predict would be the length of the respite. That would depend, he said, upon whether the Arab states remembered Israel's strength in conquering the Sinai, or its decision to withdraw right away. His personal opinion was that prospects of reaching a political agreement with Egypt were nonexistent; the two countries would remain in a belligerent state for some time and Israel would have to be ready to occupy the Sinai again, this time all the way to the Suez Canal—in order to turn it into a truly international waterway.

At the time, though, such concerns seemed remote. Exploiting the newfound tranquility, Israel's chief of staff spent a considerable time abroad. In September he went on an African tour, visiting Ghana, Liberia, and South Africa. During his three weeks in South Africa, he again underwent eye surgery in an attempt to discard his eyepatch for a glass eye. The purpose was to relieve the persistent headaches—even after surgery the pain was unlikely to disappear. He wanted the glass eye— or at least a part of him did—to prevent the invasion of privacy nearly every moment of his life. "Look at him," shouted a seven-year-old English youngster when Dayan walked into the Haifa home of Ezer Weizman's parents, "the real Captain Hook!"[1] Despite these unpleasant encounters, part of Dayan realized that the eyepatch brought him fame, a fame, he privately worried, that might evaporate with the insertion of the glass eye. Raphael Vardi, sharing a room with him in the brigade commanders course in the early 1950s, once asked Dayan why he did not have a glass eye inserted. Dayan said he had been in touch with doctors about such a step. "But there are problems, difficulties. But besides, if I have a glass eye, and I don't have the eyepatch anymore, who will know who Moshe Dayan is?"[2] The eye surgery in South Africa did not work.

BY THE FALL of 1957, Moshe Dayan—and others—contemplated what he would do after he retired as chief of staff the following January. Perhaps the most active in Dayan's cause was his wife, Ruth, despite the difficulties they were experiencing. She enjoyed easy access to David Ben-Gurion, an option she chose to exercise to determine what the prime minister had in mind for Dayan's future. Elections were two years off, and politics was an obvious career choice. Finding Ben-Gurion standing at his kitchen sink washing dishes, Ruth spoke bluntly: "Moshe is feeling a gap now that he's finishing as chief of staff, and that can be terrible for him. How do you see his future?"

Don't worry, Ben-Gurion advised her, Dayan won't get lost. "A break of some kind at this point is probably going to be good for him. He's thinking of studying at the university."

"There's talk of that," Ruth acknowledged, "but I think it's a lot of nonsense. After everything he's done, I know Moshe can't sit quietly in a classroom and read textbooks. It's just not possible, I know it."[3]

As much as she hinted, the prime minister was still disenchanted with his chief of staff's palpable dissent on the Israeli pullback from Sinai. Ben-Gurion could not overlook such disloyalty. Insubordination could not be easily rewarded with the promise of a cabinet post. Dayan would have to pay the price of a cooling-off period. That was Ben-Gurion's message to Ruth. After their conversation ended, Ben-Gurion was relieved that Ruth had not exploited their meeting to seek the prime minister's help in the Dayans' marital troubles. "I admire this woman not for what she said," he told an aide soon threafter, "but for what she didn't say."

In December and January 1958, Dayan toured Asia and Western Europe for three weeks, with stops in Thailand, Burma (where he participated in the country's Independence Day celebrations), India, Italy, France, and England. In early January Dayan and Shimon Peres, his traveling companion, arrived in India and were told at the reception desk of a certain hotel that no rooms were available. The reason: British prime minister Harold Macmillan had arrived the day before, his entourage taking up many rooms.

"You go tell Macmillan," Dayan instructed a startled clerk, "that Moshe Dayan, the man who made him prime minister of Britain, is here, and requests that one of his people vacate a room for one night." The clerk hesitated for a moment, then, checking Dayan's passport, realized that the name sounded familiar. He went upstairs. Upon returning, he announced that a room had been vacated for him.[4]

WHATEVER PATH Dayan chose, he wanted to stay in public life. In a letter to Rahel written while en route from Rome to Paris on January 13, Dayan noted that he had "considered to the best of my ability the contents of my life and the future and the different paths and all the events that I have been involved in. I don't see any way I could have changed things. I will continue to be involved in public issues. I know I have no other content or profession in my life. The society, the family— of Shimon Peres, Teddy Kollek, Ben-Gurion, Eshkol, the people at Nahalal, the army people, I know that I don't have any other acquaintances, and I can't and don't want to disconnect myself from them."

On January 28, Dayan retired as chief of staff, after serving for four years. His two most noteworthy accomplishments during that period had been the reshaping of the Israel Defense Forces into a combat-ready machine and the lightning victory in the Sinai Desert in October 1956. His legacy was the prospect for the first time of peaceful frontiers— peaceful because of the IDF's proven capacity to bring Egyptian forces to a state of collapse, not because of any sudden lessening of Arab hostility toward the state of Israel. Dayan remained in the army with the rank of brigadier general. He was replaced by one of the IDF's top tank experts, Chaim Laskov, whose appointment served notice that the army would devote itself intensely to a buildup of its armored forces.

Politics, no matter how lukewarm David Ben-Gurion seemed, was a distinct possibility for Moshe Dayan. As the hero of Sinai, he was a natural candidate; he seemed a reluctant novice. To Yael he confided that what he really wanted was some time off, freedom from the yoke of military life. "You don't really think my heart's desire is to sit around the cabinet table with Sapir and Aranne?" he asked; but then he added: "If they want me, they know how to reach me, and I'm not leaving the country."[5]

Meanwhile, he planned to study. Until then, Dayan had completed only two years of secondary education. Attending a university seemed like the perfect solution to the retired chief of staff. There were still nearly two years to the next election. He decided to take a leave of absence from the army and to study government and Middle East studies at Jerusalem's Hebrew University. (He would have preferred physics but did not feel qualified to study such a complex subject.) At the same time he would do what was necessary to complete a bachelor's degree in law at Tel Aviv University. (He gained a year's credit toward that degree for his night studies at Tel Aviv University's School of Law and Economics in the early 1950s, and eventually was awarded an under-graduate degree in law on February 27, 1959.)

Enrolling at the Hebrew University in February 1958, Dayan knew he was not the usual student, "even though I am probably the most famous in the country today, except for the young lady who was chosen Miss Israel."[6]

His two years as a student seemed like a vacation. He drove a jeep (a spade always in the rear in case he had the impulse to go digging at an archaeological site). Yael attended some of the same classes. Dayan's classmates suggested that he was not an enthusiastic scholar. During his studies he replied to a letter from a third-grader from Kibbutz Nirim: "Now, I too am a first grade student and my teachers nag at me and want me to do lots of homework. If I don't get sunstroke because of walking round without a hat, I'll still get a headache because of studying and that hurts more. . . ."[7] He did not enjoy the massive reading as-signments (his eye injury and the headaches undoubtedly added to his burden); he also complained repeatedly, especially before an examination, that it was not clear why someone should have to study and memorize facts that might not turn up in the test. Classmates acknowledge that Dayan at times asked others for answers—while the exam was in progress. Once, one professor, not certain that Dayan had seen the answer prepared for him by another student, passed the note to the former chief of staff himself!

Inevitably, student life, with its attendant freedom and leisure, began to affect Dayan's personality. The first to notice it was Yael, who found her father less appealing: "Rather than calm his restlessness, or mellow his edginess, the period of study in Jerusalem . . . produced the opposite results. Lack of responsibility made him irresponsible, and his impatience turned to arrogance. Not being at peace with himself resulted in bad headaches. . . ." He was not fun to be with. He had become, in Yael's words, "increasingly introverted, and went about systematically severing intimate friendships. His moods changed swiftly, and he reserved his more gloomy, irritable hours for the family circle."[8]

UNTIL NOW Moshe Dayan's romantic encounters had largely escaped public notice—not because they did not occur, but rather due to the IDF's practice of sheltering its soldiers and commanders from the limelight and discouraging the press from writing about anything that had to do with the personal life of a soldier. When he shed his uniform in September 1958, the press might have, had it wished, titillated the public with stories about Dayan's dalliances. Israeli journalists, however, sensing that their readers would chafe at investigative journeys into the personal lives of their political and military leaders, held back. How natural, therefore, it was for Dayan to assume that the next time he became romantically interwined with a woman, he would remain insulated from the public glare.

Then, in early 1958, he met Hadassah More. When he knocked on the door of her room in the student dormitory to borrow some blankets, he was utterly astonished to find a familiar face. He had just moved in that evening next door on the same floor. Married to Dayan's childhood chum, Dov Yermiya, Hadassah had known Dayan only fleetingly until then.

Just two weeks before Dayan knocked on her door, Hadassah and Dov had moved to Jerusalem, where she had enrolled as a student in special education at the Hebrew University. She gave him blankets and an invitation to Friday night dinner. He returned the favor by asking her to drop in on him when she got bored. They grew friendly. Dayan, realizing how strikingly attractive Hadassah was, hoped for more than friendship. "He began," she recalled, "to court me more and more persistently, and the more I refused, the more persistent he became. I actually had to avoid him so as not to be drawn into a relationship I did not really want."[9]

At that point the marriage of Hadassah and Dov deteriorated. Dov, a senior IDF commander, talked about leaving the army and joining a kibbutz, steps that Hadassah construed to mean their marriage was failing. She asked Dayan to intervene, to secure a promotion for Dov so he would remain in the IDF. Dayan tried, but in vain. Dayan's proximity to Hadassah bothered Dov and aroused his suspicions, even when the relationship of the two students remained innocent. Eventually Dov left the army and his marriage to Hadassah crumbled. In such times, Hadassah found "Dayan's neighborly presence . . . very comforting. I had someone to talk to about my sorrow. . . ." Dayan began to sense that her inhibitions had melted away. Indeed, they had. "And so I fell into Dayan's hands like a ripe fruit. I was still playing hard to get, but he already knew that all my evasions were now only a way of saying yes."

As he finally made his play for Hadassah, Dayan could not have suspected that she would turn his initial advances into one of the key scenes of a novel she would publish five years later. As Hadassah More herself acknowledged, "The first time I had relations with him [Dayan] is described in the book [*Flaming Paths*] in an entire chapter. That description, to which I tried to give the character of an ordinary novel—as if the woman were not me but someone else—did not succeed in convincing the readers. They identified me with the character of this woman and the chief of staff–student who walked with a limp they identified as Dayan."[10]

If the novel is any guide, Moshe Dayan was a passionate and forceful lover. In their first sexual encounter, "Matti Yaniv" appeared reluctant at first to take any romantic initiative. Then, with a suddenness that startled the heroine, he took her in his arms, forcefully pressed his lips on hers, and then kissed other parts of her body. She tried to extricate herself but could not. He took her to the bed, climbed on top of her, breathing heavily. When Yaniv relaxed momentarily, she wriggled out of his clutches.[11]

Hadassah has suggested that part of Dayan's motivation for a romantic fling with her went back to his childhood: "Dayan had a need for compensation for all sorts of frustration stemming from his childhood. My husband had better luck with the girls when he and Dayan were youngsters. It was as if Dayan was getting back at Dov, as if Dayan felt he had been discriminated against, and so he was trying to get back at him by having a relationship with me. . . . Dayan and Dov were very competitive toward one another."[12]

Dayan's affair with Hadassah More complicated his relationship with Rahel Rabinovitch. Once, Hadassah showed up at Dayan's student dorm room just ten minutes after Rahel had left—and Rahel found out about the visit.

"OK," Rahel said to Dayan angrily, "I'm out." She wanted to break off their relationship. "He cried and I cried, and it was very dramatic," Rahel recalled. It was just two weeks later, in May 1958, that she obtained her divorce. Walking out of the rabbinate office in Jersusalem, the first person she came upon was Dayan. He was sitting in a jeep near the King David Hotel.

"Do you realize where I'm coming from?" Rahel asked him. "I just got my divorce."

"My goodness," said Dayan, "if this were in a movie, we would go out and have a drink."

Rahel, recalling her experience of a few weeks earlier, said, "We are certainly not in the movies," and walked away. But a few days later, Dayan called her and their romance was renewed.[13]

With his romances increasingly the subject of public gossip, Dayan felt it only right that he ask Ruth if she wanted a divorce. His confused, guilt-laden feelings were communicated to Ruth in a disjointed, rambling letter he wrote to her in the winter of 1958:

> If we were to get married now, we wouldn't have done it, but this is not the choice we are facing. The question is whether to live together, or apart, and if together, how. When you married me you didn't know me well, and what I am today is totally different from the person you did know. You think my attention is divided between five-thousand-year-old antiques and corrupt young women, that I'm not devoted to the children or to you. If you think that a husband who behaves like that is not tolerable to you, the decision is fully yours. I don't regret anything that happened in the past, nor do I promise or think I can change in the future. The day you ask for a divorce, I'll grant you one, but it's entirely up to you. . . . I make no pretenses to be a model or an example, as anything to anybody. If you could accept me as I really am and not as you or your friends wish me to be, I don't have any wish to separate. Our life together can be based on mutual respect, common friends, and twenty-two years of marriage, children, and home."

He said he was sure there were couples who lived their lives "without trying something else or testing other sensations . . . I am not made this way. We can base our life on sympathy—and I don't write "love" so as not to mislead you . . . and friendship, common ideology and respect.[14]

He was not about to change his life-style even though as long as he remained a public figure he would suffer from the glare of publicity. Nothing else interested him, however, other than a public career. That is not to say that he liked politics. He did not. Politics, to him, had always been the province of his father's generation, the talkers, the meeting-goers, the speech-givers. He knew the rules but did not like the game—centered on political parties, ruled by men whose main goal was staying in power. His disaffection for political parties was matched only by the disdain he felt for the party pros, the close-knit group that ran the Mapai party machine: Golda Meir, Levi Eshkol, Pinhas Sapir, and Zalman Aranne. They stood in his mind for all that was outdated, the Diaspora, the mentality of the Jewish ghetto, the softness. Their worst sin was—in Dayan's view—their hypocrisy. They preached modesty, yet lived well themselves. They called for honesty, but they manipulated people. They encouraged Israelis to live in the Negev and the Galilee, but found homes for themselves in Tel Aviv and Jerusalem. Dayan told one of his political friends, Gad Ya'acobi, that he would never preach to anyone something that he personally was not prepared to do himself.[15]

What truly bothered Dayan was the awareness that he could not avoid the game but he could not win at it. To Yael he confided that "I can't adjust to the pattern, the hierarchy, the pace, or the style of the so-called powerful members of the party. They aren't going to change, and I'm not going to change, and sooner or later they will have their way and be rid of me. I am a thorn in their thighs, and the party routine is stifling to me."[16]

Dayan entered the political arena in the only manner he could: boldly. He began by pointing out a fact of life that few were willing to acknowledge: By the late 1950s, the state of Israel had changed. Important population shifts had taken place in the past decade. No longer were the farm settlements in outlying areas—the kibbutzim and the moshavim—the prime forces in Israeli society. No longer did the Histadrut, that mammoth labor federation that had for many years quasi-governmental powers, reign as the supreme authority. Since the early 1950s thousands upon thousands of new immigrants had reached Israeli shores, immigrants who had no trouble thumbing their noses at the settlements and the Histadrut, immigrants who, by virtue of their newly developed electoral power, had the capacity for shaping the country in one direction or another. The veteran farm settlements such as Nahalal and Ein Harod no longer symbolized the country's problems, Dayan believed. By this stage, the development towns of Beersheba, Dimona, and Ashdod did.

The Mapai party veterans were exploiting the fact that Israel, for the first time since its founding, was not experiencing intense external pressure. They were catering to the public's desire to grab new benefits—a dividend of the sudden peace and quiet. An artificial prosperity had descended upon the land in the form of higher employment levels and higher wages.

Dayan wondered how long it would take before the bubble burst. The party veterans were overpromising, the country's coffers were emptying, and soon the country would pay. It was time for him to make his voice heard. Even before leaving the IDF, he began expressing opinions on national affairs that admonished the veteran politicians. The first sign of the split between Dayan and the veterans occurred in May 1958, when Mapai held its convention. Pinhas Lavon, now the secretary-general of the Histadrut, hoped to acquire more power for himself. He wanted the Histadrut reorganized so that his position would be equal to the minister of finance. Lavon and the other party leaders were on alert against efforts by Dayan and other party "youngsters" to upstage them. Dayan fired his first real blast on May 28 before a students' club in Tel Aviv. He insisted that ineffective workers should be dismissed, wages frozen, and factories made more productive. "The men of the last generation have reached an age where they can no longer carry out revolutions," Dayan said, noting that "these men look back proudly on their achievements of 1902 . . . before we were born . . . but we are interested in 1962."

Part of the veterans' irritation with Dayan was due to his closeness to Ben-Gurion. They felt that Dayan had to be put in his place—and quickly. They would get no help from David Ben-Gurion. Before one audience on June 7 in Kfar Saba, he defended the former chief of staff, urging people to respect Dayan for his service to the country even if his views were unorthodox. Dayan revealed more of his iconoclasm to students around the country. In Jerusalem, Dayan was greeted by eight hundred Hebrew University students who packed a hall that normally seated four hundred. Some students climbed through the second-story windows in order to get in. Hitting at his theme that Israel needed a period of austerity, he blamed the youngsters in his audience for doing too little, and for eating up the money that was flowing in from abroad for economic development. What they should do was give up some of their creature comforts—and to reject those political parties that promised even higher standards of living. Heresy for Mapai—but Moshe Dayan spoke his mind.

The veterans wanted Ben-Gurion to remove Moshe Dayan from his soapbox. Eventually the prime minister agreed. He tried to hint to Dayan that civilian life was distinctly different from the IDF; it was not possible to order people about as in the army. The hint fell on deaf ears. Finally, on June 24, 1958, Ben-Gurion announced in the Knesset that he had ordered Dayan to discontinue public speeches. He had asked Dayan to delay his entry into politics until after he returned to civilian life that fall.

Dayan's participation in the forthcoming Mapai election campaign was worth many votes. He was instantly recognized wherever he went and received with great warmth—almost awe. Taking an impromptu stroll through two Jerusalem slum areas inhabited by oriental Jews, he suddenly came upon a boy outside the Sinai Restaurant who shouted, "The conquerer of Sinai is in Sinai." Because of his name and his charisma, Dayan attracted large audiences. While party veterans had power because of the party machine, Dayan's power could only come from the crowds. People sensed that Dayan had set himself apart from the party. When some rallies were over, the crowd would put him on its shoulders and cry, "Long live Dayan, down with Labor." Only two other Israelis could draw such large audiences, David Ben-Gurion and Menachem Begin. Although Dayan had neither Begin's oratorical skills nor Ben-Gurion's unique standing as Founding Father or National Prophet, he inspired great confidence.

Throughout the fall of 1958, the public saw him out of uniform. In November Dayan appeared before six hundred people at Tel Aviv's Bet Sokolov. Asked if he was prepared to lead a new movement, he ducked the question. The question got resounding applause, however. Early the next year, Dayan remarked, "The people who crawled with their rifles among the rocks of Israel for the past twenty years know as much of their country's needs as those who have spent their time sitting on the fifth floor of the Headquarters [where the Histadrut secretary worked]."[17] Such speeches did little to lessen the Mapai establishment's hatred of Dayan; indeed, dark rumblings about Dayan's supposed preference for a military dictatorship were heard.

On April 9, 1959, Mapai held a convention in Tel Aviv at the Mann Auditorium. The 1,920 delegates eagerly awaited Dayan's appearance. Thunderous applause greeted him before his remarks and afterward. When the fall campaign began in earnest, Dayan visited settlements of new immigrants known to be suspicious of his party and told them that "if you don't like Mapai, throw her out!" He prided himself on going into election districts that other politicians would not dare enter for fear of their safety. He visited Israeli Arabs. Once Dayan went to a Haifa district after new immigrants from Arabic-speaking countries had rioted. He plunged right into the district and spoke from an open-air platform.

ALL THIS TIME Moshe Dayan maintained his liaison with Hadassah More. Then one day her husband Dov discovered the truth from a mutual friend. Angry, hurt, he swore that he would kill Dayan. Instead, he chose to write a series of letters to him. In one, dated August 17, 1959, Dov accused Dayan of engaging in adultery; he bitterly used several strong epithets to describe Dayan. Hadassah had confessed that she and Dayan had been romantically involved, Dov wrote. As a result, Dov and Hadassah had separated. He appealed to Dayan to help Hadassah.[18]

Dov wrote to Dayan's wife, Ruth, pouring out his heart against her treacherous husband. Ruth answered Dov's letter on September 16, acknowledging that, had his letter arrived two years earlier, it would have seemed like a blow from which she would never recover. "But since I had the initial shock a long time ago—the same formula in a different style—I have learned to cope with it and have become inoculated against further shocks. None of Moshe's antics can shock me. I am amazed only by the fools who continue to believe in him and dance attendance on him. The illusion called 'Moshe Dayan' which I lived under for years vanished long ago. As far as I am concerned he is a sick man; he is coarse, he lacks any foundation of humanity; it's just a pity that he is allowed to infect innocent children with his illness. . . . Meantime take courage—there's a whole world out there that was created for mortals like us, too. Yours, Ruth Dayan."[19]

Dov wrote as well to Prime Minister Ben-Gurion, pointing out that Dayan was immoral and therefore unfit to hold public office. Attacking the prime minister, Dov asked Ben-Gurion why it was that he supported a hypocrite. Dov demanded that Ben-Gurion cut off his support for Dayan.

The most noteworthy of all these letters came from David Ben-Gurion to Dov Yermiya. The prime minister had replied to Dov's letter but, not satisfied, Dov wrote Ben-Gurion a second letter on September 14. The prime minister replied to this letter as well, repeating essentially what he had written in the first letter. In his second letter, dated September 19, Ben-Gurion laid down what would become one of the abiding principles of Israeli society: A public figure need not fear that marital infidelity or some other indiscretion might harm his public career. What is most remarkable about the Ben-Gurion letter is the endorsement it gave to public servants to conduct their personal lives any way they saw fit—without having to worry that their conduct could harm their public careers.

In previous generations, Ben-Gurion wrote, as well as our own, a distinction was made between intimate relationships between men and women and the public domain. "A man may be abstemious and a saint all his life and not succeed in public office, and the contrary is also true." The prime minister mentioned King David, who had slept with Batsheba, wife of Uriah the Hittite, and made her pregnant; and then, had Uriah killed in battle. But, Ben-Gurion noted: "While Nathan the prophet did go to David and courageously reprove him, still he did not declare him unfit to be king. And though every Jew knows of King David's wicked behavior toward Batsheba's husband, Uriah the Hittite, no king is more admired in Jewish legend than David."

Ben-Gurion then offered another example, Admiral Horatio Nelson, whom he described as the most admired man in British history. Nelson who defeated the French and Spanish fleets at the Battle of Trafalgar. The same Lord Nelson who, despite his affair with Lady Hamilton, enjoyed the British public's high esteem.

Instead of agreeing to force Dayan out of public life by exposing his "evil," the prime minister defended the former chief of staff. Ben-Gurion described Dayan in his letter as "the man who as a military commander has done so much for Israel."

"I feel myself bound," wrote Ben-Gurion, "rather unwillingly, to tell you that I do not find your opinion or your approach to public matters acceptable. It is impossible (and in my opinion totally unacceptable) to examine the secret, intimate life of any person—man or woman—and determine his (or her) rights and position in society in accordance with the findings." Dayan is no hypocrite, wrote the prime minister, "as he has not held, nor will he hold a position of sermonizer or castigator on intimate matters, on relations between a man and a woman; and what he has done in the service of the nation, he has done not only with great skill but also with the utmost devotion to duty: What he has asked from others he has demanded first from himself and in battle he has always stood at the head of those he commands."[20]

When Ruth Dayan spoke to Ben-Gurion in London on the same subject, urging him not to "go writing long letters to people," he replied to her: "You must get used to the idea that in the case of great men, the private and public lives will often run parallel but will never meet."[21]

Incredibly, although Dayan was a candidate for the Knesset for the first time, a former chief of staff, and an oft-mentioned candidate for prime minister, none of this became public at the time. Dayan was too much of a national hero for the media to delve into such matters. Hence, one of the more colorful episodes of the 1959 election campaign went unreported in the Israeli press.

THE NOVEMBER 3, 1959, elections marked David Ben-Gurion's greatest political triumph. His Mapai party won a record-breaking 47 Knesset seats (out of 120); that was 7 more than in the last election and 38.2 percent of the vote. Lagging far behind in second place was Menachem Begin's Herut party, with only 17 seats and 19.4 percent of the vote. Coming three years after the overwhelming Sinai victory and the ensuing years of peace and quiet along Israel's frontiers, the elections had to go well for Mapai. Ben-Gurion also added to his party's electoral strength by injecting new blood into the list of parliamentary candidates, among whom were Moshe Dayan, forty-four, Abba Eban, forty-four, and Shimon Peres, thirty-six. One sign of the changing generations was that for the first time Shmuel Dayan did not get elected to the Knesset.

Moshe Dayan made a point of saying that he had not run for the Knesset in order to sit in the members' dining room and have tea every afternoon. He wanted to be a cabinet minister, a senior one, if possible. Unlike most of the unknowns in the new cabinet, Dayan's was an internationally recognizable face. A senior post, he felt, was his almost by right. He was so well known that when he summoned Rehavam Ze'evi, then on study leave at the U.S. Army Command and General Staff College, Fort Leavenworth, Kansas, for a talk in New York City in December 1959, it set off alarm bells in the Pentagon: Israel must be planning to go to war![22]

Lessening Dayan's prospects of gaining a senior cabinet post was the fuss made by the party's veterans over Ben-Gurion's elevation of the youngsters to the Knesset. Their objections were largely directed at Moshe Dayan. What bothered them most about Dayan was his independence and his contempt for them. Both Golda Meir and Zalman Aranne had declared that they would not accept cabinet posts in the new government because the prime minister was coddling the younger generation. In fact, they were pressuring Ben-Gurion not to appoint Dayan to a senior cabinet post—either defense or foreign affairs. They had little cause for concern. Ben-Gurion was as disinclined to yield the defense portfolio as he was to push Golda Meir out of the foreign ministry. While he rejected the veterans' claim that Dayan was too irresponsible to hold a senior cabinet position, Ben-Gurion harbored his own doubts that the former chief of staff was truly ready for such high political responsibility. After intense negotiations, the oldsters got their way. It was agreed that

Moshe Dayan could be in the cabinet, but in the relatively minor position of minister of agriculture. As much as the prime minister wanted to infuse the cabinet with new blood, he could not ignore the political muscle of the veterans.

MOSHE DAYAN became a politician, and on his first day in the Knesset he found himself drinking tea in the dining room with Shimon Peres, another new deputy.

"Do you feel anything special?" Dayan asked.

Dayan did not wait for an answer. He noted how strange it was that he felt no cause for celebration. After attending the Knesset for some time, he joked to Rehavam Ze'evi about his new routine: "I get up in the morning and I begin to legislate. All the time I legislate."[23]

Becoming the minister of agriculture on December 16, Dayan served five years in the post. Next to the defense portfolio, it was the cabinet position for which he was most suitably trained. He had been a farmer, and by all accounts, a very good one. His eye was trained to recognize the various crops. His mind could easily detect when a farmer was defining a problem honestly, or trying to put one over on the new minister. Once some tomato growers surrounded him and one lashed out at him for Dayan's tomato-growing policy: "Mr. Minister, with all due respect, what do you know about tomato growing? I have twenty years of experience and I wish to say that everything you say is nonsense." Without losing his cool, Dayan responded: "True, you have twenty years of experience, but what you have is really one year of experience. You are just repeating what you learned in that time for the past twenty years."[24] Yet, he felt a natural affinity toward the farmers, and genuinely wanted to improve their standard of living.

It was not an easy job. By 1959, Israel had 2.5 million people. The hundreds of farm settlements established just after the state was founded had led to overproduction: too much milk, and too many eggs, vegetables, and fruit. The farmer had an average wage twenty to thirty percent below the national average. The worst hit were the newer settlements. As a result of the crisis young farmers were leaving the farming sector. Clearly something was needed to rescue the three hundred farm settlements. If farming policy could be centralized, gluts would hopefully disappear, as would low prices for the farmers' produce. The government had lost control over the agricultural sector, and if it was going to aid the farmers and turn their produce into exportable items, some centralized planning was inevitable. The effort to build the National Water Carrier, a project designed to help farmers irrigate arid land, would have to be intensified.

This was where Moshe Dayan thought he could contribute. Realizing how complex were the problems of farm life, Dayan instructed his legal counselor, Yossi Checanover: "Don't tell me that I cannot do what I feel is right. Tell me how I can do it legally."[25]

When he came to office, only a few marketing boards existed aimed at production planning. During his term, production boards were organized for most sectors of agriculture, with production norms devised. The boards, which were controlled exclusively by farmers, had certain policing powers, including the right to levy fines, in order to keep the farming sector efficient. These farming boards still exist today.

To resolve the problem of overproduction Dayan shut down the small farms that were located on the outskirts of the big cities. The closure was justified on the grounds that these farmers were less authentic than the Zionist ones in the outlying farm settlements. The urban farmers angrily protested Dayan's step.

Dayan's other major accomplishment was to accelerate work on the National Water Carrier and assure its completion. The carrier was a major irrigation project that had been designed to bring water from the Sea of Galilee to the Negev Desert. Planned in the early 1950s, it had been postponed under the combined pressure of the Arabs and the Americans. Dayan pushed the project toward completion, and six months after he left office in the spring of 1965, the carrier began operating.

Dayan failed miserably in one project: promoting a new kind of tomato for export, called the Moneymaker. Dayan's staunch conviction of the worthiness of this tomato—against the better judgment of the farmers—earned him the sobriquet *Aluf Hagvaniot* (The General of Tomatoes). Until then Israeli farmers had been growing a type of tomato called Merrimand. It was juicy, large, and oval, but it was not marketable internationally. Dayan's advisers searched for an alternative. They came up with the Moneymaker. True, it looked and tasted different—juiceless, fleshy, cylindrical—and it was popular abroad. To Dayan's misfortune, Israeli farmers simply would not make the transition, and he was forced to abandon the effort.

Israel was at peace. A minister could go abroad and remain there for weeks at a time without feeling that he would miss an urgent cabinet meeting. Dayan therefore invested a good deal of time in traveling. Africa was a popular place to visit. In the autumn of 1963 he was in Togo, Cameroon, the Ivory Coast, the Republic of Central Africa, and Ghana. In July 1964, he went to Malawi, Kenya, and Tanzania (then Zanzibar). He visited Ethiopia secretly so that its leader, Haile Selassie, would not be assailed by his Muslim neighbors.

There is little evidence to suggest that Dayan loved being minister of agriculture. Abba Eban, who served as minister without portfolio in that same cabinet, noted that "Dayan hated the Ministry of Agriculture because there's no history of a minister of agriculture becoming a heroic figure."[26] Dayan saw the post as a stepping-stone to greater political power, but given the mundane work of the minister of agriculture, he had to wonder whether holding the post for so long was in his favor. A few times during the five years he considered quitting but as long as David Ben-Gurion remained prime minister, he stuck it out. Ben-Gurion encouraged him to stay on, reminding Dayan that he was still young, that some day the power he was looking for would come to him. Quitting might endanger his prospects.

Even with Ben-Gurion as prime minister, Dayan's chances of rising in the cabinet were slim. An opportunity arose toward the end of 1960 when more squabbling over the Lavon Affair caused Ben-Gurion to resign (on December 25). Ben-Gurion and Lavon had been arguing over whether enough evidence existed for an official legal inquiry into the mishap. In fact, they were debating the same old issue of who gave the order that caused the mishap. Ben-Gurion wanted such an inquiry. Lavon did not. He wanted Ben-Gurion to clear him on the spot. The prime minister refused. Ben-Gurion's squabble with Lavon was regarded as an attempt to weaken Lavon, and in effect, to weaken the political power of all of the Mapai party veterans. The argument went that in bringing Lavon down, what Ben-Gurion really wanted was to boost the youngsters, chief among whom was Moshe Dayan. Conversely, the oldsters believed that clearing Lavon would have the effect of putting the youngsters in their place, of keeping Moshe Dayan and others from grabbing further political power. The last straw came when a government committee of seven ministers, set up by Finance Minister Levi Eshkol, seemingly exonerated Pinhas Lavon. Rather than call off his fight, Ben-Gurion chose to resign as prime minister in order to pursue his battle outside of government. It had been only thirteen months since he had formed a government.

Dayan and the other Mapai politicians were placed in a dilemma. Could they form a government without Ben-Gurion in it? That would have been a revolutionary thought. In discussing this problem with Mapai politicians, Dayan, of all people, suggested that he was willing. "Ninety-nine percent of my pro–Ben-Gurionism is not pro the person of Ben-Gurion," he said, "but for the identification of Ben-Gurion with the state. The state takes precedence over all, even over Ben-Gurion. If a situation arises in which Ben-Gurion decides to resign, and I consider that the good of the state demands that Mapai form a government even without Ben-Gurion, and it is given me to join such a government I shall do so." (Four years later Ben-Gurion, writing an account of this period, looked at the minutes of the December 1960 Mapai central committee meeting. He noted, smiling, "I enjoyed the words of only one person, those of Moshe. Words of understanding. He is the only one who made sense. He is a wise fellow. How could the others say that without Ben-Gurion we shall not form a government?")

Eventually, Ben-Gurion signaled his willingness to form a new government. To keep the prime minister calm, Eshkol proposed that Pinhas Lavon be fired as secretary-general of the Histadrut, and the Mapai central committee agreed. The net effect was a setback for the party veterans. Though Ben-Gurion had a partial victory in Lavon's dismissal, he paid a heavy price for this move. He no longer could count on the support of the oldsters, so bitter were they for the ouster of Lavon. At this point, he agreed to form a new government, but Mapam and Ahdut Avoda did not want Ben-Gurion as prime minister. Recommending that a new government be formed without him, Ben-Gurion proposed a number of candidates for defense minister: Peres, Dayan, and Yadin, in that order. Mapai did not leap at Ben-Gurion's offer to step down. Elections became inevitable. They were held on August 15, 1961. Mapai lost five of its forty-seven Knesset seats, due in large measure to the Ben-Gurion–Lavon feud, but it was still able to form the next government and did so under Ben-Gurion.

Though Dayan remained in the new government as minister of agriculture, he believed that he was better suited for dealing with national security questions. Not that he feared the country faced an emergency on its frontiers. Indeed, on July 23 he had told a UJA Young Leadership mission in Tel Aviv that he thought there was little likelihood of war in the next three years.

Given his reputation, Dayan was frequently quoted on these subjects, always projecting at this time a sense that Israel had little to worry about from the Arabs. On July 28, 1961, he met with Cyrus Sulzberger, the *New York Times* columnist. Sulzberger described Dayan as a "burly, sunburned, youthful-looking man with a bullet-head, strong cheekbones, large white teeth and a rather merry expression, despite the black patch. . . ." Dayan told the *Times* man that he did not think Egypt's Nasser could destroy Israel by surprise attack. "We are a weak, small country, but even if Egypt attacked, they could not prevent us from mobilizing. Unless they use atomic weapons they probably could not kill more than ten thousand people around Tel Aviv and in the morning the real war would start, and I don't think Russia is going to give Nasser atomic weapons now."[27]

ALL THE WHILE Dayan continued to see Hadassah More. But when Dayan joined the cabinet late in 1959, the affair grew increasingly complicated: She was having an affair with a well-known public figure who was married and had no intention of divorcing his wife. She did not bring up the subject of marriage. She simply did not see Dayan leaving Ruth to marry her. After her divorce from Dov Yermiya in 1961, the relationship with Dayan took a turn for the worse. Not that he stopped seeing her. As Hadassah recalled, "He would come, drink coffee or eat something, we'd talk, go to bed, chat of this and that, and part 'til the next visit; or sometimes we'd go out to a cafe or restaurant, then back again to my place and so it went on."

Until Hadassah began to rebel against this life. "I didn't see the point of this relationship, which had its accompanying frustrations." Hadassah had discovered Rahel's existence and the fact that she harbored strong claims on Dayan. It dawned on Hadassah that "on the days he was not with me, he met her, and other women too." Still, Hadassah was not put off by these other liaisons. "The knowledge that he was not willing to give up his relations with me flattered me and I didn't care about intermittent relationships he doubtless had. Moshe knew well how to divide his heart into hermetically-sealed compartments, for me, for her [Rahel], and for another woman or two, in such a way that I never felt any jealousy."[28] He never spoke to Hadassah about other women in his life—except for Ruth.

In time, Hadassah decided that she would have to end the relationship with Dayan. He himself had sensed that she wanted to break off with him when she moved to Tel Aviv at the conclusion of her studies in Jerusalem. He visited her much less frequently and she interpreted that to mean he was losing interest in her. Searching for a way to end the affair, she knew that it was unthinkable to simply announce to him that she wanted out: "I knew that for as long as he continued to want to come to me, I would not reject him."

Wanting to sever the tie, she came up with a unique solution: She would write a book about their romance (the one in which she described his passion as a lover in detail). "I was . . . vaguely aware that only such a drastic step could put an end to our relationship. And I wanted to put an end to it."

When the manuscript was ready for editing, her first thought was to show it to Dayan, and seek his permission to publish it. "I wanted to do the right thing by myself and by him." If he wanted her to burn the manuscript, she would. But after he had read it, he reacted, according to Hadassah, with great leniency: "It was a very strange meeting. Very formal. Dayan wore a suit and tie and looked as if he were receiving a guest from abroad. He told me in a matter-of-fact manner that he had read the book and that in his opinion it was very good; he added that if I wanted to publish it, I could do so because 'You've worked hard on it, I can see.' "²⁹ He had only one request: that all the passages related to the exchange of letters between Ben-Gurion and Dov Yermiya be expunged from the text; Dayan did not want to mix Ben-Gurion into his private affairs. Dayan said: "About me you can write whatever you want. But I won't have you relate to Ben-Gurion." Arguing at first on the grounds that the letters were essential from a literary point of view, Hadassah eventually agreed to leaving them out. (She also changed the name of the main character from Matti Darom to Matti Yaniv at her publisher's request.) Though the character no longer had the same initials as Dayan, the public, of course, understood who he was meant to represent.

HADASSAH WAS astonished and hurt by Dayan's indifference to the manuscript. It was "as if he attached no importance to everything I had written in the course of an entire year. Perhaps he secretly hoped that no publisher would bring out the book." "Naturally" she agreed to remove Ben-Gurion's letter and mention of him. The first publisher she approached grabbed it up. With good reason. The book's great selling point was in its titillating exposure of Moshe Dayan the womanizer, a point to which Dayan may have been indifferent but which brought great anguish to Yael: "There, printed and bound, for a few Israeli pounds, one could buy my father's body, his performance in bed, his sweet talk and intimate thoughts. . . . I was shocked by the vulgarity of it all."³⁰ But the book-buying public in Israel did not agree. When *Flaming Paths* was published in Hebrew in 1963, the book became a national bestseller; it went through three editions and sold thirty thousand copies. According to Hadassah, the forthcoming publication of the book "effectively put a complete end to my relationship with Moshe. I had freed myself from the ambivalence" that she had felt toward him. "I wanted and yet did not want to continue the relationship. He wanted to [continue] in his own way."

If Dayan wanted to keep up the relationship, he had a strange way of showing it. Though their meeting in the Ministry of Agriculture had been tranquil, the next time they met at party headquarters he was furious. He accused her of being irresponsible, of doing something that was not done. Hadassah was shocked. She tried to call his office later, but his secretary simply informed Hadassah that Dayan did not want to see her.

The book did not harm Moshe Dayan. Even if the public did identify him as the "hero" of *Flaming Paths,* no one was about to impale him for doing what King David or Lord Nelson had done. The public loved the gossip. Dayan's image was enhanced. Many excused him because he was Moshe Dayan, because they secretly envied him for living the life of Napoleon in the daytime, Don Juan in the evening. Lapping up every salacious page of *Flaming Paths,* the public helped to make Moshe Dayan larger than life. He was no longer just a military hero. He enjoyed the booty as well.

Dayan dismissed the book and the gossip as if it were an unfair invasion into his private life. To Yael he argued, "I don't consider it anybody's business, and I am not pretending to be a model husband."[31] Since he did not pretend to be faithful, he should be forgiven. Only one test should be required of him, in his view: Was he keeping his wife a prisoner at home against her will? Not at all. He had offered her the option of leaving him, separating or divorcing. If it were up to him, he hoped she would not choose any of these options. As he insisted to Yael, much of this gossip was overblown, most of it the accusations of hysterical women.

When the furor died down, Dayan emerged feeling good about himself. Had he refused to let Hadassah publish the book, a real scandal might have erupted. Nothing had really changed except that all of his antics became fair game for public comment and criticism. In the past, he had been shielded, at first by the protective shell of the IDF, then by a prime minister who used the Bible to justify the peccadillos of his cabinet ministers.

BY THIS TIME, serving as a cabinet minister no longer appeared that exciting. Nearly four years as minister of agriculture had taught Dayan that what he really wanted was a large role in the handling of Israel's national security issues. For as long as David Ben-Gurion held the defense portfolio, Dayan felt comfortable being the minister of agriculture. He knew, at least, that the defense of the country was in good hands.

Levi Eshkol replaced Ben-Gurion as prime minister in June 1963. Dayan began to grow bitter. He wanted the politicians to acknowledge that no one in the new cabinet knew as much as he about defense. Eshkol was both prime minister and defense minister; Golda Meir was foreign minister; Pinhas Sapir was minister of finance as well as minister for commerce and industry. None of these had any experience in defense matters. The natural candidate for defense minister would have been Dayan. Indeed, Shimon Peres proposed to Eshkol that he appoint Dayan defense minister, but Eshkol, undoubtedly unhappy about giving the top youngster too much political clout, balked at the idea.

Dayan was ready to leave the cabinet at that juncture. Ben-Gurion was retiring, the new government had no wish to employ his talents in defense matters, and the thought of working with production boards and technical assistance programs abroad offered little appeal.

At the last minute, Dayan stayed on. Maybe it was that he clung to the dream that Eshkol was only a caretaker prime minister, that the public would one day clamor for him to lead the country. "For many people of my generation," recalled Zalman Shoval, a longtime Dayan political lieutenant, "even before we knew him well, Dayan looked to us as the man who should become prime minister. This was based on the feeling that he was someone willing to take unconventional approaches, someone who finally was talking to us in a new voice."[32] Even Dayan's adversaries realized that the public held him in special esteem. As the minister of labor, Yigal Allon, put it: "When Dayan is hestitating, his admirers say he is thinking, but when Eshkol is thinking, his critics say that he is hesitating." If Eshkol lacked Dayan's popular appeal, he possessed greater political savvy than did the minister of agriculture. No matter how hard Dayan tried, Eshkol was not about to give up an inch of power.

It was not just Eshkol's failure to include Dayan in defense matters that bothered him. The two men had very different views on current economic matters. Dayan believed that living standards did not need to be increased, that wage demands did not have to be met. Inflation had to be curbed, production increased, and costs cut. To all this, Eshkol reacted without much enthusiasm. He felt that Israelis—after all that they had been through—could permit themselves a little relaxation, they could put on bedroom slippers, in Eshkol's neat phrase, and not always be frenetic about achieving some economic goal. Dayan countered by picking up Eshkol's imagery: The time had not yet come for Israelis to relax in their bedroom slippers. They must run even faster than they have in the past—even if they had no shoes.

The crunch for Dayan came when Eshkol backed off a promise to establish a small ministerial defense advisory committee on which Dayan would have served. To illustrate how isolated he felt in the cabinet, Dayan compared himself to the hero of a story: "Prisoners were being marched in line from the factory to the camps where they were housed. This man's comrades began to shove him, in turn, to the edge of the line, so that the outermost prisoner would push him to the edge of the steep, smooth embankment and the guards would shoot him for, apparently, trying to escape. I knew that I wouldn't be permitted to march in a line with the others in that government, I would be pushed and shoved until I stumbled. So it was better to resign before this had a chance to happen, while I was still standing on my feet."[33]

Edging toward a decision to resign in November 1964, Dayan met journalist Naphtali Lavie one day for coffee in Tel Aviv. Dayan said that he had no regrets about what he had done as minister of agriculture despite the criticism against him for proposing the Moneymaker tomato, and for ending dairy farming in urban areas. "But," he told Lavie, "I have suggestions to make on security matters too, and Eshkol is not willing to listen to me. If that's the way things are, I don't want to take the responsibility."

Did that mean he would resign, Lavie asked him?

"Draw your own conclusions," Dayan replied vaguely.

Uncertain what he should write the next day, Lavie took the risk and wrote that Dayan was considering resigning from the government. The same day Lavie's article appeared, Dayan tendered his resignation. Two hours before he turned in his letter of resignation on November 3, Dayan told Gad Ya'acobi, "I don't think Eshkol knows more than I do in defense matters. He should have made me a real partner in policymaking in those spheres. As I believe he will not do it, I will have nothing to do with this government. Eshkol is not Ben-Gurion and I'm not ready to take from Eshkol what I was ready to take from Ben-Gurion."[34]

Explaining to the prime minister why he resigned, Dayan told Eshkol that "there must be mutual trust between a prime minister and his ministers. I'm not a minister—or a person—after your own heart, and you are not a prime minister after mine."

DAYAN, who for the previous nine years had been chief of staff and then a cabinet minister, was faced with the question of what to do as a private citizen. He received a proposal from a business friend, Azriel Eynav, to let Eynav set aside sufficient funds for the next four years to finance a private office and a driver for him. No one of Dayan's status, Eynav thought, could be without an office and a driver. Dayan disagreed. He might have been able to use what was being offered, but he said no. It was then that Eynav proposed that Dayan become the head of a fishing company. Judging from the little that Dayan discussed this venture, his chairmanship of the board of the Histadrut-owned Yonah Fishing Company (which kept fishing vessels in the Red Sea) could not have excited him very much. The fact that he had to secure Prime Minister Eshkol's permission for the chairmanship gave him the distinct feeling that he had to grovel in front of his enemy. By playing hard to see, Eshkol seemed to be sticking the knife in even deeper. Around the same time, Dayan began writing his *Sinai Diary*.

Dayan's relationship with David Ben-Gurion was an increasing burden.

Supporting the Old Man in his one-man effort to nail Pinhas Lavon had been difficult, and when Dayan appeared to give less than enthusiastic backing to Ben-Gurion, the former prime minister appeared aggrieved. For his part, Dayan was bothered that Ben-Gurion stopped just short of endorsing him for the defense portfolio. Then, in the spring of 1964, Ben-Gurion offered an opinion about Dayan that was gratuitous, needless, and trouble making, and it caused Dayan acute embarrassment.

The controversial remark appeared in a newspaper interview that Ben-Gurion had given to the newspaper *Haboker*. As mentioned earlier, Ben-Gurion said that had he known Moshe Dayan at the beginning of the 1948 war, the Israeli frontiers would have been different, implying that Israel would have had more territory. He also called Dayan "the best chief of staff the Israel Defense Forces ever had," noting that Dayan's breakthrough to Lod and Ramle was "one of the most daring feats in our military history."

The impact of Ben-Gurion's remarks upon all those who had conducted the 1948 war was enormous. They took the "slur" most personally. Yigal Allon, who had commanded the Egyptian front then, complained that the country was still dismembered not because of any failure of strategy or fighting ability, but because Ben-Gurion had ordered the IDF to withdraw just as it had been about to conquer more land. Needling Moshe Dayan a bit, Yigael Yadin noted that he had had his share of failed military operations during 1948, one of which had been the abortive Beit Jalla attack. The former prime minister insisted that his comments had been meant to be off the record and, at any rate, had been taken out of context, but the damage had been done. Essentially what the Old Man did was to tout Dayan as a finer soldier than anyone else in the IDF and to infer that other Israeli military men had been inferior to Dayan. Jarred by these assaults, Ben-Gurion wrote a letter of apology to the chiefs of staff for having "stumbled over an obstacle." He insisted that he had meant to say that as a "wartime commander," Dayan had been the best among them. One wonders whether such a clarification offered any comfort to the chiefs of staff?

DAVID BEN-GURION would not let the Lavon Affair disappear. Perhaps because of his relationship with Levi Eshkol, Moshe Dayan displayed a new kindness toward Ben-Gurion and his struggle to seek justice in the Lavon Affair. After Eshkol's cabinet refused to reopen the affair in December 1964, Moshe Dayan and Shimon Peres tried the following month to mobilize support within Mapai to nominate Ben-Gurion as the party's candidate for prime minister in the August 1965 elections.

By February, Mapai was again in open revolt over the Lavon case. At the Mapai party conference in Tel Aviv that month the two factions—Ben-Gurion's and Eshkol's—vied for control of the party's executive committee. Eshkol's forces triumphed, gaining sixty percent. In a separate vote, 58.1 percent of the party voted to excise the Lavon Affair from Mapai's agenda. Continuing to dominate Mapai, Eshkol was chosen the party's candidate for prime minister in June by a vote of 179–103 of the executive committee.

The following month—on July 12—Ben-Gurion formed Rafi—Reshimat Poalei Israel, the Israel Labor List. It was to be a party that would represent Israel's younger generation, promoting modernization and the streamlining of the country's bureaucracy. To truly appeal to voters, Ben-Gurion and his lieutenants realized they needed Moshe Dayan.

Dayan, however, was most reluctant to join Rafi. Apart from any other reasons, he genuinely believed that it was time for David Ben-Gurion to leave the political arena, for the Ben-Gurion era in Israeli politics to come to a close. Dayan felt this way even though he had recently tried to make Ben-Gurion the Mapai candidate for prime minister. If Ben-Gurion insisted upon staying, there were good reasons for Dayan to steer clear of Rafi. For one thing, he told a newspaper interviewer that he was planning to retire from the political arena to settle in the desert town of Arad and run a Histadrut enterprise. He would remain loyal to Mapai "if they don't expel me." For another, he doubted that Rafi would bring the desired changes to Mapai. Why should he join a new party? His popularity in the country was a given whether he belonged to Mapai or Rafi. Most importantly, he had grave doubts that Ben-Gurion's new effort would win enough votes in the elections for Rafi to wield influence in the next government. Over coffee at Tel Aviv's Exodus coffee house, Dayan asked his cousin, Yigal Hurvitz, a new Rafi convert, how many Knesset seats he thought Rafi would win. Hurvitz replied, "fifteen to seventeen." To this Dayan said, "You should be happy if you get ten."[35] Joining Rafi, a party destined to sit on the back benches of the Knesset, would doom Dayan's prospects of becoming prime minister. Prime ministers came from the major parties—not from the tiny ones.

At one stage, both Mapai and Rafi fought over Dayan. Mapai knew Dayan's vote-getting appeal and so Eshkol urged Lova Eliav, a veteran Mapai politician, to try to persuade him to stay neutral in the Rafi-Mapai fight. Dayan was noncommittal. Eliav recalled that "Dayan's heart was not in it, only his loyalty to Ben-Gurion."[36] By the end of June, Dayan was leaning toward Rafi. If the Old Man wanted him inside Rafi, he could not resist. Still, he had demands for joining. Meeting with Ben-Gurion and his Rafi cohorts at that time, Dayan still acted hard to get.

"Ben-Gurion's two aims in setting up this list are a change in the electoral system and the establishment of a government," he said. "Neither can be achieved by an independent list." Rafi's goal, he argued, must be a change of government, not necessarily putting Ben-Gurion back in power: "The state of Israel will live on after all of us, and we must not make its existence dependent upon one person even if that person is David Ben-Gurion."

Smiling slyly, Ben-Gurion interrupted, noting: "In another two hundred years, with the help of science, man will live for thousands of years."

Dayan answered: "The question is how to get safely through those two hundred years."

During the meeting Dayan began to say "we" instead of "I." Did this mean that he had decided to join Rafi, someone asked him?

"Do you think I would have come here if I hadn't?"[37]

Ben-Gurion and Dayan then went into private consultation. The former prime minister did not want to appear to be begging Dayan to join Rafi. The Rafi list of candidates did not seem impressive to Dayan. He told Yael, "On a battlefield, a small elite unit can win over a large organized force. In the political arena, the full advantage lies with the powerful establishment. If Rafi could not achieve its aims, what was the use of founding it or joining it?" he asked pessimistically.[38] Not until September did Dayan officially join Ben-Gurion's new party, running in the seventh place on the list. Why had he accepted this relatively low spot? "Let's put it this way: a commander should lead his men into battle, but when they come to water, perhaps he should be the last to drink."[39] He was never happy inside Rafi; disdainfully, he talked about Rafi members in the second and third person, never saying "we." When the party ran into financial problems and had to ask its leaders to sign personal guarantees, Dayan refused.

On November 2 elections were held. It had been the most bitter, dirty, and expensive campaign in Israel's history. Ben-Gurion hoped Rafi would win fifteen to twenty seats. Some pundits, considering the former prime minister's towering standing in the country, actually believed Rafi would win thirty to forty seats to Mapai's fifteen to twenty. The actual results were quite a shock: Eshkol's Mapai won forty-five seats, with 36.7 percent of the vote; Menachem Begin's newly-formed Gahal party—joining Herut with the Liberal party—won twenty-six seats with 21.3 percent; the National Religious party, eleven seats with 9 percent; and Rafi, in a lowly fourth place, ten seats with 7.9 percent. Mapai's victory was considered a huge upset. Eshkol had no trouble forming a coalition—without Rafi.

The election results relegated Moshe Dayan to the back benches. This added to his unhappiness. His headaches grew more frequent and intense. He dwelt morbidly on the fact that he was getting older. "After twenty-five years in defense and five in agriculture," he told Gad Ya'acobi, "I have no such pivot now, and it's not easy."[40] Displeased at slipping from the public's mind, Dayan referred to himself as "Yael Dayan's father," a backhanded compliment to his increasingly celebrated novelist daughter. He ached for the limelight as an actor yearns for the stage. Ruth Dayan once told *Ha'olam Ha'zeh* editor Uri Avnery, "If Moshe doesn't see his name in the papers for three days running, he gets physically ill." He bemoaned private life. With Ben-Gurion abandoning the Knesset after Rafi's poor showing, Dayan and Peres were left to conduct Rafi's affairs. Dayan let Peres do the nuts-and-bolts work; Dayan determined the party's stand on issues. Dayan found the opposition role distasteful. He was an activist; debating in parliament seemed beside the point.

His most active pursuit was writing his *Diary of the Sinai Campaign 1956*, and traveling abroad to promote it during 1966. Published in October 1965 in Hebrew, the book caused consternation in Israel but won Dayan warm praise abroad. At home, he was pilloried for offering an account of the 1956 war that critics assailed as too frank. Overseas reviewers commended Dayan for his brutal honesty. Military analyst Hanson Baldwin called it "a much needed corrective to some of the earlier books on the Sinai campaign that were couched in excessive superlatives and extravagant overpraise for the tough little Israeli army."[41] British reviewer Jon Kimche echoed: "Ever since 1956, Israelis have come to believe the pretty stories about the smooth drive to the Suez, much as in earlier years they had accepted the fairy-tale version of the War of Independence. Dayan's book constituted a rude and timely awakening. Wars are no Sunday outings. They have to be fought to be won. They cost lives. The outcome is never certain. For the first time since 1956 this fact has been rammed home to the Israeli public."[42]

Infuriated Israelis did not react warmly to that fact being rammed home to them. Why was it necessary to dwell on Israeli tanks firing on one another, or commanders who disobeyed orders? Some accused Dayan of giving aid and comfort to the enemy by revealing IDF weaknesses, though the army's flaws were mild compared to those of the routed Egyptian army.

Book promotion was new to Dayan. He found the lectures he gave a strain. While in London on January 21, 1966, he wrote Rahel a wandering letter, noting that he planned to meet Ruth in Cyprus and return to Israel together; "at least we will make an impression." Then: "London was so-so. Or perhaps I was so-so. There was nothing that I worked on especially and nothing I tried to achieve." In Paris, he gave a lecture which he thought "excellent. Thank you for the grade that I have given myself. But the translation into English was terrible and destroyed the lecture. Things are blurred. I have taken a sleeping pill. Another thing, we must eat a meal together in Paris. Together, with all the tables full and you will laugh loudly, and I won't have to turn my head to see who is laughing near another table so nicely. Others will look at you and I will be jealous."

From Paris eight days later, he again wrote to Rahel, this time bemoaning his pitiful life as a Rafi politician. "Last night they took me to a very good restaurant in Paris. It was something, but not the 'something' that I am missing. What I am missing is the central axis of life. The idea that in another few days I will have to be in the Knesset in order to criticize Sapir or Eshkol, that I will have to sit as Rafi, even though it is better than sitting as Mapai, is not entirely satisfactory to me. . . . Why do I bother you? Are you missing your own problems? But then who will I bother, if not you? . . . I know that public and private activities aren't missing in my life, archaeology, but these are all marginal things. But I have been lost and I didn't have any other way—the central basis. I come back all the time to the same thing because I can't withdraw from it."

DAYAN MISSED being in a war zone. His ongoing contempt for politics seemed to be his way of acknowledging that nothing could fill the gap left by his departure from the army. Just as business tycoons needed the thrill of winning one more deal, Moshe Dayan needed one more war. "Wars are the most exciting events of life," he said some years later, the "supreme drama" because they involve death. "There is nothing more exciting or dramatic."[43] If only he could find a way to "return" to soldiering—and in doing so, grab a few headlines—all would be well again.

He found his war in the summer of 1966 in Vietnam. Dayan decided to go on an on-the-spot inspection tour of the war zone. Whatever he had to say would be listened to, reported widely, and respected. The more he thought about the idea, the more attractive it seemed. He would go under the guise of a reporter and write some newspaper articles. The articles would put him back on the front pages again. It all seemed tailor-made for him, getting briefed by senior generals, being photographed while slogging around in the mud with American soldiers. It would all seem terribly familiar, yet new.

It would have to be understood he was not making the trip to endorse the American position. Going only to South Vietnam might give that impression. So he made it clear that if the North Vietnamese issued him a visa, he would visit Hanoi as well (he had little hope of getting one). Unquestionably, the lessons he would learn could be applied back home. It was not to be ruled out that one day he might be called upon to take part in the conduct of another Israeli war: He could learn as much, he thought, from a firsthand look at the Vietnamese war as from the IDF's annual exercise. Yet, in the eyes of many, this venture was no mere exercise in journalism. The Arabs were convinced that Dayan was masquerading as a reporter to conceal some more nefarious deed. By way of response, Ahmed Shukeiry's Palestine Liberation Organization passed word that if Dayan was going to Vietnam, then some of its guerrilla fighters would go as well: They would fight on the side of the Vietcong and try to pick up some techniques that they could apply against Israel.

There was no way Dayan could escape the cold, harsh light of the criticism aimed at him. The verbal sniping came mostly from Israel's left wing, the activists who thought American involvement in Vietnam was senseless. They were shocked at the thought that Israel's most famous military figure would add his voice to America's apologists. Making the journey seemed proof that he backed the American military effort there. He must be stopped. The activists tried in various ways to have his trip canceled. The Communist party introduced a Knesset resolution on June 9 condemning the trip but that got nowhere, as Foreign Minister Abba Eban noted that the government had nothing to do with Knesset member Moshe Dayan's travels. The visits of cabinet ministers needed government approval, not those of Knesset members. Mapam party activists protested outside Dayan's home in Zahala, holding up placards that urged him to stay home. Dayan was not fazed. It was unclear to him why so many people were in an uproar over this simple exercise in journalism.

Before arriving in Vietnam, Dayan conducted his own international seminar on the subject, with stops in Paris to see the defeated French general of Dien Bien Phu and in London for a chat with Field Marshal Montgomery. Until he arrived in the United States, he could not be sure how President Lyndon Johnson's administration would take to his Vietnam journey.

He was treated well, as he noted in a letter to Rahel on July 22 while flying from New York to Los Angeles: "I am really drained physically and mentally. Each day I run around from meeting to meeting . . . in Washington the Americans received me—not the Israeli embassy. . . ." (He had been invited to meet with columnist Joseph Alsop and *Washington Post* owner Katherine Graham.) "I had the impression that [Walt] Rostow [Johnson's special assistant on national security affairs] and [Robert] McNamara [the secretary of defense] were impressed with me. . . . Ketzele, forgive me for going on with so many details in order to explain how my trip is snowballing. . . . I know that you think, as I know you, that all this [attention to Dayan] is natural and I deserve it, but God knows how things can go differently." He injected a word about American reaction to the recently published English-language version of his *Diary of the Sinai Campaign 1956:* "The publisher is licking his lips at the good reviews of the book."

Since the American book reviewers were comparing him to Gen. Archibald Wavell, the British commander of Middle East forces in World War II, and Lawrence of Arabia, it was not surprising that the American defense establishment held Dayan in great respect. Even before he had left for Vietnam, he appeared to have a firm grasp of America's military position there; his briefers were impressed. One of them, an ex-member of the Joint Chiefs of Staff, noted that "he is a man of great intelligence and depth of analysis. I have briefed dozens of important people on the same subjects, but he understood the problems, partly through military instinct and partly through research, better than any of them. In fact, he is difficult to brief because he understands everything so quickly and instinctively. He asked deeper and more probing questions about Vietnam than anyone has before or since."

For all that Dayan craved the battlefield, he was realist enough to understand that one could get killed out there. His vaunted bravery had always been genuine. Yet, no matter how many times he asserted to astonished comrades-in-arms that he had a lucky star hovering overhead, he knew better. He knew his time could come, perhaps during this trip to Vietnam. Just in case, he wanted to bid farewell to those who were closest to him. To have done so in person before leaving would have been too melodramtic. So he chose to write letters while on the American leg of his journey—to his sister Aviva, to his father, to *Ma'ariv* editor Aryeh Dissentchik, to Gad Ya'acobi, and to his friend and fellow writer, Moshe Pearlman. But the letter he wrote to Rahel was the most difficult for him to compose: "Although I wrote to you yesterday and we spoke in the morning, and wrote to you again this morning, it doesn't matter. Right? I simply wanted to tell you again how happy I was with our discussion and to hear your voice. I just wanted to hear your voice before I got to Saigon. I know that it will be a difficult period for me and not only because [Maxwell] Taylor [a presidential adviser, former American chief of staff and American ambassador to Vietnam] said to me, 'Be careful, General, there are some very hard bullets in Vietnam.' Therefore I have written many letters in the last two days. . . . I wrote not because I am a fatalist but because I want to be free of all mutual obligations and to concentrate only on one thing: the actions in Vietnam." He also wrote, while in San Francisco, that he had finally asked Ruth for a divorce. He added that she had refused, saying that one did not divorce a woman of fifty.

Nothing would seem stranger to Dayan than the American military operation in Vietnam. From the moment he arrived he could not get over the amount of firepower the Americans were expending, nor the amount of money being spent. Da Nang was not Degania, Pleiku was not Lod, and Saigon was not Jerusalem. At one stage, the American support units laid down no less than twenty-one thousand shells. "This," wrote a shocked Dayan later, "was more than the total volume of artillery fire expended by the Israeli army units during the Sinai campaign and the War of Independence together."[44] The Americans, he said on another occasion, "had more shells than the Vietcong had soldiers." Never before had he witnessed war on such a large scale. Noting that America was employing 1,700 American helicopters, each costing $3 million, Dayan could only think back to his decision as chief of staff to cancel overseas study trips for officers so that he could save seventy thousand dollars!

He spent most of his five weeks in the field, engaging in combat missions with the American troops. He ate and slept with them, washed his clothing in the muddy rivers, and insisted on being treated like a private. In few other periods of his career was Dayan so frequently photographed. He was a one-man photo opportunity. The eyepatched Israeli war hero in a whole variety of colorful poses: canteen slung over his shoulder, he is shown an American rifle by a young soldier; walking on patrol in khakis and a field hat, sometimes with a battle helmet on his head, sometimes a canteen around his waist; wading through a river. The *Sunday Telegraph* ran four photographs of Dayan on August 14 under the heading: "An Israeli general goes to the Vietnam war armed with a diary." One photo showed him shaving in the field; another, eating sweet corn on the cob, wearing an army rain coat, his boots muddied and wet; a third, bathing in a river with his eyepatch off (a rare shot indeed!); and the fourth, standing in battle gear, writing in his diary.

He behaved in Vietnam as he always did, fearlessly, cockily, acting very much as if his lucky star were shining very brightly. One platoon commander, informed that Dayan would be tagging along on a patrol, chose a route to assure that his precious visitor would not die while under his responsibility. Once in the jungle, they marched for an entire day without incident. Suddenly the Vietcong pinned them down with heavy gunfire. When the platoon commander had a moment to pick his head up, he realized that Moshe Dayan had disappeared. He searched for him, thinking the worst. He discovered the former Israeli chief of staff fifty yards away, perched on a hill, gazing down at the firefight—a sitting duck for the Vietcong, should they choose to aim in Dayan's direction. Racing to the hill, the commander was about to yell up to him, when Dayan shouted down, "Hey, what kind of commander are you? Why are you crawling down there in the dirt? You can't see anything. Come up here and see what's going on."

Such tales turned Dayan's Vietnam sojourn into a roaring public relations triumph for him. *Time* magazine described him in near-heroic terms: "Knee-deep in mud, the correspondent pushed doggedly ahead into Viet Cong territory with a U.S. Marine reconnaissance patrol. Later, he was up and at them with the Green Berets near Pleiku, then hopped aboard a helicopter to participate in a 1st Cavalry airborne assault landing." *Time* quoted an admiring American officer as saying, "He moves like a worm in hot ashes."[45]

Toward the end of his tour, he visited the American aircraft carrier *Constellation* and came away with a new appreciation of America's air power. In a letter written to Rahel toward the end of his visit Dayan noted that

> They produce the most sophisticated military actions [on the carrier]. Every hour and a half a chorus of planes leaves for bombing runs. And every hour and a half they return. Thus it is for twenty-four hours a day. There are nine stories. The ship is not dependent upon any other element to defend it from the air. To understand the American approach to security matters in the world one must see [the way it employs] its heavy industry for military actions; their planes which can reach any part of the world. And to be sovereign over them. Meanwhile I am very tired. In the cell it has been very hot. And it was impossible to sleep. And the night before I hardly slept. . . . What is strange is that I don't feel anything heavy or strange [about his activities with the Americans]. . . . Everything is new, and foreign to me, but not that much that I feel personal discomfort or unpleasantness or something like that. Ketzele, I am located at the farthest point somewhere near the China coast. Beginning tomorrow I begin to return, getting close to you geographically.

While still in Vietnam, Dayan discovered that he was to have an unexpected visitor: his wife. During a Far East tour of her own Ruth had decided to stop off in Vietnam, knowing her husband would be there. Finding him was not easy. When she caught up with him, he did not appear overjoyed.

"What in the world are you doing in Vietnam?" he asked Ruth over the phone.

"I came to see you," she said. "Aren't you a little happy I'm here?"

Dayan was cold. "A little."

They went out to a Chinese restaurant and then dancing, something they had not done for some time. Their discussion roamed over everything but the war. Ruth later described that evening as "wonderful," but Dayan was not pleased that she had appeared.[46] To Rahel, he wrote the surprising news on August 22: "Ruth has arrived here, as you imagine, it is against what I want. She obtained my timetable from the Americans through the American Embassy in Bangkok. . . . I don't think she enjoyed herself here."

Returning to Israel via the United States, Dayan held meetings with American officials who were eager to learn firsthand of his impressions. What he told them could not have caused joy. He was one of the first authoritative commentators to say that the United States had no chance of winning the war unless it captured or occupied North Vietnam. He correctly predicted that the United States would ultimately have to make an embarrassing retreat as a result of American public opinion.

From New York's Pierre Hotel he wrote Rahel in September: "Here I am completely bored. Essentially I have finished the meetings [in the United States] two days ago. It has gone better than I expected. In Washington they took care of me as if I were the family doctor with whom they were consulting about an illness in which everyone in the home is suffering from. They really listen to my opinion and to the criticism and to the conception. What needs to be and what doesn't need to be done in Vietnam. No one raised the subjects about Israel, Jordan in the meetings. The truth is that it doesn't interest them that much. So far I haven't had a free night. Tonight I finally went to a show, I don't know which one."

In the three articles he wrote for the *Sunday Telegraph* in England and *Ma'ariv* in Israel after his trip, he had much to say about American tactics. He was surprised to find the Americans forgetting some of the basic rules of engagement. Air power and artillery were used primarily for American counterattacks, not infantry. Sometimes the Americans use an exaggerated amount of firepower: "The artillery and air force are summoned to bombard an area once it is shown to be holding enemy troops—even if there is not more than one sniper."

While the Vietcong attacked when they deemed circumstances to be favorable, American forces did not attach any importance to the creation of favorable circumstances. "The American commanders just want to make contact with the Viet Cong and are convinced that once the clash developed they'll get the upper hand." As for secrecy, the Americans seemed not to worry too much about it. "The air cavalry are the perfect (though expensive) answer to the problem of mobility in the jungle. But there is one thing the Americans seem unable to do—land their units quietly, secretly, without detection. The helicopters announce themselves every inch of the way. The Viet Cong, on the other hand, may take three months to walk from the north, but they do not give themselves away."

Still, Dayan appreciated the overwhelming advantages of American firepower. When noting that the Vietcong had forgotten to take into account American artillery, aircraft, and tanks, he observed: "There is a primitive and leaden logic to warfare; in an open engagement between two unequal forces, the strong defeats the weak. The victories of the Davids over the Goliaths are rare indeed in the kingdom of tanks and guns."[47]

✦10✦

CALLED TO LEAD

THE MIDDLE EAST was sliding into war again. No one wanted it and hence few could believe that it was really happening. The period after the Sinai Campaign of 1956 had been astonishingly peaceful and productive for Israel. The country's 2.7 million Jews had grown used to feeling secure and prosperous. By late 1966, the frontiers were still reasonably quiet, with good prospects that they would remain so. Safe within its tiny 7,993 square miles, Israel had exploited the post-Sinai years to produce an economic miracle. Its growth rate had climbed ten percent every year for the fourteen years from 1950 to 1964, giving the country in that latter year a standard of living equal to Western Europe's. By 1966, the miracle had ended and Israel confronted a major recession due in part to the government's attempts to curb the then-staggering rate of ten percent annual inflation.

Just as the economic miracle proved unenduring, so too had the quiet on Israel's frontiers. The 1956 campaign, despite hopes to the contrary, had not entirely solved Israel's security problem. The "peace" that it had brought was in fact as tense as it was illusory, kept fragile by recurring incidents, especially along the Syrian-Israeli frontier, as well as by the absence of peace treaties. Events put the Jewish state once again at potential risk. The Soviets had entered the Middle East on the side of the Arab states, supporting Egypt in particular. The arms race in the Middle East had accelerated, as both Israel and the Arab countries had been furnished tanks, missiles, and jet bombers. Egypt's Nasser, though mauled badly by the 1956 defeat, had shown great resilience, gaining new popularity and portraying himself as the Arab David facing the Israeli Goliath. As if to demonstrate how tentative the post-Sinai peace was, patrolling the Sinai was a feckless group of uniformed "soldiers" called the United Nations Emergency Force (UNEF) who, as was well known to both sides, would vanish into thin air at the first indication that they were not wanted, hardly making them a guarantor of the peace.

Yet, amidst this illusory peace, no one, Moshe Dayan included, realized that the Israelis and Arabs were sitting on a powder keg that was about to go off. The first match was struck on November 12, 1966, when an Israeli unit patrolling Israel's frontier with Jordan south of Mount Hebron ran over a mine. Three soldiers were killed and six wounded. The next day Israel carried out a reprisal raid against the Jordanian village of Samoa, near Mount Hebron, from which the infiltrators had launched their attack the day before, killing twenty Jordanians and wounding thirty-five.

The Jordanians lived under the illusion that in events of this kind Egypt could be counted upon to come to their rescue. Egypt did not. Samoa showed the emptiness of Egypt's promises, and put pressure on Nasser to demonstrate his ability to take action against Israel. Egypt came under more pressure from the Syrians in early 1967. On April 7, Syria shelled three Israeli kibbutzim at the foot of the Golan Heights. In response, Israel's air force shot down six MiGs, two of them in the skies over Damascus. Angered by this obvious show of weakness, the Syrians turned to Egypt, with whom they had signed a defense pact the previous November. They demanded that Nasser send his warplanes into Syrian airspace as protection against Israel and that he take action against Israeli targets along his own frontier in the south. On May 1, Nasser announced that he would place his planes and pilots at Syria's disposal. Having grown used to the past decade of relative tranquillity, most Israelis wanted to avoid any large clash, like the one on April 7, for fear that it might provoke the Arabs into a larger confrontation. Moshe Dayan shared that view. Phoning Ezer Weizman, then head of operations for the IDF, Dayan berated him for acting so aggressively. "Are you people out of your minds? You're leading the country to war."[1]

MOST ISRAELIS still were convinced that Nasser had been so overwhelmed by the 1956 defeat that he would not dare start another round. Israel had made it clear that were Nasser to close the Straits of Tiran again, Israel would consider this an act of war, and the IDF would respond accordingly. The Israelis overlooked the fact that 1956 had been a humiliation Nasser needed to erase.

Nasser had renewed his conviction that Israel could be torn apart. The numbers appeared to favor the Arabs. Egypt, Syria, and Jordan had a combined potential military strength of 547,000 soldiers while Israel could count on 300,000 (of whom only 70,000 were in the standing army; the rest were reserves). The Arabs could field 5,404 tanks compared to Israel's 800; 900 aircraft, compared to Israel's 200. Arrayed against those 2.7 million Jews were 110 million Arabs. Israel's military posture a decade earlier had been much stronger; then Israeli and Egyptian forces in the Sinai were nearly in balance, two divisions for the Egyptians, one and a half for Israel. This time, the Egyptians seemed capable of fielding far greater forces in the Sinai.

By mid-May Nasser was ready to act. On May 12 an intelligence officer in Cairo's Soviet embassy transmitted to Egyptian intelligence "confirmation" of a Syrian report that Israel had massed troops on the Syrian frontier. With that report in hand, Nasser was ready to show Syria that it could fulfill its promises—and to demonstrate to Israel that Egypt, while down in 1956, was by no means out. He began moving thousands of troops across the Suez Canal into the Sinai, suddenly placing Israel at risk of large-scale war. The first Israeli intelligence reports of these ominous movements came during the evening of May 14 as Israel began ceremonies marking its nineteenth Independence Day. Though he had earlier doubted that the region would find itself at war, Moshe Dayan now sensed that Nasser was bent on hostilities with Israel. Nasser, in his view, had become infatuated with his words, intoxicated with power, a power derived from large quantities of tanks and planes. At an Independence Day celebration sponsored by Dayan's Rafi party, he predicted to two friends that Nasser would close the Straits, making war inevitable.

On the morning of May 16, Chief of Staff Yitzhak Rabin was host to the six previous chiefs of staff. Rabin asked them to guess the Egyptians' next moves. Dayan was the only one with a clear idea: "They'll demand the withdrawal of the UN forces, who will be obliged to obey because they are on Egyptian soil. Then if Nasser wants to go further, he will be able to seal the Straits of Tiran." No one else agreed. No one would let himself contemplate how Israel might have to react to further deterioration of its position. The very next day Dayan's prediction materialized as Nasser demanded that those UNEF troops stationed along the Israeli-Egyptian frontier from below the Gaza Strip to Eilat leave. The UNEF forces at Sharm el-Sheikh and in the Gaza Strip could remain. U Thant, the United Nations secretary-general, at first balked, saying that either his troops would all remain, or all leave. Nasser said, in effect, "Fine, then they must all leave." Two days later, on May 19, U Thant acceded to Nasser's demand and all UNEF troops left Sinai.

Then began the waiting period, a purgatory of uncertainty and fear for Israelis who had no stomach for war, but had grown increasingly convinced that war would break out, and might be catastrophic for their country. Though Israel had triumphed in 1948 and 1956, its citizens sensed that the Arabs had learned valuable lessons from their two defeats and now had the potential of breaking through Israeli defense lines. Chilling scenarios were sketched, all of which included the likelihood that Israel, even if it won the next round, would suffer twenty thousand to thirty thousand dead. News of thousands of Arabs in Cairo demonstrating wildly in favor of throwing the Jews into the sea deepened Israeli concerns. Not eager for war, its leaders turned to diplomacy, a slow process that afforded the Arabs more time to dig into the Sinai. All the while, Israelis grew more frightened.

In the present turmoil, Moshe Dayan, just turned fifty-two years old, found himself with surprisingly little to do. A mere Knesset member, he served on the Knesset Foreign Affairs and Defense Committee but played no part in the decision making, as he and his Rafi party had been in the opposition since late 1965. This was the first major military crisis confronting Israel in which Dayan could play no direct role. Field commander in 1948, chief of staff in 1956, he was frustratingly far from the action. His instincts told him that he could best serve the country, and his personal cause, by getting away from the politicians and spending time with the troops in the field. Dayan had decided to go south for the same reason that he had been on the spot when soldiers returned from reprisal raids, for the same reason that he had gone to Vietnam. The alternative was to drink tea in the Knesset dining room and coffee houses in Tel Aviv. In retrospect, heading for the front was a brilliant decision. For, all the while that pejoratives were hurled at the politicians for dithering, for procrastinating, for displaying weakness, Moshe Dayan was wrapping himself up in the one institution that might save the day— the Israel Defense Forces. While the politicians shrouded themselves in fear and worry, Moshe Dayan was crafting an image as savior. Rarely were two Israeli institutions—Moshe Dayan and the IDF—in such perfect symbiosis. Dayan inspired the army and was himself inspired by the troops.

On May 17 Dayan joined another former chief of staff, Chaim Laskov, now supervisor of harbor installations, on a visit to tank forces commanded by Armored Corps commander Israel Tal at Rafiah. Still skeptical about the value of tanks in warfare, Dayan asked Laskov what led him to boast that Israel's armored corps was the best in the world.

"Choose yourself a target within a three kilometer [two mile] range," Laskov suggested, "and we will fire a tank cannon at it. You will see what happens." Dayan did so, and the gunner fired three shells, all on the mark. "That," said a proud Laskov, "is the explanation. We are the most professional in the world."

If Dayan wished to continue touring military installations, he needed the prime minister's permission. Otherwise, commanders would be in the awkward position of having to check whether they could share sensitive military information with a mere Knesset member who happened to be a former chief of staff. Prime Minister Eshkol was distinctly cool to Dayan's request. As a former chief of staff and member of the Knesset Foreign Affairs and Defense Committee, Dayan had a perfect right to keep himself fully informed on military matters. But this was Moshe Dayan: enemy of the Mapai veterans; ally of David Ben-Gurion; leader of the youngsters. Letting him tour the bases would let him into a central position through the back door. Aharon Yariv, director of military intelligence, was sent to persuade Dayan to delay his tour for several weeks.

"Moshe, let the dust settle. At the moment the guys [the reservists] have just arrived."

"I don't want the dust to settle," Dayan replied. "I want to see them with the dust." There was no way of denying Moshe Dayan's request.

For Dayan, as for most other Israelis, the Egyptian thrust into Sinai was dangerous, but did not justify an immediate Israeli military response. Though the Egyptians had moved eighty thousand troops into Sinai, Dayan agreed with Ben-Gurion's oft-spoken thesis that Israel should avoid war unless it had a mutual defense pact with a friendly power such as the United States.

Dayan had one obligation to perform before heading south. He cabled Yael in Athens to come home at once. They had an understanding that in the event of war, he would notify her so she could be on hand. He had done so in 1956. In summoning her now, he acknowledged to himself that an Egyptian attack was likely.

On the eve of his departure, the chief of staff, Yitzhak Rabin, called on Dayan at his Zahala home to seek his advice. He gained little solace: The former chief of staff lashed into the cabinet and the IDF for effectively creating the crisis by staging provocative reprisal raids against Syria and Jordan. These raids had forced Nasser to defend his prestige by pouring troops into the Sinai. Dayan expected Nasser to close the Straits soon. In response, he suggested, the IDF should not attack Sharm right away; but hold off, and instead choose a favorable location to rout the Egyptian army. Only then should it seek to open the Straits. Rabin believed that the most favorable locale for Israel to meet the Egyptians was Gaza.

Dayan disagreed. When they parted, Dayan noted to himself that Rabin seemed tired, perplexed, dejected, definitely not impatient for battle. As Dayan predicted, Nasser announced on the morning of May 23 that he was closing the Straits of Tiran to all ships to and from Israel. From Israel's point of view, this could only mean one thing. War.

Though one newspaper the next day called upon the politicians to form an emergency government, few wanted to believe that anything so drastic as war was required. The nation's leaders, especially the prime minister and the chief of staff, looked upon an Israeli declaration of war as an admission of failing to keep the peace. Even if Egypt had poured its troops into the Sinai and could march on Tel Aviv at any minute, Israeli leaders wanted to believe that it could not happen, that Mr. Nasser was bluffing.

SETTING OFF on his journey south on May 23, Dayan felt like a little boy given a new toy. He had in fact been given a car and driver. He had donned his uniform and put on his chief of staff badge, neither of which he needed to be recognized. He did not get very far. A military policeman caught up with Dayan and gave him instructions to return to Tel Aviv for an urgent meeting of the ministerial defense committee along with opposition leaders at the prime minister's office. In the wake of Nasser's decision to close the Straits, Israeli leaders raised the idea of sending an Israeli ship on a trial sailing through the Gulf of 'Aqaba, but Washington had asked Jerusalem to wait forty-eight hours before doing so. How Israel should respond to Washington's request was the main question before the Tel Aviv meeting that morning.

"If the United States has asked for forty-eight hours, we can give it to them. But I mean forty-eight, not forty-nine," said Dayan. "If they open the Straits, so much the better. I don't believe that they will do it for us. After that delay we ought to go to war with Egypt and fight a battle that will destroy hundreds of tanks and planes. We shall have very little time—we must try to win in two or three days."

Eshkol was in no mood for such belligerent talk. He wanted to figure out how to avoid war, not pave the way for one. Israel's foreign minister, Abba Eban, had proposed that Washington be asked to provide an American destroyer to escort an Israeli vessel through the Straits. The prime minister was inclined to accept that idea. Dayan argued that such an exercise would be no test of Israel's freedom of shipping. In the end, the committee agreed to wait forty-eight hours and not to ask for an American naval escort. A decision was quietly taken to mobilize all of Israel's reserves.

To Dayan, the dithering had begun in earnest. He urged Eskhol aide Adi Yaffe not to summon him to any more meetings. "I don't want to have to attend any meeting that doesn't have the power to make a decision. I'd rather be inspecting the army units and studying the defense problems." Later that day he huddled with Rafi politicians, including David Ben-Gurion and Shimon Peres. The latter was eager to put Eskhol on the defensive, to find a way to force him to step down as prime minister. Dayan was not eager to join in such political maneuvering. He listened in growing impatience as Ben-Gurion expressed his usual nervousness that Israeli cities might become the targets of Arab attacks.

"Will the Egyptians use their missiles?" a worried Ben-Gurion asked to no one in particular.

"A missile is a plane without a pilot," Dayan responded. "The question doesn't hinge on that. The Israeli army is superb and its leadership is excellent. We can stand the test."[2]

This was precisely the kind of meeting he wished to avoid, politicians sitting around theorizing. He vowed he would not return to such forums.

As Dayan finally headed south, thousands of reservists were donning their uniforms and hitchhiking to their units. Middle-aged men were volunteering for temporary police duty, middle-aged housewives enlisting as air raid wardens. Youngsters found time to deliver the mail.

While clearly a strain for nearly everyone, the waiting period could not last long enough for one senior Israeli. Air Force Commander Mordechai Hod knew that with each passing day, Egypt was sending more of its warplanes into the Sinai. That, from Hod's point of view, was all to the good. Sixty of Israel's two hundred fighter planes were limited in range to the Sinai.

Finally, on the afternoon of May 23, Dayan reached the southern command. By this time, the Egyptians had 100,000 troops and 1,000 tanks in the Sinai, compared to Israel's 60,000 soldiers and 400 tanks. That evening he spoke with Yehoshua Gavish, southern front commander. Looking over Gavish's plans, Dayan observed that he did not know whether the plans were good or not. "I assume they're OK. But I can tell you: You will win this war. We will screw the Arabs, but you will have 20,000 to 30,000 fatalities. Everyone. The best of our youth."[3]

Agreeing that Israel would win whatever war broke out, Gavish could not believe that the IDF would lose so many soldiers. Despite the former chief of staff's morose vision of the fighting, the local front commander genuinely appreciated his presence—and, more importantly, the message he had conveyed. "He was the first one from the national level," Gavish recalled, "who came to me and said, 'You will win the war.' Until then, everyone was frightened about the outcome."[4]

If the IDF were to launch a war—and few were in favor of such a bold step—the only plan the politicians and the generals championed was a limited thrust into the Gaza Strip and northern Sinai no farther south than El Arish. This "small plan" had the advantage of keeping Israeli casualties low and of putting pressure on Egypt to end its blockade of the Straits. To Dayan's mind this plan was self-defeating. Here was Nasser thumbing his nose at Israel and all the IDF could do was try to strike a bargain with him: We will evacuate northern Sinai and the Gaza Strip, if you will permit Israeli shipping through the Straits. What if Nasser responded by telling Israel to go choke on the Gaza Strip, by ignoring the pressure, and keeping the blockade on the Straits in force? What good was a limited plan then?

As he moved from base to base, he grew more certain that war was inevitable. He felt a unique bond with his countrymen; never did he feel so close to them. He was in his own element; "His face lit up," Yael Dayan recalled. "When he spoke of the troops, of the commanders he knew; his heartbeat was with them, and all the parental love, all the camaraderie this man could summon glittered in his one eye."[5]

His presence among the troops was electrifying. Soldiers who yearned for political leadership but found none suddenly cast a happy glance at Moshe Dayan. Danny Matt, a senior commander then, recalled that "there had been a feeling that the leadership didn't have confidence in itself. There's no question that the arrival of Moshe Dayan caused a revolution in the atmosphere within the army. The army now felt capable of going to war and winning it."[6]

While the IDF's self-confidence grew, the fabric of the government was falling apart back in Jerusalem. On the morning of May 24, Gen. Avraham Yoffee, one of the three division commanders in the south, informed Dayan that the chief of staff was in bed ill, suffering from nicotine poisoning. It was true that Rabin had smoked excessively during this period but, according to even his closest acquaintances, he had suffered a near-total collapse, brought on by his being shouldered with the main responsibility for handling the crisis. Rabin had asked Weizman to replace him as chief of staff but Weizman refused. Upon hearing of Rabin's offer from Weizman, Dayan believed that the chief of operations had acted wisely; he did not want to seem to be grabbing for power.

Back in Beersheba during the evening of May 24, Dayan walked along the streets. Sidewalk café patrons noticed him and called out to him. "Moshe Dayan, Moshe Dayan." Someone tried to kiss him. Crowds formed around him. Police came and tried to extricate him. Strangers in the crowd asked him questions. Finally, a driver from the Ministry of Agriculture, spotting him in the midst of a sea of enthusiastic fans, freed him.

While that mob scene occurred, Israel's position was growing worse. Arms which Israel had ordered from France—and paid for—had been held up by French president Charles de Gaulle, who believed that delaying the arms would keep Israel from starting a war. British efforts to defuse the crisis, while well-intentioned, were of no consequence. Other West European countries such as Italy and Spain would not interfere out of fear of hurting relations with Egypt. American proposals were of no significance.

Pressure on the politicians began to mount. It was argued that if the current government could not take decisions, then a reshuffle was required, the main ideas being either a war cabinet or a wall-to-wall emergency government. A rising tide of criticism grew against Levi Eshkol, led by Shimon Peres, the secretary-general of Rafi. While numerous Knesset members outside of Mapai supported Peres's efforts, he faced serious obstacles within the prime minister's own party. Eshkol's party colleagues would not tolerate a rebellion.

Meanwhile, different scenarios were discussed. Gahal's leader, Menachem Begin, asked Peres if David Ben-Gurion, then aged eighty, would be able to take on the post of prime minister. "Able, yes. Ready, I don't know," said Peres. Eshkol refused, however, to step aside in favor of the Old Man. Begin dropped that idea but told Eshkol that Gahal was prepared to join a wall-to-wall coalition only if Dayan replaced him [Eshkol] as minister of defense. Dayan, said Begin, was "the right man in the right place." Peres shifted his efforts to securing the Defense Ministry for Dayan.

Avoiding all this political maneuvering, Dayan concentrated on visiting the troops. Whatever the cabinet decided, he wanted to be close to the action and to learn as much as he could about the IDF's state of preparedness. He had no concrete idea how he would use the information. He only knew that he wanted to be part of whatever the IDF was doing.

With the cabinet considering the possibility of going to war the next day, on May 25, Dayan asked Meir Amit, head of the Mossad, to deliver a note he had composed to Eshkol informing the prime minister of his request to Ezer Weizman to arrange for his formal entry into active military service. If Eshkol or Rabin wished Dayan to take on a certain task, he was prepared to do so. Otherwise, wrote Dayan, he would carry on visiting field units to study the army up close. These visits would enable him to speak more authoritatively on what the army could do. The memo was sent on May 25.

That evening, Dayan dined with Yael, who had arrived from Athens earlier that day, "just in time," Dayan told her. "The war may begin tomorrow with dawn, unless it is postponed again, which would not surprise me." Then he gave her some "inside information": "Make sure you're sent south. The best, of course, is Sharon's division, if you can get there!"[7] Later Dayan himself headed south. Again the war was postponed. Diplomacy was being given another try: This time Abba Eban was meeting Lyndon Johnson at the White House on May 26. On that day, Dayan heard senior officers rail against the "small plan." They were itching to take on the Egyptians. During the morning of May 26, while he was touring soldiers near Sde Boker, Dayan was summoned to meet Eshkol in Tel Aviv that evening.

Meanwhile, large advertisements appeared in the Israeli press urging that the "1956 Sinai Campaign team" of Ben-Gurion and Dayan be brought into the government. Ben-Gurion's name was mentioned as a courtesy; no one truly believed that he was fit to govern. The advertisements were aimed at bringing Dayan into the upper echelons of the government. No one was more acutely aware of the shift in public opinion toward Dayan than the prime minister, who viewed him as his greatest political threat. Eshkol sought to neutralize Dayan. Though other candidates for defense minister would be bruited about, particularly Yigal Allon and Yigael Yadin, both men were considered military heroes whose time had passed; Dayan was regarded as a military hero fresh in the public's mind, and conversant with the IDF of recent years. To the prime minister, the movement to oust him as defense minister was mean spirited. He believed that in his four years as minister of defense he had performed well; he was not prepared to let Dayan just walk in and take over. When Dayan met the prime minister at the Dan Hotel that evening, Eshkol said he wanted to set up a ministerial defense and foreign affairs committee of seven people (himself, Eban, Allon, Begin, Dayan, plus two others). Dayan said no thank you, he would not join, but if his opinion were sought, he would gladly supply it.

Labor party colleagues pressed Eshkol to appoint Allon defense minister or assistant defense minister as a way of defusing the pressure building up against him. Allon was in Leningrad. Phoning Israel Galili, his Ahdut Avoda cohort and a minister without portfolio, Allon asked whether he should return home. Galili said no, it wasn't necessary, the crisis would be over soon. That less-than-astute judgment made life all the more difficult for Levi Eshkol. The prime minister sought out military advice on appointing Dayan. Would the situation change, he asked Ariel Sharon, a division commander in the south, if Dayan were appointed defense minister?

Sharon, a future defense minister himself, was by this time fed up with all politicians and answered bluntly: "For myself, as a commander who has to lead his soldiers, it doesn't make the slightest difference who the minister of defense is. As far as Dayan is concerned, I appreciate him and his abilities tremendously. But when it comes to how my division will fight, you could invite Beba Idelson [the elderly leader of the women's labor union] to be minister of defense, you, or Dayan, or Beba Idelson, it makes no difference."[8]

Dayan was champing at the bit for action. He told journalist Naphtali Lavie that he had found the IDF well equipped and highly motivated, "but we have no national leadership that can make decisions, and this is a tragedy." Israel could not afford to simply act defensively. "We have to do something very, very drastic on our own initiative."[9]

May 27 brought more inconclusive cabinet sessions. Why, Eshkol had asked Interior Minister Moshe Haim Shapiro, did he and the other religious politicians vote against military action, yet support the hawkish Dayan? "Because we trust his judgment more than yours," was his terse, blunt reply. Eshkol was caught on the horns of a dilemma. He had the military chiefs screaming for action. He had the Soviet ambassador in Tel Aviv equally distressed, warning him not to attack the Arab states. So he did nothing.

Eshkol's rambling, stammering speech on radio on May 28 was the final straw. Every radio in Israel was tuned in to the speech, awaiting the prime minister's words. Eshkol had hoped that the speech would rally Israelis behind the government and its careful, deliberate approach to the crisis. In sounding unsure of himself, in stumbling over his words, he created alarm and deepened the political crisis around him. The next day *Ha'aretz*, reflecting widespread sentiment, argued that Eshkol was not cut out to be prime minister and defense minister in a crisis and the country would be better off making Ben-Gurion prime minister and Dayan minister of defense, with Eshkol running domestic affairs.

At this point Rafi, Gahal, and the National Religious party thought Dayan should be made minister of defense. Peres notified Golda Meir that Rafi would be prepared to dissolve itself as a party and join Mapai in a unity government. The idea of a war cabinet became less attractive; newspaper editorialists clamored for a unity government. Eshkol remained the butt of contention. When Ezer Weizman stormed out of a cabinet meeting, tore off his general's insignia from his left shoulder, and threw it on a table, news of his protest spread throughout the IDF. The military was growing restless for decisive action. Eshkol flailed, proposing that Allon and Dayan become deputy prime ministers in charge of defense under him. No one bit. What about a special defense committee of all former chiefs of staff to advise the prime minister? No one agreed.

Dayan believed that he could handle defense matters better than anyone sitting around the cabinet table, but with the Egyptians about to take action, he felt he could not afford to wait for a cabinet appointment. The most logical job was chief of staff. It was unthinkable, however, that Yitzhak Rabin would turn that job over to Dayan. That left the post of southern front commander. Dayan sensed that his appointment to that post would have an important impact on the country. Yet wherever he went the people seemed to want him in the government. In Eilat on May 30 owners of restaurants refused to let him pay for a meal. The same thing happened when he stopped for coffee at a gas station. It was Nasser and Hussein who brought the greatest pressure on the Israeli government to let Dayan in: On May 30 the Jordanian monarch flew to Cairo, where he placed his army under Egypt's command. Israel appeared to face a military threat on three fronts, Egypt, Jordan, and Syria. Late that evening Mapai held a parliamentary caucus in the Knesset with Ahdut Avoda. Speaker after speaker called upon Eshkol to give up the defense ministry, and appoint Dayan or Allon.

The next morning, May 31, Dayan visited central front commander Uzi Narkiss at his forward headquarters at the Castel, the hill five miles west of Jerusalem along the Jerusalem–Tel Aviv highway. Narkiss expressed his concern that the Tel Aviv–Jerusalem road might be cut by Arab forces at the Castel, and that Israel might have trouble defending Mount Scopus because of a lack of forces.

"Listen," said Dayan, "as for Mount Scopus, don't worry. If the Arabs come and occupy it, never mind. We are going to the Sinai. We'll get to the Suez Canal, as you know, in six or seven days. Then we will come back, the whole Israeli army, to rescue you."

"I can't agree to that," said Narkiss, indignant that Sinai should take precedence over Mount Scopus.

Dayan, acting as if he were already the minister of defense, said, "Don't bother the General Staff with this problem."[10]

Still hoping that he could keep Dayan from the defense ministry, Eshkol proposed that Dayan become deputy prime minister and Allon defense minister. Dayan rejected the offer for much the same reason he had said no to becoming deputy chief of staff in the early 1950s: He had no intention of taking a job that was purely advisory. Dayan proposed that he become southern front commander. Eshkol agreed, but he could not be sure that he could sell the idea to everyone else.

By now, events were moving swiftly toward the making of Moshe

Dayan minister of defense. Symbols became all-important. Eshkol came to symbolize what Israelis called a Diaspora complex, the sense that Israel was just another European ghetto, frightened and insecure. In contrast, Dayan was the symbol of the new Israeli, radiating trust and self-confidence in the nation and in himself. Sentiment seemed to weigh heavily in Dayan's favor. Elevating him to the defense ministry would give the Egyptians pause. It would also light a fire in his countrymen, giving them a rally point and a symbol. Rahel Rabinovitch remembered vividly what it was about the Moshe Dayan of June 1967 that captivated the citizenry: "There was in him a mixture of hero and pirate and grave-robber, of someone who had affairs with women, who had a very colorful personality. People really believed in him as a soldier. There was a belief that if Moshe Dayan would come, the whole mood would change."[11]

Although Eshkol saw the handwriting on the wall, he was furious. To turn the ministry of defense over to Dayan was to permit him to steal the limelight from the prime minister, from Rabin, from the Mapai veterans in the cabinet. It was a no-win situation for Eshkol. Were Israel to lose—it was not excluded by some Israelis—the prime minister would be blamed for showing weakness and hesitation. Were Israel to win, the new defense minister would reap all the glory.

Throughout May 31, efforts were made to appoint Yigal Allon defense minister, but they were in vain. Dayan was eager to gain some appointment, even a military one. He told Eshkol, "I am ready to be prime minister or defense minister or both. But if I am not to be put in charge of defense, then I prefer to be mobilized as commander of the southern front. I know the Sinai peninsula and the Egyptian positions in it well. To serve in the army, I would even drive a half-track."[12] Eshkol was prepared to replace Gavish with Dayan but he had trouble selling the idea to Rabin, who felt that Gavish would be unnecessarily offended.

Rabin asked Dayan whether he was prepared to submit to his authority as chief of staff. Yes, said Dayan.

Rabin then asked if Dayan in fact wanted to take Rabin's place as chief of staff.

"You are chief of staff," Dayan replied, "and I shall obey every order from the General Staff. I merely want to take part in the war, rather than watch it from the sidelines."[13] Rabin wanted time to consider what to recommend to Eshkol.

Meanwhile, Shimon Peres was having great difficulty persuading David Ben-Gurion to agree to Dayan's joining the government. To Ben-Gurion, joining an Eshkol-led government was traitorous; in his view Eshkol should be deprived of both the prime ministership and the defense ministry. Peres was more realistic, understanding there was no prospect of removing Eshkol as prime minister. It might, however, be possible to push him out of the defense ministry, if Ben-Gurion would only yield and give Peres the green light to push Dayan's candidacy.

Ben-Gurion exploded at Peres. Had they not agreed that Rafi would only join the government if Eshkol stepped down as prime minister? Finally, Ben-Gurion heard Peres out, accepted Peres's reading of the situation, and apologized to him.[14] The last obstacle to Moshe Dayan becoming minister of defense had been removed.

THE LONGEST DAY, June 1, was about to start. At 4:00 A.M., Rabin summoned Gavish to Tel Aviv. Meanwhile Dayan left that morning for a visit to the central command in Jerusalem, believing that he would likely be appointed southern front commander later in the day. When Dayan spoke to Rabin at 8:30 A.M., the chief of staff was still waiting to talk to the prime minister about the Dayan appointment. Gavish, Dayan told Rabin, could become his deputy, if he wished. Arriving at General Staff headquarters, Gavish received the news of his being replaced by Dayan as if he had been given a left uppercut.

"Why should I salute Moshe Dayan?" an angry Gavish asked the chief of staff. "I've been working for a whole month, the plans are ready. Just because of political considerations, I have to give up my job? Did I fail? The IDF isn't ready for war?"

There was little Rabin could say. For the rest of the day, Gavish and deputy chief of staff Chaim Bar-Lev toured the Sinai divisions, with Bar-Lev trying to convince Gavish to become Dayan's deputy.

Throughout the morning Dayan kept hearing from colleagues that he might well become defense minister in a day or so. He strongly doubted it. He joined Gad Ya'acobi for coffee at a Ben Yehuda Street coffee house in Tel Aviv, and expressed doubt that Mapai's veterans would let him have the post. He urged Peres later on the phone to drop his pleadings, that nothing would come of it.

The next few hours were crucial. Begin and the religious politicians agreed on Dayan as defense minister. The Mapai secretariat began meeting at 3:00 P.M. Only a few die-hard Mapai politicians endorsed Eshkol's choice of Allon as minister of defense. When Eskhol rose to speak he urged that Dayan be appointed southern front commander, insisting that Dayan himself wanted this field command. Sniping at Dayan, the prime minister suggested that Dayan would not be a good defense minister, that he would spend most of his time with the troops as he had during the 1956 war. The audience would hear none of this. Most spoke out against Eshkol and in favor of Dayan as defense minister. Some argued that Dayan's appointment as defense minister would seal the formation of a national unity government—since Rafi and Gahal were demanding Dayan's appointment as their price for joining the cabinet. Eshkol faced a full-scale rebellion. Of the twenty-four people who spoke, only five sided with his proposal to make Allon defense minister; nineteen wanted Dayan. Outside Mapai headquarters where the meeting was being held women demonstrated on behalf of a national unity government and Dayan's appointment as minister of defense. Eshkol grumpily dubbed them "The Merry Wives of Windsor." Some one hundred women shouted, "We want Dayan" and "For national security—Dayan is the man." A petition to make Dayan defense minister had aimed at one thousand signatures, but received twenty thousand.

Eshkol made one last attempt to avoid the inevitable. While the secretariat adjourned for lunch, he rushed to meet Gahal politicians to convince them to enter the government without Dayan. They refused. Only then did Eshkol acknowledge that he had lost. Allon withdrew his candidacy as defense minster. As much as Eshkol and Allon had wished that Dayan would simply go away, the public clamor was far too strong. The prime minister had attached one condition to Dayan's appointment: Yigael Yadin should become his military adviser. At 4:00 P.M. Eshkol assembled the Political Committee of the Mapai and Mapam and formally proposed Dayan replace him as defense minister. It was unanimously accepted. A Mapai politician told Dayan, "You see Moshe, at least we've appointed you minister of defense." Dayan replied: "It was the Egyptian army which did most of the work—and you did a bit too."

Eshkol summoned Dayan to tell him that he planned to recommend to the government that he be named minister of defense. Three hours later, Eshkol phoned Dayan with the news that the cabinet had just met and approved his appointment. Moshe Dayan was about to reach the peak of his public career. All that he had to do was convince his own Rafi party to join the government. Ben-Gurion was still wary. He was still concerned that Dayan would lead the country into a war it could not afford; but in the face of staunch opposition, he backed down.

"Moshe, accept!"

Smiling, Dayan said, "I'll accept on one condition, that I'll have your advice."

That sounded good to Ben-Gurion. He might still manage to convince Dayan not to go to war.

"All right. But you'll have to come to Sde Boker."

"I'm now the commander," said Dayan, "and you'll stay in Tel Aviv. That's an order." Laughter erupted in the room.[15] The phone rang. It was Eshkol inviting Dayan to his first cabinet meeting later that night.

Ben-Gurion shook Dayan's hand warmly. "Moshe, put your foot down and stand for no nonsense." At 11:00 P.M., Dayan, the new minister of defense, sat at the cabinet table for the first time, joined by two other new ministers, ministers without portfolio Menachem Begin and Joseph Sapir, both of Gahal. The main decision taken at the meeting was to begin discussing military matters more seriously at a meeting of the Ministerial Defense Committee the next morning.

At 9:00 P.M., Rabin caught up with Gavish to say, "Shaike, everything that happened this morning is canceled. Dayan is being appointed minister of defense."

By midnight Dayan was back home at Zahala. He had one more visitor. Journalist Naphtali Lavie appeared close to 1:00 A.M. with a fresh copy of the June 2 *Ha'aretz* reporting on the longest day. (Lavie had already dropped a copy off at Begin's home in Tel Aviv.) Dayan looked at the newspaper, and, almost as if he did not believe the last few hours' developments, said to himself, "I will hear it at six in the morning on the BBC." Only then would he believe what had happened.[16]

On Thursday evening, June 1, Moshe Dayan became minister of defense. In choosing him, the nation chose to go to war. For days Dayan alone among the political figures urged that the country move to the attack. Other politicians could think of a hundred reasons why not to go to war. Dayan thought Israel had to march to restore its deterrent power.

The news of Dayan's appointment electrified the public. Finally, the procrastinating was over. The nation breathed a collective sigh of relief. When Kol Yisrael broadcast the news that evening, every Israeli knew that an Israeli attack was around the corner. The fact that it would be led by Moshe Dayan exhilarated the nervous country. He inspired confidence in mothers, wives, and soldiers that the war would be won and the losses would be light.

Toasts to victory were made. Backs straightened. It was as if the war had already been won. Bonfires were lit in army camps. Soldiers sang a popular new song, "Jerusalem of Gold," which had been heard for the first time at the annual song festival only two weeks earlier. "He came at the right time," Ezer Weizman wrote. "He gave people heart and dispelled their doubts. There was something about his appearance, his speech and his confidence that dispelled gloom and replaced it with smiles, that drove away uncertainty and, in its place, created a sharp awareness that our path had been shortened."[17]

Previous wars had been led by Ben-Gurion and Yadin, Dayan and Allon. For a while it had appeared that Israel would enter the battlefield with a bunch of civilian amateurs at the helm. Thus Dayan became a hero before he had acted heroically; he was the savior of a nation that had not yet gone to war. Overseas, the Dayan appointment created excitement. The wheels of diplomacy appeared still to be turning. President Johnson hosted British prime minister Harold Wilson on June 2, but even as they mulled over possible Anglo-American moves to restore free navigation in the gulf, Israelis knew that it was too late for diplomacy.

Everything was falling into place. Even the United States, which had thus far avoided the impression that it favored an Israeli military attack, now inched toward that view. During a meeting with Mossad chief Meir Amit, Defense Secretary Robert McNamara was handed an urgent cable. The defense secretary, gazing at Amit, announced quietly that Dayan had been appointed defense minister: "I know Moshe Dayan very well. I met him when he was in Washington. I am very glad he has been appointed. Please wish him good luck from me." Then in words that had great significance, he told Amit: "Whatever decision he takes, I wish him good luck." Amit understood McNamara's comment to mean Washington had agreed with Israel's view that a preemptive strike might be necessary.[18]

The country knew only too well that the weaker the Israel government was perceived as being by the Arabs, the more likely it was they would attack. Dayan's appointment was designed to counter the impression of a weak Israeli government. Yael Dayan wrote that "the change was noticeable in every face, word, and action. As if we all got a second wind, as if a large brush had painted off the past two weeks and splashed new vivid colors and feeling into the dormant desert, the steel war machines, the spirit of the commanders, all of us." The field commanders were ecstatic. Col. Yekutiel Adam, commander of an infantry brigade, told Yael in the desert that it was the way her father would lead the IDF to victory that would be different. "Moshe is not a mystic mascot. It isn't his military genius either, as he approved of the battle plans and made only a few changes. It is a quality which can't be defined, which represents, and demands, the best in all of us."[19]

The next morning, June 2, Dayan invited Zvi Tsur, a former chief of staff, to his home for breakfsat. Tsur accepted Dayan's offer to become his assistant. There was not much time to lose. Tsur recalled that at that breakfast "it was totally clear to Dayan that the IDF would win the coming war. He talked about starting the war either on Monday or at least at the beginning of the week." His first order was to ask for a direct phone from the General Staff to his home.[20]

Upon arriving at the Defense Ministry in uniform, he requested a half-track so he could go to the front at any moment should war break out. That request disturbed his aides, who recalled his lengthy absences from the General Staff during the Sinai Campaign, but it won Dayan great plaudits from soldiers who thought it only right that the minister of defense see them in action.

At 9:10 A.M., Eshkol and the ministers of the war cabinet met at general headquarters. Also invited to the meeting were Avraham Yoffee, Israel Tal, and Ariel Sharon, the three division commanders in the south. Seated to Dayan's left, Sharon scribbled him a note: "Moshe, it seems to me the plan is still to move in phases. In my opinion we should not undertake an operation that will not break the Egyptian main forces. Gaza is not the target!" Dayan wrote back, "Arik, I've asked Yitzhak [Rabin] to meet this evening to discuss the plans."[21]

Two hours later Dayan met with Eshkol, Eban, Allon, and Rabin in the prime minister's office. This session was the one the country had waited for since May 15. The cabinet should decide on Sunday to go to war the next day, Dayan proposed, and the others agreed. At lunch with Yigael Yadin, Eshkol's new military adviser, Dayan noted that war would begin Monday.

It was time to go into the actual planning of the war. The "small" plan, limiting IDF action to Gaza and northern Sinai, held no appeal for Dayan. Nor did his "collapse" theory, which in the 1956 Sinai Campaign had aimed only at disrupting the Egyptian deployment. Israel's goal, in order to regain lost credibility, must be the destruction of the Egyptian army.

So suddenly did Dayan come on the scene that the General Staff had no time to redesign its plans to his liking. Yehoshua Gavish, retained as the southern front commander, asked Rabin which plan to present to the new minister of defense, the small one, or the large one, which called for a full offensive along several routes in the Sinai.

Present them both, Rabin instructed.

When Moshe Dayan walked into the operations room that evening of June 2, the feeling was electric. Chief of Operations Ezer Weizman remembered: "The key contribution to the whole affair was Dayan's presence and his charisma and his leadership. When he first walked into the Operations Room there was a sigh of relief as if a stone had rolled off of everyone's heart. You could have cut the air with a knife. There was leadership walking on two legs and one eye."[22] Ariel Sharon was there too and he recalled, "It was like a fresh wind. After so much confusion and so many changes, at last we were able to clarify the overall approach and make the final adjustments."[23]

Dayan asked Rabin to present the IDF's plan.

Rabin nodded toward Gavish. Which one? he asked the chief of staff. As if he were reading Dayan's thoughts, Rabin said, "The big one."

After Gavish concluded, Dayan expressed approval: "Only if we take as large a slice of Sinai as possible, and smash the Egyptian army, can we be sure of opening the Straits and removing the threat against us."

Then the new defense minister laid down some caveats. The IDF was not to enter the Gaza Strip. With its four hundred thousand Arab inhabitants, it was, in his words, "a nest of wasps." He saw no reason to seize control of the place: "Let them stew in their own juice." He laid down a similar prohibition against the IDF reaching the Suez Canal. The canal he described as a "nest of hornets," sensing that the Soviets would not stand by idle if the IDF stood on its banks.

Dayan returned home late. The house in Zahala had suddenly become filled with flowers, boxes of chocolates, and fruit baskets. Gifts from strangers arrived. Dayan's son Assi showed up on a three-hour leave from his antiaircraft gunners unit. To Dayan's family, Moshe remained less than heroic. Yael recalled that when he walked out of the bathroom in his underpants and slippers, without his eyepatch, "he hardly fit the confidence-inspiring image he represented since the previous day. Yet it was all there. The brightness in his direct look, the youthful stride as if a burden had been shed, the seriousness of a tremendous responsibility, and the bemused half-smile of self-assurance." She noted that for the first time he spoke of holding full authority, that the prime minister had turned over all military decisions to him.[24]

That evening he was interviewed by Winston Churchill, the correspondent of the London newspaper *News of the World,* and the grandson of the late British prime minister. "My grandfather needed Hitler so that he could get in power," Dayan's guest noted.

"It took eighty thousand Egyptian soldiers in the Sinai Peninsula for me to get to be defense minister." Churchill asked all the right questions, including whether war would break out. Dayan must have thought to himself, he is nice, he has a famous name, but did he really believe he would hear from Dayan the time of Israel's attack? Dayan said it was safe for Churchill to return to London. There would be no war in the next few days. On the strength of Dayan's prediction, Churchill left the country on June 4, learning the valuable lesson that defense ministers about to launch a war are unlikely to be candid with newsmen.

WITH BOTH Israeli and Egyptian armies in place and ready to spring into action, Dayan realized the IDF could not automatically catch the Egyptians off guard. Perhaps just the opposite. He had to gain the element of surprise. He had to convince the Egyptians and the world at large that Israel did not plan to go to war in the immediate future. He had managed to persuade Winston Churchill; now he had the difficult task of persuading millions.

Saturday, June 3, became the most important day of the war that had not yet started. On this day, the Jewish sabbath, the IDF was ordered to relax. Soldiers were permitted to have their children visit them in their bases. News photographers were given access to Israeli soldiers on leave. It was a summery June day and so tens of thousands of Israelis streamed to the beaches and pools. The movie houses were packed.

All these efforts at normalcy paled in comparison to Dayan's masterful stroke that afternoon, holding a news conference at Tel Aviv's Bet Sokolov and letting the international media see that war seemed to be the last thing on the minds of Israel's leadership.

By cleverly obfuscating when asked what Israel planned to do, he communicated a message to the world that an Israeli attack was not in the offing. "We are not a nation of stop-watchers," Dayan said. "I do not anticipate any major change in a month, two months, or six months, but I think we can win." Then, asked about the loss of time because of the long, drawn-out diplomatic action, Dayan said, "I accept the situation as it is. I know it is always easy to say last week we were in a better position. This is not the point. The point, I should think just now, is that it is more or less a situation of being too late or too early—too late to react regarding our chances in the miltary field—on the blockading of the Straits of Tiran—and too early to draw conclusions as to the diplomatic way of handling the matter." He kept stressing the need to give diplomacy more time to bear fruit. "The government has decided upon diplomatic steps and you have to give this a chance." Until when? "Until the government decides." There it was, at the tail end, a faint hint that Israel's patience was not unlimited, that if and when the government believed that the diplomats had exhausted their efforts, it could very well turn to other means. What Dayan did not say was that Israel's leadership had taken the decision to go to war, that the cabinet would approve the decision the next day—and that the war would soon begin.

To his countrymen Dayan sent another message. By appearing jovial and calm, by radiating self-confidence and replying to questions in a firm, resolute manner, Dayan sent word to his own people that a leadership was in place that could handle the crisis. No better illustration of this can be found than the words he uttered about Israel's ability to fight its own battles: "I personally do not expect and do not want anyone else to fight for us. . . . If somehow it comes to real fighting, I would not like American or British boys to get killed here, and I do not think we need them." In effect, Dayan had let it be known that Israel was no longer interested in outside aid, diplomatic, military, or whatever. He was sending a subtle message to his countrymen: We are capable of defeating the Arabs.

No actor could have performed better. Dayan's performance before three hundred correspondents that afternoon captured for Israel the crucial element of surprise. So successful was Dayan in conveying an air of tranquillity that many of those journalists listening to him packed their bags the next day in search of a more exciting story.

In a sense, the cabinet meetings of June 4 were a formality. Dayan's elevation to the Defense Ministry three days earlier had sealed the country's fate in everyone's minds. The decision to go to war was taken for granted. Dayan's resolution read: "The Government resolves to take military action in order to liberate Israel from the stranglehold of aggression which is progressively being tightened around Israel. The Government authorizes the Prime Minister and the Defense Minister to confirm to the General Staff of the IDF the time of action." Final Cabinet approval came at 3:00 P.M. when ten of the thirteen ministers voted their approval. The two Mapam ministers hesitated but after consultations gave their assent, making the vote unanimous. Finance Minister Pinhas Sapir was abroad. Dayan quickly phoned Rabin to say that the war could begin at 7:45 A.M. the next day. Later, Dayan flew north to meet with northern front commander David "Dado" Elazar to order him to stay put despite his personal wish to teach the Syrians a lesson. For Elazar, it was not easy. The Syrians had sent punishing artillery fire on the kibbutzim in the valley below for years; now, with Israel launching a war in the south, it seemed a golden opportunity to move against the Syrians as well. At Kibbutz Dan, the front commander pointed to the Syrian village of Za'ura and said, "That's the place I want to capture in a lightning raid, sir. It will enable me to defend the valley and serve as a springboard for a deeper penetration."

"Get used to the idea," said Dayan, "that this war is against Egypt."

"If there's a war against Egypt, there will be a war here too."

"Maybe so, but first this is a war against Egypt, and what you people have to do here is sit tight and hold out." Deeply frustrated, Elazar knew there was not much he could do—but wait and hope.[25]

Back in Tel Aviv later that afternoon, Dayan gave orders to the General Staff against attacking along the Jordanian or Syrian frontiers. Only if attacked could Israeli soldiers advance and seize key positions in enemy territory.

Dayan had one more task to perform. He could have chosen to do it himself. Indeed, he had promised David Ben-Gurion to consult with the former prime minister in his new post. Dayan did not want to see Ben-Gurion at this juncture. "I thought that he had an imperfect vision of our situation, that he was living in a world that had passed. He still admired de Gaulle, had an exaggerated opinion of Nasser's power, and understated the controlled strength of the Israel Defense forces."[26] So he asked Haim Yisraeli, a longtime Ben-Gurion aide, to inform him that Israel had decided to go to war. Yisraeli was forbidden to reveal the hour that the attack would be launched—Ben-Gurion could inadvertently tell someone about it. After hearing the message from Yisraeli, Ben-Gurion asked, "Is Moshe sure of himself?"

"Yes," said Yisraeli.

"In that event, give him my blessing."

Visibly disturbed that Dayan had not come himself, Ben-Gurion did not bother to ask when the attack would start. He only wanted to know of Yisraeli: Why did he send you?[27]

FOR BETTER or worse, this would be Moshe Dayan's war. It was as if the nation's leadership had stepped aside, and said to him: We can't do anything. Why don't you try? That gave him undisputed authority in the military field. It also would make him the most powerful figure in the country. Emerging from the shadows of David Ben-Gurion, displacing Levi Eshkol and all the other Mapai veterans, Dayan, while the number two man in the government, held sway over everyone.

On that fateful morning of June 5, the American columnist Joseph Alsop wrote a column called "The Meaning of Moshe Dayan." He compared Dayan's appointment to the Defense Ministry with the return of Winston Churchill to the British cabinet in 1939, and then suggested that the Dayan appointment was Israel's acknowledgment that the country could not wait any longer. "That is almost certainly its real meaning. Israel, it must be understood, is now struggling for very survival."

The struggle began that morning. Dayan had an early breakfast of coffee and toast at home with his family. He then joined Rahel for another coffee and croissant. Dayan brought her an old Greek jar as a gift. "He didn't say anything about the war," recalled Rahel, "but he was in a fantastically optimistic mood. He went to the counter and bought a packet of sweets and a newspaper and said: 'I'm sorry, I can't take you to the office because my time is up. I have to be in the Operations Room.' I never asked questions. . . . I looked at him and I knew something's happening."[28]

Thanks to Dayan's campaign of disinformation over the weekend, the Egyptians were under the illusion that Israel had put off plans for a military attack. They realized how wrong they were as Israel's air force thundered over Egyptian skies early that morning, swooping down and blasting the Egyptian air force on the ground. They came in two waves. In the first, from 7:14 to 8:55 A.M., 103 Israeli planes devastated 6

Egyptian airfields, 16 radar stations, and destroyed 197 aircraft. Then at 9:34 A.M. came the second wave. This time, 164 Israeli planes attacked 14 bases, destroying 107 Egyptian planes. The Egyptians lost 75 percent of their air strength—304 out of 419 aircraft—before they could absorb what was happening. Within hours of the war's start the Egyptians had lost their air cover. Although the war was not over, Israel's victory was a foregone conclusion.

Six Israeli pilots were killed, three wounded, and two taken prisoner that morning. Nine Israeli planes had been hit, but six returned safely and were reparable. While Israeli warplanes engaged Egypt, the air forces of Syria, Jordan, and Iraq attacked Israel. Syrian planes managed to bomb the Israeli towns of Tiberias and Megiddo in the north. Accordingly, a third wave of Israeli planes countered Jordan and Syria, beginning at 12:15 P.M. It destroyed the entire Jordanian air force of twenty-eight planes! Syria suffered a fifty percent loss of its air force as 53 of its 112 planes were destroyed. Ten Israeli planes were hit, five pilots were killed, two wounded, and two taken prisoner.

Preserving the secrecy of Israel's morning attacks was uppermost in Dayan's mind. He reluctantly left the air command to make what seemed like a superfluous journey to Sde Dov Airport in Tel Aviv at 8:30 A.M. to greet members of the Knesset Foreign Affairs and Defense Committee. The committee had been waiting to fly off on a previously arranged tour of the northern front. Rather than cancel the journey the night before and arouse unwanted speculation, Dayan waited until the war started before personally informing the committee that the visit had been called off. As a consolation for their inconvenience, he showed up himself and read out the communique of the IDF spokesman, broadcast at 8:10 A.M. over Israel Radio, announcing the start of hostilities: "As of this morning, stiff fighting is in progress between Egyptian air and armored forces advancing toward Israel, and our forces who have gone out to stop them." The announcement was more important for what it did not say. It disguised the central facts: Israel had initiated the fighting and was in the midst of vanquishing the Arab air forces. It sought to portray the Israeli action as defensive, designed to hurl the Arab forces back. One committee member asked who fired the first shot. Dayan would not say. Until then the sole official source for the air battle was Cairo Radio, which had bombastically declared that Egypt's air force had shot down forty Israeli planes. It said nothing of its own considerable losses.

Air Force Commander Mordechai Hod knew of Israel's overwhelming air victory by 9:00 A.M. and soon thereafter informed Dayan and Rabin. "Don't publish anything," the defense minister ordered.[29] It took considerable restraint on his part not to inform the Israeli public of the air triumph, the same Israeli public that during the waiting period had lived with nightmarish scenarios of another Auschwitz. Now there was good news to tell. Why not relieve Israeli anxieties as quickly as possible? Because, Dayan felt, the war was far from over. There was no need to encourage calls for a cease-fire before Israel's ground forces could accomplish their goals. "Why should we announce it?" he asked his assistant, Zvi Tsur, one of those who urged that Israel go public with the good news. "The Arabs still don't know what happened to them. Nothing will happen to the people in Zion. Everything will be OK anyhow. We already know that. Let's leave the Arabs in a fog and keep going."[30] Pressure grew on Dayan later in the day to announce the air triumph. Yadin had been in touch with the General Staff to say that the prime minister was deeply worried, some Israelis were beginning to panic, the country should be told how well its forces were doing. Dayan refused to change his mind. (To his aide Haim Yisraeli, however, he confided that "the war is going first class.")[31]

At 10:30 A.M., the country heard the minister of defense's voice over Israel Radio—telling them as little as possible. "At this time we do not have precise situation reports of the battles on the southern front. Our planes are locked in bitter combat with enemy aircraft and our ground forces have set out to silence the Egyptian artillery now shelling our settlements opposite the Gaza Strip and to stop the Egyptian armored forces trying to cut off the southern part of the Negev in the initial stage of the campaign. . . . They are greater in numbers but we will overcome them. They are more numerous than we. But we shall beat them. We are a small people, but a brave one."

Israel's ground forces began moving early that morning into the Sinai. Tal's troops began operating in the northern sector and soon routed an Egyptian division. They then broke through Rafiah at the southern tip of the Gaza Strip after a day of fighting, opening the coastal route and reaching the approaches to El Arish. Meanwhile, Sharon's task force broke through the fortified positions at Um Katef and reached the crossroad at Abu Agheila just before midnight. Egyptian soldiers fought hard this time but by the end of the second day (June 6), they began retreating, following Cairo's order to withdraw.

Dayan remained adamantly opposed to Israel taking the Gaza Strip. He was convinced that once Israeli troops took Rafiah and El Arish the inhabitants would simply surrender. To his regret, batteries of Palestinians began bombarding Israeli kibbutzim, requiring an Israeli military response. Rabin and Gavish persuaded him that Israel had no choice but to take the Strip. Dayan grudgingly agreed and after two days of fighting the Gaza Strip fell to the Israelis.

As the first day wound to a close, Dayan came under even more pressure to announce Israel's victories. By now he was softening. For one thing, news of Israel's air victory had inadvertently leaked during the afternoon, and though Dayan had issued instructions to offer nothing beyond a "no comment," the temptation to confirm the morning's events was becoming overwhelming. Near midnight, Dayan, coming around to Yadin's view, said, "Think of Jewish history. How many times did the Jewish people have such a victory? Not since King David and Alexander Yannai." Dayan instructed Rabin and Hod to hold a joint news conference at 2:00 A.M. and inform the world what Israel's air force had done that morning.[32]

During the early morning hours of June 7 Dayan was growing impatient at the prospect that a cease-fire might be declared before Israel could capture Sharm el-Sheikh.

"What about Sharm el-Sheikh?" he asked the chief of staff. "We'll find the war coming to an end before we get our hands on its cause!"

Dayan ordered Rabin to make sure that Israeli troops established a presence there as quickly as possible regardless of the progress of fighting in Sinai. Rabin proposed and it was agreed that Sharm would be taken that evening by a combined operation of airborne and naval forces. As it happened, the Egyptians had the night before evacuated Sharm. When Israeli troops arrived they were able to take the strategic site without firing a shot.

For Dayan, the specific cause for Israel's launching of the war was the intolerable situation posed by the closing of the Straits of Tiran. None of the other confrontation states—Lebanon, Syria, Iraq, or Jordan—had taken steps of late that warranted an Israeli assault against any of them. Toward these states the IDF was to assume a defensive posture and only go on the attack if necessary. Lebanon, with no army to speak of, was never really a factor. Syria, while it sent its air force into action in the early hours of the war, kept its ground forces in harness. Only Jordan posed a dilemma for Israel. Dayan anticipated that King Hussein might wish to intervene on Egypt's side. He ordered the Harel Brigade transferred to Jerusalem in case it was needed. Despite an Israeli warning to avoid hostilities, by midday of June 5, Jordan had unleashed a mortar and artillery attack against Jewish quarters in Jerusalem. Uzi Narkiss's forces were sent into action. This presented the Israelis, Moshe Dayan included, with the opportunity to settle some old scores. "I could see the adrenaline in Moshe working very hard," remembered Ezer Weizman. "His relationship with Jordan, his failure in forty-eight to take the areas around Jerusalem, his command in Jerusalem, his relationship with El-Tel in the early fifties, his visits to see Abdullah, all of this must have worked in his head. 'OK, you bastards, you wouldn't come to talk about this. I'll take you.' "[33]

Within hours after the Israelis counterattacked in Jerusalem, a feverish debate began about whether to take the Old City. In favor were Prime Minister Eshkol, Labor Minister Yigal Allon, and the new minister without portfolio, Menachem Begin. At midnight Eshkol phoned Dayan to say, "The government wants the Old City." Theoretically, Dayan answered, the IDF could take the Old City the next day, but he preferred a siege rather than a frontal attack, fearing that international opinion would turn against Israel for desecrating the holy places (even if Israel had not desecrated them). He preferred to wait, figuring that in time the Arabs in the Old City would simply surrender.

By 11:00 A.M., June 6, the road to Mount Scopus was clear and Front Commander Uzi Narkiss invited Dayan to travel there for a victory ceremony. Weizman flew Dayan in a helicopter, landing in a car park outside Jerusalem's Convention Center. It was a sweet moment for Dayan. He had so often urged Ben-Gurion to let the IDF take Mount Scopus after 1948 only to be told that it was too late. Now, he was driving in a jeep up the winding road to Scopus, an armored troop carrier in front and another jeep behind. After lunch, he and Narkiss proceeded to the roof of the National Library and looked out at the Old City.

"Moshe," said Narkiss, "we must go into the Old City. When do I get the OK?"

"Not now. Wait. It will fall like a ripe fruit. The Arabs will wave white flags in surrender."

On Dayan's mind were the heavy casualties the Israelis had already suffered in the fighting for Jerusalem. He wanted the bloodshed to cease. He worried too that fighting in the Old City could lead to desecration of the holy places. This would bring the Vatican down on Israel.

"Why don't you surround the Old City and we'll wait?" he asked Narkiss.

That, thought Narkiss, was a prescription for inaction. Surrounding the Old City could take a month. In the meantime a ceasefire would be declared and Israel would lose the chance to capture the walled enclave. Dayan would not budge. Nor would he yield during a cabinet meeting that day when Yigal Allon and Begin complained of his hesitancy about "liberating" Jerusalem's Old City: "I'm willing to wager that the inhabitants of the Old City will come out waving white flags within a few hours or so." The session ended inconclusively as half supported Dayan, half did not. By the morning of June 7, the advocates of taking the Old City were even more insistent. After Begin heard on the BBC that the Security Council planned to vote on a cease-fire, he phoned the prime minister to demand that the cabinet be convened at once. "I agree," said Eshkol, "speak to Dayan. If he agrees, we shall go ahead." Begin spoke to Dayan. After a few minutes, the two men agreed on the conquest of Jerusalem. So Eshkol called ministers together at 9:00 A.M. Cleverly, Dayan gave the order at 8:30 A.M. to attack the Old City even before the cabinet met. Hence, he would announce to the cabinet that plans for the capture of the Old City were already under way.

The Old City fell that morning. Public relations wizard that he was, Dayan understood that he must be there, having his photograph taken, leading the Israeli soldiers into the Old City and to the Western Wall, holiest site of the Jews. He sent a message ahead to Uzi Narkiss that he would arrive at the Lion's Gate at 1:00 P.M. "Wait for me." Narkiss had trouble complying with the order. He had already been inside the Old City with Israeli forces, but he agreed to be at the gate to greet Dayan. As the time approached, Dayan's convoy moved through the streets of the orthodox Jewish neighborhood of Mea Shearim. Chaim Herzog, the newly appointed governor of the West Bank and later president of the state of Israel, was in the convoy. He recalled how "everyone stood and waved. Dayan was sitting in the front thoroughly enjoying himself."[34]

Far, far to the south, Ezer Weizman, trying to do a good deed, had joined Israeli troops in the "taking" of Sharm el-Sheikh. At noon he put in a call to Dayan to let him know that Sharm was now in Israeli hands, only to be told that the defense minister could not come to the phone. Why not? asked Ezer. "Because he's on his way to the Western Wall."

Dayan's arrival at the St. Stephen's Gate and the subsequent historic photo of him walking jauntily into the Old City was a carefully planned and masterly executed exercise in public relations. Uzi Narkiss, who was there, credited Dayan with a "flair for ceremony and a colossal feeling for historical events." He recalled that Dayan had come to the Old City fully prepared to turn the military triumph into great theatrics. "With him were the Chief of Staff, other general staff officers, many civilians, photographers, newspaper reporters and radio broadcasters. The photographers went into the Gate first and that became the front page cover for the Six Day War in Jerusalem."[35]

For a few seconds, Dayan wanted to share the glory with absolutely no one. He wanted to enter the Old City on his own with the photographers snapping away. He eventually sensed the slight this would cause to others. "Yitzhak, you too," he called to the chief of staff. They walked a few steps, and then he looked around: "Uzi, you too," and Narkiss fell in step. Thus emerged the most famous photograph of the war: Dayan, wearing a helmet and camouflage netting, sandwiched between Rabin and Narkiss, entering the Old City.[36]

Now inside the Old City and proceeding to the Temple Mount, Dayan was unpleasantly surprised to find that an Israeli flag had been hoisted on the spire of the Dome of the Rock, the ornate Muslim holy place on the Temple Mount. It was an unnecessary act of religious insensitivity, in his view, and he immediately ordered the flag taken down. Reaching the Western Wall, Dayan found some flowers growing out of a crevice and took some as a personal souvenir. Following an old custom, he wrote a line on a page, and jammed this note between the stones.

"What did you write?" his assistant Moshe Pearlman asked.

Dayan was reluctant to say. But then he showed him: "Would that peace descend on the whole house of Israel." Later, he told Rahel that the experience of being at the Western Wall was bizarre: "I was there and yet I looked on as if I wasn't there."[37] As Dayan walked out of the Old City, he turned to Chaim Herzog and said, "It's your baby, now you take over."[38] Then back at Convention Hall, Dayan promptly ordered that the gates of the Old City be opened. He also authorized the free movement of Jews and Arabs between the two halves of Jerusalem. Few decisions that he made during the war carried graver risks; yet he was convinced that such gestures would relieve tensions and help return the city to normal.

Now it was time to report to the country the import of what had happened that morning. Dayan read from a piece of paper as Kol Yisrael broadcast his message. Everyone was asked to leave the tiny windowless room except for Rehavam Ze'evi, who held a lamp on Dayan's paper.

"This morning," said Dayan in his statement, "the Israel Defense Forces liberated Jerusalem. We have united Jerusalem, the undivided capital of Israel. We have returned to the holiest of our holy places, never to part from it again." In those few words, without checking with anyone in the cabinet, without waiting for a lengthy cabinet debate, Moshe Dayan set down the lines of Israeli policy toward Jerusalem and the other territories taken in the war. However flexible the state of Israel would wish to show itself in the coming months and years over the status of these conquered Arab lands, the phrase "never to part from it again" would ring in everyone's ears as the real Israeli policy. A reporter asked Dayan if he wanted territorial negotiations. Perhaps realizing at that early stage how controversial this issue would become, Dayan answered ambivalently, "I am ready to give peace and take peace."[39]

At a news conference on June 7 in Tel Aviv for the first time Dayan spelled out the extent of Israel's advances. "Israel," he declared, "has attained its political and military objectives. The Straits of Tiran has been opened to international navigation, and every country has a right to use it—including Egypt," he added as everyone laughed. As for the Suez

Canal, he noted that "the Israeli army can reach the canal without any difficulty, but this is not our objective. What is important for us is Sharm el-Sheikh. So why should we push on to Suez and get ourselves in international problems when it is of no interest to us?"

The question at this stage became how far the Israelis intended to go. Along the Jordanian frontier on Thursday morning, Israeli tank commander Uri Ben-Ari touched off a minor controversy when some of his troops crossed the Jordan River, alarming Jordan's commanders, who thought the Israelis were marching on Amman. Jordan's concern was unfounded. Only a few Israeli reconnaissance jeeps had crossed into Jordan via the Abdullah Bridge. Their purpose was not to serve as the vanguard of an invasion, but to aid in the blowing up of the three Jordan River bridges. Dayan apparently ordered the bridges blown to signal that the IDF was not planning to invade Jordan.

Nonetheless, a round of urgent phone calls ensued between Amman and Washington and between Washington and Tel Aviv. Dayan realized that Ben-Ari's forces must have crossed the Jordan River.

"Uri," Dayan said in a hastily put phone call, "Go back."

Ben-Ari recalled the jeeps, averting a further deepening of the Israeli-Jordanian war.

Later, noted Ben-Ari, Dayan admitted he had made a mistake, "that we should have crossed the river and gone up to Amman only to show the Arab world that we could approach and attack an Arab capital. Not to take it."[40]

DAYAN'S ORDERS against Israeli troops reaching the Suez Canal remained in force through the early phases of the war. Those orders stood little chance of being observed given the pattern of the fighting throughout the Sinai. When word came to the General Staff that Israeli forces had indeed reached the canal, Dayan's instinct was to order them back to a position twenty miles east of Suez, but after Dayan learned that the Security Council was meeting in emergency session and planning to impose a cease-fire he gave orders for two division task forces to approach the canal.

General Tal's forces, charged with preventing the retreating Egyptians from crossing the canal, reached a spot ten miles from the waterway in the early morning hours of June 8. Dayan, after consulting with Eshkol and Rabin, ordered them to take up a position twelve and a half miles from the canal. The orders were loosely given and loosely obeyed. With the expectation that the Security Council would call upon each side to remove its forces to positions six miles from the canal, Israel realized it made sense to keep its men close to the waterway, to reduce the size of the eventual withdrawal. Afterward, Dayan sought to portray the Israeli toehold on the canal as a contravention of his orders. According to his assistant, Zvi Tsur, Dayan made a point of sharing the glory with the troops. Racing after the troops who had reached the canal, Dayan was as eager as anyone to dunk his feet in the canal: "He didn't shout at them. We took off our shoes. We put our feet in the water to feel that we are in the Suez. That was in contradiction to his order. . . . Everyone wanted to reach the canal and so he was dragged along with that feeling."[41]

It was easy to be swept along. For a moment, as he helicoptered down to the canal, even Dayan began to believe that it might not be that difficult to go beyond the canal—to Cairo. Inside the chopper, he scribbled a note and passed it to his fellow passengers. None responded amid the roar of the copter blades. When everyone disembarked, Dayan turned to his companions and asked them sternly: "What I want to know is why none of you immediately scrawled no and threw the note back at me." On the note Dayan had asked whether Israeli troops should move forward and take Cairo.

THE WAR was only three days old, but Dayan could afford the luxury of taking some time to look in on the newly acquired West Bank. He realized that the Palestinian Arabs there had not taken part in the war, that most of the battles had taken place away from populated sections. The fighting that occurred was between the Jordanian armed forces and the IDF. The civilian population in the West Bank suffered virtually no casualties, a factor of great significance later when Dayan worked on normalizing relations with the local population after the war. For the moment the IDF's conquest brought the Israelis back to the places where their biblical ancestors had lived and died. Dayan wanted to retrace those footsteps.

On June 8 he journeyed to Hebron to visit the Cave of the Machpelah, the traditional burial site of Abraham and Sarah, Isaac and Rebecca, Jacob and Leah. The Arabs had forbidden Jews to enter the cave. When his convoy arrived, Dayan found the streets deserted. The mosque over the cave was guarded by a single Israeli soldier, who at first turned his rifle on Dayan's convoy. The soldier pointed to a recently written sign on the door noting that this site was out of bounds to IDF troops. When the guard realized who had arrived, he relaxed. A holster strapped to his hip, Dayan toured the premises. He ordered an Israeli flag removed from the building, then proceeded down into the area of the tombs. Dayan decided that arrangements would be made for both Jews and Muslims to pray at this shrine.

That night Dayan gave a long interview, never published, to *Time* magazine's Israel Shenker. It was noteworthy for spelling out for the first time Dayan's insights into why Israel had done so well in the first four days of fighting.

> Air power in this kind of terrain—the desert—was decisive. If you can fly a little bit higher, a little bit faster, this is of great importance. The second thing which proved better than during the Sinai campaign was this business of playing chess and seeing two steps ahead and the Egyptians were bad at chess.
>
> As long as they [the Egyptians] are in prearranged positions they are good in such things as use of terrain and field of fire. It's difficult to reach them. And during months and months they were given instruction, if not by Russians, in Russian methods. If you manage to break through then our advantage shows. Once the intelligence of the command officer comes to the fore. He has to meet new circumstances and do it very quickly. What's more important is the rear headquarters. If a new situation arises, the immediate reaction of the Arab is to call headquarters whose reaction is call Amman, which says wait a minute. By the time you get your answer the situation has changed again. If a new situation arises, no Israeli officer would dream of calling headquarters to ask what he could do. Why, this is the chance of his life—to show what he is capable of. We have to beg him to tell us what he's doing. Anyway, he is always trying to help the other fellow run the war. Only at school do we give directives and reply to questions. In the Sinai we had a thousand commanders who took decisions—and usually good ones. But if you get a thousand questions, where are you?
>
> The next factor is that the whole thing [the Arab effort] collapses because they are slow and slow to react. Had they been Germans or Russians or Americans, alright, you break through and there's a new line. Especially when you have a big theater of war and can move anywhere, and we had a big theater.

Was there not some danger, Shenker asked, that Dayan's head would be turned by the current adulation?

"I might lose my head, but only if it's cut off. I don't know about the praise. Just now I feel tired and worried. I have no feeling of gaiety about the military achievement. The only things I care about are political views and what should now be the map of the Middle East."[42]

ISRAEL WAS ambivalent about Syria. Many Israelis felt that Syria's constant shelling of the Galilee kibbutzim was reason enough to fight that week. Others such as Moshe Dayan thought it more prudent not to extend Israel's military resources too much, to deal with Egypt first, and, only if absolutely required, to take on Syria.

Even after the Syrians began shelling kibbutzim in the Galilee on June 5, Dayan's approach was restraint. Through their reluctance to enter the war on Egypt's side the Syrians had communicated their desire to stay on the sidelines. Fearful that the Soviets might come to Syria's aid if Israel lashed out against Damascus, Dayan ordered the IDF to exercise restraint. Pressure on Dayan to attack Syria came from Prime Minister Eshkol. Dayan told settlers who had experienced Syrian shelling that he would not change his mind even if it meant that some settlements along the Syrian border would have to be removed. He was concerned that the Israeli air force was too exhausted to give the ground forces sufficient support. He also feared that the attack would cost many Israeli lives.

The settlers, organized by Yigal Allon, kept up their pressure. Finally, at 7:00 P.M. on June 8, Eshkol summoned a meeting of the Ministerial Committee on Defense. At Allon's behest, a delegation from the bombed villages came to demand that Israel attack the Syrians. The delegation leaders told Eshkol, "If the Syrians keep the Heights after the war, we will leave our villages and seek peace elsewhere." Still, Dayan prevailed. So great was his influence over the cabinet that Eshkol would not put the matter to a vote.

Rabin told Elazar at midnight on June 8, "Dado, the decision is no attack." Elazar continued to argue and Rabin said he should talk to Dayan, who then got on the phone. "I know you, I understand you. I know what you want. But I also know that you're disciplined and you won't do anything that runs contrary to what we have decided." Dayan remained concerned that the Soviets might intervene and that Israel might suffer heavy losses. He also worried that, with no cease-fire yet in the south, Israel would be forced to open a second front.[43]

Then at 12:45 A.M. a cable arrived from Gavish stating that Israeli troops had arrived at the canal. Egypt announced it was agreeing to a cease-fire. Dayan recalled Elazar's words, spoken the night before: "If we don't do something on this border now, it will be a curse for generations to come." The defense minister was moving toward a decision to attack Syria, but he needed to justify the step. When an Israeli pilot reported that he had seen Syrians running away from their fortifications, Dayan thought he had found his reason. Their flight would mean that an Israeli attack would now entail fewer Israeli losses. Between 4:00 and 5:00 A.M. he asked Aharon Yariv for an intelligence update on the Syrians.

The director of military intelligence said he would check. Returning, Yariv and the defense minister had quite a tiff "because," as Yariv recalled, "Dayan wanted to be able to say that intelligence tells me that the Syrian positions are crumbling."

Dayan asked Yariv to inform Eshkol that the Syrian positions were crumbling, but the intelligence chief refused. If he had followed Dayan's orders and paved the way for an Israeli attack on the Golan Heights— and as a result of that attack numerous Israelis were killed—Yariv knew he would have been personally blamed.

Dayan had an aide inform the prime minister's military aide that "From what intelligence says, the minister of defense gathers that the Syrian positions are crumbling." It was a fine point, but it was Dayan's way of relieving Yariv of the responsibility for the attack.[44]

To Dayan much of what the settlers had said made sense to him but he had been unwilling to unleash Israeli firepower except under the best possible circumstances. Once he had been apprised by his aides in the early morning hours of June 9 that Egypt had accepted a cease-fire, those circumstances existed. He was now prepared to let the attack go forward.

Dayan asked where the chief of staff was. He was informed that he had gone home to sleep.

The defense minister then instructed an aide to get the northern front commander on the phone.

"Dado," said Dayan, "you've got the green light. Take the Syrian plateau."

"The whole thing?"

"The whole thing."

Weizman called Rabin during the night to tell him what the defense minister had decided. Meeting Rabin at headquarters in Tel Aviv, Dayan told him, "You were for [invading Syria], and I held you up. But now I've changed my mind. Otherwise everything will fall apart."

Eshkol's secretary told the prime minister of Dayan's order. Although Eshkol was infuriated, he approved the attack. "I'm not going to order the troops back."[45] The cabinet learned about Dayan's change of heart later that morning.

The Israeli attack began in earnest during the morning as the air force went into action first. An armored brigade led the Israeli ground forces into combat. Dayan constrained Elazar, ordering him not to go beyond the demilitarized zone. He did not want Syria to think that Israel was marching on Damascus. The Syrians had at their disposal five infantry and four armored brigades atop the rocky slopes of the Golan Heights. The Israelis, however, were far the superior army. By the end of the day, they enjoyed a firm foothold on the Heights. At some points during the assault Israeli infantry soldiers climbed the Heights on foot and fought hand-to-hand to take Syrian strongholds. On Saturday morning, June 10, the Israeli army carried on the attack. Dayan still refused to go beyond the line of first fortifications; but Eshkol demanded that the fighting continue until noon to remove all danger from the Huleh Valley settlements. Within a few hours the Syrian defense collapsed totally. Kuneitra, the Syrian administrative capital, fell without a fight at 2:00 P.M. By the time a cease-fire took effect at 6:00 P.M. that day the IDF had control over the entire Golan Heights up to a line that extended from the western peaks of Mount Hermon south through Kuneitra, then descended to the Yarmuk River. In all, the Israelis lost 115 men in the fighting for the Golan Heights, with another 306 wounded. The Syrians lost an estimated 2,500 men, with another 5,000 wounded.

ON A VISIT to the Suez Canal Yael Dayan found Ismalia "bathed in red poinciana trees in blossom."

"Look how beautiful," she said to her father.

"And if it weren't beautiful, it would be just as important."

Dayan looked at a few corpses of Egyptian soldiers floating in the Suez Canal. "It must be unbearable to be part of a defeated army," he said. Yael mentioned that she wanted to visit East Jerusalem soon. Dayan smiled and said, "What's the hurry? You'll be able to visit it even with your children."[46]

On June 10 Dayan paid a visit to Yehoshua Gavish in Bir Gafgafa. When he arrived, the defense minister was visibly upset. No hellos. No handshake.

"You should understand," he finally said to the front commander, "that you will be put on military trial for taking the Gaza Strip and for reaching the canal."

Gavish tried to explain why the IDF had reached the canal: There had been battles. Rabin had given his permission. Yes, this contradicted the original orders. He had no choice. Hearing Dayan, Gavish was equally furious.

"You want me to stand trial? I'll stand trial. This is what you've come to say to me—after the Sinai war? I'll stand trial and you'll hear what my defense will be."

No trial took place. Years later, Gavish, reliving those tense moments in the desert with Dayan, believed that Dayan still lived under the cloud of a Soviet threat to the canal. The defense minister feared that, if the Soviets used military force to dislodge the Israelis from the canal, Dayan would have to stand in judgment. It was best to find a scapegoat right away. Dayan chose Gavish. Once the Soviet threat dissipated, Dayan's talk of court-martialing Gavish disappeared as well.

Speaking to Israeli soldiers on June 11 Dayan summed up the fighting: "The war, the Six Day War, has ended. In those six days we liberated the Temple Mount, broke the shipping blockade and captured the Heights commanding our villages in the Galilee and the Jordan Valley. We have vanquished the enemy. We smashed their battalions and frustrated their connivings. . . . The battle has died down, but the campaign is far from over. Those who rose up against us have been defeated but they have not made peace with us. Return your swords to their scabbards, but guard and take care of them. For the day of beating them into plowshares is not yet at hand."

A NEW ISRAEL was created in six days, one that many had dreamed about but doubted could ever happen. The IDF had won a victory of immense dimensions. It now stood on cease-fire lines encompassing 27,000 square miles of territory, making the country three and a half times its prewar size. Its frontier had been cut from 611 to 374 miles. Egyptian forces were no longer in Gaza, less than fifty miles from Tel Aviv. Israel's army was within striking distance of Cairo. Gone were the dangerous salients of Latrun and Kalkilya. One million Arab inhabitants had come under Israeli occupation. Israeli troops controlled the western bank of the Suez Canal and the western bank of the Jordan River, seemingly ideal boundaries. The price for Israel had been dear: 803 dead (777 soldiers and 26 civilians), 3,006 wounded, but not nearly as steep as had been predicted and feared during the waiting period. Israel's air force, which had performed so astonishingly, lost 50 of its 200 planes. Egypt suffered 15,000 dead and 20,000 wounded, Jordan another 1,000 dead and 2,000 wounded. Some 100,000 Arabs had fled from the West Bank to the eastern side of the Jordan River.

Notwithstanding the losses and casualties suffered, euphoria gripped the Israelis, reflected in the widely felt conviction that the Arabs had no option but to agree to a durable peace. The loss of the land would, Israelis were persuaded, induce the Arabs to seek negotiations at once. The Israelis were quick to distinguish between Jerusalem and the other conquered lands: On June 15 the cabinet decided to annex the eastern sector of Jerusalem as well as the surrounding area of Mount Scopus, the Mount of Olives, Sheikh Jarrah, Sur Baher, Shua'afat, and the airport at Atarot. On June 27 the Knesset confirmed the decision. Israel would negotiate with the Arabs for the return of all occupied territory except Jerusalem: The holy city, now united under Israeli control, was to remain in Israeli hands.

The war made Moshe Dayan a hero of daunting proportions. His meteoric rise to leadership at a time when many Israelis feared the worst for their country, his unmatched record of rewriting the map of Israel in just six days, and his unfailing self-confidence dazzled both the Israeli public and the international community. In Israel's past wars the civilian leadership had been credited with the country's triumphs, the light of publicity shining largely on David Ben-Gurion. But in the Six Day War the man with the black eyepatch reaped most of the glory. Eshkol appeared as an uncertain fumbler, Rabin as a competent but bland technician. None of the other luminaries from the country's military past emerged as potential saviors. Only Moshe Dayan did.

Never had Israel looked so appealing in the eyes of the international media. Goliath had threatened menacingly, but David had not been found wanting. From the vantage point of editors and reporters, the shocking and dramatic Israeli victory invited the instant creation of a media hero. No one fit the bill better than Dayan. A wizard at public relations, the defense minister understood his position better than anyone else. Dayan orchestrated events during this period to evoke precisely the right image. The news conferences he gave before the war on June 3, and then four days later, with the war moving just as he had hoped, illustrated the point, as did the photo opportunity conceived that afternoon of June 7 at the entrance to Jerusalem's Old City. He had rushed to the Western Wall so that he could be the first Israeli leader to enter the gates of the Old City; the prime minister came hours later, by which time photo editors already had the unbeatable photo of Dayan, Rabin, and Narkiss entering the St. Stephen's Gate.

Dayan became the greatest Israeli celebrity to hit the international media. His eyepatched face was everywhere, on front pages of newspapers, the cover of major news magazines, in television film footage. His name became a household word to people who until then could not have placed Israel on a map. He became a symbol of a country, of the underdog overcoming near defeat, of the little fellow turning on the neighborhood bully and decking him with two or three solid blows. In the minds of readers and viewers, the bully was not just Egypt's Nasser, but the whole sweep of modern history that had somehow conspired against the Jewish people. Dayan, and his state of Israel, during those six days had corrected modern history, had sent a message to all the bullies in modern history. All of these symbols and emotions came together remarkably in those six days, focusing on the roundish face of an eyepatched man who had spent the weeks of the waiting period telling the Israelis, "We can do it, we can win," and then, in six days, proved that he was correct.

To many outside of Israel Dayan had taken his place in history with other military giants. In the Pentagon they described him as the greatest military strategist since Napoleon. Lt. Gen. Lewis Walt, just back from two years in Vietnam, a military hero himself, called Dayan "a brilliant tactician and strategist," and added, "I would hate to have him on the other side." Dayan's performance looked all the more dazzling in contrast with the prolonged American effort in the Vietnamese quagmire.

A curious debate arose in Israel after the Six Day War over the size of Moshe Dayan's contribution to the Six Day War victory. It was curious if only because the world at large took for granted that the defense minister had been the grand catalyst for the victory. Some of Dayan's countrymen found it intolerable that he had become a war hero. In their view he had been a Johnny-come-lately who had done very little to change Israel's fundamental military strategy. The real credit for the victory, they argued, belonged to Yitzhak Rabin, the chief of staff, who had built up the IDF into the war machine it had become on June 5. The critics were the same people who had not wanted Dayan as minister of defense in the first place.

What the critics refused to comprehend was that Moshe Dayan had made a decisive difference. Without his last-minute appointment it was not clear that Israel ever would have gone to war. As Ezer Weizman, the chief of operations, said: "We could have won this war without Dayan, but the fact is we didn't do it without him."[47]

The generals had trouble faulting Yitzhak Rabin. He had turned the IDF into what he liked to call a coiled spring, and on June 5 that coiled spring had performed with incredible efficiency and skill. The fact remained that Rabin and Eshkol had been unable to take the political decisions to move against the Arabs. The IDF had become a powerful war machine waiting for someone to turn on the switch. Dayan had played that role. Israel Tal, one of the division commanders in the south, said later: "It was a very, very good war machine, one of the most efficient war machines in history, and the credit should be given to Yitzhak Rabin. But Dayan put life and soul in it. He radiated and generated confidence and bravery and this inspired an entire nation. People literally were ready to go through fire or water or to jump from the roofs to do anything for him. Rabin provided the body, Dayan provided the spirit."[48]

Having provided the spirit for that victory, Moshe Dayan emerged as the most powerful figure in the nation. He now had the clear-cut obligation to navigate the country through the aftermath of those six crucial days.

♦11♦

EMPIRE BUILDER

A COUNTRY WHOSE survival had seemed very much in doubt had suddenly become a formidable regional power. The 1967 war had transformed the perception of Israel abroad from a country who might not exist for too many more years to the dominant military force in the Middle East. Arab countries that until the war had thought it merely a matter of time before the Jewish state would wither had to recalculate: They understood, after the licking the Egyptians and Syrians had taken, that a Jewish state would likely be a permanent part of the Middle East.

Israel's sudden worldwide recognition was personalized through its minister of defense. When an Israeli visitor to Nepal told his host that he was from the Jewish state, the man put his hand on his left eye and declared, "Ah, yes, Israel!" Two photographs graced the wall of a Thai officer in Bangkok: the king of Thailand's and Moshe Dayan's. A Rhodesian magazine polled its readers, asking who was the ideal commander for the Rhodesian army. Dayan led the field ahead of Patton, Montgomery, and Rommel. Even women's fashions fell in step: Just as the Eisenhower jacket had been worn following American achievements in World War II so too were black eyepatches sported by fashion models after the Six Day War. Good taste vanished in the veneration of Dayan: Once he received a solid-gold eyepatch with the Star of David on the front and the Biblical phrase "an eye for an eye" on the back.

No Israeli was so dissected, so scrutinized, so analyzed as the defense minister. The obsessive attention on Moshe Dayan had its effect on him. He had never seemed to like people very much, and now he grew even more impatient, even more eager to cut himself off from the masses. Perhaps inevitably, given the attention focused on him, Dayan sought to exploit his fame. If others intended to judge him as a unique institution, he would play along, following some conventions of society, violating others. Having accumulated a great deal of goodwill, Dayan found that the country gave him great latitude. More than that, it was almost as if others were congratulating him for defying society's conventions by sleeping with numerous women, by carting off archaeological treasure, by breaking the speeding laws.

A myth built up around Dayan, a myth that spoke to his uniqueness and to his belief that he had a special right to stand above the normal rules of society. That myth was encapsulated in one famous incident, actually a very minor episode in Dayan's life, but one that many Israelis heard about. It became symbolic of how Dayan behaved. On November 16, 1961, Dayan, then minister of agriculture, led a motorized column of his own car and a tractor through a detour marked by barrels. He had encountered the barrels blocking the road on the Zahala-Netanya highway near the Tel Aviv Fairground. There was a long line of cars behind him, honking away for passage. Dayan got out of the car and over the objections of the watchman, lifted several of the barrels out of the way. Returning to his car, he and the tractor then proceeded to Tel Aviv. The watchman refused to let the other cars pass.

"I just don't understand it," a frustrated Golda Meir once said of the public's constant forgiveness of Dayan's breaking the rules. "I just don't understand it." Labor party politician Pinhas Sapir put it more colorfully: "If I snatched a kiss from a grown-up woman in a dark corridor, it would mean the end of my political career, but if Dayan raped a minor on a busy street corner, he would somehow induce the crowd to cheer him for it."

As a national institution in his own right after the 1967 war, Dayan had become unquestionably the most powerful figure in the country. No wonder that what he thought, what he decided, was all-important, far more so than what Prime Minister Levi Eshkol did. Resentful of Dayan's ascending star, the prime minister fired one verbal missile after another at the defense minister. In newspaper interviews Eshkol insisted that Rabin, not Dayan, deserved the major credit for the Six Day War victory; that his government could have done very well without Dayan; that only when certain cabinet ministers "became panicky" was he brought in as defense minister. "The boasting and self-praise by one or several people about the military struggle is not dignified," the prime minister told

Yediot Aharonot on July 7 in a not-so-cryptic reference to his minister of defense. Dayan was protected against such assaults. As the then foreign minister Abba Eban noted: "He was . . . the possessor of an extraordinary charisma. There was almost nothing he could do no matter how outrageous it would be for other people, because there was a prior disposition in the public to be admiring, deferential, indulgent beyond the call of reason."[1] Letting the threat of his resignation and the automatic fall of the government hang over the cabinet table, Dayan made sure that ministers took his views into account. A cabinet minister once said that "a large cabinet majority without Dayan is not really a majority." Accordingly, newspaper editors treated Dayan with unprecedented care and attention. Whatever public utterance the defense minister made, however repetitive and rambling his speeches might have been, newspaper columns overflowed with Dayan's rhetoric. He was insulated from routine criticism. Again, Eban: "If Dayan changed his views, he was praised for intellectual resilience. If he was obdurate, he was praised for stability. He thus got the benefit of every doubt. Not that dissent from Dayan was suppressed. It was simply treated as a harmless eccentricity."[2]

Ido Dissentchik, then starting his career in journalism, got a taste of this in July 1969 when, as a reservist serving at the Abu Rudeis oil fields in the Sinai, he and his fellow soldiers were ordered to provide protection for Defense Minister Dayan at a pharaonic temple called Sirbet el Hadm. Arriving three hours later, Dissentchik and the group watched in amazement as the helicopters who had already deposited Dayan at the spot were busy putting artifacts into the chopper. Aware that the law disallowed anyone—even Moshe Dayan—to cart off such artifacts, on their return trip the group mulled over what they had seen. Someone joked to Ido: "We provided protection for a criminal act. Just like in the films: The robbers are in the bank and the security men are outside. We are accessories to a crime."

Back in civilian life, the young journalist urged his father, Aryeh Dissentchik, editor of *Ma'ariv,* to write an article about all of this "so that everyone would know what kind of person their safety has been entrusted to."

"What you tell me doesn't surprise me," the father said. "No story about Moshe Dayan would surprise me. He's capable of almost any bad action. But we won't write such things about him. We must accept Moshe Dayan as he is with both his good and his bad sides. We'll let him take whatever liberties he likes because we need him. When the day of reckoning comes, he is our support and hope. We have to swallow a lot of things so that when the day comes he will be where he needs to be, and will lead us to victory."

"At any price?" asked the son, Ido.

"The independence and security of a nation have no price," the editor answered with finality.[3]

THE POWER and prestige that Moshe Dayan enjoyed after the Six Day War gave him the political authority to shape Israel's security policies as he saw fit. A number of options were open to him. Sensing that Israel's national interests ran counter to the country trying to occupy and rule one million Arabs in the West Bank and the Gaza Strip indefinitely, the defense minister might have insisted that the Israeli army vacate these regions in orderly fashion within two months of the war. Noting that Israel had no good reason to keep its troops along the Suez Canal but did have justification for remaining at Sharm el-Sheikh, Dayan could have demanded that the IDF withdraw its forces within weeks of the war to a line running from El Arish to Sharm. Judging that Israel's only valid security interest along its Golan frontier was to keep the Syrians from firing down at the kibbutzim in the valley, the defense minister might have required a pullback of Israeli forces to positions along the western edge of the Golan plateau. Even with respect to the sticky issue of Jerusalem, he might have found a way for the city's Arabs to remain within a Jordanian political context with Israel establishing the united city as its capital. He might have defined Israel's national interests in these terms. Given his unmatchable political authority he might well have carried the day on all or most of these points—had he sought to move Israel in these directions. Israel would have been a far different country from the one that emerged after 1967, and a variety of forces, peaceful as well as violent, that were eventually unleashed, might have been altered.

One man who believed strongly that Dayan could have and should have initiated a peace initiative right after the war was Egypt's Anwar Sadat, who replaced Nasser in September 1970. He told Israeli writer Amos Elon that there was a moment after the Six Day War when Israel scuttled prospects for peace negotiations. Had Dayan understood the Arabs better, Sadat said, he would have taken the initiative himself and made a "gallant offer" to Cairo. He ought to have known, the Egyptian leader continued, that having been humiliated, the Arabs were not about to come and plead with the Israelis to dictate peace terms.[4]

To suggest that Israel's fate was entirely in the hands of Moshe Dayan in the days and weeks after the Six Day War is to personalize the Israeli-Arab conflict without taking into account the pressures, largely psychological, on Dayan at the time. It is no secret that Israel became intoxicated

by its victories and came to believe in the need to hold on to the conquered Arab lands as a way of assuring its security. In that light, the
argument goes that Dayan cannot be held responsible for Israel's decision
to cling to the conquered Arab lands. Rather, he was pulled by the sweep
of public pressure, carried along by a flood of nationalistic feeling. But
this would make Moshe Dayan a weak politician pushed along by events.
In fact, the man at Israel's defense helm knew from the start in which
direction he wished to push the country, sensed that Israel had gained
nothing from two previous withdrawals after 1948 and 1956. He was
determined not to have the country repeat those mistakes this time.

Hence, from almost the very moment he arrived on the scene to mark
the Israeli conquest of Jerusalem, Dayan had signaled that Israel had no
intention of withdrawing from its newly won territory. During and soon
after the war, the minister of defense began staking out positions about
the future status of the occupied territories before Prime Minister Eshkol
and the cabinet had the opportunity to discuss and decide these issues.
Moments after Israel had concluded its capture of the Old City, Dayan
publicly affirmed that Israel had every intention of holding on to the
newly conquered eastern portion of Jerusalem. Later he spoke of the
need to help the newly captured Gaza Strip partly under Israeli control.
In calling for the establishment of paramilitary agricultural settlements
in the West Bank, Dayan appeared to favor turning Israel's conquest
into permanent rule. Long before the other politicians began to debate
whether Israel's national interests required her to stay in the occupied
lands, Dayan had pushed Israel in the direction of empire building.
Whatever wavering he would do later, whatever concerns he felt that
Israel's hold on the territories retarded rather than guaranteed peace,
Dayan did not waver at the outset. Before the fighting died down, he
set Israel on the path of enduring occupation when he alone had the
power and authority to move the country along a different path. While
senior Israeli figures favored Israel withdrawing from virtually all of the
newly occupied lands, Dayan was moving the country, through his public
remarks, in the direction of enduring rule.

On August 2 he appeared at a ceremony on Jerusalem's Mount of
Olives for the reinterment of Israeli soldiers who had died during the
Jerusalem fighting in 1948. There he made his position clear. "We have
not abandoned your dream [of those who fell] and we have not forgotten
your lesson. We have returned to the mountain [the hill country of the
West Bank], to the cradle of our people, to the inheritance of the Patriarchs, the land of the Judges and the fortress of the Kingdom of the
House of David. We have returned to Hebron and Shechem [Nablus],
to Bethlehem and Anatot, to Jericho and the fords of the Jordan at Adam

Ha'ir." Why did he choose the path of empire? Partly because of his unflagging belief that Israel was doomed to permanent struggle with the Arab world. Neither side, he was convinced, would ever annihilate the other. The Israelis might induce the Arabs, by a show of superior military strength, to enter into peace agreements; but the signing of these accords on the part of the Arabs would be tactical. They would never lose sight of their dream of retaking all of the land on which the state of Israel existed. Peace agreements were worth pursuing, if only because they could bring a temporary peace. Permanent peace, Dayan thought, was an illusion. All of this bred in him an unfailing skepticism. Early in 1968 he said, "It has been decreed that we should live [in a state of] permanent struggle with the Arabs, and there can be no escape from bloodshed; because the real negotiations with the Arab peoples do not take place in talks of the [Middle East mediator Gunnar] Jarring type. The genuine peace negotiations have been in progress already for eighty years, here in Israel. . . . They're a type of negotiations where you settle and build, build and settle, and every so often you go to war." He offered little hope to the graduates of the IDF Staff and Command School on August 7, 1969. "The question 'What will be the end?' has been with our people for four thousand years. . . . Rest and peace for our nation have always been only a longing, never a reality. And if from time to time we did achieve these goals, they were only oases—a breath that gave us the strength and the courage to take up the struggle again. . . . The only answer we can give to the question 'What will be?' is 'We shall continue to struggle.' . . . We must prepare ourselves morally and physically to endure a protracted struggle, not to draw up a timetable for the achievement of rest and peace."

If indeed Israel had no other prospect than to engage in protracted struggle with the Arabs, the territories conquered and now ruled by Israel in the Six Day War become a strategic asset. Dayan never thought of the territories as Israel's religious or historic right. It was not the Bible that gave Jews the right to be in Hebron or Shechem or Shiloh; common military sense dictated that Israelis should cling to this land. "We have no historic right to Sharm el-Sheikh," he told newsmen in 1970, "but we have an obligation to the future to see to it that Israel be able to ship oil at Sharm."[5]

Dayan did not think that clinging to *all* of the occupied territories was necessary. The Sinai and the Golan Heights were perhaps negotiable, though he could not see yielding Sharm el-Sheikh. In an off-the-record conversation with the newspaper *Ma'ariv* on January 29, 1968, Dayan suggested that, given a choice between retaining Sharm or attaining peace with Egypt, he would prefer the former: "I don't think there is anyone on whom it is possible to rely and give him the entrance to Sharm el-Sheikh. If I had a choice between making proper peace that would require a withdrawal to the international border, or to reach an agreement accepted by both sides that would include freedom of navigation and half of the Sinai—I would prefer this to a peace agreement." He was quick to note that Egypt would undoubtedly only accept gaining control over all of the Sinai.[6]

He was equally adamant about keeping the West Bank, the Gaza Strip, and East Jerusalem. If peace were not possible with the Arabs, Israel, in Dayan's view, could not afford to yield these latter three regions. As the main architect of Israel's policies in those regions his premise was an unbending desire to stay put.

THOUGH HE STAKED out these positions early, Moshe Dayan could not dismiss the possibility that the vanquished Arabs might wish to come to the negotiating table. He would have been shocked if they had done so, but no one, including Dayan, could rule out such a step in light of the Israeli military achievements. "We are certainly happy with what we have now," Dayan said at the time. "If the Arabs want a change they should phone up."[7] He doubted they would.

Far more likely was a postwar status quo that offered Israel the prospect of moving in whichever direction it wished. That seemed to suit Moshe Dayan. The prewar rules of the game were invalid. Dayan said right away that Israel was no longer bound by the boundaries growing out of the 1948 War of Independence. The 1949 armistice agreements, in his phrase, were no longer "sacred law." The second rule to go was the one that required Israel to disengage itself from its military gains on the ground as it had in the aftermath of the 1956 war. "Dayan," recalled Abba Eban, "regarded the Six Day War as not just five days of military success but as a rather providential and substantial change in the balance of power which meant that the Arabs had proof that they had no military option. Therefore we could dictate the future settlement."[8]

Had the Arabs been prepared to bargain, had they not portrayed themselves at the Khartoum summit conference on August 29 as unbending on the question of negotiating with Israel, Dayan might well have had to reexamine his own views. At Khartoum, the Arab states were unequivocal. They issued their three famous nos: No peace with Israel, no negotiations with Israel, no recognition of Israel. After Khartoum, it was clear to Dayan and to other Israelis that there would be no phone call from the Arabs. Dayan was free to embark upon a series of measures that would solidify Israel's hold on the newly occupied areas.

Though he would steer Israel toward a larger role in the occupied areas, Dayan was ambivalent about the propriety of Israel remaining in Arab land. He firmly believed that Israel was perfectly justified in staying until the phone rang. Yet he wondered whether Israel could afford to take such an adamant stand. It might lead to another round of war. To students at the Technion in Haifa on November 8, 1967, he suggested that Israelis have to ask themselves: "Do the Arab failures and the fact that we are to be found on the bank of the Suez Canal and the Golan Heights bring the Arabs closer to a state of willingness to make peace with us? I think the answer is no. If we're not talking about what is said, about verbiage intended to serve the interests of strategy, but of real peace, then I don't think we can say that the Arab leaders are drawing any closer to peace with us as a result of the Arab states' military failure or as a result of the policies followed and the positions held by us at present."

This same theme recurred in remarks he made to more than one thousand delegates at the Rafi convention in December 1967 in Jerusalem. So great was his prestige that Dayan could speak with some understanding of the Arab view that Israel had become expansionist and not be swept off the platform: "It is natural that the Arabs should view us as expansionists, and it is also more difficult for them to accept the present situation than that before the June war. It is not enough for us to look down from the Golan Heights, see our settlements lying safe below, and say that now peace is assured. We still have to look at it also from the point of view of the Syrians, who see our troops thirty kilometers (nineteen miles) from Damascus and who do not see that as a situation guaranteeing peace."⁹ Dayan believed Israel had no alternative but to lay the groundwork for an enduring stay in the territories.

FEW IN ISRAEL had any knowledge of how to govern the one million Arabs of the West Bank and the Gaza Strip. Few Israelis had any real acquaintance with Arabs at all. Dayan did. He knew them well enough to realize that, as vital as it was for Israel's security to retain these territories, it would prove an unbearable burden to try to rule the people there. "That was where the Germans went wrong," Dayan told a friend soon after the war. "Wherever they went, they turned everything into a closed military camp."¹⁰

This was not a new thought for Dayan. At the time of the IDF withdrawal from the Sinai following the 1956 war, Dayan, still the chief of staff, told officers of the northern command: "I can imagine Syria attacking us and our being forced to occupy Damascus in order to decide the campaign, but it would not occur to us to annex Damascus. You do not just conquer areas; you also conquer populations, and it is not so simple to annex a population and to convert it into nationals of the conquering state. In this generation in particular, when it is the citizens who determine who will rule them and not the rulers who make subjects their nationals and tyrannize them, sooner or later it is the will of the people that decides and ultimately it is the population that has its way, be it in the Saar, in Cyprus, or in the Gaza Strip."[11]

Many Israelis agreed with Dayan that enduring Israeli rule over the conquered lands was in the country's best interest. Given their fears and mistrust, they could have been easily convinced that incarcerating them in prison camps was also in Israel's best interest. The idea of Jews mixing with Arabs was entirely theoretical before the Six Day War; it would not have occurred to most Israelis that West Bank or Gazan Arabs could walk down Jaffa Road on the Jewish side of Jerusalem, or swim on the beaches of Tel Aviv, or ride Israeli buses. That would happen perhaps, if at all, only in another hundred or two hundred years. It was on this point that Moshe Dayan disagreed with his countrymen. His childhood experiences, his intimate knowledge of the Galilee Arabs, had taught him that peaceful coexistence was not out of the question, that the Arabs were not going to disappear, and that some kind of accommodation must be found so that Jews and Arabs could carry on their daily lives in peace.

Accordingly, Dayan was not going to lock the Arabs of the West Bank, Gaza, or East Jerusalem in prison camps. To have done so would have been to invite internal and external pressures—and an explosion of hatred and violence from the opening days of the occupation. Moreover, he bore no hatred toward the Arabs. On the contrary, he felt empathy toward them. He disliked it when Israelis sought to dehumanize them. For that, he was sometimes called [behind his back] "Der Arabber," Yiddish for the Arab. While rejecting the role of martinet, Dayan had to decide how tightly to hold the reins, how visible Israel should be in the role of occupier, how to deal with outbursts of violence, how to treat acts of civil disobedience. It would not be an easy task.

He began with Jerusalem. Until the Six Day War the city had been divided, Jews living and working on the western side, Arabs doing the same on the eastern side. A tense, sometimes violent frontier of barbed wire and fortified emplacements laced the city. Only a few, among whom were tourists and diplomats, crossed from one side to another. Jew and Arab eyed one another, when they did, through a gun sight. After the war the barbed wire came down and Israeli soldiers established their presence on the city's eastern side. At first the IDF manned checkpoints and permits were required to cross from one section to the other. The

IDF could not fathom handling the situation any other way: Letting Jerusalem Arabs roam over to the western side was to them a nightmarish thought, conjuring up images of Arabs raping Jewish teenaged girls, knifing others, looting stores. Even if, as seemed likely, the politicians chose to annex the eastern half of the city, the security of Jerusalem appeared to warrant the isolating of Jews and Arabs from one another.

Dayan's vision of what was good for Israel led him down a different path. He saw little risk in having Jews and Arabs mingle freely. Not allowing them to mingle posed a serious risk in his view to Israel's plan to retain political control over all of Jerusalem. Dayan doubted the international community would tolerate the assertion of Israeli political control over the city if the city remained physically divided. Most Israeli politicians thought Dayan had lost his senses. Teddy Kollek, the mayor of Jerusalem, was one of them: "Who knew what smoldering hatreds might flare up if you suddenly gave Jews access to the Old City and allowed Arabs to move freely in West Jerusalem?"[12] Kollek and other Israelis urged Dayan to proceed slowly. He would not brook delay.

When Israel decided on June 28 to annex the holy city, Dayan thought the time right to bring down the barriers. Summoning Maj. Gen. Shlomo Lahat (later the mayor of Tel Aviv) back from a lecture tour in South America, the defense minister appointed him military governor of East Jerusalem, and advised him to take his new responsibilities seriously: "If there's a pogrom in the city and Arabs are killed, you'll have to answer for it. Jerusalem is important to me."[13] Dayan called the head of the Shin Bet, the internal security service, to a meeting at eight that evening and asked him how long it would take to prepare for the opening of Jerusalem to free movement. Six months was the figure that came to his mind, but knowing Dayan's impatient reputation, he said, "Two months."

"OK," said the minister of defense, "I'll give you two weeks."

He did not really mean it. Within hours Dayan gave the order to bring the barriers down—at 6:00 A.M. the next day! Gathering at the Convention Hall that evening, Israeli officials responsible for implementing the decision grumbled that the defense minister was being too hasty. "All of us felt that it wasn't necessary to open the gates," recalled one participant, Raphael Vardi, chief of staff of the West Bank military government, "that it was too early. It was dangerous and would cause many problems. We still hadn't taken full control. Jordanian soldiers were still on the eastern side. But Dayan stood his ground."[14] The next morning only a few residents crossed the city's frontier, but by the afternoon huge numbers were crossing, Jews to the Arab side, Arabs to the Jewish side. Dayan had been right. Despite the frightening predictions, all had gone smoothly.

The temptation became great to do away with other symbols of a divided city. "Every great military leader leaves his own physical imprint in the place he has conquered," Dayan said to central front commander Uzi Narkiss. "He might erect a monument. But I suggest that we dismantle the section of the Old City walls between the Nablus and New gates. It will be a sign that we were there." Not willing to bring the idea to the government himself, Dayan urged Narkiss to push for its acceptance. Narkiss, however, sensed that the government would have little appetite for knocking down the Old City walls, and never followed through.[15]

With his finely tuned antenna for Arab attitudes, Dayan knew there were certain boundaries of good taste and sensitivity beyond that Israel could not go in its emerging relations with the Arabs of these occupied territories. He understood that while conquering Arab territory had been a necessarily military measure, it was not in Israel's interest to deprive the Arabs of their right to prayer. Israel did not need the Arabs to declare a jihad, or holy war, to avenge Israeli acts against their holy places. For years the Jews had been cut off from their holy places, unable to reach Jerusalem's Western Wall or Hebron's Cave of the Machpelah. Now Israeli access was restored, making it even more necessary for Israel to assure the same access for Arabs to their holy places, the Dome of the Rock and El-Aksa on Jerusalem's Temple Mount, access which these Arabs had enjoyed for the past 1,300 years. Hence, on June 17, only a week after the war, Dayan asserted that the responsibility for the Temple Mount be in Arab hands; and that Arab Muslims would be permitted to pray there. "In the long history of the people of Israel, there are few deeds that can compare with the historical significance and profound symbolism of this act," wrote Meron Benvenisti, then the Jerusalem municipality administrator of the Old City and East Jerusalem.[16] When chief IDF chaplain Shlomo Goren, later a chief rabbi of Israel, sought to pray on the Temple Mount on August 16 Dayan insisted that Jews must not do so in order to preserve tranquillity at the site. Israelis were given access to the site for purposes of touring.

DAYAN'S APPROACH to ruling the West Bank Arabs was equally as sensitive. On the morning of June 7 Dayan had breakfast in Tel Aviv with Chaim Herzog, the newly appointed commander of military forces on the West Bank. With the West Bank falling to the Israelis, Herzog asked the defense minister, "What's our policy? What am I supposed to do?"

"You are supposed to see that everything returns to normal. But don't try to rule the Arabs. Let them rule themselves. Of course, they have to know you're the boss. It's enough that we suffer from Israeli bureaucracy. They don't deserve it. In a nutshell I want a policy whereby an Arab can be born, live, and die in the West Bank without ever seeing an Israeli official."[17] Accordingly, military command posts were kept at a discreet distance from the main Arab thoroughfares in the West Bank and Gaza. Later, however, in 1969, in response to the growing power of the fedayeen, Dayan was forced to move entire Israeli military camps into the occupied areas and have IDF soldiers patrol the streets of major West Bank towns.

He wanted normal routine restored as quickly as possible. Soon after the war he gave orders to remove roadblocks, return confiscated vehicles, permit farmers to work their fields, and restrict curfews to darkness. When he visited the West Bank town of Kalkilya he was shocked to find that one-third of the buildings had been destroyed, not by shelling, but by dynamite. He learned that the IDF had acted in reprisal for Arab sniping at Israeli soldiers. Eight hundred homes had become uninhabitable; twelve thousand residents of the town had fled, some venturing to Nablus and other nearby villages, some residing in olive groves outside Kalkilya. He ordered the town rebuilt and demanded that the refugees be permitted back home.[18]

It was critical for Dayan that the Arabs not come to regard the Israeli occupying force with the same bitter contempt as the Jews held the British during the Mandate period. For that reason, the defense minister took a personal interest in the selection of IDF officers serving in the territories, even seemingly junior ones. In contrast with the usual practice that the defense minister approves only appointments of colonels and above, Dayan insisted on personally confirming the choice of every IDF commander and deputy commander for the major West Bank towns. He knew the kind of officer he did not want, someone who resembled the current military governor of the Gaza Strip: "I don't need someone like Motta Gur, who is a good officer, but when he enters the room all the notables of Gaza have to get up as if he were a British governor-general. We are not British here. This isn't what I need. I need someone who is admired but still respected by the Arabs."[19]

Dayan was realistic enough to understand that nothing would induce the Arabs to cheerfully accept the Israeli occupation. To an audience of hundreds of mukhtars and other Arab notables, the defense minister said, "We do not ask you to love us. We ask only that you care for your own people and work with us in restoring the normalcy of their lives." Offering the Arabs the carrot, Dayan held the stick in reserve. His policy was to give the Arabs as many carrots as possible in the hope that they would believe they had much to lose by engaging in hostile acts.

When the Nablus mayor Hamdi Ka'anan came to Dayan, saying that he had to resign because he was unable to serve under an Israeli occupation, the defense minister told him that his resigning was something for Nablus residents to worry about, that he could not stop him, but that he would not replace him. "If you and the Nablus people want no public administration in Nablus, that is entirely your choice. I will not interfere with it." The mayor retracted his resignation.

In an interview with American columnist Joseph Alsop, Dayan summed up his policy toward West Bank and Gaza Arabs: "All that Israel needs is to insure that no enemy troops cross the Jordan; and for this purpose Israel only requires the use of the main roads and a few strongpoints on the heights above the river. . . . Many things [the British] cared about, we do not care about at all. If [the Palestinians] want to write protests or close their shops or schools, let them! I am not interested. But if they want fuel and teachers' salaries and electricity and everything else they need, it is up to them to cooperate with us in the very small way we need. . . . We must not interfere, become involved, issue permits, make regulations, name administrators, become rulers. For if we do, it will be bad for us. . . ." Alsop asked Dayan whether this unique system would work forever.

No, said the defense minister, no more than two to four years.[20]

By and large, the Arabs did not cooperate, but as little as they liked the occupation, they came to terms with its existence. They did so in part because they were still in a state of shock over the results of the Six Day War, and in part because of Dayan's policy of not intervening in the daily affairs of the Arabs. In all spheres, military as well as civilian, the defense minister insisted on keeping a low Israeli profile. Once, while Dayan was meeting with the local IDF commander in Nablus, some Arabs threw stones at them. Instinctively, the commander wanted to react. Should he order his soldiers to fire at the stone throwers? he asked Dayan.

"No," was the defense minister's emphatic reply.

"But," said the commander, "today they are throwing stones. Tomorrow they will throw grenades. The day after that they will kill Israeli soldiers. Why not react right from the start?"

"When they throw grenades and kill soldiers, then you can shoot them."[21]

Matters never reached that stage. Dayan's policy was unequivocal. Civilians who engaged in anti-Israeli nonviolent resistance were to be treated differently from those using violence. Dayan called the violent ones "terrorists" and was prepared to mete out all sorts of harsh measures to deter further terrorism. Their houses could be blown up. They could be deported. "Anywhere there is terror, we will put it down until the end with all possible means," he would say. Once he visited Nablus, the largest town on the West Bank, where Arabs had recently engaged in some shooting. The IDF had moved a tank into a position and shelled the house from where the shooting had occurred. Approaching the town's leaders, Dayan said, "You have to understand. If our people are hit by terrorists, there won't be one complete home left in Nablus. We will destroy Nablus totally."

These policies kept the local populace from joining the terrorist groups in large numbers. (Dayan never held Palestinian terrorists in the same contempt that other Israeli leaders did. For instance, when he was asked by a reporter some years later if he were a Palestinian would he become a terrorist, he replied that if he thought he had a chance of helping to establish a Palestinian state and defeating the Israelis, he might consider becoming one.)

Israeli soldiers were under instruction not to shoot at demonstrators. Recalled Raphael Vardi: "At one demonstration an Israeli sergeant fired into the air. Moshe Dayan himself conducted the investigation. The front commander was asked to find out why the boy shot into the air. As a result of this policy, there were no hospitalizations, no fatalities."[22] Someone found guilty of inciting demonstrators was deported; if a school held a strike, measures were taken against the strikers.

The local population remained dormant. At the time the West Bank and Gaza Arabs still hoped that one day soon the Israelis would vacate their lands; this was years before thousands of Jewish settlers would take up residence on the West Bank. Summing up Dayan's policies, Hebron mayor Sheikh Ja'abari explained that "Dayan slaps you across the face and then immediately retrieves your hat for you and places it perfectly on your head."[23]

When Israeli officials sought to use administrative detention against the Arabs, Dayan pounced on them for doing so when there was not sufficient evidence to bring the person to trial.

"I don't like this," Dayan told them. "It makes a mockery of the verdict. . . . It's written here: 'The investigators received a bad impression of him.' I'm sure that anyone who investigated me would get a good or a bad impression, but between ourselves, any investigator gets a good impression of anyone who licks his boots and a bad one of anyone who says this is his homeland."

Collective punishment irked him as well. Dayan listened impatiently in 1970 as central front commander Rehavam Ze'evi suggested sanctions against the entire West Bank village of Dura after an attack against a Jew in that village.

"Against the whole village?" Dayan asked in disbelief.
"Yes."
"What do you want? That the village should hand over the group responsible? Deal with the person against whom you have direct evidence, blow up his house, but why take action against the 3,000 villagers? . . . I'm tired of the fact that after three years you still don't understand the difference. It wasn't the whole of Dura that took part in the attack."[24]

He understood that the power of the occupier had to be used fairly. When the Israeli Egged bus company sought a monopoly over the bus lines in the West Bank, Dayan refused the request despite immense pressure on him: He asserted that the Arabs had a right to ride on their own buses. Discovering that Arabs had been taken off buses and forced to wait lengthy periods as part of IDF security checks, he ordered this practice halted. Finding Arabs waiting in the hot sun while waiting to cross the Jordan River bridges, he insisted that they be given water.

Apart from reducing the friction, Dayan realized there was virtue in encouraging freedom of movement among the West Bank and Gazan Arabs. They might derive economic benefit from being allowed into Israel, and, becoming prosperous, the Arabs might adopt a more peaceful stance toward the Jewish state. Though Arab notables begged him to cease the practice of West Bank Arabs traveling into Israel each morning to work, Dayan held his ground. "There is no way I would want to stop them," he told one of the notables, Nablus mayor Ka'anan. "If they wish to work in Israel and earn more money than they can get at home, I don't want to stop them."[25]

He was also concerned lest these Arabs feel hemmed in, unable to carry on their normal commercial and social intercourse with the Arab world. He thought it important that they enjoy free access to the Arab world on the other side of the Jordan River bridges. Dayan's attitude appeared to defy all logic. What country at war with its neighbor permits the free flow of traffic and goods across their hostile frontier? However irrational, the opening of the Jordan River bridges appealed to Dayan as a way of halting a ticking time bomb, a way of encouraging normalcy among the Arabs of the West Bank and Gaza. Creating normalcy was a means of fortifying Israel's continuing hold over these areas.

Dayan did not invent the "Open Bridges" policy though he has long been given credit for this initiative. Rather, he gave the green light after learning about it from IDF commanders. It had been a productive year for the Arab farmers, but after the war they were cut off from their markets in Jordan and the rest of the Arab world and Europe. That first summer of the occupation no one in Israel had given much thought to helping the local Arabs market their farm produce. The Arab farmers from Jenin decided to take matters into their own hands by trucking their goods to the Jordan River, then fording across, goods in tow, to the eastern bank.

WHEN ISRAELI military commanders informed the defense minister what had been occurring, his first thought was to have the crossings halted. "Stop them. They don't have permission for this," he told Raphael Vardi.[26] A few days later Dayan received a phone call from central front commander Uzi Narkiss who asked him if he wanted to see something "fantastic." Thinking it was a new archaeological site, Dayan said yes. On August 1, the defense minister and Narkiss flew to Damia, where the front commander pointed down below to a shallow part of the Jordan River where hundreds of Arab trucks loaded with tomatoes, potatoes, peaches, and apples were crossing to the eastern side. The IDF's order to cease the movement across the Jordan had been given but the Arabs were continuing anyway.

"Who approved this?" Dayan asked Narkiss, munching on a peach.

"You, now."

Dayan thought for thirty seconds and then said, "OK. Let's go down."

Senior IDF commanders were concerned that Dayan would chew them out for letting the crossings continue. Instead, he gazed at some Israeli officers checking a group of Arabs about to cross the Jordan. "You've got too much bureaucracy," he said. "You should just let this thing work."

Hearing about the crossings, Israeli generals complained. "We thought he had gone mad," recalled Ezer Weizman, then chief of operations. "We argued our heads off with him."

Weizman asked, "If we open the bridges across the Jordan, why not open the bridges to Lebanon?"

"Look," Dayan said, "There'll be a lot of pressure building up on the West Bank and this opening will be a valve."[27] The bridges were rebuilt (once Dayan obtained Hussein's approval), first the Adam Bridge near the spot where the original Jenin farmers crossed, then much later the Allenby Bridge. Eventually Dayan permitted the Arabs to take fruits, vegetables, and industrial equipment across the Jordan. "This policy may appear schizophrenic and utterly without logic," wrote Shimon Peres, "but it works, as if it were the most normal thing in the world."[28]

In time, as it became increasingly less likely that Israel and Jordan would meet at the negotiating table, Dayan took steps to tighten the country's hold over the territories. At first Dayan was hesitant about giving the local Arabs political rights. When Anwar Khatib, the former

Jordanian military governor of Jerusalem, proposed to Chaim Herzog that he organize a meeting of Arab notables in an East Jerusalem movie theater where a Palestinian entity on the West Bank would be declared, Herzog consulted Dayan. Jordan had refused the creation of such an independent entity for years. Khatib made it clear that he saw the entity as falling under Israeli sovereignty. Herzog obtained the backing of Yigal Allon, then deputy prime minister, for the plan. Dayan rejected the idea outright. The defense minister was fearful that Ahmed Shukeiry, leader of the Palestine Liberation Organization, would take over the entity. Even in those early days Dayan feared the establishment of a Palestinian Arab state arising on the West Bank and in the Gaza Strip: "I regard it as the beginning of the destruction of the State of Israel."[29] For that reason Dayan greeted any autonomy proposal with discomfort. "When I proposed autonomy except for defense, foreign relations, and finances," remembered Uzi Narkiss, "Dayan almost threw me out of the room."[30]

Dayan eventually, grudgingly, encouraged talk of Palestinian Arab autonomy, hoping that it might satisfy the Palestinians' political requirements, and that King Hussein would feel so threatened by an autonomous West Bank that he would rush to negotiate with Israel. On November 17, 1967, Dayan called a special meeting of the cabinet committee on this issue and presented his views: "We need an alternative," he said.

> We need a maneuvering option, so that we do not have only King Hussein to negotiate with. Such a Palestinian representation is needed for our maneuverability, but, who knows, maybe something will really come out of it in the form of a Palestinian entity. It is the government's policy, unanimously accepted, that Israel should not behave either as a "Russian commissar" or as a "British Mandatory official" in the West Bank and in the Gaza Strip. A "Russian commissar" is a system where the central government has spies and representatives supervising every decision and every act at every level. A "British Mandatory official" is a system where there is no foreign presence or interference at the lower echelons of the administration, but from a certain level to the top, all is in British hands. . . . Thus, for example, it is in our interest to have Mr. Hamdi Ka'anan running things in Nablus. Even if he is not "Zionist," and he openly says so, he is always preferable to an Israeli officer in charge.[31]

Several days later Dayan ordered the withdrawal of almost all functionaries belonging to the Israeli civilian administration in the occupied areas.

When in July 1968 Dayan sought to create independent administrative districts in the West Bank, he conditioned their creation upon King Hussein's approval, concerned that the king would close the bridges in retaliation. Hussein demurred, fearful that a Palestinian state would rise that would threaten Jordan's position in the West Bank.

As time went on Dayan increasingly favored linking the occupied areas with Israel. By the summer of 1968 he had proposed a plan of economic integration. He favored integrating the two labor forces and increasing Israeli investment in the territories. He would have liked to open the entire Israeli labor market to the local Arabs. Strong opposition developed on the part of Prime Minister Eshkol and Finance Minister Pinhas Sapir. Unwilling to contemplate Israel as a permanent element in the territories, the finance minister restricted the number of Arab laborers permitted to work in Israel to five thousand. Both Eshkol and Sapir worried that the inclusion of one million Arabs in Israel's political contours would threaten the demographic status of Israel's Jewish majority.

Though he harbored strong reservations about putting up Jewish settlements willy-nilly in the occupied areas, the defense minister eventually grew used to the phenomenon and became one of its ardent champions. At the beginning he seemed singularly unenthusiastic about the creation of these settlements. Jewish settlement was not permitted in the early days of the occupation, as part of Dayan's efforts to reduce friction with the Arabs. He never felt that placing Jewish settlements in the West Bank fulfilled some biblical command. Were the West Bank to become Jordanian again he would have no trouble accepting their new political context. "Let's assume that partition had taken place and I would come to Nablus or Shiloh with a visa," he said. "I would feel at home there even though the political boundary was elsewhere."[32] If settlements were to be built, he preferred them on the strategic hilltops away from densely populated Arab centers. He thought building settlements should be at the government's discretion, not left in the hands of Jewish settlers who might choose locations that the politicians felt unsuitable.

Such was the case with the settlement effort in Hebron in the spring of 1968. On the eve of Passover, April 4, ten Israeli families pretended they were Swedish tourists and registered at the Park Hotel in Hebron. The day after, Rabbi Moshe Levinger, the group's leader, announced they were reviving Jewish settlement in Hebron. They refused to be budged from the hotel. The defense minister was in a hospital due to an accident at an archaeological site, and the coordinator of activities in the territories, Shlomo Gazit, was at home observing the period of mourning for his father. No one was available who was willing to stop Levinger. A national debate ensued over the right of these families to settle in

Hebron. Influenced by the scope of public support for Levinger's settlers, the Eshkol government eventually reached a compromise under which the settlers were moved to an Israeli army base in Hebron. Dayan tried to drive the Levinger group away by forcing them to remain in cramped, uncomfortable quarters at the army base; he urged the government to have them removed, but to no avail. In time, these settlers managed to build Kiryat Arba on the outskirts of Hebron. Dayan asked the settlers to develop good neighborly relations with the Arabs. "Don't raise your children to hate them," he implored.

DAYAN DISPLAYED little interest in publicly coaxing the Arabs to the peace table. What he did do was make several dramatic, highly personal efforts—in deep secrecy—to further the peace process in the fall of 1968. One was meant to encourage Egypt's president Nasser to come to the negotiating table, the other to meet with Yassir Arafat, who became chairman of the Palestine Liberation Organization in 1969.

Dayan began these initiatives by inviting a Palestinian nationalist poet named Fadua Toukan from Nablus to his home in Zahala. The invitation became controversial because Israelis could not understand why one of their leaders entertained someone who had denounced Israel in fervid tones. Accompanying her was her uncle, Dr. Kadri Toukan, and Nablus mayor Hamdi Ka'anan. During that meeting in Zahala, Fadua Toukan asked her uncle to go see President Nasser and urge him to negotiate with the Israelis. Two months later, Dayan met the poet at Jerusalem's King David Hotel. She passed on Nasser's answer by noting that he had disapproved of her meeting with the defense minister in Zahala. Nasser told her that the American secretary of state, Dean Rusk, had urged him to reach an accord with Israel on the basis of the IDF withdrawing from all of Sinai. Nasser said no, because this kind of peace settlement did not include an Israeli withdrawal from the West Bank.

Pursuing negotiations, the defense minister offered a fedayeen prisoner his freedom if he would find Arafat and tell him that Dayan wanted to meet with him. Dayan did not indicate what the purpose of the talks would have been. He clearly sensed in Arafat a Palestinian Arab who had growing influence over the inhabitants of the West Bank and Gaza. Most likely, the defense minister wanted to put pressure on King Hussein by holding out the prospect of dealing with a Palestinian Arab alternative if the Jordanian monarch avoided the peace table. In any event, the prisoner, fearing Arafat's reaction to his serving as a messenger for the Israelis, refused.

Fadua Toukan was not through trying. She told Dayan, "I'm only a woman, but I'm no coward and I want peace. Nasser doesn't want to make peace with you. When I go to Beirut, I'll see Abu Amar [Arafat] and suggest that he meet with you. We must have peace." Dayan never found out if Toukan did go to see Arafat. She never contacted him again. He made one more attempt to see Arafat, picking another prisoner for the mission. The prisoner's allegiance was to a different political group within the Palestine Liberation Organization, not Arafat's Fatah wing, and was hardly a candidate for arranging the Dayan-Arafat talk. Dayan's efforts to see Arafat were not officially acknowledged at the time.

An Israel Radio reporter asked the defense minister how he justified meeting a nationalist Palestinian. Why, asked the reporter, should West Bank Arabs be expected to express moderate views when a nationalistic fighter is welcomed as a guest in the home of an Israeli leader?

"It was not I who made Fadua Toukan a poet," answered Dayan, "nor did I dictate her nationalistic poems to her. But since there is a Palestinian public, and since this public has poets, I suggest that the Israeli public listen to those poets who are popular among the Arabs—in order to understand them; even if they themselves are not willing to try to understand who we are and what the Zionist movement is. . . ."

DESPITE ISRAEL's overwhelming victory in the Six Day War, the Arabs would not put their arms aside. After the initial shock, Egypt put its soldiers through a period of training and rearming. By the late summer of 1967 it was ready to resume acts of violence against Israel. A major artillery exchange between Egypt and Israel occurred along the Suez Canal, forcing Egypt to evacuate tens of thousands of civilians from Suez City and Ismalia. On October 21 an Egyptian missile boat sank the Israeli ship *Eilat* thirteen and a half miles from Port Said outside Egyptian territorial waters, with forty-seven Israelis killed or missing. Israel responded by shelling the oil refineries near Suez City and setting aflame adjoining oil storage tanks. Along the entire Israeli-Egyptian front artillery exchanges took place. Then calm reigned for nearly a year.

In the fall of 1968 Egypt opened fire in the northern sector of the Suez Canal. Ten Israelis were killed and eighteen wounded. Two weeks later, Egyptian artillery hit Israeli positions along the canal for nine hours. Another fifteen Israelis were killed and thirty-four wounded. The Israeli air force went into action, blowing up several bridges on the Nile. Israeli paratroopers landed deep inside Egypt, destroying the large power station at Naj Hammadi. As with the retaliatory raids of the early 1950s, Dayan made a point of waiting at a forward command post to greet the returning force. The Egyptian bombardments had forced Israel to dig in, and during the next four calm months the IDF built up its canal positions. "We must reply with a fighting refusal to any effort to push us off of the cease-fire line," Dayan insisted. As a result Israel began building its Bar-Lev line, a series of hardened concrete and steel-reinforced bunkers along the canal. The line, completed in March 1969, was named after Chief of Staff Chaim Bar-Lev.

Dayan was never a great believer in the Bar-Lev line for much the same reason that he had not wanted Israeli troops to push to the canal during the Six Day War. One day in the Knesset he told Zalman Shoval, "We should have our defense line several kilometers [four miles] from the water. If the Egyptians try to cross the canal in force, the Bar-Lev line won't stop them. It would be far better for us to meet them deeper inside the dessert, beat them there, and push them back. Militarily, it's much wiser than to sit on the banks of the canal. We can't sit there with the entire Israeli army."[33]

Most Israeli leaders disagreed and did not want to budge from the canal. Nor did most Israelis have the appetite for another full-scale war against Egypt so soon after the fighting the previous June. Dayan sensed this lack of enthusiasm when he called together the senior air force commanders at the Ramat David air force base in April 1969.

"Listen," said the defense minister, "this thing that's happening at the canal is no good. I have in mind escalating this into something bigger and breaking it. Is the air force ready? A simple question. Are you ready to back me up? Are you ready to go to war? Full blown."

The room was quiet. Then Air Force Commander Mordechai Hod answered, "Yes, the air force is ready. But it would be much more ready in August when we get a few more Skyhawks and perhaps the first Phantoms."

Dayan's interest suddenly diminished. "I saw the glint in his eye die out," recalled Benny Peled, deputy air force commander, who was in the room at the time.

Peled said, "I don't understand this reaction of the air force. The air force is ready this afternoon. We won't be any better in August." Dayan looked at Peled and smiled, realizing that most of the men thought like Hod, not Peled, that few were disposed to engage in all-out war against the Egyptians.[34]

By July Israeli casualties at the canal reached seventy a month. Dayan intensified Israeli shelling of industrial and civilian targets across the canal and won agreement from the Ministerial Defense Committee to send the air force against Egyptian forts, gun emplacements, and SAM-2 missile sites in the northern canal sector. On July 17, for five hours

Israeli war craft bombed and strafed military targets between Kantara and Port Said, shooting down five Egyptian planes. Two Israeli planes were downed. At the end of July after an air battle in which twelve Egyptian planes were downed, Nasser fired the commander of his air force. The Egyptian leader fired his chief of staff and navy commander as well shortly thereafter.

Hoping for a respite, Dayan sought ways to put pressure on Egypt and force them into agreeing to a cease-fire: He proposed to the Ministerial Defense Committee that Israeli planes attack army bases deep inside Egypt. Twenty targets were bombed between January and March 1970. The purpose of the bombing raids, Dayan said, was to bring home to the Egyptian people the truth about the war, to suggest to them that their leaders were doing them harm. By this time Nasser had obtained Soviet troops and equipment, including three squadrons of fighter planes with Russian crews. In July Israeli and Soviet planes engaged in dogfights. Eight Soviet MiG-21s attacked an Israeli patrol plane and in the ensuing battle Israeli war craft downed five planes manned by Soviet pilots.

The War of Attrition had taken a heavy toll. Egyptian losses were ten thousand dead and wounded. In the period from the end of the Six Day War until August 1970 Israel had 721 dead, of whom 127 were civilians. Dayan was increasingly frustrated, because of the growing number of Israeli casualties, and the army's unwillingness to deploy itself in a way that might afford greater protection to Israeli soldiers' lives. The questioning began back home: Why, it was asked, were Israeli soldiers dying to protect land that the country appeared ready to give up for peace?

On trips to the Suez Canal the defense minister simply peered straight ahead at Egyptian emplacements, saying very little to the soldiers in the bunkers. Ariel Sharon, then head of the southern command, agreed with Dayan on the need to close the Bar-Lev line and take up positions farther inland. One day in the spring of 1970 they had attended a senior meeting of military men where the Bar-Lev line had been debated. They then paid a visit to an Israeli fortification opposite Port Taufiz called Mezah (the quay). Rather than take a chance that the Egyptians would spot them from the dust kicked up by their vehicles, they left their command cars and walked the last part. Egyptian shells began to land around them. Israeli soldiers ran for underground shelter. Dayan fell to the ground. Sharon was in a quandary: "Since I was the area commander, I couldn't very well take shelter myself while the defense minister was lying out in the open, so I threw myself down next to him." It hardly seemed like the place to have such a conversation but Dayan said, "Arik, this is a bad mistake." He was talking about holding on to the Bar-Lev line. "You must convince them to change the concept." Peering at Dayan, Sharon replied, "Moshe . . . you know I can't convince them. Why don't you just give them an order?"

"No. I know you'll eventually do it. Just keep at it."[35]

The conversation is remarkable. Some of Moshe Dayan's self-assurance appeared to be diminishing.

ON MARCH 18, 1968, two Israeli children were killed and twenty-seven wounded when their bus went over a mine in the Negev. The following day Dayan had spent most of the night at General Staff Headquarters planning a major reprisal for the bus attack. The Israeli attack was set for the Jordanian town of Karameh. Relaxing for a few hours, Dayan went digging at a favorite archaeological site at Azur near Holon. On earlier digs Dayan had discovered five thousand-year-old sarcophagi in the caves there. He had been laboring for some time along with his friend and spotter of the best places to dig, ten-year-old Aryeh Rosenbaum. A dirt wall caved in, sending large amounts of dirt crashing down on him, burying Dayan up to his chin. Barely conscious, Dayan thought to himself, this is it, I am going to die. He had trouble breathing. He tried to free himself but could not move. Then, grotesquely, more dirt came pouring down him. He was certain that death was near. At that point he lost consciousness.

His aide, who had been digging nearby, miraculously escaped harm. Aryeh summoned help. Sixteen-year-old Menachem Birbaum had been chasing away children who had come to gaze at Dayan's digging. Suddenly he heard the noise of the cave-in and the children shouting. He noticed that the dirt wall had fallen and Dayan had disappeared. Running home, he shouted, "A landslide has fallen on Dayan." Picking up a bucket of water and two spades, he raced back to the site of the accident. By that time his father, farmer Gershon Birbaum, had begun digging with his hands. After a few seconds he came upon Dayan's shoulder. He kept on clearing the earth away until the defense minister's face was completely clear. Able to breath, Dayan thought for the first time that he just might survive. Birbaum pulled Dayan's hand out of the earth and felt for a pulse. It was beating faintly.

"He's alive," the farmer shouted, "he's alive." His son poured water from the bucket over Dayan's face. Slowly Dayan opened his eye. Quietly, feebly, he mumbled, "Aryeh, Aryeh." He was worried only that something had happened to his aide.

Arriving soon thereafter, the ambulance drivers found Dayan lying on the ground; the Birbaums and some construction workers were standing around him. Blood was flowing from Dayan's nose. Earth clung to his clothes. Noticing the ambulance, the defense minister indicated that he wanted to get up and walk. The men would not let him. Instead they helped him on to a stretcher.[36] Riding to Tel Hashomer Hospital in Tel Aviv, Dayan asked the driver to turn off the siren but he refused.

"You may be in charge of national security," the driver said, "but I am in charge of your safety. We need the siren."

Dayan had suffered two broken ribs. His vertebrae were damaged and one of his vocal chords paralyzed. Doctors feared that his internal organs might have been damaged as well, that his liver or gall bladder might have been crushed, and that his main artery might have been harmed. Surgery was ruled out. He was put in a huge body cast. Dayan, who seemed invulnerable on the battlefield, had nearly been killed pursuing his hobby.

"HOW SOON can I get out of here?" Dayan asked soon thereafter.

Aryeh Dissentchik, the editor of *Ma'ariv*, heard the news from his son over his car radio. The editor headed for the hospital at once and was the first visitor. Professor Chaim Sheba, director of Tel Hashomer, his face strained, grave, told him: "My friend, go and pray."

"What is his condition?" Dissentchik asked.

"It is such that prayer may perhaps help him more than doctors and medicine."

When Ezer Weizman reached Tel Hashomer he became convinced that Dayan would not last long enough for him to find Ruth and bring her to the hospital.

"Has he been assassinated?" Ruth asked Weizman when he caught up with her.

"No, the trench caved in on him."

Ezer said Dayan looked "like a plane being overhauled: one wing hanging down, two tubes going in and another three siphoning the fuel out."[37] Dayan had been apprised of the list of visitors, including the prime minister and his family. He didn't like the implication.

"They've come to say good-bye to me; tell them to go back home."[38]

That same evening of the accident Avraham Biran, director of the government's Department of Antiquities, received a phone call from a journalist.

"Did you hear that Dayan was conducting another one of his illegal digs?" the journalist asked, sensing a good story. "Are you going to file a complaint against him?"

Biran, having heard that Dayan might be dying, retorted, "Do you think that my only worry is to charge the defense minister with something like this?"[39]

Dayan's accident was good news to the Fatah. The Palestinian terror group insisted that he had been the victim of a Palestinian machine gun and hand grenade attack near Holon while supervising the military buildup for Karameh. Dayan's car, they claimed, had run off the road. "Who would believe that the war criminal who then was preparing his abortive military operation, was practicing his archaeological hobby at that time in particular?" the Middle East News Agency asked.[40]

The day after the incident—while the Karameh attack was in progress—Ezer Weizman at General Staff Headquarters was told the defense minister was on the line. Weizman was convinced it was a mistake.

Picking up the phone, he heard someone grunt and wheeze. Words came out but they were unintelligible. He sounded more dead than alive. Amidst the grunts and gurgles came a few words: "Ezer, what's the news from Karameh?"

"It'll be all right. Look after yourself, Moshe."[41]

With plenty of time to think in the hospital, Dayan's thoughts went back to the time he had been wounded in his eye. He recalled sinking into a deep depression, figuring that his fighting days were over, that he might even be a cripple. Now, after the cave-in, he decided to behave differently: He would not dwell on this latest accident, would not worry how it might affect him. All he cared about was returning to work as quickly as possible.

"Now," he joked to Gad Ya'acobi, "at least I have authoritative statistics. It seems that for every thousand archaeological excavations, there is only one cave-in. If that's so I can leave here and dig another 999 times in safety. . . ."

Ya'acobi had words of reassurance. The doctors had decided that he had survived the cave-in because of his strong body and his sturdy heart.

Smiling, Dayan observed: "If I didn't dig, I wouldn't have a strong body; and if I didn't have a strong body, I wouldn't dig; and if I didn't dig, there wouldn't have been a cave-in. And then I wouldn't have needed a strong body."[42]

A few days before the accident Ma'ariv's Aryeh Dissentchik had spoken to Dayan about doing an interview. Visiting Dayan soon after the defense minister arrived home, Dissentchik saw how difficult it was for him to sit up. Dayan spoke through a loudspeaker. All Dissentchik could say was: "I understand we won't be doing the interview."

"If you're giving up the idea, so be it. I am willing to keep my promise. I'll give you one hour."

"Should I bring a photographer?" Dissentchik, in complete surprise, asked.

"Of course. Let the public see the way I am sitting and how I'm using a loudspeaker. The public has a right to know how its minister of defense looks."[43]

For several months Dayan remained in a cast to keep the backbone in the correct position. He had a special chair to help his back heal. The Arab mayors of Nablus, Hebron, and Gaza visited him, and the mayor of Kalkilya brought him oranges. His son Udi helped him, with the use of a cane, to take his first steps around the garden at home. Ben-Gurion came to see him and was shocked at how bad he looked. Dayan tried to assure him he would be fine. The visits were cheering but he remained weak and in pain. Painkillers were prescribed but Dayan took them so frequently that the physicians warned him at that pace he would become addicted in six weeks. He stopped taking them.

Twenty-one days after his injury, on April 14, just as Dayan had predicted, he returned to work, though his vocal chords were still not functioning. If he wished to speak, he whispered into a microphone. "My problem," he joked to Gad Ya'acobi, "is like the air force's—breaking the sound barrier."[44]

IN THE AFTERMATH of the Six Day War Moshe Dayan was the most popular political figure in Israel. Public opinion polls showed him leading the other choices, Prime Minister Levi Eshkol and Labor Minister Yigal Allon. Not surprisingly, Dayan was frequently described as a future prime minister. It was widely assumed that the frail, weak seventy-two-year-old Eshkol would not seek reelection in October 1969, paving the way for those two perennial rivals, fifty-three-year-old Dayan and forty-nine-year-old Yigal Allon, to compete for the top prize. Thanks to the war, the Labor party was assured of winning the next balloting. The only question was who would head its list.

Allon was given a boost when cabinet ministers expressed broad support for his peace plan that offered to relinquish some of Israel's occupied lands. Unlike Allon, Dayan was not so sure he really wanted to be prime minister. "In more than twenty years of conversation with him," said Gad Ya'acobi, "never did I hear Dayan say that he wanted or expected to be prime minister."[45] It was not that he lacked ambition. Rather, he was quite pleased to be the minister of defense. Still, he would not have minded becoming prime minister if he did not have to campaign actively for the job.

With that passive strategy, Dayan realized there were still steps he could take to improve his chances. One was taken in December 1967 when he and Shimon Peres brought Rafi back into the Mapai fold, setting the stage for the creation of the Labor party in January 1968. Only by becoming part of a larger political party and ending his link with the small Rafi group could Dayan become prime minister. Hence, he was willing to rejoin Mapai. Dayan's goal was deposing Eshkol. That was why, he explained to the Rafi convention in December 1967 in Jerusalem, that he intended to vote for the Rafi-Mapai merger.

In November of 1968 some key figures in Mapai asked Dayan if he was prepared to seek the prime ministership. "That's a question there's no point in answering," he told them. "I don't believe that members of the Labor party Central Committee [the body which chooses the party's candidate for prime minister] will change their spots and support me."[46] Toward the end of that year an independent grass-roots movement formed in support of Dayan for prime minister. He had not initiated the drive nor did he prevent it from being established. His approach was, in Gad Ya'acobi's phrase, "passive-positive." Something bothered him about the street movement. This was not the way prime ministers were chosen in Israel. Although he had become defense minister this way, through popular demand, he regarded that as an unusual situation. Israel had been on the eve of a war facing an emergency. Even then he had not initiated the public movement. He just let it happen. Though political scientists might disagree, Dayan saw in the grass-roots movement something fascist. "It's like a putsch almost," he told Yael.[47]

Launching a new movement dismayed Dayan. He knew that he was not a party animal and that he did not have the patience to run such a movement. "I do not desire to be a prime minister," he told Rahel, "because I do not desire to fight to be a prime minister."[48] If offered the post, he believed he could do a good job running the country, but he did not have the fire in his stomach to seek out the job. For all of his hesitation, predictions were that a Dayan-led list might garner as many as twenty to thirty-five Knesset seats, an enormous amount considering that Rafi under Ben-Gurion in December 1965 had only received ten. (Thirty-five seats would probably have not been enough to make Dayan prime minister but he would have had considerable political clout.)

So he remained on the sidelines, watching to see if and how the grass-roots movement might impact upon the newly formed Labor party. He had until now resisted running at the head of an independent political party, as this movement proposed. Had he wished to do so there would have been no reason to support Rafi's merger with Mapai the previous

December. The movement gathered three hundred thousand signatures, but still Dayan could not bring himself to place himself at its head openly and publicly. The pressure from the Mapai veterans was relentless, led by Golda Meir. She even showed up at a national conference of the movement to urge that Dayan not leave Labor. Bowing to the pressure, Dayan asked the movement's leaders to cease the signature-gathering campaign. His decision disappointed his lieutenants. They believed, had he tried harder, he would have become prime minister.

Dayan may well have decided not to lead an independent political movement because he retained hope of being selected by the Labor party as its prime minister candidate in the October 1969 elections. Labor could have waited to decide until the summer of that year, but Prime Minister Eshkol died on February 26, 1969. Rushing to Eshkol's death-bed upon hearing the news, Dayan broke down in tears at the sight of the dead prime minister. "You know what I've been through these last years," he said cryptically to Miriam, the prime minister's wife. She could not figure out what he meant. She thought he was referring to the suicide death of his sister Aviva on November 16, 1967. "You know how difficult it's been for me and how I understand it." Little of what Dayan said made sense to Miriam, but she realized that in his own circuitous, vague way the defense minister was trying to apologize for the political battles he had fought with Eshkol.

AFTER HIS DEATH, it was necessary for Labor to choose a successor to Eshkol. The obvious candidates were Moshe Dayan and Yigal Allon, with Dayan the clear favorite because of his great popularity in the country. A public opinion poll published in *Ha'aretz* soon after Eshkol's death showed that the public favored Dayan (forty-five percent) over Allon (thirty-two percent) for prime minister. Party leaders feared that selecting either Dayan or Allon would have split the fragile, recently created amalgam of Mapai, Dayan's ex-Rafi, and Allon's ex–Ahdut Avoda elements. Golda Meir emerged as a compromise candidate. It was assumed that Dayan could serve under Golda Meir (as could Allon), but Dayan would not be willing to serve under Allon nor might Allon serve under Dayan. Hence, the potential for a split party if either Dayan or Allon were chosen. To avoid that split they needed a compromise candidate, one who would be acceptable to all wings of the party. What the public thought did not count—it had no voice in selecting Eshkol's successor; what mattered was the choice of a handful of Labor party leaders. In Israel, upon the death of a prime minister the cabinet must resign automatically. The president of the state must then select one party to form a new government; the party with the best chance to form a government is assigned that role.

Israel Galili, the Ahdut Avoda leader, championed Allon as candidate for prime minister and he asked Pinhas Sapir to discuss the possibility of Allon being chosen with Golda Meir. Sapir said he would but he also warned Galili that the Dayan camp would oppose Allon's candidacy, which would lead to a party split; this could have disastrous consequences, Sapir said, on the elections the following fall. To give Allon the prize, Sapir reasoned, was political suicide. For one brief moment Golda Meir supported Allon's candidacy, and he might have been picked for the post had she not found out that Allon, selected by the cabinet to serve as acting prime minister on the day Eshkol died, had appealed to party leaders to make the appointment permanent. The cabinet refused and in an act of remorse for his transparent power grab, Allon hastily promised to support Golda should his own bid fail. Meanwhile Sapir was cleverly spreading the word, however premature, that both Galili and Allon wanted Golda for the prime ministership. As it became increasingly apparent that she would get the job, Dayan made convincing noises that he did not want to contest Golda's selection. That led Sylvie Keshet, a columnist for *Ha'aretz*, to write, "These two generals [Dayan and Allon] are only good to fight and frighten Arabs. But they're afraid to say 'boo' to one old Jewish lady." Few would acknowledge it, but Golda's ill will toward Dayan, dating back over the years, played a large part in her willingness to take the job when offered it. She was prepared to become prime minister for no other reason than to stop Dayan from getting the job. She had resisted Dayan becoming defense minister in May 1967 and lost that time, bowing to the people's will, but this time she vowed that "the decision on who will be the next prime minister will not be made in the street."

Though Golda was assured of getting the party's nomination, Dayan could not bring himself to make the choice unanimous. When the Labor party ministers gave her their support, Dayan was the only one to abstain; then, when the party leadership voted, his camp withheld its support but Golda soon won the backing of the leadership bureau, 40–7. When the party's Central Committee met on March 7, Golda received 297 votes, with none against, but the 45 votes from the Dayan camp abstained. Dayan later explained that he had abstained because he did not consider Golda "the kind of personality who would open new vistas in the leadership of the state and the party." Golda told everyone after her selection that she would serve as prime minister only until the October elections. Pinhas Sapir had another game plan: He was determined to prevent Dayan from becoming prime minister. Golda eventually bowed to Sapir's will and soon stopped making statements about her plans for an early retirement as prime minister.

For all of the coolness in their relationsip before the spring of 1969, Dayan developed a close working bond with Prime Minister Golda Meir. Making no changes in the old Eshkol-led cabinet, Golda kept Dayan as defense minister. Golda had no choice but to take Dayan under her wing. She was a novice in military affairs and needed him and his defense expertise. As a result, she became extremely dependent upon him in defense matters, all the more ironic considering how little she esteemed his role in the conduct of the Six Day War. Whatever she had thought of Dayan before, she now began to understand the hold he had over the nation. She fell under his spell as well. She came to trust his judgment completely. Dayan could not reciprocate but they got along. None of the bitterness from previous days marred their relationship. When it came time for the October elections, Golda was prevailed upon by party leaders to run again on the assumption that only she could prevent Dayan from becoming prime minister. The politicians worried about her health but not enough to allow her to step down. Labor suffered a minor setback in those fall elections; the Labor-Mapam alignment dropped from sixty-three to fifty-six.

✦12✦

THE DECEPTIVE CALM

THREE YEARS after the Six Day War, Moshe Dayan had become enamored with the idea of an expanded Israel. Returning any of the occupied
territories appeared out of the question. Whatever cracks in the facade
appeared, it was the minister of defense who set the course of Israeli
policy—and he would not be moved. He had grown accustomed to an
Israel that stretched from Mount Hermon in the north to the Suez Canal
in the south, providing Israelis with the kind of breathing room that had
been sorely lacking before 1967. In terms of national security, bigger
seemed better, safer. Never mind that a bigger Israel meant including
one million Arabs within the post-1967 perimeters. If the demographics
of a Jewish state that was becoming increasingly Arab worried some, it
bothered Moshe Dayan not in the least. Most Israelis, confident with
him at the defense helm, felt that if Dayan could swallow a million Arabs,
then so could they.

Three years after the 1967 war it was not difficult for Dayan to encourage a policy of permanent occupation. No Arab leader had picked
up the proverbial phone; the three nos of Khartoum were still ringing
in everyone's ears; the Arab "confrontation states" of Egypt, Jordan, and
Syria were as belligerent as ever.

Dayan could lead Israelis along a path that they found logical and
convenient to travel. Not that every Israeli saw the merit of moving into

the center of Hebron or the suburbs of Nablus, but they could fathom the security argument that Dayan preached.

To promote this policy, Dayan needed to establish in the minds of Israelis basic premises about Israel and its future relationship with the Arab world. The first premise was that the Arabs had absorbed so great a shock during the Six Day War that they would never dare attack Israel again. That assertion became the cornerstone of Israel's belief that nothing could disturb the process of establishing roots in the occupied lands. Every day that passed seemed to provide increasing evidence that Dayan could safely direct Israel into empire building at little cost to the country.

Having applied the brakes on the public movement to make him prime minister a few years earlier, Dayan by 1970 appeared content, or perhaps resigned, to play a number two role to Prime Minister Golda Meir. He was cognizant of his still-authoritative role as czar of the occupied territories, and wholly aware that his undiluted power was based in part on the fact that the major figures in the cabinet—Golda Meir, Yigal Allon, Israel Galili, Abba Eban, and Pinhas Sapir—saw eye to eye with Dayan over one crucial point: In the absence of peace agreements with the Arab states, Israel could not allow itself the luxury of vacating the occupied territories.

The prime ministership still loomed as a possibility in Dayan's future, but with elections not scheduled until October 1973, politics was on hold. A war of attrition was still raging along Israel's southern front. The country's main goal—and Dayan's—was to bring the fighting to a halt. Finally in August 1970 a cease-fire between Israel and Egypt was arranged under American sponsorship, bringing fresh hopes that serious negotiations might begin that could lead to permanent peace. Both Israel and Egypt appeared on the surface to be inching away from their previously intractable positions. Whereas before, Israel had insisted that any negotiations with the Arabs be conducted directly between the parties involved, without recourse to mediators, it was now prepared to enter into indirect talks just to get the peace process started. For his part, Nasser had insisted all along that Israel withdraw from the occupied lands before negotiations and the signing of a peace treaty. Now he backed off, indicating that he was prepared to recognize the state of Israel in return for an Israeli withdrawal from these territories.

Problems arose before the mediators could gear up for peace talks; Egypt committed serious violations of the truce by rebuilding and rearming destroyed missile sites, and establishing new missile sites in the combat zone near the Suez Canal. Israel turned to Washington at once, asking the United States, as the guarantor of the truce, to restore the status quo. Asking was not enough, in the defense minister's view. Pressure needed to be applied. One card Israel possessed was the possibility of a cabinet crisis that would lead to the fall of the Golda Meir government. The main impact of this move would be to delay the prospects of getting peace negotiations started, a prospect the United States was eager to avoid. Dayan decided to play this card.

Naphtali Lavie, Dayan's spokesman, leaked the news to several foreign newsmen that Dayan was considering resigning over the missile violations.

The leak succeeded. Washington agreed to carry out satellite flights over the canal to verify Israel's claims. Washington's efforts to verify Israel's claims went slowly, since the Americans suspected that Jerusalem might simply be trying to stall peacemaking efforts. Nor did the United States very energetically pressure Egypt to remove its missiles. When American officials urged Israel to ignore its complaints about the missiles, some Israeli politicians, including Prime Minister Meir, began talking of removing the weapons by force.

Though Dayan favored threatening a cabinet crisis in order to obtain American help, he was against Israel using force to remove the missiles. He thought restraint was in order. Looking at the Egyptian steps from a military point of view, he argued, "Moving forward the missiles gives the Egyptians an advantage they will not give up. Golda feels we should push the missiles back by force, but I don't believe the Americans would allow it. The advancement of the missiles presents us with a new state of affairs which we shall have to get used to and from which we must extract the maximum degree of benefit."[1]

On September 28, 1970, Nasser died suddenly, and peacemaking efforts were put on hold by the need to wait until his successor, Anwar Sadat, had time to formulate a new course for Egypt. Dayan was ambivalent about activating the peace process under Middle East mediator Gunnar Jarring's sponsorship. If Jarring could induce the Arabs into signing peace treaties with Israel, Dayan would applaud. The trouble with entering into peace negotiations, Dayan knew, was that ultimately Israel would have to agree to concessions. Dayan thought that Israel might find itself in a trap, sitting at a peace table and being forced to abandon the West Bank to the Arabs.

Seeking a way out of this dilemma, Dayan broached the idea of reaching an interim agreement with Egypt in newspaper interviews. The word "interim" implied that Israel and Egypt would negotiate not a full-blown peace accord that could bring Sadat all of the Sinai in exchange for a peace treaty with Israel, but rather a partial accord in which Israel would yield only some of the Sinai in return for promises of nonbelligerency.

For Dayan, the idea's appeal was its avoidance of the West Bank in the peace negotiations. American secretary of state William P. Rogers dismissed the idea, while Israel's foreign minister Abba Eban doubted it would succeed. Dayan pressed ahead, even though Washington was still wedded to the comprehensive efforts as envisioned in the Rogers Plan and the Jarring mediation. Fearing that the Jarring mission might force Israel to agree upon its final borders, Dayan on October 7 suggested publicly that Jarring need not be the only channel of negotiations between Israel and Egypt. He was inching toward a specific idea that, if accepted by all sides, would represent the first concrete diplomatic step forward since the 1967 war.

Dayan wanted Israel and Egypt to pull back their forces twenty miles from the Suez Canal. He was the first in the cabinet to propose territorial concessions in the absence of a peace treaty with Egypt. For the defense minister, an Israeli-Egyptian discussion of this plan had the great advantage of shelving Gunnar Jarring's diplomatic effort and limiting the negotiations to steps that did not require Israeli to cede all of the occupied territory in the absence of peace treaties. Pulling Israeli troops back from the canal would, in Dayan's view, let Sadat breathe more deeply, would provide the Egyptians living on the western bank of the canal with a normal life; it also would mean that Egypt would reap the economic benefit of a reopened Suez Canal. "The canal," he told his confidantes, "is an Egyptian waterway and we should enable them to run it. I can understand that the Egyptians don't want the canal under Israeli control. So we don't have to control them directly. We can be in a position that gives us enough security but at the same time gives them free passage through the Suez Canal and us free passage through the Straits of Tiran." This solution might induce Sadat to negotiate a peace treaty with Israel, or at worst, to keep the peace along the southern front.

Dayan feared that Israel's remaining on the banks of the Suez waterway would lead to war with Egypt, to far more serious fighting than the War of Attrition in 1969 and 1970. He believed that his withdrawal proposal could delay war with Egypt for as long as twenty years. Even though he would have found it surprising for Egypt to launch a full-scale war against Israel, Dayan could not rule it out, not as long as Israeli troops kept a gun to Sadat's head by remaining on the canal's eastern bank.

On October 25, when they met in the United States, Prime Minister Meir asked the American national security adviser Henry Kissinger what he thought of Dayan's pullback idea. He had not fully studied it, Kissinger said, but the idea seemed promising.[2] Pressing forward with his plan, Dayan said that Israel had to consider a new approach to political progress—what he called "more peace for less territory." To Knesset members on November 16, Dayan observed that "in the conditions in the Middle East, it may be that 'peace or nothing' is an unrealistic approach and one liable to lead to nothing more than another war." Yet Moshe Dayan's plan was not government policy. In Washington in December he could not promote the pullback plan as anything other than a "theoretical alternative" to Israel's current position of not withdrawing without a final peace accord. Did he speak for the government of Israel when he advocated this idea? No, replied Dayan, it was a "private proposal."

Prime Minister Golda Meir and several of her cabinet colleagues preferred Israel to remain at the Suez Canal as long as Egypt was hostile and would not sign a peace treaty. They relied upon the advice of Chief of Staff Chaim Bar-Lev. "We estimated," he recalled, "that if we move from the Suez Canal, in the best case the Egyptians will stay on the other side and we'll have an artillery war of attrition, and in the worst case, they'll cross and we'll have a front without an obstacle between us."[3] Under pressure, Golda and the other ministers were ready for a withdrawal of six miles from the canal but no more.

This issue represented an astonishing change in Dayan's relationship to the government. In the past he had used his personal authority to persuade the Eshkol-led government of 1967 to go to war, to formulate Israeli policy toward the West Bank and the Gaza Strip after the war, and to veer the government toward a policy of staying in the territories indefinitely. Now he faced a wall of opposition in the cabinet.

It was an anguishing time for Israel. The Americans demanded that Israel become involved in the Jarring diplomatic effort, which the Jewish state regarded as an effective agreement to withdraw to the pre-1967 lines. The Arabs made strident demands that Israel leave the occupied territories without negotiations or offering anything in return. The choices before Golda and her ministers toward the end of 1970 were unpleasant: If they opted for only a six-mile pullback from the canal, Dayan might resign, setting in motion a government crisis that could lead to its fall; if it opted for Dayan's twenty-mile pullback plan, only Dayan would be satisfied, not the General Staff, and not large segments of the country. So Golda chose not to decide.

Dayan's pullback plan gained momentum early in 1971, when an Egyptian general approached the head of the American mission in Cairo to say that President Sadat had expressed interest in the Israeli defense minister's idea. In February, Dayan spoke to Mike Wallace on the CBS news program "60 Minutes" about his pullback plan; a few days later Sadat hinted that the canal might open in the near future. Despite these vaguely hopeful developments prospects for progress were still slim. Egypt saw Dayan's interim proposal as the first step toward a total Israeli withdrawal from the territories but Dayan had put his plan forward specifically to forestall that prospect.

On February 8, 1971, Gunnar Jarring tried one more time to elicit some response from Israel and Egypt. Presenting the two sides with a document, he called for Egypt to enter into a peace agreement with Israel. Israel, for its part, would agree to withdraw her forces from the Sinai. Egypt's response: It would end the state of war but not sign a peace treaty with the state of Israel. It insisted that Israel withdraw from all occupied territories, not just the Sinai. Israel responded that it was prepared to hold peace talks with Egypt without prior conditions except for one: There would be no Israeli withdrawal to the pre-1967 lines.

Sadat also had a pullback plan. The kind of disengagement Sadat envisaged was far broader than Golda's six-mile idea or even Dayan's twenty-mile withdrawal. He wanted Israeli troops, as he mentioned to *Newsweek* on February 22, to withdraw to "a line behind El Arish"— more than halfway across the Sinai. He also insisted that United Nations forces replace the Israelis at Sharm el-Sheikh and that Egyptian military forces be permitted to cross the canal to the eastern side. All of this must take place, Sadat said, in the context of a total withdrawal as required in the Rogers Plan.

Over the next few months American diplomats sought to induce Israel and Egypt to come together on some kind of peace arrangement. Meanwhile the cabinet debated Dayan's proposal. A number of ministers agreed that Israel had to show some initiative in undoing the diplomatic logjam, but not everyone understood Dayan's pullback proposal. Yosef Burg, the veteran minister of the National Religious party, asked him, "Why did we sit for years on the bank of the canal and pay so dear a price in the War of Attrition, if the defense minister is prepared so easily to compromise on control of the canal?"

Dayan replied: "You know that from the start, also during the Six Day War, I was against the conception of being along the canal and even gave an order to our forces not to get near the canal."[4]

On March 22, at his behest, the cabinet suggested that Israeli policy was no longer anchored to the principle that not a single Israeli soldier could vacate the canal except as part of an overall peace settlement with Egypt. At that crucial cabinet meeting, the principle of a partial Israeli withdrawal in exchange for something less than a total peace was accepted. There was still disagreement over how deep into the Sinai the pullback should be. Confident of a positive outcome, Eban asked Dayan whether the defense minister was prepared to put his idea of a pullback to a cabinet vote. At this crucial juncture, though, Dayan displayed little aggressiveness, noting that unless the prime minister accepted his proposal, he would not even put it up for discussion. Eban wrote later that had Dayan shown greater zeal in pushing for the idea it could have averted the Yom Kippur War. To those who made this point, Dayan could only say, "All I can do is propose. It's a democracy and if I am outvoted, I have to accept majority decisions. If I had to resign every time the cabinet disagrees with me, I could not last as a defense minister one week."[5]

Dayan's inability or unwillingness to take on Golda Meir over the pullback idea reflected the change in his relationship to his fellow government ministers. At the time of the Six Day War and its immediate aftermath he had acted dismissively toward the cabinet, displaying indifference toward certain ministers and toward what was said at cabinet meetings. His authority over the defense field was total and indisputable. Over the years, particularly since Golda Meir became prime minister in early 1969, Dayan's power over the cabinet became diluted. It may have been due less to changes within him than to the domineering figure of Golda Meir. To be fair, she had gone through her own transformation with regard to Dayan, from utter contempt for him at the time of the Six Day War to a slavish dependence on the defense minister, relying upon his judgment and advice with regard to many aspects of defense. Still, she would not be ruled by him, and on certain notable occasions, she made this clear. One was in January 1972 when Dayan, exercising the perogative of the defense minister, proposed that Yehoshua Gavish become the new chief of staff; Golda declared that she preferred David Elazar. "Over my dead body," Dayan had said when he heard that. Eventually he capitulated, saying meekly that he had not wanted "as minister of defense to be a minority on such a problem in the cabinet." The other occasion when Golda put her foot down—and Dayan went along—was the pullback proposal.

Further efforts were made in May 1971 to ease tensions around the Suez Canal. Secretary Rogers and his aide Joseph Sisco arrived in Israel. Sensing that the existing deadlock could deteriorate into war, Dayan tinkered with the Israeli position in his talks with the Americans: Whereas in the past Israel had rejected Egypt's demand to place its forces on the eastern bank of the canal, it might be prepared, Dayan said, to accept civilians and technicians (but not military men or police as Egypt had insisted upon). Egypt still wanted its troops to take up positions on both sides of the canal. The Israeli cabinet could not accept this (though Dayan thought some Egyptian police might be acceptable). Sadat still clung to the demand that a mutual pullback at the canal would be only the first step toward a full-scale peace settlement. Unable to make such a commitment, the cabinet could not keep Dayan, however, from telling Sisco that he could live with such a notion. With the gap too wide, Rogers went home empty-handed. Sisco, in a visit to the Middle East in August, did no better.

WHILE DAYAN was becoming less aggressive in his public life, his private appetites remained unrestrained. How many women did Moshe Dayan sleep with? There were a number of answers to that question depending upon who was asked. Some, who claimed to know but really did not, said hundreds. Just as people inflated Dayan into a military legend so too did they magnify his bedroom prowess. Seeking an explanation for Dayan's seemingly unquenchable sexual appetite, a renowned neurologist suggested to Ruth once that scar tissue had formed on Dayan's brain as a result of his 1941 head wound, turning him into a sex addict! The women who had developed close relationships with the defense minister put the number of his bedroom partners at a dozen or so. As for David Ben-Gurion, Dayan's great protector, he thought the number of women Dayan slept with was none of the nation's business. Although on the surface Dayan enjoyed Ben-Gurion's protection, in private even the Old Man sought to constrain Dayan's philandering. "Moshe," Ben-Gurion had said to him once, "you can't screw around."

Dayan's womanizing is one of the accepted facts of his life. Dayan admitted as much in newspaper interviews (not, however in his memoirs); Ruth and Yael wrote bitterly but frankly about his romantic entanglements in their memoirs. (He and Ruth finally divorced in December 1971.) The Israeli public, however, curious as it was about the personal lives of its leaders, thought it wrong for the media to dig into their personal lives. Only one newspaper, *Ha'olam Ha'zeh*, wrote about Dayan's affairs, but its articles were dismissed by the rest of the media as untrue and therefore unworthy of investigation.

Though some politicians thought Dayan's antics provided a bad example to the nation's youth, on the whole he was not condemned. It was, as Yael acknowledged, a case of the public thinking he was a bastard, but being happily willing to exchange places with him. On one occasion in the late 1960s Dayan was speaking in public in Beersheba on morality and decency, when someone in the audience yelled out to him, "How can you, a man who is married and fucks other women, preach to us about morality?"

Slowly identifying the man in the audience, Dayan asked him to step forward and to repeat what he had said.

"Are you married?" Dayan asked him.

"Yes."

"If a beautiful woman came to you and said 'fuck me,' what would you do?"

The man looked at Dayan, thought for a moment, and said meekly, "I guess I would."

Dayan then shouted, "That's a real man!"

The defense minister may have deflated some of the animus toward him by acting so matter-of-factly about the subject. To friends, family, reporters, he projected an image of someone who was doing nothing that others were not doing, and who had never contended that he was innocent and pure. "In the final result," he told *Ma'ariv* reporter Tamar Avidar off the record in the early 1960s, "I didn't hurt anyone. Throughout the years I didn't start anything with a girl soldier, nor an office clerk, nor a minor. What I had, with whom I had it—was not done by rape. They agreed out of their own free will. It is my private affair."

In another country Dayan would have suffered politically, Tamar Avidar noted to him.

"I do what I do, knowing it is what I want to do, and I am not ashamed of it. There is nothing dirty in it."[6]

Ezer Weizman thought he could aid Dayan by helping him conceal his romances: "Look, Moshe, there are all sorts of rumors. Come on. I'll help you, decoys, all sorts of things." Dayan found such offers unnecessary.

"Do you think I am like all of you, running around in the dark?"[7]

Carrying on as publicly as he did, Dayan was bound to embitter those closest to him. Yael was deeply affected: "His infidelity bothered me less than his need for it, and his choice of bed partners was vulgar and in poor taste. The whole thing seemed pathetic and demeaning, lacking in either excitement or dignity."[8] His wife suffered for years. Why did she linger in marriage to him? Perhaps because she understood that Dayan was a national icon whose private peccadilloes were applauded more than condemned by the public. She too could not conceal her esteem for Moshe Dayan the national hero: "In Moshe's view, nothing was more important than Israel. In that respect, he was a shining example. Later I could have killed him. But his love for the state—that's something that I'll never forget. He treated me in a totally despicable way. I made a mistake. I should have left him long before I took the decision and left. The Moshe I knew was a difficult man, who behaved contemptibly in his relations with other people—but a great lover of Israel. It was in his soul. In his blood. And I forgave him. I forgave him everything. The terrible insult. The betrayals, his destruction of the family."[9]

Dayan's appeal to women was intriguing. It was not his physical appearance. No one described him as handsome (though in late 1970 he was named the fifth sexiest man in the world by the *London Daily Sketch*).[10] In describing Dayan's special attraction, the women who developed the closest relationships with him spoke admiringly of his personal qualities, his charm, his political power, but rarely mentioned his physical ones. Michael Elkins, the BBC correspondent in Israel for many years, was having a drink with Dayan in Beersheba when a good-looking woman came up to Dayan and said, "I'll see you later."

Elkins met the woman later and unabashedly asked, "Did you sleep with Dayan?"

"Yes," she said, and smiled.

"Why?" Elkins asked.

"Because it was like fucking a life force."[11]

Strangely, he gave the impression to his family of being old-fashioned, even prudish. Four-letter words were not to his liking, nor were references to homosexuals or prostitutes or lovemaking. In fact, the strongest words to come from his mouth would be "idiot," or "bastard," or "hell."

However prudish he was, Dayan appeared to think of most of his women as no more than sex objects. It apparently never dawned on him that some of these women might be interested in a different kind of relationship than the sexual encounters he had in mind. It also apparently never occurred to him that his refusal to contemplate marriage might induce these women to ponder revenge. Said Rahel Rabinovitch: "When it came to women he was the most innocent man I have ever met. . . . He was like a child with candy. . . . I don't think it even crossed his mind [that his lovers might seek revenge]. So these things happened. He was very upset with himself, terribly. . . . Not only for misjudging these people, but for getting involved."[12] It had been unthinkable for him that a woman might retaliate by writing a book about their affair and equally unthinkable that a woman would threaten him with a lawsuit for not keeping a "promise" of marriage.

Elisheva Zcysis was a darkly attractive twenty-two-year-old manager of a dress shop on busy Dizengoff Street in Tel Aviv who, like so many other women, became a pleasant after-hours (and sometimes during-hours) addiction for the defense minister. Their relationship began toward the end of 1968, when Elisheva called the Ministry of Defense and asked to be put through to Dayan. The minister of defense had never heard of the woman. He agreed to speak to her. She was calling, she explained, to ask Dayan to intercede with the state attorney, Meir Shamgar, who had charged her relative with forging a check. One could have imagined

another cabinet minister admonishing her that he could not interfere
with the legal system. Rather than put down the phone, Dayan suggested
they get together!

"Why on earth would you want to meet me?" Elisheva asked the
minister of defense.

"Because of your voice. You have a very interesting voice."

They met that same afternoon at a Tel Aviv restaurant, a favorite Dayan
haunt near David Ben-Gurion's house. The matter they were "discussing" was of such importance, according to the defense minister, that a
second meeting was called for—the very next day, at the same restaurant.
Dayan promised to place a call to Shamgar. He also invited her to a
cocktail party at a Tel Aviv hotel. Clearly flattered, Elisheva agreed to
attend the cocktail party, only to find herself the sole guest. Nothing
happened that day except their sharing the coffee, cake, and conversation. She agreed to visit Dayan again. When they met the next time
Dayan turned the conversation to something more personal, as she remembered it.

"Are you still a virgin?" he asked her matter-of-factly, as if he had
inquired of her whether she wanted to stroll along the beachfront.

"Yes," she acknowledged.

Dayan must have been surprised, for he asked her why she still was.

"I want to sleep with the man I'll marry."

"I'll tell you a secret. I want to marry you."

"How can that be?" Elisheva asked. "You're married to Ruth."

"I've asked Ruth for a divorce. Even if she doesn't agree I promise
you that I'll leave her and come to live with you." After acknowledging
that he had slept with many women, he said she was the "sweetest and
the most charming and that none of them had been as sexy" as she was.
It was at that point that Elisheva lost her innocence.[13]

Matters became complicated when Elisheva's mother began taping
her daughter's phone conversations with the defense minister. Her motives were unclear but she was apparently eager for Elisheva to marry a
cabinet minister. After a while Dayan tried to extricate himself from the
relationship by not taking Elisheva's phone calls. According to Rahel
(Rabinovitch) Dayan, Elisheva demanded that Dayan see her at least
once a week for a cup of coffee. So for some time, after lunching with
Rahel, Dayan went to the Hotel Yarden restaurant to have coffee with
Elisheva for half an hour.[14]

During that time, Elisheva sought out Rahel and played some of the
tapes for her simply to annoy her. As Rahel recalled: "She used to keep
my line locked. She used to call me and not close the telephone for
hours. . . . And then one day I was having dinner with Moshe, and I

told him . . . that it's been going on for a while, 'I want you to know that she's taping your conversations, and the proof that I'm telling you the truth is that you said this, and this, and this.' Shocked, Dayan called an attorney and told him that he was calling off the weekly coffee arrangement with Elisheva.

Severing ties with her, however, was not so simple. Elisheva hired an attorney in May 1970 to pursue Dayan for breach of promise. The attorney stated that unless Dayan paid 10,000 Israeli pounds—$3,300—within ten days as compensation for his breach of promise, Elisheva intended to sue.

"She won't get a penny," the minister of defense said angrily. "If she enjoyed being in bed with me, why should she do this to me?"

Rahel Dayan insisted that Dayan never promised to marry Elisheva: "How can you promise to get married when you are married? He wouldn't dream of anything like that."[15]

After lengthy negotiations between the attorneys, Dayan agreed to pay Elisheva the 10,000 pounds in exchange for her commitment not to go to court. Dayan's attorney arranged for his client to pay in installments, ending in December 1971, presumably in order to secure Elisheva's silence for as long as possible.

Five weeks after the last payment (on December 5, 1971), *Ha'olam Ha'zeh* published its first article about the liaison. Though recounting all the lurid details of the romance, the newspaper made no clear allegation that the minister of defense had compromised his post or national security. On January 23, 1972, the German news magazine *Stern* published a ten-page article on the defense minister's romance with Elisheva, an article for which she provided information.

Years later, looking back at Dayan's attempt to stifle the young woman, Rahel thought he had acted unwisely. "It was the most stupid thing. I think it was a very silly decision. . . . He should have ignored the whole thing. . . . It was so ugly. The whole thing was so stupid. So messy. . . . He paid the money and after he paid the money, she went to *Ha'olam Ha'zeh* and to *Stern* magazine and sold them the story. She showed them photostatic copies of the check, et cetera."[16]

There is an interesting footnote to this story. Just as the public would be curious about the women around Dayan, so too would the Dayan women be curious about one another. Learning about Elisheva, Rahel wanted to know what the woman in question looked like. Knowing where Elisheva worked, Rahel perched herself within sight of the dress shop: "I took a wig of dark hair, and I sat with my girlfriend and had coffee, and I thought, would I have the nerve to go in or not? As we were talking about it . . . I saw her arranging the window. And I said, 'Let's go in.

I'll buy a present. Who cares.' So we went in. And I bought something, a simple dress, and we went out. She served me. She recognized me. Two minutes after I got home, the telephone rang and she said to me, 'You think I don't know who you are. I know you. You came to spy on me.' " Rahel didn't answer, then put the phone down.[17]

(At times, the Dayan women met openly. Sometime after Dayan's death in 1981, Hadassah More greeted Rahel Dayan warmly while the latter was in the receiving line at a reception marking the publication of a book. Later, Hadassah asked Rahel if she could write a book, or at least a news article, about her.

"Do me a favor," Rahel replied, trying to end the conversation as quickly as possible, "Just leave me alone. I don't want any books about me."

Hadassah persisted. "This will be such a wonderful book. It will be good."

"Please," said Rahel with an air of finality. "Just leave me alone."[18])

Rahel Dayan thought that of all the untruths written about her in the press the most anguishing one for her had been the assertion that she and Moshe Dayan had a son. According to the tale, they sent him away to a kibbutz in order to keep the secret of their child. Rahel wished it were true, but admitted that she was not courageous enough to take this step. She did mention having a son to Moshe. He said, "For God's sake, I've got three I wish I didn't have. . . . You've got two. Together we have five. What do you need more children for?"[19]

For her, life with Moshe Dayan was thrilling and exasperating. Ironically, she shared with Ruth the unpleasant reality of Dayan's womanizing. "I would give half my life and maybe more of it, if this [affair with Elisheva Zcysis] would have been avoided. . . . How I went through this I cannot explain except that Moshe made me his partner in winning a war. . . . How he did I don't know. But the fact is he did it."[20]

Did his liaisons with other women create difficulties for her own relationship with Dayan? Rahel noted, "It would have been inhuman if it didn't. But Moshe had a way—and I don't know how he did it—he had a way of making me a part of whatever happened which . . . Look, he didn't see half as many women as the rumors go, not half. I would say to be very generous, I would say ten percent of what people say is true. It's bad enough, but . . . it's highly, highly exaggerated."

As for the trouble he endured because of Hadassah More and Elisheva Zcysis, he succeeded in making Rahel a partner in his woes to the extent that she found herself helping him. He never lied to her. Together they planned a strategy of how to get rid of the others. She recalled: "Very often people ask me how did you stand it? Eighteen years . . . you say you didn't want to get married, and you didn't want him to get divorced, this was not your aim, and we believe you, still, eighteen years to carry on such a difficult . . . love affair, is a very, very difficult thing. . . . This was really a tough time. . . . The credit goes to Moshe because he had this knack of making me so much a part of his life that there wasn't a question of either loneliness or being alone or being disconnected from anything."[21]

Although Dayan rarely talked about his women in public, toward the end of his life he became much more open. When asked whether he treated women as nothing more than objects, he replied: "I have loved no other woman the way I loved Rahel. But that doesn't mean that I regarded all the other women I met—and that I had affairs with—as technical objects. Of course, there were cases like that too. But I have not had relations with women more than other men do. But my relationships were publicized while nobody pays attention to other people's love life; because of the black patch, and because I hid nothing. If we make comparisons with today's generation, and with all I read, even if I am not an expert and I'm not interested in other people's lives, those affairs of mine were publicized out of all proportions."

Did he not think that a leader had to be exemplary?

"I am not nor do I want to be an exemplary person." However, he noted, he had never been offered a bribe, never shown preference in filling appointments. A public figure has to be measured in accordance with the manner in which he performs his office, and if he's carrying on at the same time with his neighbor's wife, it has no relevance. I once said to Ben-Gurion, if you want an exemplary person in every way, I am not a candidate for such a title. If you find fault with the way I do my job as chief of staff . . . then I am not worthy of the position."[22]

DAYAN MAY have wanted to be judged solely on the basis of his performance in office, but some would not go along with that, especially when it came to determining whether the defense minister was pillaging national treasure. The Israeli law governing archaeology was clear. It was based on the 1934 British Mandatory law that prohibited anyone from digging for antiquities without a license and which required anyone without a license who discovered an antiquity to notify the government's Department of Antiquities.

Since Dayan had never applied for a license, and even if he had, there seemed little reason to believe he would qualify for one, he most certainly appeared to be skirting, if not directly flaunting, the law. "It's correct to say he broke the law and was not prosecuted," acknowledged Avraham

Biran, the director of the government's Department of Antiquities from 1961 to 1974.[23]

When it was pointed out to Dayan that he was digging illegally, he did not stop. He insisted that he had broken no law. Archaeology officials, when asked to explain why Dayan was not prosecuted, offered a variety of explanations, mostly taking Dayan's side: Others were digging illegally, and not being prosecuted. Why should Dayan have been treated differently? "It required a lot of effort to prosecute in most cases, and it was not important. No one was holding the equivalent of the Elgin Marbles," said Avraham Biran.[24] Besides, through some of Dayan's efforts, valuable relics were saved from being destroyed by oncoming bulldozers. Finally, Dayan himself proposed in the 1960s that Department of Antiquities officials in the 1960s cart off whatever part of his collection they wished. They removed half of the collection.

Still, there was Moshe Dayan again breaking the rules that seemed to have been made for everyone but him—and getting away with it. Some among the public were amused, some bemused—and others were infuriated. In fact, no other single facet of Dayan's life, political or personal, created such bitterness in the public's mind as his archaeological raids. Nothing he would say or do to try to justify or defend his behavior had any impact whatsoever on his critics. They thought of him as no better than a criminal. Their frustration grew as they realized there was absolutely nothing they could do about Dayan's digging. It should be noted that the criticism about his digging came almost entirely from Israelis. Abroad, Dayan remained an unvarnished hero no matter how much he trivialized the law. "American Jews," said Irving Bernstein, the former executive vice-chairman of the United Jewish Appeal, "would die for a piece of Dayan's archaeology, whether it was stolen or bought."[25]

From time to time the government was asked to serve notice on Dayan to stop what he was doing, or punish him. The penalty called for in the 1934 law, still valid in the 1960s, hardly seemed a deterrent: one month in jail or a fine of twenty British pounds.

In 1964 the government's Department of Antiquities complained to the police about Dayan's alleged illegal digging, but Prime Minister Levi Eshkol's government was not prepared to put on trial the hero of Sinai simply for removing some national treasures. Knowing full well that no one would accept the offer, Dayan volunteered to lift his Knesset immunity from prosecution in order to be tried. Yigael Yadin, at the time a professor of archaeology at the Hebrew University, was irate at his colleagues for not prosecuting Dayan. "You're the criminals. Not he. If you allow him to dig, what will all the small fry do?" It was a recurring worry among the archaeological community, but the archaeologists had little clout compared to Dayan's.

In December 1971 Dayan's archaeological pursuits were again the target of public criticism. Questions were put to him in the Knesset. Where was his license? Was he not in violation of the law? Dayan defended himself on the Knesset rostrum: "I have never and do not possess a single antiquity of archaeological value that is not known to archaeologists working in the Israel Museum, in the Jerusalem and Tel Aviv universities, and in the Antiquities Department." He added that archaeologists had made free use of any item in his collection for their scientific work and exhibitions.

The Dayan archaeological collection, adorning Dayan's garden in Zahalal, would grow into one of the most important and famous in the country. The garden eventually filled up with stones and pottery and columns and pillars of granite and marble. The collection was his prize possession. He spent hours there working on his finds, allowing no one to touch or clean the objects. Among the most important works in the collection, which had over eight hundred objects, was a stone mask estimated to be nine thousand years old, the oldest work possessed by Dayan. Acquiring such a rare artifact was no accident. He had a special interest in the period before the Israelites came to the Land of Israel. He also had a reputation that allowed him to hear of unusual finds even before the Department of Antiquities.

Arab workers, upon discovering something valuable, seemed to prefer to turn to Dayan than to the Antiquities Department. Once, an Arab farmer was plowing away sand dunes at Deir el Ballah in the Gaza Strip in order to expand his orchards when he unearthed an ancient Egyptian burial ground. Knowing of Dayan's hobby, the man contacted him. Dayan arrived at the scene and wound up purchasing twenty-three giant anthropoid clay coffins shaped like mummies. They were from the late Bronze Age, 1550–1200 B.C. Some argued that Dayan should have turned the artifacts over to the state. Dayan did notify the Department of Antiquities about what he had found, but he kept the artifacts.

Dayan was no ordinary archaeologist. He had a keen sense of where to find relics. Unlike professional archaeologists, he never published any of his findings, though he made the artifacts available to any archaeologists who wished to see them. Also unlike those professionals, he actually collected relics as a hobby. He of course had advantages over other amateurs. No other amateur archaeologist could call upon IDF helicopters and soldiers—as Dayan did as minister of defense—to take artifacts back to Tel Aviv.

The anger with Dayan never abated. And none of his arguments in defense of what he did helped his cause. He contended that eighty-five percent of his collection consisted of pieces he had purchased with his own money from local and foreign dealers or from private trades. Only fifteen percent of the collection was made up of pieces he had unearthed without a license. Government archaeologists complained that, after what Dayan had been allowed to get away with, it would be nearly impossible to educate future generations to preserve antiquity sites and to prevent robberies. "What about Dayan?" they would ask. "You never cracked down on him. Why should we obey the law?" And, without any good answers, the government had little way of keeping future amateur diggers from setting up their own private archaeological gardens.

NO SUBJECT dominated Israeli politics since the early 1970s more than the occupied territories. What would Israel do about them? Annex them? Give them up? Tighten Israel's connection with them in the absence of peace arrangements? Israelis of all political stripes entered into a prolonged national debate over these questions. Dayan was the dominant personality in that debate.

Israel saw in King Hussein its only potential partner for peace with respect to the West Bank. For that reason it discouraged the formation of any independent political groups within the West Bank itself. Amman was the address for negotiations. Hussein was the odd man out, the only Arab leader prepared to talk with Israel (albeit in secret). He had his reason: A peace accord with Israel might provide him with protection against an attack from his continuing rival to the north, Syria, and he harbored a desire to regain all of the territories that he lost in the Six Day War. He had been meeting Israelis since the early 1960s. The number of meetings stepped up from 1968 to 1970 when he talked with Levi Eshkol, Golda Meir, Yigal Allon, Abba Eban, Chaim Bar-Lev, and other Israelis. Prime Minister Meir held the first of her ten meetings with Hussein in the fall of 1970.

Frequently the king asked, "Where's Moshe Dayan?" He was curious to meet the Israeli defense minister. Finally, Prime Minister Meir brought him to meet the Jordanian monarch. Hussein impressed Dayan as charming and courageous but "he does not go into things deeply, nor is he practical. His head's in the clouds when he suggests plans, agreements and solutions to Israel."[26]

The focus of the Israeli meetings with Hussein during this period was the Allon Plan. Still adamant about getting all or nothing, Hussein would not entertain anything short of the complete return of the land he had lost in the Six Day War, including Jerusalem. Under the Allon Plan Hussein would reclaim only part of his land. Hussein's rigidity turned Golda Meir increasingly hawkish.

Dayan tried to reason with the king: "You don't have to concede one inch of your soil. Let us have our settlements and military positions necessary for our security without your giving up land. Call it whatever you like, foreign presence or not. We are not interested in ruling over your people." Dayan was prepared to review the stationing of Israeli troops along the Jordan River after five years. If during this period peace prevailed in the region, those troops would withdraw. Nothing doing, said Hussein. Nothing less than total Israeli withdrawal was acceptable.[27]

According to Abba Eban, who participated in some of the Hussein meetings, Dayan was not a great fan of the dialogue with the king and at a certain point in 1970 decided to break off his personal connection. Eban recalled that Dayan once told him, "If I go, I'll just blow the whole thing up. You oughtn't to be asking me, because if I'm there, I'll blow up the whole thing. Because I don't want the king coming back to the West Bank." On one occasion, in Eban's presence, Eshkol asked Dayan to join Allon and Eban in meeting with Hussein.

"Nothing doing," said Dayan, offering the excuse that he would just cause the talks to blow up in failure. Placing the Allon Plan at the center of the discussions annoyed the defense minister. It was a plan for minimizing the annexation and maximizing the release of territory. That was against Dayan's whole conception. He thought the positions on the hill were more important than along the Jordan Valley, which was the basis for the Allon Plan.[28]

KNOWING HOW dim the prospects of obtaining a peace accord with Hussein were, Dayan supported strengthening Israel's links with the occupied areas. Because he thought his country's struggle with the Arabs would persist indefinitely, he argued that Israel should routinize life for the Arabs in the West Bank and Gaza Strip, to accustom them to an enduring period of Israeli occupation. He called this process normalization. Dayan thought it in Israel's best strategic interest to deepen its ties to these lands. Always, however, there was an overlay of religious thinking in his rhetoric, but as he was not an observant Jew, few believed that religion motivated him. Nevertheless, at times he did portray the argument for Israel's holding the West Bank in nationalistic and not strategic terms. Thus: "I know there is a Security Council Resolution 242 and there is a Rogers Plan and there is a Dayan Plan and there is an Allon Plan and there are and will be other plans. But there is one thing bigger and greater than all of them and that is the people of Israel returned to their homeland."

Early on he actually favored annexing the West Bank. On the day that Yigal Allon presented his peace plan to the cabinet in July 1967 Dayan wanted to propose that the ministers vote on his proposal to annex the West Bank. Minister without Portfolio Menachem Begin told Dayan that it would not have the support of a majority so Dayan did not press for a vote. Begin convinced Dayan that it would be better not to vote than to lose a vote on this issue.

With annexation ruled out, Dayan concentrated on intensifying Israel's role in the occupied areas. In 1969 he proposed that the government set up four Jewish cities along the ridges of the Judaen hills from Hebron to Nablus and thus break up the Arab demographic centers. These urban settlements would adjoin the major Arab towns of Ramallah, Jenin, Nablus, and Hebron. He wanted the Hebron-Beersheba area to become a single economic-administrative unit, with a second similar one in the north to include the Jewish town of Afula and the Arab town of Jenin. (When large numbers of American immigrants came to Israel in the early 1970s Dayan thought they could form the nucleus of his urban settlement program. The idea faltered when it became apparent that it would not be possible to dictate where these Americans would live.)

He was always fond of a policy of "doing" rather than talking and so the establishing of "facts" in the occupied territories, meaning Jewish settlements, appealed to him. On April 2, 1969, he told students in Haifa that

> we have the ability to initiate changes in the basic situation, changes in structure, to a certain extent. . . . Of course, we should establish Jewish and Israeli possessions in the administered area throughout, not just in the Golan, and not with the intention of withdrawing from there. These should not be tent camps which are set up and taken down. With this in mind, we should establish possession in areas from which we will not withdraw in accord with our view of the map. . . . All these things—the economic ties, the human ties . . . and the establishment of Jewish settlements and military bases in the areas—will eventually create a new land. It will not be the same map, the same structure, the same situation. . . . We must . . . try to change the basic situation every day in order to make it easier for us to attain our desired goals.[29]

He hardened his position by stating in the summer of 1971 that Israel should envisage its role in the occupied territories as that of a permanent government, "to plan and implement whatever can be done without worrying about the day of peace, which might be far away." The government must "create facts, and not confine development programs to Israel proper. . . . If the Arabs refuse to make peace, we cannot stand still. If we are denied their cooperation, let us act on our own." The defense minister's remarks, made to the army staff college, caused shock waves throughout the Middle East. His program sounded like functional annexation.

On closer examination Dayan's views on what to do about the territories during this period were ambiguous. On occasion he espoused views that appeared to counter his usual hawkish stance. For instance, in mid-June of 1970 he told newsmen that "I do not support the idea that we have an eternal deed to every piece of land here given to us by the Bible," and "we are ready to give a great deal for peace, and that includes territories." A few months later, when asked if he preferred a larger binational Israel to a small one with a Jewish majority, he replied that he preferred a larger country for defense reasons "but if it threatened the essence of our Jewish state, then I prefer a smaller one with a Jewish majority."

Given the intensity of the debate over the territories, Dayan was to become a master of ambiguity. Appearing flexible on the question of the territories was in keeping with the current political mood. The politicians were debating, but not deciding. As long as they did not decide, it was better, Dayan surmised, to appear reasonable. Some Israelis simply saw Dayan as the ultimate pragmatist. Still, Dayan in fact made dovish statements rarely. Though on the record, they pale in comparison with the quantity of statements and the emotion he invested when championing a strong Israeli role in the territories.

After the Allon Plan was shown to be a nonstarter, the national debate in Israel no longer focused on what kind of peace negotiations to hold with Jordan but what kind of role Israel should play in the territories. Dayan favored a larger one. Doves such as Pinhas Sapir, Abba Eban, and Yigal Allon preferred a smaller one. Dayan was convinced about the need for establishing "facts." In a letter he wrote on May 10, 1973, to a frequent correspondent, Yehuda Tubin, a kibbutznik from Bet Zera in the Jordan Valley, Dayan noted: "I did not say that I am in favor of settlement in all of Judaea and Samaria [the West Bank], but in specific places. . . . We have to indicate practically what should be done and what should not. With regard to settlement . . . we have to extend settlement, extend the Jewish presence in agriculture, industry, urban population, public and private sector and cooperative undertakings with Arabs in Judea and Samaria. . . . I think we should be doing more than just striving for this. In my opinion the thing can be done, too."[30]

On the other side of the debate, Pinhas Sapir, the powerful finance minister, believed that returning the territories would free Israel of an enormous burden. Therefore he was opposed to integrating the territories into Israel's economy. He worried that the Jewish state would turn into an Arab country if another million Arabs were joined to the four hundred thousand Israeli Arabs.

While the debate carried on in the cabinet, Dayan's views were winning the battle on the ground. The Golda Meir government, though unprepared to annex the territories, could not, in the absence of a peace settlement, withdraw itself from them. Hence, Dayan's program of establishing facts, of tightening economic links, of integrating the West Bank and the Gaza Strip into Israel where possible, was pursued.

By the spring of 1972 Dayan embarked on a campaign on behalf of his plan to step up Israel's role in the occupied areas, what his critics liked to call "creeping annexation." In early April he traveled around the country, speaking four to five times a week. He outlined a new proposal calling upon the government to permit Israelis to buy land from Arab owners anywhere on the West Bank. The current practice permitted the government alone to acquire land in the occupied territories. Dayan's proposal stirred further bitterness among the doves. With the October 1973 election approaching, speculation began that Dayan might be trying to improve his chance of succeeding Golda Meir by forcing the Labor party to adopt a platform that reflected his political thinking.

The year 1973 brought politics again to the forefront. For Dayan the prospects of becoming prime minister were slim. As long as he remained within the Labor party fold he could not expect to replace Golda Meir. He could only wait impatiently for her to leave the political scene. Even if she did, the same constellation of Sapir, Allon, and Galili would likely conspire to keep him from snaring the top prize. Dayan had only one small chance and that was to bolt Labor and set up his own party, joining together with Gahal and perhaps some of the ex-Rafi people.

In reality he had no appetite for trying to become prime minister within Labor or without.

Bolting the party seemed a likely option for Dayan because the impression existed that the public might well support his setting up an alternative party. One opinion poll in June indicated that while Israelis would rather have Golda Meir than Moshe Dayan as prime minister (64.2 to 27.3 percent), 51 percent said they would follow Dayan if he bolted the

Labor party.[31] Since he did not aspire to the prime ministership, Dayan sought to put his popularity to other uses.

Buoyed by the public support, Dayan was encouraged to believe he could get his way on deepening Israel's presence in the West Bank. He needled Labor politicians, reminding them that he could not be taken for granted. When the National Religious party resolved at its convention that it would resign from a government that voted to return any part of the "inheritance of the Patriarchs" (the West Bank) as part of a peace settlement, Dayan alarmed politicians by saying that his position was much closer to that of the NRP than of his own Labor party. With such threats, he managed to take the Labor party and the country down a more and more hawkish road. On May 14, he told BBC Television: "Were the problem to decide whether to give one million additional Arabs Israeli citizenship or withdraw from Nablus, I would rather withdraw from Nablus than deteriorate the entire composition of the Jewish state. I would not like to have an additional one million Arabs with three million Jews. But I think that this is not the question now. . . . The question now is whether to find some settlement with the Arabs in the West Bank by which they would stay Jordanian and we would have our ambitions fulfilled. . . . I do think that Israel should stay forever and ever and ever and ever in the West Bank because this is Judea and Samaria. This is our homeland. . . ." A few months later he said that if Israel wished to end Jewish settlement in the territories, it would have to stop teaching the Bible.

The Labor party would have to choose either to adopt Dayan's demands or reject them. That spring (of 1973) Dayan had drawn up plans to build a city and port to be called Yamit in the Rafiah approach below the Gaza Strip. The finance minister, Pinhas Sapir, tried to block Dayan's effort by denying to budget the necessary funds. Dayan was so furious at Sapir's action that the defense minister decided to press the Labor party for a clear-cut decision on the occupied territories in the forthcoming platform discussions. He planned to insist that the party platform reflect the need to expand Jewish settlement and industrial development around Jerusalem; he proposed that Israel go beyond building a military or paramilitary presence at Rafiah, that a full-blown seaport be built, as well as a densely populated town (to be called Yamit) deep within the Sinai Peninsula. He sought permission for Jews to purchase land in the occupied territories. Unquestionably implementing such a platform would constitute the effective annexation of the West Bank. Hawks and doves lined up for the final battle over the summer. As they did, another simmering question loomed in the background—not debated in public, but of crucial importance to the country. Was Israel on the verge of another war with Egypt?

THE CITIZENRY didn't give much thought to the possibility, mostly because of their faith in Moshe Dayan and his Israel Defense Forces. The country's love affair with its defense minister and its army remained constant in the years after 1967. Dayan had been so right on the eve of the Six Day War, so confident and steady during the war, that his countrymen thought him omniscient. They placed the same blind faith in the Israel Defense Forces.

A nation that had placed little importance on militarism suddenly conferred on the army's top leaders a worshipful popularity. Jokes that made the rounds at the time included:

Question: What does the Israeli army need to occupy Damascus, Moscow, and Vladivostok?

Answer: To receive an order.

Then there was the one about Dayan and Chief of Staff Elazar, looking very bored over their morning coffee.

"There is nothing to do," Dayan says with a sigh.

"How about invading another Arab country?" asks the chief of staff.

"What would we do in the afternoon?" replies Dayan.

Soldiers and officers who had been unknown until the Six Day War were sought out by journalists and publishers who wished to spread word of their triumphs. Generals were sought at cocktail parties and first nights. They showed up at fancy restaurants. Dayan and his generals were elevated to positions of supreme authority and it was firmly believed their their pronouncements were gospel. Dayan displayed an undiluted self-confidence that affected everyone around him. "Sometimes the eye was indifferent, sometimes angry, and sometimes mischievous," noted Victor Shem-Tov, a veteran Mapam party minister. "When making proposals, Dayan was sure of himself, convinced that he was right and never . . . did he say: 'Sorry, I have not been properly understood' or 'The position I took previously was wrong.' What he said was always final and decisive."[32] No one questioned his thesis that years of tranquillity and peace awaited the Jewish state. The Six Day War had restored the notion of Israeli military superiority in Arab eyes and that would be enough to deter Arab rulers from taking any foolish military steps in the future.

Israel, Dayan said often, had nothing to worry about. In March 1971, in a Weizmann Institute speech, Dayan said, "Our situation has never been better, neither militarily nor politically. . . . If war will be renewed—it will find us stronger than ever before."

Along with the self-assurance came the boasting. Thus in April 1972 the minister of defense argued that Israel was not only the "most powerful force in the area" but also "the second most powerful state in the Mediterranean basin after France."

No one took the threats of war coming from Egypt's Sadat seriously. He would have been crazy, it was said, to try to cross the Suez Canal, fortified as it was by the Bar-Lev line. If Sadat tried, Israeli military leaders promised, Egypt would take an even greater trouncing than in the Six Day War.

Yitzhak Rabin, completing a tour as Israeli ambassador in Washington, said in March that Golda Meir "has better boundaries than King David or King Solomon." On the rugged peak of Massada overlooking the Dead Sea in April, Moshe Dayan said Israel was blessed by a set of circumstances "the likes of which our people has probably never witnessed in the past and certainly not since the modern return to Zion." The first factor was the IDF, "the superiority of our forces over our enemies, which holds promise of peace for us and our neighbors." The second feature was "the jurisdiction of the Israeli government from the Jordan to Suez."

The IDF believed that the Egyptians would lie down like little lambs and never again make a fuss. Uri Ben-Ari, the veteran tank commander, recalled that Dayan believed that "even if the Egyptians attacked and crossed the canal, we would settle this very quickly. It was stupid, cocky, irresponsible, this underestimation of the enemy. The military concept was wrong: that we would destroy whoever crosses, then we would cross and fight in Egypt."[33]

Worst of all, the concept became embedded in Israel's security policies. Lova Eliav recalled that, as a member of the Knesset Foreign Affairs and Defense Committee, he joined a tour of the southern front and asked Dayan what would happen if the Egyptians crossed the canal or tried to cross.

"We'll step on them, I will crush them, let them come," he said with absolute confidence.

Dayan portrayed the plan as if Israel wanted the Egyptians to cross, that Israel would not at first put up too much resistance, but by the second day, Israel would encircle the Egyptians troops, and then on the third crush them in a massive tank battle. Based on this thinking, Eliav noted, the IDF had asked for a war budget premised on only five or six fighting days.[34]

So appealing was Dayan's concept that it was accepted at once and remained the anchor of Israeli security policy into the early 1970s. Just as the country had not wanted to believe that the Arabs would make war after Israel's triumphs in 1948 and 1956, Dayan encouraged the same hope after the Six Day War. The chilling truth was that the minister of defense did not really believe his public pronouncements that war was out of the question. As a military man he realized all too well that Egypt could not permit Israel to remain on its territory endlessly without trying to win it back militarily; nor could Egypt allow the smaller insult of Israeli troops on the eastern bank of the Suez Canal indefinitely. Worse, if Egypt would one day want to unleash its military might, Syria would as well—for Israeli troops continued to thumb their noses at Damascus by retaining a foothold on the Golan Heights. Dayan understood this situation but could not say it in public.

Why this uncharacteristic reticence? He had himself to blame in large measure. The public had come to believe that Israel was on the top of the mountain. To instill fear in the country that the Arabs might one day attack, might very soon bring on a total war, was to puncture the balloon of inner peace and contentment that had been Dayan's great achievement. To talk about the prospect of war would have meant that the minister of defense would have had to admit that the foundations of peace and security he had erected in 1967 were mere illusions. That would have meant that Moshe Dayan, the war hero, the international celebrity, the savior of the nation, was no less an illusion. No, he could not talk about war in public.

This was his public face. In private Dayan was a totally different person. He was worried that war might break out. For that reason, he had in 1970 and 1971 proposed that Israel pull back its troops from the Suez Canal. In September 1972 Dayan voted against holding a military parade in Jerusalem the following May in honor of Israel's twenty-fifth anniversary. Beginning in late 1972 until the summer of 1973 he warned the government and the General Staff on at least eleven occasions that war would break out within the next few months. On May 21, 1973, he told the General Staff: "You have to take into consideration a renewal of the war in the second half of this summer. We the government tell you, the General Staff: Gentlemen, please prepare for war in which those who threaten to start a war are Egypt and Syria." (When Zalman Shoval revealed these private warnings in 1974, Dayan told him, "Not only am I happy that you wrote it, but it's even true.")[35]

As the Israelis were convinced that chances for war in the near future were slim, they had little reason to step up their preparations for battle. Dayan and his generals firmly believed that the regular forces in the

Sinai plus the Israeli air force would be sufficient to deflect any Egyptian offensive. Accordingly, garrison units in the Sinai and on the Golan were not manned in great numbers.

Relying upon a public posture of deterrence, Israel took steps to ease the burden of military service for its war-weary population. In the summer of 1973 it announced that it was planning to reduce the length of conscript service from thirty-six to thirty-three months and that reserve duty would be cut from sixty to thirty days a year. Along with this came a cutback in defense spending from a high point in 1970, when 26 percent of the gross national product was spent on defense, to a projected 20 percent of GNP for 1973. Defense had been 40 percent of the 1970 budget but had declined to 32 percent in 1973 and would drop to an expected 14.6 percent of the budget in 1977.

When in May it appeared that the Egyptians might indeed go to war, Dayan and the IDF reacted by partially mobilizing the reserves, normally considered a prudent step if the enemy seemed intent on bellicose actions; but in the atmosphere of that spring, Chief of Staff Elazar was accused of being too cautious, and of frittering away millions of dollars. One Israeli intelligence source reported after the alert was called off that Egypt's planned canal crossing had been put off for some unexplained reason until the beginning of October. No one paid any attention to this fateful piece of intelligence.

Dayan sensed that war could come at any time. Meeting with the new air force commander, Benny Peled, on June 13, 1973, Dayan made it clear that, if it became necessary, the IDF would contemplate launching a preemptive strike against the Arabs (this time against their missile batteries, not their planes on the ground).

When Peled took over command of the air force, his lieutenants were frustrated at not having been given the chance to clear out the Egyptian missile batteries before the August 1970 cease-fire had been imposed. Peled told Dayan, "Sir, you must understand that this whole 'opera' will be conducted according to plan only if we are the initiators. There's a helluva difference between us initiating and choosing the day and the hour, the weather, the position of the sun, the right intelligence, the visibility. If we don't have that choice, the system will not work and you will have a helluva time and we shall have to take not one day, it will take three or four days, to clear those things."

Dayan said, "Benny, my dear friend, do you really think that if we believe that the Arabs are planning to attack us, the air force won't get approval to attack? Don't be a fool."

All Peled could think of saying was, "From your mouth to God's ears. So be it."[36]

EIGHTEEN MONTHS after Dayan divorced Ruth, he married Rahel. He was fifty-eight years old; she, forty-seven. The date was June 26, 1973. The Israeli press described her as the defense minister's "longtime friend and companion." Only three guests were present at the ceremony, which was presided over by the chief military chaplain, Mordechai Piron. No photographers were there. The ceremony lasted just thirty minutes and ended with toasts by the guests: Haim Yisraeli, director of Dayan's bureau; Yossi Checanover, the legal adviser to the Defense Ministry; and spokesman Naphtali Lavie.

The wedding was another wound to the relationship between Dayan and his children. Rahel had been a familiar enough fixture for years, but marrying her turned Dayan—in the children's view—into a less authentic figure, into someone less recognizable as their father. After the wedding, as Yael explained, "we all played according to new rules. A dimension of bliss had been added to his life, and who can blame a man in love. He adored her with all his heart, marveled at her beauty and charm, boasted about her cultural assets, and was carried on Eros' wings, to heights of delicate romance, with gratitude and at times disbelief. He was the frog kissed by a princess, the farm boy dwelling in a palace, the primitive being enlightened."[37]

The trouble was that the children liked the old Dayan, part-frog, part-farmboy, part-primitive. "I really believed," said Yael, "that father was best in his hooliganism. When he walked about in baggy underpants, urinated in a corner of the garden and said: 'If you don't like it, don't look! I cannot change,' he was himself. Father's charm was in the fact he did not know the difference between whiskey and cognac. Suddenly, under Rahel's influence, he boasted of knowing the difference between Bordeaux wine and Beaujolais and seemed to care for delicacies like caviar. He just wasn't authentic anymore."[38]

THE NEWLY married Dayan assured his listeners at Nahalal on July 15 that "thanks to our military superiority, our better equipment, the strategic boundaries, and the opposition of the two superpowers to a military confrontation in our region, I do not think there will be war." On that same day, just a few hours before the ceremonies in which Ariel Sharon was to formally hand over command of the southern front to Shmuel Gonen, Sharon warned Dayan, "I believe you are making a grave mistake. If we have a war here, and we might have one, Gonen does not have the experience to handle it."

Dayan could not admit to Sharon that he too worried that the situation might deteriorate. "Arik," he said confidently, "we aren't going to have any war this year. Maybe Gonen is not too experienced. But he'll have plenty of time to learn."[39] Two weeks later, on July 30, he predicted that Israel's borders would remain frozen along the 1967 lines and no major war would erupt for the next decade.[40] More upbeat talk on August 9, while lecturing to the IDF Staff College: "The overall balance of forces is in our favor and this is what decides the question and rules out the immediate renewal of the war."

IN AUGUST the issue of the occupied territories again dominated Israel's political agenda. That month Dayan hinted that he might not be a Labor party candidate for elections in the fall unless the party committed itself to strengthening Israel's hold over the occupied lands. The main proponents of the debate over the territories came from within the Labor party. Abba Eban assailed Dayan for talk of building Yamit. Arguing against such a step, Eban said Israel would be closing off its options for territorial compromise in a large segment of the Sinai.

As much as the party's doves (Eban and Sapir) did not want to give in to Dayan, they had little choice, since Golda Meir and the other party veterans insisted that a way be found to keep Dayan within the Labor party. Sapir had told Eban that if Dayan bolted the party, he might take twelve to fifteen Knesset seats away from Labor, votes which might go to a new Dayan-led independent list. Israel Galili, the minister without portfolio, and Golda's favorite wordsmith, was asked to draft a document that would bridge the gap between Dayan's views and those of the party's doves.

The so-called Galili document was published on August 23 and essentially came down on the side of Moshe Dayan, allowing him to remain within the party. Calling for a big push to be given to Jewish settlements in the occupied areas, the document urged that the number of settlements grow from forty-six to seventy-six. Dayan made it clear that the new settlements provided for by the document would all have to be inside Israel's final borders. The document called for developing Yamit, suggesting that eight hundred housing units be constructed there by 1978 for three thousand residents. Dayan was forced to make two concessions to Sapir: that the building of a major port opposite the new town in northern Sinai would be put off for three years; and that sales of Arab lands to Jews in the territories would be placed under strict control to avoid speculation. Other development projects in the occupied territories were proposed in the document as well. The cost of the document's recommendations was not provided, but Sapir mentioned that he was prepared to grant $300 million over the next four years to finance the program.

The effect of the Galili document was dramatic. The country's doves had suffered a major setback. Israel appeared further down the road of annexing the West Bank at least on a de facto basis. Dayan's prospects of succeeding Golda Meir as prime minister appeared vastly improved. Although Golda had generally sided with Dayan on his outlook toward the occupied territories, he was the winner politically. Labor had worried about losing a few seats in the fall election as a result of defections from among Dayan supporters. Now there would be no defections. And the party owed this all to Moshe Dayan.

Labor's doves were isolated. Lova Eliav termed the document "creeping annexation" but could do little more; Eban, off in South America, said lamely, "This is not a leap forward but a modest and balanced acceleration." A *Washington Post* editorial called the Galili manifesto a "permanent annexation of a major part of the territories."

In early September the Labor Party leadership's 161-member Secretariat voted 78–0 to adopt the Galili document as party policy going beyond Labor's so-called Oral Law, which had asserted that Israel would not return to the 1967 lines. The Galili document considerably expanded that Oral Law, decreeing for the first time that Israel should move quickly and decisively to stake its claim to the occupied lands. It had Moshe Dayan to thank for this new departure. To the Arabs, however, the document sent a clear-cut message that Israel was driving a nail into a coffin of peace, that the country was not prepared to negotiate over the occupied territories. The Galili document, in the view of many, brought war one step closer.

◆13◆

YOM KIPPUR SURPRISE

ON SEPTEMBER 13 Israel's air force shot down twelve Syrian warplanes in what seemed like just another Arab-Israeli dogfight. Few Israelis worried that Syria might wish revenge or unleash an all-out war. This fall was the start of the political season and keeping the peace seemed like good politics. The election campaign began picking up steam and Moshe Dayan was eager for Labor to portray itself as the party that had brought tranquillity. When Labor propagandists sought to project an image that Labor had kept the peace along the Suez Canal, that was fine with the defense minister. One newspaper advertisement showed an Israeli soldier sitting on a wicker chair on the eastern bank of the Suez Canal, looking very relaxed, with an Uzi on his knees. The ad read: "Everything is quiet along the Bar-Lev Line."

When Dayan heard about the advertisement, he phoned one of the party's propagandists, Michael Bar-Zohar at once. He was furious.

"What kind of bloody ad is that? Who said this is Bar-Lev's line? This is not Bar-Lev's line, this is my line."

Eager to placate the defense minister, the campaign team changed the caption to read: "On the banks of the Suez Canal everything is quiet." War was a remote prospect, Dayan believed, and he wanted to make sure that no one else in Labor was given credit for this "achievement."[1]

As the Jewish New Year approached, Dayan was confident that he could turn his attention to routine matters. On September 22 he traveled to Rafiah with Aryeh Nehemkin, then the secretary of the moshav movement, for a meeting with Jewish settlers. On the way back, the defense minister assured Nehemkin that the next six months would be reasonably quiet.[2] He gave much the same rosy message in a briefing to Israeli journalists that week. Yes, he acknowledged, Israel would face diplomatic trouble at the forthcoming United Nations General Assembly session, but nothing worse. The region would remain quiet.

Even as he spoke the Syrians were moving three infantry divisions, 670 tanks, and one hundred artillery batteries to their frontier with Israel. The implication of the Syrian buildup was debated at a General Staff meeting in Tel Aviv on September 24. Northern front commander Yitzhak Hofi was nervous and wanted immediate reinforcements. Much calmer were the chief of staff, David Elazar, and his director of military intelligence, Eli Zeira. There was nothing to worry about, they argued. Syria was merely setting up its defenses, fearing a major Israeli response to Syria's planned but limited reprisal for the September 13 incident. Dayan too thought that Syria would engage in limited action, if at all, but he sympathized with Hofi's frayed nerves. There was a chance that the Syrians might try to overrun some Jewish settlements. He thought it irresponsible to leave the Golan unprotected so that "before we manage to evacuate so-and-so, the Syrians have already taken over three places, women and children included."[3]

He insisted that the number of tanks along the Syrian frontier be raised from 70 to 177 and that the IDF double the number of its field artillery batteries to eight. He also decided to tour the Golan Heights lines and to warn Syria not to undertake military action. Later, Dayan's behavior toward the rising tensions in the Golan Heights that week was cited as exemplary, and indeed it was. Not only did he wisely demand that the IDF should boost its forces along the frontier, but he went to the scene for some on-the-spot checking of his own. Visits to the fronts, especially in time of extreme tension, had become his hallmark. Oddly, his visit to the Golan on September 26 was the only one he would make throughout this period.

The chief of staff was dead set against Dayan's Golan visit. "You are creating a panic by going there," he argued.

"I don't care," replied Dayan calmly, "because if the Syrians get through the lines, they are in the center of Israel."

At the Jewish settlement of Ein Zivan, in front of television cameras, Dayan pointed out that Syria had amassed at least eight hundred tanks and eight hundred guns across the frontier as well as a ground-to-air missile system that "was denser than any in the world." Israel was alert to all of this, he said, and would react to any hostile Syrian move with a "painful blow." General Hofi's nerves were less frayed. He wanted to hitch a ride back to Tel Aviv on the defense minister's helicopter. Nothing doing, said Dayan.

"Look," said Hofi, "everything is quiet."

"If it were not quiet," Dayan barked, "I would stay here. Since it is quiet, you are to stay here and make sure that the reinforcements are concluded within forty hours."[4]

Unbeknownst to the defense minister, the first hard information about fresh Egyptian measures along the Suez front began arriving in Tel Aviv. "Something was moving," Israeli intelligence men surmised over the next few days, but they termed what Egypt was doing "insignificant."[5]

The main topic on the government's agenda on Friday, September 28, had nothing to do with the Golan and Sinai fronts, but with the Palestinian Arab terror attack against a train carrying Jews from Moscow to Vienna. Five Jews and an Austrian customs official were taken hostage at the Austrian border. In exchange for their freedom, Austrian chancellor Bruno Kreisky agreed to close the Vienna transit center for Soviet Jews on their way to Israel. Over the next few days, as Israel's frontiers were being turned into potential launching pads for war, few in the government took the deteriorating situation seriously.

As fresh intelligence rolled in describing further Arab buildups along the fronts on October 2, Dayan turned to Elazar, asking him to furnish his own written assessment, a highly unusual request that appeared to reflect his mistrust of the chief of staff. "Could it be," asked Dayan, "that this exercise the Egyptians are conducting is a confidence trick?" No, responded Elazar, it was merely an exercise, Egypt would not attack on its own, nor would there be a joint Egyptian-Syrian attack.[6] Did the IDF have enough tanks in the Sinai? the defense minister asked. As part of his written reply, the chief of staff noted that there were three hundred Israeli tanks there.

Increasingly agitated about the buildups, Dayan arranged to see Prime Minister Golda Meir as soon as she returned from her trip to Strasbourg and Vienna at midnight of Tuesday, October 2. Just before meeting with her the following morning, Dayan told an aide, "I'm not sure but the indications seem to be war."

If he indeed felt that way, why did he not act as he always had and leave his desk in Tel Aviv to check the fronts for himself? Undoubtedly, deep down, Dayan did not feel that war was imminent. That is the only way to explain his subsequent laxity. For all of the criticism that was leveled against the defense minister for his behavior that week, little mention has been made of his most uncharacteristic decision to remain at his desk and rely on the reports of others. The Moshe Dayan of the

1950s and 1960s would have detached himself from the cabinet ministers and generals in Tel Aviv and raced to the scene.

He had become a victim of his own policy, the policy of self-delusion that insisted the Arabs would not dare attack Israel. The essential building block of this policy was his conviction that Israel had nothing to fear from the Arabs and, most importantly, that even if the Arabs unwisely began hostilities, the IDF would have no trouble dispensing with them quickly. Such thinking induced the IDF into a state of self-confidence that slowly turned into indolence. Just as Dayan had deluded himself, the IDF had chosen to ignore reality as well, even with evidence to the contrary. When the IDF reported to the defense minister that all would remain quiet, he had no reason to doubt them. He, after all, had articulated the idea in the first place that the Arabs were unlikely to open hostilities. Hearing this from the IDF, the defense minister had no reason to budge from Tel Aviv. All was quiet along the fronts, and bound to stay quiet. Racing to the fronts to make his own personal inspection was superfluous. He and the IDF had convinced themselves and each other that Israel had no cause for concern. Yet, in retrospect, how odd Dayan's behavior seemed. How unlike him. "The greatest mistake Dayan made," said Mordechai Hod, the former air force commander, "was that he didn't act independently and try to penetrate a little bit more deeply into what was happening inside the General Staff."[7]

Persuaded that the IDF had matters in hand, Dayan had no reason to assume that trouble was afoot for Israel. Yael was most bitter about the period and believed Dayan had been misled. "He felt that obviously he should have gone and seen every single tank, and made sure that he was in the field where he was supposed to be, but he couldn't have done it. He was not sunbathing during this time. He asked were these tanks in this and this position, and he was told yes. He took it for granted. It was inconceivable to him that people would not check and double check. This shocked him more than anything else."[8]

On Wednesday, October 3, at Dayan's behest, the prime minister called into session that band of political and military advisers known popularly as "Golda's kitchen," for the place where they usually gathered. Along with Dayan, Golda Meir, and the chief of staff were Deputy Prime Minister Yigal Allon, Air Force Commander Benny Peled, Deputy Head of Intelligence Arye Shalev (replacing the ill Eli Zeira), Golda's director-general, Mordechai Gazit, and her military aide, Yisrael Lior. This session was the first time that any forum of cabinet ministers would hear about Arab military steps. Spelling out what was known, Dayan noted that the Egyptian and Syrian measures were unusual and they were not defensive; he did not draw any operative conclusions. If he thought war imminent, he did not say. A distinctly noncrisis atmosphere prevailed, so much so that Allon suggested that the cabinet only be informed of these developments at its next regular meeting on Sunday, October 7.

Thursday, October 4, would not have been too late for Dayan to take a helicopter to the fronts and demand that the reserves be mobilized. He did not in part because he and other cabinet ministers worried seriously that mobilizing Israeli troops would be regarded in Washington as a sign of deep crisis, requiring the United States to intervene and try to work out new peace arrangements between Israel and the Arabs. What worried Dayan most was that Washington would insist that the Israelis do their part for peace by evacuating large sections of the occupied lands. Mobilization would also not sit well with Israelis, since the IDF had mobilized its reserves the previous May—and the Arabs had not launched an attack. The public considered mobilization wasteful and costly (if the Arabs did not strike). In his memoirs, Egypt's president Sadat gleefully quoted Dayan's explanation of why he had not mobilized quickly at this stage: Sadat had "made me do it twice at a cost of ten million dollars each time. So, when it was the third time round I thought he wasn't serious, but he tricked me!"[9] Finally, like all other Labor party politicians, Dayan had no appetite for appearing militant before an electorate grown used to peace. So, rather than head for the fronts, Dayan busied himself over lunch with an old friend, Rehavam Ze'evi, who only three days earlier had retired as central front commander.

"What's the matter?" Dayan asked, sensing that he had something to get off his chest.

"I suspect that we are moving toward war. And I will not be a part of it."

"What are you talking about? There's not going to be a war. Not this summer and not this fall. You're not talking to the point."[10]

That night came the first reports that Soviet advisers and their families were being evacuated from Syria. The Soviets had spread the word that their experts and families were departing out of fear of war. Persuaded, however, that Damascus could not conduct war without those Soviet advisers, Israeli analysts continued to misread what was occurring. In fact, the Soviets and Syrians were exploiting the classic military elements of deception and surprise—elements that had been ingrained into the military thinking of Moshe Dayan. This time they were using it against him. Dayan was not completely blinded. On Friday morning, October 5, he was sufficiently alarmed to order a "C" alert throughout the IDF, the highest one short of calling up reserves. The air force was placed on full alert. Even at this late stage, Dayan was confident that the IDF could respond to Arab military moves without resorting to a full-scale mobilization of the reserves.

The evening of Friday, October 5, was the start of Yom Kippur, the holiest day of the Jewish calendar. On this night even secular Jews turned to prayer, meditation, and fasting. It was the only day of the year when the country literally shut down most of its institutions and services. It was also a day that Israeli soldiers might relax their guard in response to the prevailing mood of sanctity. At 9:40 A.M. that Friday, those cabinet ministers still in town arrived at the prime minister's office for a briefing on the military situation. Attending were Dayan, Allon, Elazar, Zeira, Israel Galili (minister without portfolio), and Chaim Bar-Lev (minister for commerce and industry).

The chief of staff and his director of military intelligence wrangled over the question of whether it was possible for the Arabs to attack without further warning. Zeira believed it was, Elazar thought not. In any event, neither man thought there would be an attack. The chief of staff thought only when further evidence of an attack surfaced should the reserves be mobilized.[11] In that nonurgent atmosphere, Dayan proposed, and it was agreed, that this rump cabinet authorize the prime minister to mobilize the reserves on her own in case of fighting over Yom Kippur. The silence around the table on the question of calling up reserves was thundering. Dayan took a certain comfort from that silence later, when the criticism against him mounted. "I was not the only one to think [that the reserves should not be called up], and I did not hear anyone say that war was about to break out that day."[12]

Still, from his behavior one can sense a certain apprehension. For instance, when Golda Meir announced that she planned to spend Yom Kippur at her daughter's kibbutz in the south, it was Dayan who asked her to remain in Tel Aviv. Firmly believing that war was not around the corner, she noted that, should she be needed, she had a helicopter at her disposal. Dayan may have understood the import of what Eli Zeira had said, that there might be no additional warning, for he responded, "If there is a war, we might not be able to get you back by helicopter." Meir stayed in Tel Aviv.

If war broke out, most of the Israeli public would be taken by surprise. The government had done everything to play down the latest Arab military moves. That Friday morning Israel's military correspondents were briefed about the enemy forces massing on the fronts and "asked" not to exaggerate the significance of those moves. Details of the Arab buildup had been routinely censored from news dispatches filed by these correspondents. The public had no way to assess how serious the problem was. By now Syria had amassed 45,000 soldiers and 900 tanks along its frontier. Israel had arrayed on its side 5,000 soldiers and 177 tanks. Egypt had 120,000 soldiers and 1,200 tanks poised near its side of the canal. Israel had 8,500 soldiers and 276 tanks in the Sinai.

ISRAELIS AWAKENED on that Saturday morning of Yom Kippur, October 6, largely oblivious to what was happening along its frontiers, unaware of the growing government concern. No one could know that Mossad chief Zvi Zamir had recently left the country (to a location still not identified) to try to determine for himself how serious the Arab military threat was. At 4:00 A.M. came his ominous cable—war would break out that very day at 6:00 P.M. It was noteworthy that the first clear-cut indication of war came not from Israeli military intelligence, still largely clinging to the belief that the Arabs were merely conducting exercises, but from the Mossad, Israel's equivalent of the CIA. Perhaps, Zamir cabled, if Israel were to inform Egypt and Syria that its war intentions were known, they might postpone their planned attack.

The Mossad chief's dramatic message shocked Israeli leaders out of their slumber. They abruptly realized the awful truth: If Zamir were correct—and they assumed he was—the IDF had a mere fourteen hours to get ready for war. Vaunted, celebrated, legendary, the Israeli army had always had at least forty-eight hours warning before impending war, the forty-eight hours it needed to muster its reserve troops in time. On October 6, 1973, no matter how much it scrambled, the IDF would be forced into war with its pants down, crippled, little resembling the dynamic and frightening juggernaut of the past.

With this sobering realization Moshe Dayan and the other Israeli leaders tried to gear up for war. Hearing the news, the defense minister phoned Golda at once and then proceeded to his office for urgent consultations with the chief of staff. Meanwhile, Elazar phoned Air Force Commander Benny Peled to ask him when he would be ready and what targets he would attack should he be given the go-ahead for a preemptive strike. He replied that the air force could strike by 11:00 A.M. and that Syria would be given priority over Egypt. "If you tell me to start now, my target will be the missile sites on the Golan Heights."

By 6:00 A.M. Elazar instructed the air force commander to prepare for a preemptive strike. "I'll ask for authorization but you go ahead." When a meteorologist informed Peled that the Golan was covered in cloud, he phoned the chief of staff to say that the attack against the Syrian missiles would have to be scrubbed. "But the whole hinterland of Syria is as clear as a bell. So I'm going for the airfields, OK?" Elazar agreed, and Peled redirected his air force to plan for a preemptive strike against airfields in northern Syria by noon.

Even then, in the early morning hours of Yom Kippur, war seemed remote. "We still thought at the last moment, Sadat would recant, that he would come to his senses, that he would be frightened by the blow we would strike against him," noted Haim Yisraeli, Dayan's aide.[13] This was one of several arguments against a preemptive strike. Dayan met with the chief of staff and heard his proposal for a preemptive strike against the Syrian airfields. Dayan declared that he opposed the strike "even if it earns a ticket to paradise." Only in the event that Egypt opened fire against Israel would he condone such an action. Acting preemptively would not have helped the overall war effort, as the air force's only target could have been the Syrian airfields. What was worse, Israel would have been blamed for starting the war.

Dayan still held out hope that war could be averted. Elazar, in contrast, accepted the fact that fighting was inevitable. He favored mobilizing four divisions along with the entire air force at once. Agreeing that the air force should be called up, the defense minister thought one division for the north and one for the south was sufficient. Elazar remained firm: "I would declare a general mobilization so that the whole world will know that we are prepared for war."

"The world will believe we are prepared even if we don't call up a single man."

"Nevertheless," said Elazar, "I'm for mobilizing. I don't care what the world believes."[14]

Stuck over their disagreement, Dayan and Elazar took their differences to Golda Meir at 8:00 A.M. at her office in Tel Aviv. While precious hours were being lost, they convened and Dayan proposed that the government maintain a "business as usual" routine, refraining from evacuating the children of the Jewish settlements on the Golan. The children could be taken down from the Heights just before hostilities began.

No, insisted Golda Meir, they must be evacuated at once and not just before the action starts.

" 'Just before the action starts' is now," reminded the chief of staff.

"If you want to remove the children now," replied Dayan, "take them down now. Tomorrow, let them complain to you."[15]

Mobilization was then debated. Recalling to himself his forceful assertions to the Israeli public that war was not imminent, Dayan sensed that if Israel mobilized and the Arabs did not attack, Labor's chances in the forthcoming election would suffer. To the prime minister and Elazar, Dayan argued that if Israel mobilized before one shot was fired, it would be branded the aggressor. Under any circumstances, he expressed confidence that two reserve divisions and the air force were sufficient. If toward evening the situation worsened, he said, more troops could always be called up. However, he told the prime minister that "if you want to accept the chief of staff's proposal I will not prostrate myself on the road and will not resign; but you might as well know that it is superfluous." This was a new Moshe Dayan, letting power over defense slip away and into the hands of Golda Meir and her cabinet allies. It was a responsibility that weighed heavily on the prime minister. Now, of all times, she was aware of her lack of military experience and judgment. "My God," she anguished, "I have to decide which of them is right?" She leaned toward Elazar's view, much as she disliked overruling the defense minister. She felt that the country had to be in a position to defend itself.[16]

She ordered a mobilization of one hundred thousand men. The order went out only at 10:00 A.M. Not even then was it a full mobilization, but Elazar exploited the decision to call up more reserves than approved. Suddenly, military jeeps appeared in neighborhoods all over Israel, soldiers entered synagogues to summon men at prayer to rush to their bases urgently.

On the question of a preemptive air strike, the prime minister backed Dayan. The Nixon administration had made it clear that an Israeli first strike would make it impossible for Washington to supply Israel during the war.

An hour later, Dayan began badgering the chief of staff to find out how quickly he could release the reserves if war did not break out.

Convinced that war would break out, Elazar said offhandedly that they could be sent home in a day or two should there be no fighting.

"A hundred thousand men will hang around for a full day before they're sent home?"

"They won't hang around. They'll go down to the front. If it turns out that there's no war, we'll release them within forty-eight hours."[17]

Elazar observed that if the Syrians attacked Saturday evening and were able to break through the lines, Israel could still launch a quick counterattack and destroy the Syrian army. Hence, three divisions were necessary for the Golan front.

"What's the difference between calling them up in the evening, if war actually does break out, and not in the morning?" asked Dayan, still bothered that he had been overruled a few hours before.

"Twelve hours," snapped Elazar.

"The chief of staff," Dayan said, "wants to mobilize troops for a counterattack in a war that hasn't even begun."[18]

Throughout the morning, Dayan had been prodding the chief of staff and the military intelligence people to determine if indeed the Arabs would attack. He vacillated between a feeling that war was unlikely and a gnawing fear that Zamir's information was accurate.

At 11:00 A.M. Dayan asked Elazar whether the tanks had moved forward to the front line. Elazar said yes, that one brigade was deployed along the canal to respond to whatever might develop; two brigades were located behind. Dayan then inquired whether any order from Tel Aviv would be required before the tanks at the front could act. No, said Elazar, the battalion commander on the spot was empowered to take such action. "The defense minister understood, based on the answers he got, that everything was ready," noted his adjutant, Aryeh Brown.[19] When the war broke out three hours later, only three tanks were deployed on the front line and two brigades were fifty miles from the front.[20] Dayan's information was based upon what the chief of staff had culled from the southern command. In fact, the political and military leaders in Tel Aviv had no idea how the troops were really deployed in the south; nor did they know when the war broke out.

At noon the cabinet met and rejected the chief of staff's request for a preemptive air strike. It retroactively approved the mobilization order. Dayan suggested that the main thrust of the IDF be focused against the Syrians, but it was decided to operate against both fronts at the same time. Near 2:00 P.M. Justice Minister Ya'acov Shimshon Shapira asked: "Is there not a danger that the Egyptian attack would be advanced?"

"This is the most relevant question to be asked at this meeting. That's a danger which worries us a great deal," said the defense minister. "The Egyptians can certainly do this." As Dayan spoke, news came that Egypt and Syria had begun massive attacks. The Yom Kippur War had begun. At that moment Moshe Dayan considered it Day Seven of the Six Day War, and no different. The real war, he told newsmen, would begin the next evening when reserves reach the front lines. Then, "we will turn the area into a gigantic cemetery."

THIS WAR was different. All along the Suez Canal, two thousand Egyptian field guns fired at the sixteen hapless, largely indefensible Israeli fortifications. Stretched out at five-mile intervals, the bunkers, manned by 20 to 30 soldiers each, provided shelter to 436 soldiers, passing a quiet Yom Kippur day, war the last thing on their minds. Within the first minute some 10,500 shells had been fired. At the same time, a wave of 240 Egyptian aircraft crossed the canal. Within fifteen minutes, the first wave of some eight thousand Egyptian infantry began to attempt a crossing of the canal. By Egypt's own estimates, a canal crossing would cost them 10,000 dead; in fact they lost only 208 men.

According to most Israeli military leaders, including Moshe Dayan, had the IDF mobilized its tanks correctly, the canal crossing would have been stopped in its tracks. The tanks were not there, however, and the price Israel paid was steep. Exploiting the great distance between fortifications, Egyptian soldiers slithered in between them, out of sight of Israeli soldiers. The Bar-Lev bunkers were meant to serve as early-warning systems, a trip wire that would give enough advance warning to tank formations some miles back to move quickly into crucial defensive positions. All along the front the IDF had only eighteen artillery pieces, three of which were knocked out almost at once. Virtually unhindered, Egyptian soldiers crossed the canal at will.

While the Egyptians were storming across the canal, Syrian forces unleashed a massive artillery and air assault as the first of some 1,400 tanks moved toward the Israeli lines, crossed them, and headed across the Golan toward Israel's northern heartland.

In those first few hours of war, as Dayan and the General Staff scurried to ascertain what was happening from the vague, uncertain, and fragmentary reports, shock and despair began to set in. The unthinkable was occurring: Egyptian and Syrian soldiers who, according to conventional Israeli wisdom, would never dare to fight, were pushing across Israeli lines—and almost no one seemed to be in their way.

The *mechdal*, or mishap as the Israelis termed it later, had spread like an infectious disease into all sectors of the army. It was not only that tanks and men were not where they should have been. An entire tank battalion was missing binoculars; vehicles had not been maintained; army blankets had disappeared; orders to reinforce battle positions had not been carried out; reservists were greeted upon arrival at their units with confusion and disorder. Commanders at the top of the pyramid were no better. Amidst the fog of battle in those first few hours the chief of staff still lived under the illusion that whole tank brigades were deployed when they were not. That was not all. In the field, it took several hours for the senior officers in the southern command to agree on a time when their tanks should move into battle. All that Dayan and the generals in Tel Aviv knew was that difficult battles were in progress. The truth still eluded them.

No one was more stunned than Moshe Dayan, that genius of military deception and surprise, that his army was caught off guard. Wars began for Dayan with a Mitla Pass parachute drop or an Israeli air force raid; it was the IDF which caught its enemy off guard and unprepared. Israel could no longer use these tactical weapons: Acts that once had been touted as daring and brilliant were now called provocative and aggressive. Forced to remain in a defensive stance, the IDF continued to hold the upper hand as long as its soldiers and tanks were in the right place. Now, as the paucity of battlefield reports bitterly demonstrated, men and equipment had not been properly deployed. Had those three hundred tanks been in place near the canal, Egyptian troops would not have, could not have reached the Israeli side of the Sinai.

That they were not in place dismayed and disoriented Dayan more than any other single fact that afternoon. Over the next few days, the stigma of presiding over an unprepared army would transform him into someone unrecognizable. Where he had been decisive, he now feared giving orders. Where he had displayed such overwhelming self-confidence, he now radiated desperation and panic. One statistic, more than any other, would crush his spirit and and feed his raging sense of guilt: In that first day of fighting, five hundred Israeli soldiers died and another one thousand were wounded. Later, fighting off the critics, searching for a way to salvage what was left of his personal reputation, the defense minister denied guilt for what had happened. His reasoning was elegant, logical, masterful—others had been responsible, not him; others had led him to believe that all was well, he had no reason to doubt them. Always, others. Yet, anyone who came upon Dayan the first day of the war, or in the next few days, had no doubt how the defense minister viewed himself, viewed his responsibility for the turn of events. He had guilt written all over his face. He had guilt sketched into every physical movement, every word that he uttered.

If proof was needed of how removed from reality Dayan and the generals in Tel Aviv had become, there was their bizarre debate that first evening over whether the Bar-Lev line could be maintained. Though information was fragmentary and, in some cases, just plain wrong, some military men believed that the Bar-Lev fortifications, as sacrosanct in Israeli military thinking as any forward line had ever been, could still be saved. Undoubtedly relying upon his intuition in the absence of hard facts, the defense minister had concluded that the fortifications had already fallen, that it was too late to try to preserve them, and that all that could be done was to try to rescue the wounded. Out of that miasma of uncertainty and cloudy information Dayan correctly assessed that the real danger to Israel lay, not in the south, where hundreds of miles separated the Egyptian army from the country's main population centers, but in the north. There, Syrian troops, were they to succeed in advancing across the Golan, could move all too quickly down from the ridges and into northern Israel.

When it came time to inform the Israeli people of what had happened, the country's leaders decided to sound cautiously optimistic. Indeed, they had no choice. They did not know much about what had happened and they could not, and dared not, reveal their uncertainties. "We were not surprised," Prime Minister Golda Meir told a television audience that first evening, beginning with a monumental mistruth. "Our forces were deployed as necesary to meet the danger." Once again a mistruth was spoken in the service of caution. Soon after the prime minister's broadcast, Dayan spoke to the nation, still boastful, still persuaded that Israel was merely engaged in the Seventh Day of the Six Day War: "We shall smite the Egyptians hip and thigh. The war will end within a few days with our victory. . . . In the Golan Heights, perhaps a number of Syrian tanks penetrated across our line and perhaps they have achieved here and there some occupation, but no significant occupation. . . . Although we had a number of losses and hits here and there, the situation in the Golan Heights is relatively satisfactory, more or less, in my opinion. In Sinai, on the canal, there were many more Egyptian forces and the problem there is different altogether. . . . This is a large area. . . . There is no chance whatsoever of protecting every meter. . . . Since they began the war they succeeded in crossing the canal. . . . We are prepared for such a situation tomorrow. We should know that this is a war and we are prepared for the transition period, which is relatively short and then to rely on our forces . . . so that the Egyptian action of crossing the canal and north of the canal will end as a very, very dangerous adventure for them. We had losses but, relatively speaking, this was more or less what we estimated to be [likely in] the first day of fighting—which will end with victory in the coming few days." On the seventh and eighth day of the Six Day War, apparently.

It is difficult to imagine a less accurate depiction of Israel's military position than the one Dayan offered. Did he know the truth when he spoke? If he did, the defense minister may have decided to deceive the country in the hope that matters could be corrected soon, and his deception would pass unnoticed in the forthcoming victory. The truth was that Israel, totally unprepared, had its back to the wall, and unless it rallied its forces immediately, would face indescribable losses on the battlefield, and, perhaps the loss of sizable chunks of its territory. Later, after the war, Dayan argued that he had not been deliberately misleading: He had been genuinely convinced then that the IDF would indeed "smite the enemy hip and thigh" in short order.[21]

At 10:00 P.M., the cabinet met and heard a reasonably upbeat report from the chief of staff, despite the fact that Egypt was well on its way to putting three hundred tanks on the Israeli side of the Suez Canal. Four hours later, Dayan sought sleep, but at 4:00 A.M., two hours after going to bed, he was awakened and told that the Golan was deteriorating. A Syrian force had penetrated Israeli lines in the region of Hushniyah, eight miles south of Kuneitra, and was heading toward roads leading to the Sea of Galilee. The reports in that morning's newspapers were quite different. *Ha'aretz* said: "The Israeli army is blocking the enemy and about to counterattack"; *Davar:* "Army stops penetration into Sinai." Finding the chief of staff, Dayan expressed concern that so many Egyptian forces were streaming across the canal. Though a decision had been made to turn the air force loose against Egyptian missile sites and airfields later that morning, the defense minister urged that it be changed so that Benny Peled could send his warplanes against the Egyptian columns crossing over into the Sinai. The chief of staff preferred to go for the missile sites first.

Confronted with two hemorrhaging fronts, the defense minister chose to visit the Golan first, the more critical one in his view. Arriving there at 6:00 A.M., he heard from the commanding officer that Israel's defenses in the southern sector of the Golan had collapsed. Israeli reserve units were only expected six or seven hours later; until then the Syrians were free to advance toward the Israeli heartland. Something had to be done.

Fearing that time was running out, Dayan thought only the air force could stop the Syrians. Ordinarily, the defense minister should have found the chief of staff and passed on his instructions through him, but Dayan was unable to locate him. Seeking out Benny Peled, Dayan sought to persuade him that, despite existing plans to take out the Egyptian missiles, the air force had to move against the Syrian forces. Peled remembered that Dayan sounded "desperate."

"Benny," Dayan shouted, "the situation is grim. The Syrians are holding almost all of the Golan Heights. Your home is in danger." (That was a reference to the fact that Peled's family came from Rosh-Pina and Metulla in the north.) "There [in the Sinai], it's all sand. Here it's close to home and the Third Temple is in danger."

Acceding to Dayan's wish to unleash the air force in the north, Peled was forced to point out that "the first wave is already committed. . . . But all the other attack aircraft will be diverted up north."[22] Thirty Israeli aircraft were lost that day in the north, but Dayan's insistence that Peled turn the air power against the north bore fruit. The Syrian advance was given a major jolt.

Still, Israel's military situation never seemed gloomier. Mobilization was lagging on both the Suez and the Golan fronts, putting increasing pressure on the units already in the field. Lacking enough transport vehicles for tanks, the IDF was forced to send many tanks across the 150 miles of Sinai desert on their own engines and treads. To delay the Egyptian advances, the southern command threw reservists into immediate action even though units were understrength and only loosely coordinated. The results were frequently costly.

Rumors had spread within the IDF that the fighting in the southern part of the Golan had ended and the IDF had lost. Meanwhile in the south an armored division was being torn apart by the Egyptians. The strongholds at the canal had been surrounded and no one knew the status of the Israeli soldiers there. They were the only soldiers between the Egyptian troops and the state of Israel. At Sde Dov airfield near Tel Aviv, a general overheard Defense Minister Dayan say out loud, "We have lost the Third Commonwealth (another term for the state of Israel)."[23] If Moshe Dayan spoke like that, an IDF officer said, "then it's the end."[24]

In the past, Dayan's very presence on the battlefield had comforted soldiers. When he showed up, the men felt safe, protected, at ease. When he was around, in Iska Shadmi's colorful phrase, "he would charge your batteries." Officers greeted him with their problems, and, if he liked what he heard, his whole face would seem to explode in joy, the glint in his one eye growing brighter. If he did not, a dismissive wave of the hand, and a decision had been made. On that solemn Sunday morning, October 7, Dayan walked around the Golan spiritless, a poisonous cloud of defeat hovering above him, infecting those who once thought of him as godlike. Iska Shadmi was there, and recalled that "for the first time, the air went out at the most critical moment. We felt confidence in Dado. He encouraged us. But Dayan was broken. It was hard for him to be put back together. We had difficulty absorbing a situation in which things were not going well in the battlefield, and our God, Moshe Dayan, was the way he was."[25]

For Shadmi one episode exemplified how confused and shaken Dayan had become. It occurred on that Sunday morning after the Syrians had crossed Israeli lines in the southern sector and had nearly reached the Israeli kibbutz Ein Gev on the eastern side of the Sea of Galilee. Dayan was taking part in a debate over whether to bomb certain Syrian tanks.

Shadmi told Dayan, "Moshe, here are five Syrian tanks with ten people inside. This is what is taking up your thoughts as minister of defense? Stop dealing with this. Leave it." Never before would he have dared talk so boldly to Moshe Dayan. But the situation appeared to call for it. To ease the defense minister's burden, Shadmi offered to handle the problem on his own by organizing a force at Ein Gev and Dayan authorized him to take on the assignment.[26]

Dayan's presence in the north that morning unnerved the senior officers of the northern command. Ordinarily, had he given them orders on the spot they would have implemented them without question. This time, seeing him in a mood of despair and frustration, they did not. At one stage Dayan turned to division commander Dan Laner and ordered him to prepare the Jordan bridges for demolition. Laner realized that this meant the IDF was going to abandon the Golan. Without uttering a word of assent, Laner found the northern front commander, Hofi, and told him of Dayan's instructions. They turned to the chief of staff, who told them that no bridges were to be wired for demolition.[27]

Dayan flew to Tel Aviv for meetings with the General Staff. Aharon Yariv, the former director of military intelligence, saw him then and thought he looked like "a broken man."[28]

The defense minister next flew south. Just before landing at 11:40 A.M. at Um Hasheiba, the southern command's forward post near the canal, southern front commander Shmuel "Gorodish" Gonen advised Dayan to turn back as there had been Egyptian commando units in the hills near there. (Gonen, who replaced Sharon as front commander in July, had been a highly competent field commander in the Six Day War.) Dayan disregarded the suggestion. From the moment that he walked into the command post, the generals there sensed that a frightening change had come over him. "He was in panic," remembered Uri Ben-Ari, just appointed deputy front commander. "When he entered the room, panic accompanied him. He was not his usual self, studying the situation quietly and giving orders. He seemed very insecure. Asking silly questions. Making very silly remarks. Not taking responsibility."[29] Another witness was Rehavam Ze'evi. "His disposition was at its worst that day—complete defeatism, believing that everything was lost."[30]

Listening to the generals' grim reports of Egyptian tanks and soldiers massing on the eastern side of the canal, of the IDF's inability to thwart their crossing, Dayan said simply, "This is war. Withdraw to the high ground." Taking a map, he traced a line east of Refidim to Abu Rudeis on the Gulf of Suez, advising against holding armored battles near the canal, instead urging that the IDF consolidate behind a new line and block the enemy at the foot of the hills, twelve to nineteen miles east of the canal.

"It's clear," he began, "that priority will be given to the Jordan Valley and Tiberias. Sinai isn't that important. Twenty miles more, forty less— it's less important than the north. You'll get more air support, but only tomorrow morning. The water line must be abandoned, and everything transferred to the [new line]. . . . There's no point in building on the strongholds, and it's a pity to break through to them. It's not logical. I don't see that the situation will change. The men in the strongholds should try and break out by night."

"What about their wounded?" asked an officer.

"The healthy should try and cross the lines. The wounded? There's no alternative. Let them be taken captive."

An odd silence fell on the room. The generals found his talk shattering. This was not the Moshe Dayan of old. They had been nurtured on his military wisdom, on his aggressiveness. He had been their teacher, they his pupils. He had instilled in them the unflagging belief that one never gave up the battle, that no matter what its losses, a unit had to go forward. If there were wounded, they were never to be left to die or be taken captive. This was not the Dayan of the 1967 war. As difficult as it had been to absorb the shocks of the opening hours of battle Saturday and Sunday, the commanders found Dayan's uncharacteristic behavior even more startling, and therefore all the more unsettling. As he had taught them in earlier days, they were firmly against caving in. "The situation is indeed serious, but not desperate," General Gonen suggested. "We won't retreat voluntarily."[31]

Nor would they permit the defense minister's defeatist stance to affect their thinking. They made it clear that he was no longer welcome in the command post. As if he understood the way the wind was blowing, the defense minister sought to reassure his listeners, to let them know that he had not come to impose his views on them. "What I said was advice at ministerial level. Of course everything must be coordinated with Dado." (That phrase, "ministerial advice," would come to haunt Dayan. Until the war, he had virtual carte blanche to handle any defense issue; now he had voluntarily abandoned decision making to his subordinates.)

Flying back from Sinai to Tel Aviv, Dayan thought to himself that he had never felt such anxiety. The country was in danger, "and the results could be fatal if we did not recognize and understand the new situation in time, and if we failed to suit our warfare to the new needs."[32]

Reaching Tel Aviv at 2:30 P.M., the defense minister saw his aide Haim Yisraeli and explained that there was no immediate prospect of throwing the Egyptians back to the other side of the canal. "Perhaps we can do this but it will cost us many casualties. It's not worth it. We should remain on the second line."

"We can remain on the second line?" Yisraeli asked him, wondering whether the IDF could even do that.

"Forever," Dayan answered in English.[33]

Dayan then saw the chief of staff. If the generals in the south would not listen to him about the need to withdraw, perhaps Elazar would. "This is a war for the Third Temple," he told him, hoping to dramatize his message, "not for Sinai. We must withdraw to Sharm el-Sheikh.

Sharm el-Sheikh is the important thing: We must deploy on the second line at the passes."

The chief of staff was angry and dismayed. "Even if we must deploy on the second line," he asked, "why should we evacuate the Gulf [of Suez]?"

"Perhaps not evacuation, but we must fight a delaying battle there."

It must have dawned on both men that a day earlier they had been debating how many Israeli troops to mobilize; the situation had deteriorated to the point today where they were debating whether to withdraw from one front. That afternoon the chief of staff heard Gonen talk eagerly of staging an immediate counterattack. Elazar was lukewarm to the idea. Gonen was enthused because division commander Ariel Sharon had arrived with his troops and one hundred tanks deep in the Sinai. Sharon favored an immediate canal crossing. It appeared absurd: The Bar-Lev fortifications had been given up that morning; the reserves had not yet all arrived. Shouting down Gonen's plans for a counterattack, the chief of staff thought it better to wait for an Egyptian attack first. Against this background, the defense minister went to see Golda Meir at her Tel Aviv office at 3:30 P.M.

He found her and her colleagues, Yigal Allon and Israel Galili, hopeful of a quick, triumphant outcome for the IDF. Only that morning the chief of staff had told them that in a day or two the war would be over and Israel would be the victor. Later he had been confident that the IDF could launch a counterattack on Monday. In contrast, the defense minister had reached a nadir of despair and remained convinced that the IDF had to pull back in the Sinai to a new line. To anyone coming into contact with Dayan, he appeared so distraught, so confused, that the proposal appeared less a military tactic and more a first step toward quitting.

Arguing against a counterattack in the south, Dayan said that "the Sinai is not Degania." It was not necessary to fight for every inch of the desert as he and others had fought for his kibbutz in 1948. Regrouping behind a new line and waiting for the reserves to arrive made better military sense to him.

Golda Meir found Dayan's gloomy account shocking, disturbing. At 4:00 P.M., she turned to her chief of staff, who was still brimming with optimism. Though earlier he had opposed a quick counterattack, he could not let Dayan and his pessimism influence the cabinet deliberation. Elazar, sensing himself in competition with Dayan, did a quick about-face. He reported that Gorodish was confident that the IDF could turn the battle around. "If we let him counterattack, by evening there won't be a single Egyptian on this side of the canal." Offering no further resistance, Dayan gave the chief of staff an opening. He wanted to make sure he understood, said Elazar, that if he went south and became convinced there that the counterattack was feasible, he had the green light to proceed.

"I doubt the forces are ready," replied Dayan, "but if you are persuaded that it's possible to do it, we'll support you."[34] With no support for his own withdrawal proposal, Dayan at least wanted to give the impression that he remained in charge. He in fact was not. The defense minister certainly demonstrated that by giving power to the chief of staff to conduct a battle Dayan did not think worth fighting. Only a few hours earlier he had been in the south and concluded that the troops were unprepared for a counterattack.

The prime minister asked Yigal Allon for his opinion. He supported Elazar. She turned to Galili. More support for the chief of staff. Golda then fell in line behind Elazar's plan. Dayan was isolated. She rejected retreat, opted for staying put and trying to resist the Arabs. She asked the chief of staff to go south and give her his assessment; she also decided to seek out Chaim Bar-Lev, a former chief of staff, and send him north for his assessment.

It had become a very frustrating situation for Dayan, who thought he knew what should be done. Observing him during these first few days of the war, his daughter remarked later at how frustrated he had been at having his ideas so quickly discarded. "He always believed in the Sinai as a big buffer zone, not as something we should lose blood over. When he suggested withdrawing to a second line . . . and found that those who opposed him regarded the canal as if it were a Wailing Wall, and thought that we should kick the Egyptians back across the canal at whatever cost, he was very frustrated. He thought this a mistaken military concept. He truly felt that sitting on the canal was not some sacred national goal. That's why he was gloomy. . . . At a certain point he felt that he was not really in control. He felt he was one hundred percent right."[35]

DAYAN NEXT conferred with Golda privately. He seemed absolutely despondent.

"Golda," he began with great emotion, "I was wrong in everything. We are heading toward a catastrophe. We shall have to withdraw on the Golan Heights to the edge of the escarpment overlooking the valley and in the south in Sinai to the passes and hold on to the last bullet." If the Arabs offered Israel a cease-fire, Israel ought to consider accepting it. He passed on one piece of advice that would earn him much credit later on: Priority should be given to the north, where the situation was grave.

Ten kilometers more or less in the Sinai made no difference, he told her, but the north was different. Syrian tanks were threatening the heart of the country, and something must be done immediately. It is no wonder that later Golda Meir described Dayan's horrifying portrayal of events "the most pessimistic prediction I had yet heard."[36] She had never heard anyone, let alone Moshe Dayan, speak in such depressing terms.

Though Dayan's supporters insisted later that he had not panicked, others in the government and the IDF managed to convey the impression that he, alone among the senior Israeli leaders, appeared to question the army's ability to withstand the Arab attacks. Soldiers were not supposed to panic. Elazar and Bar-Lev, also generals, had not lost their nerve. No one—other than Dayan, it seemed—truly believed that the Egyptians might advance beyond the positions they had taken in the opening hours of the war and march on to Tel Aviv! Indeed, those around Golda Meir offered testimony that Dayan had even talked of surrender.[37] After her private conversation with Dayan, the prime minister closed the door behind him and wept openly. Her aide Lou Kaddar asked her what was the matter.

"Dayan wants to talk about the conditions for surrender," Golda Meir intoned.

No direct evidence exists to suggest that the defense minister actually used the word "surrender." However, Lou Kaddar, Golda Meir's aide at the time, insisted that the prime minister had quoted the defense minister as using the word. The most likely explanation is that the prime minister, upon hearing Dayan speak of the need to withdraw along both fronts and to consider an immediate cease-fire, interpreted his views as those of a man talking about surrender. Dayan vigorously denied he had spoken of surrender.

Again, Dayan sought out the prime minister. The defense minister thought the only honorable step was to resign. "In all sincerity and friendship," he told her, "if you think there is somebody more capable of handling the duties of defense minister, then give it to him. If I was prime minister and thought the defense minister had to be changed, I wouldn't hesitate a moment. It will be a mistake on your part if you don't do what you think right." Dayan said he felt guilty over two matters: He had not seen the war breaking out on Yom Kippur and he had not taken into account the weaponry Sadat had concentrated along the frontier. "I think," he went on, "that I can continue to conduct the war until the end but if you are prepared to accept my resignation, I submit it to you immediately."

All Golda could say was "God forbid!" No matter how convinced she had become that Dayan was a different person, and that perhaps he should be replaced, she knew that dismissing the defense minister would encourage demands that she herself be replaced. For, if the defense minister was guilty of letting the war happen, was not the prime minister as well?

Later Sunday afternoon, the prime minister summoned Chaim Bar-Lev to talk about his going north. He found her sitting at her desk with her head between her hands. She looked as if she were carrying an awful burden on her shoulders. She was. It was not just the pain of the war but the shock of witnessing an unimaginable change in Moshe Dayan. Dayan, she noted sadly to Bar-Lev, had feared the worst for Israel; he worried that the Egyptians might penetrate deeply into Israel; that the Syrians might cross the Jordan; and that eventually Israel would have to ask for a cease-fire. "Well," the prime minister went on, "the surprise by the Arabs I can understand, it has happened before in history, but Moshe Dayan, I cannot understand, how has he collapsed?" Bar-Lev was stunned to hear about Dayan: "He, an international security figure, had reached the conclusion that all was lost and we would have to fight till the last bullet." Golda's discontent infected Bar-Lev. He thought to himself that Israel would somehow cope with the Arabs, but he could not understand how Dayan had concluded that matters were so desperate. Soon Bar-Lev would head north—to find out if indeed Israel had to fight to the last bullet.

Before leaving, Bar-Lev asked the prime minister to make sure that Dayan and Elazar approved of his going. That done, Bar-Lev went off.

"I appreciate this very much," Dayan told him. "Perhaps you'd like my army shirt."

There was no need, Bar-Lev replied, he was not going to enlist.[38]

Dayan faced a cabinet that wanted to believe that the war's opening was an illusion, that Israel would bounce back quickly: "The ministers breathed a sigh of relief [upon hearing the chief of staff say that he could push the Egyptians back]. They could not bear to think that we lacked the power at any moment to throw the enemy back to where they were some thirty hours earlier."[39] The ministers believed fervently that the IDF had the resources to repel the Egyptians (even if at this stage the defense minister did not), because over the years Dayan had convinced them that the IDF would never falter. Just as he had educated his soldiers to remain in the battle no matter how difficult it was going, not to retreat, Dayan had educated these politicians into believing that the IDF could not be pushed back by the Arab armies.

On Sunday evening Elazar presented to the southern command a proposal for an armored counterattack, employing several hundred tanks, to be conducted the next day against Egyptian forces in the Sinai. If all went well, he promised, the counterattack would be a turning point. The attack failed, and Dayan was furious with himself for not fighting harder to have it postponed. It became clear that more time was needed to allow for the reserves to be properly integrated into the units.

That same evening, Bar-Lev phoned Golda Meir to say that "the situation is bad. Perhaps very bad, but not desperate." He saw no reason to build a second defense line on the westerly ridges across the Golan. Plans were going ahead, he noted, for an IDF counterattack to begin on the next morning—Monday.

Back in Tel Aviv Bar-Lev found the prime minister as preoccupied with Moshe Dayan as with the war. Putting her right elbow on her desk and moving her arm from side to side, she uttered, "The great Moshe Dayan! One day like this, one day like that!"[40] One day euphoric, certain that Israel was invincible, another day deep in despair and defeatism. He had been her rock, but that had been in the past. Now, she, an old woman of seventy-five, had to conduct a war without Moshe Dayan's guidance, relying upon her own instincts.

BY THIS POINT the chief of staff had become the supreme military authority. Dayan simply refused to get involved. On Monday, October 8, at 6:00 A.M., Ariel Sharon eagerly sought approval for an early canal crossing. Hoping to gain influence, Sharon sought out Moshe Dayan, even though this meant going around Elazar. Sharon phoned Dayan: "We have to cross, we have to cross," the division commander insisted. All Dayan would say was: "I don't intervene."[41]

As the country began to sense the scale of the tragedy that had befallen Israel, demands were heard not only for an official probe, but for Dayan's resignation as well. Zalman Shoval, then a member of the opposition Likud party and a close friend of Dayan's, put a stop to these moves by securing Likud leader Menachem Begin's agreement not to make such demands. In Begin's view the entire government was responsible for the outbreak of war, not a single minister, even the defense minister.

By Monday evening, the country's politicians were still in shock. The Knesset Foreign Affairs and Defense Committee convened for a briefing from Aharon Yariv, the former director of military intelligence who was acting as an assistant to the chief of staff. Yariv placed two maps before the members, one of the northern front, the other of the southern front. The enemy was colored red, Israel blue. Lova Eliav, one of the members, remembered that "we had seen that the Egyptians had crossed the Suez Canal in God knows how many places. And the Syrians were overlooking the Kinneret." Someone noticed that the map showing the eastern front with Jordan indicated that it had been left almost defenseless. The last of the tanks had been sent to the north and south.

One Knesset member asked Yariv, "This is not what's happening. This is what you think in the worst case scenario can happen?"

"No," said Yariv sadly, "this is what's happened!"

Suddenly several members shouted: "We want Dayan. We want Dayan." They simply did not believe Yariv, and wanted to hear the minister of defense. Later that evening Dayan appeared before the committee. Eliav recalled that he seemed very pale. Dayan confirmed Yariv's description of Israel's military situation. The defense minister left the meeting, his moroseness and depression hanging like a black cloud over the room. The stunned deputies remained silent after he left. One committee member observed, "In another army, this man should have gone into another room, found a pistol there, and we should have heard a shot."[42]

Dayan did not look for a pistol, and when the question was asked of him much later whether he had contemplated suicide, he replied angrily that he had not. Yet a number of senior IDF commanders who saw him during that first week of the war became convinced that he may have wished upon himself the relief of a combat death. Uri Ben-Ari was only one of a number of the generals who voiced such a belief: "All of us had the feeling that Dayan was looking to get killed. . . . There was no other way than to believe that he wanted to commit suicide."[43]

In the early morning hours of Tuesday, October 9, Dayan flew to the Sinai. He viewed the previous day as wasted, all due to the failed counterattack. He thought that Gonen should be replaced by either Sharon, Tal, or Bar-Lev. A decision was soon taken to give Bar-Lev overall command of the southern front.

Later that morning, Dayan met the prime minister and noted that Syria had fired ground-to-ground missiles against Israeli settlements for three nights in a row, and that this action could not go unanswered. The defense minister wanted to bomb military targets in the vicinity of Damascus. The prime minister gave her approval. During this morning an Israeli counterattack on the Golan Heights was under way.

As late as Tuesday afternoon the Israeli public had still not been told the full truth. The political and military leadership knew that the war would not end quickly in an Israeli triumph. They were reasonably confident Israel would win, but it would take a good deal longer than a few days, and would undoubtedly cost many lives. Dayan thought the country should know this awful truth. He prepared to convene the nation's editors in an off-the-record session to let them know how serious the situation was. Later that night he planned to tell the whole country on television.

The editors met at 3:00 P.M. at the Bet Sokolov in Tel Aviv, and Dayan had asked Air Force Commander Benny Peled to brief the editors first. Before the meeting Dayan put his hand on Peled's shoulder: "Benny," he said to him emotionally, "the Third Temple rests on your shoulders." Again, Dayan was speaking as if the country might fall and again others heard him.

The press briefing was dramatic. Shortly before it began, Peled had learned that his pilot son had been shot down over the canal. The air force chief had given him up for lost. As Peled spoke, someone passed a small piece of paper intended for Peled, but Dayan read it first. "Your son has been rescued," was its brief, happy message. Dayan interrupted in midsentence and announced that the commander's son had been rescued. *Davar* editor Hannah Zemer began to weep. (Later, stories would appear suggesting that editors had begun crying when they heard Dayan's dismal report, but the tears had come in happiness over the news about Peled's son.)

Dayan thought it was time for the nation to know the truth. (A transcript of the off-the-record briefing was released in February 1974, apparently to counter the claims that Dayan had broken down during the early part of the war.[44])

He believed that the Syrians were no longer a serious threat since the IDF had gone on the offensive in the Golan that morning. The Sinai was not secure, however, and Israel had to regroup its forces on a second line in the south. Dayan was now confident that Israel could turn its attention to the Egyptians, freed of the burden of a deteriorating Syrian front.

Though Dayan deserved much credit for seeking to tell the truth, the press conference merely encouraged the feeling that he had lost his touch. While the chief of staff was talking about "breaking the bones" of the Egyptians, about counterattacking, the defense minister was asserting the need for retreat. He dropped a bombshell. The Bar-Lev line had been evacuated, "partly in orderly fashion and partly not. We have given it up."

He admitted that "the halo of superiority, the political and military principle that Israel is stronger than the Arabs and that if they dared to start a war, they would be defeated, has not been proved here."

He predicted that "we will finish off the Syrians and then the Jordanians will not enter the war; neither will the Iraqis. . . ." Yet he noted sadly, "I asked for this meeting, so that we should not live in different worlds . . . and this evening on television I want to tell this to the people. . . . If one were to say that all this came as a shock, there would be truth in it."

Herzl Rosenblum, editor of *Yediot Aharonot*, asked Dayan whether he thought there was any point in repeating his remarks on television.

Yes, he indicated, if only because the fall of the Bar-Lev strongholds will soon become known: "We are at war, and everybody is saying: 'Well?' I want to be able to look the public in the eye; I don't want to be suspected . . . of deceit, of trying to gloss over things. I will try to say it all elegantly. I will also say that this isn't a situation in which we are controlling developments with our stopwatches."[45]

Several editors seriously doubted the wisdom of Dayan appearing on television that evening. They feared that public morale would be jolted by the defense minister's gloomy assessment. Herzl Rosenblum reminded Dayan that history was full of wars that had changed direction overnight; that if a defense chief announced at the start of the battle that all was lost, the nation would panic and there would be a wave of suicides. Rosenblum called the prime minister, but could not reach her; so instead he phoned Menachem Begin, who eventually got through to her. Golda Meir agreed that Dayan should not appear on television. She told Dayan that the nation was still in the thick of battle, "so there is no need to tell the people the whole story. The truth at this moment might change and not be the final truth." Dayan sensed the prime minister's troubled mind and agreed not to appear. It was decided that Aharon Yariv would replace the defense minister. With a blend of optimism and realism, Yariv provided a calming voice to the country. He hinted at the bitter truth without sending the country into a panic. Said Yariv: "Let's not delude ourselves with rapid and elegant conquests. The situation is neither simple nor easy. The war is likely to go on, but let's not think in terms of danger to the population of Israel." This marked the first time that the public heard that the war would not be a six-day one, that it would take longer, perhaps much longer.

Later, Dayan's willingness to reveal the truth won praise from division commander Avraham Adan: "In the long run, hiding the whole truth from the public caused greater harm to national morale and confidence in the leadership than the short-term advantage gained by not revealing the true picture."[46] *Ma'ariv* editor Aryeh Dissentchik, visiting his son at Sharm el-Sheikh, recalled the off-the-record briefing with Dayan that day: "I saw him with his pants down. He didn't even have balls. . . . He crumpled. He was beaten and defeated. We thought he'd raise our morale a bit but he made us melancholy. It's lucky for us that Golda wouldn't let him appear on television. He would have announced our surrender."[47]

Around this time Dayan received some blunt advice from his spokesman, Naphtali Lavie. Sensing the mood in the country, Lavie urged Dayan to resign. "The prevailing mood in the country blames you," he told him honestly. Dayan, of course, had already offered to resign, and the prime minister had rejected his offer.

After a grim cabinet session on Tuesday, the defense minister flew south. He was furious that the counterattack had gone so poorly. He gave orders to the Israeli forces to array themselves in a defensive posture, since full priority was still being given to the north. The Egyptians appeared content with their gains and were not trying to push farther north.

In the north there was great danger that the Syrians might advance to the edge of the Golan plateau overlooking the Jordan Valley. From there they would be in an ideal position to dominate the roads leading up to the Golan Heights. That would enable the Syrians to prevent Israeli reinforcements from moving up from the Jordan Valley.

Wednesday, October 10, was the first day that Dayan stopped worrying whether the IDF might not be able to keep the Arabs from entering into Israel. At midday he met the General Staff in Tel Aviv, where future efforts along the northern front were being discussed. The chief of staff was eager to push farther into Syria, so that IDF forces would be within artillery range of Damascus to show what a heavy price it would pay for starting the war. Also, with Syria neutralized, Israel could concentrate on the Egyptian front. Dayan was concerned about possible Soviet intervention if the IDF pushed too close to the Syrian capital. Again the two men went to Golda with their differences, and again she took the chief of staff's side. The drive deeper into Syria was planned for the next day.

DAYAN AND THE GENERALS began to debate the strategy for stalling the Egyptian drive. By now most of the Egyptian army had crossed over into the Sinai, but two armored divisions remained on the western side of the canal. The IDF's senior command debated whether to cross to the western side of the canal at once and deal with the two divisions on the Egyptian side; or to let them cross into the Sinai and try to destroy them. Uri Ben-Ari, the deputy front commander, and Dayan debated the point heatedly. Ben-Ari thought the IDF should wait for the Egyptians to cross over into Sinai first, then fight them. Only then should the IDF cross over to the western side of the canal. Dayan wanted the IDF to cross to the western side of the canal right away. Ben-Ari remembered: "He didn't believe that Israel would be allowed to fight for too much longer. With the Egyptians sitting on our side, Dayan wanted Israel to obtain some achievements."

Finally, Dayan said, "I'm for [crossing to the western side of the Canal at once], but I don't have to make a ministerial decision. That's your decision." Years later, Uri Ben-Ari was amazed at his open disagreement with the defense minister at that time. He, nor anyone else, would have dared speak to him so directly in earlier days.[48]

By Friday, October 12, plans were gearing up for an Israeli crossing to the canal's western bank. Although less than enthusiastic about the plan, Dayan said he would not "wage a jihad against it." He doubted that the crossing would change the war or that it would force the Egyptians to propose a cease-fire. With the chief of staff supporting the crossing, Dayan brought their differences once again to the prime minister and her cabinet advisers. The meeting convened at noon.

Bar-Lev favored the crossing as the only strategic step that could change the situation. "Everything else means we just sit there, shoot, and get shot at. If we manage to cross with two or three divisions, we can force a cease-fire upon the Egyptians."

Dayan replied angrily, "Listen, a cease-fire is none of your business. You are a military man. A cease-fire is a political decision. Leave it to the politicians." Mossad chief Zvi Zamir delivered information that more Egyptians forces were crossing into the Sinai. It was no longer necessary for Israel to decide whether to cross over the western side of the canal. The IDF would deal with the Egyptians crossing over first and then undertake its own canal crossing.[49]

Meanwhile, Gen. Ariel Sharon applied heavy pressure on Dayan to press for a canal crossing right away. Since the prevailing thinking was to let the Egyptians come across into the Sinai first, Sharon appealed to Dayan to do something, but the defense minister simply referred him to the General Staff. Sharon got Yael on the phone and urged her to tell her father that "the whole division here is champing on the bit. My horses are ready for war. You remember the picture—like the eve of the Six Day War. Explain that to him. He must understand that there is enough initiative here to bust up this Egyptian business. Otherwise it will finish as is, and we'll have a cease-fire in this critical situation. He must understand that there's no connection between Syria and Egypt. Here we have to take the intiative."

Eventually the defense minister told Sharon, "Your opinions and attitudes are acceptable to me. You'll succeed in getting from Command HQ whatever you want. Keep pressing them till they accept your opinion. You will convince them." Sharon got nowhere with the command headquarters. The order was to wait for the Egyptian armor to cross the canal first.[50]

On October 14, after the Egyptians had sent 1,000 tanks into the Sinai, an armored battle took place and Egypt lost 250 tanks. That set the stage for the Israeli canal crossing to the western side the next night of October 15–16.

At 5:00 P.M. on October 15 the first tanks under Sharon's command rolled out of Tasa toward the Suez Canal. Four hours later only two hundred paratroopers had actually started to cross the waterway. Heavy fighting with the Egyptian forces on the eastern bank of the canal prevented Sharon from sending his troops over the water speedily. The battle continued and by 9:00 A.M. on October 16 only thirty tanks and two thousand men had reached the western bank. Dayan worried and considered ordering the men back. Bar-Lev and the others reassured him. Eventually an Israeli bridgehead was established on the canal's west bank and Israeli troops advanced to within sixty-three miles of Cairo.

When the Israelis were firmly ensconced on the Egyptian side of the canal, Dayan went to visit the troops. He became the first cabinet minister to cross over into "Africa," as the Israelis dubbed the Egyptian side. Deeply moved, Dayan shook soldiers' hands and then noticed some Egyptian prisoners, one of whom had been crying, "Musa Dayan is here!" One prisoner stood up. Another prisoner saluted and extended his hand to the defense minister. He asked for water and treatment for their wounded. Complying, Dayan turned to nearby officers and reminded them to follow the Geneva Convention. No longer did Moshe Dayan appear gray, with sunken cheeks. Now and again a smile came to his face. His self-confidence appeared to be returning.

ISRAELIS FOUND it odd to have their army on the eastern bank of the Suez Canal, only sixty-three miles from Cairo. Dayan thought it strange and unsettling. "Almost every day I visit the units on the other side of the canal," he told Gad Ya'acobi after the war, "I can't free myself for a moment from the thought: 'What are we doing here?; after all, this isn't the Western Wall.' When something is necessary, you have to do it. But you always have to think if it's really necessary."[51]

As the tide of the battle turned in favor of Israel by the third week of fighting, the Soviets pressed Washington to help in arranging a cease-fire. American secretary of state Henry Kissinger was asked by the Soviets to come to Moscow. The joint Russian-American efforts bore fruit in Security Council Resolution 338, formally adopted by the UN on October

22. It called for a cease-fire, for the implementation of Resolution 242, and for negotiations towards a just and durable peace in the Middle East to start at once. Neither the Israelis nor Egyptians actually stopped fighting, and fire was exchanged for another thirty-six hours, which led to Soviet threats of direct intervention if the U.S. did not force Israel to abide by the UN cease-fire resolution. In response, Kissinger persuaded President Nixon to place the American military on alert, a step that forced the Russians to back down. The fighting between Israelis and Arabs finally ended on October 25 after a second cease-fire was called.

Dayan was impressed after his initial meetings with the American secretary of state. "Whatever you think of him," he told newsmen at a briefing, "you have to admit that this fellow puts things into gear and gets things moving. Our business is now on the move. Whether we like it or not, and I like it, there is no stagnation. . . . Whether this will bring real peace I don't know, but it won't be in two stages like before . . . stop firing and then wait for years."

At the end of the Yom Kippur War, Israeli troops had advanced deep into Syria and Egypt. Once again, the IDF had demonstrated that the Arabs could not defeat Israel, but the cost was monumental. The Arab states, remembering those first heady days of war when their troops overran Israeli positions with ease, claimed victory, despite their perilous position on October 25. For Israel the victory was marred by high casualties: 2,552 soldiers dead and another 3,000 wounded. In no other war except the 1948 War of Independence had so many Israelis fallen.

Israel's military accomplishments were formidable, particularly in light of the shock and surprise at its start. In 1967, Israel had destroyed 100 of the 450 Syrian tanks. In 1973, 1,000 of the 2,000 Syrian tanks were destroyed. The Israeli air force downed 200 of the 410 Syrian planes this time and took out half of the Syrian missiles. As for the southern front: In 1967, Israel had knocked out 700 of the 1,000 Egyptian tanks; in 1973, it destroyed 1,000 of the 2,600 Egyptian tanks. Israel's air force knocked out of action 180 of Egypt's 230 planes in the first hours of the Six Day War; this time, Egypt lost 240 of its 680 planes.

In sum, Israel destroyed 2,500 Arab tanks, shot down 400 Arab planes, crossed the Suez Canal, captured a stronghold on the peak of Mount Hermon in the north, and advanced to within twenty-five miles of Damascus. On the Israeli side, a staggering 107 planes and 840 tanks had been lost. Later, Dayan noted that no army had ever managed to destroy thousands of enemy tanks and hundreds of warplanes with fewer casualties.

IN NOVEMBER 1973 Moshe Dayan remained defensive about his behavior on the eve of the war. "Not a single person foresaw that war would break out until the morning of Yom Kippur, and that is why the mobilization of reserves was not ordered," he observed on November 14 at a meeting of army officers. He added that he had not thought there would be a war, but he had not heard anyone else say that war was imminent.

After the war, supporters of the defense minister argued that he had never abandoned hope, never truly thought that the IDF was defeated, that he had been misunderstood. Yet too many witnesses heard Moshe Dayan make apocalyptic remarks to put much stock in what his defenders sought to convey. He did portray Israel's military situation in the bleakest terms. As events would prove, his portrayal was just plain wrong. In time, the country would not only recover, but would also end the war in some cases in a superior military situation than before the fighting. Some of Dayan's colleagues refuted arguments that the defense minister had suffered a psychological collapse at the outset of the war; they could not forgive him, however, for adopting a defeatist manner. "Look," noted archaeologist Yigael Yadin, the former chief of staff, to Chaim Yisraeli, "Dayan never collapsed. Dayan was much more optimistic than I was. Dayan stood with his two feet on the ground. But I have one complaint about Dayan: A leader should give off a spirit of hope. To say that we are winning. Dayan never said that."[52]

By suggesting that Israel's survival was in doubt during those first days of the Yom Kippur War the defense minister offered his critics the ammunition they needed to portray him as desperate. Abba Eban, then foreign minister, recalled hearing from Golda Meir "that Moshe more or less collapsed. Golda told me that Moshe had shown signs of weakness, and vacillation and despondency. . . . He was talking about the destruction of the Third Temple."[53] An accusing finger was eagerly pointed at Dayan. By seeming weak and uncertain, he was slowly digging a political grave for himself, offering himself up as the main figure responsible for Israel's calamity.

In those first few weeks after the war the public reserved its judgment of Dayan. For good reason. Thousands of Israelis were still mobilized at the fronts. While the war was technically over, sporadic shooting continued, distracting the people at home, preventing them from concentrating on the political aspects of what had happened. Public opinion polls were indecisive; while one poll indicated that 64.3 percent of the public had absolute confidence in the defense minister, another showed that only 36 percent thought he should continue in his post.

Slowly, as the public and the politicians absorbed the pain and suffering the war had caused, they turned their wrath on one man—Dayan. "You should become a gardener the rest of your life," Lova Eliav told him bitterly, "putting water on the flowers of the graves of the soldiers who fell."[54] Sixty people signed a public statement and published it on November 20 in *Ha'aretz*, contending, "We see Minister of Defense Dayan as directly responsible . . . for the failues which occurred on the eve of the war."

Conscious of the growing storm, friends of Dayan urged him to take the drastic step of offering to resign as minister of defense. Dayan continued to have the undiluted support of the prime minister and her cabinet. When Justice Minister Ya'acov Shimshon Shapira had recommended at war's end that Dayan quit, the cabinet rallied around Dayan, and forced Shapira out instead, for having the nerve to suggest that the defense minister step down. Gad Ya'acobi and novelist Yizhar Smilansky told Dayan that were he to offer his resignation, he would instantly be asked to withdraw it and, with the support of the Labor party and the public, be rehabilitated. Should he not volunteer to resign, they said, the criticism against him would mount and he would be forced to step down at a later date. None of what anyone had to say fazed the minister of defense. He had approached the prime minister about his stepping down but she had refused to accept his offer to quit. Why should he have to offer it again? Ya'acobi and Smilansky explained that Golda Meir's acceptance of his offer would have been an admission of her own guilt as well, and she would have had to step down. Dayan was unmoved by such logic.

"I have behaved perfectly," he told his visitors. "I have functioned properly. I don't feel that I have to come to any conclusions."[55]

Still the criticism would not go away. An open letter was published in *Yediot Aharonot* condemning Dayan for what had happened: "You have prided yourself that you attained your high office by the will of the people. But the people are loath to see you continue. Strange are the ways of destiny. The entrance of Egyptian divisions into Sinai in 1967 brought about your appointment then and their return in 1973 calls for you resignation now."

The families of those men who had fallen thought him directly responsible for their losses. The cries of "murderer" accompanied Dayan wherever he went. It saddened him, but he knew there was not much he could do.

The government came under increasing pressure to order an official probe into the war. Such a commission was not to Dayan's liking. He told Yoseph Checanover, the legal adviser to the defense ministry, that no judge could examine what had happened during wartime and take into proper account the kind of pressures commanders came under. He was aware that if his objections to the commission became known people would think that he had something to hide.[56]

On November 21, the government appointed a five-member commission of inquiry with a mandate to investigate the intelligence information prior to the war, the evaluation of this information and the decisions taken by the military and political authorities, the IDF's deployment, its state of readiness before the war, and its operations up to the containment of the enemy. Significantly, the panel had an obligation to probe not only military personnel but the political figures as well, including Moshe Dayan.

The chief justice of the Supreme Court, American-born Shimon Agranat, was named to head the panel. Other members were Supreme Court Justice Moshe Landau, State Comptroller Yitzhak Nebenzahl, former chief of staff Yigael Yadin (then a professor of archaeology at Jerusalem's Hebrew University), and former chief of staff Chaim Laskov (then the IDF ombudsman).

Dayan's appearances before the commission were held in secret. The defense minister's main purpose at the hearing, according to one confidante, was "to prove that he had been cautious before the war. He wanted to show the commission that he had based his decisions on the information and answers he had obtained from the military. As far as the Golan Heights was concerned, he had done his best."

Dayan's request on October 2 that Chief of Staff Elazar put his assessment of IDF readiness in writing proved valuable to Dayan. He later submitted that document to the commission as evidence that he had the word of the chief of staff in writing that the army was properly deployed on the eve of battle.

Toward the end of the first session, Agranat put a tough question to him. Dayan had banked on the fact, provided by Israeli intelligence, that Egypt would not attack unless it received long-range bombers, and that Syria would not attack without the Egyptians. Nevertheless, Agranat said, Dayan was still afraid Syria might attack. So why was he surprised by the ultimate attack on both fronts when he possessed intelligence that was correct? Dayan was taken aback by the question. At that point, before the defense minister could answer, another panel member suggested they hear the response the next day. According to one panel member, that was a key moment in the proceedings. Agranat could have required the defense minister to answer on the spot, but he did not think of the probe as the equivalent of a trial where it might benefit to surprise the witness. The panel wanted to be fair to Dayan. It was willing to give him time to prepare his answer.

When the commission reconvened the defense minister was ready with his succinct answer. When northern front commander Hofi had expressed concern that the Syrians might attack, he was thinking of a move against one or two Jewish settlements on the Golan, not an all-out attack. Therefore Dayan had not considered the possibility of a full-scale war, he told the panel. The commission found Dayan's answer to be logical.

The commission also asked him why, with Egyptian and Syrian forces arrayed in defensive positions along the fronts, it was not taken into account that they could have quickly changed to offensive deployments, as Russian tactics taught? Dayan replied that Israel knew about the Russian tactics, but the Egyptians had spread a rumor that they were about to engage in military exercises. It seemed as if they were not bent on attacking Israel. Dayan conceded that the rumor was designed to deceive the Israelis. The military intelligence people had said they too had considered the Russian tactics, but believed the Egyptians were only on exercise. The commission found Dayan's answer acceptable. On the whole, Dayan fared well before the panel. The members were impressed with his integrity and honesty, according to one panel member.[57]

Dayan, of course, could not know how the commission had responded to his presentation. He was pessimistic. Following one appearance, he thought that at least one member, Dr. Nebenzahl, would damn his performance.[58] Despite his fears about Nebenzahl, Dayan became confident that he would emerge vindicted by the Agranat Commission, and he believed that such a verdict would clear him in the minds of the public. For that reason, when aides came to him and urged him to go public with a more concrete version of how he had behaved just before and during the early days of the war, the defense minister refused. For one thing, such disclosures would have meant divulging secret material, which he felt duty-bound to avoid. For another, he would have had to place blame on the IDF and its senior commanders, hardly a pleasant exercise for a minister of defense. Finally, with wars of attrition being fought on both fronts he had no appetite for embroiling himself further in controversy. Aides urged Dayan to allow them to leak information to the Israeli press. He would have none of it. "The Agranat Commission will exonerate me. The people will accept it. And that's it."[59]

WHILE THE COMMISSION of inquiry debated the fate of Moshe Dayan and other Israeli leaders, the public would have a chance to register its

views in the forthcoming elections on December 31, postponed from
October because of the war.

Increasingly, acquaintances of Dayan came to him and urged him to
resign. Leaving a cabinet meeting one day, a young woman, undoubtedly
the widow of a fallen soldier, cried out to Dayan, "Murderer!" The word
affected him deeply. Later he wrote, "It was a dagger in the heart. I
knew that never in my life had I ordered a military operation in which
I myself was not prepared to take part. . . . But this was my own private
truth, and I could never, nor would I ever try, to explain this to the
young woman."[60] Michael Bar-Zohar was one of those who spoke plainly:
"Moshe, you created the feeling in Israel that we are not going to be
attacked by Egypt." The defense minister remained confident that the
Agranat Commission would exonerate him. Bar-Zohar agreed, but added,
"Yes, because they won't ask the right question: 'Who created this feeling
in Israel?' "[61]

On November 28 the Labor party Central Committee approved the
original prewar list of candidates by a vote of 256–107 with 30 abstentions.
At a meeting a week later on December 5 the prime minister, sensing
the growing turmoil within the public and the Labor party, asked for a
vote of confidence through a secret ballot. She wanted anyone who
wished to propose another candidate for prime minister to do so.

At the December 5 committee meeting, Dayan made it clear that he
was prepared to resign as defense minister if Golda Meir so wished, and
he would remove himself from the Labor party's list of Knesset candidates, if the party so wished. These were safe offers. Dayan knew that
the prime minister had no intention of dismissing him as defense minister;
nor did she, as head of the Labor party, have any intention of dropping
him from the candidate list. Protecting Dayan was essential for her own
job security.

"Even if I am not to blame for anything, and someone in the army is,
even then I bear parliamentary responsibility. But what am I to do? To
come to the prime minister and say, 'Madam, there was a mishap here?
At least I am convinced that it was a mishap. I am responsible for this,
directly or indirectly before the Knesset. I'll do anything you want. If
you want to accept my resignation and there is someone else who can
do better—please do.' I am not glued to my seat. If they want to press
charges of criminal negligence, Chief Justice Agranat is more of an authority than any party ideological circle. Justice Agranat at least will
examine the facts and hear all the sides."[62]

The committee meeting lasted into the evening. Speaking last, the
prime minister stood by her defense minister. If she were to repair the
harm done to her and to her government's reputation over the war, she

had to keep her prewar cabinet intact. This meant making sure that Dayan was not dismissed by the party. She argued that under Israeli law all government officials were collectively responsible for all actions. There was no separate parliamentary responsibility for each minister. She wrapped her own future up with Dayan's: If the party wanted her as prime minister, it had to leave her the option of selecting her own ministers. The message was clear. A vote was taken resulting in a resounding triumph for Golda Meir and Moshe Dayan, 293–33 with 17 abstentions.

Soon thereafter Dayan invited himself to see the prime minister at her home in Jerusalem. He wanted to assure her that he would not struggle against a decision to dismiss him if she came to the conclusion that he must go. If the Agranat Commission found even the slightest blemish on his record, he would resign at once, he said. She assured him that she had not hesitated for a moment over whether to reappoint him defense minister in the postelection government, should Labor win. To others, the prime minister acknowledged that if Dayan were to resign, she too would have to step down. She had no intention of letting that happen.

Just six days before the elections, Dayan continued to do well in public opinion polls, though the polls were contradictory. In one poll only seventeen percent said they had little or no confidence in Dayan as defense minister. When people were asked to choose between Dayan and a list of other candidates for the post (Allon, Bar-Lev, Rabin), Moshe Dayan defeated all adversaries, most overwhelmingly.

On election eve tension was high. No one could be sure how voters would feel so soon after the war. The results indicated that the voters were distraught about the government's handling of the war, but not enough to toss them out of office. The Labor-Mapam Alignment dropped six seats but still, with fifty-one seats, was in the strongest position to form the next government.

DAYAN WAS CONFIDENT that Israel could negotiate some kind of peace accord with Egypt, what with the IDF only sixty miles or so from Cairo. "They tried to get territory by force and they failed," he told newsmen, "and now we are sitting on the western side of the Bitter Lake. They have almost no choice."

Early in December Dayan was in Washington working with Kissinger on ways to bring about a peace agreement with the Arabs. The defense minister presented him with the official Israeli government position on a disengagement of forces accord, part of which included Israeli opposition to a return to the pre-1967 war lines. Dayan's personal view, as he communicated it to Kissinger, envisaged an Israeli withdrawal to a line six miles west of the Mitla and Gidi passes, some twenty miles east of the Suez Canal. For its part, Egypt would have to agree to substantial demilitarization near the canal. Dayan and Kissinger got along well and the secretary of state came to think of him as the most innovative of all Israeli negotiators, though he described him privately as "an acquired taste."[63]

During December Kissinger traveled to the Middle East to prepare the way for a peace conference that would bring some stability to the region and implement the goals of Resolution 338. The peace conference was convened in Geneva under joint American-Russian auspices on December 21, 1973. Israel, Egypt, and Jordan attended; the Syrians refused to come and the PLO was not invited. The conference lasted two days.

Four days later, Dayan expressed some optimism that the Egyptians just might be prepared to enter into a partial peace agreement with Israel, which would represent a great departure from their past policy. Speaking to newspaper editors and military correspondents at the Bet Sokolov in Tel Aviv, the defense minister noted that until the October war, the Egyptians had not been prepared for a partial accord on reopening the Suez Canal unless it was part of a general agreement that included an agreed-upon timetable for a complete Israel withdrawal from occupied Arab lands. After the Yom Kippur War, however, he said, "they are now ready, even anxious, to discuss separation of forces and are preparing for the reopening of the Suez Canal and normalization of the area. I told Motta Gur, the Israeli military attaché in Washington and his country's representative in Geneva, not to mention the words 'partial agreement' in Geneva, or any other phrases earlier rejected by the Egyptians. They could talk about disengagement or withdrawal but not partial agreement."

As an outgrowth of the Geneva conference, Kissinger embarked upon the first of his "shuttle diplomacy" missions in the Middle East, flying back and forth between Egypt and Israel for eight days in January 1974. Though the negotiations were difficult, Dayan understood that Egypt's Anwar Sadat would settle for nothing less than including a portion of the Sinai as part of the agreement: He would have to show that his "victory" in the early days of the war had brought Egypt tangible results. During the shuttle, while Dayan was entertaining Kissinger at a garden party at the defense minister's home in Zahala, Dayan, Kissinger, his aide Joseph Sisco, and Chief of Staff Elazar retired to Dayan's bedroom and spread a large map out on the double bed. The secretary of state began explaining why Sadat had objected to the forward line Israel had proposed for its own troops. Dayan cut Kissinger's explanation short: "If I were Sadat, I too would not have agreed to a line so close to the Gulf of Suez." Taking a pencil, Dayan drew a new Israeli line farther back from the Gulf of Suez. Dayan and Kissinger knew that Sadat could never accept such a concession if it came from the Israelis. So the secretary of state presented it to him as an American proposal. The Egyptian leader gave his assent.[64]

Through Kissinger's efforts, the two sides signed a separation of forces agreement on January 18. Israel agreed to withdraw from the west bank of the Suez Canal to a distance of fifteen miles from the eastern bank. Egypt in turn agreed to limit its military presence on the east bank to seven thousand troops, thirty-six artillery pieces, and thirty tanks. UN troops were placed between the two sides in a buffer zone.

IN THE DECEMBER 31 election, the Labor party had won by the narrowest margin in its history, as the disgruntled voters had not yet been aggressive enough to bring about substantive political change. However, during the first two months of 1974, the tide of protest had grown, shapeless, leaderless, but angry and persistent. The movement began among the soldiers, acutely aware of the state of the IDF's unpreparedness at the outbreak of war. They had been gradually returning from the fronts since November and December. By early 1974 most of them were home, anguished and horrified at what they had witnessed; returning to normal life was unthinkable to those who had seen firsthand the IDF's mishaps and the heaviest war casualties in twenty-five years.

The protest movement was initiated by a young captain named Motti Ashkenazi, the commanding officer of "Budapest," the northernmost stronghold on the Suez Canal, the only one near the canal that had not fallen to the Egyptians. He hurled many accusations at the government, but his fury was focused at Moshe Dayan. During his one-man demonstrations outside the prime minister's office in Jerusalem, Ashkenazi repeatedly called for Dayan's resignation. Placards at the rallies read: "Grandma—your defense minister is a failure and 3,000 of your grandchildren are dead." And, "We've had enough of Dayan." The protesters chanted, "The minister of defense is the minister of shame." Ashkenazi said that "in any civilized country, the man who bears responsibility for such a major disaster [as the Yom Kippur War] would have resigned promptly." On February 12 some four thousand people demonstrated outside the prime minister's office.

Gradually the movement grew, though still retaining its amorphous character. Israel had never witnessed public outrage on such a scale. At first rallies attracted hundreds, then thousands. It was as if the December elections had not taken place, as if the commission of inquiry was not sitting and deliberating. The protest movement was not a political one; it had no policy for reform, no list of candidates; it had a single issue: the removal of the government.

The new mood did not effect immediate political change. With its strong conservative bent, the Israeli political system was far too well entrenched to surrender easily. Yet the protests did cause the prime minister increasing difficulty in putting together a coalition government after the elections. With seven fewer Knesset seats, she had less room for maneuver in dealing with the smaller parties. Beset with defense problems, she took over two months to form a government.

TRY AS SHE MIGHT to keep Dayan in her government, to salvage something of her own reputation, Golda Meir could not contain growing public anger. The matter came to a head on February 18 at a closed-door session of senior army officers meeting to discuss the war. During one session a colonel on the Israeli liaison team with the United Nations rose to assail the entire government, Dayan especially, for the war. In the audience were Dayan, the prime minister, and the chief of staff. Dayan felt that the colonel had no business interfering in a political matter such as who ought to be minister of defense. A reprimand was in order. Yet the prime minister and the chief of staff sat in silence, giving their tacit approval to what had been said. On February 25 Dayan announced that he would not serve in the new Golda Meir government. The incident at the army officers meeting was given as the main reason for his decision.

Dayan came under pressure to retract his resignation. Even Henry Kissinger sought to persuade him to change his mind. He viewed the defense minister as essential to a continuation of the Israeli-Syrian peace talks that had accelerated in the wake of the Israeli-Egyptian separation of forces accord. Dayan's decision seemed firm.

It was undoubtedly reinforced when on February 28 he spoke to a gathering at Mount Herzl in Jerusalem in honor of the 162 Israeli soldiers missing after the war. As he spoke, an agitated man and woman began shouting, "Murderer, criminal! You sent our sons to death!" Dayan seemed to pause for a fraction of a second but then continued his slow and somber reading. The shouting persisted. Golda Meir stood nearby with her head bowed.

The prime minister was still insistent that Dayan join the new government. During one cabinet meeting she sent Shimon Peres a note saying she was very disappointed that Dayan considered himself no longer in office. Then at a subsequent meeting of the Labor party Central

Committee, she turned to Dayan and Peres: "You have no right to go."[65]

Thoroughly confounded by these events was Dayan's purported replacement, Yitzhak Rabin. It eventually dawned on him what had happened. "Naive as I was," he wrote later, "it never occurred to me that my appointment [in March 1974] was really no more than a ruse to lure Dayan back into the cabinet. I was led further astray when Dayan sent me a warm and friendly note congratulating me on my appointment and adding that he thought it was a good choice."

On the morning of March 5 Dayan phoned Rabin to ask whether he should sign certain documents or leave them for Rabin to sign upon assuming office. Rabin replied that he was not yet defense minister. To which Dayan countered, "Listen, I know politics. The Central Committee is going to approve the appointment of all the ministers today, and you are going to be defense minister."[66]

Yet when the committee met later that day in Tel Aviv, it urged Golda Meir to continue to form a government and asked Dayan to return to office. Its appeal was not necessary. Sometime during the day information had arrived in Israel that the Syrians were about to launch an all-out attack, and the government met in emergency session. Dayan agreed to return as minister of defense in Golda Meir's new government. "I could not have received a nicer present," the prime minister told Dayan when she heard the news of his intended return. In any event, the Syrians did not launch an attack. On March 10 the prime minister finally presented her new cabinet to the Knesset.

As for Dayan, he was still uncomfortable about staying in office. The public outcry against him was building. How much longer could he hold on? Soon, the Agranat verdict would be made public. If he were exonerated, would that quiet the turmoil? Or ignite it? It seemed as if the entire country was rising up against him.

Some remembered that his public record had begun before October 6, but their voices were not shrill like the demonstrators' outside the prime minister's office. Those who supported him were heard from sparingly. One who did go public was a fifteen-year-old American-born Israeli named Ellen Ross from Kibbutz Gadot in northern Israel. She undoubtedly represented the views of many non-Israelis who wondered why such a fuss was being made about a national hero. In a moving letter written to the *Jerusalem Post* on March 12 she wrote that she always viewed Dayan as Israel's greatest champion and as the symbol of the state. "I never felt afraid living here in Israel. We had our government and our army to protect us and when I thought of that, the face I saw in my mind was Dayan's. And I was not alone."

When she found after the 1973 war that he had been turned into a scapegoat, she felt shock and then rage. "Dayan was not alone in making a mistake during the war. Surely his uniquely brilliant past record can allow him one human failure, even if it did have tragic consequences? . . . I know that Moshe Dayan does not need me, that my approval or my condemnation is less then nothing to him. But I need him, and so does Israel. A house divided cannot stand."

IN EARLY APRIL the Agranat Commission's long-awaited interim report was ready for publication. Of all the bodies judging him after the war, Dayan had the most confidence that the Agranat panel would treat him fairly. Certainly he could expect sympathy from the two former chiefs of staff, he believed. With regard to at least one of them, Chaim Laskov, he was certainly right. "We won't let them get Dayan," Laskov told one acquaintance.

Published on April 2, the report exonerated Golda Meir and Moshe Dayan and laid the blame on Chief of Staff David Elazar, recommending that he quit. The report also recommended that the southern front commander, Gonen, be suspended from active duty pending the completion of the inquiry into the war; and that four intelligence officers be relieved of their posts. Gonen insisted that Dayan was responsible for Israel's reversals in the early phases of the war.

Dayan read the report in Golda Meir's office and again asked if she wished him to resign. Unlike previously, she said simply, "This time it must be the decision of the party." Dayan asked Justice Minister Haim Zadok for a legal ruling on whether the Agranat Commission report required him to resign. Zadok replied that resignation was a political act, not a legal one. Dayan did not have to quit, in Zadok's view.

Reading the report, Minister without Portfolio Israel Galili was astounded. Galili had been actively involved in formulating the powers of the Agranat Commission and noted later that "we took particular care not to impose on the commission any restraint that would prevent its ascertaining the responsibility or guilt or blamelessness of the political echelon." Finding that the commission had drawn no conclusions about Dayan, Galili called it "a grave, an inexcusable injustice that the men in uniform alone should have been singled out for all the blame."[67]

When the report was formally submitted to the government, the chief of staff resigned. At a tense cabinet meeting, with Dayan present, Elazar contended he had been treated unjustly, implying that the defense minister should have shared responsibility with him for the war. How, the chief of staff wondered, could the commission blame him for not mobilizing the troops, but not blame Dayan? One cabinet minister snidely remarked that Dayan had always been willing to take credit for success, but apparently not for failure.

In dealing with Dayan, the panel asked whether the mishap was due to his personal negligence. It laid down one important criterion for judging political leaders, including Dayan: If a minister's advisers had been unanimous in a recommendation, and if that advice turned out to have been a mistake, that minister had to be judged not guilty. Also, a minister could be judged innocent if he followed the advice of one of his advisers who had dissented from the consensus, and that adviser had been proven correct. When the northern front commander had expressed unhappiness with the Syrian troop buildup—in effect, offering a minority viewpoint that had eventually been proven correct—Dayan had thought it wise to call for reinforcement along the northern frontier. Impressed at how Dayan had reacted on this point, the commission excused the defense minister.

It did not fault him for accepting at face value the intelligence reports that suggested that the probability of war was low. Nor did it fault him for the fact that the IDF had been unprepared for war. That was the purview of the chief of staff. Thus he was judged by a different standard. The only valid criterion for judging a military leader, in the commission's view, was to determine whether he had deployed his troops correctly so as to defend against a surprise attack. Elazar had not. The commission therefore had recommended that Elazar be relieved of his post. The commission, examining the written report of October 2 that Dayan had elicited from Elazar on the state of IDF readiness in the Sinai, had been impressed that Dayan had done all he could to find out if the army was properly prepared.

Writing of Dayan in its report, the commission noted in part:

> The central question is whether the defense minister was negligent in carrying out his duties on matters that were within his area of responsibility.

It took into account the following: That Dayan had no special assessing mechanism and received assessments from the General Staff; that on May 21, 1973, he had warned the General Staff to prepare for war in the second half of the summer; that operational details on the deployment of soldiers were the responsibility of the chief of staff, not Dayan.

> The problem which particularly occupied us was whether the defense minister, on Friday, October 5, should have reached an assessment different from that of the chief of

intelligence and the chief of staff. . . . The minister was en-
titled to rely on the strength of the regular army including
the air force to stop the enemy and on the statement of the
chief of staff that the state of alert in the regular
forces . . . was adequate to meet the situation on that
day. . . . We weighed with great seriousness all these matters and reached the conclusion that by standards of reasonable behavior required by the one holding the post of
defense minister, the minister was not required to issue
orders additional to or different from those proposed to him
by the General Staff in accordance with joint assessment and
consultation between the chief of staff and chief of intelligence. . . .[68]

"We do not feel called upon to give our views on what can be considered the Ministers' parliamentary responsibility." The Agranat panel
refused to speculate on the delicate question of whether the special
qualifications or personal experience of any minister—in this case Moshe
Dayan, who had served as chief of staff—should have led him to reach
a conclusion at odds with what was unanimously presented to him by
the military staff.

The commission's verdict on Dayan was a shock to the public.

By asking the questions that it had chosen to ask, the panel emerged
with answers that made the defense minister seem merely an outside
observer of the military scene. The Agranat report praised him for responding effectively to the Syrian buildup before the war but overlooked
the fact that Dayan had done nothing to deal with the Egyptian buildup.
The way the panel described Dayan's role in the defense establishment,
he was not the number one official, he was an unimportant bureaucrat.
It forgave Dayan for being misled by all of his intelligence advisers, who
had suggested that the probability of war was low. It forgave him because
a consensus existed on the probability of war.

It was not as if the intelligence community had kept the buildup from
Dayan. He knew, as he had known on the eve of the 1967 war, that
thousands of troops were gathering at the fronts. He did not react in
1973, fixated as he was by a mind-set that the Arabs would not attack
and the IDF could handle anything. The commission knew of Dayan's
mind-set, knew he had been the architect of that mind-set, and knew
that the intelligence community had been swayed by Dayan's conviction
that the Arabs would not dare attack. The commission knew too of Dayan's great fear of mobilization, that it might be branded provocative, that
it might unleash a war. Still, the commission avoided blaming Dayan.

The public did not. The nation was not in sympathy with the Agranat report. Demobilized soldiers began demonstrating again, calling upon Dayan to resign. The Labor party newspaper *Davar* charged the commission with "flagrant discrimination" in its treatment of Dayan and Elazar. Students, academicians, writers, and artists published their views in newspaper advertisements, insisting that Dayan step down. For his part, Dayan could understand the swelling of public emotion against him. "I don't blame the people," he told his spokesman, Naphtali Lavie. "They could sleep at night because I was in charge and they were disappointed. They cannot understand how things went wrong. I can't share with them all I feel about what went wrong. Agranat didn't charge me because they had the full picture. I could share information with Agranat, but I couldn't share it with the people."[69]

The defense minister also became the focus of an intense and bitter struggle within the Labor party. If Dayan were not fired as minister of defense, one wing of the party, the former Ahdut Avoda faction, planned to stage a rebellion. On the other hand, if Dayan were to be forced out, his own former Rafi wing threatened to stage a walkout. In either case Golda Meir would not be able to form a strong government. The party had sent the prime minister a clear signal. She had reached the end of the road. Now, after months of refusing to accept Dayan's resignation, she finally concluded that he should voluntarily step down. When he did not, the prime minister on April 10 stunned members of the Labor party Knesset and Leadership Bureau by announcing that she was resigning. No one tried to dissuade her. Her resignation meant in effect that the entire government had resigned, including Defense Minister Moshe Dayan.

◆ 14 ◆

REHABILITATION AND

PEACEMAKING

IN ECLIPSE, his vaunted reputation shattered, Moshe Dayan was cast into the political wilderness. His final days as defense minister were spent putting the finishing touches on the Israel-Syria separation of forces accord, signed on June 1, 1974, which required Israel to withdraw its forces slightly to the west of the prewar lines. Two days later he left office as Golda Meir's discredited government gave way to one formed by the Labor party, but with Yitzhak Rabin at its head. Shimon Peres succeeded Dayan as defense minister; Yigal Allon became the new foreign minister.

Though deprived of the defense ministry, Dayan remained a Knesset member, a post that had the singular attraction of keeping him involved, however minimally, in political life. Indifferent toward the life of a parliamentarian, Dayan rarely took part in debates. (He went abroad on occasion to lecture, garnering $4,500 a speech, including expenses.) His few Knesset appearances were taken up with subdued meetings in the members' dining room, a life he had once promised himself he would never lead. He had no real choice. Wishing to detach itself from the Yom Kippur War leadership, the Rabin-led Labor party did what it could to keep Moshe Dayan removed from the levers of power.

The media, which had once been unable to get enough of him, sensed that Dayan's star was flickering, and stayed away. He seemed to sense that the country wanted to hear from him as little as possible. He gave few speeches, appeared little in public. Devoid of political power for the first time in seven years, Dayan rationalized that the phone not ringing in the middle of the night was a relief, that staying home, rather than rushing to an office each morning, had its benefits.

He had none of the joys or consolations of someone newly retired. He lived a form of exile in Zahala, an exile he believed to be unfair. A defensiveness took hold of him. No criminal was he, no guilt should he feel over the war. He could look widows in the eye and feel no troubled conscience. If the public at large had been unforgiving, the Agranat verdict had discerned no wrongdoing. If only the public would follow the lead of the Agranat commissioners. It would not, as Dayan was reminded graphically when he tried to lecture. For example, when he appeared at Bar-Ilan University, bereaved parents, angry and grieving, turned the hall into a dangerous, ugly place. Dayan looked at their faces and felt their anger. Once the public had reached out to him as if he were a holy man. Now he was the devil incarnate. Violence seemed about to erupt at any moment, but Dayan refused to allow the security guards to clear the families from the hall. That might have suggested he could not look into their faces and reject their message. Instead, the guards pulled him off the stage just in time. Those who were at Bar-Ilan that day realized that, try as he might, Dayan would carry the cross of the Yom Kippur War for the rest of his days. In fact, every Independence Day, families of the war's fallen showed up at Zahala to remind Dayan that they had not forgotten, not forgiven.

Dayan sought to act as if the families had not come, willing them away, hoping to erase the past. Yet etched on his face, more bony, more leathery, more pained, was a sadness that betrayed his awareness of their presence and message. It was that sadness that compelled him to look for vindication. "I'm sure that I was right and behaved right," he said in his BBC film biography in April 1981. "I can even look straight into the face of a mother who says I murdered her son."

He spent a good deal of his time in the years after the war engaging in a craft he had always loved, writing. In February 1974 the British publisher Weidenfeld and Nicolson offered him the handsome sum of $460,000 to write his memoirs, and once he left office in June he began the task. It occurred to Dayan that, while his career had been filled with challenge and adventure, the only part that truly interested him—at least in the recounting—were the later years. He turned to Yael and asked her to write a draft of the period up to 1948. To her first draft he would add "my own flavor."[1] He offered to pay her. Yael at first balked at helping her father; she was about to start another novel, and she questioned whether part of someone's memoirs should be crafted by a relative. Might that not rob the book of its authenticity? Fatherly pressure was applied—if Yael did not agree to do her part, the memoirs would not get done—and eventually the two Dayans embarked on the project.

Meanwhile, Middle East diplomacy was on hold. The pace had been so intense during the past year that a cooling-off period appeared in order. Time was needed to test the two separation of forces accords and to determine whether further progress toward peace was possible. American attention was focused on the trauma of deciding whether to unseat a president for the first time in its history. Despite these constraints, the new prime minister, Yitzhak Rabin, hoped to secure a series of limited accords with the Arabs, convinced that a comprehensive peace was unrealistic. Aiming as well at a limited accord, Egypt demanded the return of both the Mitla and Gidi passes as well as the economically significant Abu Rudeis oil fields in southern Sinai. In return, Israel required an Egyptian promise of nonbelligerency.

Reflecting a certain optimism alive in Israel, Dayan sensed that this country and Egypt might be able to strike a bargain. "Contrary to what happened after past wars," he suggested, "the United States and the Soviet Union are not prepared this time to settle for a cease-fire. They are not going to leave the problem alone. They want a settlement, and they are pushing for it together. And there is no better mediator than Kissinger."

Even the American secretary of state's zeal in the spring of 1975 could not induce the Egyptians to provide the needed promise of nonbelligerency. Israeli-Egyptian negotiations broke down. By fall, however, Cairo had softened its position, promising not to use force against Israel for the duration of the agreement. This promise was part of the Sinai II interim agreement that was approved by the Knesset by a 70–43 vote on September 3. Voting against it was Moshe Dayan. Stung by the Yom Kippur War, Dayan believed that Israel could not afford to withdraw without an unconditional Egyptian pledge of nonbelligerency, something not contained in the Sinai II accord. Dayan argued from the Knesset rostrum that the Egyptians did not seem at all interested in ending the state of war. "We are making concessions—very significant concessions—but are getting nothing in return from the Egyptians. What we are getting is compensation from the Americans in lieu of Egyptian concessions. Well, this is good for Egypt but bad for Israel."

DAYAN HAD a peripheral involvement in the Entebbe hijacking during the early summer of 1976. On June 27 Israeli passengers aboard an Air France jet were hijacked by Palestinian Arab terrorists to Entebbe,

Uganda, a country that was 2,620 miles away from Israel and hostile to the Jewish state. The terrorists were demanding the release of "freedom fighters" from jails in Israel and three other countries. One suggestion made during the afternoon of July 4 by a member of Rabin's cabinet (as well as by Defense Minister Peres, Chief of Staff Motta Gur, and some military officers) was that Moshe Dayan should go to Uganda to help negotiate the release of the hostages, in view of his previous close friendship with Idi Amin, the president of Uganda. Rabin, who later termed the idea "truly bizarre," could not agree, fearing that Amin might simply humiliate the former defense minister as he had done others in the past, or even hold him prisoner too. "My reaction," wrote Rabin later, "bordered on disbelief. Placing a famous and important individual like Moshe Dayan in the hands of Uganda's unpredictable tyrant? Further strengthen the blackmailers' hand and leave ourselves absolutely no room to maneuver? Obviously I rejected the proposal and the subject was dropped."[2]

Another approach was accelerated, a daring rescue plan of the hostages. Peres was eager to find out what Dayan thought of the idea. He tracked down his predecessor at a restaurant where Dayan and Rahel were dining with Australian visitors. Asking the others to excuse them, Peres took Dayan aside to a secluded table and outlined the rescue attempt. "It's a beauty of a plan!" Dayan remarked.[3] Dayan's encouraging words were what Peres had been waiting to hear. He now felt confident about sending IDF soldiers off to Entebbe. On the evening of July 4 the rescue was successfully carried off.

That fall Dayan tried his hand at running an afternoon newspaper called *Hayom Hazeh*, Hebrew for "This Day." It appeared for the first time on September 1, 1976, and was self-described as "Zionist and independent." With Dayan as editor in chief, the newspaper was expected to hew to a hawkish editorial line. Unenthusiastic about its prospects, Dayan confessed that it would be a miracle if it succeeded. He limited his involvement in the newspaper to presiding over meetings on how to write editorials. His name was not enough to woo advertisers, and the newspaper folded after only three months.

Then toward the end of November Dayan spoke publicly about the most sensitive issue within Israel's defense establishment—Israeli nuclear weapons. For years Israeli leaders refused to acknowledge that Israel had such weapons, and indicated only that Israel would not be the first to introduce nuclear weapons into the region—an implied threat that Israel would, if attacked by nuclear weapons, retaliate in kind. News reports from time to time mentioned Israel's nuclear capability, but Israel's policy of not publicly boasting of its nuclear weapons remained in force. It was that policy that Dayan suggested should be changed.

To a dinner of the Advertisers Association in Tel Aviv on November 30 he decried Israel's reliance on the tank and asserted that Israel should develop "the nuclear option." Asked why he spoke about an Israeli nuclear option, Dayan said, "The option is no secret and I don't think things should be covered up." He disagreed with those Israeli military leaders who wanted to purchase thousands and thousands of additional tanks. "The idea that Israel has to have 10,000 tanks is destructive." Sweden, he noted, maintained a nuclear option and no one called it an aggressor. So did France. Israel should do so too, he said. "Then should the Arabs decide one day to throw against us the thousands of tanks and missiles they are accumulating, we'll be able to tell them 'We can destroy you too.' "[4]

As part of an interview with *Time* correspondent Marlin Levin on March 23, 1976, Dayan, in an unpublished section, had been asked why he so forcefully advocated a nuclear option for Israel. He answered that "Israel has got to the point where we cannot really increase our conventional forces. According to published figures, we have three times as many tanks as France. We cannot really tie our balance of forces to many more additional quantities of conventional arms. You reach a point with conventional arms that they are just as dangerous as nuclear power. Israel has no choice. We cannot physically, financially, economically with our manpower go on acquiring more and more tanks and more and more planes. Shortly you'll have all of us maintaining tanks and oiling them."[5]

Only a figure of Dayan's stature could have addressed the subject of Israeli nuclear warfare in public without incurring public censure. If Dayan hoped to start a public debate on the subject, he did not succeed. Defense Minister Peres and Foreign Minister Allon let it be known that they disagreed with Dayan; they believed that Israel could in fact tolerate a prolonged conventional arms race; for that reason, it had no need to publicly acknowledge it was in possession of a nuclear option.

ISRAELI ELECTIONS were scheduled for the fall of 1977, but a political crisis occurred, altering that timetable. The trouble began when three American F-15 fighter planes landed late one Friday afternoon in December 1976. The introduction of these, the most advanced warplanes yet developed, into the Israeli air force was sensational military news. Acquiring the F-15s was a major achievement for Israel, and Rabin arranged for a welcoming ceremony at Ben-Gurion Airport, complete with government leaders and top military men. The fact that the planes would be landing less than an hour before the onset of the Sabbath in Jerusalem and seventy-four minutes before its onset in Tel Aviv meant that those attending would be driving home Friday evening , thus desecrating the Sabbath. When Rabin's coalition partner, the National Religious party, protested, the ensuing controversy led the prime minister to resign and call for elections to be advanced to May 17.

The political turmoil breathed new life into Moshe Dayan's political career. For nearly three years he had stayed on the sidelines, but now he intimated that he wanted to return to Labor's inner circle. Having served under such luminaries as David Ben-Gurion and Golda Meir, he told acquaintances, he no longer wished to be sidestepped by the lesser lights, Rabin and Peres. Dayan passed word through his former aide Haim Yisraeli that if he were not included in the Labor party's election leadership team—the party's leading cabinet ministers if Labor took power—he would consider himself free to bolt the party. In the winter of 1976 that threat did not have the same effect as in earlier years. Labor party leaders felt no need to lift Dayan into the leadership. In the days leading to Labor's convention on February 22, Peres challenged Rabin as an alternative candidate to Rabin for prime minister. Assuming that Peres would win the party's nomination, Dayan suggested himself as a candidate for foreign minister in the Peres government. Peres made no promises.[6] In any event, Rabin narrowly defeated Peres to become the party's candidate for prime minister.

The Labor party's main opponent in the election was the right-wing Likud party, headed by Menachem Begin, a former leader of the Irgun and for years the head of the political opposition. Yigael Yadin's new Democratic Movement for Change (DMC) appeared to be capturing a sizable portion of the votes—some even forecast that it could win as many as fifteen to twenty seats in the Knesset. Public opinion polls in mid-March indicated that Rabin was almost certain to win the prime ministership on May 17, but the race was likely to be close.

Still shunted aside by Labor, Dayan now thought it wise to explore other political options. His strongest personal associations had been with Labor, but on the ideological level he felt closer to Menachem Begin's right-wing Likud party. For that reason, he made it clear to Begin that he was prepared to join a Begin-led cabinet. Dayan told the Likud leader that he did not want to be "second fiddle" to anyone—but Begin. He would accept any post in a Begin-led government.[7] Only a promise from the Labor party leadership that none of the West Bank would be ceded without another election kept Dayan from bolting to Likud before the 1977 election.

Dayan identified easily with Begin's steadfastness toward the West Bank though he was uneasy about the Likud's hopes to annex the region. However, according to Dayan's spokesman Naphtali Lavie, Dayan found

Begin's oratorical style bounding on cheap theatrics, and winced at his bombast and hyperbole. What was more, he had little respect for Begin's understanding of the Arabs: He doubted that Begin could negotiate with the Arabs without offending their pride.

In the spring, with the election campaign at its peak, Dayan was ready to join Likud, but he needed assurances from Begin that a Likud government would not annex the West Bank. Dayan brought Begin a document which, if he signed, would enable the former defense minister to join a Likud-led government. The document stated that "as long as there are negotiations between Israel and the Arab states, no Israeli sovereignty will be extended to the administered territories or parts of them. That includes the West Bank." The document went too far for Begin. He refused to sign, fearing that potential Likud votes would be lost if word spread that Begin had promised not to annex the West Bank. Still, Begin suggested to Dayan that the two men leave the door open, in other words, that, if Likud won the election, they could talk again.

Meanwhile, events were conspiring to help Likud to victory. Early in April a political earthquake occurred when the Israeli newspaper *Ha'aretz* discovered that Leah Rabin, the wife of the prime minister, had kept an illegal foreign currency account in the United States after he had retired as Israeli ambassador to Washington and had returned to Israel. In response, on April 7 Rabin announced that he was resigning from office and withdrawing as Labor's candidate for prime minister. A few days later Peres was named as the Labor party nominee for prime minister. Rabin took a leave from his office as interim prime minister, and Peres took his place.

Few had expected the Likud to triumph on May 17. But the 1.8 million Israeli voters who went to the polls that day produced a revolution, rejecting the Labor party, which had been in power for the entire twenty-nine-year history of the state. They voted into office the Likud, which had been in opposition all that time. Menachem Begin finally became prime minister after eight unsuccessful attempts. The final results of the election gave the Likud forty-three Knesset seats (four more than in 1973); the Labor Alignment won only thirty-two (nineteen fewer than in 1973); and the Democratic Movement for Change, fifteen, a remarkable achievement for a party only six months old. The National Religious party (NRP) won twelve seats, two more than in 1973; the rest of the seats were shared among nine other parties. Begin was able to form a new government supported by the Likud, the NRP, Agudat Yisrael (with four seats)—and Moshe Dayan.

For Begin to select Dayan as his foreign minister seemed almost inconceivable to many. On election day Golda Meir dismissed the constant speculation that Dayan might defect from Labor. He was capable of nearly everything, she told Gideon Rafael, the former director-general of the Foreign Ministry, but he would not leave the party.[8] Even Begin himself had sounded as if he had no intention of appointing Dayan as a Likud minister. Receiving a delegation of bereaved parents shortly before the election, he reassured them he would never appoint Dayan as minister of defense or to any post that touched on defense matters in the slightest degree.

Still, Begin badly wanted Dayan. On Saturday morning, May 21, Begin offered Dayan the post of foreign minister. For Begin the choice was not so startling at all. He had long admired Dayan. To the prime minister designate, the IDF was the key to Israel's existence and to its security, it was the instrument that had brought Jewish liberation, and no one symbolized the Jewish army more to him and to countless others than Moshe Dayan. Unsurprised by Begin's offer and eager to take the job for his own reasons, Dayan still wanted to ascertain that he was not joining a government that would disrupt whatever dim prospects existed for peace negotiations by immediately announcing that it would annex the West Bank. Dayan also made it clear that, since he had been elected on a Labor party ticket, he might give up his Knesset seat. Begin noted that he had not offered Dayan the cabinet post to gain a parliamentary seat. Dayan promised to give an answer after Begin's response on annexation.

Begin could have chosen one of his cronies in his Herut party (the main party in the right-wing Likud Bloc). Their political obeisance was guaranteed; instead he chose a maverick, an independent spirit, a man who owed nothing to Likud, who seemed to owe nothing to anyone. He chose a man who only four years earlier had, in the eyes of many in his country, been responsible for Israel's most calamitous war. None of this bothered Begin. "Yes, Dayan has lost standing as a leader here in Israel," Begin explained to his aide Yehiel Kadishai, "but in the world— both to our friends and our enemies—he remains a symbol. He is the man with the eyepatch! He stands for staunch Zionism. He stands for strength." Dayan was, in Begin's words, "a man whom no foreign dignitary would dare meet without checking to make sure his pants are pressed!"[9]

Such considerations were important to Begin, who had been delegitimized by some of his political rivals until now as a former terrorist and future warmonger. Dayan's international recognition and prestige would purchase legitimacy abroad for Begin's government; Dayan would soften Begin's reputation and make him palatable to world leaders. Some in the Likud rankled at the idea that Begin needed Dayan because of his international popularity. "What we need as foreign minister now," Begin's new foreign press adviser Shmuel Katz told him, "is not a popular person but somebody who is prepared to be unpopular.[10]

To Begin, those who had articulated Israel's foreign policy of late had suffered from a faintness of heart. He was particularly appalled at the treatment Rabin had received that March at the White House with President Jimmy Carter. After promising Rabin that he had no intention of voicing his private view that Israel should withdraw from the occupied lands except for minor adjustments, Carter went ahead and said the same thing in public soon thereafter. In appointing Dayan, Begin hoped to avoid such difficulties in the future. Should Israel and the Arabs negotiate seriously about Israel's final frontiers, Dayan ranked among the most skillful of Israel's negotiators, his experience dating back to the 1948 war.

Ariel Sharon, who served in the first Begin government as minister of agriculture, theorized that Begin chose Dayan in order to add one more militant figure to the list of Ezer Weizman and Sharon himself. Including Dayan would strengthen the Arab belief that Israel was preparing for war, and induce the Arabs to negotiate before it was too late.[11]

The choice of Dayan, and Dayan's willingness to serve in a Begin government, aroused a good deal of public concern and criticism, and some of Begin's own Likud members recoiled at the prospect of finding themselves allied with the man whom many blamed for the early reverses of the 1973 Yom Kipper War. Begin was adamant.

For the next few days Dayan considered the offer. He seemed inclined to take it, but worried about the public reaction. He sought Rahel's advice. He sensed that she was mostly concerned at his having to suffer further public criticism. To him the appointment made eminent sense. No matter how little he liked politics, no matter how unambitious he claimed to be, he thrived only when in power. He was not meant to sit on the back benches of parliament, make speeches, and drink tea in the Knesset dining room. He had not enjoyed his political banishment these past few years. In choosing him to be foreign minister, Begin was offering Dayan the chance to return to the central arena of public life and, more importantly, political rehabilitation.

The timing was auspicious. Dayan had a premonition that something was afoot in Middle East diplomacy. He could not put his finger on it, but he sensed that Egypt was eager to seek the return of all of its lost territory in the Sinai. Israel might soon become involved in peace negotiations. Dayan told Naphtali Lavie that he would hate not to be involved in such peace talks. Indeed, his presence might be crucial to the outcome. "This is something I can't resist."[12]

He did not. During the night of May 22–23 Begin was rushed to the hospital with a suspected heart attack. On that morning of May 23, Begin, from his hospital bed, gave Dayan the final assurance that there would be no sovereignty imposed over the occupied lands while peace negotiations were in progress. Dayan accepted the job. That same morning Dayan asked Ezer Weizman, who had been designated by Begin to become the new defense minister, to visit him at Zahala. Concerned that Begin might be unable to take office, Dayan proposed that Weizman become prime minister; he was prepared to serve under Weizman as foreign minister. Weizman was flattered, but Dayan's concern was overblown. Begin was suffering only from exhaustion. After six days he was released from the hospital. Weizman wondered whether Dayan ever regretted his haste in summoning his former brother-in-law on May 23.[13]

Still, some Israelis found the Dayan appointment reprehensible. Sixty people who had lost relatives during the Yom Kippur War demonstrated outside Begin's Tel Aviv home. When Begin and Dayan showed up, they booed them and even threw stones. One day in late May one thousand demonstrators gathered outside Herut headquarters in Tel Aviv to shout slogans for and against, but more against, the Dayan selection. Some seven hundred anti-Dayan protesters held signs saying "Fascism Won't Work," "The Likud and Dayan Equals Failure," and "Enough, Enough, Enough of Dayan." Another three hundred were on hand urging Dayan on. One of their placards read: "For the Sake of Israel, We Need Dayan." On the day Begin presented his cabinet to the Knesset, Israelis picketed on the Knesset lawn. Motti Ashkenazi was there, renewing his crusade to keep Moshe Dayan from public life. "There may be a statute of limitations for theft of antiquities, but not for responsibility for the deaths of 3,000 young men," one placard read. Overall the public appeared to have mixed views about the selection. One poll showed that 40.5 percent were disenchanted with Dayan becoming foreign minister. Yet another 39.5 percent favored the selection. Labor party members were, however, quite decisive.

Dayan's selection was "like lightning in the middle of the day," suggested Chaim Bar-Lev, Labor's campaign manager.[14] Having done all that they could to push Dayan into a corner, the party's leaders nonetheless took his defection as a huge personal insult. It was not enough that he had gone over to the enemy; in deciding to remain in the Knesset, his seat had been lost to Labor. Dayan had asked for expert advice and found that there was ample precedent for keeping his seat. Israel Kargman, the former chairman of the Knesset Finance Committee, called Dayan's defection an act of political prostitution and rank treachery.

Forgotten was the fact that Dayan's connections to the Labor party had been tenuous at best. What was more, Dayan had always had little enthusiasm for political parties, Labor included. If others thought he was a traitor, it did not bother him. He could only feel comfortable in a party if its platform and ideology conformed with his. Such thinking was anathema to many in Labor and to one person in particular it was like stabbing a knife in her back.

Undoubtedly Golda Meir's fury was based in part on a feeling of resentment: She had been banished as well from public leadership after the Yom Kippur War, but she was remaining outside, and Dayan was being brought back to a leadership position. It did not seem fair. She could not strike back at an amorphous public, but she could strike back at Moshe Dayan. So when he sought to pay a courtesy call on the party's elder stateswoman, she always had some excuse why they could not meet. Finally, he got the message.

Begin won Knesset approval for his government on June 20, 1977. There had been rumors that the Labor party would seek to disrupt Dayan's maiden speech either by loud taunts or a mass walkout. Friends advised him not to speak, to wait a few weeks until tempers cooled. He said no. When he spoke, there were loud taunts. Cries of "Shame" and "Resign" were heard, but there was no mass walkout. He had survived the storm.

DAYAN COULD NOT wait to search for partners in peace negotiations. Egypt was the main target. He believed that Anwar Sadat needed an agreement with Israel if only to gain large amounts of needed American aid. To probe for potential peace partners, Dayan knew that he would have to engage at first in secret diplomacy. So frequently did he do so that Naphtali Lavie once quipped that the job of Dayan's media adviser consisted entirely of concealing the events taking place from the media.[15]

Following the Sinai II accord of September 1975 an attempt had been made to work out a further interim accord between Israel and Egypt. Sadat eventually moved away from that concept, believing that there should be a comprehensive peace worked out between Israel and the various Arab states—not just Egypt. In this way, Egypt would not be attacked by other Arabs for gaining special advantage in a separate peace with the Jewish state. Begin too sensed that the time for interim agreements was over and he sought to find out if it would be possible to reconvene the Geneva conference. Begin met Carter in the White House on July 19 and proposed that Israel and the United States try to revive Geneva.

At first, Dayan was hardly methodical. He visited leaders whenever he saw the faintest spark of hope. The initial opportunity for secret diplomacy arose very soon after he took office in June. Dayan asked Azriel Eynav, his businessman friend, to help him breath some life into Israeli-Indian relations. The two countries did not have diplomatic relations. Seemingly in a good position to forge ahead, Eynav had recently developed close connections to powerful Indian political figures. Once Eynav had contacted the Indian prime minister Morarji Desai and won his approval for Begin or Dayan to visit him, Dayan informed Begin of the unofficial invitation. Such an invitation seemed close to a snub to the formalistic Begin. He insisted upon a formal invitation. Eynav was not put off. He composed his own telex to the Israeli prime minister, inviting Begin or Dayan to India, and signed it Azriel Eynav on behalf of Desai. Begin approved. He urged Dayan to accept the invitation. The foreign minister left in secret on August 14.

All twelve first-class seats on an Alitalia jet had been rented by Eynav for Dayan and his party (including three security guards). To protect the secret, Dayan removed his eyepatch and put on a wig, mustache, and sunglasses. "Azriel," Dayan said, nursing a dry martini as their plane departed for India, "if this succeeds, you have made history which Ben-Gurion, Sharett, and Golda did not succeed in doing." Indeed, there had never been an invitation to an Israeli leader from the Indian prime minister before.[16]

Dayan could not contain his glee upon landing and noticing a battalion of Indian soldiers saluting him. Entering a large black Mercedes, he turned to Eynav and said in English, "You made it. We did the impossible." A nervous Eynav answered, "Wait and see."

Boarding a Soviet-made Ilyushin plane, Dayan flew to New Delhi. He wanted to take off his sunglasses and put back on his eyepatch. Eynav said no, it was too soon. They were taken to a villa in the suburbs. Walking down some steps to take a drink before visiting the prime minister, Dayan slipped and lost consciousness for a brief moment. Eynav and the guards were beside themselves. "What are you excited about?" Dayan asked, coming back to life a few seconds later. "It happens." Eynav cautioned Dayan to drink only water, no more alcohol.

Soon Dayan was greeted by the Indian prime minister. Their talk was cordial and eventually Desai agreed to consider establishing diplomatic relations with Israel. Unfortunately for Dayan, word of his secret visit to India was leaked to *Time* magazine. When a brief reference to it was made in its October 3 edition, Desai phoned Eynav to say that the disclosure was bound to hurt him politically, and no further meetings could be held. Officially, both Israel and India denied that Dayan had held such a meeting.

EIGHT DAYS AFTER sitting down with the Indian prime minister, Dayan was on another crucial secret diplomatic mission—spending two days with Jordan's King Hussein in London on August 22 and 23. For the sake of the king, Dayan had to keep their meeting a secret even from the foreign minister's British bodyguards. Leaving his hotel, Dayan headed to a house, remained there for a few moments, left by a back door, got into a waiting car, and then proceeded to a private home, where he met Hussein. Meanwhile, newsmen were tracking down rumors of a possible Dayan-Hussein meeting in England. An Israeli embassy spokesman, suggesting that Dayan had arrived for a "quiet evening," did what he could to pour water on the rumors. "We don't need London for that. There is the Jordan River."

Dayan noticed a change in Hussein since the last time he had seen him in the early 1970s. The foreign minister hoped to sound out Hussein on a political settlement of the West Bank. The king seemed to Dayan withdrawn and subdued. His style of speaking was terse, he answered questions with only a yes or no. Why the king acted in this way was not clear. Perhaps, thought Dayan, it was because the Arab countries, via the 1974 Rabat decision, had recognized the PLO as the sole authorized representative of the Palestinians, hence replacing Hussein. That decision had pulled the carpet out from under Hussein's once dominant position in the West Bank.

Hussein had great respect for Dayan, considering him a man of extraordinary military talent, thinking that he, as a military man, had much in common with him. Hussein's message was clear: He would not force himself on the Palestinians. Dayan asked Hussein if he thought a division of the West Bank between Jordan and Israel might serve as a basis for an Israel-Jordan peace treaty. Hussein said no. Partitioning the West Bank would mean Hussein had accepted that part of the West Bank would be joined to Israel. He would be counted as a traitor. The only solution, he stressed, was for Israel to return to the pre-1967 war borders. Privately, Dayan saw Hussein as a spoiled child, someone who had always been given everything he wanted and so expected everything served up to him on a silver platter.

GIVEN HUSSEIN'S hard line and the Arab insistence that the PLO was the sole representative of the Palestinians, Dayan thought there was little chance of achieving a negotiated settlement on the West Bank and in the Gaza Strip. He placed his hopes on Egypt as the most likely partner for peace with Israel.

A crucial break came when the foreign minister received an invitation in early September 1977 to visit King Hassan of Morocco. Again, the visit was to be secret. Some time before, the king had chatted with a member of Israel's Mossad, presumably on the prospects of achieving some fresh understanding between Israel and Egypt over the Sinai.

This trip was not Dayan's first visit to Morocco. He had been there in 1953 on his way to England to attend the senior army officers' course. Now he was no tourist. The king greeted Dayan at the royal palace at Marrakech. At Dayan's request, Hassan sent a message to Cairo suggesting a high-level Israeli-Egyptian meeting. It was Dayan's view that the meeting could be between Begin or himself, and Sadat or Hosni Mubarak, the Egyptian vice-president. Within four days of Dayan's return to Jerusalem, word came from Cairo that the Egyptians were ready for such talks. The king informed Dayan on September 9 that Egypt had suggested either a Sadat-Begin summit or a lower-level meeting between Egyptian deputy prime minister Hassan Tuhami and Dayan. Despite Dayan's reservations, Begin was prepared to go straight to Anwar Sadat. Egypt, however, had second thoughts about a summit at this stage.

Dayan asked Meir Rosenne, the Foreign Ministry's legal adviser, to begin drafting a possible Israeli-Egyptian peace treaty. Rosenne's working draft contained forty-six points and was sent on to Washington and Cairo for perusal. Soon after, President Carter penned a letter to Anwar Sadat, appealing to him to test Menachem Begin's good intentions to accede to an early revival of the Geneva peace conference.

Arrangements went ahead for a secret meeting between Foreign Minister Dayan and Deputy Prime Minister Tuhami on September 16. Washington was to be kept in the picture. Dayan was due to be in the United States on September 18 for the opening of the United Nations General Assembly. No one noticed his vanishing act in Brussels. The plane that was supposed to have taken him on to the United States took off without him. He was driven to Paris, and then flown by private jet to Morocco. Donning the "secrecy kit" composed of a wig, mustache, and sunglasses, Dayan arrived in Morocco this time wondering whether the Egyptians were ready to offer true peace to Israel. He was confident that if they were, Israel would return all of Sinai to them.

"Do you really want peace?" Dayan asked Tuhami when they first met.

"At least as much as you do," was the Egyptian's reply.

Tuhami was a frightened man, fearful that his life was in danger for meeting an Israeli leader, even in utmost secrecy. Only Sadat and Mu-

barak knew of his visit to Morocco. He explained that Sadat would agree
to open a dialogue with Israel, but only after Begin agreed in principle
that Israel would withdraw from all of the occupied territories—the Sinai,
Golan Heights, West Bank, and Gaza Strip. King Hassan urged Tuhami
not to be so rigid, not to expect that Israel would agree to such a precondition. Tuhami took a tough line. The Egyptian president, he said,
was not prepared to shake the hand of Menachem Begin as long as there
was one Israeli soldier on Arab soil. (On Hassan's advice, Tuhami
amended the phrase to be "Egyptian soil.")

Dayan suggested this was no way to begin negotiations. What if the
Israeli prime minister did not agree to such a demand? Did that mean,
Dayan asked, that there would be no further meetings of this kind? All
Tuhami would do was repeat that Begin had to commit himself to with-
drawing from all the occupied territories. Don't count on it, Dayan re-
plied.

Begin, the foreign minister said, would certainly want to meet at the
highest Egyptian level without committing himself to anything. Then
Dayan expressed his "firm belief that we could arrive at a suitable arrangement with Egypt."

Had Dayan promised Tuhami that Israel would withdraw from all of
Sinai at this point? Clearly the Egyptian deputy prime minister gained
that impression from his talks with the foreign minister. Those who have
read the minutes of the Dayan-Tuhami meeting insist that Dayan did
not make such a commitment. By asserting that the foreign minister had
committed Israel to such a withdrawal, the Egyptians found it easier to
explain why President Sadat had entered into dialogue with Israel two
months later.

Dayan and Tuhami agreed that they should meet again in two weeks.
Dayan agreed to report to Begin on Sadat's request that Israel commit
itself to withdraw from the territories as a prior condition for continuing
the talks. When Dayan did so, Begin refused to give any such pledge.
The prime minister did agree that Dayan should meet again with Tuhami
in two weeks. As it turned out they would not meet then, but only in
another two and a half months.

ON SEPTEMBER 18, 1977, Dayan flew to New York. There to attend the
UN General Assembly, he had a larger purpose, working out preparations
with Washington for the planned Geneva peace conference. Uninformed
about the Dayan-Tuhami meeting, the Americans pressed ahead toward
Geneva.

On September 19 Dayan met American secretary of state Cyrus Vance in Washington and then with President Carter in the White House. Carter was in a belligerent mood, angry at listening to television statements by Agriculture Minister Ariel Sharon declaring that Israel planned to settle hundreds of thousands of Jews in Jewish settlements in the occupied territories. Dayan took the brunt of Carter's anger. Such statements, the president said, could keep the Palestinian Arabs from joining peace talks. Israel, he added, was more stubborn than the Arabs. "You put obstacles on the path to peace." This was a refrain Carter would utter often in the near future.

Dayan angrily replied that Israel did not think the settlements were illegal nor had it ever hidden its contempt for American peace plans that required it to withdraw from most of the occupied lands. What was preventing peace, Dayan suggested, was the Arabs, not Israel, by refusing to reconcile themselves to Israel's existence. He was prepared to recommend to Begin that no more civilians be permitted into the settlements; only uniformed Israelis would be allowed into military sites. (When Dayan forwarded this idea to Begin, the prime minister turned it down.)

The gap between American and Israeli views was wide. The president had demanded that the Palestinians be represented at Geneva. Up until this time, the Israelis had opposed the idea of a separate and independent Palestinian Arab delegation at Geneva, arguing that this would pave the way for a Palestinian state. Israel insisted that the Palestinians be part of a delegation of an Arab state. Carter, however, also demanded that Israel accept a Palestinian entity or homeland on the West Bank and in the Gaza Strip. Dayan made it clear that Israel would never accept such a Palestinian state, nor would it talk to the PLO.

On September 29 American officials presented Dayan the draft of a joint declaration that the U.S. and the USSR would issue as their Middle East policy. It called for the resumption of the Geneva conference no later than December 1977, with the U.S. and the USSR serving as cochairmen; it called for the participation of all parties, including "those of the Palestinian people." The next day Dayan passed on to Vance Israel's displeasure with the document, interpreting Carter's policy to mean that Israel would have to abandon most of the occupied territories and negotiate with the Palestine Liberation Organization on the establishment of a Palestinian state. Sensing that there was no way to avoid a direct confrontation with President Carter, Dayan decided to try to mobilize American public opinion on Israel's side. He gave one interview after another and initiated five major conferences of Jewish activists in five large Jewish centers—New York, Chicago, Los Angeles, Atlanta, and Miami.

Speaking to three hundred United Jewish Appeal leaders in Chicago, Dayan said: "We are being told by Carter and Vance that if we want peace, we must accept the Arab terms—we must give up the Golan Heights, the Sinai and the West Bank. Maybe there will be peace if we do all that but there will be no Israel. We are not going to accept this . . . ."

As for allowing a Palestinian state to rise on the West Bank, that would be nothing less than "sowing the seeds for future destruction. We will not accept the PLO. We will not talk to them. We will not negotiate with them. We will not accept the American position that we talk to them. And we will go to Geneva only with the understanding that the U.S.-Soviet joint statement is not binding."[17]

From his sickbed in Tel Aviv, Prime Minister Begin urged Dayan to suspend his talks in the United States, but the foreign minister convinced him that he should stay on and renew his conversations with American officials. For six hours during the evening of October 4 Carter and his aides again met Dayan, this time in New York. The president remained throughout the evening except when he had to appear at a dinner engagement.

Carter wanted to talk about the American-Soviet declaration. Dayan preferred to talk about the Geneva conference. Dayan raised the question of whether Israel could go to Geneva without accepting the two-power declaration or if the declaration was regarded by the U.S. and the USSR as the basis for Geneva.

No, said Vance, accepting the joint declaration was not a precondition for Israel attending Geneva.

The two sides then wrangled over the composition of the Arab delegation. Israel had favored delegations representing individual Arab states. Carter pressed Dayan to accept the concept of a united Arab delegation; that delegation would include PLO members who were not well-known. (Dayan quipped that by the time they reached Geneva they would be very well known.) "I have only one eye," Dayan said, "but I'm not blind." Acknowledging Israeli sensitivity on the PLO issue, the Americans agreed secretly to let the Israelis have veto power over which Palestinians would be able to attend Geneva.[18]

Prepared to concede that a unified Arab delegation could attend Geneva—rather than separate ones, each affiliated with a different Arab state—Dayan slyly asked President Carter not to give the impression that Israel had offered the concession voluntarily. Carter should make it appear that the U.S. had forced the idea upon Israel and it had reluctantly accepted. "If the Arabs know it comes from us they will certainly reject it," Dayan told Carter. "You should say that we object, and then you can try to force it on us." Carter agreed to the notion of a unified delegation.[19]

Returning from dinner at 9:30 P.M., Carter asked Dayan if he would accept an Israeli withdrawal to the pre-1967 war lines within the framework of a peace treaty. "You once said you had been against the capture of the Golan. Have you changed your mind?"

The clock could not be turned back, was Dayan's only response.

No withdrawal whatsoever? asked Carter.

That would be putting it too strongly, said Dayan.

Having toured the United States and rallied American Jewish opinion behind Israel, Dayan was in a strong position. He exploited that position, threatening Carter and his aides with activating American Jewry against the administration unless the president helped Israel by opposing an independent West Bank and committed himself to giving Israel more economic and military aid. It was an implied rather than a direct threat, but it worked. Carter had been stunned and impressed with the reaction of American Jewry. Originally Vance had wanted the U.S. and Israel to state their positions separately after the October 4 session. Dayan insisted on a joint statement and got it.

Accordingly, by the end of the evening, Carter, Vance, and Dayan had hammered out an American-Israeli working paper and joint communiqué. The two sides had agreed to a unified Arab delegation that would include Palestinian Arabs. Both the unified delegation and the inclusion of Palestinian Arabs in something other than an individual Arab delegation were concessions to the American side. The Americans had not gotten all they had wanted: Their hope was to have the Palestinians represented in a delegation of their own. In a concession to the Israeli view, working groups would be formed later to negotiate and conclude separate peace treaties between individual Arab states and Israel. In another concession to Israel, the West Bank and Gaza would be discussed in a working group limited to Israel, Jordan, Egypt, and the Palestinian Arabs (Syria and other Arab states were barred from participating in talks over the West Bank and Gaza).

Begin was not too pleased with Dayan's performance. To his mind, the American-Israeli working paper had gone too far in allowing the PLO into the Geneva conference by agreeing to negotiate with Palestinian Arabs. "I do not intend to be confronted with any more faits accomplis!" Begin thundered to colleagues when apprised of what Dayan had done.[20]

Eager to keep the momentum going, President Carter sought to make history by arranging for Moshe Dayan to meet his counterpart, Egyptian foreign minister Ismael Fahmi, next day in New York. To Fahmi, Carter noted that it would represent the climax of his career to arrange such a meeting. To his astonishment, the Egyptian foreign minister agreed to the encounter. When Carter proposed that Camp David be the venue and that the meeting be kept secret, Fahmi refused. He did not trust the Israelis not to leak it. It should be public. Carter was stunned.

Then Fahmi produced the catch. He said he planned to bring PLO leader Yassir Arafat to meet Dayan. Not to bring him would make a mockery of such a meeting—for the content would focus on the Palestinian issue.

"This is not possible," Carter repeated to himself. "This is not possible." With one of the linchpins of Israeli policy not to negotiate or recognize the PLO, Dayan, of course, was not about to agree to a meeting at which Chairman Arafat participated.

Two days later, unbeknownst to President Carter, Henry Kissinger proposed that Fahmi meet the Israeli foreign minister. The former American secretary of state had in mind the Rockefeller estate outside New York City as the secret venue. Fahmi never mentioned Carter's nearly identical proposal, but simply rejected the offer.[21]

Back in Israel, Dayan listened to Begin's objections to the American-Israeli working paper and therefore doubted that it would win cabinet approval. The prime minister, however, dropped his reservations and the paper was approved by the cabinet on October 11. Some cabinet ministers apparently feared that Dayan might leave the government, inducing a political crisis, if he was not supported. Begin had the same fears.

The fear that Menachem Begin and the cabinet had of Dayan was reminiscent of the political clout the foreign minister once enjoyed when he had been in Labor governments. On what was that clout based in 1977? Certainly not his political following. He had only a handful of supporters in the Knesset. In truth, the fear was unfounded, but there nonetheless.

PUBLICLY, Dayan's peacemaking had been aimed at resurrecting the Geneva conference. His private efforts were designed to lure Egypt into negotiations. Though he had urged a high-level Israeli-Egyptian meeting to Hassan Tuhami, he could not have known that Anwar Sadat was considering a plan that would provide that meeting in the most dramatic format imaginable.

Sadat had grown increasingly annoyed that precious time was being eaten away in the attempt to reach Geneva. He wanted to cut through the delays and obstacles, to plunge into direct negotiations with the Israelis. By early November he had an idea of how to do it. He had decided what no Arab leader had dared to do until now: He would breach the greatest taboo for any Arab leader.

On November 9 Sadat addressed the Egyptian parliament and said that he was prepared to go to the Knesset in Jerusalem if that would help prevent a single Egyptian son from being killed or wounded in battle. Israeli leaders could not decide if he was serious or if this was just another throwaway line used by Arab leaders to make them sound peace-minded. Meeting the next day with the American ambassador to Israel, Sam Lewis, Dayan reflected Israel's disbelief at Sadat's remarks by making only one brief, positive reference to the idea of a Sadat visit.[22]

Taking President Sadat at his word, Prime Minister Begin replied he was ready to meet the Egyptian leader. Sadat, in response, indicated that he was ready to go to Israel for a few days to address the Knesset and talk to its members about setting up a real peace between Israel and the Arabs. Four days later, on November 13, Begin issued an official invitation to Sadat to come to Jerusalem for talks on a permanent peace between Israel and Egypt.

Like many other Israelis, Dayan reacted to the news with suspicion. On November 13 he told his aides that the visit might be an alibi for war, or could precipitate a slide to fighting. The question for Israel was whether it would have to pay for the visit in real estate. A few days later, sensing that something historic was in progress, Dayan shifted to a more positive tone. "If the visit took place." he said, "it would have great importance."

On November 16, three days before Sadat was due to arrive in Israel, Dayan told Israel Radio that Israel should be ready with a response to Sadat's speech in the Knesset. If there was the smallest spark of hope that Egypt would sign a separate peace with Israel, Dayan said he would recommend that Israel do so immediately without waiting for the Geneva conference. More than any other Israeli, Dayan knew how significant the Sadat visit would be. Only a few months earlier he had listened to Hassan Tuhami pass on Sadat's disinterest in shaking Menachem Begin's hand until all Israeli soldiers had left Sinai. Sadat had abandoned that demand. He had also apparently abandoned the demand that Israel commit itself to withdraw from the Sinai as a precondition to his holding a summit with Begin. All of this left Dayan amazed: In his fondest hopes he imagined only unofficial, unpublicized contacts with Arab diplomats, but not with Sadat, and not in the Knesset in Jerusalem.

Saturday evening, November 19, 1977, was a night all Israelis would remember. A plane carrying the first Arab leader to ever publicly visit

Israel landed at Ben-Gurion Airport near Tel Aviv. Israeli political figures crowded next to one another at the foot of the plane waiting for the first glimpse of Anwar Sadat. Accompanying him on his historic flight were media superstars Walter Cronkite and Barbara Walters. One of the first Israelis Sadat greeted was Dayan. "Don't worry, Moshe. It will be all right," he said, as if he had read Dayan's concerned mind that somehow Sadat was intent on tricking the Israelis. Trailing behind Sadat was Hassan Tuhami, who did not greet Dayan like a long lost friend. "You said you were waiting for a phone call," he told the foreign minister. "Here we are."

Few Israelis that evening thought Sadat had tricks up his sleeve. Lining the streets along that his motorcade progressed through Jerusalem, thousands greeted him as if he were a hero returning from battle, as if his very presence in the country meant that peace between Israel and Egypt had been formally declared.

In a way it had—and all the rest were details that had to be formalized. Still, much work needed to be done until both Israel and Egypt could be satisfied that peace was in fact at hand. Dayan drove back with acting Egyptian foreign minister Dr. Boutrus Ghali from Ben-Gurion Airport to the King David Hotel in Jerusalem, Sadat's headquarters during his three days in Israel. The conversation was polite and pleasant, but too much had passed between their countries for them to become immediate friends. Ghali stressed that Egypt could not make peace with Israel on its own. In return, Dayan said he doubted that Jordan and the Palestinians would sit at a peace conference, and in that event, Egypt would have to be ready to sign a separate peace with Israel. "Are you ready for a separate peace?" Dayan asked bluntly. No, said the Egyptian. Looking ahead to President Sadat's Knesset speech the next day, Dayan said that Israel would appreciate it very much if the Egyptian president did not mention the PLO; if he did, Begin would be forced to bring up the PLO Covenant and its clause that called for the end of the state of Israel. Ghali promised to pass the message on to Sadat. (Dayan never found out whether his personal appeal had been the reason, but Sadat did not mention the PLO in his Knesset speech.)

On Sunday, November 20, Dayan joined a working lunch with Sadat. The Egyptian leader opened the discussion by noting that he had already laid down his conditions for a peace agreement and he had nothing further to add. Now he merely wished to know if Israel was prepared to agree to his terms. Dayan was forced to say that Sadat's busy schedule in Jerusalem left little time for actual negotiating. Well then, said Sadat, they must begin on this trip and continue at a later stage. The two men spoke politely to one another but no special chemistry arose, as it did between the Egyptian president and Israel's defense minister Ezer Weiz-man. To Sadat and the other Egyptians, Dayan symbolized more than any other Israeli the humiliating defeats of 1956 and 1967. Even when Sadat and Dayan exchanged pleasantries about Dayan's three "visits" to Egypt, the Egyptian leader blurted out in all honesty: "I tried to catch you three times!"[23]

Dayan realized that the real stumbling block was Egypt's disinterest in a separate peace with Israel. "Mr. President," Dayan asked Sadat, "What would you like us to say in our address of reply so that your visit here should be a success and not a failure?"

"I want you to speak sincerely and to tell me what you are prepared for and what you are not prepared for."

Dayan sought Sadat's views on the American-Israeli working paper, but Sadat had no interest in such a discussion.

"Forget it, it doesn't interest me. The working paper doesn't interest me. I want to talk about peace and not about the working paper."

"I understand," said Dayan, trying to introduce a little levity, "you are interested in the working and not the paper."

"Well said, that's it exactly, Moshe."

The highlight of Sadat's dramatic visit to Jerusalem was his appearance before the Knesset at 4:00 P.M. that Sunday, televised around the world live. "I have not come here for a separate agreement between Egypt and Israel," he said. He had not come to seek a partial peace—merely to terminate the state of belligerency. Nor had he come for a third disengagement agreement in Sinai or in the Golan or in the West Bank. He urged the complete withdrawal of all IDF troops from occupied Arab lands and the establishment of a Palestinian state. Defense Minister Weizman leaned over to Dayan and passed him a note: "We've got to prepare for war." Then Sadat promised an end to fighting. "Tell your sons that the past war was the last of wars and the end of sorrows." Dayan had heard the Egyptian's hard-line words, but he nonetheless thought it might be possible to do business with the man.

When it was his turn to speak, Prime Minister Begin said Israel wanted peace treaties with the Arabs that would end the state of war. Everything was negotiable, he said. (Despite such a declaration, few imagined Begin to mean he would give up the West Bank.)

That evening at dinner Sadat gloomily told Dayan he was disappointed that Begin had rejected his proposals in his speech. Dayan said no, Begin had not done that, he had said that everything was negotiable, including Jerusalem. Sadat could not have expected Begin to say, "Aye, aye, sir!" to everything he had sought, Dayan told Sadat. Trying to sound en-couraging, the foreign minister then said, "The way to advance is to continue the talks, and, believe me, you won't be sorry." It was clear that Sadat was not eager to invite Israeli leaders to Egypt for those talks under present circumstances. "As long as you hold conquered Egyptian soil I do not want any Israeli visitors in my country," he told Dayan. In response to Sadat's gesture of coming to Jerusalem, Israelis were encouraged to return the gesture to Sadat—perhaps by returning a small piece of Egyptian territory unilaterally. Ariel Sharon had proposed in the cabinet that Sadat, upon his arrival, be offered Egyptian civilian administration of El-Arish and the right of passage on the roads leading to the city. Begin liked the idea, but Dayan did not. He felt that Sadat was not coming to Israel just to get a small morsel of land. Moreover, it would do Sadat more harm than good, for the Arabs would only accuse him of engaging in a separate peace with Israel.

As Sadat was about to return to Egypt, Dayan composed a limerick-style jingle:

> A great wind came suddenly
> And the bells of peace chimed
> Courageously,
> President Sadat
> In Israel landed
> Did it happen or was it a dream?[24]

For days after Sadat left Israel, Dayan and his countrymen pondered that question—did the Egyptian president really come to Jerusalem, or was it a dream? It was no dream, but it was also no panacea for the problems that separated Israel and Egypt. Sadat searched for ways to keep the momentum alive. Soon after returning to Cairo, the Egyptian president called for a conference that would pave the way for the Geneva conference, inviting all those countries who had attended the original one four years before in December 1973.

Sadat saw virtue in maintaining direct contact with Israel. He proposed that Dayan once again meet Hassan Tuhami in Morocco, and that the meeting be kept secret. The foreign minister left for Marrakech on December 2. He proposed Egyptian sovereignty over all of the Sinai, demilitarizing the area east of the Mitla and Gidi passes, and permitting the Israeli settlements to remain under a United Nations flag. This sounded unappealing to Tuhami, who argued that it was not to reach such an accord that Anwar Sadat had risked the ire of the Arab world. Furthermore, there could not be any Israeli-Egyptian agreement without a parallel resolution of the Palestinian issue.

Tuhami presented his own handwritten proposal to Dayan. In it Egypt still insisted that any Israeli-Egyptian arrangement would have to include a resolution of the conflict with all the other Arab states. Dayan asked him whether Egypt was ready to make peace with Israel even if the other Arab states did not. All Tuhami would say was that "we would have to await developments." Dayan left Morocco depressed. His talks with Tuhami had not advanced the peace process very much. Perhaps, thought Dayan, more progress could be made if Washington were to become involved.

By the time the next serious step between Israel and Egypt was taken—the Begin-Sadat summit at Ismalia on December 25—Dayan was in a foul mood. He felt that Sadat's gesture of visiting Jerusalem would be of little value if the Egyptians were not prepared to understand that a comprehensive peace was out of the question. Israel could only make peace with Egypt at this stage. Dayan's mood remained morose as he landed at Ismalia along with Begin and Weizman.

"Look," he said to Begin as they were driving toward President Sadat's holiday residence, "not a single Israeli flag. Not even a banner to welcome us."

The Ismalia talks did not go smoothly. There was still no movement at all on the crucial issues. Begin put forward Israel's peace proposals, and Sadat rejected them. Sadat replied with the familiar Egyptian position demanding a total Israeli withdrawal from the occupied Arab lands, Palestinian self-determination, and no separate peace.

Begin still thought it a good idea for Israel and Egypt to issue a joint communiqué, spelling out the points on which there had been agreement and on which there had not been, and announcing that working committees would continue to try to resolve the areas of disagreement.

"Why should we?" barked Dayan. "We are sitting in Sinai, and the Suez Canal, and on the Golan Heights. If he likes it—fine and good! If not—then not! What does all this mean? There's no flag! No welcome posters! We are not invited to Cairo! Either we issue a communiqué about an agreement, or we leave without it."

When the subject of a joint communiqué came up, the Egyptians insisted it include a statement in favor of Palestinian self-determination, but the Israeli negotiators were only willing to include a statement that Egypt wanted a Palestinian state while Israel championed Palestinian autonomy. In the end no joint communiqué was issued. Begin and Sadat did agree, however, on establishing joint committees, one for political and civil affairs, the other for military affairs. That was all that emerged from the summit.

At one stage Sadat asked Ezer Weizman how old Dayan was. Sixty-three, Weizman answered incorrectly. Dayan was in fact sixty-two.

"He looks like he's in his seventies," Sadat said, "The Six Day War made him old."

When Dayan returned from Ismalia, his depression about the state of the peace process reached an all-time low. Egypt would only make peace if Israel did what it was not prepared to do—withdraw from all the occupied lands.

Over the next few months many discussions were held between Israel and the United States, and between Egypt and the United States. Dayan would visit the United States on several occasions. No real progress was made. The joint Egypt-Israel working committees, the only positive outcome of the Ismalia summit, began to function. When the political committee met at the Hilton Hotel in Jerusalem on January 15, 1978, it proved fruitless. Five days later a sorrowful Foreign Minister Dayan told Israel Television that "if Sadat really wants an Israeli commitment to withdraw from all territories occupied in sixty-seven before negotiations begin, then the situation is a dead end."

IT STAYED that way for quite some time. When Ezer Weizman met Anwar Sadat in Cairo, in March 1978, the Egyptian president asked him for a clear declaration that Israel would agree to the principle of a full withdrawal. Once that was given, all else could be resolved. Weizman suggested that Sadat talk to Dayan.

"I don't think that's a good idea. Not yet. The time has not yet come for me to receive Dayan. Dayan can't keep a secret."

That was not true, said Weizman, but Sadat refused to invite the foreign minister.

Not much would change over the next few months. Indeed, between January and July, Israel and Egypt refrained almost entirely from direct talks. For some time Washington had been sending officials to Jerusalem and Cairo to formulate a declaration of principles, but in vain.

Dayan told Vance that the best way to advance peace negotiations was to abandon the search for a formula of principles and concentrate on substantive peace proposals. To that end the United States proposed a tripartite Israel-Egypt–United States conference at Leeds Castle in England for the summer. A spark of hope was ignited when the session got under way on July 18. Heading the Israeli delegation was Foreign Minister Dayan. His counterparts were Secretary of State Cyrus Vance and Foreign Minister Mohamed Ibrahim Kamel.

Entering the conference room at Leeds that first day, Dayan could not bring himself to chat amiably with the Egyptian delegation. Matters had not reached such a friendly stage. Instead, he spotted an ancient

Egyptian stone relic and spent time gazing at it, ignoring the Egyptians.

Kamel adhered to the familiar Egyptian line: no separate Israeli-Egyptian peace; self-determination for the Palestinians; Israeli settlements and military bases must be abandoned. Dayan listened to these demands once again, but this time he asked the Egyptians if they regarded Israel's proposals (envisaging only a separate Israeli-Egyptian peace) as a basis for a settlement. If they did not, Israel might well regard itself free to cancel the proposals. The Egyptians were shocked. All they could manage to say was that the West Bank was the main subject at Leeds, not the Sinai. It was that look of shock in the Egyptians' faces that gave Dayan hope. Perhaps a separate settlement might be achievable after all.

Dayan asked the Egyptians if they were prepared to consider a territorial division of the West Bank along the lines of the Allon Plan. They said no. Dayan formulated Israel's position at these talks in a memo to Vance. Begin was annoyed at the part that stated that Israel would be ready to consider a proposal for a peace treaty based upon a concrete territorial compromise. To Begin, that seemed to go too far, hinting that Israel might actually yield some occupied lands. Still, the cabinet backed Dayan.

The Americans grew to admire Dayan's supple mind at Leeds. During a dinner discussion on the Jewish settlements, Dayan told William Quandt, a member of the National Security Council: "Look, you're not going to get Begin to say that Jews have no right to settle in the West Bank. You're not going to get me to say that either. I understand it's a problem. The trick is to find an agreement on this one that is not a challenge to our right to settle [and to] construct an arrangement whereby in practical terms we won't create new settlements."

Quandt was suitably intrigued. One approach, said Dayan, would be to say that under the scheme of Palestinian self-government the state-owned lands (the only lands used for Jewish settlement) would pass to the control of the self-governing authority, which would then hold the lands in trust, and be barred from selling them to anyone, Palestinian or Israeli. Israel would not be able to build new settlements, but it would not feel itself discriminated against. "We can live with that. Even Begin can live with that. It's just when you say that a Jew has no right whereas an Arab does that it really gets to us. But if you set things up right, you will have the effect that you want." Afterward, Quandt thought of Dayan as a man who was trying to solve a problem.[25]

Nine months after Sadat's visit to Jerusalem the peace process remained in stalemate. Carter launched a fresh initiative in August to undo that stalemate, inviting Begin and Sadat to join him at the mountain resort of Camp David the following month.

Camp David was to be an American experiment in diplomacy. Getting the parties to agree to come together in the private, isolated surroundings of Catoctin Mountain in Maryland, seventy-two miles from Washington, D.C., was itself an accomplishment. Once they arrived, they would undergo a series of subtle pressures to maximize the prospects for success. The greatest one was the very visible presence of the president of the United States. Here was Jimmy Carter, the man with a thousand pressures a day haunting him, committing himself to spending as much time as necessary at Camp David to fashion a Middle East peace accord. Laying his personal prestige on the line, Carter sent a clear signal to his guests: Don't waste my time. No one would want to. So failure to reach agreement carried with it a high price indeed—angering the American president. The secluded nature of Camp David, with its electrified fences and electronic security devices, was wonderfully designed to remove outside pressures—the ticking of a stopwatch, the persistent questions of a waiting, voracious press. No one was supposed to worry about catching a plane, no one had to think about issuing a stream of communiqués. The parties could devote their time and energy exclusively to resolving their differences. Carter insisted that no one leave Camp David, in this way preventing leaks to the press. There would be only one spokesman, presidential spokesman Jody Powell.

Not all the parties to the Middle East conflict would be there. Jordan stayed home, as did Syria, Saudi Arabia, and the Palestinians. Their absence placed Sadat in the awkward position of seeking a comprehensive peace even though other Arab states refused to attend the peace talks. Still, as he arrived at Camp David, Sadat was bent on obtaining that comprehensive peace—and nothing less.

Even without all of these pressures, Moshe Dayan had an incentive to make sure that Camp David was a success. Playing a major role in fashioning a peace treaty between Israel and Egypt could salvage his tarnished reputation, and it could assure that his career did not end at a low point of personal guilt and pain. It could guarantee that Dayan's last role would be that of peacemaker. What better way to vindicate his claim that there was more to Moshe Dayan than his record in the Yom Kippur War. With much to gain from a positive outcome, and much to lose from a failure, the foreign minister had a great incentive to try harder, to search relentlessly for formulas that might break impasses, not to admit failure, not to give up. Others at Camp David, such as Menachem Begin and Anwar Sadat, had a large personal stake in Camp David as well. To Begin and Sadat, principles were not to be abandoned simply for the expediency of reaching a political agreement. For Begin, it was the principle of preserving Eretz Yisrael (the land of Israel). For Sadat, it was regaining every inch of his lost Sinai Peninsula. Dayan too had principles, but they had more to do with assuring Israel's security and with making sure that Egypt offered a genuine peace in exchange for the territory Israel would cede.

Oddly enough, it was Dayan, rather than Begin, who seemed the most wedded to the Sinai, who seemed the least willing to surrender it in its entirety. For years Dayan had asserted that he preferred Sharm el-Sheikh to peace, though of late, as prospects for peace with Egypt improved, he refrained from making such an assertion. Ideologically speaking, Menachem Begin thought of the West Bank as indispensable—a part of Israel's homeland that could not be severed. He harbored no such thoughts with regard to the Sinai. Dayan, on the other hand, had led Israel into the Sinai in 1956 and in 1967—and he had been forced to retreat both times against his better judgment. To relinquish Sinai one more time without an Egyptian guarantee that this time there would be lasting peace seemed absurd. For a true peace, Dayan was willing to jump into the icy waters. He simply wished to make sure he was not drowned.

THESE WERE not your usual diplomats in pinstripes and three-piece suits. The dress code at Camp David was informal, bordering on the leisurely. Jimmy Carter brought along his faded jeans. Even Menachem Begin, rarely seen without a suit and tie, dispensed with the business attire and unbuttoned his shirt. Cyrus Vance wore his large heavy sweater. The Egyptians, however, stuck to coats and ties. No faded jeans or baggy sweaters for them. As part of the effort to make Camp David seem like one large summer camp, everyone was given a blue windbreaker with "Camp David" written in gold letters on it. Like other "summer camps," there was ample time for long walks amidst the forested mountains, or tennis or Ping-Pong, or even football. None of those sports appealed to Dayan, not with his one eye. While Begin and Brzezinski, Carter's national security adviser, played chess, and others played tennis, Dayan preferred solitude. Sitting through the long meetings afforded little time to think through sticky problems. It was not Dayan's style to seek out the others, even the Israelis, and engage in small talk. It was either substance or nothing. He went on long walks despite being in constant pain. His back hurt him, as did his eye. He was slowly losing his sight.

By the time he reached Camp David, President Sadat may well have realized that he would have to give up his demand for a comprehensive Middle East settlement. The only success possible at Camp David was forging the one agreement he had forcefully resisted until now—a separate peace with Israel. If he could disguise whatever emerged as part of a comprehensive peace arrangement, it might work. He had Jimmy Carter's solemn promise that the other Arab states would not assail Sadat for going his separate way. It was still a mighty risk. Nonetheless, Sadat deemed it a risk worth taking—if he could reclaim every inch of Sinai and empty that desert of every last vestige of Israeli presence— thirteen Jewish settlements and two airfields.

MENACHEM BEGIN, leader of the Israeli delegation, took decisions after consulting with his advisers, Moshe Dayan included. Matters were not put to a vote. Begin listened, then decided. Begin's lawyer-like formalism contrasted sharply with Dayan's suppleness of mind. The foreign minister's long familiarity with American negotiating patterns, American personalities and language, gave him a distinct advantage over the more provincial Begin. Although he was as devoted as Begin to holding on to the West Bank and the Gaza Strip, Dayan differed from him in negotiating style, a difference that made the prime minister appear rigid, the foreign minister flexible. Dayan was more driven to find formulas that would be acceptable to the other side. Begin had more of a "take it or leave it" outlook. Others in the Israeli delegation picked up on this difference between the two men. Aharon Barak, a member of the Israeli delegation who was then the attorney general, said: "There is a game that children play with a little car. The car goes to a wall and then the moment it hits the wall it changes direction. It goes to another wall, hits another wall, changes direction. It's never stuck. This is my image of Dayan. He never became stuck in a corner and said, 'Uh-uh, that's it, take it or leave it. We go home.' "[26]

CAMP DAVID OPENED on Tuesday, September 5. The negotiations were, in Dayan's words, "the decisive, most difficult and least pleasant stage in the Egypt-Israel peace negotiations."[27] Monumental concessions by both Israel and Egypt were necessary before any political settlement could be within grasp. All of this would be anguishing for the participants. Even for Moshe Dayan, the search for solutions would vex his soul: "There were times when only by clenching teeth and fists could I stop myself from exploding."[28]

The prime minister was eager to weigh in with an Israeli proposal early on. He feared that the Americans might introduce their own proposal without the benefit of having seen an Israeli one. Dayan cautioned Begin against submitting an Israeli proposal too quickly. It was better to wait for an Egyptian one. In this way, Israel would avoid encouraging early American compromise proposals. The prime minister agreed. Sadat presented his proposal at his first meeting with Carter at 3:00 P.M. Wednesday, September 6. It was no different from Sadat's proposals in Jerusalem. When Dayan learned of Sadat's proposals, he rejected them out of hand. "The Egyptians are behaving like landlords, as if they had occupied the West Bank and the Old City, as if nothing had happened."[29] The Israeli delegation thought the conference might end before it had gotten started. Dayan suggested that an Israeli counterproposal be prepared, but not submitted lest it be considered an ultimatum.

On Thursday, September 7, Begin and Sadat squabbled about the Egyptian document. Carter proposed coming up with an American proposal for further discussion. On Friday night, September 8, Under Secretary of State Hal Saunders came up with an American proposal in the form of a Framework for Peace in the Middle East. Sadat was still adamant against agreeing to a separate peace with Israel. The Framework for Peace therefore had to embrace Israeli peace accords with all of the other Arab states as well.

On Sunday at 4:00 P.M. the U.S. presented its seventeen-page proposal to Israel. Dayan noticed that although the document dealt with the West Bank, Gaza, and the Palestinians, it said nothing about Jewish settlements in the West Bank, and very little about the Sinai. Listening to Israeli reaction to their proposals later Sunday evening, the Americans were disappointed to find Israel unwilling to give up any part of the West Bank. Dayan tried to sound conciliatory: "We are not after political control," Dayan said, "if it looks that way to you, we will look at it again."[30]

Such statements perplexed Brzezinski: "Superficially, Dayan seemed like a reasonable man. . . . But he was in some ways more devious than Begin. You knew with Begin more clearly what he wanted to convey. Dayan was less inclined than Begin to put his cards on the table. There was a strangely elusive quality about Dayan. . . . While I more or less knew what made Begin and Weizman tick, I never had that feeling about Dayan. I always saw him in a fog." Still, he suggested that "Dayan may have been less inclined to dig in his heels than Begin. . . . One had a feeling that Dayan had an instinctive appreciation of the ambiguities and nuances of the Arabs."[31]

The Israeli-American meeting did not break up until 3:00 A.M. By this time President Carter had begun to search for ways to break through Menachem Begin's ideological wall. He sought out Moshe Dayan. Carter found Dayan "level-headed" whereas Begin was "unreasonable." Had the foreign minister (or Defense Minister Ezer Weizman, for that matter) headed the Israeli delegation, Carter was sure he would have been able to reach agreement without difficulty. Inviting Dayan to walk with him, the president made it clear that he thought Sadat had been far more forthcoming than Begin and he asked the foreign minister to do what he could to bring the prime minister around.

At this juncture, the thirteen Jewish settlements in the Sinai appeared a major obstacle to a peace agreement. Both Begin and Dayan were reluctant to part with them. Though relatively few Israelis lived on them, they took on symbolic meaning and, according to Zbigniew Brzezinski, "were an external reflection of a much deeper issue: the West Bank. If the Israelis gave up settlements even in the Sinai they felt that would lead to them giving up the West Bank."[32] Dayan had proposed to Zbigniew Brzezinski that the settlement issue be put off until all other issues were resolved at Camp David and won his agreement on that point.

Dayan now asked Carter to try to persuade Sadat to take title of the settlements but to permit Israelis to live there for some time longer. (The next day, the Egyptian president rejected that idea outright.) From Carter, Dayan learned that Sadat had toughened his stance on the West Bank and the Gaza Strip. He now insisted upon deploying Egyptian army units in Gaza and the West Bank pending a final decision on the areas' status. Dayan turned the idea down flat. Realizing that the first American document talked mostly about the West Bank, President Carter thought a second one was needed to focus on the Sinai. Dayan encouraged him to draw one up. Even if Sadat did not accept it, it would help clarify and define the issues. Carter said he would have one prepared and present it to both delegations. This meant a major turning point in the discussions. The Americans were moving toward the conclusion that the only realistic approach was to strive for an Israeli-Egyptian peace and to shelve the other issues as unrealizable at this stage. As daybreak approached, the American president watched sadly as Dayan, his eyesight seriously impaired, nearly walked into a tree. "My heart went out to him. I considered him a friend and a proper ally."[33] He sensed that Dayan had become a key to success. Others in the Israeli delegation still clung to old positions. Dayan had made it clear he was interested in moving beyond them.

THE AMERICANS found Dayan appealing, and used him to soften up Begin, because the foreign minister had an ability to sense what the Arab side wanted and needed, while Begin did not. None of the others in the Israeli delegation puzzled as much about what Anwar Sadat really wanted. Why had he taken a certain position? And what could Israel do to make him change his position? "Dayan would not ask in front of Begin," noted William Quandt, "but would take an American aside, and ask what's making Sadat tick. Is he serious? Is this a bluff? Is this for domestic consumption?[34]

Dayan had a special curiosity about the Arab mind, and a familiarity as well. This came from his direct negotiations with Abdullah el-Tel and with Arab representatives on the Mixed Armistice Commission. It came from countless conversations with Arab personalities in the occupied territories after 1967. It came from being a shrewd observer of what the Arabs said and what they did. It came from thinking a great deal about his adversaries. "He really had the capacity," noted Alfred Atherton, then the assistant secretary of state for Near Eastern Affairs, and a member of the American delegation at Camp David, "to put himself in their shoes, or in their mind-set and see how they looked at a problem."[35]

Sam Lewis, the American ambassador in Israel and a member of the American delegation, found it easier to talk to Dayan than to the prime minister "because Begin would lapse into stereotypes, never having conversed with a West Banker or Gazan until late into his prime ministry. Dayan could change position without any sense of personal ego involved. He was very results-oriented." To move Begin with arguments was tough, he only moved when he assessed he had to move. Then, said Lewis, Begin would find his argument, "whereas you could sell Dayan an argument. He was intellectually engageable in a way that Begin wasn't."[36]

According to Jimmy Carter, "Dayan would quite often try to tell us what the Palestinians would accept or would not accept. He knew them. He had grown up with them. And so we looked at his assessments as authoritative."[37]

Though Carter and Dayan had concluded their talks in an upbeat mood, the rest of the Israeli delegation was filled with an impending sense of failure. By Tuesday, September 12, the prime minister had passed word that he would only give the talks three more days. To Israeli delegation members Dayan advocated restraint. He knew that Carter was busy drafting a new document that would concentrate on the Sinai. More time was needed to determine whether Sadat would give way under the president's influence. However, as a tactic, Dayan reflected the Israeli sense of gloom to the Americans. He was playing on Carter's deep desire for a successful finale to Camp David. Bumping into Sam Lewis, Dayan told him casually that he was scheduled to return to Israel the next day. To Lewis the news was startling and terrifying. The implication was that the Israelis had abandoned hope. Lewis reported back to Carter at once. The Americans realized they had less time than they thought. The pace quickened.

Later that day, Begin felt he would not be able to sign the American document. His main objection was the principle that territories could not be obtained by force. Begin had insisted that Israel had not acquired the West Bank by force but in self-defense. He quickly won agreement from the rest of the delegation. A few moments later, Cyrus Vance entered the Israeli cabin to say that there would be a new American document after Carter met Sadat. "There is no need to hurry," said Vance, aware that the Israelis had threatened to pack their bags. "Patience is a virtue."

Throughout Wednesday Carter worked, aided by Egyptian and Israeli officials, trying to hammer out an American compromise document. It became increasingly apparent that the issue of Jewish settlements in the Sinai was the main sticking point. On Thursday, September 14, Carter asked to see Dayan and Barak that morning, and told them, "You must agree to the removal of the Sinai settlements, and that way we will get a peace treaty."

MEMBERS OF both the Israeli and American delegations thought it wise to arrange for Dayan and Sadat to meet alone. Sadat had the power to make decisions on the Egyptian side. Dayan had a special ability to influence Begin. Perhaps if the two men put their heads together, progress could be made. From nearly the time they arrived at Camp David, Carter had pushed for such a meeting. As early as September 6 Carter spoke in praise of Dayan to Sadat. "It is my experience that he has particularly distinguished himself with proposals that have contributed to extrication from complicated situations. He is a creative thinker."[38]

Now, eight days later, Weizman had a proposal for Sadat. "My dear friend," he told the president, "it's ten months since you arrived in Jerusalem, and I haven't given you bad advice yet. If you want to get this damn thing out of the mud that we're stuck in, call Dayan and talk to him."

For Sadat, sitting down with Moshe Dayan was perhaps the single most difficult step he would take—other than embarking on his visit to Jerusalem. Conquerer of Sinai in 1956 and 1967, symbol of a militant, aggressive Israel, Moshe Dayan was a reminder of the years of humiliation Egypt had experienced. Through those years the Egyptians had caricatured him as the devil, evil incarnate, a monster, and now their leader had to decide whether to engage him in conversation—one man talking to another. It seemed almost too much for Anwar Sadat to do.

For Dayan, the problem was not talking to Sadat. He knew that he could do that. The problem was figuring out how to break down the barrier between them. He, after all, was an Israeli, and Sadat was an

Egyptian. Talking to Sadat was not the same for Dayan as talking to Shimon Peres or Ezer Weizman.

Finally, that Thursday afternoon Sadat and Dayan met. Sadat opened by saying that he saw no solution on the horizon and he would like to hear from Dayan what could be done.

Dayan replied that while Begin was a strong man, he could not oppose the Knesset and the Israeli people, "particularly on the matter of settlements. On that question we cannot compromise."

Sadat then complained that the Israelis had exploited Sadat's concessions to Carter to speed up normalization and put off the final status of the West Bank—by asking for more concessions. "Tell Begin," Sadat told Dayan, "there is no sense in torturing Carter anymore if you are not empowered by Israel to remove the settlements."

Then Sadat offered a sweetener, hinting that he would agree to full diplomatic relations with Israel nine months after a peace treaty. All Israel had to do was withdraw the Sinai settlements.

The choice for Israel became clear to Dayan: holding the Sinai settlements or peace. He and Sadat had avoided the thornier Palestinian issue. The Egyptian president had concentrated on the Sinai settlements, leading the foreign minister to understand that Israel had moved far closer to a peace settlement with Egypt. Sadat had hinted that he was prepared to go for a separate peace.

"Concentrate on the Sinai issues," Dayan told other members of the Israeli delegation after he left Sadat. "I'm sure this is what Sadat really wants." As long as Israel demonstrated suitable flexibility on the Sinai, Dayan sensed that Sadat would accept a "fig leaf" for the West Bank and the Gaza Strip—words, but not commitments. At this juncture, Avraham Tamir, head of the IDF's Planning Division, proposed that Ariel Sharon, the minister for agriculture, and the man in charge of Jewish settlements, phone Menachem Begin to say that he gave his blessing to the evacuation of the Sinai settlements if that would bring peace.

On Friday, September 15, Carter heard from Dayan that he and Sadat had held an unsatisfactory meeting. The U.S. president believed that his mission was on the verge of failure. Sadat declared that he intended to leave, but Carter urged him to stay another day or two. Dayan returned to the Israeli delegation and informed them that Carter intended to end the conference in two days, on Sunday night. He planned to meet with both houses of Congress and the press on Monday, and very likely blame Israel for the failure of Camp David.

Until Saturday, September 16, Begin had remained against withdrawing the settlers; Dayan had been prepared to promise withdrawal after an extended period. The foreign minister now sensed that Israel would have to yield them to gain peace with Egypt. Alfred Atherton asked Dayan why he had urged the building of Yamit, a major settlement in northern Sinai, if he knew he would eventually have to abandon it. "We never thought the Egyptians would make peace," Dayan said. "Now that they are making peace, we have to give it up."[39]

Finally, on Saturday evening came the breakthrough. Begin announced to Carter that "if it is the settlements in Sinai that are an obstacle to peace, I will submit the matter to the Knesset." He would recommend that party discipline be suspended so that members could vote their consciences. The prime minister said he would respect whatever the Knesset decided.

It was still not over. The entire peace conference threatened to come unhinged over an unexpected flap related to Jerusalem. Without the Egyptians requesting it, the Americans had prepared a letter for President Carter to write about the status of Jerusalem. It was to be attached to the framework agreement. Apparently Washington had deliberately left this, the most sensitive of all subjects to Israel, to the last so that Begin and his colleagues would have no choice but to agree to it. To the Israelis it seemed a clear-cut move to set the stage for the removal of the Old City from Israel's control. On this point Begin said he was prepared to leave for home—without signing any agreement.

Hearing this, Dayan warned the Americans that if they insisted on setting out in detail the American position on East Jerusalem, Begin would simply pack his bags and go home. Carter said that the paper on Jerusalem was intended to clarify the American position on this issue. Did Dayan mean that the United States could not publicly state its own national position?

Not answering the question directly, the foreign minister sought to explain that Begin could not associate himself with an agreement that included such an American statement. For the first time, Dayan said, the Americans had taken their own independent stand on an issue. The Israelis would not have come to Camp David if they knew that the U.S. was going to announce its position on Jerusalem.

At this stage matters became worse when Brzezinski reported that Sadat had revived an old demand that an Arab flag fly on an Arab mosque on the Temple Mount. "Maybe Sadat wants an Arab flag above the Knesset building too," said Dayan disdainfully. Dayan was annoyed and would go to the barricades on this issue.

Finally a compromise was reached. The Israeli delegation said that it would accept a reference to the American position on Jerusalem as presented at the United Nations. As Carter spoke with Sadat, it was agreed that the Egyptian president would write Carter a letter that outlined the Egyptian position on Jerusalem. Begin would do the same stating the Israeli position. Carter would then respond in letters based on statements regarding Jerusalem that had been made by two American ambassadors to the UN. No longer was it an American position that was being independently stated and recorded in the agreement. By including Israel's position in the accord it would be clear that Begin and his colleagues had not paved the way for the Israeli abandonment of part of Jerusalem.

By late Sunday afternoon the agreement was at hand. To Carter, much of the credit belonged to the Israeli foreign minister: "There is no doubt that Dayan was very receptive to the offer of peace and progress that President Sadat was making. Quite frequently, almost invariably, when we sought agreement on some issue, Begin would be the most recalcitrant member of the Israeli delegation. And Dayan would work with Begin to induce him to make the necessary compromise. I can say that the basic terms of the Camp David accords were hammered out substantially under the influence of Moshe."[40]

One agreement was the framework for a peace treaty between Israel and Egypt, requiring Israel to relinquish all of Sinai, its settlements and airfields. The United States was committed to building two airfields for Israel replacing the two in the Sinai before the final withdrawal of the IDF. Sinai would not be demilitarized—as Israel had once hoped—but a sizable buffer zone would exist between the two armies. Egypt promised to normalize relations much earlier than at first envisaged: Nine months after the first IDF withdrawal, ambassadors would be exchanged.

The second document was a framework agreement for peace in the Middle East. It foresaw peace between Israel and all Arab countries, but focused on the West Bank and Gaza. Israel promised to permit full autonomy for the Palestinian Arab residents of the West Bank and the Gaza Strip. In language that Israel had never before agreed upon, the document said that the solution must recognize the legitimate rights of the Palestinian people and its just demands. Autonomy would be good for only five years. Israel could still demand sovereignty over the regions.

The Camp David accords were remarkable achievements, paving the way for the first peace treaty between Israel and an Arab state. Documents had been forged after both parties had made major concessions. Egypt had compromised on its original demand that there would be no separate peace; that Israel would have to agree as well to withdrawing from the rest of the occupied Arab lands. Israel had compromised on its insistence on clinging to the Jewish settlements and the airfields. Both sides could agree in the end because, other than Israel's promise to withdraw from Sinai, nothing else had been enshrined in stone. As one of the architects of the accords, Aharon Barak, said: "The beauty of Camp David is that everything is open. We didn't say Palestinian state. We didn't say no Palestinian state. We just left it open. Camp David is a process. It's a document that creates a process, it's not a document that is aimed at creating results. Because it was clear that while we could agree on the process we couldn't agree on the results."[41]

BOTH ISRAEL and Egypt were confident that a peace treaty could be signed within three months. Still, there remained the Knesset vote on the Jewish settlements. Looking ahead to the Knesset vote, Dayan said, "In the next few weeks, each of us will take stock, will think of himself, of his family, of his children. It will be one of the great moments of the state of Israel, of its self-examination, of its assessment of the future." The Knesset, in recess, was specially convened for the debate on September 25. Geula Cohen, a right-wing firebrand, noisily sought the floor at once to demand that Begin resign. She was quickly expelled from the chamber. Begin and Peres spoke and the Knesset then adjourned for two days. When the vote was taken, it was 84–19 in favor of withdrawal of the settlements, with 17 abstentions. One of those who abstained was a member of the National Religious party, Yehuda Ben-Meir. Dayan sent him a note saying: "By abstention shall the righteous live."[42]

The Blair House Conference was called in October for the three parties—Israel, Egypt, and the United States—to try to grind out the details of the peace treaty. Little progress was made and it became clear that the signing of the treaty would not fall within the stated three-month period.

Begin and Sadat extended an invitation to Carter to visit them in early March to try to finalize the details of the peace treaty. The president spent a few days in Cairo starting on March 8, and on Saturday evening, March 10, arrived in Israel. The formal talks began the next morning. Vance revealed to Dayan that Egypt was demanding liaison officers between Egypt and Gaza. On oil supplies—another crucial issue for Israel—Vance informed Dayan that Washington was proposing a ten-year agreement with Israel in which Egypt would sell to the United States the production from the Sinai oil fields at the market price, and the U.S. would sell that oil to Israel for the next ten years. Egypt was also insisting the peace treaty not supersede its defense treaties with other Arab states. Israel thought the new peace treaty should. Begin had threatened the night before in his talk with Carter to take the proposed treaty to the

Knesset for discussion and approval before signing it. The president had balked at this as an unnecessary delay. The American delegation led by Carter met with Israeli officials, including Dayan, and the president urged quick approval of the treaty. Begin was angry too that he had reached agreement with Carter on the "supersedence" issue and on the target goal of one year for ending the autonomy negotiations and obtained his government's approval, but now Cairo was unwilling to go along. Israel also was dissatisfied that Egypt wanted to establish autonomy first in Gaza, rather than the West Bank. That night the Israeli cabinet met from 11:30 P.M. until 5:30 A.M. A number of concessions was made on these issues but when Vance was informed of them, he said he saw no point in going to Egypt unless Israel agreed as well to the stationing of Egyptian liaison officers in Gaza.

On Monday, March 12, at 10:30 A.M., Carter met with the entire cabinet. The atmosphere was tense and bitter. The president was scheduled to leave the Middle East the next day and his hopes of securing a signed peace treaty seemed to be slipping away. Carter insisted that Israel agree to Egyptian liaison officers in Gaza to enable Egypt to support the autonomy program. Begin noted that the Camp David accords made no mention of such officers and Israel would not agree to them. On the oil question, some cabinet ministers were troubled at Israel having to purchase Egyptian oil through an American firm, signifying a continuation of the Arab boycott against Israel. They felt that the oil should be sold directly to Israel. The meeting ended and Carter then appeared before the parliament. A raucous Knesset followed with Geula Cohen being removed for her constant shouting at Begin (she accused him of conceding too much to Egypt). The Knesset ended at 2:00 P.M. and the cabinet reconvened in Begin's office. Carter passed word that he was leaving the next morning. The cabinet broke up at 6:30 P.M. with no further meetings scheduled. It appeared that the presidential visit to the Middle East to secure the peace treaty had been derailed.

A few cabinet ministers remained behind, frustrated in the knowledge that only two issues remained to be resolved: the liaison officers in Gaza and the oil supplies. One minister proposed a new formula on the oil question and Dayan won Begin's approval to take the idea to Vance. Dayan and Vance met privately for the next few hours. Dayan urged the American secretary of state to try to convince Sadat not to insist upon the liaison officers in Gaza. He stressed that once Israel had started pulling back from the Sinai and normal relations existed, any Egyptian would be able to travel to Gaza on an Israeli visa. These ideas appealed to Vance but he needed Israel's cooperation on the oil question. Dayan said that he understood that the Egyptians could not agree at this time to sell Israel oil on a long-term basis and at a preferred price.

Hearing this, Vance knew they were on the verge of a breakthrough. However, if Israel were to agree to the Egyptians' supplying Israel oil via the Americans, Israel would need two commitments: one, an American guarantee that Israel's oil needs would be satisfied for the next twenty years, rather than ten; two, the inclusion of a clause in the peace treaty that Israel had the right to purchase oil directly from Egypt, without which the Egyptian boycott of Israel would have remained in force. Vance was on the phone to Carter several times. Dayan persuaded Vance to ask Carter to invite Begin to see the proposals and to take them to the cabinet. Meanwhile, Dayan would make sure to have told Begin that a cabinet majority existed for the proposals. The foreign minister was optimistic. Vance was ecstatic: "When we shook hands at the elevator, I thanked heaven for Dayan and his patience, imagination, and courage."[43] Returning to his hotel, Dayan told Rahel: "The crisis is over."

It almost was. The next morning, March 13, Dayan phoned Begin and informed him of his talk with Vance. At 7:00 A.M. over breakfast, Vance showed the foreign minister how the Americans had incorporated the new proposals into the draft of the peace treaty. On the oil question, the U.S. had agreed to a guarantee of fifteen years and if after that period Israel could not obtain oil from other sources, the United States would supply it. Vance and Dayan then entered the president's hotel suite. Carter had invited Begin, who was already there. Carter made sure to present the clause focusing on oil supplies as an American proposal. Begin said the new proposals would need the cabinet's approval. First he wanted Carter to obtain Sadat's agreement. Then he would take the proposals to the cabinet. Carter agreed. From the president's look Dayan had the impression that Carter felt all obstacles had been cleared away. Carter left at 1:00 P.M. for Cairo. The following morning, Wednesday, March 14, Begin convened the cabinet and reported that Carter had phoned from Cairo airport to report a satisfactory response from the Egyptian leader. Sadat had agreed to the new text dealing with the conflict of obligations over treaties and had approved the draft of a joint letter that did not mention Egyptian liaison officers in Gaza. The cabinet agreed to the peace treaty. On March 20 the Knesset followed suit by a vote of 95-18, with 2 abstaining.

The ceremony marking the signing of the peace treaty was originally to take place jointly in Cairo and Jerusalem. Sadat changed his mind and instead it was held on March 26 in Washington, with the Egyptian president and the Israeli prime minister present and signing for their countries (Carter signed as well for the United States). Witnessing the ceremony, Dayan thought the speeches of Carter, Begin, and Sadat were only mediocre; the three had spoken so much during the past few months on the importance of peace that there was almost nothing new left to say. Still, Dayan could not help but be impressed with the significance of the event—the signing of the first peace treaty between Israel and an Arab state!

◆ 15 ◆

NEARING THE END

Now THAT the peace treaty was signed, and the arduous negotiating sessions were behind him, Moshe Dayan could turn to a long-delayed problem—his personal health. For more than a year he had been feeling out of sorts, finding it strenuous to walk up a flight of stairs or climb a hill. Almost any physical effort, such as the kind he was used to in fixing up his garden at Zahala, seemed too much. Still, he could not place himself under a doctor's care. He had committed himself to a few weeks in the Far East and so on April 23 he left for a seventeen-day jaunt to Nepal, Burma, Singapore, and Thailand. When he returned he asked his doctors to find out what was wrong. A series of tests were done and nothing was found at first. Then on June 21 an X ray was taken and Dayan was diagnosed as having a growth in his colon. Cancer? he asked the doctors. They would not say, not until they could operate. They advised that the surgery take place as soon as possible. Dayan phoned Rahel at home and told her the news. Thoughts of death crept into his mind. He tried to act calmly about it.

Still, the awful anticipation before the doctors would find out whether the growth had spread to other parts of his body had to be faced. Perhaps it was no coincidence that the next night he dreamed of climbing a hill and trying desperately to reach the top, where he hoped to find a haven. "I am exhausted, and the going is hard," he recalled, "but I continue to climb without pause. The track I follow is known to me, and so is my objective. I am clambering up the hillside just north of my village of Nahalal, the site of the village cemetery."[1]

The operation took place on Sunday, June 24, and the news was good. The cancer had not spread. His recovery period went smoothly and quickly. Among his visitors was Egyptian minister of state for foreign affairs Boutrus Ghali, who noticed that the foreign minister's voice had become quite hoarse. Don't worry, Dayan joked with him, Israelis had heard enough of what he had to say already.

Sitting there in Tel Hashomer Hospital, Dayan felt a need for a summing-up of his life. He turned to poetry, always a solace for him, often affording him the best means to get across his true feelings to those closest to him. The poem he wrote was for Rahel and his three children. It was so personal, it revealed so much of him, that he decided it was better they not see it during his lifetime. He called it "At the End of the Day":

> *Come, my three children and Rahel, and let us sit*
> *together around the stone in the garden.*
> *I find myself at my nightfall, the wind is blowing from*
> *the sea.*
> *My days were not devoted to you. I was never the*
> *perfect father.*
> *I followed my own path, never exposing my grief and*
> *joy.*
> *I lived my own life.*
> *Only two things I could do:*
> *Sow, plow and reap the wheat and*
> *Fight back the guns threatening our homes.*
> *Let each of you cultivate our ancestors' land, and have*
> *the sword within reach above your bed. And at the end*
> *of your days, bring it down and give it to your children.*
> *And now, let each of you take his bundle and*
> *walking stick to cross his Jordan in his own way.*
> *My blessings be with you, do not let the hardships of*
> *life paralyze you.*[2]

He had sown, and he had fought back the guns threatening his home long enough. It was not that he wanted to leave the position of authority he had held for the past few years, nor to cease being foreign minister. Yet the authority had been ebbing away from him, the power to accomplish what he had wanted to do. He had been there at the crucial moments when Israel carved out the first peace treaty with an Arab state. Not just any Arab state, but Egypt, the most powerful, most important, most crucial.

He had been there joining the other Israeli leaders in a solemn pledge that the peace treaty with Egypt would not be the end of the road, but only the beginning; that Israel and Egypt and the United States would turn their attention next to the Palestinian Arabs, turn their attention to the negotiations spelled out in the peace treaty that would aim at full autonomy for these inhabitants of the West Bank and Gaza. The words were not there as a trick or a deception or a fig leaf, at least not in Moshe Dayan's view. They were there, but not to set the stage for an Israeli withdrawal from the West Bank and the Gaza Strip. Dayan had long been against such a development. The words of Camp David were designed to bind Israel to thoughtful, constructive peace talks that could not be swept under the carpet; that would allow Israel and the Palestinian Arabs to meet halfway, to work out terms for peaceful coexistence. Dayan favored holding such talks at once.

Yet no sooner had the ink on the peace treaty become dry than Menachem Begin began to sweep autonomy under the rug. He began deftly, not announcing it in public for all to hear and argue and criticize, when Moshe Dayan volunteered to head the Israeli delegation to the autonomy talks scheduled to begin soon. Dayan did not push himself on Begin, he did not say, "Appoint me or I quit." That had never been Dayan's style. He said instead, "You can appoint me or anyone else."

That was exactly what Begin did. He appointed Yosef Burg, one of the great veterans of the Israeli political scene, but not a man experienced in foreign policy or defense matters. Burg was the interior minister, and for Begin the choice seemed safe. Dr. Burg would not call rump cabinet sessions into being as Moshe Dayan had done back in February. Nor would he go off and meet with PLO sympathizers in the occupied territories as Dayan had been doing of late. Dr. Burg would not stomp and holler the way Dayan would if Begin took his time in dishing out autonomy to the Palestinians.

It took Dayan some time before he realized what Menachem Begin was doing. Dayan was the foreign minister, but when it came to the critical issue facing the country—the fate of the Palestinian Arabs in the territories—he had little influence over policy. To be sure, he was a member of the autonomy delegation, but then again so were a handful of other ministers such as Shmuel Tamir and Moshe Nissim. Slowly but surely, Menachem Begin had become his own foreign minister, making his own policy, setting the pace. That pace was very, very slow.

Through the summer of 1979 and into the fall Dayan swallowed the bitter pill of isolation, of being neutralized. He watched and listened as his cabinet colleagues harped on him, passed the word to their favorite journalists that Moshe Dayan was a bit too liberal for their taste, a bit too eager to give away the store to the Egyptians and the Americans, a bit too eager to turn over the West Bank and the Gaza Strip to Yassir Arafat and his henchmen. Had not Dayan hustled off to the Gaza Strip to meet Dr. Haider Abdel-Shafi, that well-known supporter of the PLO? Just a few days later, Dayan again closeted himself with a leading West Bank Communist, Dr. Ahmed Hamzi Natsche. The implication was that Dayan was trying to sell these men his own proposal that Israel should allow the Palestinian Arabs to establish autonomy without negotiating its nature with the Israelis (unilateral autonomy). Dayan would only say that if you want to know what the Arabs are thinking, you do not make appointments with the Jews. You talk to the Arabs. Few among Begin's supporters thought it a very acceptable explanation. They did not want Dayan "interfering" with the autonomy issue. He should stick to improving Israel's relations with countries in Asia or Africa. Dayan would have none of that. It seemed odd timing: Dayan had not been willing to resign on the big issues of the past. He did not resign when Golda Meir and Bar-Lev and Galili turned him down on the Sinai pullback, or when the guilt tore at his consciousness at the time of the Yom Kippur War, or when the widows were screaming murderer outside his house. How strange, now, simply because he had nothing to do, he entertained thoughts of quitting.

The years had taken their toll on him. When things had gone wrong in the past, he had the inner strength, physical as well as mental, to ride out difficulties and, if not to fight, at least to wait until the storm had passed. Sixty-four years old, racked by illness, his one good eye failing, confronting the terrifying prospect of going blind, he did not have it in him to wait out the storm.

He resigned in late October 1979. He was bowing out, he told the reporters, because "there must be a foreign minister with views acceptable to the government who can express the government's views on foreign policy—about relations with the Arabs, which was the focal foreign policy issue."

In penning his resignation letter to the prime minister, Dayan made much the same point: "It is not possible for a foreign minister to perform his function properly without him being personally engaged, involved and being among the formulators of Israel's policy on this question (the relationship to the Arabs of the areas). It is no secret to you that I differ over the manner (the technique) and the substance whereby the autonomy negotiations are being conducted, and this applies, too, to a number of activities performed by us on the ground."

Indeed, he and Begin did differ over the manner and the technique and the substance. For that reason, the prime minister did not beg Dayan to reconsider, he just said he was sorry. In reality he was not. By this time Menachem Begin did not need legitimacy and respectability, as he had in May 1977. Menachem Begin had stood up to Jimmy Carter and to Anwar Sadat and had emerged from the pain and suffering of giving up settlements in the Sinai with the support and blessings of his followers. Now he did not need Moshe Dayan (or Ezer Weizman, for that matter, who resigned as defense minister the following June).

Dayan left, but not quietly. He embarked on a one-man campaign to try to convince the country that he was right and Menachem Begin was wrong. Dayan thought that he knew how to get the peace process back on track. He spoke out in favor of unilateral autonomy, a first step toward unhinging the Israeli occupation. "We should start," he told *Time* magazine, "by giving a lot, by withdrawing the military administration, even though we get nothing in return. We would pull out our military forces, unless of course the PLO took over and what we had planned as a peaceful region suddenly turned into a base for terrorism. Then we would come back with a stronger force.

". . . And even if the autonomy talks fail, about 90 percent of what I am describing we could do unilaterally. There never would have been open bridges between Israel and Jordan if we had waited for King Hussein's signature; not even Henry Kissinger could have negotiated that one."[3]

A year later he was ready to put his proposal to the test. Let the Knesset vote on it. If approved, Menachem Begin would be on notice and would have to respond. It was a brilliant piece of strategy. Unfortunately for Dayan, the prospects were slim, if only because he faced the formidable presence of Begin. To the prime minister unilateral autonomy was a recipe for disaster. In his view Dayan's machinations were a sly attempt to move toward autonomy and therefore represented no progress at all. When Dayan brought his plan before the Knesset in late December 1980, Begin got up on the Knesset rostrum and said the plan was worthless, a diversion from the Camp David accords.

Yes, said Dayan, it was a diversion all right, but a diversion was necessary to give the Palestinians what they were supposed to get out of Camp David, and to make sure that Mr. Begin did not drop a bombshell and annex the whole West Bank when no one was looking. Dayan's proposal was doomed from the start. The Knesset was in Begin's pocket and Dayan had little political clout anymore. The Knesset voted it down, not by a wide margin, only 43–39, but enough to send a signal to Moshe Dayan. Let Begin manage the pace of autonomy. Mind your business. "One day they will yet deign to bend down and take my proposal out of the wastebasket," he told his colleagues back in the Knesset dining room.

IN RETROSPECT, Moshe Dayan might have wished that he had gone back to Zahala and finished out his days writing another book. (He wanted to write a book about the 1967 war that would be called "The Guns of Ras-Natsrani".) He discussed this book project often with Rahel. If his one eye did not fail him, it might have been a satisfying way to depart from the political arena. He was not ready for such a quiet life. For one thing, he felt quite well. The doctors had been right. The cancer had not spread. His mind was sharp and there was one more battle to fight.

If Menachem Begin was going to keep autonomy in the deep freeze, the battle was far from being over. As long as he had breath in him, he would remain in the arena and fight for those ideas that he believed in. He always had said to himself, and to anyone who was listening, that he knew best how to resolve the problems of the Arabs. Never did he believe it more than now. So he vowed to stay in politics.

The wisest course for him to take would be to sneak back into the Labor party. That had always been his natural home. A man of fewer complexes, a man who asked himself what was in his own best interest, would have rung up Labor party leader Shimon Peres and asked to be let back in. Moshe Dayan felt too much bitterness toward Labor politicians—too many of them had failed to rally behind him while the public hauled him out to dry after the Yom Kippur War. Too many of them had called him a traitor when he had become Begin's foreign minister. He would not beg, but he would wait to see if Labor sought him out.

So he waited through the winter of 1980–81, but when the phone did not ring, he passed word to a few of his political allies that he was considering forming his own political party to run in the June 1981 elections. Perhaps he would find a receptive audience for his thoughts on unilateral autonomy. Perhaps he would touch a nerve.

The initial soundings were positive. The first polls asking how Moshe Dayan would do at the head of his own ticket looked good indeed. Some said twenty-two Knesset seats. Some said seventeen. Some said fifteen. A good deal of seats for a new party.

IN MARCH Dayan visited Cairo for three days, a visit packed with emotion for him, coming in peace to the capital of the country against whom he had fought so often. He met with Anwar Sadat and other Egyptian officials, and waded into the Khan Khalili market in Cairo's old city. A milling mob surrounded him. Brushing aside his security men, Dayan grabbed for outstretched hands. An eerie silence fell over the area of the Pyramids and the Sphinx when Dayan visited there later: The entire area had been cleared by police of everyone but the official party.

INSTEAD OF going home to Zahala in the spring of 1981, Moshe Dayan formed Telem, a political party that was designed for one purpose only—to promote the cause of Moshe Dayan. Telem—a Hebrew acronym for State Renewal party—might as well have been called the Dayan party. It was his show and his show alone. A few of his most loyal followers picked up stakes and left their old parties and joined forces with Dayan. Mostly the list he put together contained a lot of political unknowns. It did not matter. It did not matter what the actual Telem platform was, left, right, centrist. It only mattered that Dayan would run at the head of the ticket.

To be sure, there were arguments, heated ones, over the Telem platform. Ironically, Dayan was drifting to the political left—at least in the eyes of some of his former political cronies, such as Yigal Hurvitz. When Dayan wanted to slip into the platform a willingness on the part of Telem to let the PLO come to a peace conference on the Arab refugees (if it would drop terror and endorse UN Resolution 242) the far right within Telem went apoplectic. Dayan gave in on that one—the expression "PLO" was dropped and the platform instead used the more innocuous phrase "representatives of the refugees." Dayan was prevailed upon to change the statement that "Jordan would have the right to raise Jerusalem" in peace talks to "Jordan would have the right to raise holy places."

On the most sensitive issue of all—Israel's nuclear option—Dayan might have been tempted to include some reference to the ideas he had been tossing around, largely in private, that it was time for the country to declare itself capable of building a nuclear weapon. Dayan's reasoning had been largely based on his growing fear that Israel was running out of money to pay for all the tanks and planes and bullets and artillery shells. Nuclear deterrence seemed much cheaper than pursuing the conventional arms race. Such thinking may have been wise and prudent and practical, but few were ready to turn the question of Israeli nuclear weapons into a no-holds-barred national debate. Now that he was out of office and there was little likelihood that he would ever hold public office again, Dayan savored the luxury of speaking his mind on this delicate subject. In the past, as chief of staff, later as minister of defense, he would have ordered the military censor to throw such public speeches into the garbage. He would have threatened jail to any senior Israeli official who wished to enunciate such policies in public. Though he was out of office, and the subject remained taboo, Dayan still had that untouchable quality to him. In the spring of 1981 he was still eager to launch that debate. Upon reflection he decided that doing so during an election campaign would expose him to fresh criticism. Why provide the ammunition? He squelched the urge of some in Telem to include a clear-cut nuclear weapons position in the platform.

Even before the balloting took place postmortems were being offered. Dayan was moody, tyrannical, he was not running the campaign diligently. Worst of all, he refused to answer the critics who challenged him as a soldier, a politician, a human being. One day the Yom Kippur War was dredged up. The next day, his flaunting the law in accumulating archaeological treasures. On another day, the sky-high lecture fees and payments for newspaper interviews he had accepted. The public relations people at Telem told Dayan forthrightly: You've got to fight, you've got to return the fire. Tell them what you think. The public deserves to hear from you. He did not have the heart. He did not believe it would make any difference. He saw no reason to respond when he had done no wrong.

When the voters seriously thought about the election they concluded that Dayan was not for them. It is not clear why Dayan did so well in the early public opinion polls. Many Israeli politicians have found that the voters love them six months before the election, but like them much less as they approach the ballot box. The same was true of Dayan. As the June 30 election approached, Dayan nose-dived in the polls, and with only a few weeks to go some predicted he might get as few as two Knesset seats.

Dayan's silence on the issues forced the public to judge him largely on his physical appearance, which was not good at all. He looked like the image of death: a gaunt, thin, frail body, lined face, ill-fitting clothes, and the sad, almost pathetic look that seemed to say: "What the hell am I doing here?" The public knew that a nearly blind, physically weakened shell of a man was acting out a pathetic play in which he was the one tragic character. If he would not get off stage, they would have to send him a message. When he called rallies, they did not show up. Once, when he found out in advance that not even fifty people had come to one of his appearances in Jerusalem, Dayan sent word ahead that he had been called away suddenly for urgent consultations. Everyone saw through the charade. It was only a matter of time and then the voters would have the final say.

On June 30 they voted to return Menachem Begin to office but not by a large margin. The prime minister had been in trouble going into the election, and it appeared that Shimon Peres and the Labor party had a reasonable chance of regaining office. Then came the dramatic Israeli air raid against the Iraqi nuclear reactor three weeks before the election. The Likud eked out a victory, getting forty-eight Knesset seats to Labor's forty-seven. While the voters were lining up to choose Likud or Labor, they stayed away in droves from Moshe Dayan and his Telem party. Two Knesset seats were all he got. Dayan was humiliated. He was sorry that he had run. He was sorry that he had dragged all of his friends and admirers through the muddy waters of politics for such meager results.

In July he went off to the United States. Glaucoma had developed in the "good" eye and the doctors thought laser surgery might help. Little came of it. He had developed a cataract as well, but the risks of the eye being adversely affected by surgery were too great and so it was left alone. Around this time he took an active interest in purchasing an apartment. He did not tell Rahel the real reason he was interested in one. He simply pressed her to look for one. In the back of his mind, according to Rahel, Dayan realized that she would have to sell the home in Zahala after his death and use the proceeds to live on. At first Rahel did not suspect the true reason behind the search for the apartment. She argued that she did not see why they needed to spend the money. In the end, he found a place in a Tel Aviv high-rise and paid $235,000 for it, putting the apartment in her name. She asked him if he wanted to look at the apartment before she signed for it. His face grew contorted and he shouted, "I don't want to see it." Then she knew why he had purchased it.[4]

SOON AFTER Dayan's return to Israel, Gad Ya'acobi came to see him. Ya'acobi found him exhausted, his eye red. He was in great pain. He mentioned the pain, which was unusual. Ya'acobi had rarely heard Dayan talk about his physical ailments. He knew how much he must have been suffering. Ya'acobi's mind was on politics. He wanted to secure Dayan's agreement for Telem to link forces with Ya'acobi's Labor Alignment. Together with the Citizens Rights Movement they would then have fifty Knesset seats. Perhaps, together with some of the other parties, Peres could then ask the president for the mandate to form the next government. Dayan said that he had already told Prime Minister Begin that Telem would not join him in a new government. Their differences over the West Bank and the autonomy were too serious. "I haven't initiated talks with anyone," Dayan told Ya'acobi. "Do I have any divisions?" Not with only two Knesset seats, he was told. "But it seems to me that with you [the Labor Alignment], in principle, we can come to an understanding."[5] Dayan said he would recommend to the president that Peres form the next government. However, the president asked Begin, since he appeared to have the best chance to form a government. Ultimately, Begin set up a coalition with sixty-one Knesset members supporting it.

In August Gad Ya'acobi came back to Dayan with a new offer. Would he be interested in formally joining the Labor party? Dayan said yes, but it would have to be Telem joining, not just Moshe Dayan. Ya'acobi and some others in Labor made soundings, but the results were largely negative. The kibbutz movement, Ahdut Avoda, and others still had not forgiven Dayan his defection to the Likud. When Ya'acobi brought back the findings, Dayan was irate. He informed his Telem party colleagues that if they wished to find a place in Labor, they could. He was no longer interested.

THE NEXT few months brought the mental anguish of a man with few friends looking in on him, an anguish compounded by the fear of going blind. When Dayan felt well, he talked about writing another book, this one about Jewish heroes. Hannah Senesh, Meir Har-Zion, and Yonatan Netanyahu were mentioned as subjects. He saw a little bit of himself in them and he hoped that others did as well. He would enjoy writing about their exploits.

Those close to Dayan sensed his end was near. One day in August his son Assi phoned him. He and his father had been estranged for years. Dayan had had almost no contact with him. Assi asked if he could come over. He wanted to borrow $1,500 from his father. He had never asked him for money before. But now he needed it, and with his father's reputation for wealth, Assi thought he could afford it. Assi had read the newspapers. They described Dayan in dire terms. Assi planned to exploit this meeting to let his father know with all the frankness and brutal honesty that he could muster what the years of estrangement had meant to him, why he, as a son, had not wanted to have anything to do with him. Assi looked around at the interior of Dayan's home and thought to himself that his father now lived like an Arab sheikh. Assi also noticed the sharp contrast between the opulence and the "half-dead" figure standing near him.

Despite his father's physical appearance, Assi began his monologue. Sometimes he spoke in the past tense, as if his father were already dead.

"My God, it's true, you are going to die. Listen, I want to tell you a few things. . . . I want to tell you that you were OK, you were quite a father till the age of sixteen. Since then just one thing I remember, that you are an SOB, you are the worst person, full of yourself, full of shit. You are the one who invented screwing as a national item; who sends his bodyguard to give my kids chocolate on their birthdays. They don't know much about you. But I'll tell them. That you were a practical man, without any great vision like Ben-Gurion. . . . You are the generation that lost sight . . . of what we were. You made this country after the Six Day War into a little fascist fraction, a little SS-trooping nation with the nationality on our identity cards being Jewish. . . . You're trying to be something you are not. You have changed this whole state into a racist one. Everything B.G., who was God for you, said, you did exactly the opposite, because at a certain point you thought you were David the King. But one thing you should remember: You were always like Iago—stuck to the asses of prime ministers, always. Begin, Golda, even Eshkol. You were so obedient, like a good Roman general. But you were afraid of Caesar.

"You could have saved the Yom Kippur War. You had a good idea and you should have resigned. If you had vision you would have seen it was endless, [the chances for peace] really gone. But you said no. [You] listened to Golda . . . and that's why it happened, the Yom Kippur War.

"You started to hate everybody, you made us into losers. We behaved according to your standard of ethics.

"Anyhow I want you to know that I simply hate your guts. So when you die, remember there's one person who thinks of you as a fake, as a killer. I understand that you were trying to get a peace with Egypt but it was to compensate, it was your conscience—because if you really knew anything about peace you could have brought it many years ago. You could have become a prime minister many years ago. You . . . created the best army in the world, i.e., the best killers. Better than the Germans and Rommel, and you contributed nothing to this land. If you did contribute, you ruined it. You didn't listen to B.G. You didn't read enough books. You were so . . . busy, you don't know what Zionism is all about. [You think it is] everything to do with selfishness and nothing to do with the country. . . .

"You were interviewed in the paper and you said that if you could live again you'd never have a family. I hope you understand what that means to me. That I am your mistake. Things have changed. Now you are my mistake. I had to go through being your son for quite a while. Till the age of twenty-one. Then I found a way out of it—[there were] people who tried to appreciate me for whatever I am. And they did. It worked. Films, et cetera. I was busy."

Until this point Dayan had just listened without the strength or the will to interrupt. As the words poured out, tears began to form in his eye. All that the father could think of saying was, "I can't answer you now in a way that will explain everything. The money is there. Take it from Rahel." Assi did. They would meet again when the end was being counted in minutes.[6]

DAYAN'S HEALTH deteriorated in the fall. Friends who saw him then recalled how frail he looked. His mind, however, was active. He always had the time and the patience to provide one more analysis of the Middle East situation. His friends were saddened at his being nearly blind. It was worst for him when he was in a dark room and suddenly emerged into the daylight, or when a lit room abruptly became dark. For a long time he had had trouble reading and often had asked Rahel or her daughter Orna to read to him. Rahel or a bodyguard hinted about what was in front of him.

Then on October 6 came a psychological blow: the assassination of Anwar Sadat. Despite his launching of the Yom Kippur War, Sadat's death brought no rejoicing to Dayan. Both men were graduates of Camp David, colleagues in a peace process that linked them both indelibly to the historic Israeli-Egyptian peace treaty.

And now one of the architects of that treaty was dead. Dayan worried that the treaty might not survive. He showed up at the Egyptian embassy to pay his respects, and wrote an opinion column, his last, appearing on October 16. In it he warned his countrymen not to let the treaty collapse.

In the week after Sadat's death Dayan heard from a few acquaintances from the past. The phone rang less and less now. Eli Rubinstein, Dayan's former aide, had been in touch with him on the Saturday night after Sadat's killing, and they talked emotionally about how this might affect the peace process.

One subject now was always on his mind—death. He knew that his physical condition was a signal of what was to come sooner or later. He thought in terms of months, not weeks, or days. He was interviewed on Israel Radio on October 6. "I don't see death as something negative or threatening," he said. "In the end I will lie on the hill in Nahalal with my family and others. Why do you think death is a terrible thing? All through my life death passed close to me and it never frightened me."

It did not frighten him now, but he knew it was near. He looked around in the darkness of his home and saw the signs. Gad Ya'acobi phoned him one night. He was leaving for the United States and he wanted to come over to say farewell. Was he free? "Yes," said Dayan remorsefully, "no one comes to see me." When Ya'acobi approached the house it was nearly dark inside, only a small light. He heard tiny footsteps and realized later that it was Dayan feeling his way along a wall, nearly blind, groping for the front door. Ya'acobi asked why there were no lights in the house. Dayan answered that it made no difference. "I can hardly make out the difference between light and dark. I don't see anything at all. I can only tell light from dark with difficulty. I don't see anything. I see your image as if it were a spot. That's in the light. I am almost totally blinded, but I won't endure this much longer."[7]

Sensing that, Dayan spoke from his heart. He knew that he was at the end of his life and he was very pessimistic about the state of Israel, about the lack of an agreement with the Palestinian Arabs and the fact that autonomy negotiations had been given over to Israeli officials who, in his view, did not know how to deal with the Arabs. He was gloomy too that Israel was getting involved in Lebanon. That, he said, would be a terrible mistake. Lebanon was like Vietnam. "I hope," he told Ya'acobi, "that you and your generation will be able to change the situation, but I'm not sure. I am very worried." As he walked out the door, Ya'acobi realized that he had just listened to a man at the end of his life.

Early in the week of October 12 Dayan experienced new pains in his chest. He shrugged them off, as he did with most of the pain he had suffered through the years. Moshe Pearlman came by to see him. Pearlman had helped him with his book, *Breakthrough*, and now they were supposed to talk about his new book project on Jewish heroes. Instead Dayan talked about the graveyard plot in Nahalal where he would be buried. Rarely had he mentioned his parents. Now, knowing the end was near, they too were on his mind. Pearlman found the conversation worrisome. Dayan had always been a fighter. Now the fight seemed to have gone out of him.

Then late Thursday night the chest pains were so intense that Rahel phoned the hospital. An ambulance was dispatched. As it was driving to Zahala, Dayan was arguing with Rahel that he did not want to go. After an hour he relented and was taken to Tel Hashomer Hospital in Tel Aviv. Prime Minister Begin was informed that Dayan had been hospitalized. "I have seen him on television," the prime minister said, referring to Dayan's appearance a few days earlier commenting on the Sadat assassination, "and he looked to me so bad that I thought he was going to die. His face was the image of a skull covered with skin." Some of the doctors feared that Dayan would not survive the night, but Friday morning he seemed back to his old self, eager to read the newspapers and write some letters.

At noon he suffered a serious heart attack. The children were called to his bedside. He was hooked up to machines. They found him alert.

Assi thought he was working himself up to say how bad a father he had been; perhaps he would ask the children for forgiveness.

"I want to tell you that there's a good chance that I'm dying. But I think I'll go to New York for another operation."

"You'll be all right," said Yael encouragingly. "Just be strong."

Such talk made Dayan angry: "You are such an idiot. Philosophy shit. Thank God I'm leaving this place." Assi and Udi left the room. Assi said to his brother. "Let's go. He's going to die. You want to watch it?"

During the late afternoon Dayan had been sleeping off and on, drugged on sleeping pills. Then at seven in the evening he awoke and wanted to try to go to the bathroom himself. The doctors had told Rahel not to let him try. He spotted a wheelchair and grabbed for it. He missed and fell to the floor with Rahel clinging to him. He lost consciousness. A half hour later the doctors told Rahel and Yael that Moshe Dayan was dead.

REACTION CAME from a variety of quarters. Prime Minister Begin broadcast a eulogy, calling Dayan "a pioneer and a soldier" and likening him to the biblical heroes of Joshua and Gideon, Jonathan and David. "For he was their brother, their son or grandson. Their blood flowed through his veins." Hosni Mubarak, the new leader of Egypt, received the news "with deep sorrow." The Soviet government newspaper *Izvestia* gave his death two paragraphs, saying that Dayan had taken part in "aggressive" wars against the Arabs. Perhaps the most poignant comment came from Shimon Peres: "He never copied anyone in his life and he can never be copied." The greatest tribute came from Anwar Nusseibeh, the former Jordanian minister of defense, who said that one could not help but like and respect Dayan. "I wish we had had him on our side."

He was buried that Sunday, October 18, in a ceremony that was simple, as he had wished. No eulogies were spoken, just his sons saying the mourner's kaddish, the Jewish prayer for the dead. Israeli leaders came, as did foreign delegations, including an Egyptian one. "Who could ever have imagined," Ezer Weizman said to Ruth, "that there would be an official Egyptian delegation, led by its minister of state for foreign affairs, Boutrus Ghali, at Moshe's funeral in Nahalal?" William French Smith, the attorney general, headed the American delegation. The coffin was wrapped in a prayer shawl and the national flag. It was borne by six generals. An aide-de-camp displayed Dayan's military decorations on a velvet cushion. Yael stood next to Rahel. Ruth stood on the other side of the grave near President Yitzhak Navon. Menachem Begin laid a wreath at the grave on behalf of the government. So did Tal Brody on behalf of the Maccabi Tel Aviv basketball team that Dayan followed faithfully. Also present were members of the bedouin el-Mazarib tribe, who still lived at the foot of Givat Shimron.

MOSHE DAYAN was a man of wealth and in his last years he had to decide where that wealth should go after his death. The obvious beneficiaries were Rahel and his three children. In fact he had taken steps while alive to protect Rahel from others who might lay claims to his assets. Those assets had once included the house at Zahala, his antiquities collection, and some assorted real estate. Even before his death, he had turned over half of the house to Rahel, and had deeded the collection (which he estimated to be worth $2 million to $2.5 million) over to her. Though he had already turned over a large part of his assets to Rahel, Dayan used the will to reassert his intent that she was to be his chief beneficiary, again trying to shield her from other claimants.

It had been assumed while Dayan was alive that he would treat Rahel and the children as equitably as possible. At least so the children thought. Rahel knew differently. She knew that Dayan had prepared at least four wills in the past few years, all of them leaving the children out completely. (Copies of these wills were shown to the author.) Rahel also knew that on August 28, 1975, Moshe Dayan had deeded the archaeology collection to her, thus making her the beneficiary of the bulk of his assets before he died. Nonetheless, Rahel urged Dayan to leave the children something.

As the week of mourning approached the end, Dayan's lawyer called Yael and informed her that other than a piece of land and half an apartment, all of Dayan's assets had been left to Rahel.

Soon everyone gathered in the lawyer's office in Tel Aviv. The will was read. Rahel was the chief beneficiary. The three children were given the quarter of an acre of land their father had owned. Udi's children were given half an apartment. Also, in the will, Dayan had asked to be buried in Nahalal, to avoid graveside eulogies, gun salutes at the funeral, and to make sure that nothing was named after him. He made a request of everyone: Please don't take the will to court in case there was disagreement.

Rahel says that Dayan warned her that she might come under pressure to change the will, but under no circumstances was she to bend under that pressure: "You must not give them a penny," he had said. "If you do, you will be a wicked woman 'till the end of your life. If you give them nothing, after three months they will get tired of it and that will be the end of it."[8]

Rahel sensed that, no matter what her husband had said to her, she must make some effort to alleviate the blow. She offered to give the other half of the apartment (Udi's children were to get one-half under the will) to the Dayan grandchildren. In other words, each grandchild would receive one-fifth of a half of an apartment. Rahel had conditions for this: The children must promise not to do anything that would hurt Dayan's name or hers.

Yael was dumbfounded and would make no deals at this juncture.

At this point the attorney produced a copy of two documents. One was a letter Dayan had written to the children. The other was a copy of the poem he had penned while in the hospital after his cancer surgery.

The letter from Dayan, dated February 1980, read:

> Dear Yula, Udi and Assi,
> I thought it proper to add a few clarifying words to the will . . .
> . . . It isn't a secret that my heart is damaged. All the treatments and medications haven't been effective and it may suddenly cease to beat (maybe during my sleep)—what is referred to as a heart attack.
> If this happens soon, Rahel will continue, I hope, to live for scores of years. She is healthy and ten years younger than I am. This is why I decided to leave her the money we have jointly. . . . As to you, one generation younger than Rahel and myself, I believe that each of you will be able to take care of himself and his family. Yours, Father.[9]

Yael dismissed the letter bitterly as the work more of an accountant than a father. When the lawyer had broken the news to her on the phone, Yael penned a letter to Rahel, several pages long, which she now distributed to those in the room. It was essentially a plea to Dayan's widow that she display a generosity to the children that Dayan had not done in the will.

> How a wise man like Father, who managed his life so well, didn't think all the way—a generation ahead, when he came to settle his after-death affairs—I'll never understand.
> What are we to tell our children?
> The children I'm supposed to bring up in the light of his memory, to be like him—patriots, brave, wise, proud of him—what do I tell them about morality and justice, of parents taking care of children? What do I tell them about generosity? . . . They'll have photographs, his books, some

> letters and they will look from the outside in on everything
> that was his that will now belong to your own grandchildren.
> What do I tell them?
> My love for my father remains untouched; not so my
> respect. . . . Father's will does not "honor" him and doesn't
> add to your "dignity" either. The archaeological collection
> should be made available to the public; the house—at least
> after your lifetime—should remain in the family. . . . So
> what he didn't do when alive, maybe we'll do after his death,
> letting justice and fairness win. . . .[10]

Rahel read the letter and abandoned whatever intention she might have
had of offering more to the children.

When the Dayan children met their own attorney, he said he was
encouraged by the fact that Rahel had made an offer. The children should
try to negotiate an even better settlement.

Thirty days after Dayan's death the mourners again gathered at the
graveside. Udi did not come this time. He had closeted himself in his
room and written a long letter to his father that would be published the
following May. In its way it was just as devastating an indictment as the
one Assi had made in person to his father the previous summer. Udi's
written "J'accuse" opened with the reading of the will: "Forty-five minutes after entering the office we left the room three shamed remnants
and one millionairess." Addressing his father as "you" throughout, he
dismissed Dayan's writings as "dry military journals," in which his involvement was small. He belittled his father's rise in the military as well
by suggesting that Dayan would have advanced no further than platoon
commander in England. Udi also scoffed at the archaeological diggings
as a mere collection of "lousy jars." And he denounced Dayan as an
unfaithful husband, an incompetent general, and a man driven by greed.
In one bitter passage Udi wrote that his father had recited kaddish, the
Jewish prayer for the dead, "three times too often for someone who never
obeyed half of the ten commandments." He then accused his father of
having written books about Israel's wars purely for profit, of cultivating
the image of a simple farmer while frequenting expensive restaurants,
and even of making money out of his battle with cancer. If people are
saddened by such a eulogy, wrote the son, they should keep in mind
that he too was disappointed to have had such a father. Rahel's influence
over his father clearly annoyed Udi. "From the day you brought this
woman to your home, your hair was being cut and your power gone."[11]

Meanwhile, Rahel decided to sell the antiquities collection, leading
critics to insist that she turn the relics over to the state without financial

gain to herself. Rahel countered that Dayan had made it clear to her that the collection could be sold in order to provide for her after his death. That was why he had deeded the antiquities to her in 1975. She had offers for the collection that were higher than the price to which she eventually agreed. She preferred to keep the collection in Israel. In the end, she sold it to the Israel Museum for $1 million on the condition that it be known as the Moshe Dayan Collection. Most of the funds were provided by Laurence A. Tisch, the head of CBS. Rahel sold the house in Zahala as well, for $400,000.

She came under pressure from the children to act more generously toward them. She considered Yael's letter an insult, and she did not want to budge. "It's a terrible letter," she said. Emissaries were sent. Yael sent lawyer Ron Caspi and Zalman Shoval to see her. But she stood her ground.

"This is unheard of," Caspi said.

"Look," Rahel answered, "this is Moshe's will."

"I'm going to take the will to court."

"Look," said Rahel, "you can only take it on one ground. That Moshe was insane."

"I'll do that."

"Go ahead."

Then Rahel came under even more pressure from high-powered loyalists to the children. One of those friends proposed that Rahel provide $150,000 to be divided among the three children.

Rahel thought this might be the end of it. So she agreed on condition that she receive a letter of thanks from the children for the money. And she wanted their written statement that they would respect their father's memory. She received two letters in the spring of 1982 but was later disappointed to find that Udi had written his diatribe against his father. By that time, she no longer had the heart for a fight. "What could I do? Take them to court? Ask for the money back?"[12]

What she gave the children was done, she said later, under duress. She knew she had no choice. But under different circumstances, had Yael not written the letter, "that horrible letter," as she called it, had there been a different atmosphere among them, she might have acted differently, more generously. "Without all this viciousness, I might have considered something, some sort of settlement or whatever. By now, if I have to burn whatever is left after me, I wouldn't leave them a penny! This is finished. What they did to Moshe and what they did to me. It's disgusting."[13]

So this was how Moshe Dayan left the world: his wife and children arguing bitterly about dividing his spoils.

AFTERWORD

IN THE DECADE after Moshe Dayan's death Israel passed through further tension and violence. In June 1982, seven and a half months after he died, Israeli forces invaded Lebanon to remove Palestinian Liberation Organization fighters who had been attacking northern Israeli towns and settlements. Three years later most of the IDF left Lebanon, its mission accomplished. In December 1987 Palestinian Arabs on the West Bank and in the Gaza Strip began an uprising, known as the Intifada: Rock-throwing Palestinians confronted rifle-toting Israeli soldiers in daily violent confrontations. Hoping to eject IDF troops from the occupied lands and gain political independence, the Palestinians continued their Intifada into the early 1990s. Then, from January 17 to February 28, 1991, Iraq engaged in war against Israel, aiming Scud missles at the country's population centers. Despite the Lebanon war, despite the Intifida, despite the Iraqi missle war, Israel's peace treaty with Egypt, signed in Marach 1979, has survived.

The survival of that peace treaty may be Moshe Dayan's greatest legacy.

It is a fitting tribute to Dayan that when Israelis think of him now they dwell mostly on his knack for creative diplomacy, the kind he exercised as Jerusalem commander in 1948 and as Israeli foreign minister in the late 1970s. They wonder what legerdemain he might have employed to resolve current Middle East problems had he been around today.

What would he have thought of the Intifada? Would he have changed his mind and advocated a Palestinian state? Would he have urged that Israel negotiate with Yassir Arafat and the Palestine Liberation Organization?

Dayan undoubtedly would have understood that the Intifada was inevitable. For all that he tried to suppress Palestinian political feelings, Dayan was only too aware that Palestinians would one day resort to increased violence to attain a state and to disgorge the IDF from their midst. For years he fought against a Palestinian state and refused to negotiate with Yassir Arafat and the Palestine Liberation Organization. Yet Dayan was a great pragmatist, and toward the end of his career he had given a strong indication that he was moving toward dialogue with the PLO: When he championed unilateral autonomy for the Palestinians on the West Bank and in Gaza, he was fully aware that such a step could lead to Palestinian statehood, but he was not deterred.

Surveying the Israeli-Palestinian conflict today, Dayan would have been saddened at the way events had dealt a blow to his "open gates" policy for Jews and Arabs. He had believed that Jews and Arabs had no choice but to learn to live with one another. For twenty years—between 1967 and 1987—the relative peace and quiet that prevailed on the West Bank and in Gaza appeared to suggest that Dayan's policy was feasible. It was all illusion. The Intifada, raising the level of violence between Palestinians and Israelis to a new high, closed the two communities off from one another: Israelis no longer visited the West Bank, Gaza, or Arab Jerusalem as they routinely had. Palestinian Arabs no longer frequented Jewish Jerusalem. Whereas once Dayan preached a policy of integrating the West Bank, Gaza, and Israel, a decade after his death Israelis talked more and more of the virtue of separating themselves from the West Bank and Gaza. It would not have surprised Dayan to find that a solution to the Israeli-Palestinian conflict remains elusive.

Dayan would have been pleased that the army he had helped to shape was stronger than it had ever been, the most potent force in the Middle East. Though Israel's relationship with the United States had its ups and downs, Washington still made sure that the Jewish state had the armaments it needed to retain a qualitative edge over the Arabs. Moreover, thousands of highly skilled Soviet Jewish immigrants had arrived in the early 1990s, deepening the nation's self-confidence. In recent years Syria and Iraq had constituted the two main military threats to Israel.

At the time of Dayan's death, Saddam Hussein's Iraq had been engaged in a war with Iran for over a year. Nine years later, in the summer of 1990, Saddam invaded Kuwait, triggering a crisis that brought a half million American troops to Saudi Arabia and its surroundings. Shortly after America went to war against Iraq on January 16, 1991, Saddam Hussein launched his Scud missiles at Israel, hoping to lure the Jewish state into the fighting. The United States urged Israel not to retaliate against Iraq for those missile attacks. An Israeli retaliation might have forced Saudi Arabia, Syria, and Egypt to drop out of the coalition of military forces arrayed against Iraq and join Iraq in fighting the Jewish state. That would have made it far more difficult, if not impossible, for the United States to carry on its quest of forcing Iraq out of Kuwait. The whole nature of the Persian Gulf crisis would have changed from one in which America and its Arab coalition partners were lined up against Iraq in order to resolve the Kuwait question to one in which America was forced to side with Israel against an Iraqi-led Arab coalition.

Had he been alive for this crisis, Moshe Dayan would not have been surprised that Washington had cautioned Israel against intervening in the Persian Gulf war, but it seems reasonable to assume that Israel's policy of restraint—of not retaliating against Iraq for the missile attacks— would have pained Dayan. The need to retaliate, if attacked, in order to preserve Israel's deterrent capability, was an important part of Dayan's military thinking. Yet, as a warrior who was also a statesman, he would have understood the political considerations that compelled the United States to urge Israel to refrain from combat. It would not have been easy for him to watch his country absorb a military blow without responding. One can hear him asking what possible justification there was for Israel to sit quietly. Still, had he been able to look on as America decimated the Iraqi armed forces, Dayan probably would have thought Israel's restraint was in fact the proper thing to do. After all, there would be one less Arab military power around to go to war against Israel. That would have pleased Moshe Dayan.

NOTES

CHAPTER 1

1. Shmuel Dayan, *The Promised Land* (London: Routledge and Kegan Paul, 1961), p. 4.

2: Shmuel Dayan, *On the Banks of the Jordan River and the Sea of Galilee* (Tel Aviv: Massada Press, 1959), pp. 160–61.

3: Dvorah Dayan, *In Happiness and Grief* (Hebrew) (Tel Aviv: Massada Press 1957), p. 292.

4: Dvorah Dayan, *Pioneer* (Tel Aviv: Massada Press, 1968), p. 22.

5: Shmuel Dayan, *The Promised Land*, p. 16.

6: Ibid., p. 64.

7: Dvorah Dayan, *In Happiness and Grief*, pp. 331–41.

8: Ibid., p. 18.

9: Binyamin Zarhi, interview with author, July 31, 1989.

10: Shmuel Dayan, *The Promised Land*, pp. 76–77.

11: *Yediot Aharonot*, "Dayan—The Man We Didn't Know," October 15, 198?

12: Ibid.

13: Avino'am Slutzky, interview with author, August 14, 1989.

14: *Yediot Aharonot*, "Dayan—The Man We Didn't Know," October 15, 1982.

15: Ibid.

CHAPTER 2

1: Binyamin Zarhi, interview with author, July 31, 1989.

2: Ruth Dayan and Helga Dudman, *The Story of Ruth Dayan: . . . Or Did I Dream a Dream?* (New York: Harcourt Brace Jovanovich, Inc., 1973), p. 16.

3: Ibid., p. 20.

4: Ruth Dayan, interview with author, November 26, 1989.

5: Moshe Dayan, *Story of My Life* (New York: William Morrow and Company, New York, 1976), p. 39.

6: Ibid., p. 41.

7: Ruth Dayan, *The Story of Ruth Dayan*, p. 60.

8: Yael Dayan, *My Father, His Daughter* (New York: Farrar Straus Giroux, 1985), p. 28.

9: Ruth Dayan, interview with author, November 26, 1989.

10: Yossi Harel, interview with author, April 24, 1989.

11: Ruth Dayan, *The Story of Ruth Dayan*. The quotes from Ruth Dayan's letters to Moshe appear in Ruth's memoirs, p. 66.

12: Ruth Dayan, interview with author, November 26, 1989.

13: Ruth Dayan, *The Story of Ruth Dayan*, p. 59.

14: Avino'am Slutzky, interview with author, August 14, 1989.

15: Ibid.

16: Ruth Dayan, *The Story of Ruth Dayan*, p. 54.

17: Moshe Dayan, "Dayan Talks Candidly About Himself and His Ideas," interview with the *Observer* (London), January 16, 1972.

18: Moshe Dayan, *Story of My Life*, p. 45.

19: Ibid., p. 47.

20: Ruth Dayan, *The Story of Ruth Dayan*, pp. 62–63.

CHAPTER 3

1: *Ma'ariv*, "Dayan's letters from Acre Jail," October 1, 1982.

2: Ibid.

3: Ruth Dayan, *The Story of Ruth Dayan*, p. 78.

4: Shmuel Dayan, *The Promised Land*, p. 112.

5: Ben Feller, interview with author, July 2, 1989.

6: *Ma'ariv*, "Love Letters from Acre Jail," October 1, 1982.

7: Shmuel Dayan, *The Promised Land*, p. 122.

8: Ruth Dayan, interview with author, February 28, 1989.

9: Yael Dayan, *My Father, His Daughter*, p. 46–47.

10: Ibid.

11: Moshe Carmel, interview with author, May 7, 1989.

12: Moshe Dayan, "Dayan Talks Candidly About Himself and His Ideas," interview with the *Observer* (London), January 16, 1972.

13: Ruth Dayan, *The Story of Ruth Dayan*, p. 101.

14: Eliahu Lankin, interview with author, January 24, 1990.
15: *Jerusalem Post*, "The Rise and Fall of Moshe Dayan," April 12, 1974.
16: Iska Shadmi, interview with author, April 24, 1989.
17: Zalman Shoval, interview with author, June 27, 1989.
18: Moshe Dayan, *Story of My Life*, pp. 82–83.
19: Ruth Dayan, *The Story of Ruth Dayan*, p. 112.
20: Israel Gefen, interview with author, March 26, 1989.

CHAPTER 4

1: *Haboker*, "Interview with David Ben-Gurion," March 6, 1964.
2: Avino'am Slutzky, interview with author, August 14, 1989.
3: Yohanan Pelz, interview with author, April 4, 1989.
4: Ibid.
5: Israel Gefen, interview with author, March 26, 1989.
6: Moshe Dayan, *Story of My Life*, p. 99.
7: Ibid., p. 98.
8: Israel Gefen, interview with author, March 26, 1989.
9: Raphael Vardi, interview with author, February 7, 1989.
10: Israel Gefen, interview with author, March 26, 1989.

CHAPTER 5

1: Ezer Weizman *On Eagles' Wings* (London: Weidenfeld and Nicolson, London, 1976), p. 92.
2. Ruth Dayan, *The Story of Ruth Dayan*, p. 149.
3: Avi Shlaim, *Collusion Across the Jordan* (Oxford: Clarendon Press, 1988), pp. 444–45.
4: Ibid., pp. 459–60.
5: *Ha'aretz*, "With Dayan, About Dayan," May 22, 1981.

CHAPTER 6

1: Yosef Almogi, interview with author, May 2, 1990.
2: Avraham Adan, interview with author, April 13, 1989.
3: Moshe Dayan, *Story of My Life*, p. 161.
4: Meir Har-Zion, interview with author, July 30, 1989.
5: Uri Ben-Ari, interview with author, June 7, 1989.
6: Ariel Sharon with David Chanoff, *Warrior: The Autobiography of Ariel Sharon* (New York: Simon and Schuster, 1989), pp. 73–76.
7: Yehoshafat Harkabi, interview with author, December 16, 1988.
8: Sharon, *Warrior*, p. 108.
9: *Bamachane*, "Dayan Address to Army Officers," September 5, 1955.
10: Moshe Dayan, *Living with the Bible* (New York: Bantam, 1978), p. 81.

CHAPTER 7

1: Matti Golan, *Shimon Peres, A Biography* (London: Weidenfeld and Nicolson, 1982), p. 30.

2: Rahel (Rabinovitch) Dayan, interview with author, January 17, 1989.

3: Shlomo Gazit, interview with author, January 26, 1989.

4: *Yediot Aharonot*, "The Moshe Dayan I Knew," October 23, 1981.

5: Ibid.

6: Raphael Vardi, interview with author, February 12, 1989.

7: *New York Times Magazine*, "Moshe Dayan: Reflections on a Life of War and Peace," May 4, 1980.

8: Neora Bar-Nor, interview with author, February 26, 1989.

9: From a lecture to army officers published in *Bamachane* and reported in the *Jerusalem Post*, "Dayan: Officers' Ability to Attack is Paramount," Sept. 15, 1955.

10: Iska Shadmi, interview with author, April 24, 1989.

11: Yael Dayan, *My Father, His Daughter*, p. 90.

12: Israel Gefen, interview with author, March 26, 1989.

13: Moshe Dayan, *Story of My Life*, p. 165.

14: David Ben-Gurion, *Israel: A Personal History* (New York: Sabra Books, 1972), pp. 427–28.

15: Moshe Dayan, "Israel's Borders and Security Problems," *Foreign Affairs*, January 1955, pp. 1–18.

16: Gideon Rafael, *Destination Peace, Three Decades of Israeli Foreign Policy, A Personal Memoir* (London: Weidenfeld and Nicolson, 1981), pp. 42–43.

17: Ibid.

18: *La'isha*, "Moshe Dayan—Loving Women," October 26, 1981.

19: Rahel (Rabinovitch) Dayan, interview with author, January 17, 1989.

20: Ibid.

21: Uzi Narkiss, interview with author, December 27, 1988.

22: As noted in Mordechai Bar-On's planned book, "Defense and Foreign Policy of Israel: 1955–57" (based upon his doctoral dissertation submitted to Jerusalem's Hebrew University in 1989).

23: *Davar*, "Intelligent, Brave and Original—A Year After Moshe Dayan's Death," October 14, 1982.

CHAPTER 8

1: Uzi Narkiss, interview with author, January 27, 1989.

2: Yael Dayan, *My Father, His Daughter*, p. 125.

3: Mordechai Bar-On, interview with author, December 21, 1988.

4: Meir Har-Zion, interview with author, July 30, 1989.

5: Moshe Dayan, *Diary of the Sinai Campaign 1956* (London: Sphere Books, 1966), p. 36.

6: *Yediot Aharonot*, "Working with Dayan," October 19, 1981.

7: Shlomo Gazit, interview with author, January 26, 1989.

8: Uzi Narkiss, interview with author, December 21, 1988.

9: Shlomo Gazit, interview with author, January 26, 1989.

10: Moshe Dayan, *Diary of the Sinai Campaign 1956*, p. 40.

11: Ibid., p. 43.

12: Uzi Benziman, *Sharon: An Israeli Caesar* (New York: Adam Books, 1985), pp. 71–74.

13: Moshe Dayan, *Diary of the Sinai Campaign 1956*, p. 59.

14: Moshe Dayan, *Story of My Life*, p. 233.

15: Rahel (Rabinovitch) Dayan, interview with author, February 26, 1989.

16: Noted in the *Jerusalem Post*, "The Secrets of Mitla Revealed," October 31, 1986.

17: Moshe Dayan, *Diary of the Sinai Campaign 1956*, p. 65.

18: Rahel (Rabinovitch) Dayan, interview with author, January 17, 1989.

19: Yehoshua Gavish, interview with author, August 1, 1989.

20: Moshe Dayan, *Diary of the Sinai Campaign 1956*, p. 17.

21: Meir Amit, interview with author, June 28, 1989.

22: Rahel (Rabinovitch) Dayan, interview with author, February 26, 1989.

23: Moshe Dayan, *Diary of the Sinai Campaign 1956*, p. 94.

24: Mordechai Bar-On, interview with author, December 21, 1988.

25: Rahel (Rabinovitch) Dayan, interview with author, February 26, 1989.

26: Aryeh Nehemkin, interview with the author, March 27, 1989.

27: *Time*, "A Bloody Good Exercise," November 19, 1956.

28: This episode is recounted in Ruth Dayan, *The Story of Ruth Dayan*, p. 199.

29: Rahel (Rabinovitch) Dayan, interview with author, January 17, 1989.

30: Weizman, *On Eagles' Wings*, p. 158.

31: This episode is recounted in Yoram Peri, *Between Battles and Ballots: Israeli Military in Politics* (New York: Cambridge University Press, 1983), pp. 2–3.

CHAPTER 9

1: Ezer Weizman, interview with author, August 16, 1989.

2: Raphael Vardi, interview with author, February 7, 1989.

3: Ruth Dayan, *The Story of Ruth Dayan*, p. 202.

4: *Ma'ariv*, "I Do Not Lower My Head," June 9, 1967.

5: Yael Dayan, *My Father, His Daughter*, p. 136.

6: *Jerusalem Post*, May 26, 1959.

7: *Ma'ariv*, "I Do Not Lower My Head," June 9, 1967.

8: Yael Dayan, *My Father, His Daughter*, pp. 136–37.

9: Hadassah More, interview with author, August 20, 1989.

10: Ibid.

11: Hadassah More, *Flaming Paths* (Tel Aviv: Kotz Publishers, 1963), p. 79.

12: Hadassah More, interview with author, June 19, 1989.

13: Rahel (Rabinovitch) Dayan, interview with author, June 11, 1989.

14: Yael Dayan, *My Father, His Daughter*, p. 141.

15: Gad Ya'acobi, interview with author, March 29, 1989.

16: Yael Dayan, *My Father, His Daughter*, p. 154.

17: *Jerusalem Post*, "Dayan Takes 'Hard Look'," January 8, 1959.

18: *Ha'olam Ha'zeh*, "The Secret Documents of the Yirmiya Affair," January 5, 1972.

19: Ibid.

20: Ibid.

21: Ruth Dayan, *The Story of Ruth Dayan*, p. 203.

22: Rehavam Ze'evi, interview with author, April 17, 1989.

23: Ibid.

24: Azriel Eynav, interview with author, April 16, 1989.

25: Yoseph Checanover, interview with author, April 12, 1989.

26: Abba Eban, interview with author, August 20, 1989.

27: C. L. Sulzberger, *Seven Continents and Forty Years* (New York: Quadrangle, 1977), p. 327.

28: Hadassah More, interview with author, August 20, 1989.

29: Ibid.

30: Yael Dayan, *My Father, His Daughter*, p. 148.

31: Ibid., p. 146.

32: Zalman Shoval, interview with author, June 27, 1989.

33: *Yediot Aharonot*, "Why Did Dayan Not Become Prime Minister," October 19, 1981.

34: Gad Ya'acobi, interview with author, March 29, 1989.

35: Yigal Hurvitz, interview with author, August 1, 1989.

36: Arie Lova Eliav, interview with author, April 18, 1989.

37: *Yediot Aharonot*, "Dayan from the Personal Point of View," November 27, 1981.

38: Yael Dayan, *My Father, His Daughter*, p. 166.

39: *Jerusalem Post*, "Moshe Dayan: Why I Joined Rafi," October 9, 1965.

40: *Yediot Aharonot*, "Dayan from the Personal Point of View," November 27, 1981.

41: *New York Times Book Review*, "Tough Little Army," August 14, 1966.

42: *Jewish Observer and Middle East Review*, "The Moral of the Dayan Diary," March 25, 1966.

43: British ITV, "This Week," February 3, 1972.

44: Moshe Dayan, *Story of My Life*, p. 301.

45: *Time* (People section), August 19, 1966.

46: Ruth Dayan, interview with author, February 28, 1989 and *The Story of Ruth Dayan*, pp. 186–87.

47: *Sunday Telegraph*, "Dayan at the Vietnam War," October 21, 1966.

CHAPTER 10

1: Ezer Weizman, interview with author, September 4, 1989.

2: Michael Bar-Zohar, *Embassies in Crisis* (Englewood Cliffs, NJ: Prentice-Hall, 1970), pp. 63–64.

3: Yehoshua Gavish, interview with author, August 13, 1989.

4: Ibid.

5: Yael Dayan, *My Father, His Daughter,* p. 171.

6: Danny Matt, interview with author, June 28, 1989.

7: Yael Dayan, *My Father, His Daughter,* pp. 170–171.

8: Sharon, *Warrior,* p. 185.

9: Naphtali Lavie, interview with author, December 20, 1988.

10: Uzi Narkiss, interview with author, January 10, 1989.

11: Rahel (Rabinovitch) Dayan, interview with author, February 26, 1989.

 12: Bar Zoher, *Crisis,* pp. 170–71.

13: Yitzhak Rabin, *The Rabin Memoirs,* p. 74.

14: Shimon Peres, *From These Men* (New York: Wyndham Books, 1979), pp. 102–105.

15: Dan Kurzman, *Ben-Gurion, Prophet of Fire* (New York: Simon and Schuster, 1983), pp. 542–43.

16: Naphtali Lavie, interview with author, December 20, 1989.

17: Weizman, *On Eagles' Wings,* pp. 209–10.

18: Dennis Eisenberg, Uri Dan, and Eli Landau, *The Mossad, Israel's Intelligence Service: Inside Stories* (New York: New American Library, 1978), p. 163.

19: Yael Dayan, *My Father, His Daughter,* pp. 174–75.

20: Zvi Tsur, interview with author, July 19, 1989.

21: Sharon, *Warrior,* p. 186.

22: Ezer Weizman, interview with author, September 4, 1989.

23: Ariel Sharon, *Warrior,* p. 186.

24: Yael Dayan, *My Father, His Daughter,* p. 177.

25: Hanoch Bar-Tov, *Dado* (Tel Aviv: Ma'ariv Book Guild, 1981), p. 96.

26: Moshe Dayan, *Story of My Life,* p. 350.

27: Chaim Yisraeli, interview with author, January 26, 1989 and Michael Bar-Zohar, *Crisis,* p. 194.

28: Rahel (Rabinovitch) Dayan, interview with author, February 26, 1989.

29: Mordechai Hod, interview with author, September 10, 1989.

30: Zvi Tsur, interview with author, July 19, 1989.

31: Chaim Yisraeli, interview with author, January 26, 1989.

32: Yuval Ne'eman, interview with author, July 18, 1989.

33: Ezer Weizman, interview with author, September 4, 1989.

34: J. Robert Moskin, *Among Lions* (New York: Ballantine Books, 1982), p. 322.

35: Uzi Narkiss, *The Liberation of Jerusalem* (London: Vallentine, Mitchell, 1983), p. 262.

36: Uzi Narkiss, interview with author, January 10, 1989.

37: Rahel (Rabinovitch) Dayan, interview with author, February 26, 1989.

38: Moskin, *Among Lions,* p. 322.

39: Ibid., p. 318.

40: Uri Ben-Ari, interview with author, June 7, 1989.

41: Zvi Tsur, interview with author, July 19, 1989.

42: *Time,* unpublished interview with Moshe Dayan, June 8, 1967.

43: Bar-Tov, *Dado,* p. 101.

44: Aharon Yariv, interview with author, May 1, 1989.

45: Bar-Zohar, *Crisis,* p. 251.

46: Yael Dayan, *My Father, His Daughter,* p. 185.

47: Ezer Weizman, interview with author, September 4, 1989.

48: Israel Tal, interview with author, July 17, 1989.

CHAPTER 11

1: Abba Eban, interview with author, August 20, 1989.

2: Abba Eban, *An Autobiography* (Tel Aviv: Steimatzky's, 1977), p. 494.

3: *Ma'ariv*, "From my Archives," May 29, 1981.

4: Amos Elon, *Flight into Egypt* (Garden City, NY: Doubleday, 1980), p. 199.

5: *Jerusalem Post*, "A Profile of Moshe Dayan," October 17, 1986.

6: *Ma'ariv*, "Dayan—In January 1968: On the Borders and on the United States," November 13, 1981.

7: *Ha'aretz*, "The Number You Dialed is not Connected," April 22, 1968.

8: Abba Eban, interview with author, August 20, 1989.

9: *New York Times*, "Dayan's Political Star Rising: Policy on Arabs is Moderate," December 18, 1967.

10: Aryeh Nehemkin, interview with author, March 27, 1989.

11: *Jerusalem Post*, "The Lessons of Sinai," November 8, 1959.

12: Teddy Kollek, with Amos Kollek, *For Jerusalem* (Tel Aviv: Steimatzky's, 1978), p. 200.

13: Rafik Halabi, *The West Bank Story* (New York: Harcourt Brace Jovanovich, 1981), pp. 29–30.

14: Raphael Vardi, interview with author, February 12, 1989.

15: Uzi Narkiss, interview with author, January 22, 1989.

16: Meron Benvenisti, *Jerusalem: The Torn City* (Jerusalem: Isrratypset Ltd., 1976), p. 277.

17: Chaim Herzog, interview with author, July 13, 1989.

18: Jom Kimche and Dan Bawly, *The Sandstorm: the Arab-Israeli War of 1967* (London: Secker and Warburg, 1968), p. 225.

19: Amnon Cohen, interview with author, January 15, 1989.

20: Joseph Alsop, "Moshe Dayan's Motto," *Washington Post*, December 8, 1967.

21: *Yediot Aharonot*, "The Rise and Fall of the 'Moshe Dayan for Prime Minister' Movement," October 23, 1981.

22: Raphael Vardi, interview with author, February 12, 1989.

23: Halabi, *The West Bank Story*, pp. 63–64.

24: *Kol Ha'ir*, "When the Occupation Was Young," December 9, 1988.

25: Amnon Cohen, interview with author, January 15, 1989.

26: Raphael Vardi, interview with author, February 12, 1989.

27: Ezer Weizman, interview with author, September 4, 1989.

28: Shimon Peres, *David's Sling* (New York: Random House, 1970), pp. 268–69.

29: Rael Jean Isaac, *Israel Divided* (Baltimore: Johns Hopkins University Press, 1976), pp. 150–51.

30: Uzi Narkiss, interview with author, January 22, 1989.

31: Shlomo Gazit, "Early Attempts at Establishing West Bank Autonomy," *Harvard Journal of Law and Public Policy*, Vol. 3, No. 1, 1980. Gazit quoted from the official protocol of the November 17, 1967 meeting.

32: *Jerusalem Post,* "A Profile of Moshe Dayan," October 17, 1986.
33: Zalman Shoval, interview with author, June 27, 1989.
34: Benny Peled, interview with author, July 14, 1989.
35: Ariel Sharon, *Warrior,* p. 230.
36: *Yediot Aharonot,* "This Is How Dayan Was Rescued from the Debris," March 21, 1968.
37: Weizman, *On Eagles' Wings,* p. 259.
38: *Yediot Aharonot,* "We Have Been Orphaned," October 23, 1981.
39: Avraham Biran, interview with author, May 7, 1990.
40: UPI, Cairo, reported in the *Jerusalem Post,* "And Now—the Fatah Put Dayan in Hospital," March 24, 1968.
41: Weizman, *On Eagles' Wings,* p. 260.
42: *Yediot Aharonot,* "Dayan from the General Point of View," November 27, 1981.
43: *Ma'ariv,* "From My Archives," February 11, 1977.
44: *Yediot Aharonot,* "Dayan from the General Point of View," November 27, 1981.
45: *Yediot Aharonot,* "30 Days Since Moshe Dayan Died," November 13, 1981.
46: Ibid.
47: Yael Dayan, interview with author, June 22, 1989.
48: Rahel (Rabinovitch) Dayan, interview with author, February 26, 1989.

CHAPTER 12

1: *Yediot Aharonot,* "Never Did I Send Soldiers into Battle That I Wasn't Prepared to Enter," October 23, 1981.
2: Henry Kissinger, *White House Years* (Boston: Little, Brown and Co., 1979), p. 1280.
3: Chaim Bar-Lev, interview with author, June 19, 1989.
4: *Ma'ariv,* "From My Archival Memories," January 27, 1978.
5: Yael Dayan, *My Father, His Daughter,* p. 203.
6: *Ma'ariv,* "Dayan: Flesh and Blood," November 13, 1981.
7: Ezer Weizman, interview with author, August 17, 1989.
8: Yael Dayan, *My Father, His Daughter,* pp. 148–49.
9: *Ma'ariv,* "Love Letters from Acre Jail," October 1, 1982.
10: London, *Jerusalem Post,* "Dayan Named 5th Most Sexy Man," November 6, 1970.
11: Michael Elkins, interview with author, December 2, 1988.
12: Rahel (Rabinovitch) Dayan, interview with author, June 11, 1989.
13: *Stern,* "The Woman Who Has Moshe Dayan in Her Hand," January 23, 1972.
14: Rahel (Rabinovitch) Dayan, interview with author, June 11, 1989.
15: Ibid.
16: Rahel (Rabinovitch) Dayan, interview with author, November 19, 1989.
17: Rahel (Rabinovitch) Dayan, interview with author, June 11, 1989.
18: Ibid.
19: Ibid.

20: Rahel (Rabinovitch) Dayan, interview with author, November 19, 1989.

21: Rahel (Rabinovitch) Dayan, interview with author, June 11, 1989.

22: *Ha'aretz*, "With Dayan, About Dayan," May 22, 1981.

23: Avraham Biran, interview with author, May 7, 1990.

24: Ibid.

25: Irving Bernstein, interview with author, May 16, 1989.

26: *Ma'ariv*, "Dayan's Direct Line," October 19, 1981.

27: *Jerusalem Post*, "Talking to Hussein," April 19, 1985.

28: Abba Eban, interview with author, August 20, 1989.

29: *Ha'aretz*, "Dayan Speaks to Students," April 2, 1969.

30: Copies of Tubin-Dayan letters were supplied to the author by Yehuda Tubin.

31: *Jerusalem Post*, "Most Prefer Golda to Dayan, But not if Labour Splits," June 28, 1973.

32: *Al Hamishmar*, "Victor Shem-Tov Talks about Moshe Dayan," October 23, 1981.

33: Uri Ben-Ari, interview with author, June 7, 1989.

34: Arie Lova Eliav, interview with author, April 18, 1989.

35: Zalman Shoval, interview with author, June 27, 1989.

36: Benny Peled, interview with author, July 14, 1989.

37: Yael Dayan, *My Father, His Daughter*, p. 228.

38: *People*, "Yael Dayan and Camelia Sadat Pay Literary Homage—of Sorts—To Their Famous Fathers," November 11, 1985.

39: Ariel Sharon, *Warrior*, pp. 270–71.

40: *Time*, "Waiting in the Wings," July 30, 1973.

CHAPTER 13

1: Michael Bar-Zohar, interview with author, February 27, 1989.

2: Aryeh Nehemkin, interview with author, March 27, 1989.

3: Bar-Tov, *Dado*, p. 236.

4: Naphtali Lavie, interview with author, January 8, 1989.

5: Yeshayahu Ben-Porat et al, *Kippur* (Tel Aviv: Special Editions, 1973), pp. 17–19.

6: *Yediot Aharonot*, "On October 2 Dayan Asks about Egyptian Deployment," September 16, 1983.

7: Mordechai Hod, interview with author, September 10, 1989.

8: Yael Dayan, interview with author, June 22, 1989.

9: Anwar Sadat, *In Search of Identity, An Autobiography*, (Glasgow: Fontana/Collins, 1978), p. 289.

10: Rehavam Ze'evi, interview with author, April 17, 1989.

11: Israel Tal, interview with author, July 19, 1989.

12: The Insight Team of the Sunday Times, *Insight on the Middle East War* (London: Andre Deutsch, 1974), p. 55.

13: Chaim Yisraeli, interview with author, February 13, 1989.

14: Bar-Tov, *Dado*, pp. 276–79.

15: Ibid., pp. 284–89.

16: Golda Meir, *My Life* (Tel Aviv: Steimatzky's, 1975), pp. 358–59.

17: Bar-Tov, *Dado*, pp. 292–93.

18: Ibid., pp. 276–79.

19: Aryeh Brown, interview with author, February 14, 1989.

20: Ibid.

21: In a talk to newspaper editors and military correspondents, Bet Sokolov, Tel Aviv, December 25, 1973.

22: Benny Peled, interview with author, July 14, 1989.

23: Bar-Tov, *Dado*, p. 325.

24: Aharon Yariv, interview with author, May 1, 1989.

25: Iska Shadmi, interview with author, April 24, 1989.

26: Ibid.

27: Bar-Tov, *Dado*, pp. 312–13.

28: Aharon Yariv, interview with author, May 1, 1989.

29: Uri Ben-Ari, interview with author, June 7, 1989.

30: Rehavam Ze'evi, interview with author, April 17, 1989.

31: *Ma'ariv*, "Gonen: Dayan Was a Broken Man," September 22, 1976.

32: Moshe Dayan, *Story of My Life*, p. 500.

33: Chaim Yisraeli, interview with author, February 13, 1989.

34: Aryeh Brown, interview with author, February 14, 1989.

35: Yael Dayan, interview with author, June 22, 1989.

36: Meir, *My Life*, pp. 360–61.

37: Robert Slater, *Golda: The Uncrowned Queen of Israel*, (Middle Village, NY: Jonathan David Publishers, 1981), pp. 241–42.

38: *Yediot Aharonot*, "How I Was Sent to the Golan Front," September 16, 1983.

39: Moshe Dayan, *Story of My Life*, p. 501.

40: Chaim Herzog, *The War of Atonement, October, 1973* (Boston: Little, Brown and Co., 1975), pp. 117–18.

41: Michael Bar-Zohar, interview with author, February 27, 1989.

42: Arie Lova Eliav, interview with author, April 18, 1989.

43: Uri Ben-Ari, interview with author, June 7, 1989.

44: *Jerusalem Post*, "Dayan—The Situation on Oct. 9," February 15, 1974.

45: Ibid.

46: Avraham Adan, *The Yom Kippur War* (New York: Drum, 1986), pp. 173–74.

47: *Ma'ariv*, "We Are All Guilty—Except Moshe Dayan," May 29, 1981.

48: Uri Ben-Ari, interview with author, June 7, 1989.

49: Chaim Bar-Lev, interview with author, May 8, 1989.

50: Uri Dan, *Sharon's Bridgehead* (Tel Aviv: E. L. Special Edition, 1975), pp. 92–95.

51: *Yediot Aharonot*, "Moshe Dayan from a Personal Point of View," December 4, 1981.

52: Chaim Yisraeli, interview with author, February 13, 1989.

53: Abba Eban, interview with author, August 20, 1989.

54: Arie Lova Eliav, interview with author, April 18, 1989.

55: Gad Ya'acobi, interview with author, June 14, 1989.

56: Yoseph Checanover, interview with author, April 12, 1989.

57: The material on Dayan's testimony before the secret panel was obtained from a panel member who insisted on remaining unidentified.

58: Chaim Yisraeli, interview with author, February 13, 1989.

59: Aryeh Brown, interview with author, February 14, 1989.

60: Moshe Dayan, *Story of My Life*, p. 607.

61: Michael Bar-Zohar, interview with author, February 27, 1989.

62: *Jerusalem Post*, "Dayan: Would Resign if Golda So Desired," Dec. 6, 1973.

63: Richard Valeriani, *Travels with Henry* (Boston: Houghton Mifflin, 1979), p. 203.

64: Matti Golan, *The Secret Conversations of Henry Kissinger* (New York: Bantam, 1976), pp. 142–43.

65: Golan, *Shimon Peres*, pp. 142-43.

66: Rabin, *The Rabin Memoirs*, p. 186.

67: *Yediot Aharonot*, "Interview with Israel Galili," October 27, 1978.

68: *Jerusalem Post*, "Agranat Commission Blames Elazar, Gonen, Zeira, 3 Others," April 3, 1974.

69: Naphtali Lavie, interview with author, January 8, 1989.

CHAPTER 14

1: Yael Dayan, *My Father, His Daughter*, pp. 222–23.

2: Rabin, *The Rabin Memoirs*, p. 223.

3: Golan, *Shimon Peres*, p. 182.

4: *Jerusalem Post*, "Dayan: Atoms, Not Tanks, Should Defend Israel," November 30, 1976.

5: Unpublished part of *Time* interview with Moshe Dayan, March 23, 1976.

6: Chaim Yisraeli, interview with author, February 13, 1989.

7: Yehiel Kadishai, interview with author, June 6, 1989.

8: Rafael, *Destination Peace*, p. 317.

9: Ned Temko, *To Win or Die, A Personal Portrait of Menachem Begin* (New York: William Morrow, 1987), p. 199.

10: Shmuel Katz, *The Hollow Peace* (Jerusalem: The Jerusalem Post, 1981), pp. 12–13.

11: Ariel Sharon. *Warrior*, pp. 394–95.

12: Naphtali Lavie, interview with author, December 27, 1988.

13: Ezer Weizman, *The Battle For Peace* (New York: Bantam Books, 1981), p. 310.

14: Chaim Bar-Lev, interview with author, June 19, 1989.

15: *Yediot Aharonot*, "Never Did I Send Soldiers into Battle That I Wasn't Prepared to Enter," October 23, 1981.

16: Azriel Eynav, interview with author, April 16, 1989.

17: *Time*, "On the Hustings with Moshe Dayan," October 17, 1977.

18: William Quandt, interview with author, May 23, 1989.

19: Zbigniew Brzezinski, *Power and Principle* (New York: Farrar Straus Giroux, 1983), p. 107.

20: Weizman, *The Battle For Peace*, pp. 284–85.

21: Ismail Fahmi, *Negotiating for Peace in the Middle East* (Baltimore: Johns Hopkins University Press, 1983), pp. 236–39.

22: *Jerusalem Post*, "Did it Happen or Was it a Dream?", November 13, 1987.

23: Ibid.

24: Ibid.

25: William Quandt, interview with author, May 23, 1989.

26: Aharon Barak, interview with author, August 9, 1989.

27: Moshe Dayan, *Breakthrough: A Personal Account of the Egypt-Israel Peace Negotiations* (London: Weidenfeld and Nicolson, 1981), p. 153.

28: Ibid.

29: Eitan Haber, Zeev Schiff, and Ehud Yaari, *Year of the Dove* (New York: Bantam, 1979), pp. 232–33.

30: Brzezinski, *Power and Principle*, pp. 260–61.

31: Zbigniew Brzezinski, interview with author, May 15, 1989.

32: Ibid.

33: Jimmy Carter, *Keeping Faith, Memoirs of a President* (New York: Bantam Books, 1982) p. 379.

34: William Quandt, interview with author, May 23, 1989.

35: Alfred Atherton, interview with author, May 23, 1989.

36: Sam Lewis, interview with author, May 24, 1989.

37: Jimmy Carter, interview with author, June 22, 1989.

38: Haber et al., *Year of the Dove*, pp. 224–25.

39: Alfred Atherton, interview with author, May 23, 1989.

40: Jimmy Carter, interview with author, June 22, 1989.

41: Aharon Barak, interview with author, August 9, 1989.

42: Moshe Dayan, *Breakthrough*, p. 194.

43: Cyrus Vance, *Hard Choices* (New York: Simon and Schuster, 1983), p. 250.

CHAPTER 15

1: Moshe Dayan, *Breakthrough*, pp. 296–97.

2: Quoted in Yael Dayan, *My Father, His Daughter*, pp. 286–87.

3: *Time*, "Dayan's Vision of Coexistence," November 5, 1979.

4: Rahel Dayan, interview with author, November 19, 1989.

5: *Yediot Aharonot*, "30 Days Since Moshe Dayan Died," November 13, 1981.

6: Assi Dayan, interview with author, December 20, 1989.

7: Gad Ya'acobi, interview with author, June 14, 1989.

8: Rahel Dayan, interview with author, November 19, 1989.

9: The letter is quoted in Yael Dayan, *My Father, His Daughter*, pp. 274–75.

10: Quoted in Yael Dayan, *My Father, His Daughter*, p. 275.

11: *Ma'ariv*, "Life as a Sideshow," May 27, 1982.

12: Rahel Dayan, interview with author, November 19, 1989.

13: Ibid.

INDEX